SOX Compliance with SAP® Treasury and Risk Management

 PRESS

SAP PRESS is a joint initiative of SAP and Galileo Press. The know-how offered by SAP specialists combined with the expertise of the Galileo Press publishing house offers the reader expert books in the field. SAP PRESS features first-hand information and expert advice, and provides useful skills for professional decision-making.

SAP PRESS offers a variety of books on technical and business related topics for the SAP user. For further information, please visit our website: *www.sap-press.com*.

Sönke Jarré, Reinhold Lövenich, Andreas Martin, Klaus G. Müller
SAP® Treasury and Risk Management
2008, 722 pp.
978-1-59229-149-6

Sabine Schöler, Olaf Zink
SAP® Governance, Risk, and Compliance
2008, 312 pp.
978-1-59229-191-5

Aylin Korkmaz
Financial Reporting with SAP®
2008, 672 pp.
978-1-59229-179-3

John Jordan
Product Cost Controlling with SAP®
2008, 572 pp.
1-978-159229-167-0

Arjun Krishnan, Alamanda Balaji Kumar

SOX Compliance with SAP® Treasury and Risk Management

Bonn • Boston

ISBN 978-1-59229-200-4

© 2009 by Galileo Press Inc., Boston (MA)
1st Edition 2009

Galileo Press is named after the Italian physicist, mathematician and philosopher Galileo Galilei (1564–1642). He is known as one of the founders of modern science and an advocate of our contemporary, heliocentric worldview. His words *Eppur si muove* (And yet it moves) have become legendary. The Galileo Press logo depicts Jupiter orbited by the four Galilean moons, which were discovered by Galileo in 1610.

Editor   Stephen Solomon
Copyeditor   Jutta VanStean
Cover Design   Jill Winitzer
Photo Credit   Getty Images/Martin Diebel
Layout Design   Vera Brauner
Production Editor   Kelly O'Callaghan
Typesetting   Publishers' Design and Production Services, Inc.
Printed and bound in Canada

All rights reserved. Neither this publication nor any part of it may be copied or reproduced in any form or by any means or translated into another language, without the prior consent of Galileo Press GmbH, Rheinwerkallee 4, 53227 Bonn, Germany.

Galileo Press makes no warranties or representations with respect to the content hereof and specifically disclaims any implied warranties of merchantability or fitness for any particular purpose. Galileo Press assumes no responsibility for any errors that may appear in this publication.

"Galileo Press" and the Galileo Press logo are registered trademarks of Galileo Press GmbH, Bonn, Germany. SAP PRESS is an imprint of Galileo Press.

All of the screenshots and graphics reproduced in this book are subject to copyright © SAP AG, Dietmar-Hopp-Allee 16, 69190 Walldorf, Germany.

SAP, the SAP-Logo, mySAP, mySAP.com, mySAP Business Suite, SAP NetWeaver, SAP R/3, SAP R/2, SAP B2B, SAPtronic, SAPscript, SAP BW, SAP CRM, SAP Early Watch, SAP ArchiveLink, SAP GUI, SAP Business Workflow, SAP Business Engineer, SAP Business Navigator, SAP Business Framework, SAP Business Information Warehouse, SAP inter-enterprise solutions, SAP APO, AcceleratedSAP, InterSAP, SAPoffice, SAPfind, SAPfile, SAPtime, SAPmail, SAP¬access, SAP-EDI, R/3 Retail, Accelerated HR, Accelerated HiTech, Accelerated Consumer Products, ABAP, ABAP/4, ALE/WEB, BAPI, Business Framework, BW Explorer, Enjoy-SAP, mySAP.com e-business platform, mySAP Enterprise Portals, RIVA, SAPPHIRE, TeamSAP, Webflow und SAP PRESS are registered or unregistered trademarks of SAP AG, Walldorf, Germany.

All other products mentioned in this book are registered or unregistered trademarks of their respective companies.

Contents at a Glance

1	Business and Functional Overview	19
2	Controls in SAP ERP	51
3	Inbound Electronic Banking in SAP ERP	91
4	Outbound Electronic Banking in SAP ERP	137
5	Positive Pay and Payment Card Processing	179
6	Cash Management & Liquidity Forecasting	225
7	Financial Risk Management: Foreign Exchange and Derivatives	275
8	Investment and Debt Management	317
9	Tools and Techniques for Internal Controls in SAP ERP	361
10	Special Topics in Treasury Management	395

Contents

Foreword 15
Preface 17
Acknowledgements 21

1 Business and Functional Overview 23

1.1 ERP Treasury Systems: A New Era? 23
1.2 Standalone Workstation or ERP Treasury System? 24
1.3 Key Drivers and Challenges for Treasury Management 27
1.4 The Sarbanes-Oxley Act of 2002 and its Impact on Treasury Governance and Operations 29
    1.4.1 Section 302 — Corporate Responsibility for Financial Reports 29
    1.4.2 Section 404 — Management Assessment of Internal Controls 31
    1.4.3 Control Frameworks and SOX 32
    1.4.4 Other Important Regulations that Impact Treasury 33
1.5 SAP ERP Treasury Functionality 34
    1.5.1 Implementation Timeline for SAP ERP Treasury and Risk Management 35
    1.5.2 SAP ERP Treasury and Risk Management — Powerful but Underutilized 35
    1.5.3 SAP ERP Cash Management 40
    1.5.4 SAP ERP Financial Risk Management 43
    1.5.5 Master Data and Market Data 48
    1.5.6 Key Drivers and Benefits 51
    1.5.7 The Bottom Line 52
1.6 Summary 53

2 Controls in SAP ERP 55

2.1 Control Framework and Objectives 55
    2.1.1 The Need for Controls 55
    2.1.2 Control Frameworks 56
    2.1.3 COBIT and Information Technology Systems 58

2.2	Risk and Internal Control		59
	2.2.1 Risk/Control Matrix		59
	2.2.2 Types of Risks		59
	2.2.3 Treasury-Specific Risks		60
2.3	Control Mechanisms in SAP ERP		61
	2.3.1 Architectural Elements of Control in SAP ERP		62
	2.3.2 Authorization Concept		68
	2.3.3 Configurable Authorizations		76
	2.3.4 SoD and Sensitive Access Control		79
	2.3.5 Audit Trail and Change Documents in SAP ERP		80
	2.3.6 Accounting Integrity in SAP ERP		85
	2.3.7 Reports and ALV		87
	2.3.8 Workflow Technology		88
2.4	Summary of Controls in SAP ERP		89
	2.4.1 Systemic or Built-in Controls		90
	2.4.2 Configurable Controls		90
	2.4.3 Programmable Controls		91
	2.4.4 Manual Controls		92
2.5	Risk/Control Matrix		92
2.6	Summary		94

3 Inbound Electronic Banking in SAP ERP 95

3.1	The Inbound EBS Process Flow		95
3.2	Banking Structure and Master Data		97
	3.2.1 Banking Structures		97
	3.2.2 Bank Master Data		100
	3.2.3 Master Data Key Controls		104
	3.2.4 Configuring Electronic Bank Statements		106
3.3	Straight Through Processing (STP)		112
	3.3.1 Polling Bank Files		114
	3.3.2 Preprocessing		114
	3.3.3 Bank Balance Mismatch Error		116
	3.3.4 Automatic Matching and Clearing		117
	3.3.5 Custom Program Using Field KFMOD		118
	3.3.6 Bank Polling and File Transmission		122
3.4	Prior Day Bank Statements		122
	3.4.1 Creating Test Files for Upload		125

		3.4.2	Posting Matching and Reconciliation of Bank Statements ...	126
		3.4.3	Controls for Prior Day Statements	128
	3.5	Bank Reconciliation and Control		129
		3.5.1	Post-Processing	129
		3.5.2	Displaying an Electronic Bank Statement	132
		3.5.3	Manual Bank Statement	133
		3.5.4	Deleting and Archiving Bank Statements	137
	3.6	Summary of Controls for Inbound Electronic Banking		139
	3.7	Summary		140

4 Outbound Electronic Banking in SAP ERP 141

		4.0.1	Key Drivers and Benefits	141
	4.1	Master Data Structure and Controls		143
		4.1.1	Bank Master Data	143
		4.1.2	Vendor Master Data	145
		4.1.3	Dual Authorization Control	147
	4.2	ACH Payments		148
		4.2.1	Electronic Formats	148
		4.2.2	ACH Formats	149
		4.2.3	ACH User Exits	151
		4.2.4	User Exits for ACH Formats	152
		4.2.5	Prenotification	152
		4.2.6	Key Controls for ACH Transmissions	153
	4.3	Wire Transfers		155
		4.3.1	Wire Types and Formats	155
		4.3.2	Repetitive Codes	156
		4.3.3	Types of Wire Transfers	159
		4.3.4	Cash Concentration	160
		4.3.5	Wire Payments to Treasury Partners Using Transaction FRFT	162
		4.3.6	Online Free Form and Non-Repetitive Wire Payments	163
		4.3.7	Key Controls for Wire Transmissions	166
	4.4	The Payment Medium Workbench (PMW)		166
		4.4.1	Creating a New File Format for Outbound Payments	167
		4.4.2	Linking the New Format to a Payment Method	170
		4.4.3	Configuring the PMW	173

4.5	File Transmission	176
	4.5.1 Communication Options	176
	4.5.2 Security Procedures	177
	4.5.3 Testing procedures	177
	4.5.4 Key Controls for File Transmissions	178
4.6	Using Workflow to Route Authorizations	178
4.7	Implementing Outbound Banking in SAP ERP: Lessons Learned	179
4.8	Summary of Key Controls	180
4.9	Summary	181

5 Positive Pay and Payment Card Processing ... 183

5.1	Positive Pay	183
	5.1.1 Process Overview	184
	5.1.2 Preprocessing of Files	185
	5.1.3 Detailed Process Steps	186
	5.1.4 Implementing Positive Payee	190
	5.1.5 Controlled Disbursement in Positive Pay	191
	5.1.6 Summary of Key Controls	192
5.2	Lockbox Processing	193
	5.2.1 Accounting Controls in the Lockbox Process	196
	5.2.2 Simulating Lockbox Processing	198
	5.2.3 Summary of Key Lockbox Controls	205
5.3	Procurement and Credit Card Processing	207
	5.3.1 Overview of Process	207
	5.3.2 Payment Card Industry (PCI) Data Security Standards	208
	5.3.3 PCI DSS Requirements and SAP ERP	210
	5.3.4 Key Design Considerations	211
	5.3.5 Key Configuration Steps	212
	5.3.6 Key Authorization and Encryption Controls	217
	5.3.7 Summary of Credit Card Controls	223
5.4	Escheatment	224
	5.4.1 The Escheatment Process	224
	5.4.2 Company Accounting and Reporting Requirements	225
	5.4.3 SAP ERP and Escheatment	225
	5.4.4 Accounting for Escheatment in SAP ERP	227
	5.4.5 Overview of Key Escheatment Controls	227
5.5	Summary	228

6 Cash Management & Liquidity Forecasting ... 229

- 6.1 Cash Management ... 230
  - 6.1.1 Intraday Bank Statements ... 231
  - 6.1.2 Inputs Required for Daily Cash Positioning and Liquidity Forecasting ... 236
- 6.2 Reporting ... 256
  - 6.2.1 Daily Cash Positioning ... 256
  - 6.2.2 Liquidity Forecasting ... 259
  - 6.2.3 Liquidity Planner ... 260
- 6.3 Controls for Cash Management ... 260
- 6.4 In-House Cash (IHC) Management ... 263
  - 6.4.1 IHC and Intercompany Processing ... 264
  - 6.4.2 Cost/Benefit Considerations in Implementing IHC ... 265
  - 6.4.3 Process Overview ... 266
  - 6.4.4 Master Data ... 267
  - 6.4.5 Integration with Cash Management ... 273
  - 6.4.6 Authorization Management ... 276
  - 6.4.7 Controls for IHC ... 277
- 6.5 Summary ... 277

7 Financial Risk Management: Foreign Exchange and Derivatives ... 279

- 7.1 Master Data for FX Transaction Management ... 282
- 7.2 Master Data for Transaction Processing ... 283
  - 7.2.1 Product Categories ... 283
  - 7.2.2 Product Types ... 284
  - 7.2.3 Transaction Types ... 284
  - 7.2.4 Flow Types ... 286
  - 7.2.5 Update Types ... 288
  - 7.2.6 Links Between Transaction Management and Accounting ... 288
- 7.3 Master Data for Transaction Management ... 289
  - 7.3.1 Business Partner (BP) ... 290
  - 7.3.2 Trader ... 295
  - 7.3.3 Bank-Related Master Data ... 295
- 7.4 Master Data for Accounting, Valuation, and Reporting ... 296
  - 7.4.1 Portfolio ... 296

		7.4.2	Valuation Areas	296
		7.4.3	Market Data	297
	7.5	Workflow Management		297
	7.6	Transaction Management		298
		7.6.1	Transaction Management Menu	300
		7.6.2	Front Office	300
		7.6.3	Back Office	306
		7.6.4	Accounting	308
	7.7	Hedge Management		309
		7.7.1	Hedge Management Menu Options	311
		7.7.2	Hedge Management Steps	311
		7.7.3	Hedge Documentation	316
		7.7.4	Hedge Accounting and Periodic Processing	317
	7.8	Integration with Cash Management		317
	7.9	Market Data Management		318
	7.10	Summary		319

8 Investment and Debt Management ... 321

	8.1	Master Data Structure		322
		8.1.1	Product Types	322
		8.1.2	Global Settings for Securities	323
		8.1.3	Transaction Types	323
		8.1.4	Securities Account	325
		8.1.5	Class Data	326
		8.1.6	Business Partner	329
	8.2	Transaction Management		330
		8.2.1	Money Market Fixed Term Deposit Example	330
		8.2.2	Securities Bond Purchase Example	337
		8.2.3	Month End Accounting	339
		8.2.4	Valuation of an Open Contract	341
	8.3	Market Data Management		344
		8.3.1	Transaction Data Feed	345
		8.3.2	Master Data Feed	346
	8.4	The Analyzers		348
		8.4.1	Analyzer Functionality	349
		8.4.2	Valuation and Mark to Market	349
		8.4.3	Limit Management	355

8.5	Integration with Cash Management	361
8.6	Reporting	362
8.7	Summary	363

9 Tools and Techniques for Internal Controls in SAP ERP ... 365

9.1	Management of Internal Controls (MIC)	366
	9.1.1 Basic Prerequisites	366
	9.1.2 MIC Technical Implementation Considerations	367
	9.1.3 MIC Features	368
	9.1.4 Process Flow for a MIC Project	371
	9.1.5 Customizing Settings for MIC	372
9.2	Audit Information Systems (AIS)	377
	9.2.1 Areas Supported by AIS	379
	9.2.2 Process Flow for AIS	380
	9.2.3 Steps to Implement AIS	383
	9.2.4 AIS OSS Notes	384
9.3	GRC AC and Other SOX Compliance Systems	385
	9.3.1 SAP GRC components	385
	9.3.2 Other SOX Compliance Systems	386
9.4	Managing a SOX Audit from the Treasury Perspective	386
	9.4.1 SOX Audit	386
	9.4.2 Best Practices for a Treasury SOX Audit	391
9.5	Reporting, Audit Trail and Documentation	392
	9.5.1 Reporting	392
	9.5.2 Audit Trail	395
	9.5.3 Documentation	396
9.6	Summary	398

10 Special Topics in Treasury Management ... 399

10.1	Upgrading SAP ERP	399
	10.1.1 Key Drivers for Upgrading	399
	10.1.2 Types of Upgrades	400
	10.1.3 Using a Phased Approach to Upgrading	401
	10.1.4 Factors to Consider in the Upgrade Decision	402
	10.1.5 Steps in the Upgrade Process	404

		10.1.6	Key Process Steps	405
		10.1.7	Project Methodology	411
	10.2	Archiving		417
		10.2.1	Archiving Process Flow	419
		10.2.2	Support Tools for the SAP Data Archiving Process	420
		10.2.3	The Business Need for Archiving	423
		10.2.4	Potential Control-Related Issues for Archiving	423
		10.2.5	Access to Archived Data	427
	10.3	New Treasury-Related Functionality in SAP ERP		427
		10.3.1	Frontend Trading Platform Integration	427
		10.3.2	Exposure Management	428
		10.3.3	New Product Types	430
	10.4	Summary		431
	10.5	Conclusion		431

The Authors 433

Index 435

Foreword

ERP systems have always come with great promise to simplify processes, eliminate work and improve controls. Yet, when you talk to users, you find that many times after the installation process has been completed, not much has changed from the old way of doing things. There may have been marginal improvements, and perhaps a few process modifications. But most installations do not lead to significant changes. Once the basic installation is complete, people tend to go on with things the way they had been done before. Part of the reason is that people just don't realize the full functionality of the ERP system they just installed. This book can change all that. This book can help you realize more of the potential, and get more benefit from that major investment you've made. The authors, Arjun Krishnan and Alamanda Balaji Kumar, are not people who are writing about theoretical ideas. They have actually done the things they write about. They have delved into the heart of SAP ERP and maximized its potential. And because they understand the operation issues from the user perspective, as well as the technical issues from the IT perspective, they have developed solutions that work for both.

I've worked for 3 companies that installed ERP systems. One of those installed SAP ERP just prior to me joining the company and I was fortunate that Arjun Krishnan was one of the people involved in that installation. Although I was a 'user' with many years of accounting and treasury experience, I often had to ask Arjun to explain to me why he had set the system up the way it was. I alternated between thinking it was an ingenious system and then wondering why it worked the way it did. But it always came back to an implementation design that was structured so well, with so many internal checks and balances, that it eliminated some reconciliations and greatly simplified others. And it eliminated a lot of manual effort. As someone who is always concerned about integrity of systems and processes, the way Arjun set up SAP ERP to work provided me with a great sense of confidence. As Arjun so aptly expresses it in the book, SAP ERP provides integration, automation and control, leveraging one-time data entry and straight-through processing to ensure data integrity as well as efficiency.

I learned a lot from Arjun and he raised my expectations about what an ERP system should do. At a company I worked for later, we installed a different ERP system. When I asked our IT people and the installation consultants for some of the functionality we had used in my prior company I got a lot of blank stares. People didn't know if the system could do those things, and in fact, they had never heard of an ERP system having those capabilities. But I knew it could, because Arjun had found a way to do it.

I have to recommend this book for anyone who wants to help their company get the most out of their SAP ERP system. And that makes it a valuable career advancement tool as well. Within the pages of this book you're going to find ways to make your daily tasks much more efficient. Even if you don't have SAP ERP, this book is a wonderful thought-starter. You'll see how SAP ERP can be used to do many things in ways you haven't thought of. Even if you aren't using SAP as your ERP system, this book can get you started thinking about ways to get more out of the system you do have.

To get the most out of SAP Treasury and Risk Management, use this book to find out how you can do things better, easier, faster and with greater accuracy and accountability. Along the way, you'll probably find that you've made your entire ERP investment better, as well.

Brad Larson
VP Treasurer
Pamida Inc.

Preface

Introduction

This book is more than a review of SOX compliance and controls in the context of SAP ERP Treasury and Risk management. Because the control environment is closely tied to business process and best practices, it is also a practical guide to leveraging SAP ERP's Treasury and Risk Management functionality, based on the authors' many years of actual experience implementing SAP ERP Treasury systems. It focuses on the key business issues and challenges faced by treasury and financial managers in their day-to-day business, and how SAP ERP can help to meet those challenges.

This book provides the convergence between two critical business requirements: treasury business processes, and SAP ERP system compliance with the Sarbanes-Oxley Act.

Most public corporations to which SOX applies have implemented or are in the process of implementing Enterprise Resource Planning systems like SAP ERP, where technology, functionality and business processes are integrated seamlessly across the enterprise.

From a control standpoint, this provides great opportunities, as well as a number of challenges. One of the most critical areas where strong SOX controls and effective business processes are required is in the area of treasury management. The primary reason for this is because treasury is typically responsible for managing the cash flow requirements of the organization as well as the financial risks associated with such management.

Further, treasury also tends to be responsible for a lot of the high value transactions and transfers that typify the business requirements of most corporations. With the increasing globalization of business, the need for good management and internal controls has become even more critical. Additionally, new regulatory requirements like SEPA and Basel need to be complied with in Europe and other parts of the world.

The primary focus of this book is to provide an understanding of the business processes, tools and techniques involved in the Treasury & Risk Management, and Cash & Liquidity Management applications as implemented in SAP ERP, and how relevant internal controls can be built into the system to make it compliant with the Sarbanes-Oxley Act and other regulatory requirements.

Additionally, key integration points between Treasury, SAP ERP Financials, and other components will be explained, so that controls are integrated throughout the entire functional business supply chain. The book addresses controls and processes in the context of the latest system that SAP has to offer, namely SAP ERP ECC 6.0 and the NetWeaver architecture.

How the book is organized

The book focuses on providing a tutorial for treasury and finance professionals charged with bringing SOX compliance to an existing or planned Treasury implementation and maintenance. The chapters employ a "macro to micro" pedagogy in the knowledge transfer, focusing first on the processes, then expanding the discussion to incorporate information on the specific applications and tools, followed by a summary of the associated controls. The "macro to micro" pedagogy allows the book to be modular, in the sense that individual chapters can be used on an ad hoc basis as reference or tutorial as necessary during the course of an implementation and maintenance.

Chapter 1 provides an overview of key SAP functionality, SOX, and other statutory and governance requirements relevant to treasury. It discusses current issues in treasury management and how the SAP ERP system can be leveraged to meet those challenges.

Chapter 2 provides an overview of key control concepts and control mechanisms used within SAP ERP. It covers the different types of controls available in an integrated system and how they can be leveraged to facilitate compliance with SOX and other regulatory requirements

Chapter 3 describes the key business processes involved in Inbound Electronic Banking in SAP ERP, covering prior day electronic bank statements, reconciliation and controls, and how straight through automated processing can be achieved in the upload, posting, matching, clearing and reconciliation of electronic bank statements.

Chapter 4 covers all the important aspects of outbound electronic banking business processes and related controls in SAP ERP, including Domestic (U.S.) and International Electronic fund transfers, Automated Clearing House (ACH) payments, Cash Concentration and Bank-to-bank transfers. The use of powerful tools like the Payment Workbench (PMW) to create custom file formats will be explained

Chapter 5 covers some key treasury processes that involve electronic banking, like the Positive Pay cycle for check payments, lockbox processing for incoming remittances, Payment Card processing and Escheatment in SAP ERP.

Chapter 6 covers Cash Management, Liquidity Forecasting, In-House banking, and current day bank statement processing.

Chapter 7 covers foreign exchange risk management and derivatives and related transaction management, hedge management and accounting, payment processing, and market data integration.

Chapter 8 covers transaction management for investment and debt, using examples from the Money Market and Securities sub-components, master data, data feed and integration, and how the analyzer tools are used in the key areas of valuation and limit management.

Chapter 9 covers the additional tools available to further enhance and facilitate SOX compliance for SAP ERP Financials like Management of Internal Controls (MIC), Audit Information System (AIS), and SAP GRC Access Control.

Chapter 10 covers the special topics of upgrading and archiving that are of particular importance to existing SAP ERP users. The book concludes with key new functionality available in SAP ERP ECC 6.0 of special relevance to treasury and not covered elsewhere.

Intended Audience

This book will be of particular relevance to Treasurers, Chief Financial Officers, Controllers, Treasury Directors, Cash, Risk Management and Financial Managers, Treasury and Finance Consultants, Project Managers, Internal and External Auditors, Treasury and Finance users, and Systems Security and Controls staff.

From an SAP ERP project implementation perspective, this book will provide guidance with respect to design, testing and implementation of treasury processes and related controls in the various project phases.

This book will also be useful for Treasury consultants responsible for configuration of the system, as it covers key business scenarios, and provides relevant information around tables, programs and transaction codes used in those processes. Finally, it can be used as a useful training tool for users as it explains key treasury business processes that they are familiar with, in the context of how they are executed and managed in the SAP ERP system.

Acknowledgements

I would like to thank Jawahara Saidullah of SAP PRESS for providing us the opportunity to write this book, Stephen Solomon of SAP PRESS for his help and guidance in getting the book completed, and my co-author Balaji for his cooperation and support. My sincere thanks go to my many friends and colleagues in the treasury and SAP world who have shared their knowledge and experience with me, in particular Brad Larson and Odette Go, from whom I have learned so much. Lastly, I would like to thank my family for all their love, patience, encouragement and support in fulfilling my dream of finally getting this book written.

Arjun Krishnan

I am deeply indebted to all those who supported me in this endeavor, in particular Jawahara Saidullah and Stephen Solomon from SAP PRESS for providing me with this wonderful opportunity to write a book. I convey my special thanks to my treasury mentor, Shirley Waltmire, and my friends Dan Wilson, Todd Hagan, Stephen Graber, Ravi Gona and Sarah Sears for their valuable inputs. I would also like to thank my co-author, Arjun, for his cooperation and constructive insight. Finally, I would like to take this opportunity to thank my wife Viji and sons Vignesh and Bharath, who supported and motivated me in the arduous journey of writing this book.

Alamanda Balaji Kumar

The opinions in this book are those of the authors only, and do not reflect the opinions of the authors' employers or clients.

Chapter 1 provides an overview of key treasury functionality in SAP ERP, and SOX and other statutory and governance requirements relevant to treasury. It discusses current issues in treasury management and how the SAP ERP system can be leveraged to meet those challenges.

1 Business and Functional Overview

Treasury departments are more and more frequently playing a critical role in the overall governance of corporations. Although they tend to be small, treasury departments' responsibilities encompass key functions within an organization, such as cash management, liquidity forecasting, financial risk management, foreign exchange and investment management, and all of the related controls and processes. With the advent of the Sarbanes-Oxley (SOX) legislation and other regulatory requirements such as the Basel accords and Single European Payments Authority (SEPA) in Europe, a greater degree of responsibility exists with regard to the approval authorization and reconciliation requirements of transactions and the accuracy and integrity of their entry in the prime books of record, for example SAP ERP.

1.1 ERP Treasury Systems: A New Era?

The typical corporate treasury department is a small group of people that attends to treasury functions in a manner fairly isolated from the other functional groups within an organization. This is because treasury management and operations are highly specialized, and treasury staff interacts primarily with banks, brokers, and the capital markets. This is particularly true when the treasury department is linked to a bank or broker through a treasury workstation supplied by the broker.

The typical treasury day starts early in the morning before the business day begins and well before banks and capital markets open for the day. Bank balances need to be updated, cash positioning based on intraday information relating to check presentations performed, and lockbox receipts, cash concentration receipts, wire transfers, and Automated Clearing House (ACH) payments completed so investment and borrowing requirements can be ascertained prior to the markets opening. Furthermore, foreign exchange transactions need to be ascertained and set up based on a review of current market rates and opportunities, and short term investment decisions need to be made based on current market information, all before the markets and banking systems start commencing operations for the day.

In the current, fast-paced business world, where timely information access is of critical importance, companies are looking to leverage their information systems to provide integrated and real-time information to be able to make decisions in an effective and efficient manner. This was and will continue to be the promise of ERP systems. A second, equally critical need has developed over the course of the last decade. A spate of corporate scandals has resulted in increased regulatory compliance and enhanced corporate governance requirements. This has translated into very stringent standards for internal control requirements that can only be satisfied through high levels of automation of — and integration between — business processes. Organizations with an array of different systems that do not communicate with each other and where a lot of manual reentry of data takes place are increasingly at risk of non compliance with those regulations.

This is particularly true of the treasury function, for two key reasons. First, although perceived to be isolated and specialized in its functionality, treasury is usually at the end of the financial supply chain; it is where every financial transaction is converted into cash or its equivalent, and it therefore plays a role in all significant financial transactions. Thus, a dependency exists between treasury and all of the functional areas in the financial supply chain that precede it, in terms of appropriate approvals, authorizations, and segregation of duties (SoD). Therefore, integration between these functions has taken on a critical importance. Second, treasury is usually responsible for high-value wire payments that typically require multiple authorizations at the highest levels within an organization. This again requires a timely and effective process that can be provided by using workflow in an integrated ERP environment to manage hand off of a transaction between different functional areas, and in turn enabling compliance with SoD requirements, a key component of sound internal control.

1.2 Standalone Workstation or ERP Treasury System?

One of the biggest questions facing treasurers today is whether to migrate existing standalone treasury systems to an ERP system such as SAP ERP, or, if manual

Microsoft Excel-based processes are being automated, whether to install a standalone workstation or an ERP-based system.

Powerful arguments exist for using a standalone treasury workstation. They have been around for a long time, are built to meet specific functional needs, and allow treasury to work more or less independently of the rest of the organization. Typically, a banking partner that enables direct online access for payment processing and intraday information provides the treasury workstation and software. Banking information can then be uploaded for accounting and reconciliation purposes.

ERP systems on the other hand are expensive, complex, and time- consuming to implement. The return on investment (ROI) is realized in the medium-to-longterm, rarely in the short term. So why are corporations increasingly turning to ERP systems for their treasury, banking, and financial risk management requirements? The answer is simple: *integration*, *automation,* and *control*. We will look at these important factors throughout the course of this chapter because they need to be considered in any decision between treasury workstation and platform.

We mentioned earlier that treasury departments tend to work on their own, and in isolation from the rest of the organization. This is becoming increasingly impractical for two important reasons. First, treasury is taking on a much more critical role in the overall governance of a corporation. CEOs and CFOs are looking to treasury for input into major decisions with respect to liquidity, corporate financial management, risk management, and best business practices. Secondly, because of SOX legislation and requirements regarding internal controls and SoD, authorizations and financial processes need to be redesigned to allow appropriate hand off between functions, as a transaction flows through the financial supply chain. ERP systems provide the integration between functions in a seamless way and include robust controls using tools such as workflow and security around authorizations. Later in this chapter, we will look at how SAP ERP is able to integrate treasury functionality with other key functions of the business and the many tools available to provide strong internal controls.

The other key advantage of an ERP system lies in its ability to automate the financial supply chain to allow for STP in many areas of finance and treasury management. We will review in detail how STP can be used in SAP ERP in key areas such as electronic banking and transaction management. In particular, we will look at examples of how to include strong authorization controls using workflow, and leverage built-in systemic controls during transaction processing.

1 Business and Functional Overview

The Treasury component in SAP ERP is an integral part of the SAP ERP suite of applications, and benefits from all aspects of integration with the accounting, accounts payable, and accounts receivable functionalities that are part of the Financial Accounting component, as well as the Purchasing, Sales and Distribution (SD), Materials Management (MM), and Production components and applications that form part of the larger integrated supply chain functionality within SAP ERP.

Unlike with manual systems or standalone treasury workstations, with an ERP system it is not necessary to re-input data into the main books of accounting record, or build interfaces with legacy systems for transferring such data. Furthermore, in manual systems and workstations, additional reconciliation and control mechanisms have to be incorporated when data has to be re-entered or transferred from another external system.

In an integrated system such as SAP ERP, data needs to be entered only once to be available throughout the system as it flows through the financial supply chain. For example, purchase order information that has been entered into the system is available in its subsequent flow through documents such as the goods receipt, invoice, and payment request, and through to final clearing and reconciliation in the electronic bank statement.

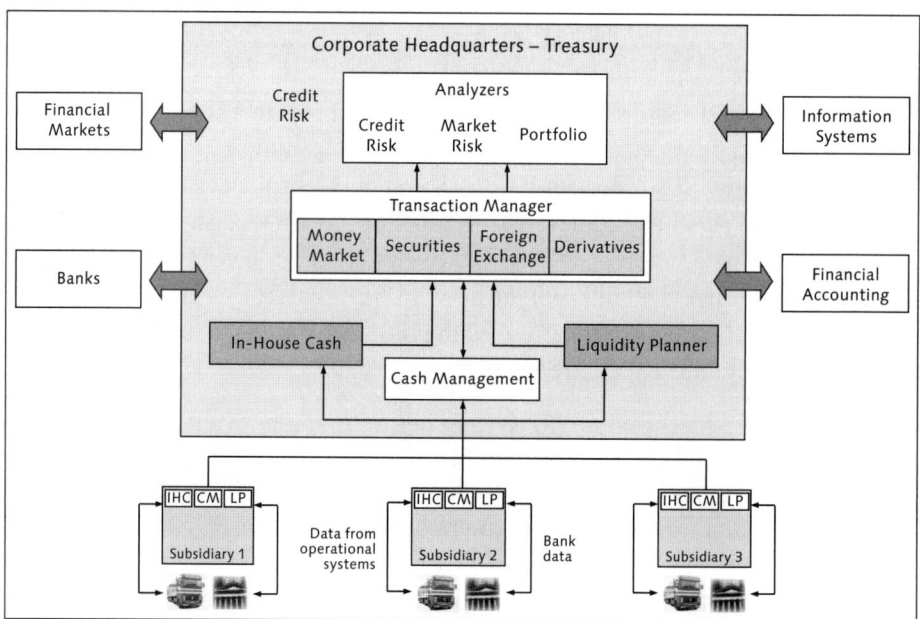

Figure 1.1 Integrated Treasury Management with SAP ERP Systems

Thus, the goal for ERP treasury systems is to build all of the functionality of stand-alone workstations into an integrated enterprise-wide system that leverages all of the benefits of automation, integration, and STP while providing all of the functionality for the highly specialized and increasingly sophisticated requirements of treasury departments. Figure 1.1 shows an integrated model of functionality provided with SAP ERP. We will look at the key components that make up this model as we progress through the chapters of this book.

1.3 Key Drivers and Challenges for Treasury Management

The new millennium has brought with it serious challenges in the areas of corporate finance, treasury, controls, and governance. These are having a large impact on how corporations are organized and managed, and how they conduct their day-to-day business. In fact, when this book was written, the U.S. (and world) economy was facing an unprecedented liquidity and financial crisis, arising out of the sub prime mortgage credit problems that had been building up over the previous years. Additionally, international trends such as globalization, outsourcing, off shoring, increased regulation, and harmonization of and compliance with international standards have also been changing the way businesses operate and behave. Post 9/11 anti-terrorist funding and anti-money laundering laws have brought greater scrutiny over domestic and international funds transfers. Regulatory legislation such as SOX in the U.S., SEPA in the European Union, and also the Basel accords are increasingly defining best practices and requirements with respect to internal controls, corporate governance, funds transfer, and banking requirements.

Key trends such as globalization and off shoring of many functions require a new way of conducting business, bringing with them a host of new challenges and opportunities. In a global environment, there is a need for ensuring synergy and common practices and procedures, while at the same time providing enough flexibility to address potentially diverse local and regional needs.

Global corporations are accountable for all of their operations, and there is increased responsibility for safeguarding the value of corporate assets, especially in a multi-currency environment. There is also a need for control over and consolidation of cash and liquid assets, whether centrally or regionally, increasing inter-company, intra-company and intergroup transactions, national pooling, and cross border fund transfers, just to name a few. And all of these need to be accounted for, in the prime books of record.

1 | Business and Functional Overview

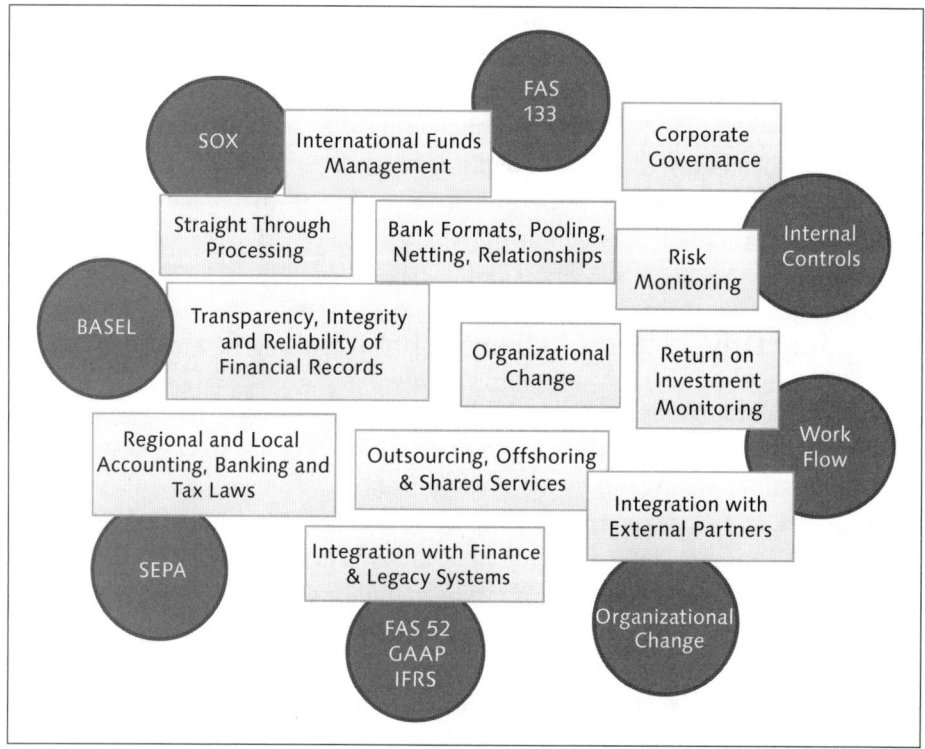

Figure 1.2 Challenges and Opportunities for Treasury

As shown in Figure 1.2, the new millennium has brought with it many challenges and opportunities for the treasury management function.

Additionally, accounting standards such as GAAP's FAS 133 in the U.S. have created new challenges in the areas of accounting for and documenting of the use of derivative instruments within a corporation for financial risk management purposes. Harmonization between and compliance with U.S. and international accounting standards such as International Financial Reporting Standards (IFRS) are also affecting the accounting and reporting of business transactions and their underlying processes.

Major global corporations based in the U.S. will need to comply with GAAP and IFRS, and many subsidiaries located outside of the U.S. will have to provide country-specific local financial statements for legal and tax purposes to satisfy the requirements of their respective home countries. These local financial statements, and cash flow and other reports may be required in multiple currencies and in different formats and possibly different languages. Countries such as China have strict regulations with respect to cash transfers and also have stringent documentation requirements to support requests for any treasury-related activities. The increasingly complex international environment we operate in demands sophisticated information technology systems to support it.

1.4 The Sarbanes-Oxley Act of 2002 and its Impact on Treasury Governance and Operations

The SOX act of 2002 was introduced to strengthen investor confidence in companies registered with the U.S. Securities and Exchange Commission (SEC), through requirements for better corporate governance and through setting standards for accountability and greater accuracy and reliability in an organization's financial records as reported to the SEC.

The SOX act has had a significant impact on the way corporations conduct their day-to-day business, with sections 302 and 404 being of particular importance and relevance to treasury processes, practices, control systems, and governance.

In this chapter, we will review the key requirements of the SOX compliance requirements as they relate to treasury, and describe the control frameworks used in its application from both a process and systems perspective.

1.4.1 Section 302 – Corporate Responsibility for Financial Reports

Section 302 of the SOX act states that the principal executive officer or officers, and the principal financial officer or officers, or persons performing similar functions, certify in each annual or quarterly report filed or submitted to the SEC under either section 13(a) or 15(d) of the SEC act of 1934 that:

- The signing officer has reviewed the report:

    Based on the officer's knowledge, the report does not contain any untrue statement of a material fact, or omit to state a material fact necessary in order to make the statements made, in light of the circumstances under which such statements were made, not misleading.

    Based on such officer's knowledge, the financial statements, and other financial information included in the report, fairly present in all material respects the financial conditions and results of operations of the issuer as of, and for, the periods presented in the report.

- The signing officers:

Are responsible for establishing and maintaining internal controls.

Have designed such internal controls to ensure the material information relating to the issuer, and it consolidated subsidiaries is made known to such officers by others within those entities, particularly during the period in which the periodic reports are being prepared.

Have evaluated the effectiveness of the issuer's internal controls as of a date within 90 days prior to the report.

Have presented in their report their conclusions about the effectiveness of their internal controls based on their evaluation as of that date.

- The signing officers have disclosed to the issuer's auditors and the audit committee of the board of directors (or persons fulfilling the equivalent function):

All significant deficiencies in the design or operation of internal controls which could adversely affect the issuer's ability to record, process, summarize, and report financial data and have identified for the issuer's auditors any material weaknesses in internal controls.

Any fraud, whether or not material, that involves management or other employees who have a significant role in the issuer's internal controls.

- The signing officers have indicated in the report whether or not there were significant changes in internal controls or in other factors that could significantly affect internal controls subsequent to the date of their evaluation, including any corrective actions with regard to significant deficiencies and material weaknesses.

From a treasury standpoint the above section will have a significant impact in the following key areas:

- Many corporations are implementing a sub-certification process that may require treasurers and other key members of treasury management to sign off on the adequacy and accuracy of transactions and records that are impacted by treasury.

- The Act establishes the need for ongoing incorporation, development, enhancement, and monitoring of internal controls to provide assurances with respect to the accuracy and integrity of the financial records and statements issued. This needs to be a continuous improvement process.

- Treasury operations are involved with key areas such as banking, cash management, and financial risk management that also involve other functions within an organization. The appropriate design of business processes and integration between functions takes on a new degree of importance in light of SOX compliance.

- There is an increased onus on treasury staff for fraud detection, prevention, and reporting. Treasury is typically responsible for maintaining bank relationships and controls for check and electronic fund transfer payment processing, where there is the most potential for fraudulent activity. A heightened level of scrutiny is now required to ensure that adequate control systems are in place for fraud prevetion and detection.

- The certification of financial statements and reports include results of cash flow and cash forecasts. The preparation, review, and validation of these almost certainly involves the treasury department. Section 302 also goes beyond financial reports to include non-financial information such as controls for operations and compliance with other laws and regulations.

- Section 302 also applies to subsidiaries of a corporation registered with the SEC. This is of particular importance if treasury has operations in many different regions of the world. The impact of globalization on treasury operations is far-reaching, especially with respect to the movement of funds across borders and the legal and tax implications specific to various countries and regions of the world.

- The SOX act places an equal emphasis on disclosure controls as it does on preventative and detective controls in the design of business processes and procedures.

1.4.2 Section 404 — Management Assessment of Internal Controls

> **Key Term: Section 404**
>
> Section 404 specifies requirements for certification of internal controls as described here:
>
> - (a) RULES REQUIRED: The SEC shall prescribe rules requiring each annual report required by section 13(a) or 15(d) of the SEC act of 1934 to contain an internal control report, which shall:

> ▶ State the responsibility of management for establishing and maintaining an adequate internal control structure and procedures for financial reporting; and
>
> ▶ Contain an assessment, as of the end of the most recent fiscal year of the issuer, of the effectiveness of the internal control structure and procedures of the issuer for financial reporting
>
> ▶ (b) INTERNAL CONTROL EVALUATION AND REPORTING: With respect to the internal control assessment required by subsection (a), each registered public accounting firm that prepares or issues the audit report for the issuer shall attest to, and report on, the assessment made by the management of the issuer. An attestation made under this subsection shall be made in accordance with standards for attestation engagements issued or adopted by the Board. Any such attestation shall not be the subject of a separate engagement.

From a treasury perspective, Section 404 has had a major impact on audit practices and procedures, as well as on the entire framework of internal controls and designs over business process and procedures within a corporation, as follows:

▶ Because attestation needs to be made by external auditors, all new implementations of treasury systems or processes will need their involvement and sign off with respect to the adequacy of internal controls.

▶ Tools need to be developed and maintained to provide ongoing evaluation of the effectiveness of internal controls through reports, and transparency of the books of financial record and other information that fall within its purview.

▶ Documentation and audit trails of all treasury-related transactions need to be maintained so that they can be accessed and reviewed as part of the ongoing evaluation and attestation.

▶ Through the attestation, confidence needs to be ensured in the information technology systems that record, store, and move treasury data internally and outside the organization.

This book concerns itself primarily with treasury business processes and with building effective internal controls around them. We will look at the processes, tools, methodologies, and controls provided by SAP ERP to facilitate these in Chapter 2 and the rest of the book, where specific treasury business functionality is addressed.

1.4.3 Control Frameworks and SOX

Complying with SOX relates primarily to the requirements for controls within an enterprise. Its successful implementation requires using appropriate control frameworks that can be used to design, implement, evaluate, and monitor both processes and information technology systems. The Committee of Sponsoring Organizations (COSO) framework is used for accounting procedures and controls, and the Control Objectives for Information and Related Technologies (COBIT) framework for information technology systems.

Committee of Sponsoring Organizations (COSO)

COSO — also known as the Treadway Commission, after it's founding chairman's name — is a voluntary private sector organization set up originally in 1985 to improve the quality of financial reporting through business ethics, effective internal controls, and corporate governance. It was updated in 2004.

COSO is the internal control framework recommended by regulatory and industry bodies for use for SOX compliance purposes. It satisfies the SEC criteria for compliance and provides an evaluation methodology with respect to accounting procedures and controls. It is widely used by companies required to comply with SOX.

Control Objectives for Information and Related Technologies (COBIT)

COBIT is an open standard published by the Information Technology Governance Institute (ITGI) and the Information Systems Audit and Control Association (ISACA). It is an IT control framework built in part on the COSO framework.

We will review control structures in the chapters that follow, and look at how the SAP ERP system provides functionality in accordance with these frameworks.

1.4.4 Other Important Regulations that Impact Treasury

SEPA is an initiative of the European Payments Council (EPC), whose primary goal is to create a single Euro zone for electronic payments within the European Union's (EU) member countries.

Single European Payments Authority

All electronic payments within this zone will be considered domestic — and not cross-border — which will greatly simplify the process of making electronic fund transfers. It will make fund transfers cheaper and more efficient, and provide for STP of electronic payments because there will be no distinction between national and international borders within the EU. Additionally, it will provide greater visibility of money flows, enabling better monitoring of funds transfers for illicit activities such as money laundering and terrorism funding.

SEPA will impact all banks operating in 31 countries: the 27 EU member states, three other European economic area countries (Liechtenstein, Iceland, and Norway), and Switzerland. A heavy investment in technology will be necessary to support SEPA payment instruments, and to have these technologies in place by 2010.

Companies will have the opportunity to consolidate their payment processing into one platform, using standard formats and common data fields across the Euro zone. Using SWIFT and IBAN numbers will be mandatory for all electronic fund transfers within SEPA. In Chapter 8, the chapter on Outbound Banking, we will look at how you will need to configure SAP ERP to ensure compliance with SEPA requirements.

Basel Accords

The Basel accords deal mostly with international banking standards and regulations relating to capital maintenance requirements that are designed to protect banks from financial and operational risks. Although the Basel accords apply mostly to banking organizations, companies and their treasury departments need to be aware of any direct or indirect impact to their own operations as a result of liquidity requirements or risk exposure through their relationships with banking partners. The recent failure of major banks and brokerage houses in the U.S. as a result of the financial and liquidity crisis will have major ramifications on banking relationships for global corporations. Most corporations are currently in the process of evaluating these relationships, as well as assessing the extent of their risk exposure in the fallen or teetering financial institutions.

1.5 SAP ERP Treasury Functionality

The SAP ERP system provides a wide range of treasury functionality through its Financial Supply Chain Management (FSCM) suite of applications. We will review the evolution and development of this functionality.

1.5.1 Implementation Timeline for SAP ERP Treasury and Risk Management

Most companies implementing SAP ERP initially focus on setting up the core Financial Accounting application and Controlling component. Although cash management, electronic banking, and payment processing are an integral part of SAP ERP Financials, they are seen as "treasury" functions and are typically not fully implemented to leverage all of the available functionality. After the core functions are implemented and working smoothly, the focus shifts to enhancing functionality within SAP ERP Financials, as well as to taking the next logical step in integrating the enterprise, namely by implementing Treasury and Risk Management functionality. The investment in ERP systems is very significant, and it is essential that all of its functionality be leveraged and optimized to enable a profitable ROI, and to reduce the payback period. ERP systems are complex, and the benefits accrue over time, as the learning curve is mastered, existing functionality is optimized, and new functionality is added. As mentioned previously, with increasing governance and regulatory requirements being placed on corporations, the next logical step is to look at how to leverage the powerful treasury and risk management functionality of SAP ERP from a controls and SOX compliance standpoint.

1.5.2 SAP ERP Treasury and Risk Management — Powerful but Underutilized

The SAP ERP Treasury and Risk Management functionality in SAP ERP Financials is powerful but — in our experience — highly underutilized. To a large extent, this is because there is a general lack of understanding of the features SAP ERP has to offer, especially in the area of electronic banking and payment processing. This book seeks to bridge that gap, and we will be looking at this functionality in detail in later chapters. Corporations start to consider Treasury when their core components are working smoothly, or when they would like to migrate from a manual system or standalone treasury workstation to leverage the benefits of integration. The factors affecting the choice of a standalone treasury workstation or Treasury will be considered in the next section.

Introduction

The evolution of treasury functionality within SAP has an almost direct co-relation to the increasing influence of treasury and its functions within the organization. The early versions of Treasury were essentially add-ons and bolt-ons, providing limited integration with the rest of the components. As the architecture of SAP software improved, so did the functionality within the Treasury components, enabling a greater degree of integration with the rest of the SAP suite of applications, as well as leveraging integration external to the enterprise. The evolution and maturity of the Treasury functionality is shown in Figure 1.3.

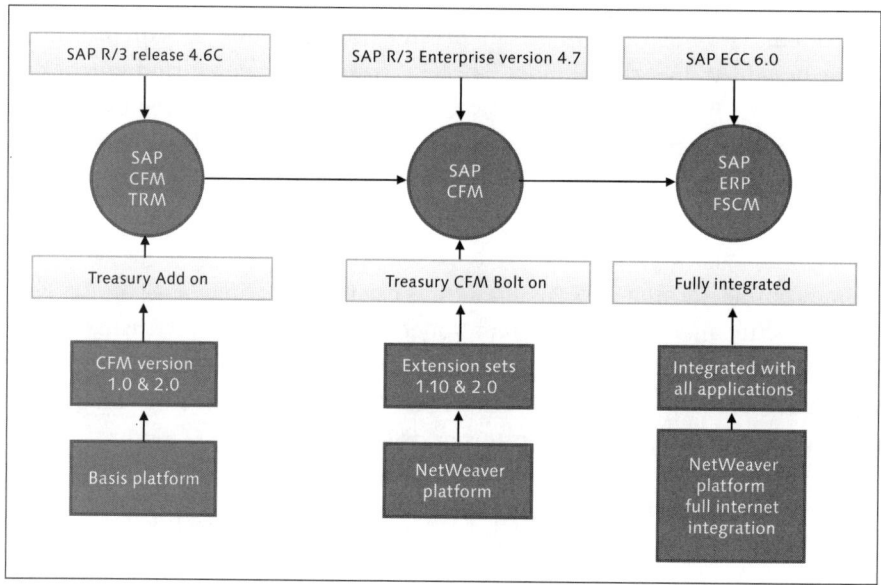

Figure 1.3 Evolution of the SAP Treasury Architecture

The SAP NetWeaver Platform and Treasury

When SAP introduced the NetWeaver platform with the SAP R/3 Enterprise version, it meant the inclusion of powerful tools, applications, and functionality for leveraging the Internet as a means of conducting business within and outside of the enterprise. This has had a significant impact on the development of treasury functionality within SAP. As new laws and accounting requirements such as SOX and FAS 133 came into being, there was a need for treasury to incorporate the ability to send and receive information between itself and banks, counterparties, market data providers, vendors and customers externally, and to leverage functionality such as workflow, increased security and controls internally. The NetWeaver platform in SAP ERP ECC 6.0 provides the tools and technologies to leverage the Internet (e.g. SAP Enterprise Portal), SAP NetWeaver Business Intelligence (SAP NetWeaver BI) (e.g. reporting, analysis), and SAP NetWeaver eXchange Infrastructure (SAP NetWeaver XI) for external communication, secure data transfer, and file transfer management. In this section, we will look at how SAP NetWeaver XI in particular can be used as a powerful tool for optimizing Treasury functionality in areas such as external communication, STP in electronic banking, and trading foreign exchange and securities transactions.

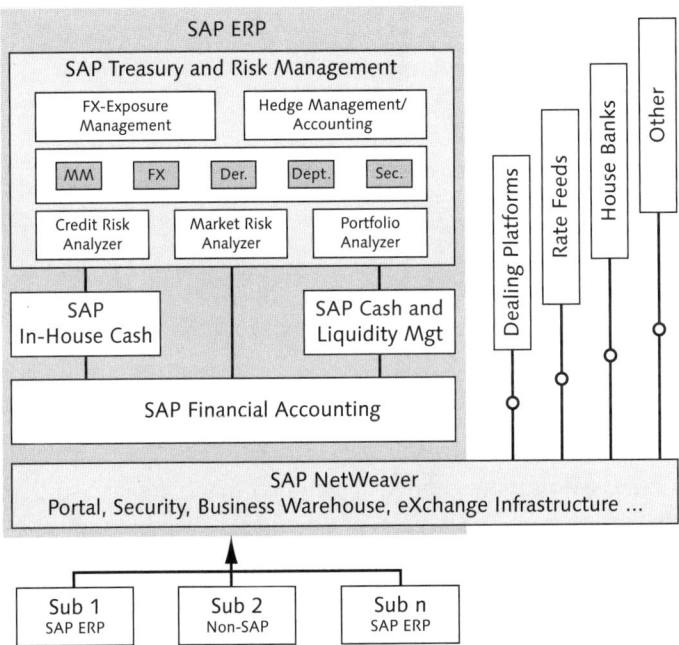

Figure 1.4 Treasury Integration in SAP ECC 6.0

Figure 1.4 provides an overview of how the SAP NetWeaver platform forms the basis for a myriad of functionality, with applications for file communication, interfacing with market data providers and banking partners, as well as applications for web-based functionality and reporting. The NetWeaver platform was introduced with SAP R/3 Enterprise version 4.7, and is the standard for all SAP ERP versions going forward.

Financial Supply Chain Management in SAP ERP ECC 6.0

With the release of SAP ERP Central Component version 6.0 (SAP ERP ECC 6.0), full integration between Treasury and rest of the functional modules was achieved. All of the key treasury-related components and functionality have been reorganized and placed under the application menu heading FINANCIAL SUPPLY CHAIN MANAGEMENT (FSCM), as shown in Figure 1.5. This book is based on Treasury functionality provided in SAP ERP ECC 6.0.

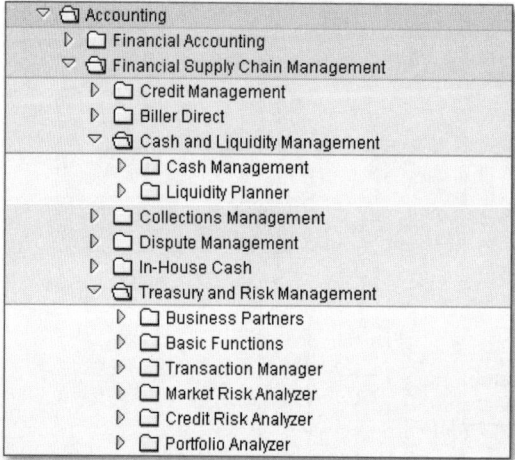

Figure 1.5 The Financial Supply Chain Menu in SAP ERP ECC 6.0

The menu options for transaction management have been made generic so that they apply to all financial transactions, regardless of whether they are money market, foreign exchange, security, or derivative transactions. Under the old Corporate Finance Management (CFM) menu, specific product types were provided in the menu path under their appropriate headings, such as money market, securities, and so on. As shown in Figure 1.6, the generic Transaction FTR_CREATE enables access to all transaction types.

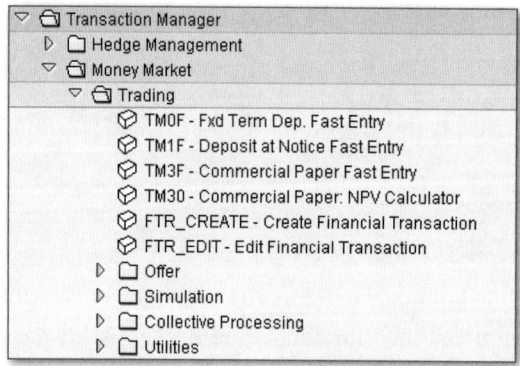

Figure 1.6 Transaction FTR_CREATE

Transaction FTR_CREATE is new and provides a flexible entry screen for any product type. Furthermore, it can be set up with a default value as shown in Figure 1.7. The selection of SECURITIES as the default financial transaction results in securities-specific options being available in the input fields.

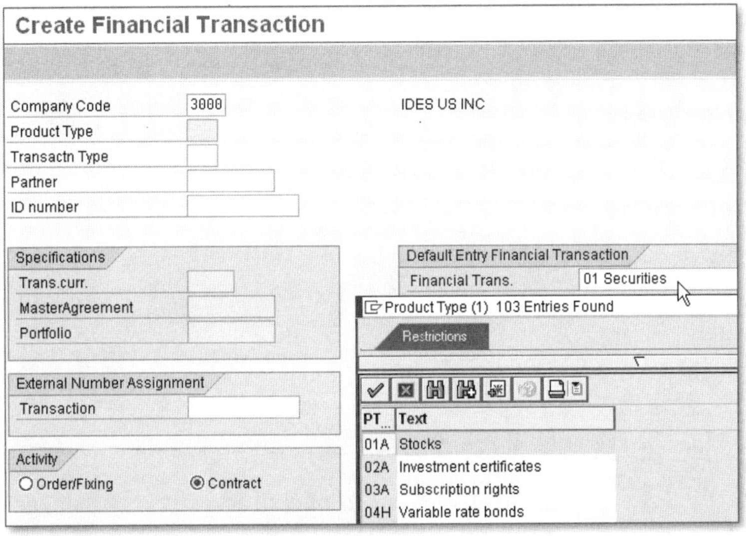

Figure 1.7 Generic Input Screen to Create a Financial Transaction

New to the FSCM menu is the DEBT MANAGEMENT tab under the TRANSACTION MANAGER menu item. Debt instruments can also be handled through the MONEY MARKET and SECURITIES menu areas, this additional option consolidates all debt-related products, master data, reports, and activities. That multiple different ways to access functionality exist is common to SAP ERP menu options, and the menu options are often available through multiple menu paths.

The FSCM functionality can be grouped into three areas, which in turn contain key areas of Treasury functionality, as follows:

- **Cash and liquidity management**
  - Cash positioning
  - Cash and liquidity planning and forecasting
  - Inbound and outbound electronic banking
  - In-house cash management
  - Payment processing

- **Financial risk management**
  - Investment and debt management
  - Foreign exchange management
  - Derivatives
  - FAS 133 compliance and hedge accounting
  - Payment processing
  - Exposure management
  - Limit management and compliance
  - Market data management
- **Credit risk management**
  - Credit Management
  - Biller Direct
  - Collections Management
  - Dispute Management

In the chapters that follow, we will cover key aspects of cash and liquidity management as well as financial risk management in terms of functionality and controls. Credit management is outside of the scope of this book and will not be covered.

1.5.3 SAP ERP Cash Management

All of the benefits of an ERP system would be of little use if the system could not provide the same functionality as the standalone workstations built specifically for treasury functions. SAP ERP provides most of that functionality, and it is also continuously being improved. In addition, new functionality is built and implemented through upgrades and version releases. We will now provide you with an overview of this functionality, which will be explained in further detail in subsequent chapters.

Inbound and Outbound Electronic Banking

As we had previously mentioned, although a lot of electronic banking functionality in SAP ERP exists in the Financial Accounting component, it is one of the most underutilized areas because of a lack of understanding of the wide range of features available within SAP ERP.

Electronic banking in SAP is feature-rich and lets you automate end-to-end processes relating to inbound and outbound banking. Because of the strong integration between Treasury and the other SAP ERP components, this automation can be extended throughout the financial supply chain in Procure to Pay, Order to Cash, and other enterprise-wide processes. This also lets you build strong systemic and user-defined internal control features throughout each process.

SAP provides full end-to-end functionality for polling daily electronic bank statements, positive payee processing, electronic funds transfers, and lockbox processing, with full integration internally as well as with the external banking environment. An overview of this functionality is provided in Figure 1.8.

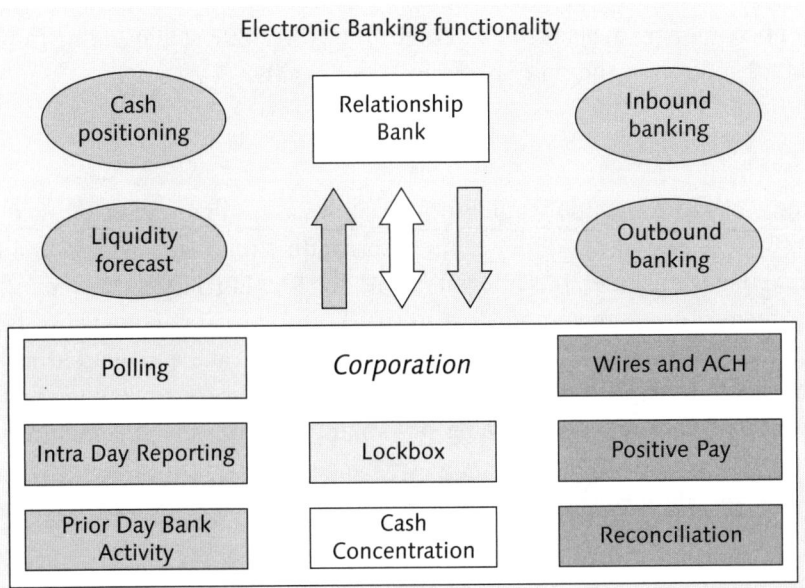

Figure 1.8 Electronic Banking Functionality in SAP ERP

Cash Management and Liquidity Forecasting

Cash management and liquidity forecasting provides the ability to bring together all cash-relevant information available in the system, as well as intraday banking information, to enable flexible reporting in a real-time mode for the following purposes:

- Daily cash positioning to determine borrowing or investment requirements in the immediate term.

- Medium to longer term cash and liquidity forecasting.
- Cash concentration and controlled disbursement requirements determination.
- Inter-group and intra-company transfers.

Liquidity Planner

The Liquidity Planner integrates planning functionality that uses both plan and actual data to provide dynamic views through the SAP ERP system as well as through its Business Warehouse (BW) reporting component. It extends standard cash management and liquidity forecasting functionality to enable greater visibility of transactions being posted to the books of account and to utilize that information as a basis for building projected liquidity plans. It replaces the Cash Budget Management component available in older releases of SAP ERP, while adding fully integrated cross-enterprise liquidity planning functionality.

In-House Cash

The In-House Cash (IHC) component lets organizations act as their own banker for internal group transactions, and allows them to conduct internal business in an efficient and effective manner. It is integrated with the SAP ERP Financial Accounting and payment processing components so that both internal payments can be simulated if desired. Similarly, payments to external parties can be made centrally or on behalf of group subsidiaries. This functionality provides strong ROI because of the opportunity to reduce the number of banking relationships, banking fees and commissions, and losses due to foreign exchange currency conversion. Additionally, it lets you automate the entire intercompany accounting and transaction process.

Functionality within IHC is summarized as follows:

- Collect on Behalf
- 3rd Party Payment on Behalf
- 3rd Party Payment Optimization
- Internal Payments
- Internal Payment Optimization
- Netting

- Net Cash Settlements
- Cash Pooling

1.5.4 SAP ERP Financial Risk Management

Financial risk management functionality in SAP ERP provides treasury with the ability to manage contracts relating to investment, debt, and foreign exchange transactions.

Transaction Management

These transactions can be hedged using derivatives, and be accounted for and documented in compliance with the requirements of FAS 133. An overview of the key financial instruments and derivatives supported within SAP ERP is provided in Figure 1.9.

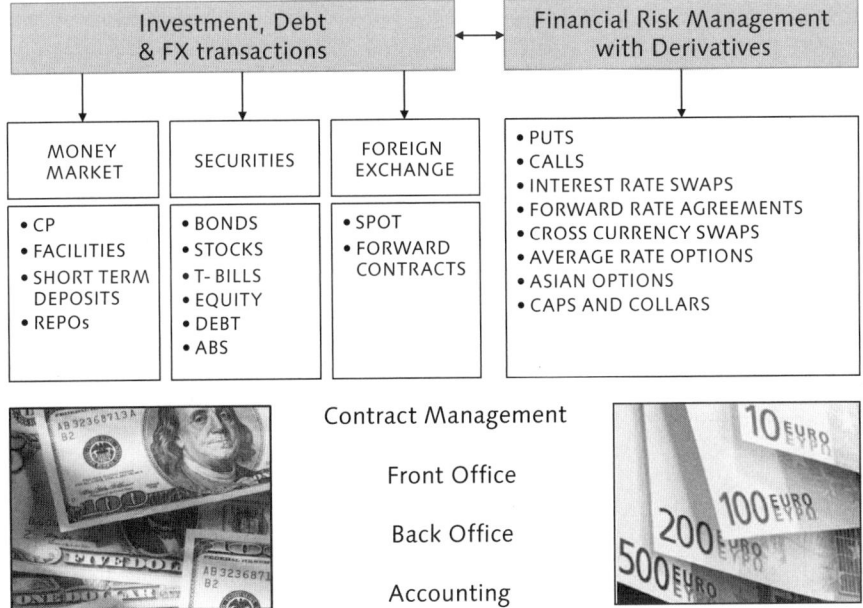

Figure 1.9 Treasury Management Functionality

The transaction management supply chain is split between front office, back office, and accounting, providing the tools and controls to be SOX complaint, especially with respect to SoD requirements. The various functions supported in the three areas are shown in Figure 1.10. All processes and functions are controlled through mechanisms such as release and authorization controls, which are built into key areas where they may be required. Additional examples of treasury controls — such as limit management or automatic payment block until released — are also available to further enhance controls relating to treasury management processes.

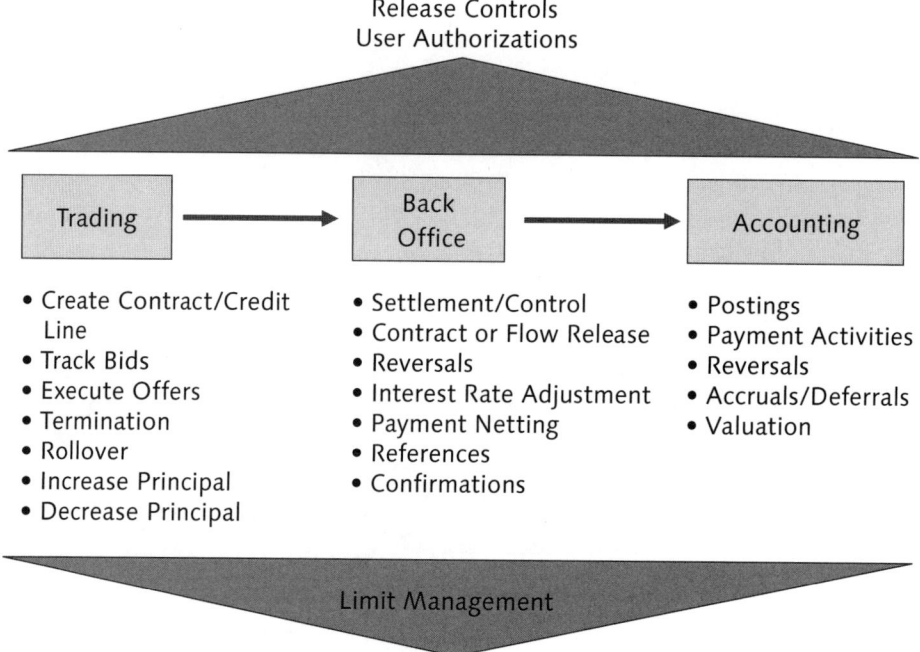

Figure 1.10 Transaction Management Functionality

Hedge Management

A key concern in foreign exchange management is the requirements for hedge management and hedge accounting under FAS 133. SAP ERP supports full compliance with these requirements. Although this functionality has been available since early releases of SAP's ERP software, only recently has the functionality been enhanced considerably. This is especially true since the introduction of the NetWeaver platform, which provides greater integration opportunities with market data providers and counterparties, as well as the ability to leverage the Internet as an efficient and secure means of user-friendly data access and communication. Different aspects of this functionality are illustrated in Figure 1.11.

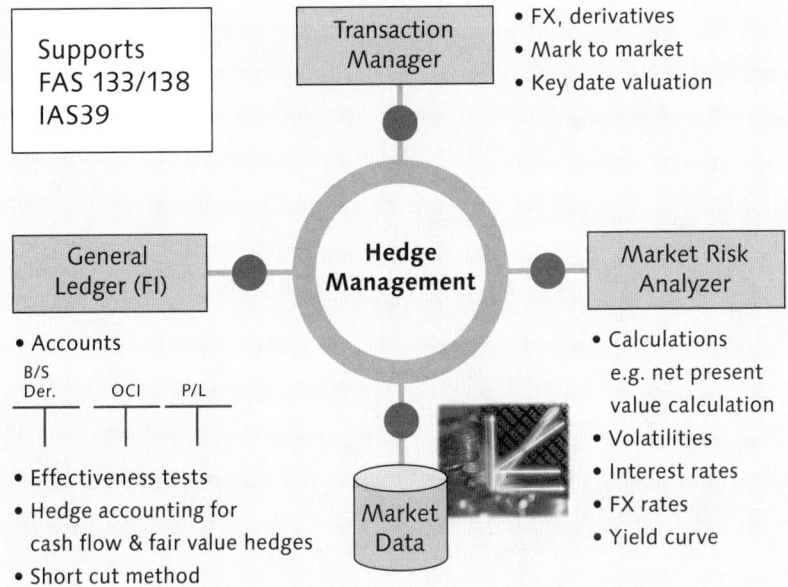

Figure 1.11 Hedge Management Functionality

Risk Analyzers

The FSCM suite includes three analyzer tools that support transaction management within SAP ERP. They all come with an abundance of optional features, but there is certain functionality within the market risk and credit risk analyzer components required for transaction management processing — for example, mark to market calculations and limit management tools. In this section, we will focus on these aspects of the analyzers.

Market Risk Analyzer

The Market Risk Analyzer provides the tools for the calculation of mark to market valuation, download of interest, foreign exchange and volatility rates, and Value at Risk (VAR) analysis, just to name a few. SAP ERP uses discounted cash flow in conjunction with yield curve information to calculate mark to market valuations. It also provides the tools to automatically import and populate SAP ERP with daily market data that is used by the system to execute daily transactions within FSCM. A sample of the menu options available for the MARKET RISK ANALYZER is provided in Figure 1.12.

1 | Business and Functional Overview

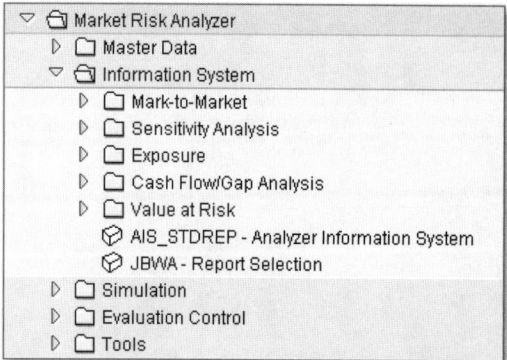

Figure 1.12 Market Risk Analyzer Menu Options

Credit Risk Analyzer

The Credit Risk Analyzer provides limit and risk exposure management capability in the execution of securities purchases and redemptions. This allows corporations to keep within their investment guidelines as set out by its board of directors or investment committee. A sample of the menu options for the CREDIT RISK ANALYZER is provided in Figure 1.13.

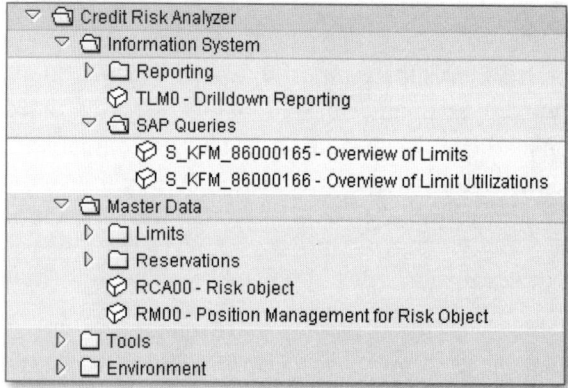

Figure 1.13 Credit Risk Analyzer Menu Option

Options for limit management are available through the credit risk analyzer, and can be based on single or multiple criteria for managing limits, as shown in Figure 1.14. For example, a dollar limit can be established by transaction type for a specific trader, and controlled through limit management and authorization checks.

46

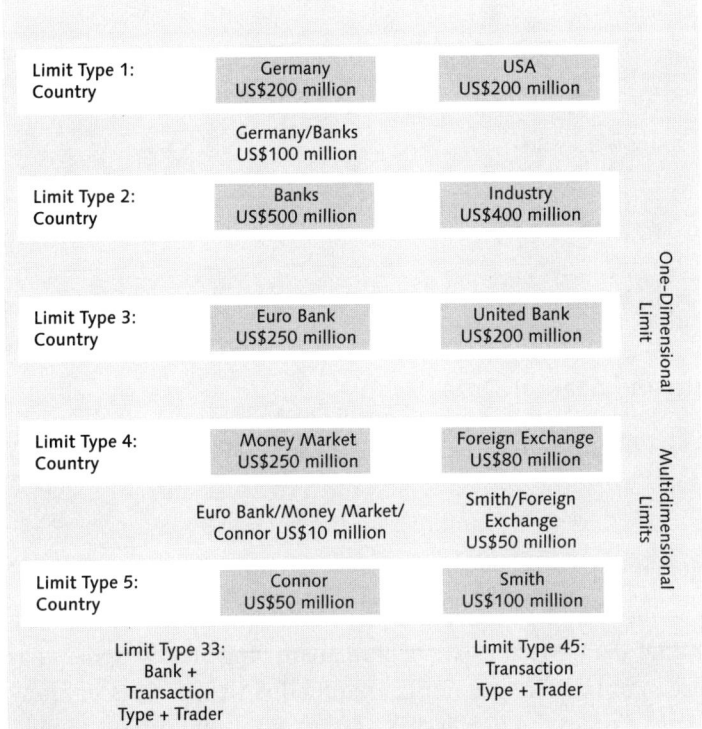

Figure 1.14 Combination Criteria for Limit Management

Portfolio Analyzer

The Portfolio Analyzer provides the tools to calculate the performance of a corporation's investments through benchmarking, analysis of sectors, yield curves, interest rate spreads, and maintenance of a yield book to compare such performance with pre-defined benchmarking indicators and attribution analysis. The list below provides a summary of the more useful features of the Portfolio Risk Analyzer:

- Measure ROI
- Benchmarking
- Actual vs target performance measurement
- Attribution of performance
- Evaluations based on portfolio structure
- Grouping of investments into different categories

A sample of the menu options for the PORTFOLIO ANALYZER is provided in Figure 1.15.

1 | Business and Functional Overview

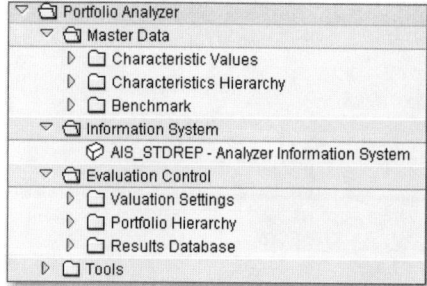

Figure 1.15 Portfolio Analyzer Menu Option

1.5.5 Master Data and Market Data

Master data refers to an organization's foundation data that typically is set up only once.

Master Data Management

Vendors, customers, house banks, bank accounts, or counterparties, and so on typically comprise master data. Master data is permanent, and is only updated as changes to the data occur, or when it is no longer required. SAP ERP accesses many different types of master data in the processing of transactions within its components and functions. Figure 1.16 provides a comparison between master data and transactional data as it is used in SAP ERP.

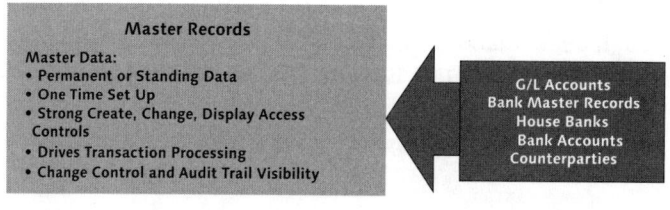

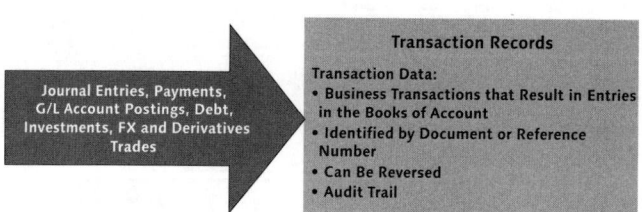

Figure 1.16 Master Data Compared to Transaction Data

48

SAP ERP uses a special type of master data called business partner (BP). This is of particular importance and relevance in treasury management processing in SAP ERP. A BP master data record is created and can be assigned different roles, for example vendor, creditor, counterparty, or depositary bank. Although general data is common, the assignment of specific roles provides tabular screens required for that particular role, as shown in Figure 1.18. Typical treasury roles are issuer, counterparty, depositary bank, paying bank, and treasury partner.

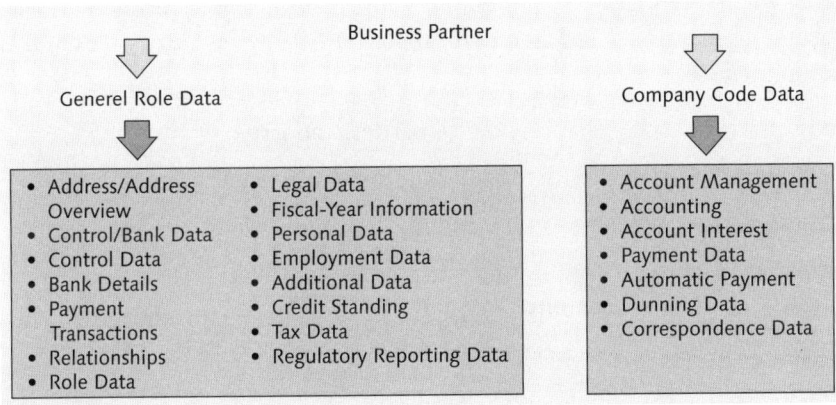

Figure 1.17 Business Partner Master Data Views

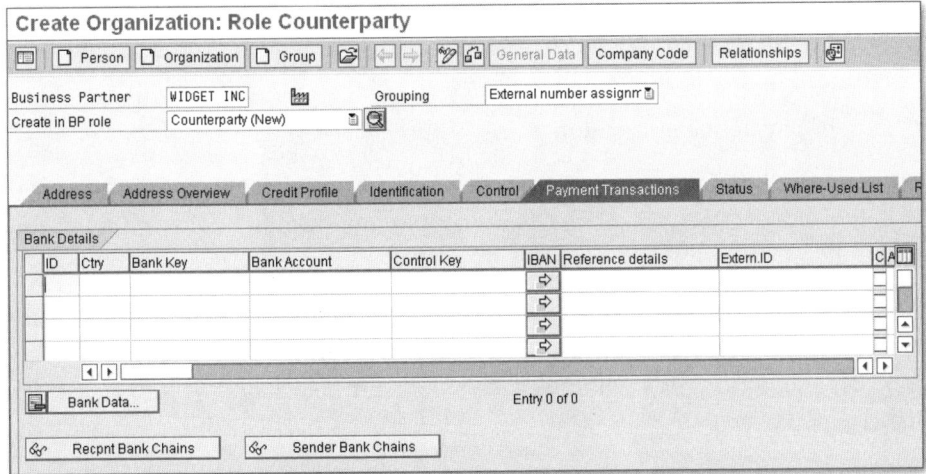

Figure 1.18 Business Partner in Role Counterparty

Controls for the creation, update, and maintenance of master data maintenance are of critical importance as you will see in later chapters. We will look at BPs in detail in the chapter on financial risk management, Chapter 7.

Market Data

We have looked at the importance of integration not only within the enterprise, but outside of the enterprise as well. This is of particular importance for treasury operations, which are highly dependent on daily, real-time feeds of market data, in the form of transactional and (sometimes) master data as well. Examples of this information include:

- Business partners such as banks, counterparties, and issuers
- Bank account master data with SWIFT code and bank key information
- Securities class, securities accounts, and CUSIP numbers with relevant security information
- House banks and bank accounts
- Exchange rates
- Volatilities
- Interest rates and yield curve information
- Security prices
- Ratings information
- Financial information
- Deal or payment confirmation

The external interfaces with these various market data providers can be set up through SAP NetWeaver XI for two-way communication, both inbound and outbound.

Although direct trading through SAP ERP by linking directly to FX and securities markets is not prevalent, the SAP NetWeaver platform provides all of the tools for this functionality. We will look at this model in the chapters on financial risk management.

1.5.6 Key Drivers and Benefits

The key drivers for decision-making with respect to the choice of treasury systems revolve around efficiency and automation, integration, controls and compliance, and decision support. The benefits with respect to each of these drivers are summarized in Figure 1.19 for electronic banking and cash management, and in Figure 1.20 for financial risk management.

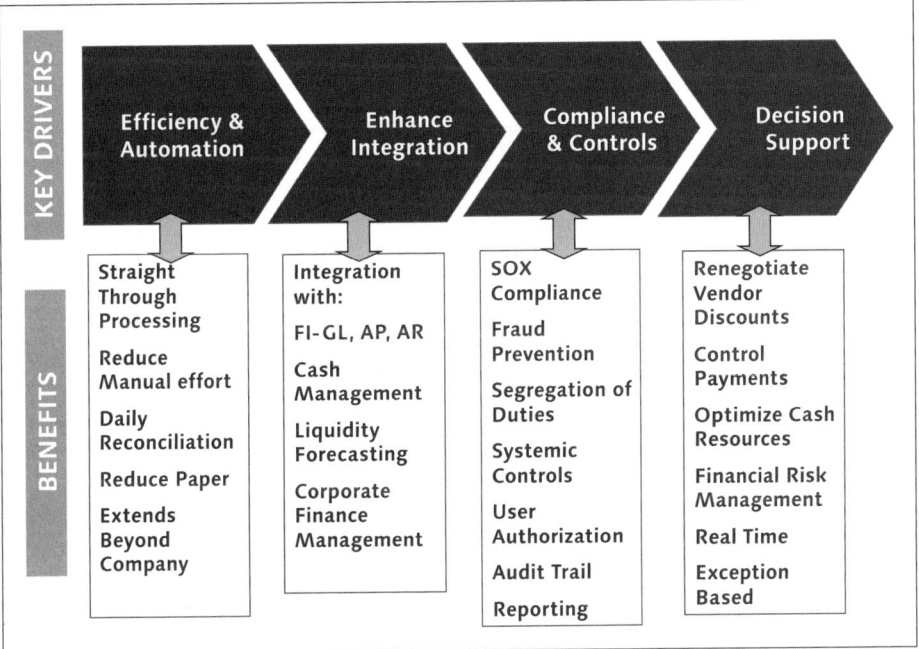

Figure 1.19 Electronic Banking and Cash Management Drivers and Benefits

> **Note**
>
> Cost/benefit analysis plays a very important role in the decision to move to an enterprise system such as SAP ERP. After the move to an ERP-based treasury system has been made, a continuous improvement process is necessary to leverage the benefits and bring down the total cost of ownership (TCO) over time. For example, the introduction of ACH electronic payments to vendors (replacing check payments) will result in a reduction of cash float for many organizations. However, this should also provide an opportunity to renegotiate vendor discount terms to offset the loss of float time. The certainty of receiving their payments on time electronically is a big driver from the vendors' point of view, who can also plan their cash requirements.

1 | Business and Functional Overview

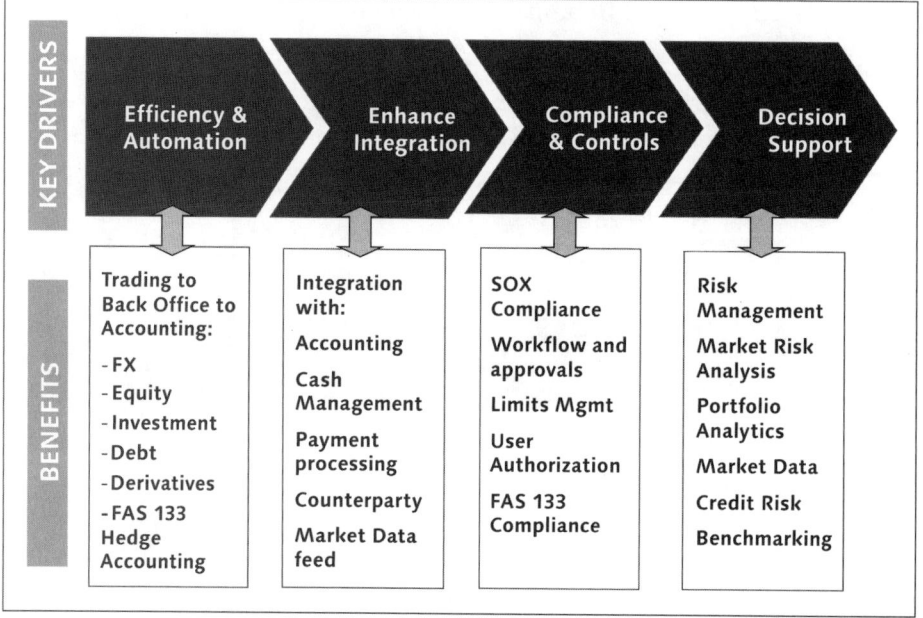

Figure 1.20 Financial Risk Management Drivers and Benefits

1.5.7 The Bottom Line

ERP systems are expensive, complex, and difficult to implement. From a treasury perspective, when one is used to standalone or customized tools that focus on one specific functionality, it is not surprising that there is reluctance to switch to an ERP treasury system. There is also no question that the ROI from an investment in an ERP system will accrue not in the immediate or short term, but in the medium to long term. It is only over time, as the organization and systems mature and the learning curve decreases, that the real benefits of an integrated global system will be realized.

Ultimately, every treasury organization will have to make the decision of which path to choose based on their individual department requirements, or more often on overall corporate strategy and direction. We hope that this book will provide the tools and information to organizations to make that decision, in the overall context of the controls and business processes that drive daily treasury business operations and management.

Overall, the SAP Treasury components provide most of the standalone workstation functionality within an integrated environment. And although correct design and implementation are of utmost importance, the true benefits of an integrated ERP system such as SAP ERP will be realized over time.

1.6 Summary

This introductory chapter provided you with an overview of the need for integrated treasury functionality within an organization in the context of new challenges and responsibilities being placed on corporate treasury functions. We reviewed key functionality available within SAP Treasury to meet those challenges, and provided criteria for deciding what will be in the best interest of your organization. In Chapter 2, we will look at the control environment within SAP ERP that provides the backdrop to subsequent chapters on treasury business functionality within the SAP ERP system.

Chapter 2 provides an overview of key control concepts and control mechanisms used in SAP ERP.

2 Controls in SAP ERP

As we have seen in Chapter 1, the SOX Act lays down very specific requirements with respect to maintenance of good internal controls, identification of weaknesses in internal controls, fraud prevention, and the accuracy and integrity of the financial books of record. In designing good business processes and related internal controls, it is important to understand the nature of risks faced by corporations, which often operate in a global environment.

2.1 Control Framework and Objectives

What control frameworks can be used to mitigate such risks? How can an ERP system such as SAP ERP help to provide an environment that allows corporations to build appropriate control mechanisms as part of daily business and transaction processing performed by corporations? We will attempt to answer these questions as the chapter unfolds.

2.1.1 The Need for Controls

The need for strong internal controls in an organization has always been a significant factor in the way corporations have done business, and has impacted and influenced internal and external accounting and auditing practices. With the spate of corporate scandals and fraudulent financial reporting and practices that were revealed in the first few years of this millennium, a greater sense of urgency and importance has developed in the entire area of internal control and corporate governance in organizations.

Strong internal controls are necessary for the following reasons:

- Regulatory compliance with SOX and other related national and international requirements by governments, regulators, and standard-setting bodies.
- Prevention and detection of fraud and error.
- An increasingly complex global business environment that is dynamic and constantly changing.
- Rapid advances in information technology and the impact on business processes and transaction processing.
- Changes in corporate culture and governance.
- Increased responsibilty and accountability of corporate officers, boards of directors, and audit committees with respect to public financial records, reports, and statements.

2.1.2 Control Frameworks

As mentioned previously in Chapter 1, the two control frameworks most widely used for SOX compliance are COSO (for accounting and business process controls), and COBIT (for information technology systems and security controls).

Although SOX does not specifically address IT controls, IT systems are so entwined in supporting the complex business processes of most corporations that the COBIT framework is used extensively in supporting SOX compliance within a corporation. Control frameworks provide the guidelines and benchmarks that enable corporations to design adequate and appropriate internal control systems. They also enable standards and regulation-setting bodies such as the SEC, Public Company Accounting Oversight Board (PCOAB), American Institute of Certified Public Accountants (AICPA), and The Institute of Internal Auditors (IIA) in establishing generally accepted accounting and auditing standards, as well as regulatory and statutory requirements.

The COSO Control Framework

COSO was originally formed with the primary objective of identifying factors that cause fraudulent financial reporting, and to make recommendations to reduce its incidence. COSO has established a common definition of internal controls, standards, and criteria against which companies and organizations can assess their control systems.

The COSO framework defines internal control as a process, put into effect by an entity's board of directors, management and other personnel, and designed to provide reasonable assurance regarding the achievement of objectives in the following categories:

- Effectiveness and efficiency of operations.
- Reliability of financial reporting.
- Compliance with applicable laws and regulations.

According to the COSO framework, internal control consists of five interrelated components. These components provide an effective framework for describing and analyzing the internal control system implemented in an organization. They are as follows:

- **Control environment**
  The control environment sets the tone of an organization, influencing the control consciousness of its people. It is the foundation for all other components of internal control, providing discipline and structure. Control environment factors include the integrity, ethical values, management's operating style, delegation of authority systems, and the processes for managing and developing people in the organization.

- **Risk assessment**
  Every entity faces a variety of risks from external and internal sources that must be assessed. A precondition to risk assessment is establishment of objectives, and thus, risk assessment is the identification and analysis of relevant risks to the achievement of assigned objectives. Risk assessment is a prerequisite for determining how risks should be managed.

- **Control activities**
  Control activities are the policies and procedures that help ensure that management directives are carried out, and that the necessary actions are taken to address risks to the achievement of the entity's objectives. Control activities occur throughout the organization, at all levels, and in all functions. They include a range of activities as diverse as approvals, authorizations, verifications, reconciliations, reviews of operating performance, security of assets, and SoD.
  The following are key types of control activities and their objectives:

- **Preventative**
  Focus on preventing errors or exceptions, and are implemeted using appropriate policies and procedures, approvals and authorizations, security access controls, and SoD.

- **Detective**
  Designed to identify errors and exceptions after they have occurred. These can be identified through audit trails, reconciliations, exception reporting, change controls, and internal and external audit reviews.

- **Manual**
  Made possible through instituting procedures that require physical intervention by a person or persons. These can provide a very flexibile and effective control environment, but can be bypassed due to error or intentionally.

- **Automated or systemic**
  Provided through information technology. They are highly reliable and consistent. If they are not designed, implemented and monitored properly, they could also be consistently wrong.

▶ **Information and communication**
Information systems play a key role in internal control systems because they produce reports, including operational, financial, and compliance-related information that make it possible to run and control the business. In a broader sense, effective communication must ensure information flows down, across, and up the organization. Effective communication should also be ensured with external parties, such as customers, suppliers, regulators, and shareholders.

▶ **Monitoring**
Internal control systems need to be monitored--a process that assesses the quality of the system's performance over time. This is accomplished through ongoing monitoring activities or separate evaluations. Internal control deficiencies detected through these monitoring activities should be reported upstream and corrective actions should be taken to ensure continuous improvement of the system.

2.1.3 COBIT and Information Technology Systems

COSO deals primarily with accounting and business process controls, and does not provide guidance on information technology systems, although it is included as one of the five components within the information and communication objective.

For most organizations to comply with the requirements of information technology systems controls, the COBIT framework is used.

The COBIT framework is a set of best practices for information technology management created by ISACA and ITGI in 1992. It provides managers, auditors, and IT users with a set of generally-accepted measures, indicators, processes, and best practices to assist in maximizing the benefits derived through the use of information technology and in developing appropriate IT governance and control in a company.

In this and in subsequent chapters we will use both of the discussed frameworks in the context of treasury business applications in SAP ERP.

In the next section, we will discuss the role of risk in the determination of internal controls.

2.2 Risk and Internal Control

2.2.1 Risk/Control Matrix

The assessment, evaluation, or development of a control must be based on the risk exposure to a corporation of a particular business process or activity. This assessment is often made through the development of a risk/control matrix. Both the SEC and PCOAB have encouraged a top-down risk-based approach for the evaluation of the internal control environment in an organization. We will be looking at key treasury business processes in SAP ERP to enable the development of risk/control matrices for each key activity and process.

2.2.2 Types of Risks

Companies are exposed to a wide range of risks inherent in the normal course of business operations that could have an impact on treasury business processes. These can be summarized as follows:

- Changes in the operating environment due to growth, mergers and acquisitions, divestments, and scope of operations.
- Changes in personnel, policies, business processes, and internal re-organizations and corporate re-structuring.
- Implementation of new information technology systems.

In assessing risk, it is important to first identify the risk, then estimate its impact and materiality, and finally to assess its probability of occurrence.

2.2.3 Treasury-Specific Risks

Treasury departments face a variety of risks in their day-to-day business through the specialized nature of their function, as well as through their increasing integration with other functions within the organization, especially finance, accounts payable, and accounts receivable.

Examples of key risks specific to treasury applications for companies, either in an enterprise-wide integrated or a manual or stand alone system environment, are as follows:

- **SoD**
  Appropriate SoD between front and back office and key handoffs between functional groups. SoD is one of the most important and critical controls from a SOX compliance perspective. It is of particular relevance in an integrated system such as SAP ERP, where users will have access to common functionality across the enterprise. For example, in payment processing, vendor payments are typically made by the accounts payable department, whereas high value treasury wire payments are made by the treasury department.

- **Authorizations and approvals**
  Treasury departments are usually responsible for executing high value, low volume wire payments that may require special authorizations, often at the highest levels of the organization.

- **Integration with other functions**
  In a standalone treasury environment, treasury transactions will need to be reinput into the books of record. Thus, there will need to be additional reconciliation and checks and balances to ensure the integrity of the books of account.

- **Electronic banking**
  With increasing opportunity for both inbound and outbound electronic banking, organizations are trying to fully automate their banking processes and integrate them with their financial system of record. With increasing STP of transactions, a need exists for automatic or systemic controls and exception-based error processing.

- **External treasury and banking relationships**
  Treasury is responsible for maintaining relationships with diverse treasury partners such as banks, brokerage houses, market data providers, loan providers, investment portfolio custodians, just to name a few. It is important to ensure that all relationships and operating procedures are authorized, documented, and updated regularly.

- **Need for up-to-date real-time information**
  Treasury operations are dynamic in nature, requiring real-time up-to-date information for many activities such as, for example, cash positioning, investment, borrowing, foreign exchange and interest rate risk management, and market rates.

- **Intercompany transactions**
  Intercompany transactions are usually executed by treasury through funds transfer.

- **Treasury technology**
  The specialised nature of treasury operations has resulted in many different systems technology offerings, each with specialized functions. This poses a challenge in terms of technology integration, and input and reconciliation with the prime books of record.

2.3 Control Mechanisms in SAP ERP

For all of its functionality, SAP ERP is essentially an accounting system and the prime book of record for all of an organization's transactions. The focus of the SOX Act also leads to the books of financial record. To enable compliance with SOX requirements, SAP ERP includes many forms of control in the system. In this section, we will discuss the main control features and how they are used. These will be revisited later in the book as we look in detail at the individual treasury business processes, and how these controls can be used to ensure compliance with SOX, audit, and other regulatory requirements.

SAP ERP includes four key control mechanisms, as follows:

- Systemic or built-in controls
- Configurable controls
- Programmable controls
- Manual controls

Any or all of these mechanisms in combination can be used within a business process to mitigate risks and meet control objectives as identified in the risk control matrix for that process. We will now discuss each of these mechanisms in detail, along with the key related controls available in SAP ERP and examples of where they can be of relevance for treasury business processes. The controls can be preventative or detective in nature. They can be further classified into financial- or information technology-related controls. These classifications are helpful when building a risk/control matrix, as discussed further in Section 2.5, Risk/Control Matrix.

2.3.1 Architectural Elements of Control in SAP ERP

From a controls as well as a functional perspective, it is important to understand how the SAP ERP system processes data. All information that enters the system is stored in tables because it is a table-driven database system. All functionality is provided through program code, and users can run the corresponding programs by either executing an associated transaction code, or by executing the program directly.

Transaction Codes

A transaction code is a shortcut to access a particular program. Transaction codes can be standard (i.e. delivered in the system), or user specific (i.e. tied to a custom program or requirement). The transaction code is fundamental to the authorization concept and security access that will be discussed further in Section 2.3.2, Authorization Concept.

For example, SoD can be achieved by restricting user access to certain functions, which is in turn achieved by restricting access to the underlying transaction driving those functions.

Transaction codes can be used to execute specific functionality through a selection screen, program, configuration settings, or report. They usually are four-digit alphanumeric characters, but can sometimes be very long, especially when they are report-driven. A transaction code can be executed in the input screen in the top left-hand corner of the SAP ERP screen, as shown in Figure 2.1, where executing Transaction code FF7A brings up the selection screen for a cash management report.

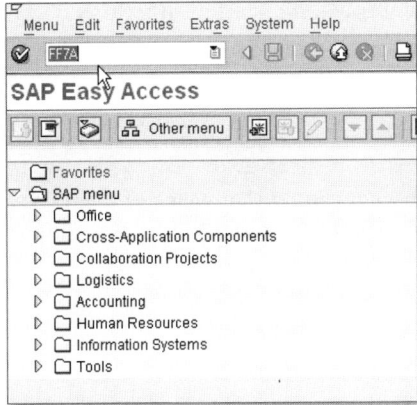

Figure 2.1 Executing a Program with a Transaction Code

The resulting screen for accessing the cash management report is shown in Figure 2.2.

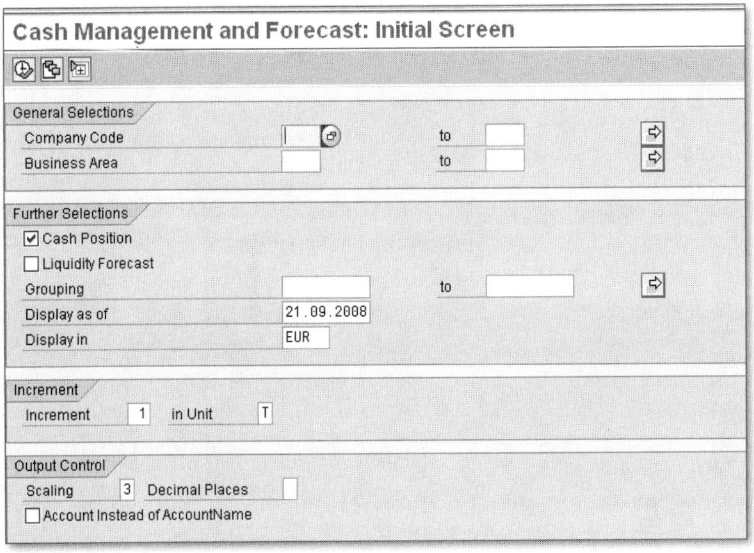

Figure 2.2 Report Screen for Transaction FF7A

Table-Driven Data

All transactional and master data is stored in tables. These may be temporary or permanent, and they can be linked together through common key index key fields.

This structure enables the powerful integration between different functions that is at the core of the SAP ERP system. Data within a table can be viewed using Transaction SE16 or SE16N.

> **Note: Transaction Codes with "N" Attached**
>
> Newer versions of transaction codes sometimes have the letter N attached to them. For example Transaction FEBAN is the updated version of old Transaction FEBA that allows post-processing of incoming electronic bank statements.

To view the contents of Table T012K, which contains house bank information, execute Transaction SE16N. This calls the table input parameters screen, as shown in Figure 2.3.

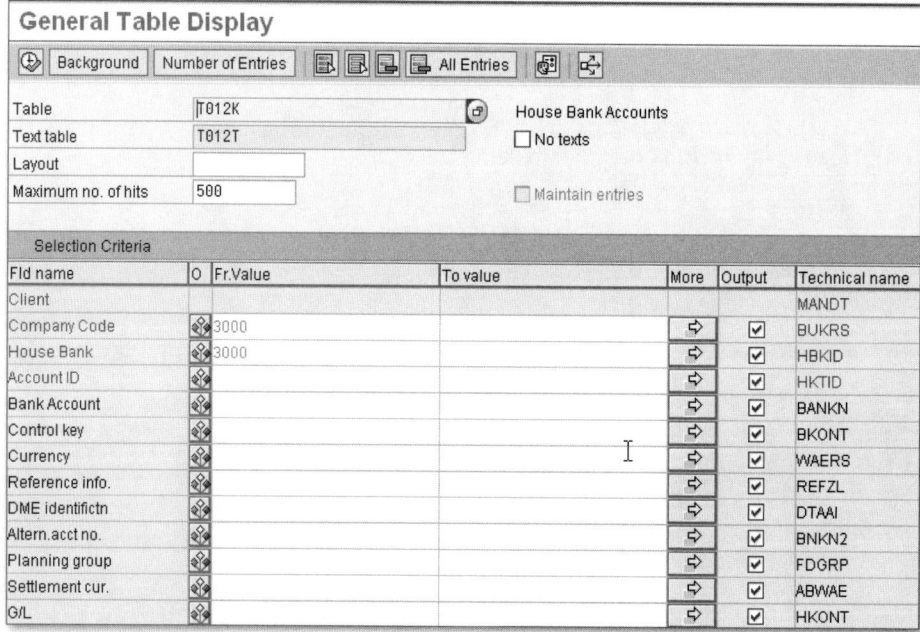

Figure 2.3 Table Input Parameter Screen Accessed Using Transaction SE16N

To view the contents of Table T012K, enter the table name in the TABLE field and identify any specific selection criteria by field name. In this case COMPANY CODE and HOUSE BANK have been selected. On execution, the resulting table entries are displayed, as shown in Figure 2.4.

Control Mechanisms in SAP ERP | 2.3

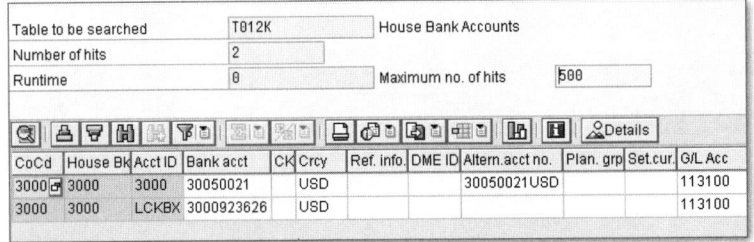

Figure 2.4 Detailed Table Entries for Table T012K

In SAP ERP, field names that comprise tables are identified by a combination of table name and field name, joined by a hyphen. For example, the field name for Company Code is BUKRS, and is identified in Table T012K as T012K-BUKRS.

Programs and User Exits

Transactions call SAP ERP programs that execute and provide the desired functionality. Programs can also be run using Transaction SE38, which allows a user to run the program in foreground or online mode, or as a background job that runs immediately or is scheduled for a particular time. For example, to execute the function for uploading electronic bank statements, enter Transaction SE38, then enter "RFEBKA00" in the PROGRAM field, and execute as shown in Figure 2.5.

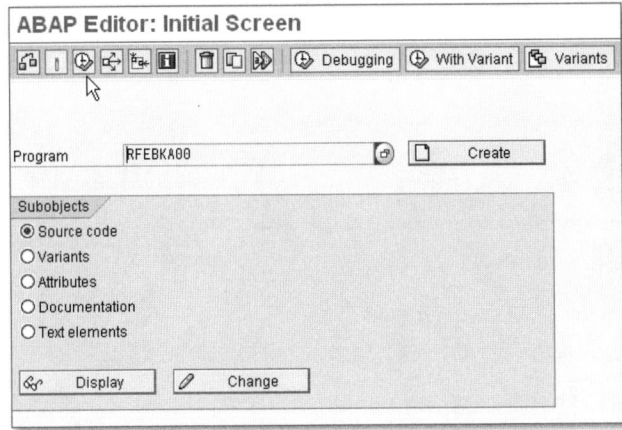

Figure 2.5 Executing a Program Using Transaction SE38

The resulting selection screen is shown in Figure 2.6.

65

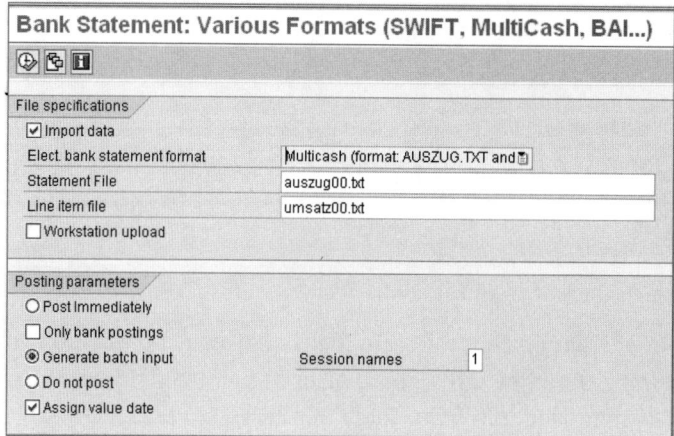

Figure 2.6 Selection Screen for Program RFEBKA00

Transaction SE38 also lets you view the program source code or documentation relating to the program. For example, to view documentation for program RFFOUS_T (U.S. ACH payment format), the documentation can be retrieved as shown in Figure 2.7.

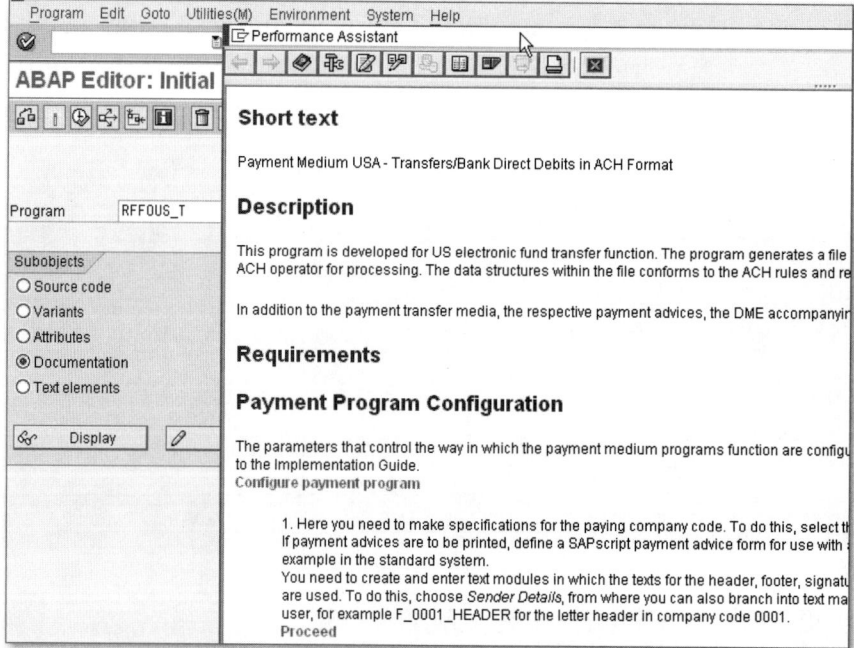

Figure 2.7 Documentation for Program RFFOUS_T

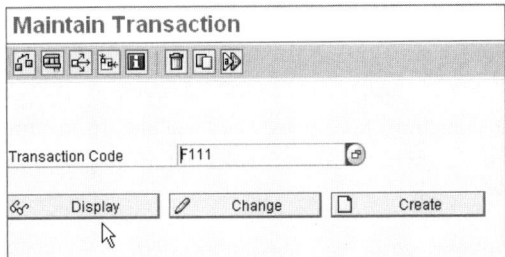

Figure 2.8 Viewing Transaction Details Using Transaction SE93

A useful method to determine what program lies behind a particular transaction code and that also provides a dashboard of functions relating to the program is Transaction SE93. For example, to obtain details about Transaction F111 (the treasury payment program), execute Transaction SE93, and enter "F111" in the MAINTAIN TRANSACTION input screen, as shown in Figure 2.8.

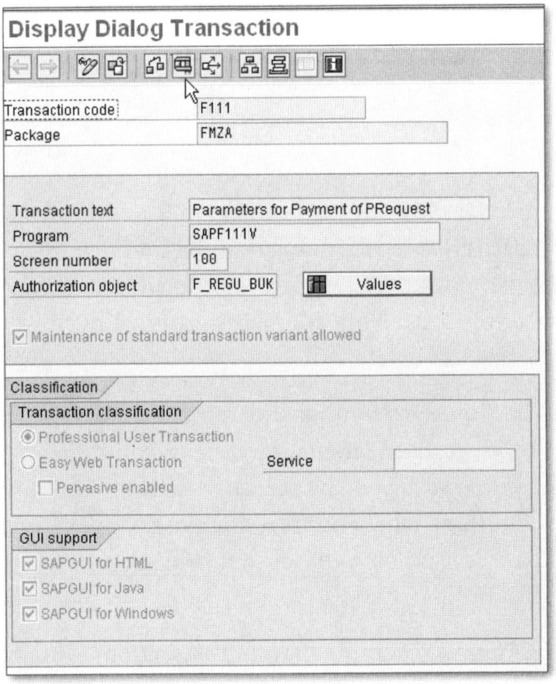

Figure 2.9 Report Screen Showing Transaction F111 Details

The resulting screen provides many details with respect to the transaction, as shown in Figure 2.9. Along with a description of the transaction itself, it provides information on the underlying program. Double-clicking on the program name will drill down into the actual program code. Running the test indicator, which is located where the cursor is pointing in Figure 2.9, executes the transaction. It also contains information relating to authorization objects it uses, a critical component of control in SAP ERP. We will discuss authorization objects in detail in the next section, Section 2.3.2, Authorization Concept.

Along with standard programs, SAP ERP contains user exits. These allow users to include custom code to tailor a program to specific requirements. SAP does not recommend, however, that original programs be changed. Instead, they provide various methods that enable organizations to enhance the existing functionality. Where specific function modules or user exits are not available, SAP recommends that a custom version of the original program be created by copying the original and renaming it using the letter Z before the program name, and then amending the program code as required.

On account of the very specialized nature of treasury operations, customization is carried out in many areas of SAP ERP to better represent the organization's business requirements.

2.3.2 Authorization Concept

The authorization control mechanism in SAP ERP is fundamental to almost all aspects of controlled access to transaction and program execution and data management in SAP ERP. It is a crucial component of the governance, risk, and compliance (GRC) requirements to ensure proper SoD and access control over key information assets.

The authorization concept in SAP ERP protects transactions, programs, data, and services from any unauthorized access. Authorizations are usually controlled by the team responsible for SAP ERP system security. The security team (or administrator) assigns authorizations that determine which transactions a user can execute in the SAP ERP system, after they have logged on to the system and authenticated their identity via a legitimate user ID and password.

The authorization concept in SAP ERP uses a combination of transactions, authorization objects, and authorization values to control access to transactions. These can then be assigned to users through single and composite roles and profiles that make it easier for the security team or administer to implement. Authorizations can be designed based on an organization's business processes and functions. In this way, authorizations are essential tools to implement appropriate SoD within and between functions and business processes.

Authorization Check

An *authorization check* refers to the process of validating a user with respect to a particular transaction, and is described later using Transaction FF.6 (create, change, or display electronic or manual bank statement in a company code) as an example. The mechanism through which an authorization check is made is called an *authorization object*.

Authorization Object

Tables USOBT and USOBX contain the authorization objects related to transactions, and can be viewed using Transaction SE16N, as shown in Figure 2.10.

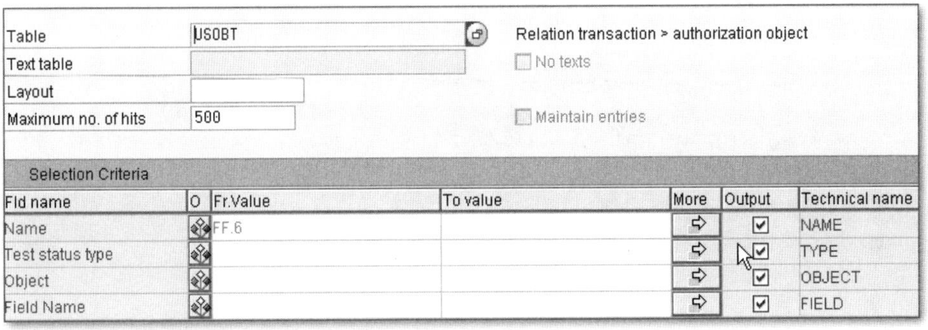

Figure 2.10 Viewing Authorization Objects Through Table USOBT

The resulting table entries, shown in Figure 2.11, specify that Transaction FF.6 uses authorization object F_FEBB_BUK (company code bank account statement). The object consists of the activity and company code fields (field names ACTVT and BUKRS).

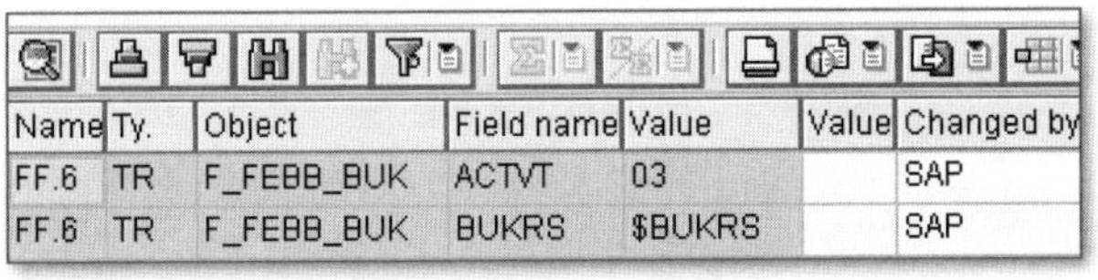

Name	Ty.	Object	Field name	Value	Value	Changed by
FF.6	TR	F_FEBB_BUK	ACTVT	03		SAP
FF.6	TR	F_FEBB_BUK	BUKRS	$BUKRS		SAP

Figure 2.11 Authorization Objects for Transaction FF.6

Object F_FEBB_BUK controls authorizations to maintain bank statements in a company code. The activity field controls the list of possible values that specify whether a user can create (01), change (02), or display (03) the bank statement within a company code.

> **Note**
>
> Security setup using the authorization concept is a technical implementation, and is usually administered by the SAP Basis security team. However, from a functional treasury perspective, it is important to understand how the authorization concept can be used to build effective controls. More important, it is treasury management and users who will need to provide the key inputs into the design of the authorization system through defining roles, activities, transactions, and processes that treasury users will need to conduct their daily business operations.

The authorization object is inserted in the program that runs when the transaction is executed, as shown in Figure 2.12. It is a powerful systemic programmable control.

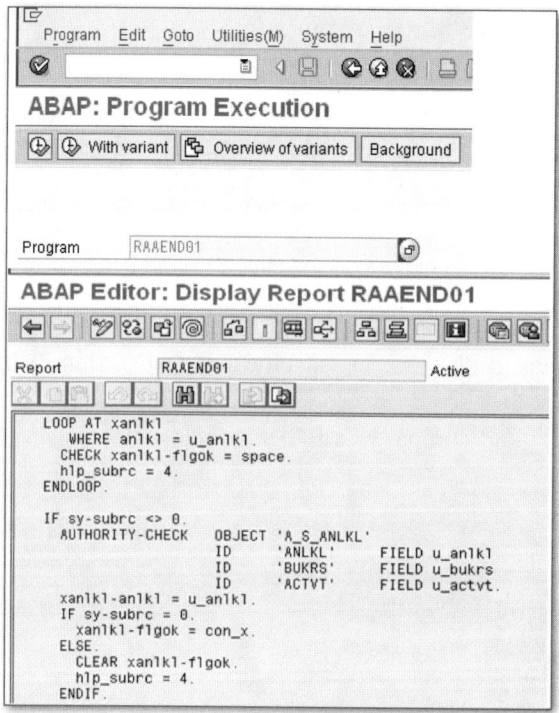

Figure 2.12 Authorization Check Within a Program

The user executing the transaction will be subject to the authorization check when the underlying program executes.

Table TOBJ provides details with respect to fields that are active for a particular authorization object, as shown in Figure 2.13.

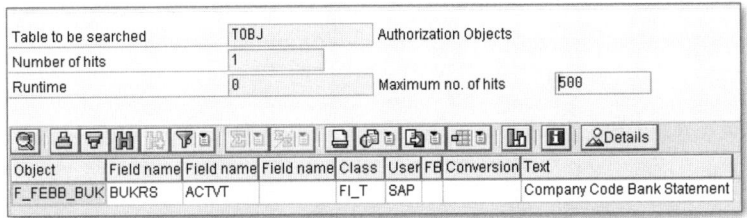

Figure 2.13 Field Names Active for Authorization Object F_FEBB_BUK

Activities

Activities (field name ACTVT) control the actions a user is allowed to perform and is linked to the authorization object. Table TACT contains the list of activities available for use in the system. A sample of available activities is shown in Figure 2.14.

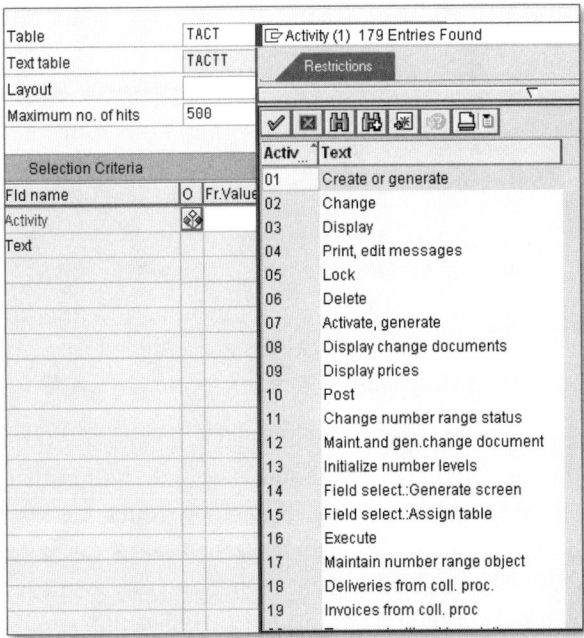

Figure 2.14 Available Activities for Controlling User Actions in the System

Authorization Group

An authorization group allows extended authorization protection for particular objects, such as access to master data. Figure 2.15 provides an example of how an authorization group can be used to control who can process a particular BUSINESS PARTNER master record. Authorization groups are freely definable and usually occur in authorization objects together with an activity, and are used to make additional restrictions on authorizations (e.g. for document maintenance).

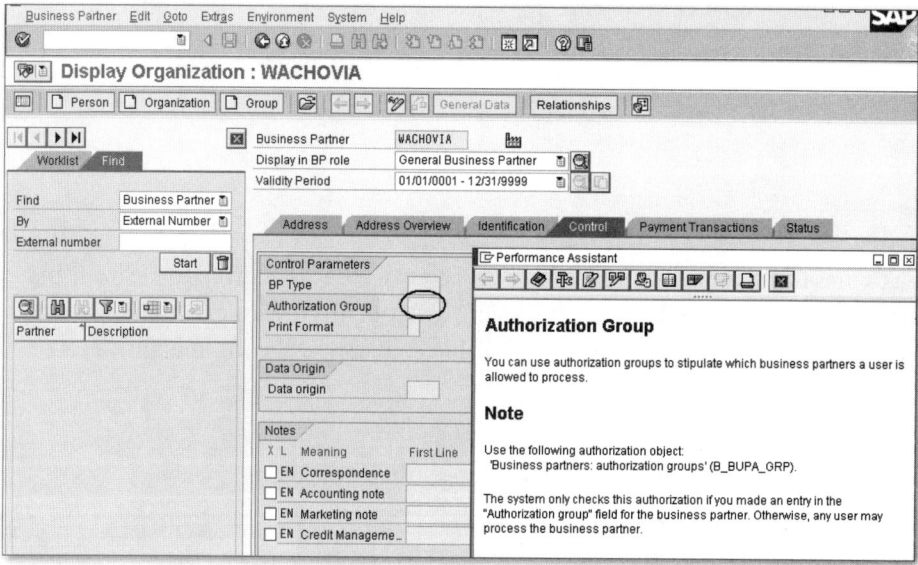

Figure 2.15 Assigning an Authorization Group to a BP

Roles

Roles are used as part of the authorization concept to define functions and responsibilities that translate into specific transaction codes. Users are assigned to roles that then enable them to execute the functions allowed for that role.

From a functional standpoint, treasury departments will need to define roles for their staff, and establish what transactions each role should have, and within that role, what activity is permissible (for example, create, change or display). These roles then need to be tested against each other to ensure that the transactions and authorizations within them do not violate any SoD rules. Once treasury management has decided on roles and responsibilities, the security team will set up appropriate access security in the system, based on the requirements established.

Control Mechanisms in SAP ERP | 2.3

> **Note**
>
> It is important to ensure that thorough testing of security access is part of any SAP Treasury implementation, and is usually conducted during the integration test cycle phase of the implementation.

Transaction SUIM provides a useful dashboard for viewing all aspects of the authorization concept in SAP ERP, as shown in Figure 2.16.

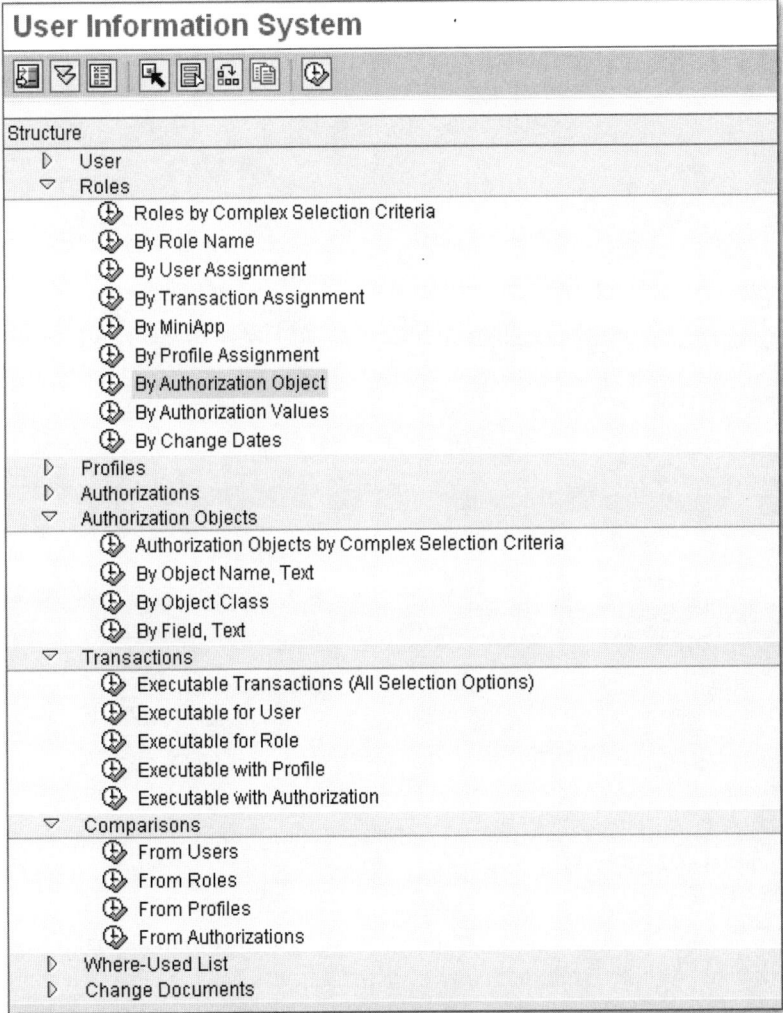

Figure 2.16 Authorization Concept Dashboard Using Transaction SUIM

Roles, objects and transactions authorized for particular functions that are set up in the system can be viewed from the dashboard. For example, the cash manager role can encompass various duties relating to cash management, treasury management, and limit management, as shown in Figure 2.17, which in turn provides a dashboard of information tabs relevant to the role. Under the role of cash management, the cash manager will need the ability to CHECK AND RECONCILE BANK ACCOUNTS, as shown in Figure 2.17.

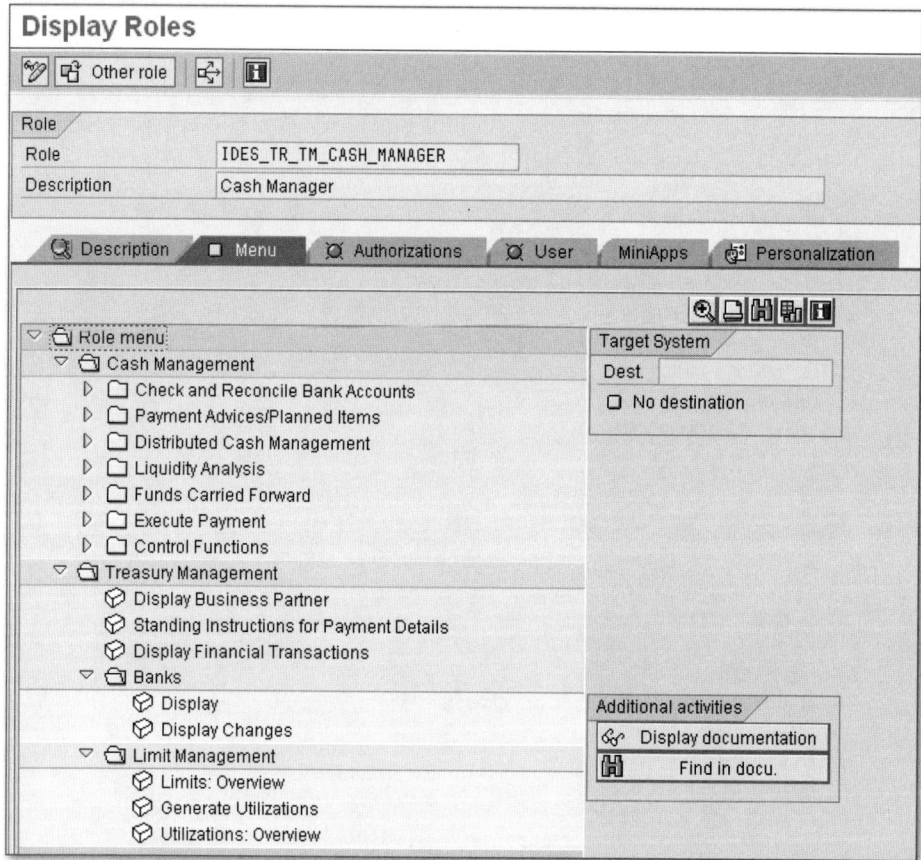

Figure 2.17 Dashboard for Cash Manager Role

Finally, the tasks under CHECK AND RECONCILE BANK ACCOUNTS contain actual transaction codes that need to be executed to trigger the activity, such as POSTPROCESS BANK STATEMENTS AND CHECKS (Transaction FEBAN) or DISPLAY BANK STATEMENT (Transaction FF.6), as shown in Figure 2.18.

2.3 Control Mechanisms in SAP ERP

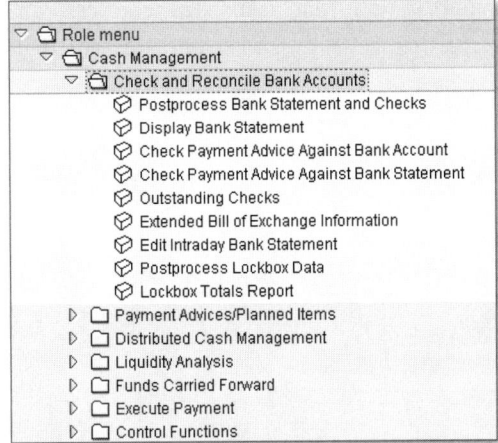

Figure 2.18 Functions Allowed by the Cash Manager Role

Figure 2.19 displays the transactions executable by the Cash Manager as identified by role IDES_TR_TM_CASH_MANAGER.

Transactions in Menu of IDES_TR_TM_CASH_MANAGER	
Transaction Code	Transaction Text
F.75	Extended Bill/Exchange Information
F110	Parameters for Automatic Payment
F111	Parameters for Payment of PRequest
F8BT	Display Payment Requests
F8BV	Reversal of Bank-to-Bank Transfers
FEBA	Postprocess Electronic Bank Statmt
FF-1	Outstanding Checks
FF-7	Planned Item Journal
FF-8	Payment Advice Journal
FF.3	G/L Account Cashed Checks
FF.4	Vendor Cashed Checks
FF.6	Display Electronic Bank Statement
FF.7	Compare Payment Advices
FF.8	Print Payment Orders
FF.9	Post Payment Orders
FF.D	Generate payt req. from advices
FF/1	Compare Bank Terms
FF/2	Compare value date
FF/9	Compare Advices with Bank Statement
FF$3	Send planning data to central system
FF$4	Retrieve planning data
FF$5	Retrieve transmission results
FF$L	Display transmission information
FF$S	Display transmission information
FF63	Create Planning Memo Record
FF6A	Edit Cash Mgmt Pos Payment Advices
FF6B	Edit liquidity forecast planned item

Figure 2.19 Transaction Codes Relevant to Cash Manager Role

75

Another important role in the treasury department that needs strong access controls for allowable transactions is that of the TRADER, shown and described in Figure 2.20.

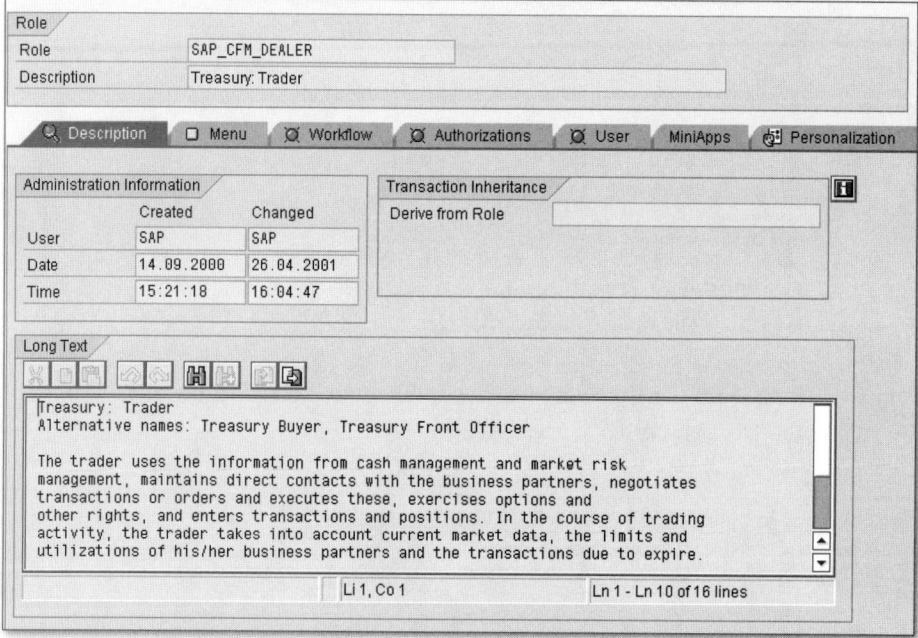

Figure 2.20 Example of Setup of a Role for a Treasury Trader

> **Note**
>
> The access protection system must ensure that only authorized individuals have access to the system and to particular data. For achieving precise application security concerning authorization, and to protect confidential data against unauthorized access, it is very important to focus on all aspects of security as part of an implementation.

2.3.3 Configurable Authorizations

In areas where controls specific to certain transactions are critical, authorizations can be configured within the system specific to the particular function, object, or person. For example, in front office trading, a trader can be authorized to trade only in certain products.

TRADER 01 is created through the configuration menu, and as shown in Figure 2.21, is assigned to specific contract types.

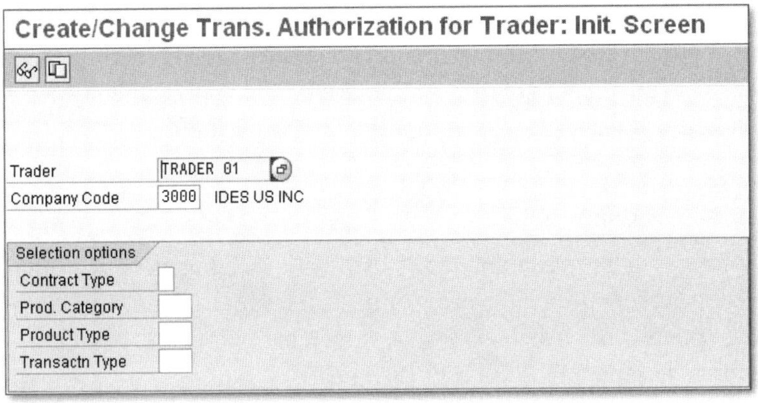

Control Mechanisms in SAP ERP | 2.3

Figure 2.21 Creating Trader Authorization for Specific Contract Types

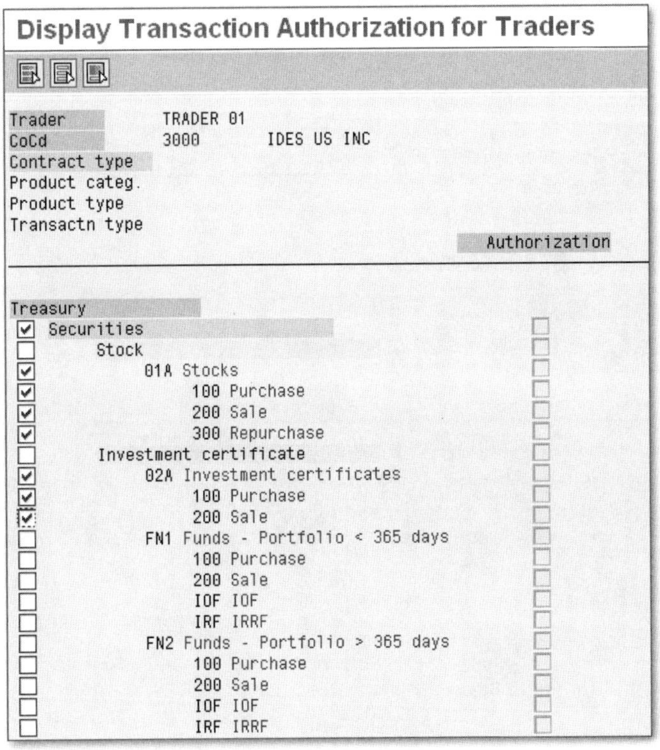

Figure 2.22 Contract-Specific Authorization for Trader

The resulting screen allows the selection of contract types within the system. For example, as shown in Figure 2.22, TRADER 01 can be set up to only trade in certain

77

securities as selected under the AUTHORIZATION column. Needless to say, there must be proper SoD to ensure that traders do not have access to set up these configuration options, and such configuration should be done by a completely separate and independent functional area in accounting or the back office.

Business Partner Access Controls

Configurable controls are also available for BPs external to the business, to authorize payment processing for specific types of contracts relevant to them. For example, the BP bank in the role of COUNTERPARTY, as shown in Figure 2.23, has a number of bank accounts designated in different currencies.

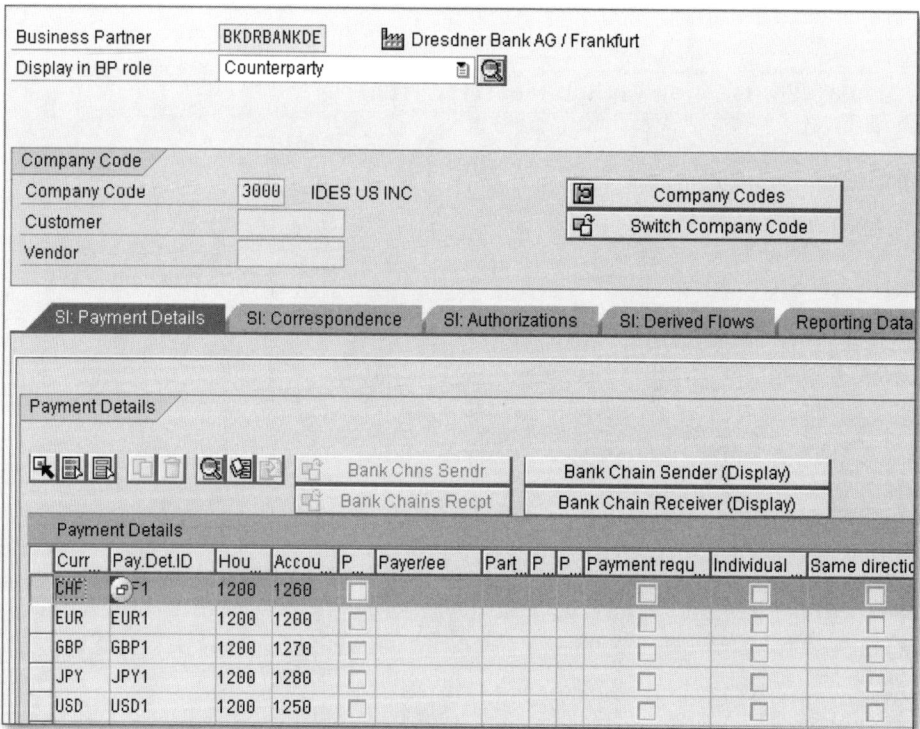

Figure 2.23 Assigning Contract Authority to BPs

The BP is only authorized to use its CHF currency bank account to purchase fixed term deposits, deposits at notice, and commercial papers, as shown in Figure 2.24.

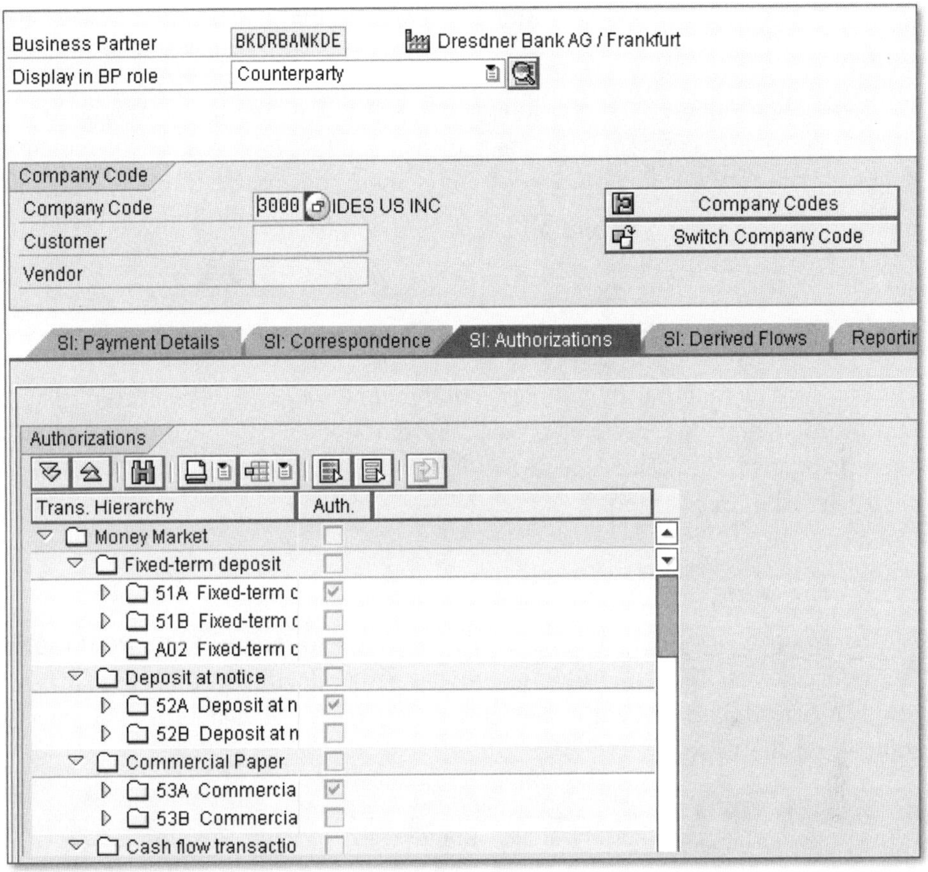

Figure 2.24 Contract Types Authorized for BP

In addition to facilitating SoD through programmable and configurable authorization checks, the SAP ERP system also has a configurable feature called sensitive access or dual control.

2.3.4 SoD and Sensitive Access Control

Proper SoD is a powerful internal control tool. It allows an independent authorization or validation of a transaction or entry in the financial records, thus reducing the possibility of fraud or error. For example, the person who is entering a wire payment request in the system should not also be the person to authorize and release it for payment.

In addition to using the authorization system, SAP ERP has built-in SoD functionality in sensitive areas of transaction management, so that it is possible to configure dual approval and release requirements for elements of a transaction. We will look at examples of dual control in payment processing in Chapter 4 and subsequent chapters.

2.3.5 Audit Trail and Change Documents in SAP ERP

The presence of an audit trail is a key requirement of a good internal control system from an audit perspective, as well as from a detective control perspective. There are many tools available in SAP ERP to maintain proper audit trails and these are discussed in this section.

Change Documents

All changes to master data and transaction data are tracked in SAP ERP through *change documents*. This is accomplished via change document objects managed using Transaction SCDO. Figure 2.25 shows an extract of change document objects through this transaction.

BP_SI_0001	Business partner - Standing instructions: Payment detail
BP_SI_0002	Business partner - Standing instructions: Correspondence
BP_SI_0003	Business partner - Standing instructions: Transaction auth.
BP_SI_0004	Business partner - Standing instructions: Derived flows
BUPA_ADR	Business partner: Addresses
BUPA_BANK	Business Partner: Bank Details

Figure 2.25 Change Document Objects in Transaction SCDO

Table TCDOB provides the settings with respect to whether a change document object is active, as shown in Figure 2.26.

Control Mechanisms in SAP ERP | 2.3

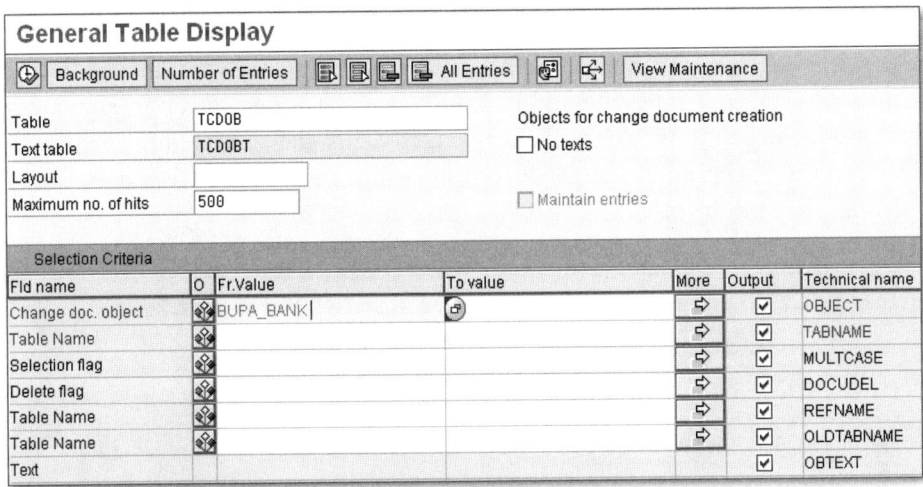

Figure 2.26 Table TCDOB Containing Change Document Objects

Figure 2.27 confirms that the change document object BUPA_BANK is marked as active.

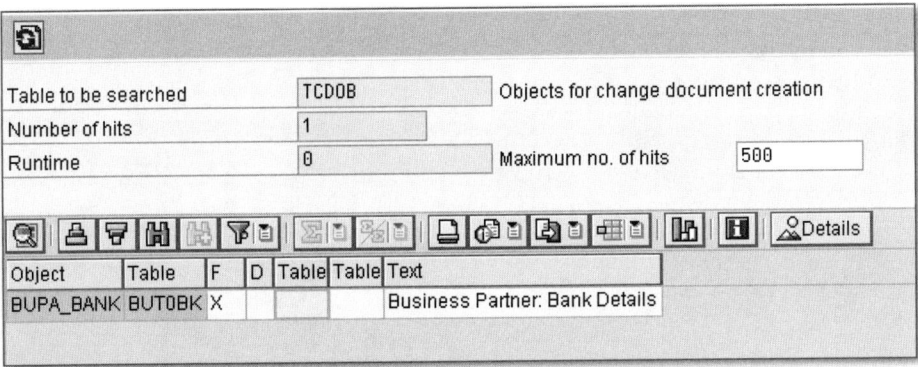

Figure 2.27 Change Document is Active for Object Business Partner: Bank Details

Next, we will look at several methods for setting up audit trails through change history tracking in SAP ERP.

Table Logging

Every Transaction, document, or entry made in the system by a user is recorded with the user name, and date and time of creation. Changes made to key tables can also be logged in the form of change documents and reviewed through standard reports. In certain instances, document change rules can be created to specify whether they can be modified or remain locked.

Table logs can be evaluated using Transaction SCU3 or program RSTBHIST using Transaction SE38. The initial selection screen is shown in Figure 2.28.

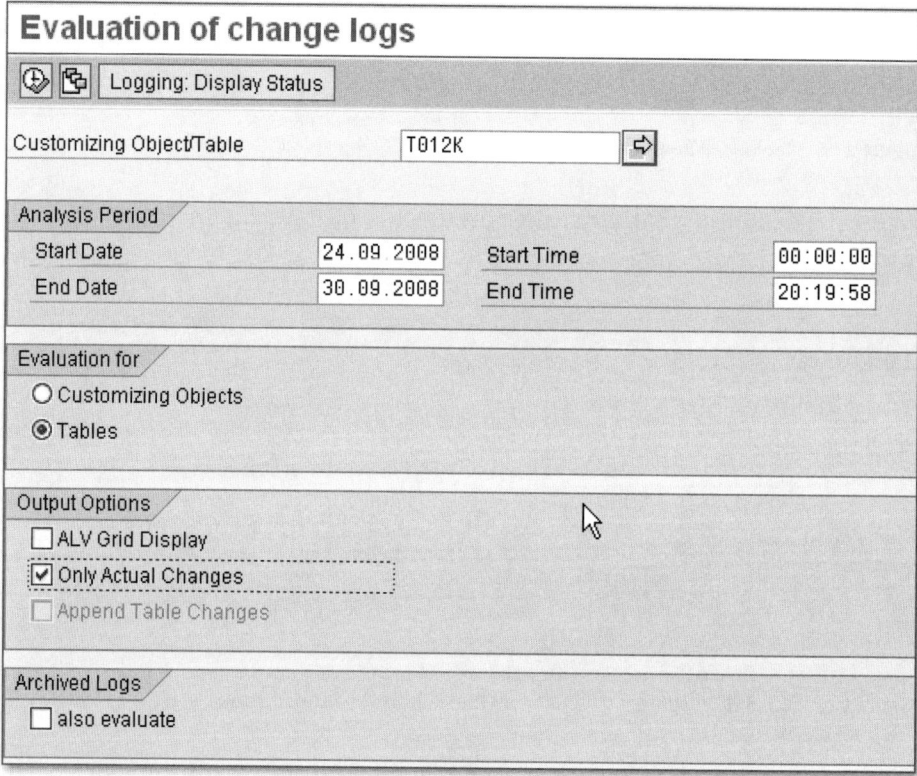

Figure 2.28 Evaluation of Change Logs for Table T012K

If table logging is not active in the system, a pop-up screen will appear, as shown in Figure 2.29.

2.3 Control Mechanisms in SAP ERP

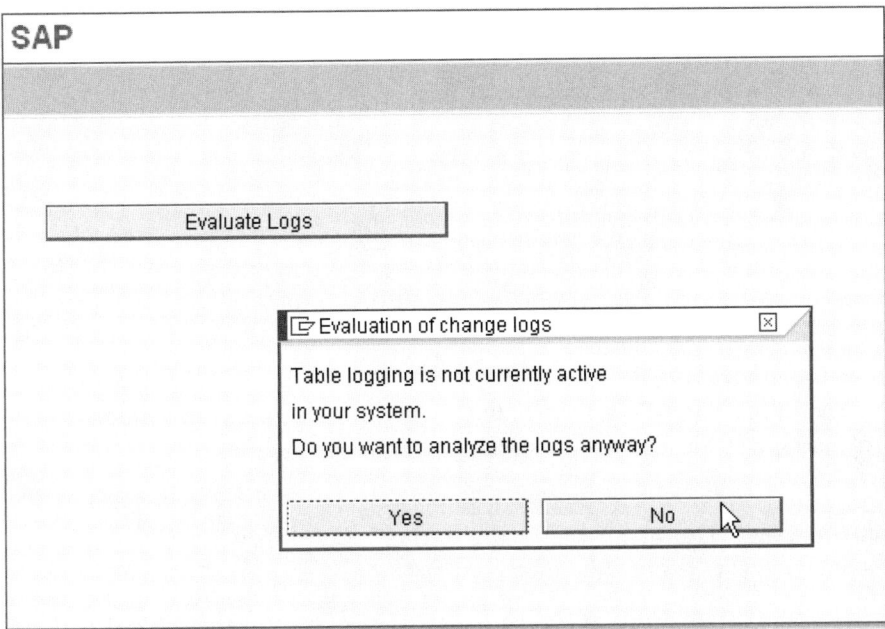

Figure 2.29 Transaction SCU3 to evaluate logs

To activate table logging, program RSPFPAR has to be run using Transaction SE38. In the resulting screen, the input field profile parameter needs to be populated with the setting REC/CLIENT as shown in Figure 2.30.

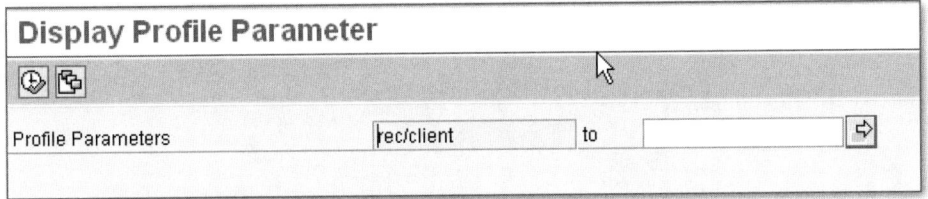

Figure 2.30 Activating Table Logging

On execution of the program, the status of table logging — either ON or OFF — will be displayed, as shown in Figure 2.31.

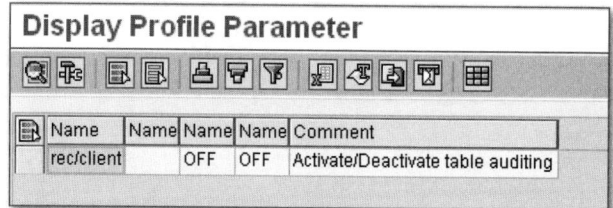

Figure 2.31 Executed Program RSPFPAR Showing Table Logging Off

Document Field Control

Transaction OB32 provides the ability to create field-specific document change rules. The initial selection screen provides fields available in the vendor or customer master data that can be controlled, as shown in Figure 2.32.

AccTy	Trans.type	Fld name	Co	Field Label
K		BSEG-ZUONR		Assignment
K	A	BSEC-BANKL		Bank Key
K	A	BSEC-BANKN		Bank Account
K	A	BSEC-BANKS		Bank Country
K	A	BSEC-BKONT		Bank control key
K	A	BSEC-NAME1		Name
K	A	BSEC-NAME2		Name 2
K	A	BSEC-NAME3		Name 3
K	A	BSEC-NAME4		Name 4
K	A	BSEC-ORT01		City
K	A	BSEC-PSTLZ		Postal Code
K	A	BSEC-STRAS		Street
K	A	BSEG-AUFNR		Order
K	A	BSEG-BVTYP		Partner Bank Type
K	A	BSEG-EBELN		Purchasing Document
K	A	BSEG-EBELP		Item

Figure 2.32 Field-Specific Document Change Rules Using Transaction OB32

By clicking on a specific field name, it is possible to specify whether a field name can be changed, as shown in Figure 2.33.

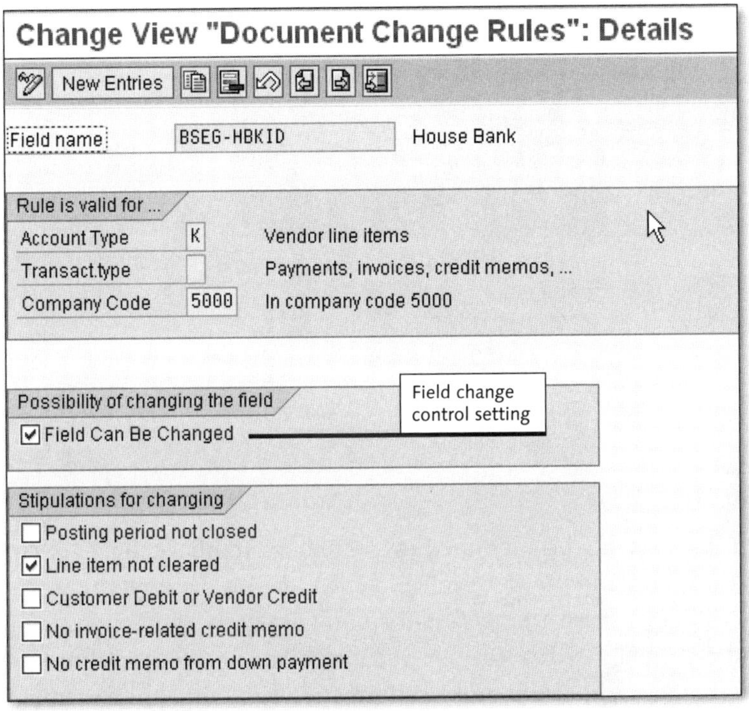

Control Mechanisms in SAP ERP | 2.3

Figure 2.33 Field Change Control Setting Using Transaction OB32

2.3.6 Accounting Integrity in SAP ERP

Document Control

A journal entry will not post unless the debits equal credits. All sub ledgers have a reconciliation account to which manual postings can't be made. Instead, a mirror posting automatically occurs every time there is an entry in the sub ledger. After a document has been posted, it can't be deleted. If it needs to be changed, it must be reversed, and will get its own document reference number. Similarly, although the text or descriptive line items in a posted document can be changed, key items such as the amount, posting parameters, and so on can't be changed. Figure 2.34 shows the four sub ledgers in finance: ACCOUNTS PAYABLE, ACCOUNTS RECEIVABLE, ASSET ACCOUNTING, and BANK ACCOUNTING. These sub ledgers integrate with the general ledger (G/L).

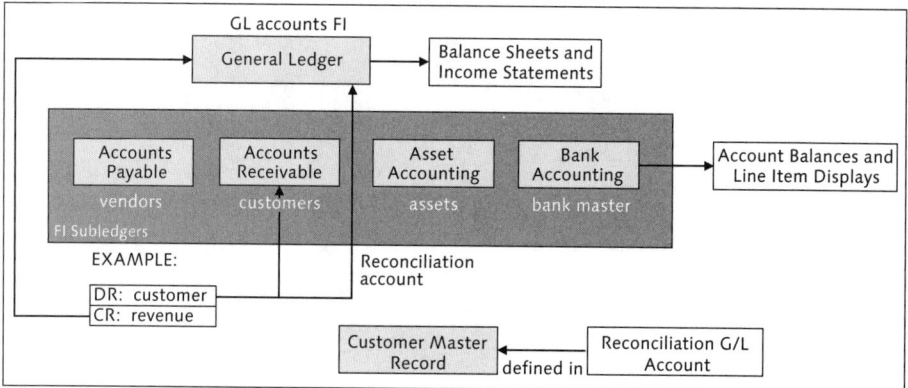

Figure 2.34 G/L Integration with the Finance Sub Ledgers in SAP ERP

Document Numbers

Every document that is created is identified by a number. Number ranges are created during configuration and can be specified depending on the type of transaction or document. They can also be assigned automatically by the system internally, or created externally by the user. A document has header and line item information that provides a full audit trail of information relating to the document, including when it was created and by whom, as well as reference, posting, and clearing information, if applicable.

Use of Clearing Accounts

Clearing G/L accounts are used extensively in SAP ERP to facilitate STP, exception-based reporting, and error management. Because the system can be configured to automatically post transactions based on specific rules, clearing accounts must be set up to capture any transaction that did not follow a posting rule. This often happens in the inbound electronic banking process, when information provided by the bank may change, resulting in a transaction not recognizable by the system. Another example of how clearing accounts facilitate control and reconciliation is when funding transfers or cash concentration between banks take place. Both receiving and sending banks have clearing accounts, and in many cases it may be the same clearing account. If funds are sent but not received, or are in transit, an unreconciled or unmatched item will remain outstanding in the clearing account. This will raise a red flag that will require follow up action.

Figure 2.35 provides an example of how clearing works in the SAP ERP system when an investment is purchased. When a payment request is created, it is held in a clearing account until it is approved and payment is released. It then clears the payment request clearing account, and moves to a bank clearing account, waiting for the electronic bank statement that will confirm payment settlement. When the electronic bank statement is received, the bank clearing account will be cleared. The clearing account is thus an important tool for monitoring exceptions, as well as for in-transit funds transfers.

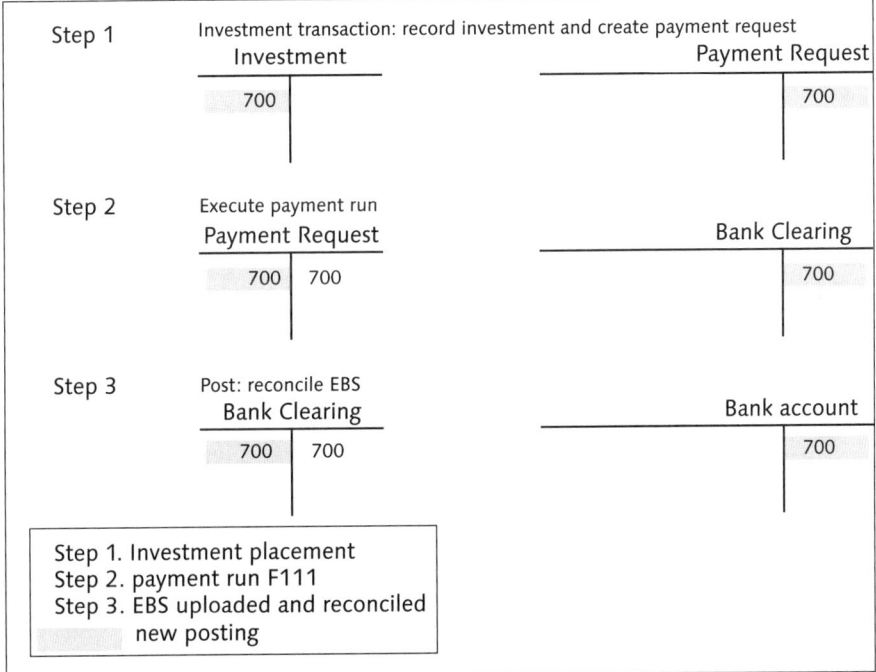

Figure 2.35 Clearing Account Example

2.3.7 Reports and ALV

The SAP ERP system includes an extensive range of standard reports that provide a variety of control features, including audit trail, analysis functions, the ability to download information in various formats, and the creation of variants that can be run when desired. Because reports are run using programs, these can also be customized to meet specific user needs. We will see many instances of standard and custom reports used by treasury as we progress through the book.

2.3.8 Workflow Technology

SAP ERP provides an efficient cross-application tool — SAP Business Workflow — which enables integrated electronic management of business processes through business workflow. SAP Business Workflow is fully integrated into SAP ERP, enabling specific business process flows to be coordinated and controlled across functions within an enterprise.

Although workflow has many applications, it is particularly useful in treasury management for approvals and release-based authorizations for the myriad treasury transactions that invariably involve financial settlement of one form or another. Integration of release management strategies can be customized for treasury processes through workflow.

Triggering Events

Workflow can be used for approvals as well as to report errors and exceptions through e-mail. Workflow is activated by a triggering event that could result in an email to the appropriate person for an authorization or review. A triggering event could be the execution of a transaction code or any other function in the system, such as saving a document or transaction. For example, in the creation of a foreign exchange forward contract, the saving of the contract that creates a transaction in the system could trigger an e-mail to the treasury manager for his approval or rejection. An approval automatically changes the status of the transaction to Released, enabling the next stage in the business process to proceed. A rejection could require the transaction to be reversed, or a request for more information before approval is provided. These rules can be built into the workflow using standard templates, or, as is more often the case with treasury transactions, through customizing the workflow using ABAP or Java program code if the workflow is web based.

Release Strategy

The release strategy is based on the dual-control principle and can be performed by one, two, or three authorized users. Release procedures and release conditions can be customized for specific products and transaction types. Another useful feature is the ability to generate workflow reports that provide details of what was released, by whom, and when. The principle of dual control for releases is shown in Figure 2.36.

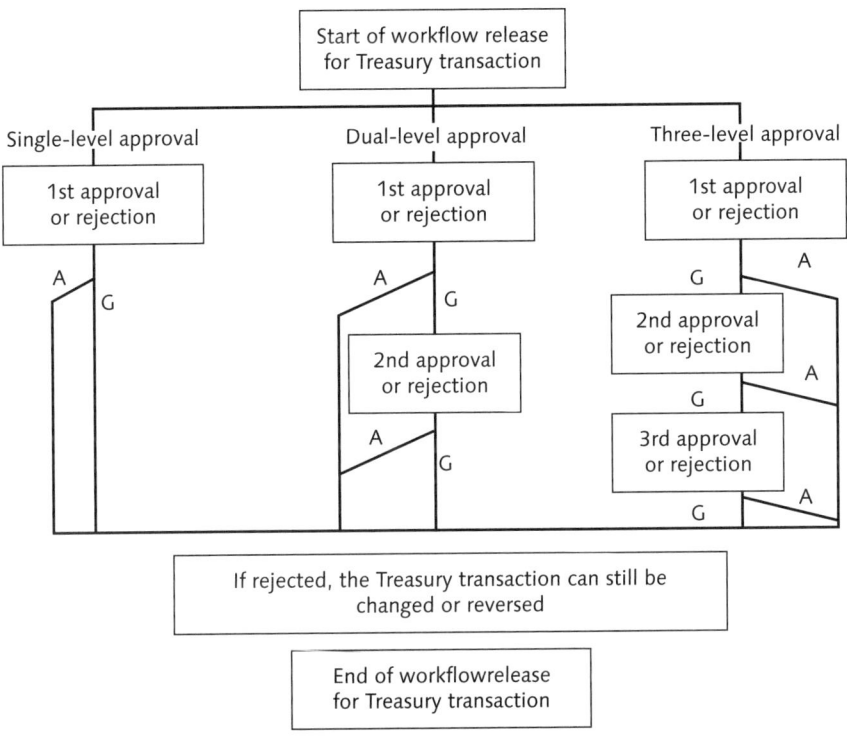

Figure 2.36 Dual Control Release Through Workflow

Treasury Applications

The use of workflow and release strategy has many applications in treasury. For example, a release strategy is mandatory for creating or changing a BP before treasury transactions can be executed with them.

2.4 Summary of Controls in SAP ERP

The previous sections covered the key principles and tools that are used by SAP ERP to maintain sound internal control at the level of sophistication required to comply with SOX and other regulatory legislation. The following is a summary of the various controls available, classified by whether they are systemic, configurable, programmatic, or manual. These controls will be referred to or elaborated upon in later chapters in the context of specific treasury business processes.

2.4.1 Systemic or Built-in Controls

Systemic controls are built into the SAP ERP software as part of its standard functionality. They can be preventative or detective in nature:

- **Preventative**
  - Pop up information messages
  - Information, warning, or hard errors issued by the system
  - Document posting and accounting integrity
  - Automatic synchronization between main and sub ledgers
  - Only reversal of posted documents allowed, not deletion
  - Clearing documents need to be reset and reversed
- **Detective**
  - Audit trail and change history
  - Drill down capability
  - Error logs
  - E-mail notification of spool logs
  - Transaction logs

2.4.2 Configurable Controls

Configurable controls are set up in the SAP ERP system through the configuration menu, which allows users to configure settings out of a suite of options that are specific to the organization's business:

- **Preventative**
  - Transaction execution
  - Master data maintenance
  - User defined validation
  - Access to master data
  - Controls for master data
  - Security controls
  - Password controls

- Dual controls with sensitive access fields
- Release controls
- Limit management
- Payment blocks
▶ **Detective**
  - Table logging

2.4.3 Programmable Controls

Programmable controls require development of specific program code using the ABAP or Java programming language, or the use of function modules or user exit programs provided by the SAP ERP system and built into existing programs for use by the organization:

▶ **Preventative**
  - Function modules and user exits
  - Validation rules
  - Customized programs
  - Custom reconciliation or audit program auto reconciliation
  - Use of clearing accounts
  - Workflow with email triggers
  - Custom transaction codes
  - Execution control
  - Audit table updates
  - Email alerts
  - Interface with external validation
▶ **Detective**
  - Dashboards
  - Exception reporting
  - Standard reporting
  - Audit tools such as VIRSA, MIC and AIS

2.4.4 Manual Controls

Manual controls are developed and implemented internally by an organization, and are an essential part of sound internal control policy. They are used together with the other forms of control described previously:

- **Preventative**
    - Approvals and authorizations
    - Policies and procedures
    - Maintenance of documentation
    - Physical security for passwords
- **Detective**
    - Daily and monthly reconciliation
    - External validation
    - Evaluation of balances
    - Post-processing of errors
    - Review of clearing accounts

> **Note**
> All different forms and types of controls described in this section should be used in combination with one another to create multiple and compensatory controls to provide a robust internal control system.

2.5 Risk/Control Matrix

The concept of strong internal controls for treasury has always been an integral part of good financial practice in an organization, as well as a requirement for internal and external audit purposes. With SOX compliance requirements this becomes an essential component of all key treasury business processes. An effective tool for evaluating SOX compliance is the creation of a risk/control matrix for key business processes within treasury. The format of a risk/control matrix may vary with different organizations but the key components are described in this section. It is up to each individual organization to decide what is most appropriate and relevant for their business. The risk/control matrix may comprise the following key components:

- **Identification**
  Name and description of the business process, owner, and period of evaluation.

- **COSO objective**
  Description of the key control objective from the COSO framework, and period of evaluation.

- **Process evaluation**
  Summary of evaluation, status of evaluation, and the evaluator's comments on the effectiveness of the process.

- **Controls evaluated**
  List of controls for evaluation, period and status of evaluation (e.g., authorization, SoD, completeness and accuracy, and reconciliation).

- **Risk identification**
  List of risks identified, period of evaluation, and effectiveness and adequacy of control.

- **Approval and sign-off document**
  The risk/control matrix needs to be signed off by the manager responsible for the process, and approved by the treasury director or treasurer.

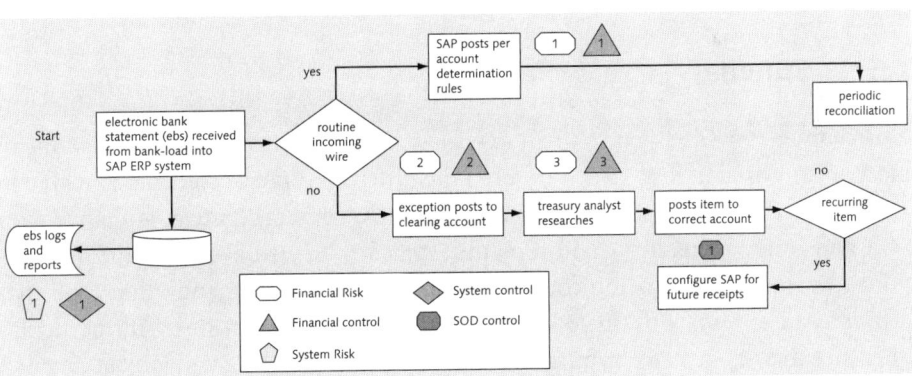

Figure 2.37 Process Map Example for Incoming Treasury Wires

- **Process flow diagram**
  A process map of the business process, identifying financial risk and control points, as well as information technology risks and control features. This map also needs to identify key integration points when there is handover between key functions, for example within the treasury department, between front and back office, or between treasury and the finance department. Figure 2.37 provides an

example of a process map for receipt of incoming wires. Table 2.1 explains the risks and mitigating controls that were observed in the process map.

Control list	Control type	Mitigation of risk
1. Account determination rules set up, authorized, and tested.	Financial, preventative	Yes
2. Exception recorded in clearing account.	Financial, detective	Yes
3. SoD between transaction processing and configuration set up.	Financial, preventative	Yes
4. No log of ebs not uploaded.	Systems, detective	No

Table 2.1 Risks and mitigating controls

The risk/control matrix should be signed off by the process owner when completed, and approved by executive management. It can be expanded to provide as much detail as is required to satisfy the compliance and documentation requirements as established by management.

2.6 Summary

This chapter provided you with an overview of key control concepts and control mechanisms used in SAP ERP. It covered the different types of controls available in an integrated system, and how they can be leveraged to facilitate compliance with SOX and other regulatory requirements. It also reviewed systemic and transactional controls, authorization concepts, audit trails, workflow, and other tools that can be used to enhance controls and improve business processes with particular reference to SAP Treasury applications. Next, in Chapter 3, we will look at detailed treasury functionality available in Inbound Electronic Banking in SAP ERP, relating to key business processes and the control mechanisms surrounding them.

Chapter 3 describes the key business processes involved in inbound electronic banking in SAP ERP, covering prior and intraday electronic bank statements, reconciliation and controls, and how straight-through automated processing can be achieved in the upload, posting, matching, clearing, and reconciliation of electronic bank statements.

3 Inbound Electronic Banking in SAP ERP

Electronic bank statements (EBS) can be automatically polled, uploaded, posted, and reconciled daily in SAP ERP. Prior day statements update the FI general and subsidiary ledgers and record the previous day's activity for accounting purposes. Intraday statements can be uploaded for daily cash positioning purposes. Bank statements are ready to be polled from the bank's host computer system at the beginning of the day. These are typically polled via the internet using *file transfer protocol* (FTP) and loaded into a company's host directory. Polling can be scheduled to automatically poll and upload using a script program or file transmission software or the SAP NetWeaver XI interface.

3.1 The Inbound EBS Process Flow

The inbound EBS process flow typically includes the following key steps:

1. Bank statements (prior and current day) are polled from the bank using automated polling software.
2. The incoming bank files are loaded into SAP ERP and preprocessed using a custom program.
3. When the file preprocessing is complete, the main upload program RFEBKA00 is triggered automatically using a bank-specific variant. A user exit XF01U01 can be used for additional preprocessing and to automate account assignment and posting.
4. An internal check takes place to ensure that the bank statement is in sequence.

5. On successful upload of the bank statement, posting to the financial records or cash management reports will take place depending on whether they are prior day or current day statements.

6. If there are any errors, post-processing can take place through Transaction FEBAN for correction and posting.

7. At end of the day a, G/L clearing program — Transaction F.13 — can be run for all bank clearing accounts, to clear all matching transactions out of open items into cleared items. This will leave only uncleared items in the accounts, which will need to be investigated and corrected along with the post, using clearing Transaction F-04.

An overview of the process is summarized in Figure 3.1. In this chapter, we will review each of these steps along with the key controls surrounding each sub-process.

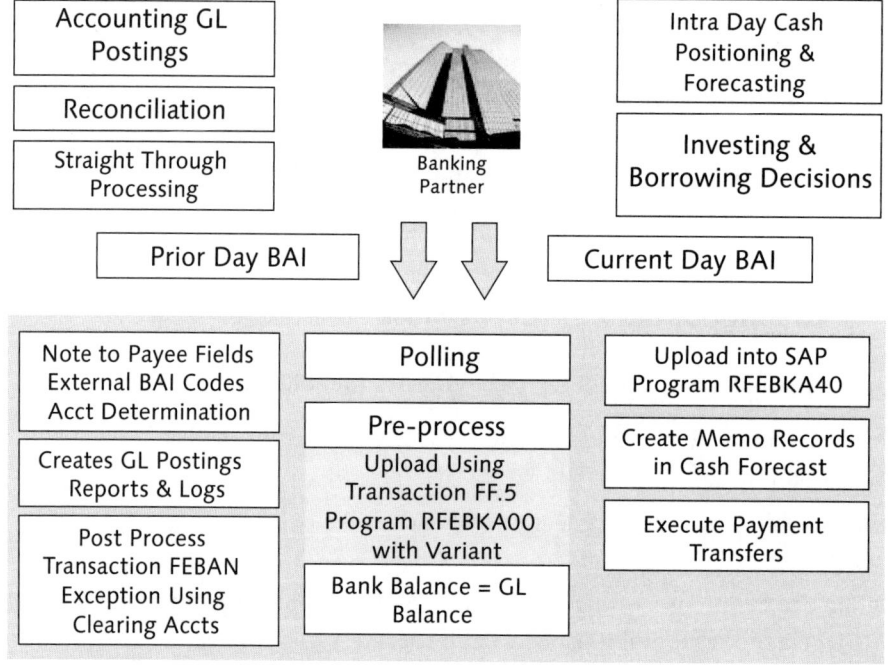

Figure 3.1 Overview of Inbound Electronic Banking

3.2 Banking Structure and Master Data

The correct design of the banking structure and proper master data and accounting setup in SAP ERP is of utmost importance from a controls perspective, as well as to enable and optimize automated straight through processing.

3.2.1 Banking Structures

Every bank account is represented by a G/L account in the financial records. When an EBS is uploaded and posted in SAP ERP, one side of every transaction posts to this G/L account. This account will always reflect the balance per the last bank statement uploaded successfully in the system. The other side of the entry will post to the respective G/L or sub ledger account, depending on the accounting assignment and posting rules set up in the system.

The way the bank account is set up will affect the design of the G/L structure and clearing accounts. There are two types of account structures that can appear in an EBS. With the first, a physical bank account is unique and equates to one logical account. Examples of this are a checking account, a cash concentration account, a Zero Balance Account (ZBA), or a disbursement account.

The second type is called a *sub-account structure*. With this type, there is one physical account that contains many different logical accounts. Sub-account structures are common in retail organizations that, for example, have many stores in a certain region, and although there is only one bank account for the region (represented by one G/L account and one physical bank account), store deposits made into that account need to be identified by a sub-account that equates to a store location or outlet. The posting rules for a sub-account structure need to be able to accommodate this setup.

The advantage of the sub-account structure is cost savings in terms of maintaining only one account. On the other hand, more upfront one time configuration and setup work is involved to correctly identify the sub-account and post it to the correct G/L account.

We will look at the details of how posting takes place later in this chapter. The most important point to note is that any item that does not get posted to a specific G/L or sub ledger account will be posted to a clearing account.

Clearing accounts are used extensively in the automated EBS process of SAP ERP, and are used to capture unmatched items and inter-company bank account transfers, which when complete will offset each other in the clearing account.

The design of clearing accounts is important because SAP ERP uses account masking to define posting rules. For example, the same posting rule can be applied to all accounts ending with 2, which, if the chart of accounts has eight digits, will be shown as +++++++2 in the account assignment table.

Although you could have multiple clearing accounts for a bank, we recommend an approach that uses one clearing account per "family" of bank accounts. This is a particularly strong control feature when ZBA accounts are rolled up to a master account or for transfers between different accounts within the same bank. This applies to, for example, controlled disbursement, cash concentration, or funding purposes, as explained in the next section.

ZBA Account Structure

The ZBA account records all banking activity for the day. At the end of the day, the bank automatically transfers the balance on the account to a designated master bank account, leaving a zero balance in the sending account. If a company has many ZBA accounts, they can all be represented by a single G/L account because the balance of all ZBA accounts will be zero at the end of the day, regardless of the number of accounts.

However, if a large number of ZBA accounts are uploaded, the system will not be able to detect a missing statement (usually done through a balance mismatch check; see Section 3.3.3, Bank Balance Mismatch Error). This is because the opening and closing balances will always be zero. By using a common clearing account between the ZBA accounts and the master account, any missing statements will be detected because both the ZBA accounts as well as the master account will post one side to the same clearing account. If a ZBA statement is missing, there will be an unmatched item on the clearing account, because the master bank account will reflect the transfer, and post to the clearing account. This same concept can be used to track and reconcile inter-bank transfers, and determine any cash in transit between bank accounts.

> **Note: ZBA Clearing Accounts**
>
> When a company maintains multiple ZBA accounts under one bank key, one clearing account is adequate to control transactions within the ZBA and between the ZBA accounts and their master account.

For example, if you have multiple accounts with bank A, you can designate the G/L account range 100000 to 100009 for bank A, and assign G/L accounts as shown in Table 3.1:

Bank G/L Account Structure	G/L Account
Bank A Disbursement account	100000
Bank A ZBA Accounts (25 accounts)	100001
Bank A Clearing Account	100002
Bank A Master Account	100005
Bank A Checks Outstanding Account	100009

Table 3.1 Designating and Assigning G/L Accounts

For bank B, you could designate the G/L account range 100010 to 100019, and so on. It is important to remember that to use account masking effectively, all clearing accounts should end with 2, all ZBA accounts with 1, and all master accounts with 5.

Typically, at the end of the day, the G/L clearing program is run in batch mode for all clearing G/L accounts, to clear all matched items so that only unreconciled or unmatched items will remain in the clearing account. These need to be researched and cleared out through the post with clearing Transaction.

> **Note**
>
> Clearing bank accounts are a key component in ensuring integrity, accuracy, and completeness of the inbound banking process, and should be designed and used correctly for optimal control.

Sub-Account Structure

As mentioned previously, the sub-account structure uses only one physical bank account, represented by one G/L account, but can have multiple logical accounts reporting within the same bank account. In the EBS, the bank will need to identify the sub location (store, retail outlet, or plant) using the note to payee field. The account determination rules can be set up to post sub-account information to respective G/L or sub ledger accounts.

If the information is not consistently reported by the bank, or the bank uses a different reference, a preprocessing program can be used to reformat the file to enable SAP ERP to upload and post the information automatically.

3.2.2 Bank Master Data

The successful processing of EBS is dependent on the correct setup of key bank master data in the system. Additionally, it is imperative that adequate controls for access/create/change/display to bank master data are incorporated from a SOX compliance perspective.

House Bank

The house bank is the highest level of master data in the banking structure within SAP ERP and is defined by company code. It is defined with alphanumeric five-digit characters, as well as a numeric field for the bank key. In the U.S., the house bank equates to the nine-digit routing or ABA number. In Europe and Asia, either numeric keys or the SWIFT code is used as the bank key or routing number. The numeric bank key identifies the house bank in an incoming electronic bank statement. SAP ERP recognizes the incoming statement based on the entries in the house bank table for the bank key or routing number. There must be strict controls for the access, create, and change functions relating to house bank master data. The house bank can also be used to set up an in-house bank, for intra- and inter-company transactions. We will discuss in-house banking in detail in Chapter 6.

House banks are created using Transaction FI12 or by using application menu path: FINANCIAL ACCOUNTING • BANK ACCOUNTING • BANK ACCOUNTS • DEFINE HOUSE BANKS. Bank accounts with the same routing number are set up below the house bank.

The resulting screen is shown in Figure 3.2, where you can see the house banks created under company code 3000. These entries can also be verified through the house bank Table T012K.

Banking Structure and Master Data | 3.2

Dialog Structure	Company Code		3000	IDES US INC	
▽ House Banks					
Bank Accounts	House Banks				
	House bank	Bank ctry.	Bank Key	Bank name	
	3000	US	134329042	Citibank	
	3050	US	123123123	Citibank	
	3200	US	238100235	Mellon Bank	
	3400	US	123445678	Chase Manhattan Bank	
	55555	US	000000005	TEST BANK	
	9999	US	000000001	Test Bank 2	
	BOA	GB	6800	Bank of America	
	BOFA	US	938573829	Bank of America	
	CHASE	US	121000358	Chase Manhattan Bank	
	CITI	US	021000089	Citibank	
	DBKA	US	222222222	Demobank Americas (IHC)	
	DBKE	DE	11111111	Demobank Europe (IHC)	

Figure 3.2 House Banks Main Screen

The house bank that represents the bank key or routing number is created at the company code level. In the detail screen, settings for Electronic Data Interchange (EDI) and Data Medium Exchange (DME) can be maintained, in addition to address and contact information, as shown in Figure 3.3.

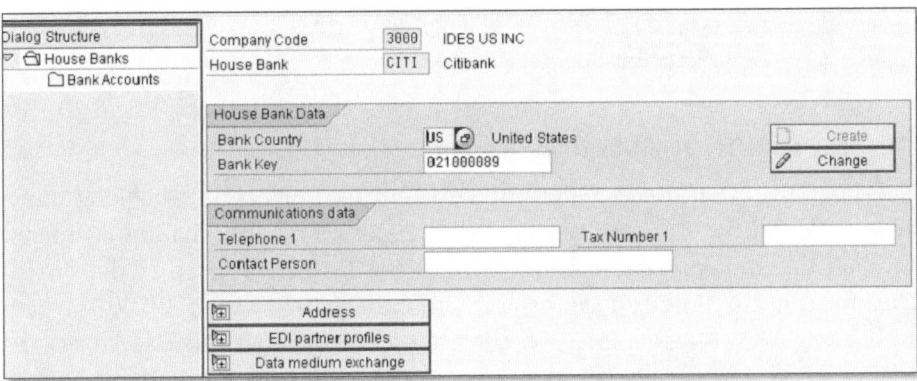

Figure 3.3 House Banks Detail Screen

By clicking on the buttons for EDI PARTNER PROFILES and DATA MEDIUM EXCHANGE, access is provided to configure detailed settings with respect to EDI PARTNER NUMber, eligible EDI payment methods (EDI COMP. PYT MTHDS), and PARTNER PROFILES. As shown in Figure 3.4, similar information can be set up for DATA MEDIUM EXCHANGE information that will appear in the outbound classic payment formats. These will be described in greater detail in Chapter 4.

Because settings such as EDI-compatible payment methods need to be set up to enable a payment to be sent via EDI, control over create or change access to house bank master data is an important aspect of internal control.

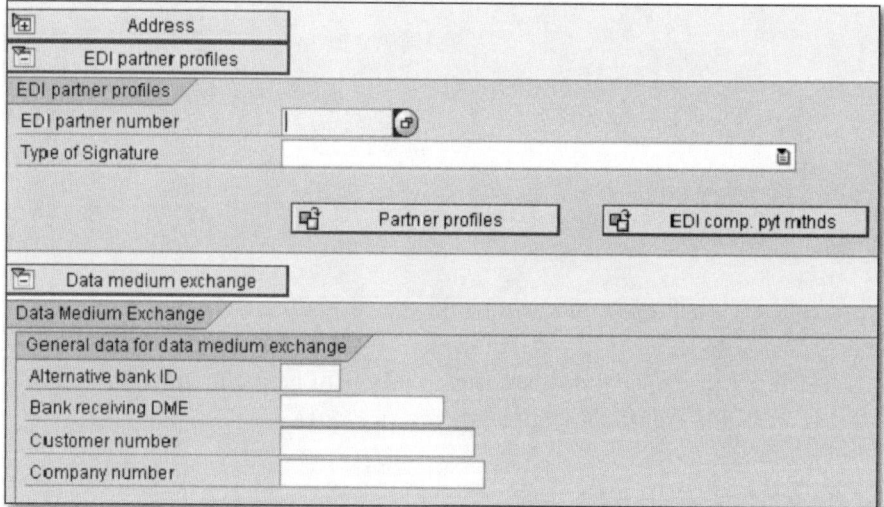

Figure 3.4 House Bank DME and EDI Setup

Company Code Tax Identification Number

The Tax ID is often used to identify the company in electronic banking transactions, especially U.S. ACH payment transactions. This information is entered through the Implementation Guide (IMG). The IMG is the area of the system used for configuration, and can be accessed through Transaction SPRO. The path is SPRO • SAP REFERENCE IMG • FINANCIAL ACCOUNTING (NEW) • GLOBAL PARAMETERS FOR COMPANY CODE • ENTER GLOBAL PARAMETERS • (SELECT COMPANY CODE) • ADDITIONAL DATA.

The entry screen for tax ID information is shown in Figure 3.5.

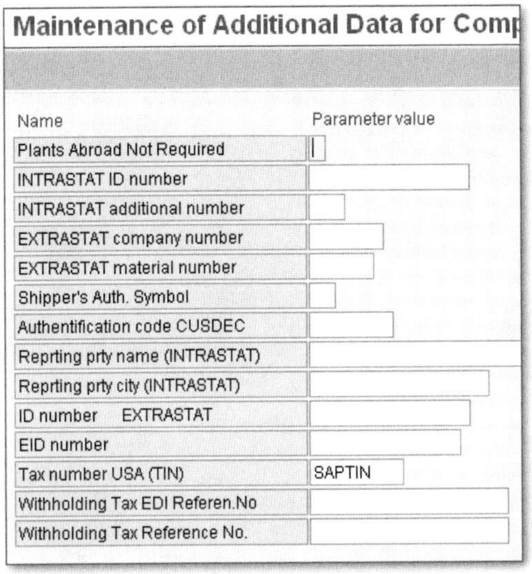

Banking Structure and Master Data | **3.2**

Name	Parameter value
Plants Abroad Not Required	
INTRASTAT ID number	
INTRASTAT additional number	
EXTRASTAT company number	
EXTRASTAT material number	
Shipper's Auth. Symbol	
Authentification code CUSDEC	
Reprting prty name (INTRASTAT)	
Reprting prty city (INTRASTAT)	
ID number EXTRASTAT	
EID number	
Tax number USA (TIN)	SAPTIN
Withholding Tax EDI Referen.No	
Withholding Tax Reference No.	

Figure 3.5 Configuring Company Tax ID

Bank Account

The bank account is the next level down from the house bank, and equates to each actual individual bank account the company operates. The master data has a field for the G/L account to which all transactions relating to this account will post when uploading the EBS. If implemented correctly, the balance on this G/L account will always equal the balance per the last bank statement uploaded into SAP ERP relating to this account. The other important field is the currency field that enables bank accounts to be maintained in multiple currencies. Company-specific bank accounts are created using the same path as when creating house banks, because they are created at a level below these. Figure 3.6 shows the bank accounts created under house bank CITI. These can be viewed in Table T012.

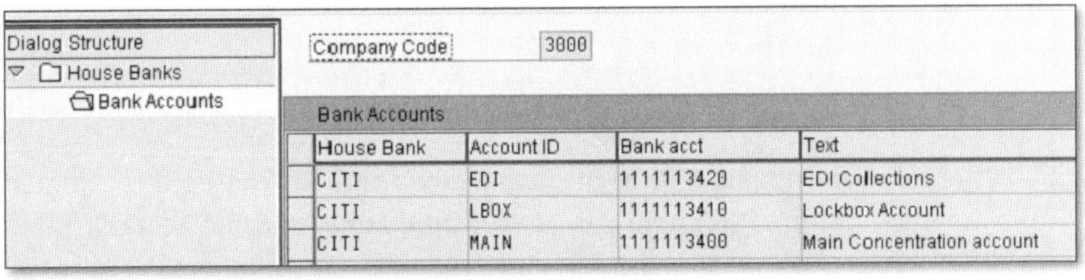

Dialog Structure
▽ ☐ House Banks
    ☐ Bank Accounts

Company Code: 3000

Bank Accounts

House Bank	Account ID	Bank acct	Text
CITI	EDI	1111113420	EDI Collections
CITI	LBOX	1111113410	Lockbox Account
CITI	MAIN	1111113400	Main Concentration account

Figure 3.6 Bank Accounts Summary Screen

103

The BANK ACCOUNTS detail screen enables key bank account information to be entered that is used by the rest of the application, both for inbound and outbound electronic banking. The G/L account for the BANK, CURRENCY, SWIFT CODE, and IBAN number are all important fields that are maintained in this screen, as shown in Figure 3.7.

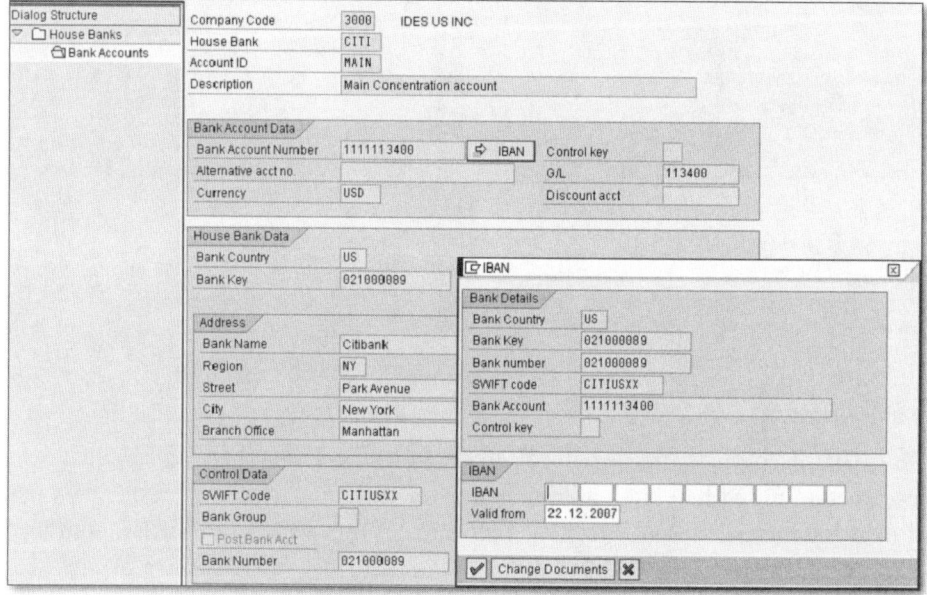

Figure 3.7 Bank Accounts Detail Screen

3.2.3 Master Data Key Controls

The importance of appropriate controls for master data setup can't be overemphasized, especially in the area of electronic banking. Important controls range from process checks, SoD, approval procedures, workflow, change control, and systemic checks.

Country-Specific Checks

Country-specific checks are a form of systemic control that can be incorporated through configuration. The menu path to set up country-specific checks is: IMG • SAP NETWEAVER • GENERAL SETTINGS • SET COUNTRY-SPECIFIC CHECKS. The menu path is shown in Figure 3.8.

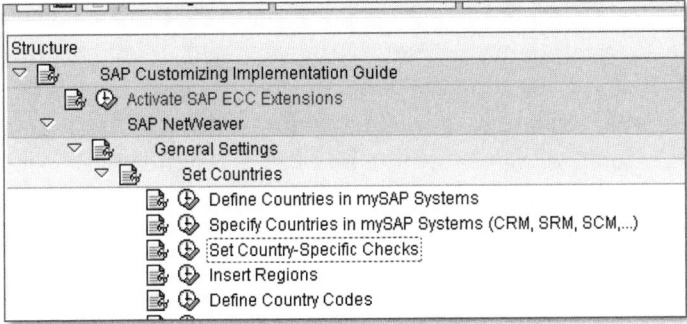

Figure 3.8 Setting Country-Specific Checks for Bank Account Data

The resulting input table screen and field settings that can be controlled are shown in Figure 3.9.

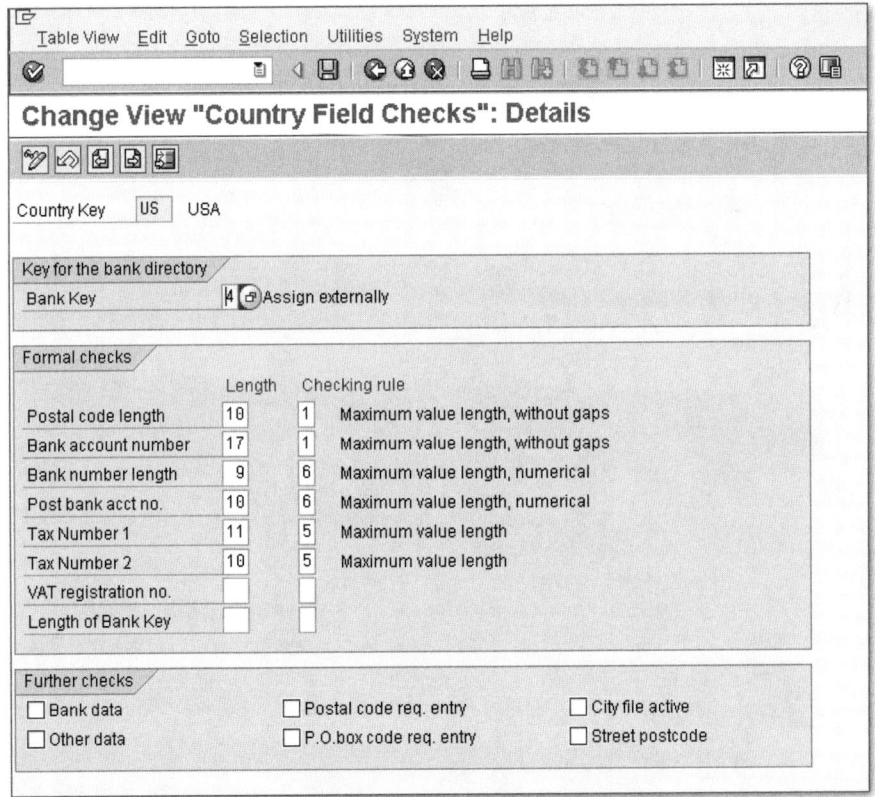

Figure 3.9 Setting Field-Specific Checks for Bank Master Data

Country-specific checks can be tailored according to the specific rules prevailing in a country. For example, in the U.S., the ABA or routing number can only be nine digits in numeric format, and the setting can be configured to exactly match this requirement. If a value of a different length or containing a character is entered in the master data, the system will not allow it to be created, resulting in an error message.

3.2.4 Configuring Electronic Bank Statements

Using the available configuration options fully is key to enabling STP of the EBS, from polling the bank through to posting in the financial records. The path to the configuration is IMG • ACCOUNTING • FINANCIAL ACCOUNTING • BANK ACCOUNTING • BUSINESS TRANSACTIONS • PAYMENT TRANSACTIONS • ELECTRONIC BANK STATEMENT • MAKE GLOBAL SETTINGS FOR ELECTRONIC BANK STATEMENT, as partially shown in Figure 3.10.

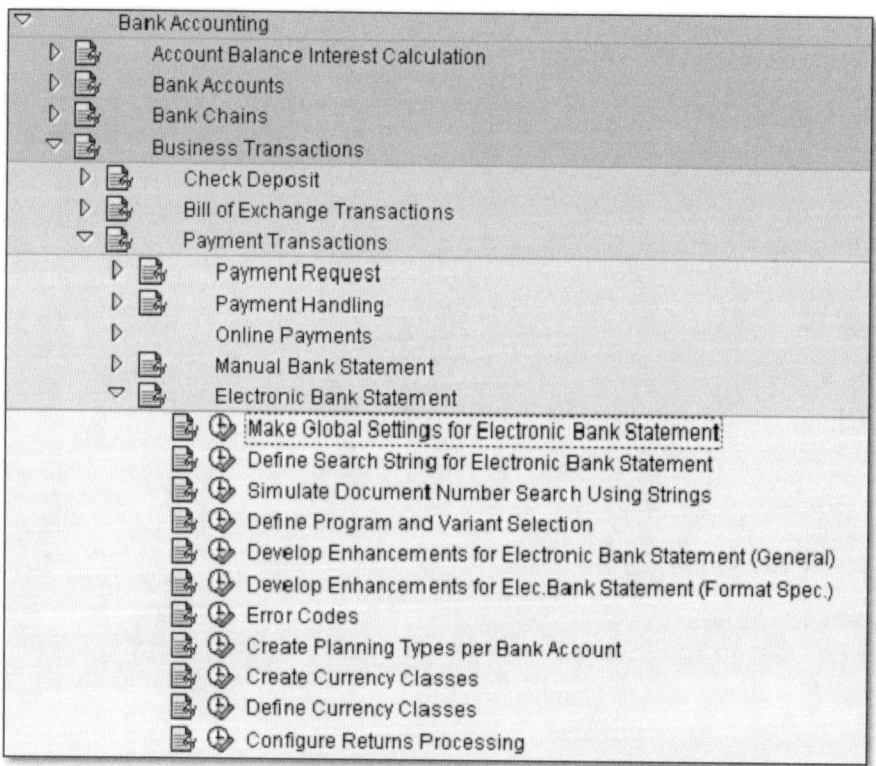

Figure 3.10 IMG Menu Path for EBS Configuration

The incoming EBS is identified by SAP ERP through the bank header information, that is, the bank routing number and bank account number that was configured during the house bank master data setup. The EBS identifies each transaction in the file with an external three-digit Bankers Administration Institute (BAI) code. BAI codes using the BAI format are prevalent in the U.S.; in Europe and Asia SWIFT codes are typically used. These codes are linked to posting rules that are assigned to G/L and sub ledger accounts. The posting rules can be further refined through the use of account modification and use of the note to payee or bank reference field, where the bank provides details with respect to the specific transaction.

The key areas that need to be configured are described next.

Create Account Symbols

Account symbols describe transactions that can be posted to either the debit or credit side, based on a predefined posting rule. Account symbols need to be created to be able to set up the appropriate posting rules, through linking each account symbol to a G/L account or multiple G/L accounts. They are set up through the CREATE ACCOUNT SYMBOLS path, as shown in Figure 3.11.

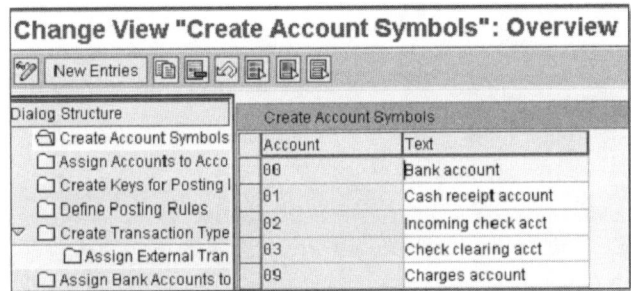

Figure 3.11 Creating Account Symbols

Assign Accounts to Account Symbols

Account symbols that are used in posting rules need to be assigned to G/L accounts, as shown in Figure 3.12. These account symbols are either assigned to specific G/L accounts, or masked to enable more generic postings. In the latter case, the system retrieves an account number and uses it for posting but overlays it with the mask set up during configuration. For example, as shown in Figure 3.12, the account symbol US WIRE PAID will post to the G/L account taken from the bank master, but will replace the last character with a "2" because the masking rule that has been set up is +++++2. So whenever the electronic bank statement has an external transaction code that is linked to a posting rule that contains the account symbol US WIRE PAID, it will post to 110002, and if Citibank had a G/L account 222000, it would post to G/L account 222002.

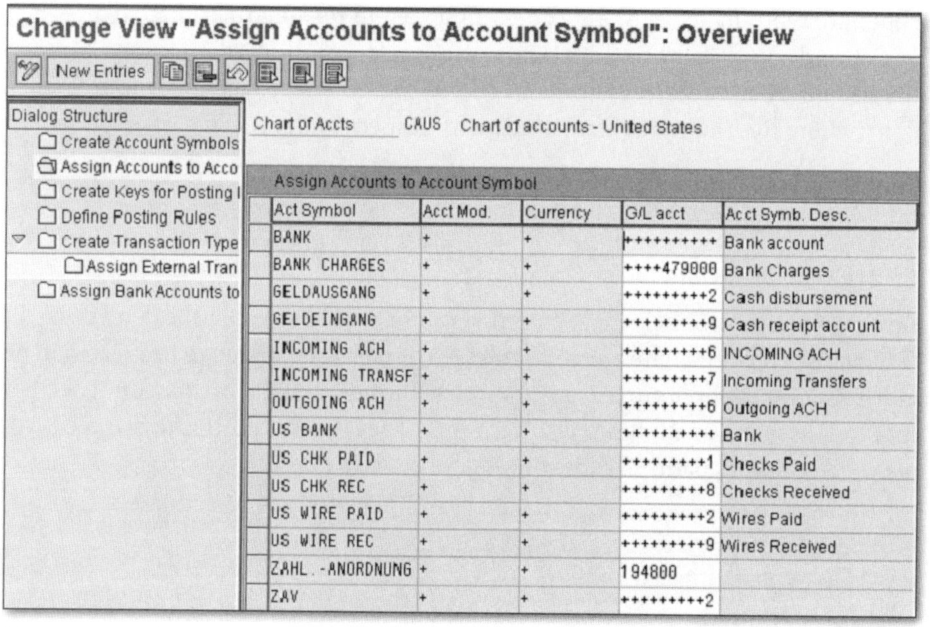

Figure 3.12 Assigning Accounts to Account Symbols

> **Key principle: One side of every EBS transaction will post to the G/L bank account**
> The G/L account designating the actual bank balance is configured during the bank account setup. One side of every transaction received for this bank through the EBS will post to this account. The balance per the bank G/L account should always equal the balance per the last uploaded EBS for that bank account.

Further refinement is possible through the use of account modification in column ACCT MOD. The entry in this column is tied to the field KFMOD. If the system encounters an entry in the note to payee field in the incoming bank statement that matches the KFMOD entry, then posting will take place based on the rule set up in the table. For example, as shown in Figure 3.13, if an entry for US WIRE PAID is received with a value of INSCE in the EBS NOTE TO PAYEE field, instead of using the account masking rule and posting it to G/L account +++++2, it would post to G/L ACCT 479555.

Banking Structure and Master Data | 3.2

Chart of Accts	CAUS	Chart of accounts - United States			

Assign Accounts to Account Symbol

Act Symbol	Acct Mod.	Currency	G/L acct	Acct Symb. Desc.
BANK	+	+	++++++++++	Bank account
BANK CHARGES	+	+	++++479000	Bank Charges
GELDAUSGANG	+	+	++++++++++2	Cash disbursement
GELDEINGANG	+	+	++++++++++9	Cash receipt account
INCOMING ACH	+	+	++++++++++6	INCOMING ACH
INCOMING TRANSF	+	+	++++++++++7	Incoming Transfers
OUTGOING ACH	+	+	++++++++++6	Outgoing ACH
US BANK	+	+	++++++++++	Bank
US CHK PAID	+	+	++++++++++1	Checks Paid
US CHK REC	+	+	++++++++++8	Checks Received
US WIRE PAID	+	+	++++++++++2	Wires Paid
US WIRE PAID	INSCE	+	++++479555	Wires Paid
US WIRE REC	+	+	++++++++++9	Wires Received
ZAHL.-ANORDNUNG	+	+	194800	
ZAV	+	+	++++++++++2	

Figure 3.13 Account Modification of Account Symbol

We will revisit this functionality in Section 3.3.5, Custom Program Using Field KFMOD, to create a powerful tool that enables a high level of automatic posting using a combination of the NOTE TO PAYEE field and the ACCOUNT MODIFICATION field.

Create and Assign Posting Rules

The next step is to create posting rules that use the account symbols as debit and credit indicators. Posting keys are created and assigned to posting rules as shown in Figure 3.14.

Posting rule	Text
0001	Cash inflow via interim account
0002	Check credit memo through bank
0003	Check deposit via interim account
0004	Direct check deposit
0005	Check (debit memo)
0006	Bank transfer (debit memo)
0007	Clearing transfer: Outflow
0008	Clearing transfer: Inflow
0009	Account charges

Figure 3.14 Creating Keys for Posting Rules

Posting rules are created using posting rule keys together with account symbols, as shown in Figure 3.15.

Define Posting Rules								
Posti	Pos	Posting	Special	Acct (Debit)	Compr	Posting	Special	Acct (Credit)
002	1	40		US BANK	☐	50		INCOMING TRANSF
003	1	40		US BANK	☐			OUTGOING ACH
004	1	40		US BANK	☐	50		INCOMING ACH

Figure 3.15 Creating Posting Rules

Create Transaction Types

Every EBS format must have at least one *transaction type* that identifies it uniquely. The transaction type provides the link between a particular format and the EBS statement configuration in SAP ERP. For example, as shown in Figure 3.16, the transaction type BAI2 represents the U.S. BAI format statements.

Trans. type	Name
BAI2	US BAI2 Transaction
BANCOESP	Banco Español
BRADESCO	BRAZIL: BANCO BRADESCO
ES_CSB43	Spanish codes for elect.acct statment
FEBRABAN	
FI-CAX	Swift MT940 (standard-Germany)
FICABAI2	US BAI2 Transaction
FIDES	FIDES Switzerland
FIN	Finland: Merita
FRANCE	French codes for elect.acct statment
IHC	
ITAU	BRAZIL: BANCO ITAU
JP	Japanese codes for elect.acct statement
MT940	Swift MT940 (standard-Germany)
RE	Immobilien

Dialog Structure:
- Create Account Symbols
- Assign Accounts to Acco
- Create Keys for Posting I
- Define Posting Rules
- Create Transaction Type
  - Assign External Tran
  - Assign Bank Accounts to

Figure 3.16 Creating Transaction Type

Transaction type BAI2 is then linked to the company's chart of accounts, posting rules, routing numbers, and external transaction codes, to provide the link between the external EBS and the internal configuration settings to enable posting of the EBS in the books of account.

Assign External Transaction Types to Posting Rules

We are now ready to link the external EBS with the configuration set up in the SAP ERP system. External transaction codes are each assigned to a posting rule, as shown in Figure 3.17. Standard algorithms are available to allow for matching and clearing for special types of processing, for example check number matching (where cashed check details are reported through the EBS). Additionally, *planning types* can be assigned to the external BAI codes. Planning types are used in cash management and liquidity forecasting, and will be explained further in Chapter 6.

External tra	+/-	Posting	Interpretation Algorithm	Planning	Processing Type
009	-	0012	001: Standard algorithm	AB	my entry
051	+	0001	001: Standard algorithm		Dummy entry
115	+	001	000: No interpretation		Dummy entry
142	+	004	001: Standard algorithm		Dummy entry
168	+	004	000: No interpretation		Dummy entry
175	+	001	000: No interpretation		Dummy entry
195	+	002	001: Standard algorithm		Dummy entry
196	+	002	001: Standard algorithm		Dummy entry
197	+	001	000: No interpretation		Dummy entry
254	+	008	000: No interpretation		Dummy entry
275	+	006	000: No interpretation		Dummy entry
281	+	USZ+	000: No interpretation		Dummy entry
399	+	008	000: No interpretation		Dummy entry
475	+	007	000: No interpretation		Dummy entry

Figure 3.17 Assigning BAI Codes to Posting Rules

Assign Bank Accounts to Transaction Types

The final link in the basic configuration chain for EBS upload is assigning the bank key of the house bank to the transaction type. These can be generic to all bank accounts falling under the house bank, or they can be set up for specific bank accounts only. This provides great flexibility in being able to process EBS differently; even within the same house bank structure, if desired. Figure 3.18 shows the assignment of bank accounts to transaction type.

3 | Inbound Electronic Banking in SAP ERP

Dialog Structure	Assign Bank Accounts to Transaction Types									
☐ Create Account Symbols	Bank Key	Bank Account	Trans. ty	Currency cl	P	Su	Co	Cash Mana	Worklist	N D D
☐ Assign Accounts to Acco	10050033	88884444	FI-CAX		☐					☐
☐ Create Keys for Posting I	11111111	+	IHC		☐					☐
☐ Define Posting Rules	123123123	111111111	MT940		☐					☐
▽ ☐ Create Transaction Type	123123123	55552222	FICABAI2		☐					☐
☐ Assign External Tran	1234567890	12345678901	FRANCE	FRANCE	☐					☐
🗐 Assign Bank Accounts to	134329042	30050021	BAI2		CL	☐				☐
	20050000	10000100	MT940		☐					☐

Figure 3.18 Assigning Bank Key to Transaction Type

It is also an important configurable control because the bank key will need to be entered in this table and assigned to the appropriate transaction type to enable the system to successfully upload the statement.

An overview of the configuration logic is shown in Figure 3.19.

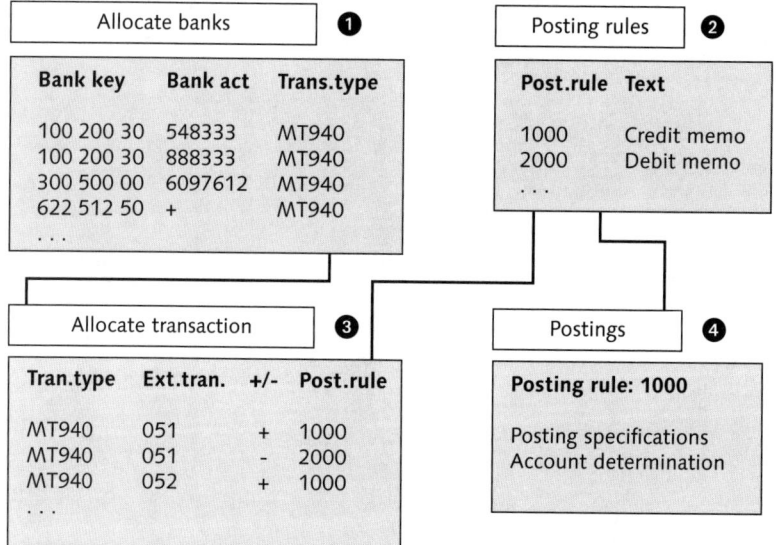

Figure 3.19 Overview of EBS Posting Logic

3.3 Straight Through Processing (STP)

STP, a term usually associated with automation of the capital markets' trade process and settlement, is one of the many benefits of having an integrated enterprise resource planning (ERP) system such as SAP ERP. It refers to the ability to conduct an entire end-to-end business process electronically, without the need for rekeying or manual intervention. Several areas in SAP Treasury are very conducive to STP, and we will cover these in the relevant chapters of this book. One area is the import, upload, posting, clearing, and reconciliation of EBS, where the STP can be as high as 97% of all transactions processed, with only 3% of transactions needing post-processing or manual intervention. From an internal control perspective, the greater the degree of STP, the greater the control over the process and assurance of the accuracy and integrity of the financial records and process. With inbound electronic banking, a high percentage of STP is achievable through a combination of configuration, integration, automation of file processing, use of available standard programs called user exits or custom user defined programs, and where appropriate, the use of workflow. Shortly, we will describe the key steps to automating the inbound EBS process, together with the inherent controls that need to be configured to ensure the integrity of the process.

The goal is to achieve 99% STP of transactions, measured by the number of transactions that need manual clearing or post-processing, as a percentage of the total throughput of transactions.

The number of uncleared or exceptional items is a red flag for auditors, and a robust automated process provides them with additional assurance with respect to the integrity and accuracy of transaction flow. We have seen STP as high as 97%, and we will discuss some of the tools to enable achieving this goal.

The following describes a typical flow scenario for the processing of inbound EBS:

1. The file is polled from the bank.
2. The bank file is received into the company's system and preprocessed.
3. The file is uploaded into SAP ERP after clearing a sequence check through balance matching.
4. The EBS is created in SAP ERP.
5. The transactions in the EBS are posted in the system.
6. Transactions are automatically matched and cleared or posted.
7. Errors are post-processed using Transaction FEBAN.
8. A G/L clearing program Transaction F.13 is run at the end of the day to clear matching items.

We will describe each of these steps in the following sections.

3.3.1 Polling Bank Files

Bank files are usually ready for polling in the early hours of the normal banking business day. Polling is scheduled for a particular time, to be agreed upon with the bank. It is good practice to schedule multiple polls within a time window, especially if polling takes place between the company and multiple banks. This will ensure that should there be a delay on the bank side in creating the files within the agreed time frame, a later poll will capture and poll the bank statement file.

The bank directory is polled using communication, scripting, and polling software to load the raw file into the company's internal file directory. Encryption and decryption software is typically used for additional security to safeguard the confidentiality of the inbound files.

3.3.2 Preprocessing

The incoming files are usually based on standards such as the BAI or SWIFT formats and can be in ASCII or text file format. Although bank formats are supposed to be standard, in practice, each bank applies the standards differently in subtle ways. For example, the NOTE TO PAYEE field may be in the fifth field for one bank and the sixth field for another bank. Because banks deal with many customers, it usually is not easy to get them to change their format. It is much easier to control the format internally, and use a preprocessing program to change the field contents to a format that will enable error-free upload into SAP ERP.

Another important argument in favor of using a preprocessing program is the fact that the banking environment is very dynamic, with mergers between banks taking place on a regular basis. Banks are also regularly upgrading their systems, and along with these changes come changes to formats and processing procedures. In most cases, a preprocessing program allows the changes to be accommodated internally, without affecting the overall process or requiring a complete rebuilding of the process or system.

Pre-processing examples

Typically, the preprocessing program is written in ABAP code and is inserted prior to the program that uploads and posts the bank statement. The preprocessing program reads the raw inbound file received form the bank, and processes it by bank name, making the necessary changes and outputting a new file with a different extension. This file is then uploaded into SAP ERP. The original file is archived for future reference.

To make this process automatic, the upload program in SAP ERP should be preceded by the preprocessing program. The upload program is activated by an event that is triggered when the preprocessing program for the specific bank or group of banks is completed.

The following is a list of common tasks performed by the bank preprocessing programs:

- Move information between comma delimited fields.
- Parse note to payee information if extraneous information is added to company-specific data that might be recognizable by SAP ERP for matching.
- Bank key numbers that are populated with leading zeroes in the raw file. The bank key in the house bank must match the bank key in the incoming EBS header data exactly; otherwise the upload will fail
- Populate specific note to payee information that can be used for matching through account modification.
- Identify sub-account numbers within a sub-account structure bank statement file.
- Bank account numbers that are populated with leading zeroes in the raw file. Again, these must match the bank account number in the incoming EBS exactly. Another configurable option is the ALTERNATIVE ACCT NO. field in the bank master data setup, as shown in Figure 3.20, which would have the same effect.

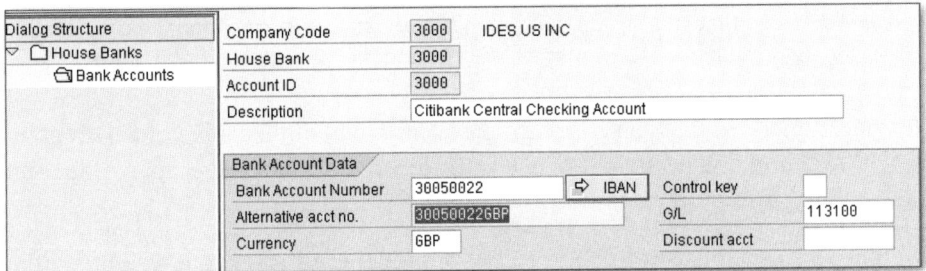

Figure 3.20 Use of Alternate Account Number Bank Key in House Bank Master Data

In Figure 3.20, because the currency is designated in GBP, the bank may add the currency to the bank account number in the incoming EBS. This will not match the entry in the bank account number field, and the EBS will not upload. This error can be prevented by entering the matching entry in the ALTERNATE ACCOUNT NO. field. As indicated previously, this can also be achieved through the preprocessing program, through program code.

3.3.3 Bank Balance Mismatch Error

The upload and processing of bank statements is a fully automated process. When bank statements are uploaded, SAP ERP performs a check to ensure that the opening balance of the uploaded statement is equal to the closing balance of the last statement in the system. This ensures that the statements are uploaded and posted in sequence. This is important from an accounting, control, and reconciliation perspective.

When the EBS is imported into the system, upload Program RFEBKA00 performs the bank balance statement check as follows: The system derives the opening balance of the incoming statement and compares it to the closing balance of the previous statement in the system. In the event of a mismatched balance, the statement will be rejected.

Unfortunately, the standard SAP ERP system is set up to only issue a warning if there is a balance mismatch. In an automated process, this means that the statement will upload and post, regardless. From an internal control perspective this is not acceptable and could make reconciliation more difficult. It may also give rise to audit issues.

> **Important Note**
>
> We recommend that you change the warning error to a hard error within the program so that the out of sequence statement will be rejected during automated processing.

It is recommended that you create a copy (Z program) of the bank upload Program RFEBKA00 and amend it as discussed previously, to use for the upload of bank statements.

In the event of a mismatch due to an out of sequence or erroneous statement, the responsible staff will need to contact the bank to obtain the correct statement and upload it manually, or to request operations support to rerun the batch job after the missing file is polled from the bank.

In large, global corporations it may not be practical to stop the upload for one missing or out of sequence statement, especially if there are numerous banks loading in multiple time zones. In this case it may be appropriate to allow the upload. However, the preprocessing program should be amended to provide detailed reports of exceptions, and a stringent process for prompt correction and reconciliation must be in place.

3.3.4 Automatic Matching and Clearing

SAP ERP lets you enable and optimize STP in the inbound EBS process in many ways, including through configuration, standard delivered programs or user exits, and tools. We will discuss these, as well as a very effective method to enable a high degree of STP. They can be controlled by the user department using a combination of the note to payee and account modification functionality.

> **Key Term: Note to Payee or Bank Reference Field**
>
> The note to payee or bank reference field contains information returned by the bank that provides customer-specific information with respect to the transaction on the bank statement. It is a key field that, if properly filled in, enables the automatic identification, matching, and clearing of incoming bank receipts and payments.

Electronic bank statements are uploaded and posted into SAP ERP using Program RFEBBU00. In the U.S., the EBS use a standard BAI format that allows individual transactions to be posted based on the external transaction code. Banks in Europe and Asia instead use four-digit alpha SWIFT codes to identify transactions. Postings in SAP ERP are affected by linking these external transaction codes to posting rules that specify the debit and credit postings. However, BAI codes can be quite generic in their description, and can be used differently by different banks in terms of their classification of a transaction. Also, if a bank is not sure what a transaction relates to, they will default it to a miscellaneous BAI code that will need to be further identified. Otherwise the transaction will by default post to a clearing account, and will need to be manually post-processed.

The automatic posting, matching, and clearing of EBS transactions takes place through any one or all of the following settings:

- Using the external (BAI) or bank code as described in Section 3.2.4, Configuring Electronic Bank Statements.
- Using account symbols with masking as described in Section 3.2.4, Configuring Electronic Bank Statements.

- Using the search string functionality in the IMG. The menu path is the same as shown earlier in Figure 3.10, IMG • ACCOUNTING • FINANCIAL ACCOUNTING • BANK ACCOUNTING • BUSINESS TRANSACTIONS • PAYMENT TRANSACTIONS • ELECTRONIC BANK STATEMENT • DEFINE SEARCH STRING FOR ELECTRONIC BANK STATEMENT / SIMULATE DOCUMENT NUMBER SEARCH USING STRINGS. This functionality was available in earlier versions but has been strengthened considerably in SAP ERP ECC 6.0. It uses similar logic as the customized version described in the next bullet point and in Section 3.3.5, Custom Program Using Field KFMOD, and is — in our opinion — a better alternative because it provides a lot more flexibility and ease of user maintenance.

- Using the field KFMOD in combination with the EBS user exit and custom table. This method is highly recommended, because it provides a great deal of flexibility, can be controlled by user departments, and can be easily maintained as new transactions need to be identified uniquely and assigned to posting rules.

> **Note**
> Creating a user-maintained custom table to identify note to payee information in combination with the standard EBS user exit and account modification rules provides the greatest flexibility for auto matching and clearing.

3.3.5 Custom Program Using Field KFMOD

In many instances, a detailed description is available in the detail line of the EBS, which is transferred into the note to payee field (FEBRE-VWEZW) in SAP ERP. Three lines of note to payee information are available, which are transferred from the EBS to Table FEBRE, as shown in Figure 3.21.

Table to be searched	FEBRE	Reference record for electronic bank statement line item
Number of hits	39	
Runtime	0	Maximum no. of hits	500

Shrt key	MR no	CRN	Payment Notes
42	1	1	INV1004
42	2	1	CHECK 0085275 001860703
42	3	1	MISC BANK FEE PITTSBURGH PA

Figure 3.21 Table FEBRE Holds Bank Note to Payee Information

A user exit (ZXF01U01) is available within the bank statement upload and posting program (RFEBBU00) that will allow account assignment based on unique strings in the note to payee field. The account assignment for the unique field is set up in IMG Configuration, as described in Section 3.2.4, Configuring Electronic Bank Statements.

An internal table within the custom program leverages the note to payee (bank reference field) and links it to the KFMOD account modification configuration. This allows a greater level of auto posting on incoming EBS transactions. The table is user-maintained, and can therefore be updated based on new transactions that need to be linked to existing KFMOD account posting entries. This enables a very high level of STP for EBS clearing. If additional account postings need to be maintained for field KFMOD, these need to be set up through configuration, as explained previously in Section 3.2.4, Configuring Electronic Bank Statements. The functionality can be designed based on the following assumptions:

- The program uses a custom internal table.
- The internal table needs to be maintained by authorized users.
- The KFMOD account determination line in the EBS user exit needs to be active and maintained.
- Account modification setup in the table will be specific to a combination of company code, house bank, bank account, and transaction code. The inclusion of company code is optional, depending on company-specific requirements.

Custom Program Logic

The user exit can be programmed to allow automatic assignment of incoming bank transactions based on the information provided in the note to payee field. The logic for the program is described in the related box.

> **Program Logic for Linking Note to Payee Information to Field KFMOD**
> - When a specific company code (FEBKO-BUKRS), bank (I_FEBKO-HBKID), and bank account (I_FEBKO_HKTID) are encountered,
> - For a specific external transaction code (FEBEP-VGEXT),

- Read SAP ERP table for a specific line (index) of the note to payee field (TABLE T_FEBRE INDEX N (FEBRE-RSNUM)
- Search for a unique subset of a string within the line (T_FEBRE-VWEZW)
- If the subset is found, populate the account modification field (E_FEBEP-KFMOD) with a designated five-character field.
- The five-character field is linked to an account assignment in the IMG.

The program logic flow is illustrated in Figure 3.22.

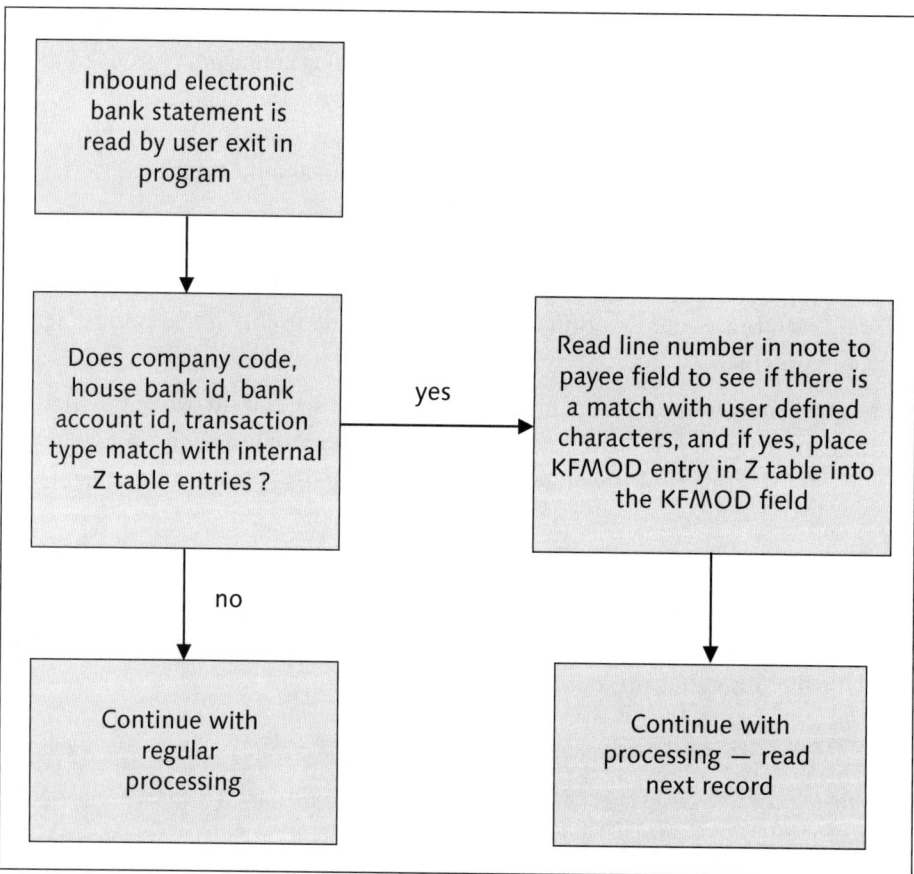

Figure 3.22 Account Modification with Note to Payee Program Logic

This logic is contained in user exit ZXF01U01, which is available for Program RFEBBU00 to allow account modification.

The custom table provides the requisite details to the program in the user exit that will allow account modification and posting to take place.

The program will call the following fields from the custom table:

1. COMPANY CODE (BUKRS)
2. HOUSE BANK ID (HBKID)
3. BANK ACCOUNT ID (HKTID)
4. EXTERNAL TRANSACTION CODE (VGEXT)
5. NOTE TO PAYEE INDEX (RSNUM)
6. UNIQUE LOOKUP STRING
7. MAPPING FIELD

This example results in an entry in the custom table, as shown in Table 3.2.

COMPANY CODE	HOUSE BANK	BANK A/C	EXT T-CODE (BTC)	INDEX	LOOK UP FIELD	MAPPING TO ACCOUNT ASSIGNMENT
3000	CITIBK	CHK01	399	3	MISC BANK FEE	FXFEE

Table 3.2 Custom table results

In the SAP ERP configuration mapping field, FXFEE will be assigned to the G/L account to which the transaction must post. The program in the user exit will access the information in the custom table Z_NOTE_TO_PAYEE_TABLE while processing each record in the inbound electronic bank file, and populate the KFMOD field when it finds matching criteria for house bank, external transaction code, and specified note to payee string. The user exit will receive and process one record at a time. The user exit must be activated. The program will use Boolean logic to search for the lookup field. As long as the information in the note to payee field is consistent, this method can be used to identify and post to specific G/L accounts.

Custom Table Maintenance and Security

Entries in the table have to be made in conjunction with SAP ERP configuration, as well as analyzing the incoming electronic bank statement file for specific note to payee content and index information. It is recommended that appropriate treasury users are authorized to maintain the custom table system in production, using Transaction SM30 with appropriate authorization access, or through a Z transaction. A new security authorization group should be created for the custom transaction. There must be appropriate SoD between configuration access and user access for maintaining the custom note to payee table.

3.3.6 Bank Polling and File Transmission

Typically, polling takes place from multiple banks, depending on the number of bank relationships maintained. Because polling is automated, each incoming bank needs to be set up as a variant. The program will then process each bank in order, as specified in the batch job that runs the upload program.

The polling software needs to be scheduled to run at a specific time in the morning when the files will be ready on the bank servers. Access to the bank servers will be controlled through a company user ID and password. These need to be provided to the script program. Banks typically require passwords to be changed after a specific time period, usually three months. It is important to designate an authorized treasury manager who can change the passwords. If the passwords are not changed within the bank's deadline, the polling will fail. This is one of the primary reasons for polling failure, and therefore something to be aware of.

A batch job will be required for each bank upload and processing that is scheduled, based on the latest time the polling can be completed.

> **Note**
> Bank host passwords need to be changed periodically. Authorized users must change the password on or before the due date, or polling will fail.

3.4 Prior Day Bank Statements

SAP ERP supports a variety of incoming electronic bank statement formats. These are shown in Figure 3.23. The most common EBS formats are BAI in the U.S and

Multicash and SWIFT (MT940) in Europe and Asia. A number of country-specific formats, such as Multicash, that support the Bank Communication Standard (BCS), are available in SAP ERP. Many global corporations sometimes use a bank or third party as a consolidator or value added network (VAN), to preprocess and consolidate various files and formats from different banks into one file for upload into SAP ERP. However, companies can also create their own preprocessing programs, and any number of statement files and formats can be uploaded automatically through the use of variants in the bank upload program.

Electronic bank statement format	Short text
M	Multicash (format: AUSZUG.TXT and UMSATZ.TXT)
I	SWIFT MT940 international format (field 86 unstuctured)
S	SWIFT MT940 with field 86 structured
E	ETEBAC format (France)
D	DTAUS format (Germany)
C	CSB43 format (Spain)
R	CSB43 format (Spain), reference fields together
B	Cobrança/Pagar Itau - Brazil
1	Cobrança/Pagar Bradesco - Brazil
A	BAI format
F	TITO format (Finland)

Figure 3.23 Sample of Supported Bank Formats

The screen shown in Figure 3.24 shows the settings required for the upload of prior day statements. Transaction FF.5 with an appropriate bank variant, (Program RFEBKA00) is used to upload and post the EBS.

> **Note**
>
> You should build a frontend preprocessing program prior to uploading bank statements. This will provide you with flexibility in a continually changing and dynamic global banking environment.

3 | Inbound Electronic Banking in SAP ERP

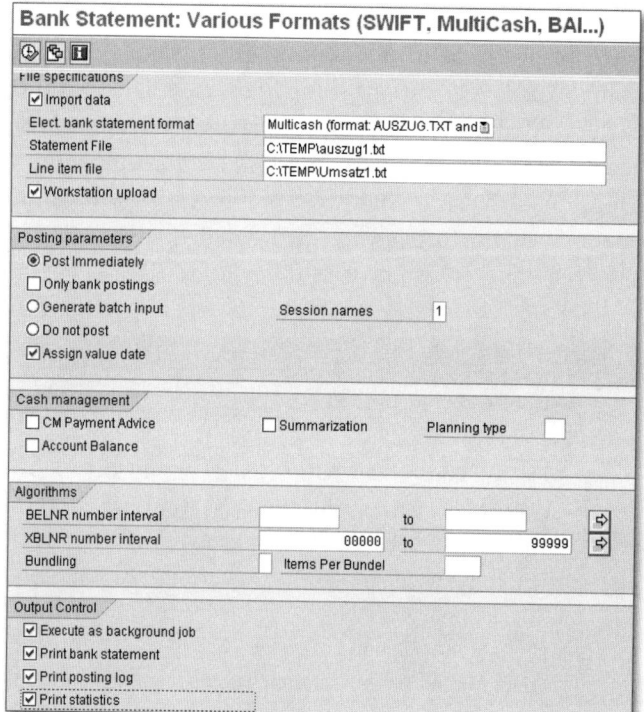

Figure 3.24 Prior Day Bank Statement Upload Program Transaction FF.5

After uploading the EBS into the system, it can be viewed using Transaction FF.6, as shown in Figure 3.25.

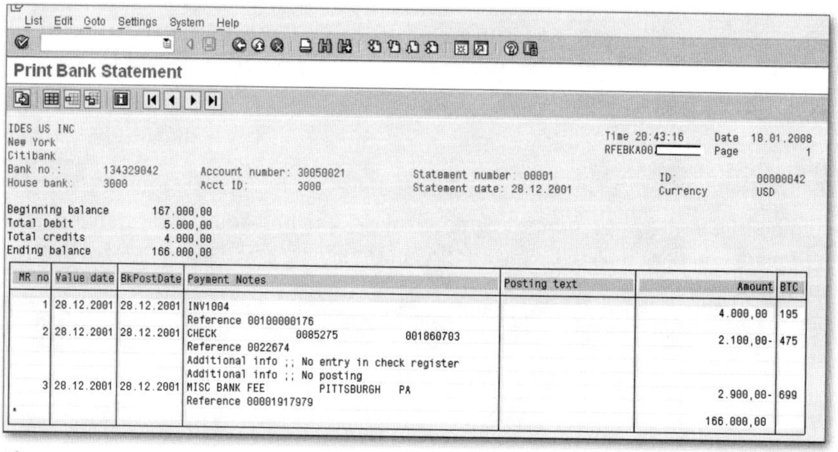

Figure 3.25 EBS Extract

124

The column BTC denotes the bank's external (BAI) transaction code reference. Note to payee information is available in the column PAYMENT NOTES. Note to payee information is stored in Table FEBRE, in up to four lines. Bank statement details are stored in Table FEBKO.

3.4.1 Creating Test Files for Upload

Implementing an electronic banking system requires receiving the files in electronic format from the bank so that you can set up the current configuration in SAP ERP. Program RFEBKATZ creates open items and bank statement files in Multicash format that can be used to configure the system and test it prior to receiving actual test files from the bank.

Executing Program RFEBKATZ creates a bank statement file for upload, as well as open items that will clear against the incoming bank statement file. The results of the test program are shown in Figure 3.26.

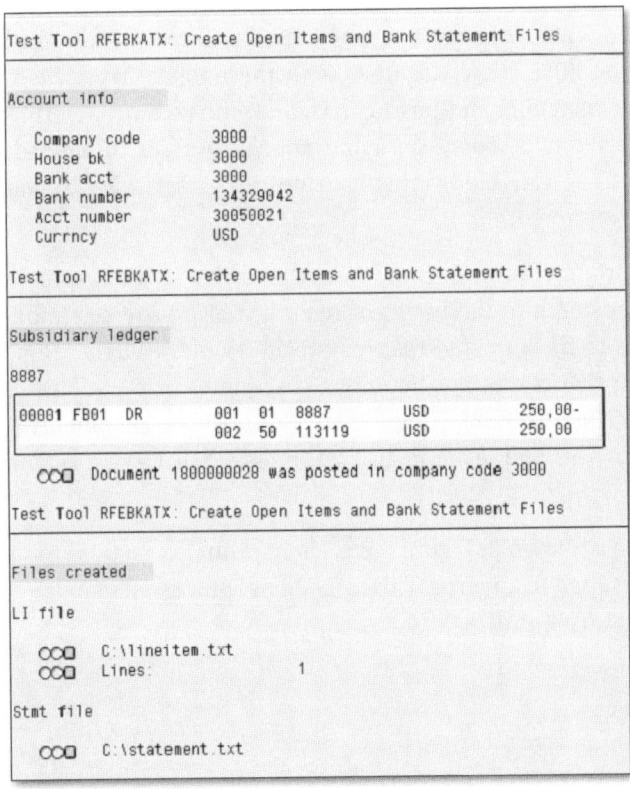

Figure 3.26 A Bank Upload Scenario Created by Test Tool Program RFEBATX

The resulting bank statement — after it has been uploaded and created — can be viewed using Transaction FF.6, as shown in Figure 3.27.

```
Citibank
Account holder  SAP test program RFEBKATX
Bank no.:        134329042      Account number: 30050021    Statement number: 00003       ID:              00000051
House bank:      3000           Acct ID:        3000        Statement date:   28.01.2008   Currency         USD

Beginning balance      166.000,00
Total Debit                 0,00
Total credits             250,00
Ending balance        166.250,00
```

MR no	Value date	BkPostDate	Payment Notes	Posting text	Amount	BTC
1	28.01.2008	28.01.2008	Invoice number 1800000028 Invoice date 26.01.2008 Paul Johnson SPRINGFIELD Business partner;; Paul Johnson SPR.. Partner bank number 123445678 Partner account 2222222229	Beginning balance	166.000,00 250,00	051
					166.250,00	

Figure 3.27 Electronic Bank Statement After Upload into SAP

3.4.2 Posting Matching and Reconciliation of Bank Statements

BAI external transaction codes are three-digit numbers used to identify individual transactions reported on the EBS. These, together with the note to payee field, form the basis of automatic matching and posting based on the account determination rules that have been set up through configuration. After successful upload, a posting log provides details of transactions that have posted successfully, as well as any errors that were encountered.

The posting log is an important control document that provides an audit trail of all transactions that have posted into the books of record. It also provides information on errors that need to be corrected that may relate to master data setup. For example, a G/L account that is set up to require a cost center may not have a cost center assigned to it. When the EBS program tries to post the statement, it will not find the cost center. This will result in an error message that a cost center assignment is required.

An example of a posting log is shown in Figure 3.28. There is one correctly posted transaction, and one that resulted in an error. This can be post-processed manually, as described in Section 3.5.1, Post-Processing.

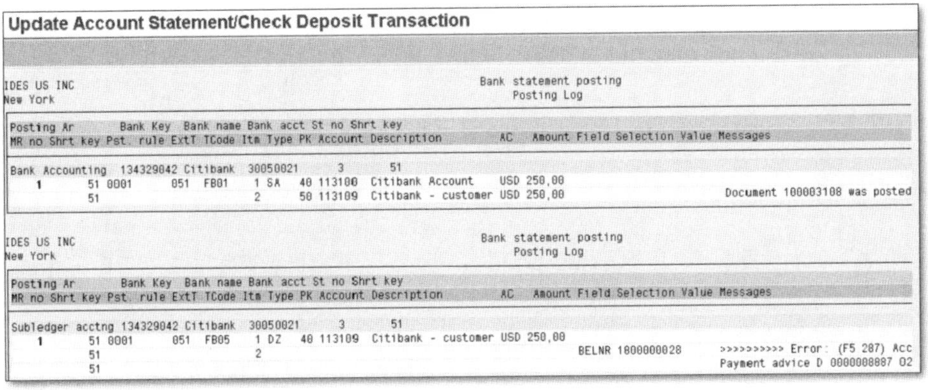

Update Account Statement/Check Deposit Transaction

```
IDES US INC                                             Bank statement posting
New York                                                    Posting Log

Posting Ar        Bank Key  Bank name Bank acct St no Shrt key
MR no Shrt key Pst. rule ExtT TCode Itm Type PK Account Description        AC   Amount Field Selection Value Messages

Bank Accounting  134329042 Citibank  30050021      3       51
    1       51 0001       051  FB01    1 SA   40 113100  Citibank Account    USD 250,00
            51                         2      50 113109  Citibank - customer USD 250,00            Document 100003108 was posted

IDES US INC                                             Bank statement posting
New York                                                    Posting Log

Posting Ar        Bank Key  Bank name Bank acct St no Shrt key
MR no Shrt key Pst. rule ExtT TCode Itm Type PK Account Description        AC   Amount Field Selection Value Messages

Subledger acctng 134329042 Citibank  30050021      3       51
    1       51 0001       051  FB05    1 DZ   40 113109  Citibank - customer USD 250,00
            51                         2                                     BELNR 1800000028     >>>>>>>>>> Error: (F5 287) Acc
            51                                                                                    Payment advice D 0000008887 02
```

Figure 3.28 Posting Log on Upload of EBS

In addition to the posting log, a table of statistics is created that provides a summary log of transactions, as shown in Figure 3.29. This represents a useful audit trail from a control perspective, and can be used by auditors and persons responsible for posting, clearing, and reconciliation of the bank statement.

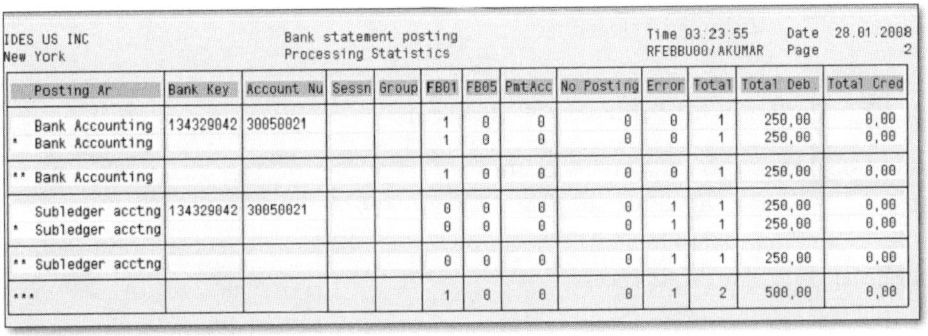

IDES US INC — Bank statement posting — Time 03:23:55 — Date 28.01.2008
New York — Processing Statistics — RFEBBU00/AKUMAR — Page 2

Posting Ar	Bank Key	Account Nu	Sessn	Group	FB01	FB05	PmtAcc	No Posting	Error	Total	Total Deb.	Total Cred
Bank Accounting * Bank Accounting	134329042	30050021			1 1	0 0	0 0	0 0	0 0	1 1	250,00 250,00	0,00 0,00
** Bank Accounting					1	0	0	0	0	1	250,00	0,00
Subledger acctng * Subledger acctng	134329042	30050021			0 0	0 0	0 0	0 0	1 1	1 1	250,00 250,00	0,00 0,00
** Subledger acctng					0	0	0	0	1	1	250,00	0,00
***					1	0	0	0	1	2	500,00	0,00

Figure 3.29 Posting Log on Upload and Posting of EBS

Posting details in the EBS are available in Table FEBEP, as shown in Figure 3.30.

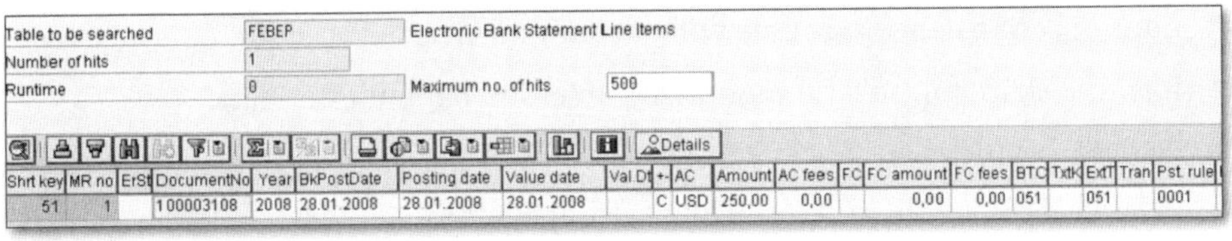

Table to be searched: FEBEP — Electronic Bank Statement Line Items
Number of hits: 1
Runtime: 0 — Maximum no. of hits: 500

Details

Shrt key	MR no	ErSt	DocumentNo	Year	BkPostDate	Posting date	Value date	Val.Dt	+-	AC	Amount	AC fees	FC	FC amount	FC fees	BTC	TxtK	ExtT	Tran	Pst. rule
51	1		100003108	2008	28.01.2008	28.01.2008	28.01.2008		C	USD	250,00	0,00		0,00	0,00	051		051		0001

Figure 3.30 Posting Log Details in Table FEBEP

Note to payee information, a critical component of automatic matching and clearing, is available for viewing in Table FEBRE, as shown in Figure 3.31.

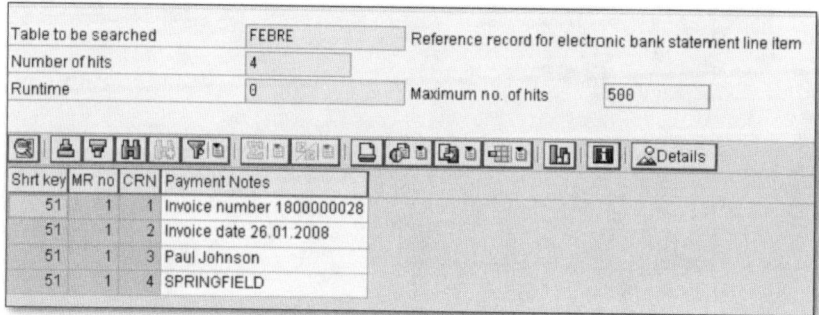

Figure 3.31 Note to Payee Information in Table FEBRE

Note that each line in the note to payee field is identified as a row number from 1 to 4. These rows are used to identify specific information for the purpose of matching and clearing incoming EBS transactions. See Section 3.3.6, Bank Polling and File Transmission, for a description of how this information can be used for automatic matching and clearing.

3.4.3 Controls for Prior Day Statements

Controls for prior day statements are very important because these transactions post to the books of record; unposted or unreconciled items will affect the accuracy of the financial statements. The following are the key areas for ensuring sound internal control for the process:

- Define and implement a process for monitoring polling exceptions and escalation procedures.
- Use clearing accounts to capture exception items that must be reconciled daily — or at least periodically — depending on volume.
- Control zero balance accounts with a common clearing account.
- Institute strict controls for authorized access to bank master data.
- Segregate duties between key functions such as master data creation and maintenance, transaction processing, and reconciliation.
- Review the posting log and Transaction FEBAN to ensure all transactions are posted.

- Reconcile bank statements and ensure that all clearing accounts are balanced.
- Investigate items that post to the clearing account because the system cannot recognize the transaction. These should be identified and set up for STP in the future, using the methods outlined in section 3.3.5, Custom Program Using Field KFMOD.
- Control access to preprocessing programs and file directories where raw and preprocessed bank files are stored.
- Restrict access to configuration settings for EBS.
- Ensure that balance mismatches result in a hard stop error where possible. Alternatively, ensure that adequate compensatory controls are in place to track and reconcile out of sequence bank statements and ensure that the financial books of record are updated.

3.5 Bank Reconciliation and Control

Bank reconciliation is a straightforward process in SAP ERP. Because one side of the EBS always posts to the G/L account designated for that bank account, the balance per the bank statement uploaded into the system will always equal the balance per the G/L. Any in transit items will represent internal bank transfers or cash concentration movements that have not had both sides of the transaction reflected. For example, there could be a delay in uploading the statement for the receiving bank, but the sending bank statement has been uploaded. In this case, an unmatched item will exist in the clearing account for that family of banks that represents an in transit amount and that will need to be added to the bank reconciliation.

For reconciliation purposes, reporting of bank balances and in-transit accounts can be performed through cash management reporting, by grouping the appropriate family of bank G/L and clearing accounts. We will discuss the setup of cash management reporting in Chapter 6.

3.5.1 Post-Processing

Any errors encountered by the posting program will result in an error log, as shown in Figure 3.28. These can be corrected in post-processing, using Transaction FEBAN. The initial selection screen is shown in Figure 3.32. The available options let you select specific statements by date, or you can select a group of statements for collective processing, including specific header and item data.

> **Note**
>
> The EBS upload process consists of two distinct steps that are usually executed in sequence through the variant in Transaction FF.5. The first step in the process is the actual upload of the bank statement into the SAP ERP system. This creates a bank statement and populates the various tables with EBS information. The second step is the actual posting of the transactions in the books of record. It is important to make this distinction to be able to isolate causes of failure in the EBS process. If the EBS doesn't upload, this indicates a problem with the upload program not recognizing the bank identification in the incoming file header. This can't be post-processed and the file will simply be rejected. After the file is uploaded, any errors in the posting process will go to post-processing.

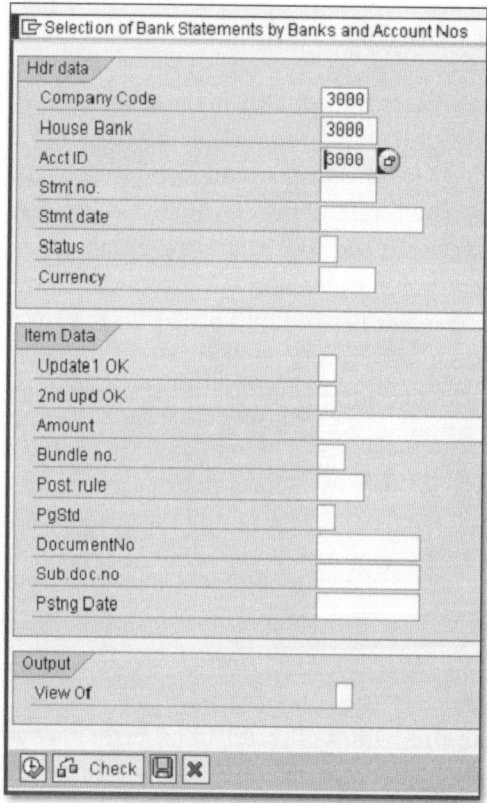

Figure 3.32 Initial Screen for Transaction FEBAN

After executing the selection, the resulting screen will indicate in red any items that need post-processing, as shown in Figure 3.23.

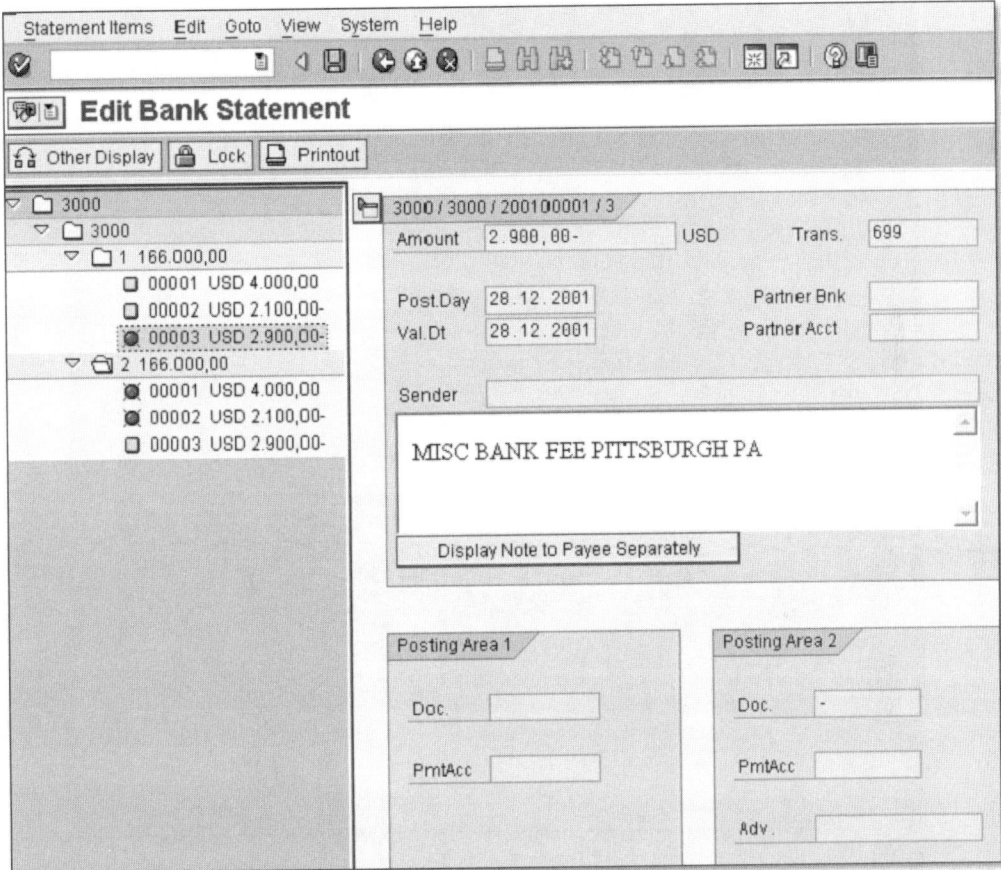

Figure 3.33 Transaction FEBAN Detail View

Clicking on the transaction with errors provides details about any missing information that needs to be provided. You can provide the information online, and after you do, the transaction will post and the red bullet will change to green. An example is shown in Figure 3.34 where an error message indicates that the posting period is not open.

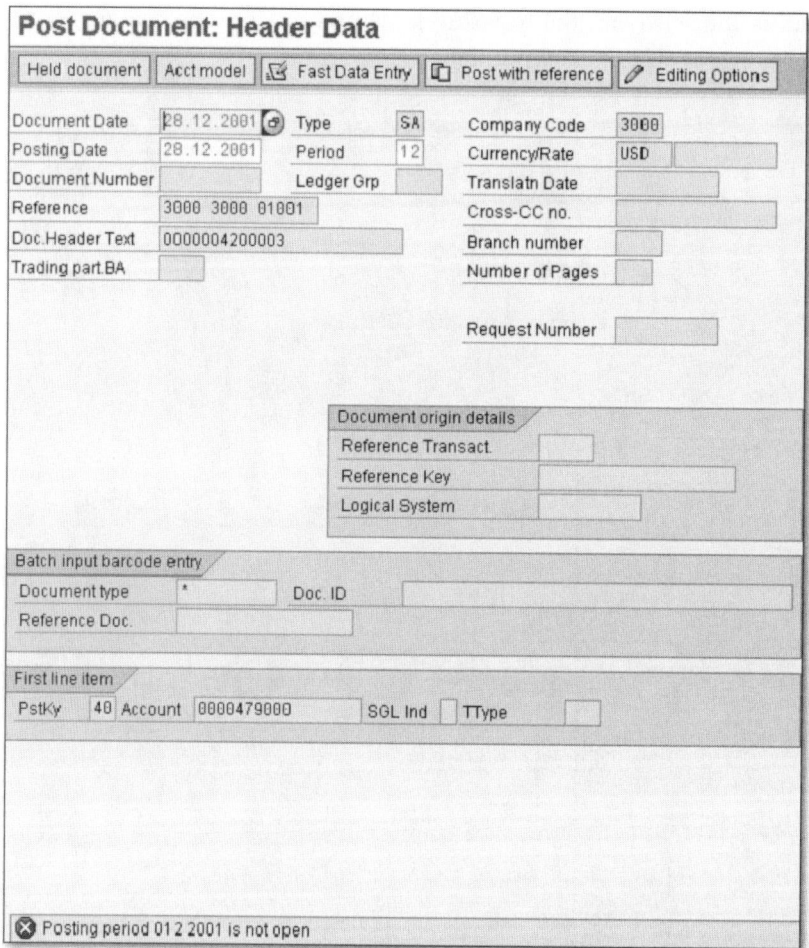

Figure 3.34 Error Resolution Using Transaction FEBAN

3.5.2 Displaying an Electronic Bank Statement

An EBS can be displayed using Transaction FF.6 or using the application menu path FINANCIAL SUPPLY CHAIN MANAGEMENT • CASH AND LIQUIDITY MANAGEMENT • CASH MANAGEMENT • INCOMINGS • ELECTRONIC BANK STATEMENTS • FF.6 DISPLAY.

This step is performed after importing the EBS through Transaction FF.5 or application menu path FINANCIAL SUPPLY CHAIN MANAGEMENT • CASH AND LIQUIDITY MANAGEMENT • CASH MANAGEMENT • INCOMINGS • ELECTRONIC BANK STATEMENTS • FF.5 IMPORT.

You display bank statements to facilitate reconciliation and for audit trail and record keeping purposes. An example of a bank statement uploaded into SAP ERP is shown in Figure 3.35.

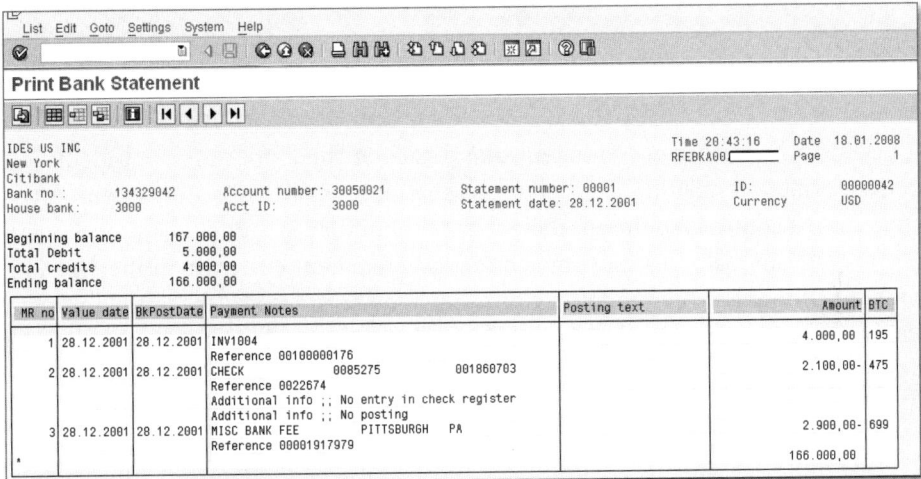

Figure 3.35 Display EBS Transaction FF.6

Bank statements can be archived or deleted as discussed in Section 3.5.4, Deleting and Archiving Bank Statements.

3.5.3 Manual Bank Statement

In some instances, an EBS is not available because of problems at the bank, or because of a corrupted or incomplete file that can't be recovered. To address this, SAP ERP provides the ability to manually enter a bank statement based on a paper statement.

The manual bank statement is uploaded using Transaction FF67 or application menu path FINANCIAL SUPPLY CHAIN MANAGEMENT • CASH AND LIQUIDITY MANAGEMENT • CASH MANAGEMENT • INCOMING • MANUAL BANK STATEMENT • FF67 ENTER.

The initial selection screen provides a view of statements currently available in the system, as shown in Figure 3.36. A new statement is generated by clicking on NEW STATEMENT.

3 | Inbound Electronic Banking in SAP ERP

Manual Bank Statement Overview						
Copy New Statement						
Bank Account						
CCode	Name of bank		Bank Key	Acct		Curr
1000	Deutsche Bank Gruppe		50070010	10000100	EUR	EUR
1000	Deutsche Bank		62030050	7002335300	EUR	EUR
3000	Citibank		134329042	30050021	USD	USD

Figure 3.36 Overview of Bank Statements Using Transaction FF67

To create a manual bank statement, the details of the bank statement identification information need to be specified, as shown in Figure 3.37. It is important to note from a control standpoint that statement number, statement date, and opening and closing balances must match the last statement currently in the SAP ERP system. Otherwise, the program won't allow you to proceed. This is an important control feature to ensure that bank statements are entered in sequence.

Process Manual Bank Statement

Overview | Planning types

Bank Key	134329042	Citibank
Bank Account	30050021	Citibank Central Checking Account
Currency	USD	American Dollar
Statement Number	4	
Statement Date	29.01.2008	

Control

Opening Balance	166.250,00
Closing Balance	166.550,00
Posting date	29.01.2008

Selection of Payment Advices

Planning type	
Statement Date	
Planning date from		Planning date to	
Characteristic	

Further Processing

☐ Bank postings only

Figure 3.37 Initial Entry Screen for Manual Bank Statement

After entering the correct control and sequence data, the next screen lets you enter actual bank transactions, as shown in Figure 3.38. Because the opening and closing balance have been entered in the initial screen, the cumulative balance in the detail screen must match the difference; otherwise the program will not let you post the bank statement. This is another example of an inherent, important accounting control feature that is built into the system.

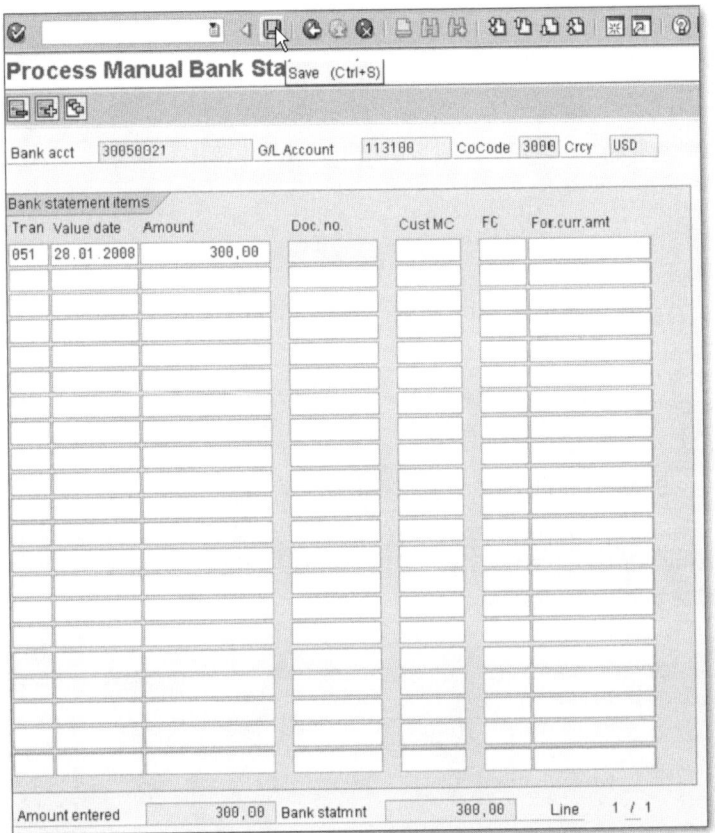

Figure 3.38 Input Screen for Manual Bank Statement Entry

Manual bank statements use internal codes configured in the SAP ERP system instead of the external BAI codes used by the incoming electronic bank statements discussed earlier.

The path for configuring manual bank statements is IMG • ACCOUNTING • FINANCIAL ACCOUNTING • BANK ACCOUNTING • BUSINESS TRANSACTIONS • MANUAL BANK STATEMENT. Internal codes are configured in this screen, as shown in Figure 3.39.

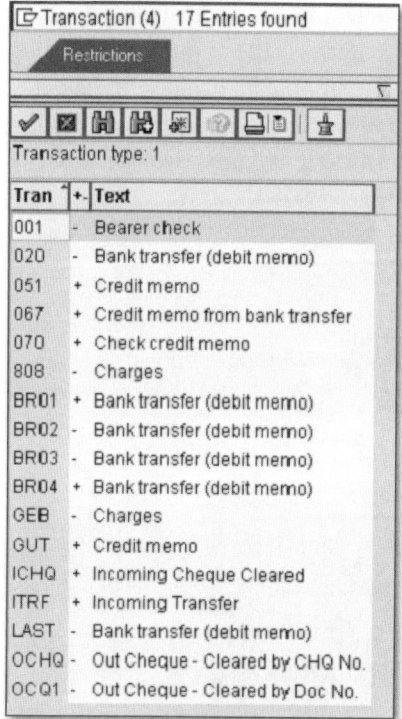

Figure 3.39 Internal Account Symbols for Manual Bank Statement Entry

After successful posting, a manual bank statement is created that provides an overview of the posting, as shown in Figure 3.40.

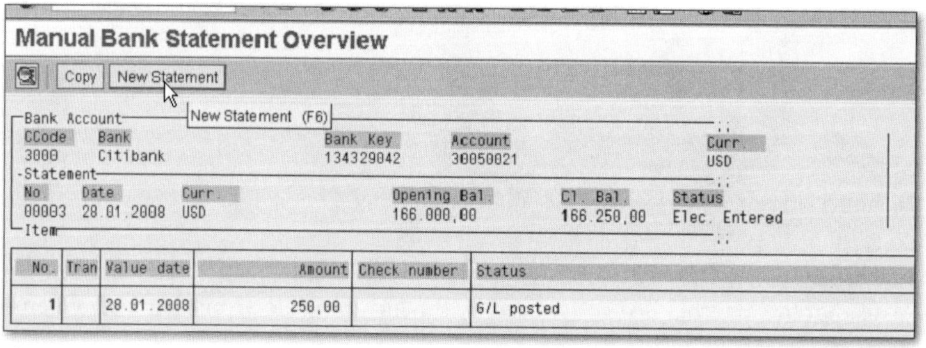

Figure 3.40 Manual Bank Statement Report of a Created Statement

The resulting posting log is shown in Figure 3.41.

Posting Ar	Bank Key	Account Nu	Sessn	Group	FB01	FB05	PmtAcc	No Posting	Error	Total	Total Deb	Total Cred
Bank Accounting	134329042	30050021			1	0	0	0	0	1	300,00	0,00
• Bank Accounting					1	0	0	0	0	1	300,00	0,00
•• Bank Accounting					1	0	0	0	0	1	300,00	0,00
Subledger acctng	134329042	30050021			0	0	0	0	1	1	300,00	0,00
• Subledger acctng					0	0	0	0	1	1	300,00	0,00
•• Subledger acctng					0	0	0	0	1	1	300,00	0,00
•••					1	0	0	0	1	2	600,00	0,00

Figure 3.41 Posting Log for Manual Bank Statement

3.5.4 Deleting and Archiving Bank Statements

It is recommended that you keep all inbound EBS files and bank statements in the system for at least the current and previous year. Depending on the company's data retention strategy, bank statements, bank master data, and transaction data can be archived in SAP ERP, or deleted if necessary.

Archiving

The transactions shown in Table 3.3 can be used for archiving bank-related data in SAP ERP.

Transaction	Data Archived
F61A	Bank master data
F66A	Electronic bank statements

Table 3.3 Transactions used for archiving bank-related data

Deletion

There may be instances where bank statements need to be deleted from the system because they are out of sequence or incorrect. Program RFEBKA96 is used to delete a bank statement from the bank data buffer. The program is executed using Transaction SE38 or SA38, as shown in Figure 3.42.

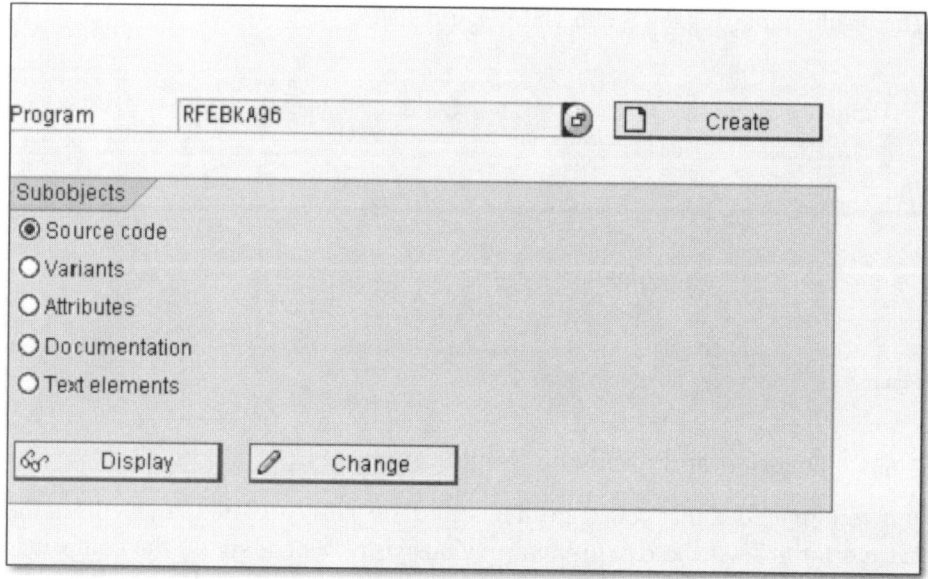

Figure 3.42 Program RFEBKA96 for Deletion of Bank Statements

The resulting selection screen requires selection of the type of data to be deleted, for example electronic or manual bank statement, check deposit transaction, lockbox or account balance. If an electronic or manual bank statement is selected for deletion, the statement ID needs to be entered in the selection screen, as shown in Figure 3.43.

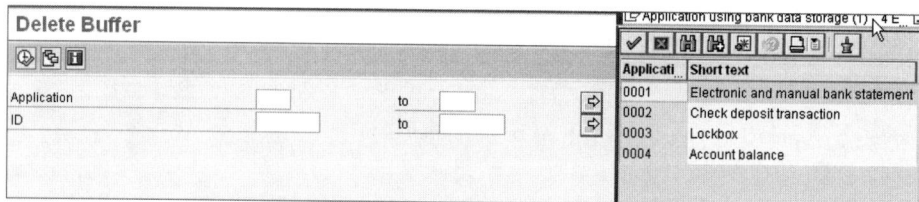

Figure 3.43 Input Screen for Bank Statement Deletion Program RFEBKA96

The statement ID can be determined by executing Transaction FF67, and then setting the indicator that the statement should be deleted, as shown in Figure 3.44.

Summary of Controls for Inbound Electronic Banking | 3.6

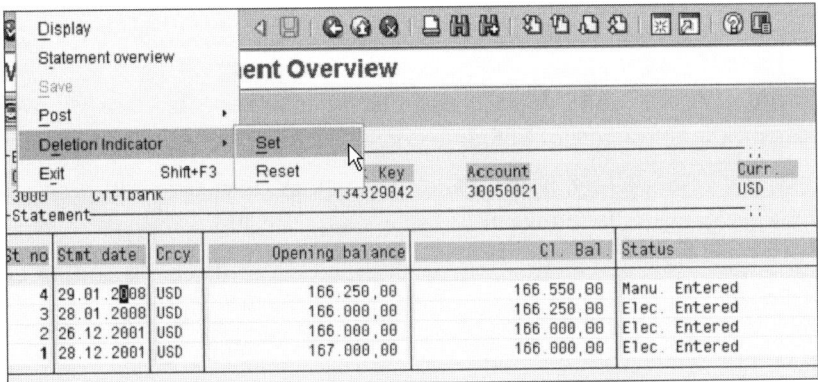

Figure 3.44 Bank Statement Overview Before Deletion

The resulting screen, shown in Figure 3.45, shows that the statement has been deleted.

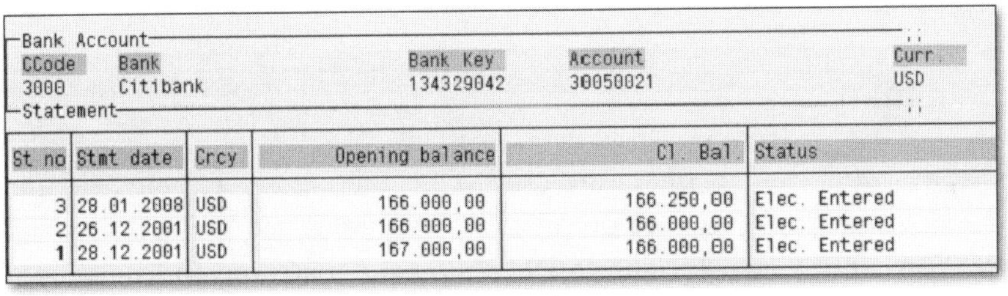

Figure 3.45 Bank Statement Overview After Deletion

It is important to note that strict controls must be in place for deleting bank statements. This includes restricted access to the transactions enabling deletion, controls to ensure proper authorization was obtained to delete a bank statement, and effective SoD to ensure that persons with access to creation or deletion of bank statements don't also have access to transaction processing or post-processing activities.

3.6 Summary of Controls for Inbound Electronic Banking

This chapter covered many key controls inherent in the inbound EBS process. These can be summarized as follows:

139

- Formal documentation of correction and escalation procedures in case of polling or upload failures.
- Reconciliation on a periodic basis of clearing accounts and in transit flows, depending on the frequency of EBS uploads.
- Regular review of all polling, upload, and posting logs, as well as post processing activities, to ensure the books of record are accurate and complete.
- Set up of automatic email alerts of anycritical failures in the bank polling or upload process.
- Establishment of security and access controls for inbound files, file directories, master data, and password change access.
- Establishment of strict SoD between key functions and monitoring of change management logs, especially for key master data.
- Establishment, documentation, and maintenance of risk/control matrices of key business processes for SOX compliance purposes.

3.7 Summary

In this chapter, we looked at the entire process for inbound electronic banking, and how to leverage the system to optimize STP. We reviewed several tools and techniques to enable a high hit rate for the automatic matching and posting of EBS transactions, making full use of the bank's note to payee or bank reference field. We also looked at how the banking and accounting structure design and configuration plays an important part in strengthening and enhancing controls for the inbound banking process. In Chapter 4, we will look at the outbound side of electronic banking in SAP ERP.

Chapter 4 covers key business processes involved in outbound electronic banking and payment processing in SAP ERP.

4   Outbound Electronic Banking in SAP ERP

Electronic banking in SAP ERP is feature-rich with a diverse range of functionality that allows for the automation of end-to-end processes related to outbound banking. Owing to the significant integration between SAP Treasury and the other SAP ERP applications, this automation can be extended throughout the financial supply chain in Procure to Pay, Order to Cash, and other enterprise-wide processes. It can also be extended beyond the enterprise to vendors, suppliers, and customers. This integration makes it easy to build strong systemic and user-defined internal control features throughout the process.

Almost every type of payment media is available within SAP ERP for electronic payment setup, creation, processing, and transmission. A powerful utility called Payment Workbench enables the creation of file formats in SAP ERP without any programming knowledge. Domestic and international ACH, Fedwire (U.S.), and international formats such as SWIFT (MT100, MT103, etc.) are fully supported.

Vendor master banking information supports Bank Identifier Code (BIC) — also called SWIFT address — and International Bank Account Number (IBAN) formats. Since January 1, 2007, providing the valid BIC and IBAN numbers of the receiver's account is mandatory for all international Euro payments within EU member states, Norway, Iceland, Liechtenstein and Switzerland, irrespective of value.

The ability of vendor master banking information to include BIC and IBAN is of particular importance when SEPA rules come into effect for electronic fund transfers to and from the European Union (EU) zone.

4.0.1   Key Drivers and Benefits

One of the foremost benefits of initiating outbound payments within SAP ERP comes as a result of its integration with the frontend finance and business functions such as sales, purchasing, and materials management. All transactions are initiated, recorded, authorized and approved prior to payment. The payment process automatically executes these payments based on due dates. The cycle is complete when the outbound transactions settle, are reflected in incoming bank statements, and post to clearing accounts for reconciliation with the original entries in the G/L and sub ledgers. Because SAP ERP is the prime book of record, from a control standpoint, approvals, checks, and balances can be provided throughout the system at key handoff points, as the transaction moves through the financial supply chain process.

This is one of the major advantages over the standalone treasury workstations that are often used by companies to make electronic fund payments. As part of that process, all transactions have to be reentered into the prime book of record, and additional external as well as manual controls need to be built to ensure their integrity and accuracy. Using SAP ERP in this manner reduces the time and expense associated with any duplicate processes.

An overview of the outbound banking process cycle in SAP ERP is shown in Figure 4.1. Financial transactions, after they're recorded, are selected automatically by the system through daily or weekly payment runs, which propose items for payment based on due dates. SAP ERP uses a payment method designated by an alpha character to identify and link to a specific form of payment media such as check, ACH, wire, and so on. These payment methods are in turn linked to the appropriate disbursement bank. Checks, wires, and ACH are the most common form of payment media and SAP ERP supports all format types, including the ability to create custom formats if required.

Electronic payments are sent to the bank for further processing. The settled transactions are reflected in the incoming bank statements that can be reconciled and cleared against the originating transaction in SAP ERP. Adequate controls need to be built into the entire cycle to ensure that transactions are authorized, verified, accurate, and reconciled, with proper checks and balances and SoD between key functions and processes to prevent error and fraud.

Although check processing is predominantly a manual process using the postal system, in the U.S. it could include a fraud prevention service called Positive Pay that uses electronic bank file transfers. Positive Pay will be discussed in detail in Chapter 5.

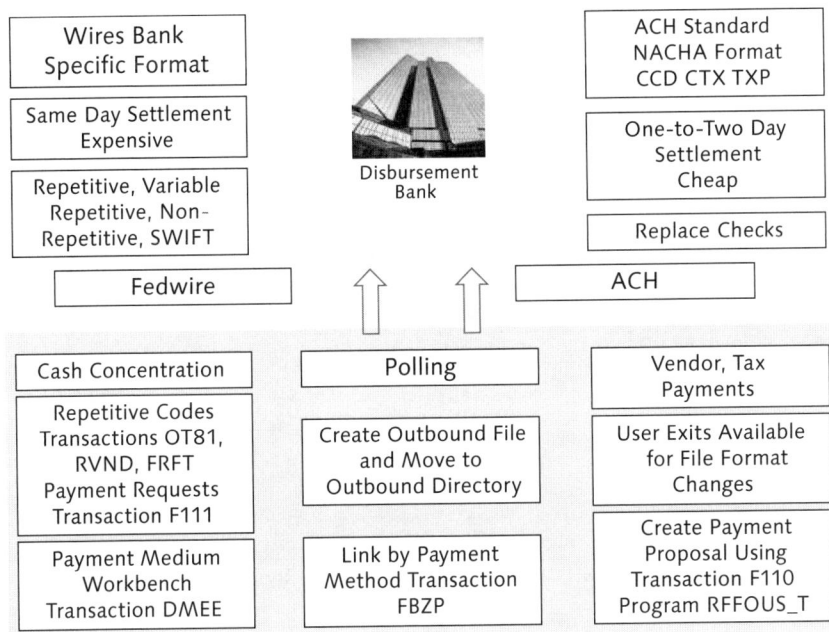

Figure 4.1 Overview of Outbound Electronic Banking Functionality

4.1 Master Data Structure and Controls

All transactions in SAP ERP access master data in one form or another. Master data is usually set up once and can be added to, changed, or deleted. Appropriate controls for master data are essential in order to ensure the integrity and accuracy of transactional data, and to prevent fraud and unauthorized use. This is especially important with respect to bank-related master data.

4.1.1 Bank Master Data

The correct setup and structure for bank master data is key to accurate processing and control over transactional data in SAP ERP. From an outbound banking perspective, strict access, security, and authorization controls for the create, change, and display functions must be in place. Transaction FI12 provides access to house banks and all related configuration to which access must be strictly controlled.

Figure 4.2 shows the authorization objects available for controlling access to house banks and payment methods.

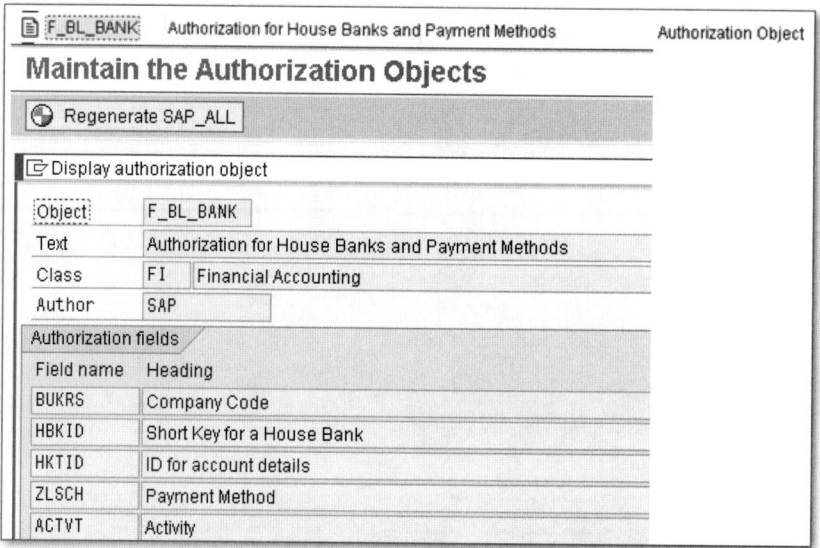

Figure 4.2 Authorization Object for House Banks and Payment Methods

Authorization object FI_BL_BANK enables you to restrict access to any combination of CREATE OR GENERATE, CHANGE, DISPLAY, DELETE, and DISPLAY CHANGE DOCUMENTS, as shown in Figure 4.3.

DISPLAY CHANGE DOCUMENTS is an important setting from an audit trail standpoint, because it tracks details of any changes made to master data, such as the identity of the user making the change, the date of the change, the old value, and the new value.

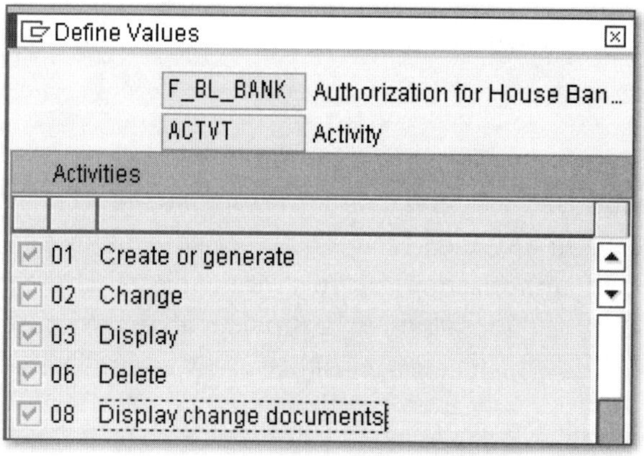

Figure 4.3 Authorization for Change Activities

Other important authorization objects used in payment processing are shown in Figure 4.4. Key among these are the authorization objects F_RPCODE for repetitive codes (covered in Section 4.4.2, Repetitive Codes) and F_PAYRQ for payment requests.

	Financial Accounting	Object Class
FI		
F_BKPF_VW	Acc. Document: Change/Display Default Vals for Doc.Type/PKey	Authorization Object
F_PAYRQ	Authorization Object for Payment Requests	Authorization Object
F_WORKQ001	Authorization Object for Work Queue	Authorization Object
F_ACT_EBPP	Authorization Object for the Activities (EBPP)	Authorization Object
F_T011E	Authorization for Financial Calendar	Authorization Object
F_INVRPGIR	Authorization for GR/IR Journal (Inventory Info System)	Authorization Object
F_BL_BANK	Authorization for House Banks and Payment Methods	Authorization Object
F_RPCODE	Repetitive Code	Authorization Object

Figure 4.4 Authorization Objects for Payment Processing

4.1.2 Vendor Master Data

Banking data relevant to the vendor is entered in the PAYMENT TRANSACTIONS section of the vendor master. The fields available include the IBAN and SWIFT codes. The screen is shown in Figure 4.5.

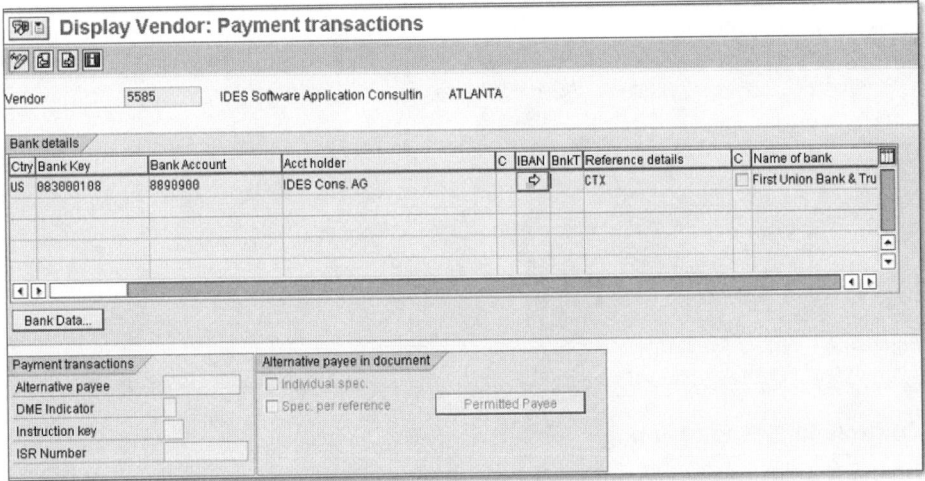

Figure 4.5 Vendor Master Bank Data Screen

The PAYMENT TRANSACTIONS ACCOUNTING screen in the vendor master is used to link the payment method types available to the vendor, and to provide default values for automatic payment, such as house bank, and payment terms. A number of fields are available that enhance controls for vendor payment processing, such as PAYMENT BLOCK, GROUPING KEY and TOLERANCE GROUPS, as shown in Figure 4.6.

If the vendor is set up for payment by check, the field CHK CASHING TIME can be configured to calculate the average check cashing time based on actual value dates. This information can be useful for cash forecasting purposes as we will see in Chapter 6.

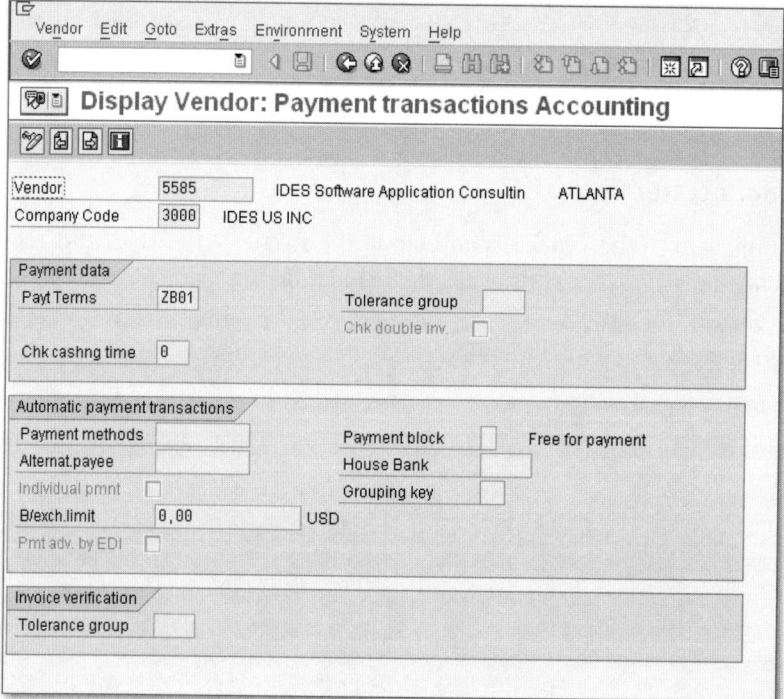

Figure 4.6 Vendor Master Payment Transactions Accounting Screen

Controls for Setup of Foreign Vendors

Creation of new foreign vendors and customer master records should be analyzed from the perspective of meeting the Office of the Foreign Assets Control (OFAC) and Anti-Money Laundering (AML) requirements.

4.1.3 Dual Authorization Control

A useful control feature available through configuration is the ability to define certain fields as *sensitive*. This results in activating dual control over any change activity relating to that field.

Defining Sensitive Fields for Dual Control

For example, if you define a field in the customer/vendor master record as "sensitive," the corresponding customer/vendor account is blocked for payment if the entry is changed. The block is removed when a second person with authorization checks the change and confirms or rejects it. This is a very useful control tool, especially where high dollar-amount payments are involved that need additional scrutiny and approval release.

Configuring a Sensitive Field for Dual Control

The menu path to configure a sensitive field for dual control is IMG • FINANCIAL ACCOUNTING • ACCOUNTS RECEIVABLE AND ACCOUNTS PAYABLE • VENDOR ACCOUNTS • MASTER DATA • DEFINE SENSITIVE FIELDS FOR DUAL CONTROL (VENDOR).

In Figure 4.7 the ALTERNATIVE PAYEE field has been defined as sensitive in the Customizing table. If the accounting clerk responsible changes the entry in this field in the customer/vendor master record, the account is blocked for the payment run until a second person with authorization confirms the change to the master data.

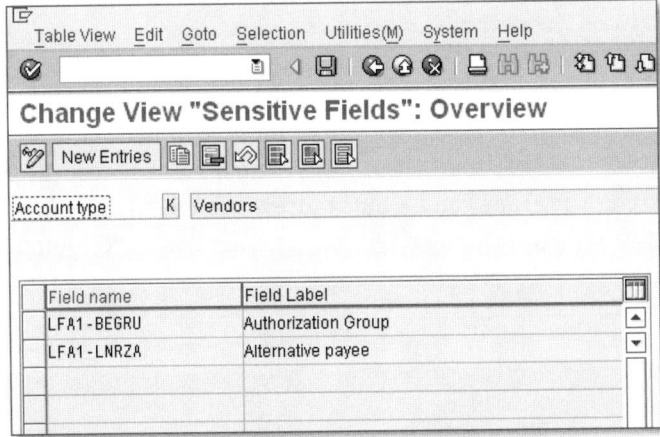

Figure 4.7 Setup of Alternative Payee as Vendor Sensitive Field

4.2 ACH Payments

ACH transfers are the cheapest and most effective methods of transferring funds electronically. In the U.S., they are the most common form of making electronic payments to vendors. International ACH has also been introduced recently by some banks and is gaining acceptance as a means of international funds transfer. ACH transfers settle in one or two days, depending on the arrangements made with the disbursement bank. Most vendor payments are made through this medium, and whenever payments can be planned in advance, we recommend the use of ACH over wire transfers and checks because it is cheaper and more efficient. It is true that by replacing checks with ACH payments, companies will lose the benefit of check float as a means of working capital. However, we have seen that most companies, when switching to ACH, renegotiate discount terms with their vendors to compensate for the benefits accruing to the vendor. (See note on how replacing checks with ACH will save you money.) ACH payments are controlled through the payment program relating to Transaction F110 and are usually executed by the accounts payable group.

> **Note: Replacing Checks with ACH Will Save You Money**
>
> Although you may lose check float time when replacing checks with ACH, you can renegotiate discount terms accordingly. Furthermore, using ACH is less expensive. Most vendors prefer to receive their payments through ACH for the overall benefits of certainty of timing, efficiency, and integration with their own accounting systems.

4.2.1 Electronic Formats

Flat File Format

Two types of file formats are most commonly used for the creation of electronic output media. The first one is a flat or text file format. With this format, the information is created using ASCII-readable text. Files of this format are the most common and are the easiest to create. They can be transmitted through any medium, such as FTP, e-mail, or host-to-host computer systems. Standard SAP ERP output files are in text file format.

EDI-Enabled IDOCs

The second type of file format is proprietary to SAP ERP and is called Intermediate Documents (IDocs). IDocs are platform-independent and self-contained, enabling transfer of data between SAP ERP and non-SAP ERP or legacy systems. IDocs are available in standard EDI-enabled ANSI X12 and EDIFACT formats that support most of the formats required for outbound payment processing. Most major banks now accept IDocs directly, and translate them internally. If not, the IDocs must be converted to standard EDI types before they are sent to the bank. IDocs can be transferred to the bank using FTP or VPN connections. They can and should be encrypted prior to sending to the bank. Bank master data and payment method configuration must be EDI-enabled. The variant that produces standard IDocs is RFFOEDI1 and is substituted for the classic RFFOUS_T program in the payment program, as well as the link to payment method in bank determination configuration using Transaction FBZP.

4.2.2 ACH Formats

SAP ERP supports all standard National Automated Clearing House Association (NACHA) formats for ACH payments — also called standard entry classes — as described in the following list:

- **Corporate Trade Exchange (CTX)**
  The format designated for corporate to corporate trade payments. It is the most common form of ACH payment in the U.S. and uses multiple addenda records (see the note on addenda records) to store invoice information detail relating to a payment.

- **Cash Concentration or Disbursement (CCD+)**
  The format used to transfer funds intra-company for concentration or disbursement purposes. It contains an addenda record for additional information, but there is also a CCD version that does not have an addenda record.

- **Pre-arranged Payment or Deposit (PPD)**
  The format used primarily for salary payments.

- **Tax Payment (TXP)**
  The format used for tax payments. It uses the addenda record for providing additional information. Most states in the U.S. accept the TXP format for the remittance of sales, use and other taxes.

4 | Outbound Electronic Banking in SAP ERP

> **Note: The Addenda Record**
>
> The addenda record is a freetext space allowing up to 80 characters of descriptive data. Both the CCD+ and TXP formats allow the addition of an addenda record. The CTX format allows multiple addenda records, up to 9999 records of up to 80 characters each. The addenda record in SAP ERP is in ANSI X12-compatible format and contains detailed information relating to the payment, such as invoice reference number, gross, discount, and net amount,
>
> The program RFFOUS_T in SAP ERP controls the ACH payment process using the previously discussed NACHA formats. SAP ERP has provided user exits — or each line item in these formats — to enable company- and bank-specific information to be populated in the format. A special user exit exists to add the addenda (7 records) to the appropriate formats and to amend it for specific company use.

> **Key tip: Vendor Master Setting for ACH Format**
>
> Use the REFERENCE DETAILS field to populate the ACH standard format if you are using it in conjunction with the classic payment program RFFOUS_T.
>
> If you are using the CTX format, enter "CTX" in the REFERENCE DETAILS field (see Figure 4.8). Otherwise, you will not be able to create the output in the desired format.

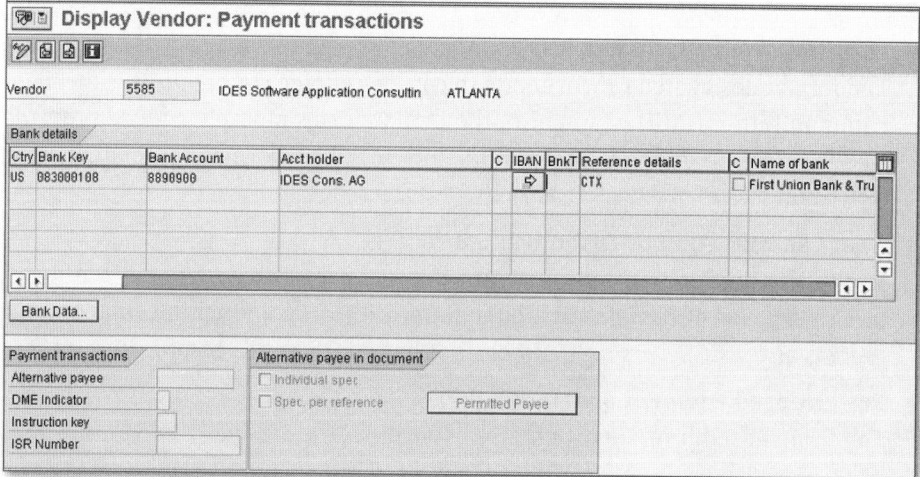

Figure 4.8 Enable CTX Format in Vendor Master

4.2.3 ACH User Exits

A user exit is an SAP ERP program that allows custom programming code to be added to standard SAP ERP functionality. Although the various NACHA formats for ACH payments are standard, they still need to be modified to suit a particular disbursement bank's requirements. SAP ERP provides a user exit within the main ACH Transaction RFFOUS_T for each record in the ACH file format, that is, header, batch, detail, addenda, and batch control. The details for each user exit are provided in Table 4.1.

One of the biggest advantages of using the CTX format with addenda record is that the addenda record can store invoice reference details such as gross, discount, and net amounts, as well as customer reference information, and so on. The recipient vendor will be able to import the addenda information directly into their accounting system if their bank and accounting system support electronic transmission of the addenda record data. This greatly reduces paperwork and automates the reconciliation process for both the sending and receiving company. An ACH extract in the CTX file format is shown in Figure 4.9.

```
101 031100851113555555506051514244094101BANK ABC
5200TTM LLC         DIRECT DEPOSIT      1135555555CTXACCT PAY   APACH 060516    1031100350000001
6221220002476802052532      0000112000              0005VENDOR A INC            1031100350000001
705ISA*00*NV           *00*NV           *ZZ*NV           *ZZ*NV           *060515*1420001000001
7054*&*00400*000000000*0*P*?/GS*RA*NV*NV*20060515*1424*0*X*004020/ST*820*0001/BPR*I0002000001
705*1120.00*C*ACH*CTX*01*031100351*DA*0300956661*1134008324**01*122000247*DA*6402050003000001
7052531**VEN/ENT*1/RMR*OI*KLM-05-01-06**1120.00*1120.00*0.00/SE*5*0001/GE*1*0/IEA*10004000001
                                                                                 00050000001
705*000000000/
6223222716278000607182      0000120150              0005VENDOR B INC            1031100350000002
705ISA*00*NV           *00*NV           *ZZ*NV           *ZZ*NV           *060515*1420001000002
7054*&*00400*000000000*0*P*?/GS*RA*NV*NV*20060515*1424*0*X*004020/ST*820*0001/BPR*I0002000002
705*1201.50*C*ACH*CTX*01*031100351*DA*0300956661*1135555555**01*322271627*DA*1000600003000002
7057185**VEN/ENT*1/RMR*OI*LCH-5.5.06**1201.50*1201.50*0.00/SE*5*0001/GE*1*0/IEA*1*00004000002
                                                                                 00050000001
70500000000/
820000001200444271860000000000000000002321501134008324                          0311003500000001
90000010000020000001200444271860000000000000000000232150
9999999999999999999999999999999999999999999999999999999999999999999999999999999999
9999999999999999999999999999999999999999999999999999999999999999999999999999999999
9999999999999999999999999999999999999999999999999999999999999999999999999999999999
9999999999999999999999999999999999999999999999999999999999999999999999999999999999
```

Figure 4.9 ACH Extract in CTX Format

The addenda record has a prefix of 7, and will contain all of the invoice details relating to the payment. It can accommodate up to 9,999 invoice records.

In the next section, we will provide you with details on the function modules used to customize each record line in the CTX format.

> **Note**
>
> The addenda record "7" user exit must be activated to enable the use of the addenda record in the CTX transaction. See Section 4.3.4, User Exits for ACH Formats, for more details.

4.2.4 User Exits for ACH Formats

The user exits for ACH are available using Transaction SE37. To display the user exit code, enter the function module name and execute it. The function modules are shown in Table 4.1.

Function Module	Structure	Description of Record Line
EXIT_RFFOEXIT_100	DTAMUSFH	File header record -1
EXIT_RFFOEXIT_101	DTAMUSBH	Batch header record -5
EXIT_RFFOEXIT_102	DTAMUSCCD	CCD detail record -6
EXIT_RFFOEXIT_103	DTAMUSCTX	CTX detail record -6
EXIT_RFFOEXIT_104	DTAUMSADD	Addenda record -7
EXIT_RFFOEXIT_105	DTAMUSBC	Batch control record -8

Table 4.1 Function Modules for ACH Formats

These user exits can be called if any company-specific information or special fields or data need to be provided in any particular line record. For example, if you need to show multiple invoice details in the CTX format, you must activate and program the user exit for the addenda record.

4.2.5 Prenotification

Prenotification is the process of sending an ACH payment (a prenote) — using a non-dollar (zero) amount — to a vendor's bank account to validate the routing, type of account, and account number at the vendor's financial institution.

Although SAP ERP has the ability to create a prenote using a standard SAP ERP program (see below), it is strongly recommended that you use the regular ACH payment process to send a small test amount to each vendor before switching them to live ACH transaction processing. An amount of $0.10, for example, would be appropriate. We have found that verifying with the vendor that the $0.10 was actually deposited in the vendor's bank account is the surest way to know that the end-to-end process is working correctly.

If preferred, prior to commencing live transactions a prenote file can be created in SAP ERP using Program RFKKPNFC00, as shown in Fig 4.10.

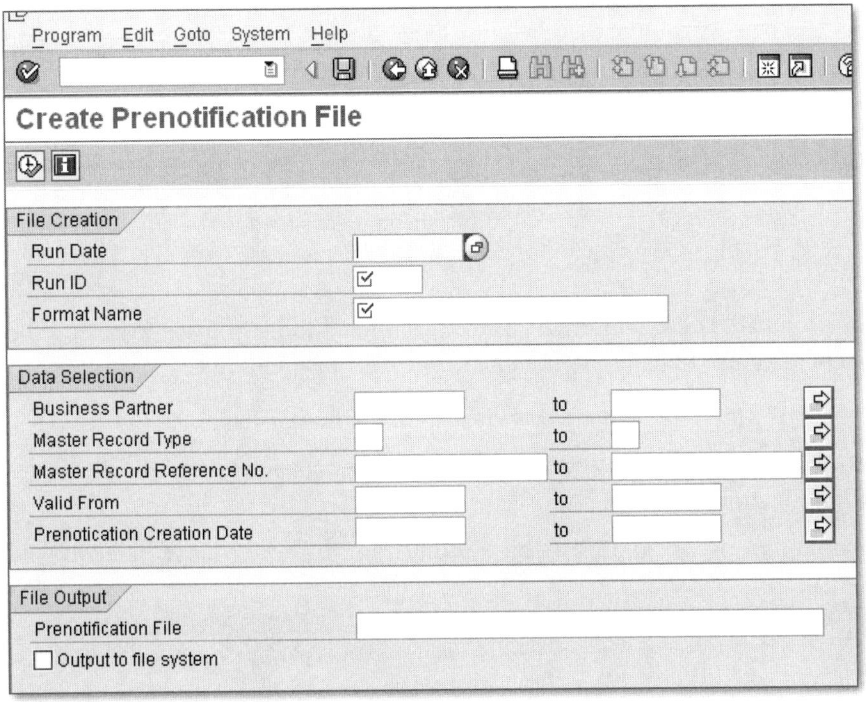

Figure 4.10 Creating a Prenote File in SAP ERP

> **Note**
>
> To test an ACH file transmission to a vendor prior to going live (pre-notification), send a real transmission for a very small amount, so the end-to-end process can be tested, including actual receipt of the money in the vendor's bank account.

4.2.6 Key Controls for ACH Transmissions

The ACH outbound transmission is the last step before data actually leaves the SAP ERP system and the company's host system. Because the payment is in electronic form, with a settlement time of one to two days, it is important that adequate controls are in place for the payment to ensure that it is authorized, secure, and accurate and can't be altered during processing. The payment file is generated based on the payment run of all open vendor invoice items. The payment program has many built-in, systemic checks that rely on bank and vendor master data and payment method configuration. Additionally, approval processes exist that ensure that the vendor invoices selected for payment are authorized, approved, and not blocked for payment for any reason. There are also controls for the actual creation, storage, and transmission of the file to the bank. Finally, the payment is settled and reported back to the company through intraday and prior day bank statements, for reconciliation, clearing, and recording in the financial ledgers of SAP ERP.

> **Definition: ACH Recalls**
>
> A *recall* is a manual request to have an ACH transaction returned to the originator, after it has posted to the receiver's account and after the ACH reversal.

The following are the key internal controls that need to be in place to ensure the secure creation and transmission of electronic ACH payment files:

- Establish controls for access to vendor and bank master data.
- Ensure adequate SoD between master data maintenance and transaction processing functions.
- Obtain appropriate approval and authorization for invoices selected for payment.
- Transport payment processing variants through the system so they can't be changed in the production system.
- Optimize the use of built-in master data checks such as duplicate invoice, tolerance limits, allowable payment methods, and default house bank.
- Use dual control, workflow, and authorization control to enhance internal control and SoD.
- Report daily ACH batch control totals via touch phone entry service.
- Establish a process for recalls (see the box on ACH recalls for a definition).

> **Key Tip: View Field Definitions and Documentation to Optimize Functionality**
>
> Review each field available in the master data using the F1 help key to determine how it can be used to enhance built-in systemic checks and provide optimal functionality.

4.3 Wire Transfers

In many cases, despite using SAP ERP software for many years, companies do not use the wire transfer functionality of SAP ERP. This is mostly because of a lack of understanding of the available features and the perception that the convenience and security available through a standalone workstation provided by and linked to the disbursement bank is superior. This, however, is not accurate. Although the initial setup does require careful planning and execution, outbound wire processing in SAP ERP is flexible, robust, and fully integrated with accounting and payment processing functionality. It also has the additional advantage of being able to leverage workflow for multi-level authorizations, which is particularly important because wire transfers often are high value, low volume transactions.

Although ACH is the recommended form of electronic funds transfer (EFT) in situations requiring lower cost and one- to two-day settlement, when same-day settlement is required, wire transfers are the most efficient and secure form of money transfer. Also, most EFT payments outside of the US are wires using the SWIFT format.

In the U.S., domestic wires use the Fedwire system and international wires use the SWIFT network. SAP ERP can be configured to set up wire transfers using specific payment methods for each type of transfer. Transfers are executed using the standard payment processing functionality, as with the other types of payment media.

Wire payments are executed through payment programs relating to Transaction F111 for treasury payments and Transaction F110 for accounts payable transactions.

4.3.1 Wire Types and Formats

Wires can be set up as repetitive, variable repetitive, and non-repetitive. One of the issues with wire transfers is that although all banks use the same payment networks, they do vary in their format requirements. This is one of the main reasons many companies prefer to use the standalone, bank-provided workstation. The Payment Medium Workbench (PMW), described in detail in Section 4.5, lets you create various formats that can be linked back to the payment method for processing.

Section 4.3, ACH Payments, referred to the classic payment formats available in SAP ERP. The PMW settings are used as an alternative to the classic format. This means that for any particular payment method, you can only use one format type (i.e., either the classic program or the PMW settings).

> **Key Concept: Classic Payment Programs vs. PMW**
>
> Using the PMW for payment processing is an alternative to using the classic payment program RFFOUS_T. It also needs to be configured and linked to the appropriate payment method and variants.

4.3.2 Repetitive Codes

A *repetitive code* is a unique alphanumeric code assigned by the disbursement bank to other bank accounts of the company or its vendors. The repetitive code is linked to all of the relevant banking information required to execute a wire transfer of funds, and is maintained in the disbursement bank's repository. When a company issues a wire transfer it only needs to include the repetitive code in the file. The disbursing bank will know where to route the payment based on the information it has relevant to the code.

Typically, the only wire payments that treasury is authorized to execute are cash transfers between intra-company bank accounts. SAP ERP has functionality for making such transfers using repetitive codes issued by the bank, which — along with other systemic and configurable controls — ensures that monies can only be transferred internally by authorized groups.

To configure repetitive codes, use Transaction OT81. The menu path to the transaction is shown in Figure 4.11. The first step is to set up the repetitive code of the recipient bank.

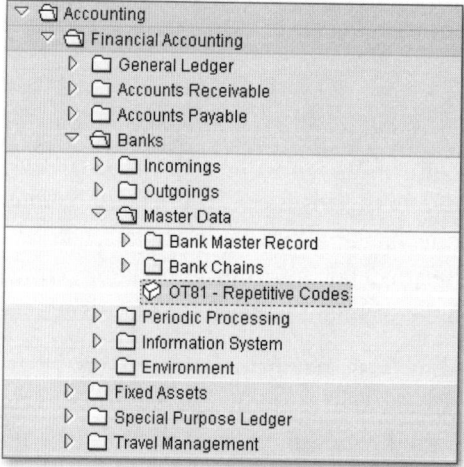

Figure 4.11 Menu Path to Create Repetitive Code

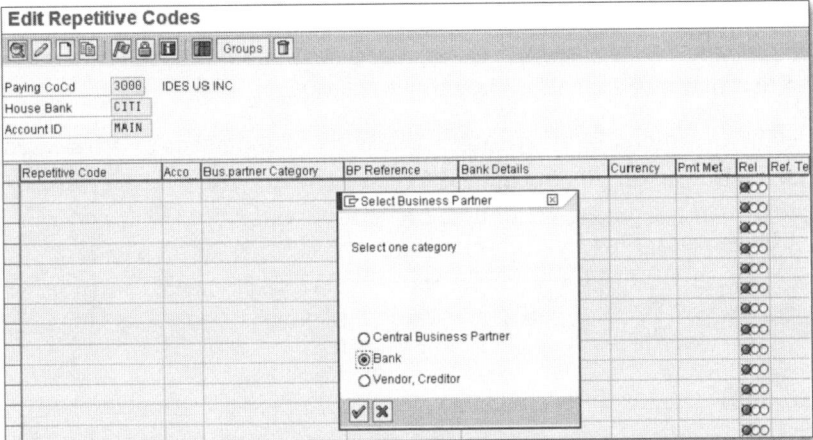

Figure 4.12 Repetitive Code Selection Screen for Type of Business Partner

Create Repetitive Code

Repetitive codes can be created for wire transfers to any of the following BPs: central BPs, banks, vendors, or creditors. The relevant selection screen is shown in Figure 4.12.

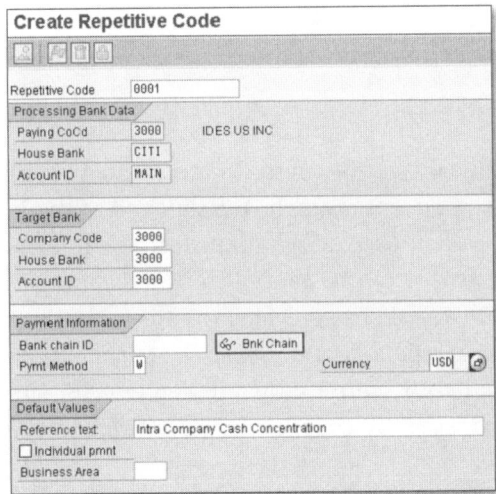

Figure 4.13 Create Details for BP Repetitive Code

The repetitive code is created for a specific BP or bank. The example in Figure 4.13 sets up the parameters for an intra-company bank to bank cash concentration

4 | Outbound Electronic Banking in SAP ERP

transfer. The repetitive code is linked to the sending bank, the target bank, the payment method, and the currency. There is also provision for standard reference information text that will appear in the wire transfer file.

After the details are entered, the repetitive code is saved and needs to be released so that it can be used, as shown in Figure 4.14. This release should be executed by someone other than the person creating the repetitive code.

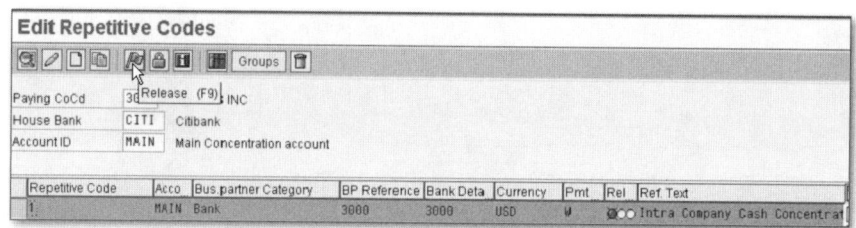

Figure 4.14 Review and Release Repetitive Code

After a successful release, a green button under the column RELEASE STATUS will confirm that the repetitive code is available for use, as shown in Figure 4.15.

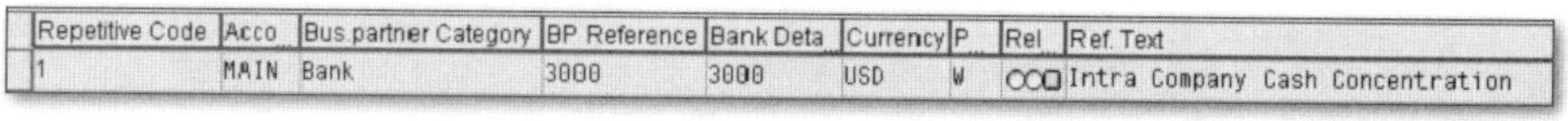

Figure 4.15 Repetitive Code Released and Ready for Use

Repetitive Code Group

A *repetitive code group* enables an additional layer of controlled access to a set of repetitive codes by a specific functional group. For example, treasury and accounts payable — the two functions that most often execute wire transfers — can each be assigned to a group. Access to these groups can be controlled by assigning the appropriate authorization object security access that prevents the treasury group users' access to the accounts payable list of repetitive codes, and vice versa. A new group can be created by clicking on the GROUP button shown in Figure 4.16. The group is named and then assigned to the repetitive code, as shown in Figure 4.17.

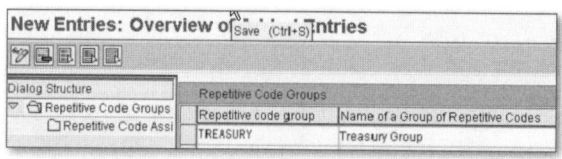

Figure 4.16 Create Repetitive Code Group

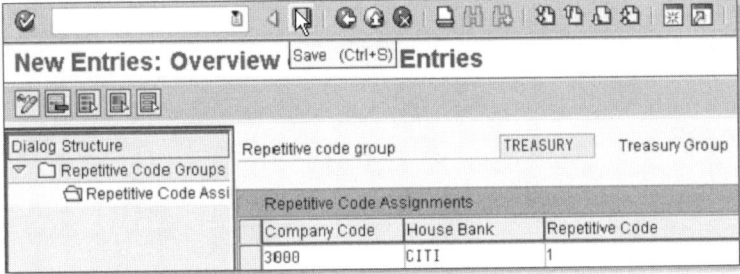

Figure 4.17 Assign Repetitive Code to Group

4.3.3 Types of Wire Transfers

As mentioned previously, wire payments can be repetitive, variable repetitive, or — in exceptional cases — non-repetitive. Formats for each type differ, so each type needs to be assigned its own payment method. The formats can be created and set up using the PMW, as described in Section 4.5, The Payment Medium Workbench (PMW).

The process of creating a wire involves setting up the vendor and bank master data, creating and releasing the repetitive code for the vendor, bank, or BP, and assigning the repetitive code to a group.

Using groups to segregate repetitive codes between internal and external partners allows SoD and authorization controls to ensure that the group that handles cash concentration (typically treasury) can't handle payments to external partners (typically accounts payable), and vice versa.

After the setup is completed, the transaction can be created depending on the transaction option being used. The wire needs to be created, resulting in a payment request that can be released and then paid through the treasury payment program Transaction F111.

In the following sections, we will discuss the two main forms of outbound wire transfers using Transaction FRFT: cash concentration within the company's internal banks, and payments to external treasury partners. Transaction FRFT can be used for all three types of wire formats, and is linked to the payment program through unique payment methods.

We will then describe the use of Transaction RVND to create free form and non-repetitive wires to vendors and creditors, and the controls surrounding them.

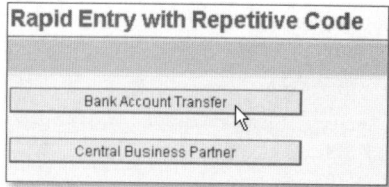

Figure 4.18 Selection Screen for Cash Concentration Wire Transfer

4.3.4 Cash Concentration

Cash concentration refers to the transfer of funds between an organization's multiple bank accounts for the purpose of pooling, netting, or concentrating for funding disbursement or investment activity. The selection screen is shown in Figure 4.18 and is accessed using Transaction FRFT. Click on the BANK ACCOUNT TRANSFER button to create bank-to-bank fund transfers.

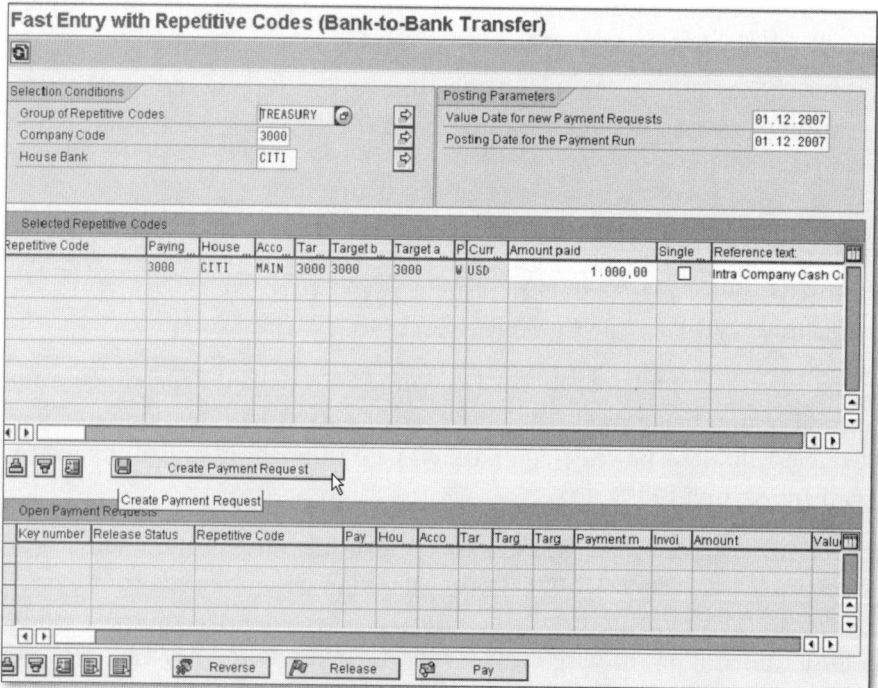

Figure 4.19 Create a Bank-to-Bank Wire Transfer

The input parameters are entered in the resulting screen, as shown in Figure 4.19. The repetitive code, group, and house bank information are entered automatically because the repetitive code reference will bring up the details based on the initial setup, including the reference text. The only field that needs to be completed is the AMOUNT PAID. This is an example of a repetitive code where only the amount and the date change with each new transaction.

After saving, the transaction and payment request is created, as shown in Figure 4.20.

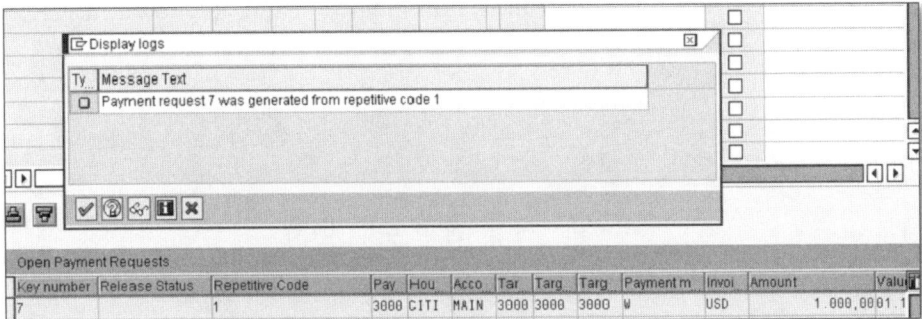

Figure 4.20 Create the Payment Request

The payment request now needs to be released. This is an important review and control feature that allows for SoD between creation and release of the wire. The process can be streamlined through workflow, with the CREATE and RELEASE functions triggering the workflow. Figure 4.21 shows the selection of the payment request for release.

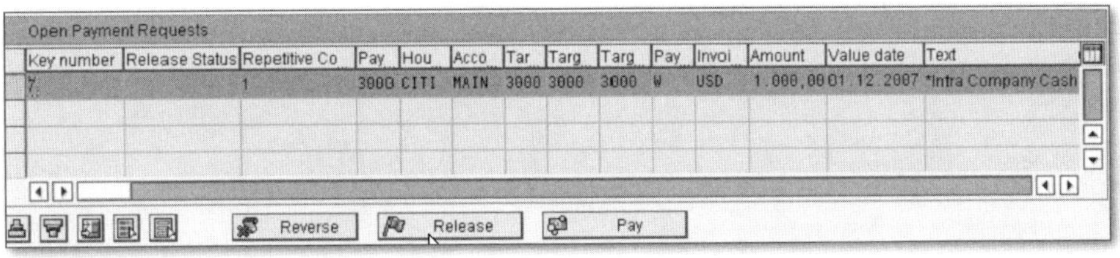

Figure 4.21 Releasing the Wire

After successful release by the authorized user, the message log confirms that the payment request has been released, as shown in Figure 4.22.

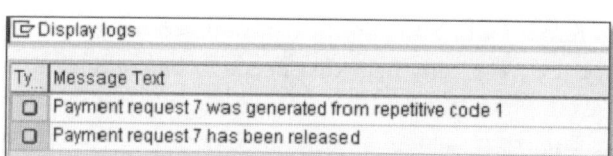

Figure 4.22 Wire Release Confirmation

After successful release, the payment request can be routed back to the payer. Clicking on PAY triggers the start of the payment program, as shown in Figure 4.23.

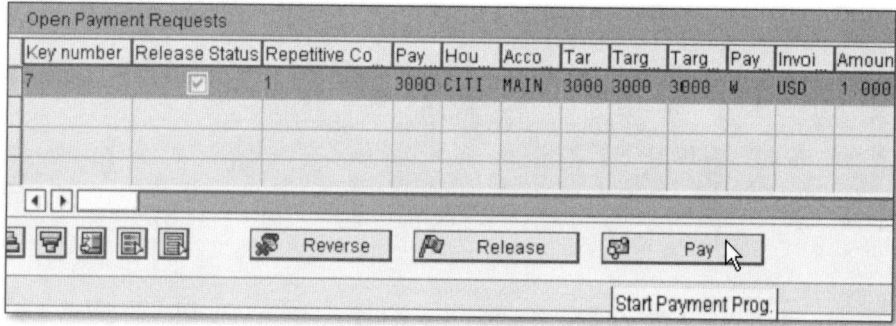

Figure 4.23 Pay Wire

The payment program creates a payment run, and a confirmation that the selected payment requests were paid with a payment run displays in the logs, as shown in Figure 4.24. This payment run can then be executed as normal, using the payment program Transaction F111 to create the outbound wire.

Ty	Message Text
☐	Payment request 7 was generated from repetitive code 1
☐	Payment request 7 has been released
☐	The selected payment requests were paid with payment run 01.12.2007, 00001R

Figure 4.24 Payment Run Created for Further Processing

4.3.5 Wire Payments to Treasury Partners Using Transaction FRFT

Wire transfers to treasury partners are set up and executed the same way as described for cash concentration, by selecting a vendor or BP in Transaction FRFT, and creating a payment request, release, and payment run. The repetitive codes are set up with the vendor-specific details, and are released and assigned to a group using Transaction OT81, as described earlier.

4.3.6 Online Free Form and Non-Repetitive Wire Payments

Free form or non-repetitive wires can be created using Transaction RVND. However, it is recommended that you use repetitive codes whenever possible. The controls for free form or non-repetitive wires must be very strong because these wire types do not need vendor master and payee bank information set up as master data. It is also strongly recommended that the release of the payment request be assigned to someone other than the person creating the wire payment request. The selection screen for creating free form wires is shown in Figure 4.25.

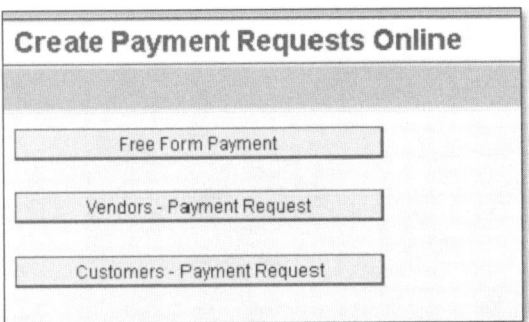

Figure 4.25 Online Free Form Payment Request Creation

Online Free Form Payment

As mentioned previously, Transaction RVND can be used to make payments to vendors and BPs as an alternative to the Transaction FRFT process described in the previous sections. Although the free form payment does not require any master data to be set up, it does require a bank account to be set up using Transaction FI01.

Free form payments are useful for emergency payments, although the controls and authorizations for them need to be very stringent. Payment release controls can be incorporated as described later in this section. The payment request is converted to outbound electronic media using the Transaction F111 payment program for wires.

Vendor Payments Using Transaction RVND

Figure 4.26 provides an example of how Transaction RVND can be used to make payments to vendors through the creation of a payment request and then running the Transaction F111 payment program for wires.

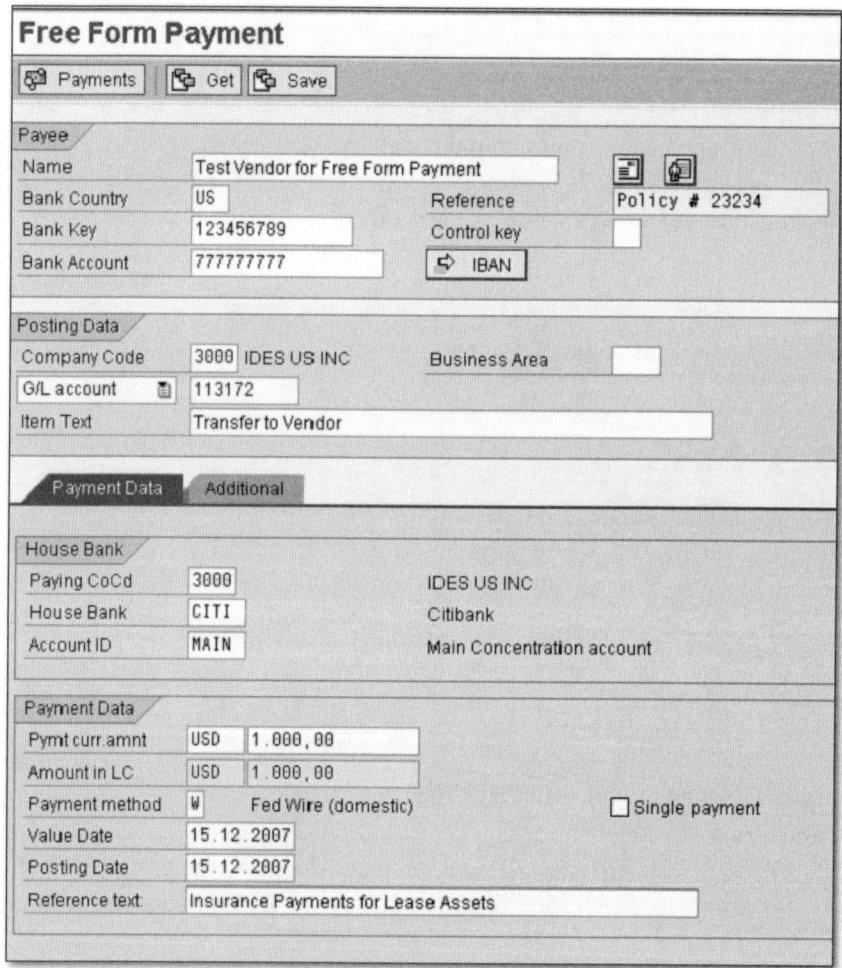

Figure 4.26 Free Form Wire Details for a One-Time Vendor

Controls for Transaction RVND

Online-generated payment requests can be released when they are created, provided that the user has authorization for the company code and authorization object F_PAYRQ for activity 02 (change). It is recommended that a second person have access to perform the release after the payment request has been created by the first user. Figure 4.27 shows the options for controlling access to completing the wire transaction through release, restricted document types, and processing steps.

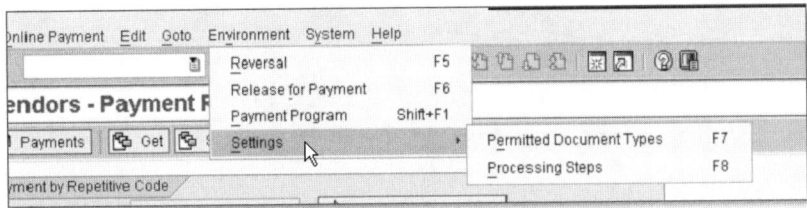

Figure 4.27 Controls for Transaction RVND

The path to specify the controls to be used with respect to Transaction RVND is IMG • FINANCIAL ACCOUNTING • BANK ACCOUNTING • BUSINESS TRANSACTIONS • PAYMENT TRANSACTIONS • ONLINE PAYMENTS, as partially shown in Figure 4.28.

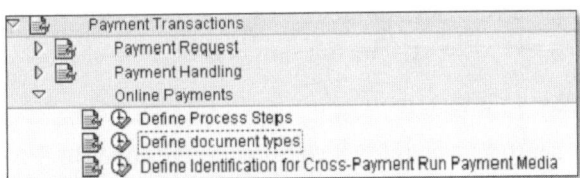

Figure 4.28 IMG Path to Set Up Online Payment Controls

Figure 4.29 shows the sequence of controls that can be set up. This allows for effective SoD between the various key steps in the process.

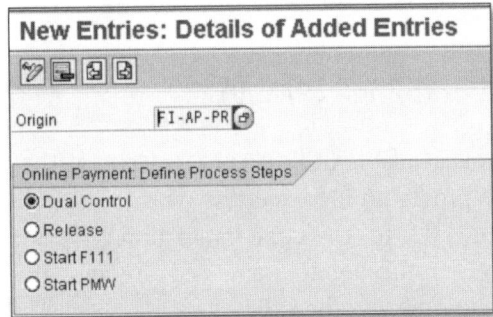

Figure 4.29 Define Process Steps for Online Payments

Figure 4.30 provides an example of controls that can be incorporated through configuration. In this example, only document types KZ will be eligible for payment processing through online payments.

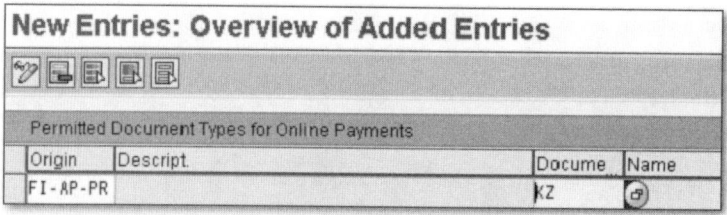

Figure 4.30 Specify Allowed Document Types for Online Payments

4.3.7 Key Controls for Wire Transmissions

Wire transfers require the most stringent of controls because they typically are low-volume, high-value transactions, and often one off payments to one-time vendors. Wire transfers are settled on the same day as transmission; therefore, it is essential that payments reach the intended partner, and in the right amount. The following are the key controls to be considered for wire transmission in SAP ERP:

- Require repetitive code for all wire transfers.
- Implement strict controls for setup and maintenance of repetitive codes in SAP ERP and with the disbursement bank.
- Segregate types of wires between accounts payable and treasury, and assign repetitive codes accordingly by group.
- Report daily wire batch control totals via touch phone entry service.
- Validate wire payment settlement through intraday reporting.

4.4 The Payment Medium Workbench (PMW)

The PMW is one of the most useful tools available in SAP TRM. It lets you configure custom file formats without any programming expertise. This is valuable because in many cases, bank file formats differ for the same transaction type. For example, in the U.S., domestic wires are sent through the same Fedwire network, but each bank has different file formats that need to be adhered to.

4.4.1 Creating a New File Format for Outbound Payments

The PMW is accessed using Transaction DMEE. The change function for this tool is client-independent; therefore, special access may need to be provided when a new format is being created. Figure 4.31 shows the INITIAL SELECTION screen.

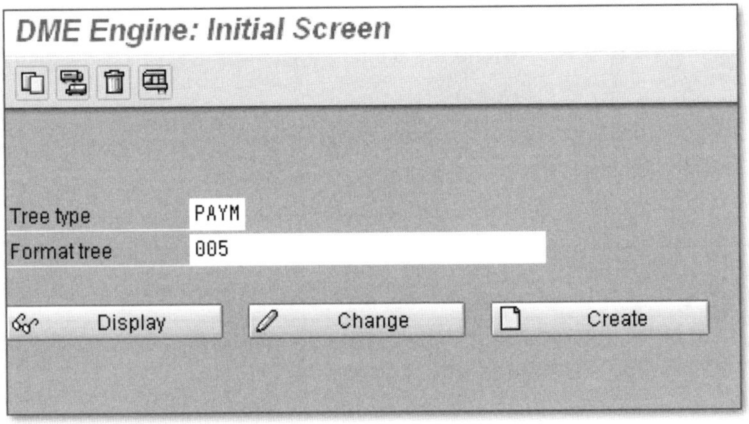

![DME Engine: Initial Screen showing Tree type PAYM, Format tree 005, with Display, Change, and Create buttons]

Figure 4.31 PMW Initial Screen

The DMEE FORMAT TREE follows the structure of the file, with a file header, detail record, and file trailer. Each node and sub node can be customized. Figure 4.32 shows a sample format tree.

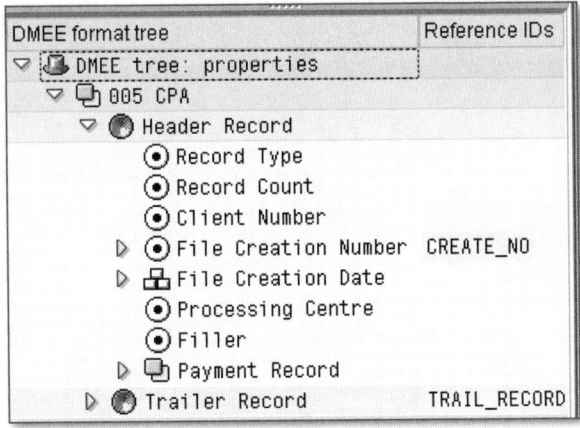

Figure 4.32 Extract of a DMEE Tree Structure

Each node can be set up with specific attributes that call fields in SAP ERP tables such as bank account number, routing number, amount, and son, and can accommodate constants, or access program code. Figure 4.33 shows an example where the payment amount is linked to field RWBTR in Table FPAYH.

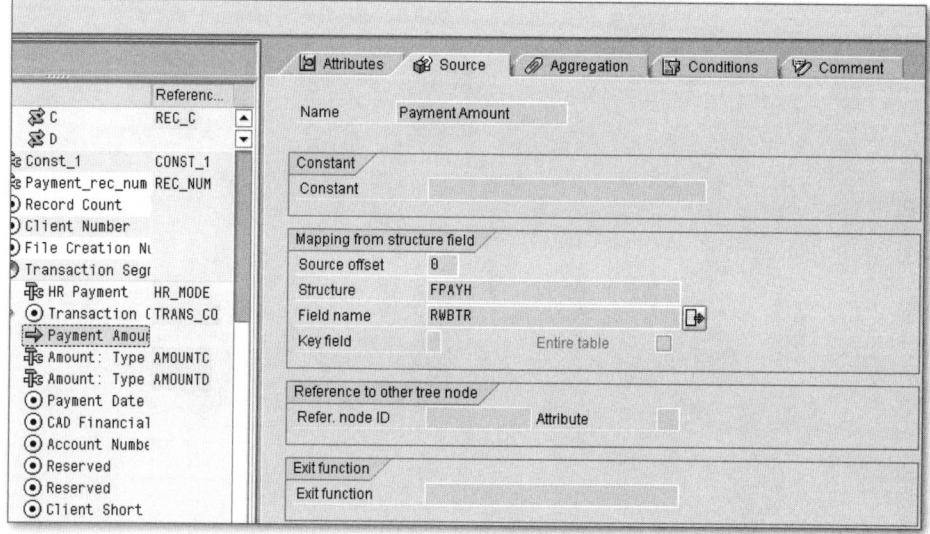

Figure 4.33 DMEE Node Attributes

Because the format needs to exactly match the bank's requirements, a test tool exists to create the output based on the format tree, which can then be corrected based on the output results. The test tool is executed from the DMEE initial screen as shown in Figure 4.34.

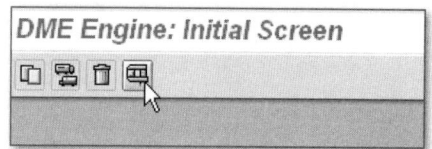

Figure 4.34 DMEE Test Tool

The resulting template is based on the format tree. It allows the input of test data based on the field parameters in the file format, as shown in Figure 4.35.

The Payment Medium Workbench (PMW) | **4.4**

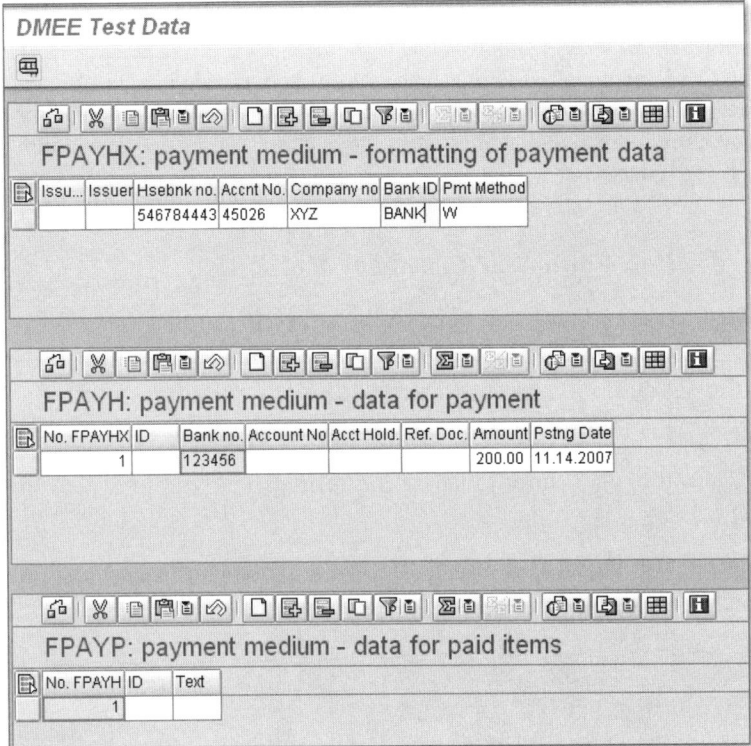

Figure 4.35 DMEE Test Data Template

After execution, the file format results are output as shown in Figure 4.36.

```
Data Output
A000000001XYZ         000100732100000
C000000002XYZ         0001
4300002000000000000123456       00000000000000000000000000
Z000000003XYZ         0001000000000000000000000000002000000000000010000
```

Figure 4.36 DMEE Test Output File

The test output can be compared to the bank's required format. Any changes that are required can be made in the format tree, and retested until the formats match exactly.

169

4 | Outbound Electronic Banking in SAP ERP

> **Note: Using the Test Tool Reduces Bank Format Approval Cycle Time**
>
> Because the bank has to approve the format before the system can go live, the format specifications must match exactly. Otherwise, formats will be returned by the bank for correction. This cycle time can be reduced by using the test tool, because it can confirm the exact matching specification.

4.4.2 Linking the New Format to a Payment Method

After the file format has been created, it needs to be linked to the specific payment method, and assigned a variant that will allow for the automatic execution of the payment processing (as described previously in the sections on cash concentration and treasury partner payments).

In this section, we will explain how to select the format type and link it to the payment method:

1. Execute Transaction FBZP (Figure 4.37). The screen that displays provides access to payment method setup and configuration.

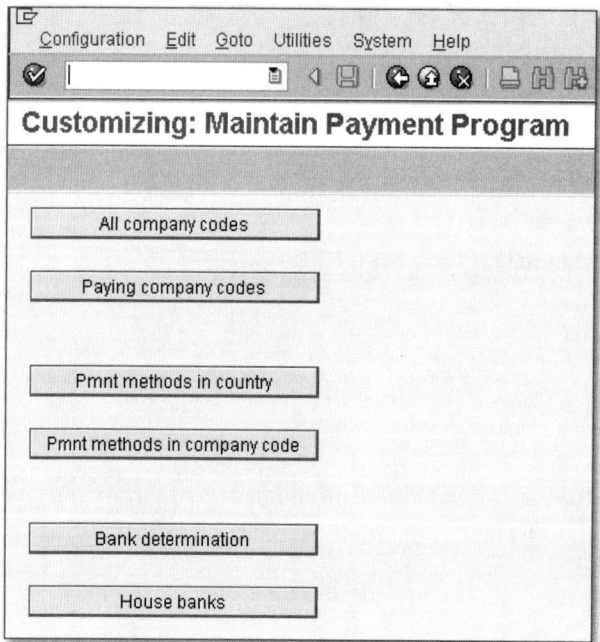

Figure 4.37 Payment Program Configuration Transaction FBZP

2. Next, select CoCd and Pmt m... and double-click on payment method W, Fed Wire (domestic) (Figure 4.38).

Maintenance of Company Code Data for a Payment Method				
CoCd	Name	City	Pmt m	Name
3000	IDES US INC	New York	0	Biller Direct - Collection
			1	Biller Direct - Credit Card
			8	Bank Debit (passive payment)
			9	Bank Credit (passive payment)
			A	ACH
			C	Check
			D	Fed Drawdown
			I	Payment via IHC (Internal)
			J	Payment via IHC (External)
			S	Single Check
			T	Bank transfer
			U	Internat'l Bank transfer (in)
			W	Fed Wire (domestic)

Figure 4.38 Selection of Company Code and Payment Method

3. Click on the Pymt meth in ctry button (Figure 4.39).

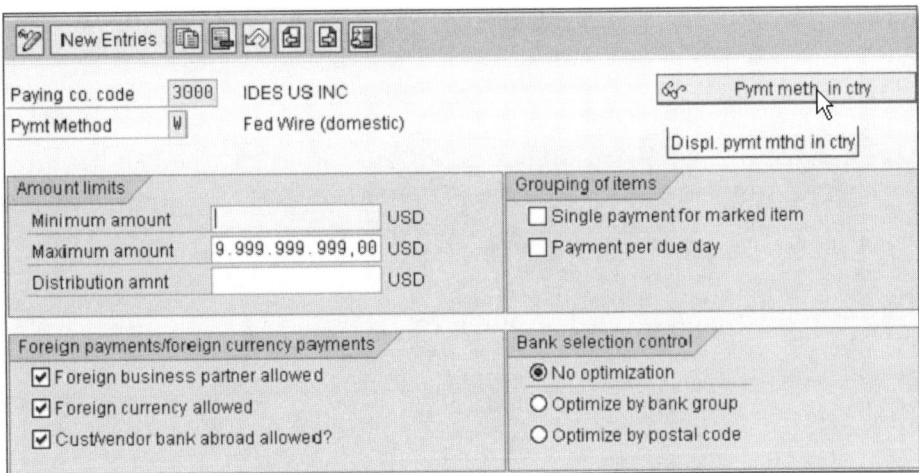

Figure 4.39 Selection Screen for Payment Method in Country

4. Select the USE PAYMENT MEDIUM WORKBENCH radio button. (Figure 4.40). This is where you specify whether to use the classic payment programs or the new PMW.

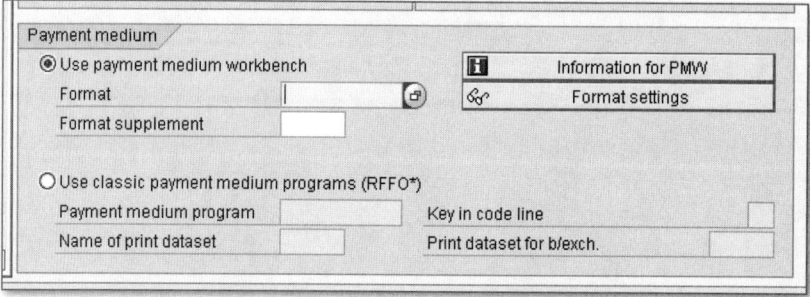

Figure 4.40 Selection Screen to Use Payment Medium Workbench

5. In the FORMAT field, enter the format that has been created. (Figure 4.41). You can access your selected format settings and other related configuration by clicking on the FORMAT SETTINGS button.

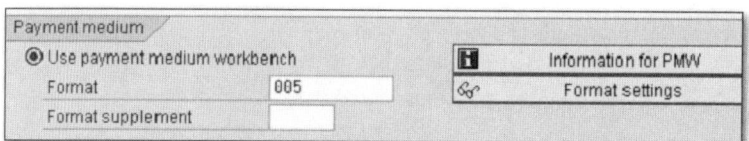

Figure 4.41 Input Field for New Format Created

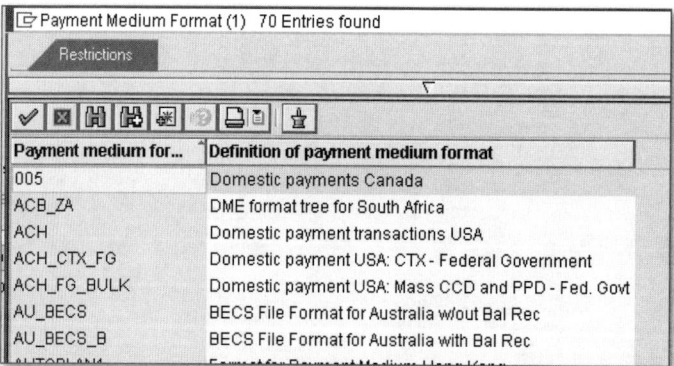

Figure 4.42 Example of File Formats Delivered

Figure 4.42 shows a screen print of several formats that are delivered with the SAP ERP system. These can be copied and renamed, and then amended to conform to user-specific requirements. The simplest way to transport the new formats is to use the download/upload file option provide in the initial DMEE screen.

If you want to use the classic payment format (Program RFFOUS_T), select USE CLASSIC PAYMENT MEDIUM PROGRAMS (RFFO*), as shown in Figure 4.43.

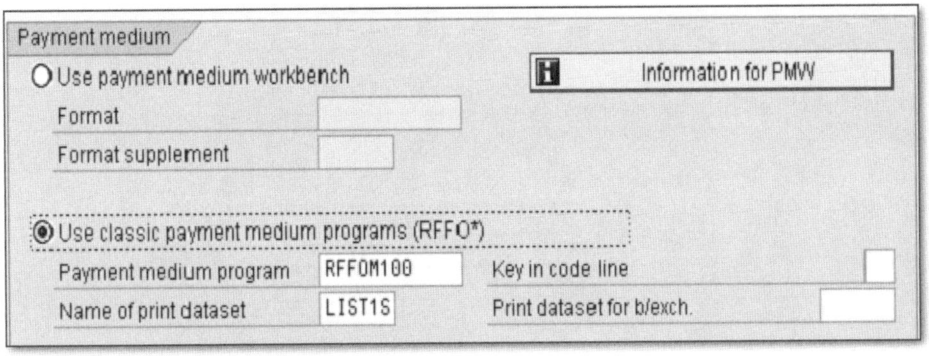

Figure 4.43 Classical Payment Format Setting

The next section explains the final step of connecting the new format and the payment method with the payment processing cycle.

4.4.3 Configuring the PMW

After the file format has been created, it needs to be linked through configuration to the payment method. This, in turn, controls the payment processing that results in the payment media electronic output to a specified outbound directory when a wire transfer is executed.

The process comprises creating a variant with the appropriate parameters and then assigning this variant through configuration to the newly created format, using Program SAPFAYM. The sequence of steps is described in this section.

1. First, execute Program SAPFAYM using Transaction SE38 or SA38, and then enter the parameters as shown in Figure 4.46. Note the field that provides the directory path for the outbound file created by the payment run.

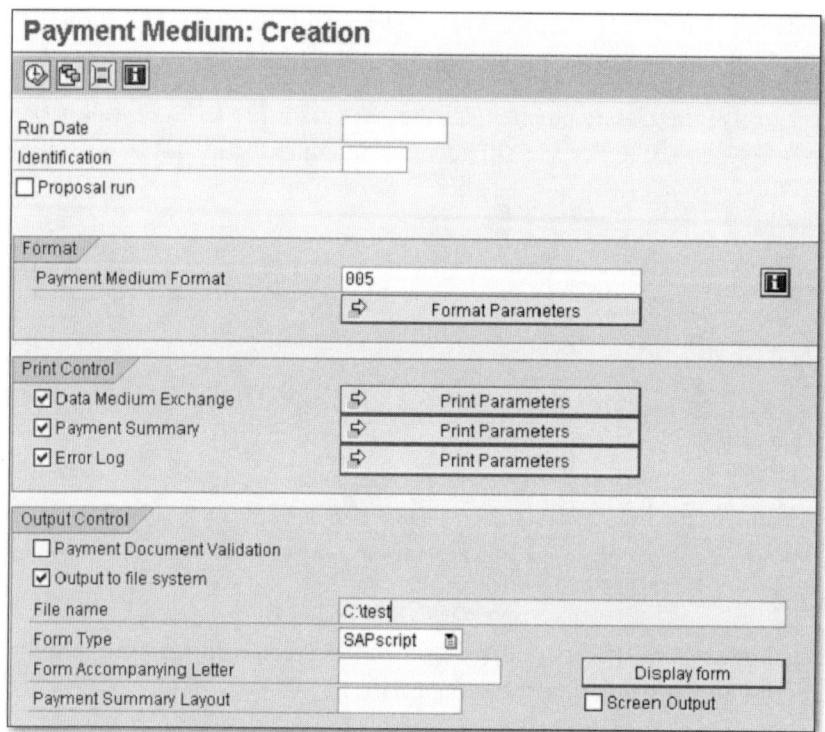

Figure 4.44 Create Variant Using Program SAPFAYM

2. Next, create a name for the variant and click on the SAVE button (Figure 4.45).

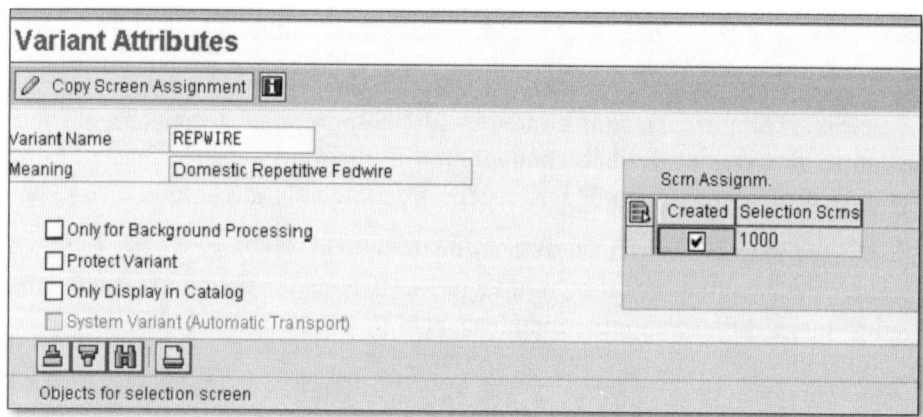

Figure 4.45 Create Name for Variant for Payment Method Wire Format

3. The newly created variant then needs to be assigned in Customizing in the IMG. The menu path, as partially shown in Figure 4.46, is as follows: IMG • FINANCIAL ACCOUNTING • ACCOUNTS RECEIVABLE AND ACCOUNTS PAYABLE • BUSINESS TRANSACTIONS • OUTGOING PAYMENTS • AUTOMATIC OUTGOING PAYMENTS • PAYMENT MEDIA • MAKE SETTINGS FOR PAYMENT MEDIUM FORMAT AND NOTE TO PAYEE TO PAYMENT METHOD • CREATE/ASSIGN SELECTION VARIANTS.

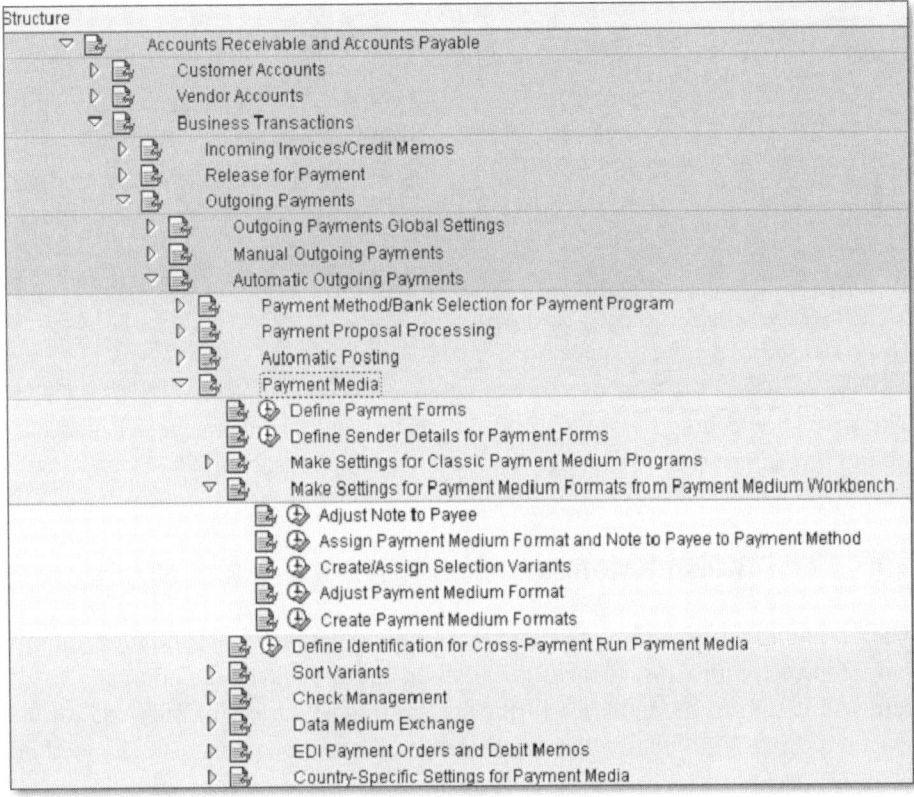

Figure 4.46 Menu Path to Assign Variant in the IMG

4. Select CREATE/ASSIGN SELECTION VARIANTS, click on the newly created payment medium format, and select VARIANT. The variant will appear in the dropdown list, and should be selected. Click on the EXECUTE button to create the link. (Figure 4.47).

4 | Outbound Electronic Banking in SAP ERP

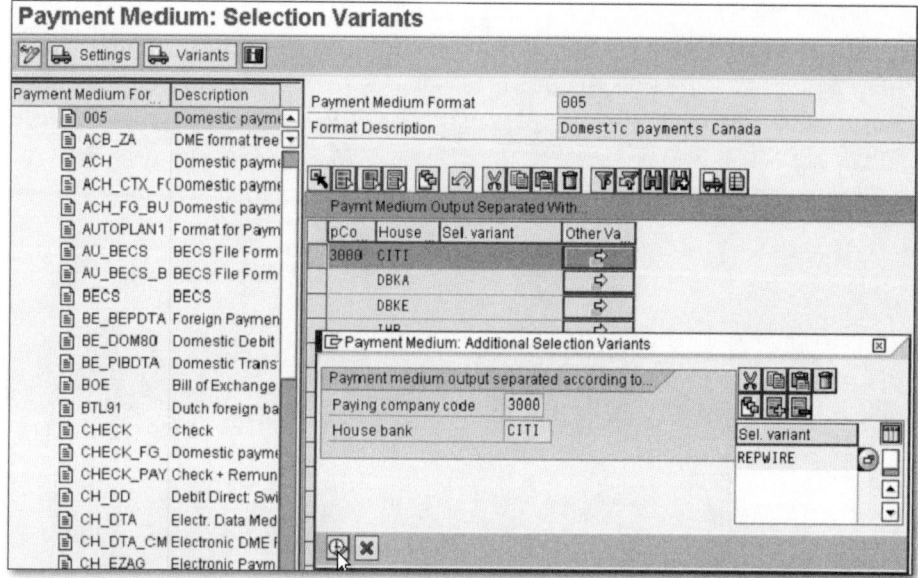

Figure 4.47 Assign Variant REPWIRE to Format 005

The wire should now be available to be created and output to the selected outbound directory when executing payment program Transaction F111.

4.5 File Transmission

The outbound transmission of electronic payment files is the last and most important step in the process. It takes place when the file leaves the company's system and is sent to the bank for further processing. A variety of methods can be used within SAP ERP that will be discussed in this section. Whatever the method of transmission, it is imperative that strict controls are built around the entire process.

4.5.1 Communication Options

Many communication options exist for outbound transmissions, ranging from simple to extremely complex, depending on the environment and technology used. It is important to emphasize that it is the controls surrounding the communication method being used, and its reliability and robustness, that will decide its ultimate effectiveness. We have seen daily inbound and outbound polling from over 20 banks using a simple polling software and FTP over the Internet, to more complex environments that use middleware such as SAP NetWeaver XI (see the box on SAP NetWeaver XI), to not only conduct inbound and outbound polling, but a perform a variety of other preprocessing and file management functions.

> **Key Term: SAP NetWeaver Exchange Infrastructure (SAP NetWeaver XI)**
>
> In simple terms, SAP NetWeaver XI allows one application to send data to another application. It is an integral part of the SAP NetWeaver architecture. Although SAP NetWeaver XI is a complex middleware tool capable of performing many tasks, it has a very good file transfer management component that can be used for inbound and outbound transmissions between a company and bank, as well as other data providers such as Bloomberg and Reuters.

4.5.2 Security Procedures

Security for the file transmission process is an important part of effective internal controls for SOX compliance. Adequate security for both access and integrity controls relating to the file transmission process must be in place. Access controls restrict who has access to data, files, and systems, and integrity controls are used to protect data to ensure completeness and accuracy. They also ensure that data can't be changed during the end-to-end process. These controls can be implemented through use of passwords, encryption and decryption algorithms, error logs, email alerts, validation messages, and — where warranted — through dedicated connections.

4.5.3 Testing procedures

Testing of communication to and from your bank, and of the formats required by the bank, is a critical part of the implementation of outbound banking in SAP ERP.

Communications testing is required to test your file delivery method and to ensure that you can transmit data and files successfully and securely between your company and bank.

File format testing is required to ensure that your files comply with the file format specified by the bank for the specific type of transaction, such as NACHA for ACH, Fedwire for US wires, SWIFT for international wires, BACS in the UK, and so on. Although all of these formats are standard in that the file specifications are established by the respective sponsoring organizations, in our experience, every bank has its own interpretation of the format and therefore specifies its own requirements to conform to its internal systems and procedures. SAP ERP provides all of the previously mentioned formats but also provides tools to modify the standard formats to be able to meet specific bank requirements.

File delivery and file format testing must be successful and signed off on by the bank before proceeding to prenotification and planning for go-live to commence.

4.5.4 Key Controls for File Transmissions

Security controls for file transmission are very important to ensure that the files can't be accessed and changed or manipulated after creation. Because the files contain payment instructions and banking information, they must be encrypted to protect the data during transmission until they have reached the desired destination. Integrity controls must ensure that the files are sent and received in its entirety. The following are some of the key controls to be incorporated into the process:

- Control access to directories holding outbound files.
- Ensure outbound files are encrypted prior to transmission.
- Review exception log files for systemic or repeating errors that need to be fixed.
- Schedule all outbound jobs and agree on a schedule with the bank. Scheduled times need to meet bank and Fedwire deadlines for receiving wire and ACH transmissions.
- Test each format that will be used by the company. For example, if standard entry class formats CTX and PPD are used, both should be tested and approved independently.

4.6 Using Workflow to Route Authorizations

Workflow can be used very effectively in these processes to route authorizations. This is particularly true for low-volume, high-value payments that need to obtain senior management approval, and that then have to be routed through several departments or significant handoffs of data because of SoD and authorization control requirements. In Chapter 7, which focuses on financial risk management of foreign exchange and derivatives, we will look at a detailed example of how workflow can be used. The example will include approvals for wire payment processing.

4.7 Implementing Outbound Banking in SAP ERP: Lessons Learned

After electronic banking is implemented in SAP ERP, the benefits of automation, integration, and STP will greatly enhance the efficiency and effectiveness of banking processes, as well as strengthen overall enterprise-wide controls. It is important to recognize that a well-implemented system is vital to optimizing these benefits.

The following is a list of key lessons learned about implementing outbound banking in SAP ERP that will greatly facilitate a smooth and effective implementation:

- Meet with your bank's or external partner's project team right from the start of the project and have weekly calls to monitor progress on formats, interfaces, testing, and procedures.
- Engage key business stakeholders in finance and other departments early on, especially G/L, accounts payable, accounts receivable, treasury, audit, and legal.
- Ensure change management as it is a critical part of the implementation.
- Request your bank to provide its approved formats, create and test these formats, and obtain sign off that they meet bank requirements (bank standard formats will almost always require some preprocessing or customization).
- Build in adequate time frames for setting up, testing, and bank approval of file delivery communication interfaces and file formats.
- Plan and document key internal controls relating to SoD, business process flows, and authorizations, and test them end-to-end in the system.
- Establish and document verification procedures with the bank, as well as the timing of file transfers and bank processing deadlines, and daily operational monitoring procedures.
- Agree on timing and cut off procedures with the bank for go-live.
- Agree on post go-live monitoring and cut off dates for transition from project to operational mode, before the project is signed off as completed.

4.8 Summary of Key Controls

Controls for outbound banking are critical to the process because company payments are involved. Key controls need to be maintained, tested, documented, and monitored. The following is a summary of the key controls discussed earlier.

As part of bank relationship management, it is important to document all procedures and processes agreed with your banking partners:

- Maintain all documentation relating to the setup and operation of all forms of payment media between the company and the bank, including legal contracts and service level agreements (SLAs).
- Establish a process for telephone verification of payment totals to be notified to the bank.
- Establish fax/email confirmation of payment totals received by the bank.
- Set up a process for the handling of exception items that failed outbound transmission.
- Establish a process for reversing erroneous or duplicate transactions.
- Develop a list of contact names and information between the bank and the company, as well as of mutually agreed upon escalation procedures.

Establishing robust controls for file transmission will provide strong assurance with respect to the integrity and security of payment processes:

- Ensure secure file transmission with file encryption and decryption for outbound payment transfers.
- Implement procedures to ensure monitoring of transmission of outbound files.
- Provide the appropriate reconciliation staff with logs of SAP ERP batch jobs relating to outbound file transfers.
- Ensure that outbound payment files can't be manipulated prior to transmission to the bank.
- Develop and implement backup procedures to protect yourself against failure of outbound payment processing in SAP ERP.

Documenting all procedures and processes will provide evidence and assurance of strong internal controls that can be validated and tested:

- Document all key business process flows, controls, and handoffs of data.
- Create a risk/control matrix for key business processes.
- Segregate duties between accounts payable and treasury staff with respect to payment processing and reconciliation of outbound electronic fund transfers.
- Ensure adequate SoD between requestors and payers.
- Develop and deliver appropriate training for treasury and accounts payable staff for the outbound payment cycle process.
- Ensure adequate controls for the creation of repetitive codes for wire transfers.
- Ensure adequate controls of master data with respect to authorization access, keeping in mind SoD between key handoff points.
- Test process controls periodically to ensure they are working as intended.

Regular reconciliation will provide assurance that the books of financial record are accurate, and ensure that unauthorized activity has not taken place:

- Ensure daily or otherwise regular reconciliation of bank accounts and clearing accounts for unclearcd items, and develop and implement an escalation process for unresolved issues.
- Consider separate bank accounts for ACH, wire, and direct debit transactions. Additional restrictions can be placed on a bank account, such as no direct debit ACH, only ACH and wire payments, only deposits, and so on.
- Consider establishing limits for high-value transmissions, with additional special approvals required for exceptions.
- Perform regular reconciliation of daily outbound payments and direct debits with the originating documents in SAP ERP.
- Ensure balances in clearing accounts are reconciled and cleared.

4.9 Summary

In this chapter we covered all of the important aspects of outbound electronic banking business processes and related controls in SAP ERP. We reviewed domestic (U.S.) and international electronic fund transfers and ACH payments, cash concentration, and bank-to-bank transfers. We also explained how to use the PMW to create custom file formats.

In Chapter 5, we will cover topics in electronic banking that are of particular importance and relevance to treasury departments — in particular, U.S. treasury departments.

This chapter covers treasury processes that involve electronic banking, such as the Positive Pay cycle for check payments, lockbox processing for incoming remittances, payment card processing, and escheatment in SAP ERP.

5 Positive Pay and Payment Card Processing

Positive Pay is one of the most powerful tools available to combat check fraud. It is a service offered by most of the major banks in the U.S. and Canada. The standard Positive Pay service allows the bank, prior to honoring a check to a payee, to match the date, check number, and dollar amount of each check presented for payment against an electronic list of checks previously authorized and issued by the company.

5.1 Positive Pay

With the advent of increasingly sophisticated digital imaging technology that allows for the near-perfect fraudulent copying of checks, an enhancement to the basic service has been developed, called Positive Payee, which features the addition of the payee name to the list of items to be matched. The addition of payee name match is strongly recommended for any organization implementing a new Positive Pay service or enhancing their existing service. Adding the payee name as match criteria is a major deterrent to check fraud and considerably strengthens the controls for check fraud prevention.

> **Note: Executing an SAP Program**
>
> SAP programs are executed using Transaction SE38. They can be run online, or scheduled as a background job. Most bank-related jobs are scheduled because the intent is to automate the end to end process. Exceptions or errors in processing are available for post-processing through job logs that can be monitored or e-mailed to the responsible persons.

5 Positive Pay and Payment Card Processing

Using Positive Pay, if any of the required items do not match, the payment needs to revert back to the company issuing the check for appropriate authorization.

Positive Pay processing is provided as standard functionality within SAP ERP, and can be fully automated end-to-end. Because the Positive Pay service is provided by banks, formats may differ from bank to bank. Some preprocessing of outbound and inbound files may be required to conform to bank formats. As part of the preprocessing, it is possible to add the payee name field to convert the file into Positive Payee format. An overview of the process is shown in Figure 5.1.

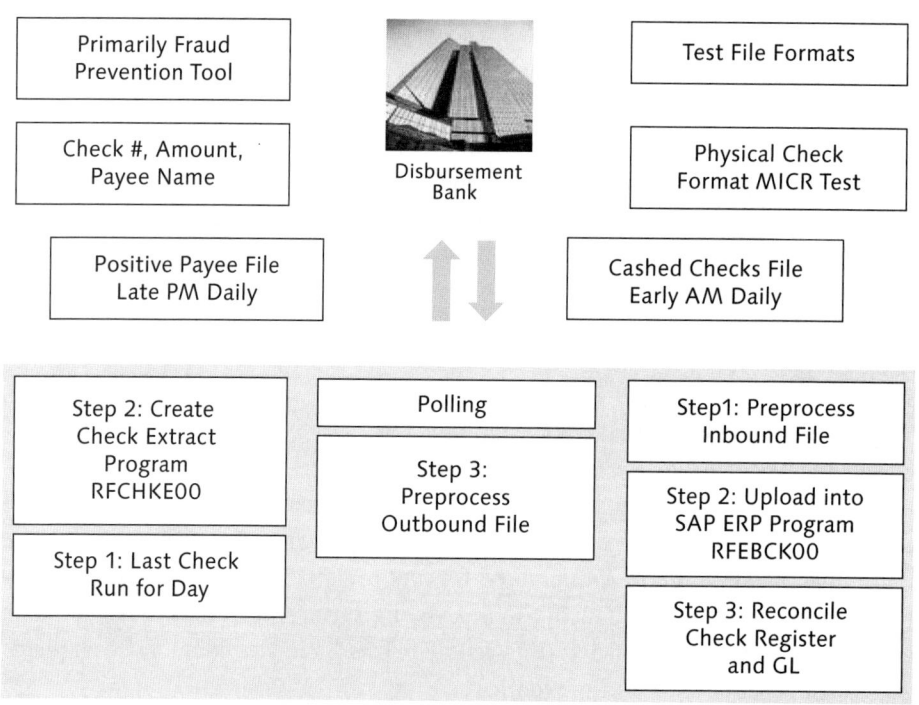

Figure 5.1 Overview of Positive Pay

5.1.1 Process Overview

Typically, a company will have many check payment runs during the day. After the last check run of the day, a standard SAP program RFCHKE00 is run as a scheduled batch (background) job that creates an electronic file of all checks issued that day.

> **Tip: Timing of Creation and Transmission of Positive Pay Files**
>
> Estimate the time the for the last check run of the day, and keep in mind that sometimes you may have to run an emergency check run late in the day. Ensure that the batch job creating the Positive Payee file runs well after the latest possible time that your company could conceivably cut a check. In our experience, anytime after 8pm works well. The file needs to be received by the bank prior to the start of the next business day.

The outbound file created by the program will need to be preprocessed to ensure that header information conforms to the receiving bank's format, and to add the payee name to the detail level.

The electronic Positive Payee file that is created by the scheduled job is sent to an outbound directory and then to the bank — through another scheduled job — using your company's polling software (typically FTP via the Internet). The bank's host computer receives the file, which is then available for use in matching checks cashed by payees.

The file processing cycle completes when the bank sends a daily electronic file of cashed checks back to the company. Typically, this is received early in the morning, around 7am, prior to first presentment of checks for clearing. The file is polled from the bank's host directory and the cashed check file is placed by the polling software into its own internal directory. It is then uploaded into SAP ERP through a scheduled batch job using Program RFEBCK00.

5.1.2 Preprocessing of Files

Both outbound and inbound files may need to be preprocessed to conform to the bank format, or to add Positive Payee. This is done by creating a copy of the SAP ERP standard program (usually preceded with a Z to denote a custom program), which can be amended to conform to specified standards. For example, Program RFEBCK00 will become ZRFEBCK00, and all batch jobs need to be scheduled using the Z program.

> **Note: Obtain Bank Formats from the Positive Pay Service Bank**
>
> The Positive Pay service bank needs to provide the formats for the outbound Positive Pay file and the inbound cashed checks file. The outbound file from SAP ERP must conform to the bank format, and can be changed to add the payee name field if the bank provides Positive Payee service. Similarly, the inbound cashed check file from the bank needs to be changed to conform to SAP ERP format to enable automatic upload, posting, and clearing. Both of these changes are achieved through preprocessing using a Z version of the standard SAP ERP programs specified.

5.1.3 Detailed Process Steps

At the end of the check processing day, an electronic extract of all checks issued for the day is created using Program RFCHKE00, as shown in Figure 5.2. For a successful run, the file name with the number of checks extracted will display on the screen or job log.

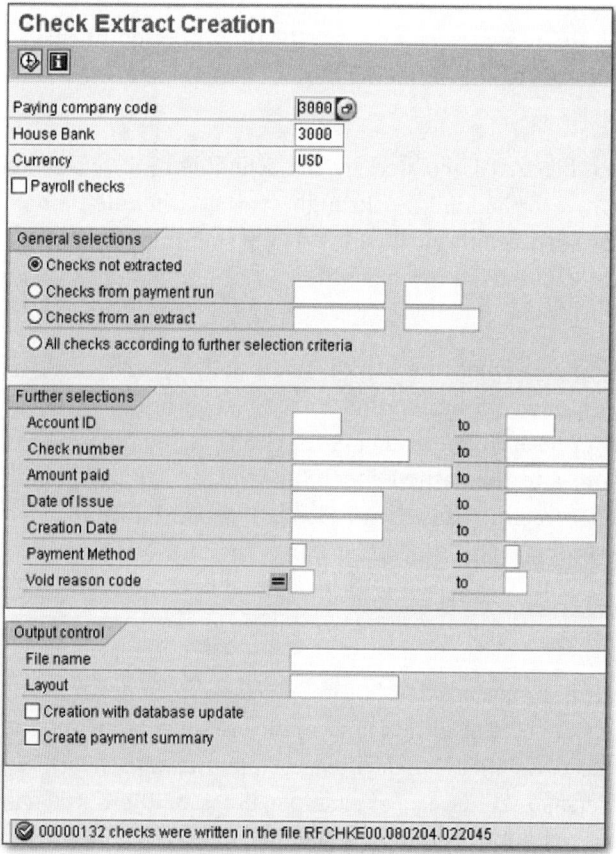

Figure 5.2 Create Check Extract Using Program RFCHKE00

An extract of the actual file is shown in Figure 5.3. The format needs to be based on the specifications provided by the bank. If the required format does not match the format provided by the standard program, then it can be modified appropriately by creating a Z version of the SAP ERP program as explained previously. Formats must be validated through test transmissions sent to the bank for confirmation.

```
134329042      IDES US INC              20080204022045 00000000000001320000132000000032737887120
30050021       00022678     00022678    Fremont Supplies              00000000000019700020020820000
30050021       00022682     00022682    Adams Inc.                    00000000000356780002003100700
30050021       00022686     00022686    Adams Inc.                    00000000000453550002003101000
30050021       00022689     00022689    EGS America                   00000000005441721020041220000
30050021       00022690     00022690    NJ Electronics                00000000007009221020041220000
30050021       00022691     00022691    MicroElectronics              00000000002154143002004122000
30050021       00022692     00022692    Atlanta Electronics Supply    00000000004569730020041220000
30050021       00022693     00022693    Tucker Industries             00000000005610796020041220000
```

Figure 5.3 Extract File Created with Positive Payee Information

Issued checks also need to be recorded in the check register, as shown in Figure 5.4. The balance in the checks outstanding account must always match the balance per the check register. Transaction FCHR lets you view the check register. The menu path is as follows: SAP MENU: ACCOUNTING • FINANCIAL ACCOUNTING • ACCOUNTS RECEIVABLE • ENVIRONMENT • CHECK INFORMATION • CHANGE • ON LINE CASHED CHECKS.

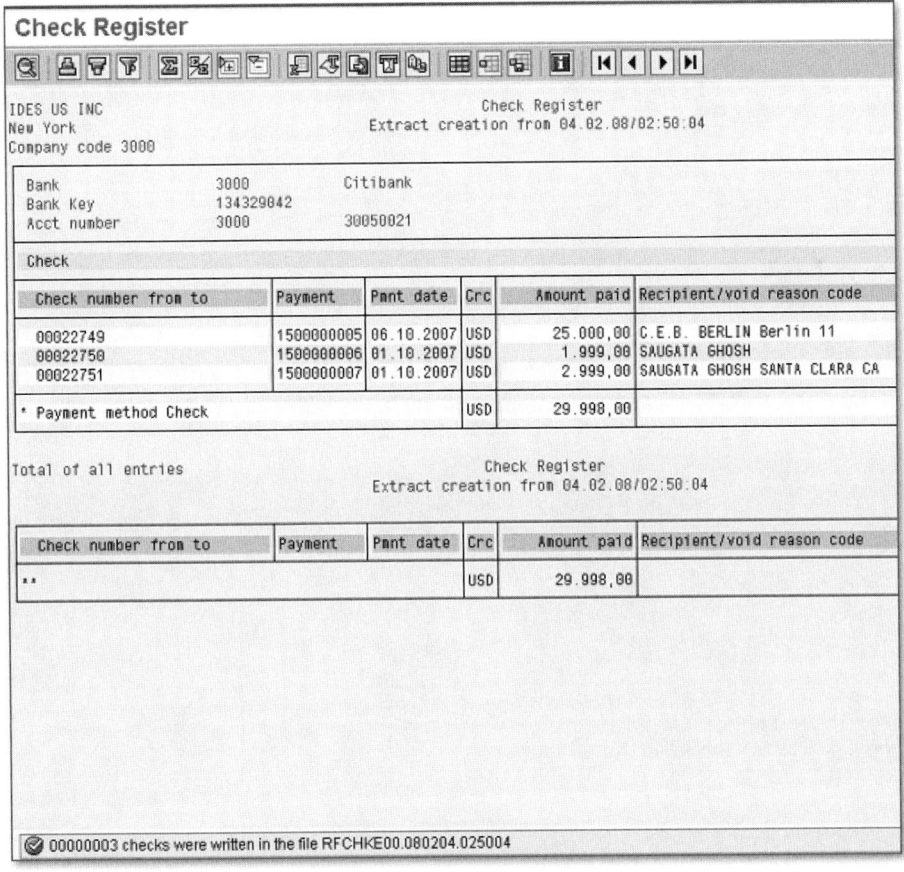

Figure 5.4 Extract of Check Register Transaction FCHR

When checks are cashed by a payee, the bank validates the information on the check with the Positive Pay file, and on successful validation clears the check. At the end of the day, the bank sends an electronic file of all encashed checks, called the encashment or cashed checks file. This file is received in the company's host directory and uploaded into SAP ERP. It may be necessary to preprocess the inbound bank file to enable successful upload into SAP ERP.

The screen for the cashed check file upload program is shown in Figure 5.5.

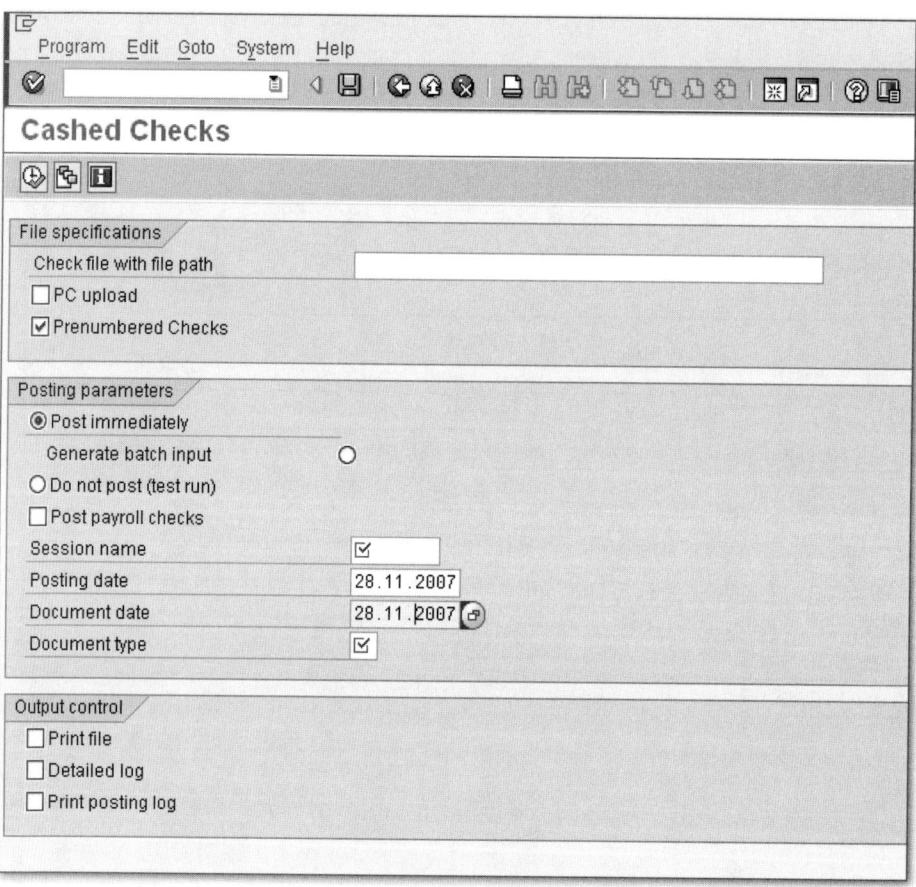

Figure 5.5 Cashed Check File Upload Program

The menu path for the check upload program is SAP MENU: ACCOUNTING • FINANCIAL ACCOUNTING • BANKS • INCOMINGS • CASHED CHECKS • EXECUTE.

The successful upload of the cashed check file results in updating the SAP ERP check register with the checks cashed and date of encashment. This is shown in Figure 5.6.

Bank	3000	Citibank					New York	
Bank Key	134329042							
Acct number	3000		30050021					

Check								
Check number from to		Payment	Pmnt date	Crcy	Amount paid (FC)	Recipient/void reason code		Enca./void
22664		2000000068	31.01.1997	USD	950.700,00	Henderson Inc. Philadelphia PA		
22665		2000000069	31.01.1997	USD	29.260,00	World Wide Computer Warehouse San Jose		
22666		2000000070	31.01.1997	USD	3.875,65	Phoenix Supplies Wilmington DE		
22667		2000000071	31.01.1997	USD	21.387,11	Pyramid Systems Santa Clara		
22668						voided by ODABASHIAN - Page overflow		14.02.1997
22669		2000000072	31.01.1997	USD	1.134.012,35	TetPak Inc. Chicago, IL		
22670						voided by ODABASHIAN - Form closing		14.02.1997
22671		1500000000	24.10.2001	USD	5.300,00	Another One Time Mendota Heights MN		
22672-22673						voided by ODIGHIBOR - Test printout		30.12.2001
22674		2000000032	28.12.2001	USD	2.100,00	Abbott Building Supplies, Inc.Wayne PA		
22675						voided by ODIGHIBOR - Form closing		30.12.2001
* Payment method Check				CAD	2.150,00			
				USD	32.737.887,12			

Figure 5.6 Updated Check Register with Encashment Details

Also, the G/L account of outstanding checks is reduced by the amount of the checks cashed, as described in Section 5.1.3. This is an important control feature that ensures that the check register balance of outstanding checks will always be equal to the balance of outstanding checks in the G/L.

Next, an entry is created in the bank clearing account reflecting the total amount of checks that will be presented for clearing the same morning for controlled disbursement, cash flow, and funding purposes. This is an additional control feature to ensure reconciliation of flows between the controlled disbursement account and transferring bank account. When the EBS is received, reflecting the actual settlement of monies cashed, the bank clearing account is debited and the bank account is credited, completing the process. The accounting cycle for Positive Pay is shown in Figure 5.7.

5 | Positive Pay and Payment Card Processing

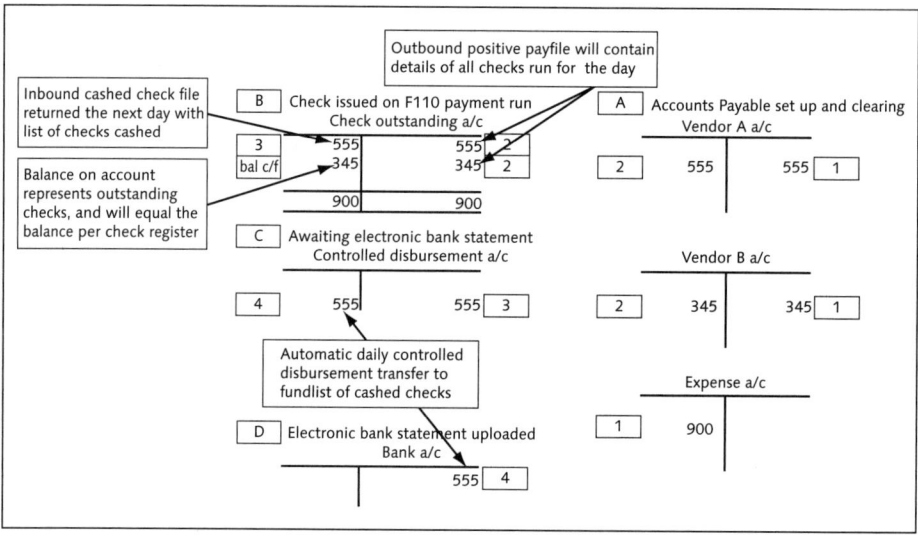

Figure 5.7 Accounting Flow for the Positive Pay Cycle

5.1.4 Implementing Positive Pay

The setup of Positive Pay service within a company entails detailed planning and execution, especially because electronic files are being transmitted to and from the Positive Pay bank partner.

The following is a list of several key considerations for planning an implementation of Positive Pay:

- Set up a project team together with the bank.
- Obtain bank file formats for outbound and inbound files.
- Define exception procedures, file transmission times, escalation procedures, key contacts, and other policies and procedures between the company and the bank.
- Create and test inbound and outbound formats with the bank.
- Set up and test inbound and outbound file transmission capabilities.
- Create and test preprocessing programs.
- Schedule batch jobs.
- Plan for cutover and go-live.

> **Note: Test Positive Pay Through the Entire Bank Process**
>
> Test Positive Pay through the entire banking system in both the test and live system, including testing an unauthorized check to ensure that it fails Positive Pay. Banks typically have to switch on their Positive Pay service, and sometimes omit to do so on the go-live date. It is also good practice to force an exception at least once a year to ensure Positive Pay is working.

5.1.5 Controlled Disbursement in Positive Pay

Typically, funding of daily cashed checks is done using controlled disbursement. This is an important control and funding mechanism available to companies through their bank. Based on the Federal Reserve's early morning presentment schedule, banks will be able to determine the exact dollar amount of checks being cashed. This will match the total of the daily cashed checks file sent to the company as part of the Positive Pay cycle. Based on prior arrangements, this amount is automatically transferred by the bank out of the company's funding account into the check disbursement account to fund the checks cashed during the previous day.

> **Key Tip: Controlled Disbursement Amounts Available in Intraday File**
>
> Controlled disbursement amounts that go through presentment are also available on inbound intraday electronic bank statements for cash positioning and planning purposes. Intraday banking is covered in detail in Chapter 6.

This allows the company to plan its daily investment and borrowing requirements because it will know the exact amount of the checks being cashed. Effective implementation of controlled disbursement results in the following benefits:

- Reduction of costs by adding the ability to reduce interest expense for borrowing.
- Automation and accuracy of check funding and elimination of need to forecast daily check clearing amounts.
- Reduction of administrative work involved in executing daily funding transfers.
- Ability to each day invest excess balances that would otherwise be idle, and obtain increased ROI. Alternatively, reduction of excess borrowing costs.

5.1.6 Summary of Key Controls

The Positive Payee service is one of the most effective control mechanisms for check fraud. In this section, we will provide you with a summary of the key controls that need to be in place when implementing a Positive Payee process to maximize its benefits.

As part of bank relationship management, it is important to document all procedures and processes with respect to the Positive Pay cycle as agreed with your banking partner:

- Maintain all documentation relating to the setup and operation of Positive Pay between the bank and the company, including legal contracts and SLAs.
- Develop a list of contact names and information for communication between the bank and the company, as well as escalation procedures.
- Set up process for disposition of exception items that failed Positive Pay.
- Develop and deliver appropriate training for treasury and accounts payable staff for the Positive Payee cycle process.
- Implement procedures to ensure monitoring of transmission of outbound and inbound files.
- Develop and implement polices with respect to imaging and archiving of checks.
- Establish a process for reversing erroneous or duplicate transactions.
- Test Positive Pay through the entire cycle in test and live environments, including negative testing to ensure unauthorized checks fail Positive Pay.
- Negative test at least once a year to ensure Positive Pay service is working.

Establishing robust controls for file transmission will provide strong assurance with respect to the integrity and security over payment processes:

- Ensure secure file transmission with file encryption and decryption for outbound and inbound Positive Pay files.
- Implement procedures to ensure monitoring of transmission of outbound and inbound files.
- Provide appropriate reconciliation staff with logs of SAP ERP batch jobs relating to outbound and inbound file transfers.

- Ensure that outbound Positive Pay files can't be manipulated prior to transmission to the bank.
- Develop and implement backup procedures to protect yourself against failure of inbound and outbound file transmission.
- Develop and implement backup procedures to protect yourself against failure of the Positive Pay cycle in SAP ERP.
- Segregate duties between accounts payable and treasury staff with respect to payment processing and reconciliation of outbound electronic fund transfers.
- Develop and deliver appropriate training for treasury and accounts payable staff for the Positive Pay cycle process.
- Ensure adequate controls of master data with respect to authorization access, keeping in mind SoD between key handoff points.
- Test process controls periodically to ensure they are working as intended.

Regular reconciliation will provide assurance that the books of financial record are accurate, and ensure that unauthorized activity has not taken place:

- Perform daily or otherwise regular reconciliation of outstanding checks, bank accounts, and clearing accounts for uncleared items, and implement an escalation process for unresolved issues.
- Ensure balances in clearing accounts are reconciled and cleared.
- Create a risk/control matrix for Positive Pay business processes.
- Develop a process for incorporating manual, cancelled, and voided checks into the Positive Pay cycle, through timely entry into the SAP ERP system.
- Segregate duties between accounts payable and treasury staff with respect to payment processing and reconciliation of the check register.
- Document all procedures and processes to provide evidence and assurance of strong internal controls that can be validated and tested.

5.2 Lockbox Processing

Lockboxes are used primarily in the U.S. where customers mail checks to a designated post office (P.O.) address, maintained by the company's bank. The received checks are collected by the bank, deposited into the company's designated bank account, and an electronic version of the deposit details is created and sent to the company. This file is uploaded into SAP ERP, and matched and cleared against customer accounts in the Accounts Receivable module of SAP ERP. SAP ERP then creates payment advices out of each line entry in the file, and performs matching and posting functions based on clearing algorithms set up in configuration. The process is usually fully automated using batch jobs for receiving, processing, and posting the incoming files.

Post-processing capabilities are provided to clear unmatched items. Banks can also provide ACH and wire deposit details in the lockbox file in addition to checks, if so requested by the company.

The key steps in the lockbox process cycle are as follows:

1. Customers send checks through the mail to their designated lockbox. The bank then creates an electronic version of the deposits in a standard BAI2 format. Next, the file is transmitted to the company for storing and upload into SAP ERP.

2. The file is received by the company into its host directory. It needs to be preprocessed to enable upload into SAP ERP. The preprocessed file is uploaded and processed in SAP ERP through execution of the lockbox import program (Program RFEBLB00). This is usually done overnight in background mode, although the program can also be run online.

3. The import program matches each receipt in the electronic file to the customer account information available in SAP ERP's Account Receivable component. Matching and clearing takes place depending on the amount of information available in the lockbox file. Four levels of matching and posting take place, as follows:

   ▶ **Applied fully**
   Takes place when a customer number and invoice-specific information is available that enables a direct match with an invoice number in the customer's open item accounts receivable.

   ▶ **Partially applied**
   Takes place when some but not all of the items are matched because of a missing invoice number or other missing information relating to the amount (requires BAI2 format).

   ▶ **On account**
   Takes place when a customer is identified but no other information is available. In this case, the system posts to the customer on account, but with-

out clearing any specific invoices. Even if the lockbox file does not contain a customer reference, the system may be able to identify the customer by matching the MICR number on the lockbox receipt with the number in the customer master data banking information.

▶ **Unidentified**
Takes place when there is no reference information at all. In this case, the amount will post to a clearing account that will need to be identified and posted to the correct customer account.

Posting takes place in a two-step process on upload. First, all amounts post to a clearing account. Second, when a match is found, amounts post to the accounts receivable sub ledger. Any unidentified amounts remain in the clearing account, for post-processing.

4. Post-processing and reconciliation of unmatched and uncleared amounts is the last step in the process. The upload program provides a detailed posting log, sorted by the four categories of matching described in the previous step. Post-processing of any unmatched or uncleared amounts is done manually using Transaction FEBA_LOCKBOX. The menu path is ACCOUNTING • FINANCIAL ACCOUNTING • BANKS • LOCKBOX • REPROCESS.

Figure 5.8 shows the lockbox processing cycle in SAP ERP.

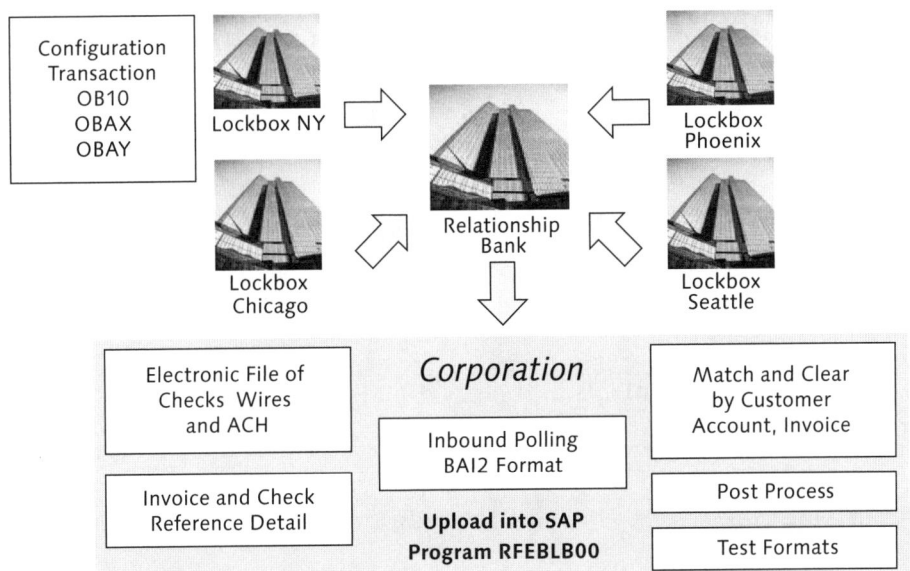

Figure 5.8 Overview of Lockbox Processing

The menu path for processing lockbox transactions is shown in Figure 5.9.

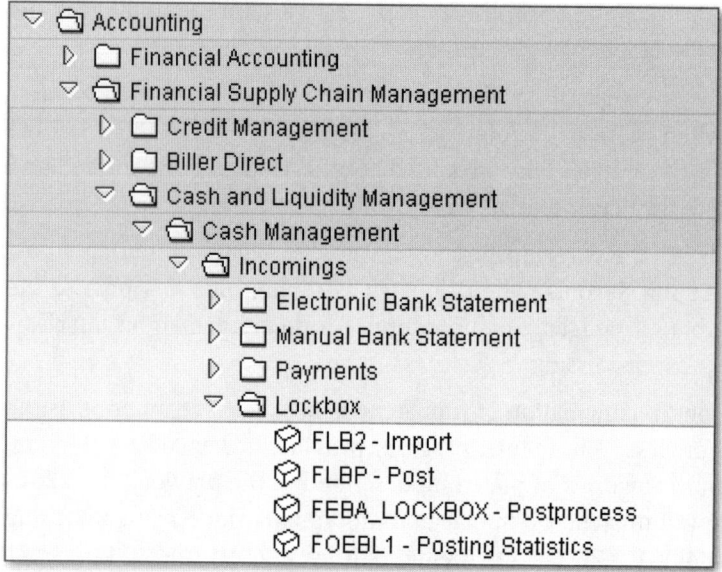

Figure 5.9 Lockbox Application Menu Options

> **Note**
>
> Ask your lockbox bank to include electronic fund receipts such as ACH-CTX and wire remittances in the lockbox file along with check information received. Electronic ACH receipts — especially in the CTX format with detailed addenda information containing invoice details — will result in a high hit rate of matching and clearing with customer open item receivables.

Lockbox information can also be added to the customer master, as shown in Figure 5.10. This provides an added measure of control to ensure the correct matching between an incoming lockbox file and the customer record.

5.2.1 Accounting Controls in the Lockbox Process

The lockbox processing cycle can be fully automated in SAP ERP. The inbound lockbox file is typically polled late in the evening or early in the morning, depending on when the bank agrees to have the file ready for the day's lockbox collections.

Lockbox Processing | 5.2

The inbound file can be automatically preprocessed and uploaded using batch programs. The accounting postings within SAP ERP are controlled and passed through clearing accounts to ensure that all transactions are processed, and that all lockbox receipts per the lockbox file are also received subsequently from the bank. This is achieved through the accounting posting that posts the consolidated total of receipts to the bank clearing account. This account is cleared when the EBS is received, showing the total deposits. These should match and clear the entry in the clearing account, unless the amounts don't match. In this event, it is an exception item and needs to be followed up with the bank.

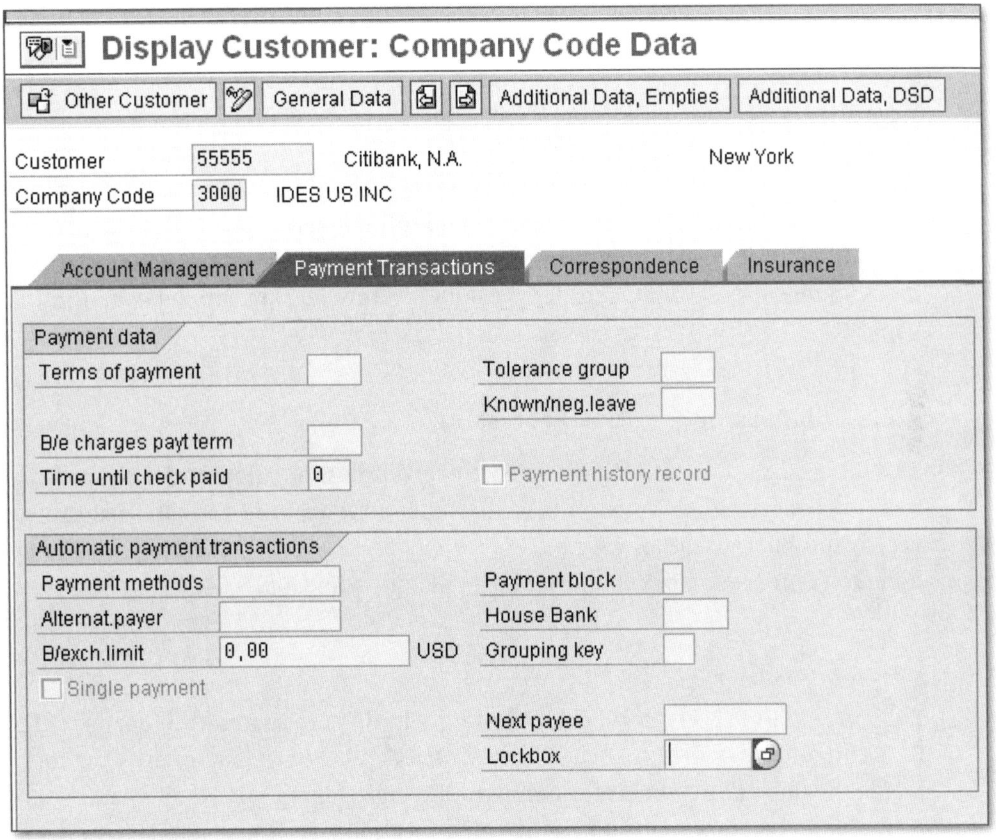

Figure 5.10 Lockbox Identification in the Customer Master Record

197

5 | Positive Pay and Payment Card Processing

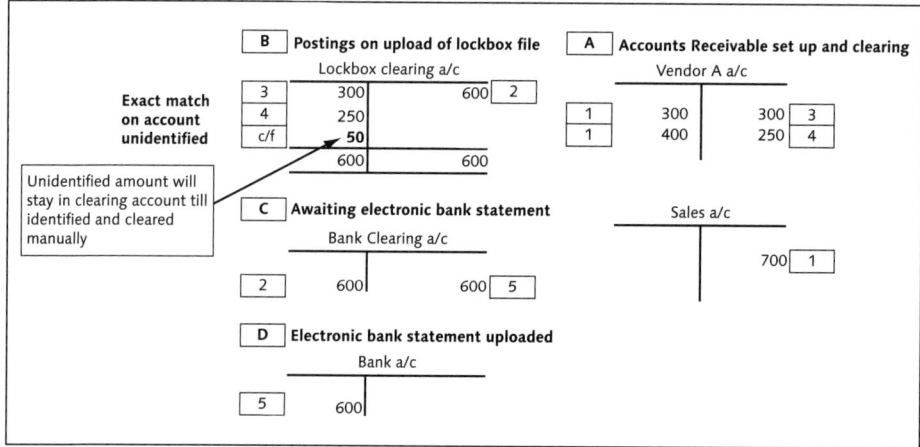

Figure 5.11 Accounting Postings in the Lockbox Process

As shown in Figure 5.11, the lockbox clearing account (box B) controls all entries that are uploaded from the file. Any unidentified receipts will remain in this account, and will need to be post-processed. The other control is the bank clearing account (Box C), which ensures that all lockbox receipts are deposited in the bank.

5.2.2 Simulating Lockbox Processing

SAP ERP includes a set of programs that enable the simulation of the entire lockbox process, including creation of a test upload file in BAI2 format. This can be very helpful because it forms the basis for any preprocessing that may need to be done to the inbound lockbox format provided by the bank.

Creating Test Files for Upload

Program RFEBLBT2 creates lockbox test data in BAI2 format with filename GHL-BOX and other parameters such as DESTINATION and ORIGIN that identify the lockbox in the file. The key fields for input are shown in Figure 5.12. These parameters are set up in configuration and control identification, account assignment, clearing account posting, and other settings to enable successful file upload, matching, and clearing.

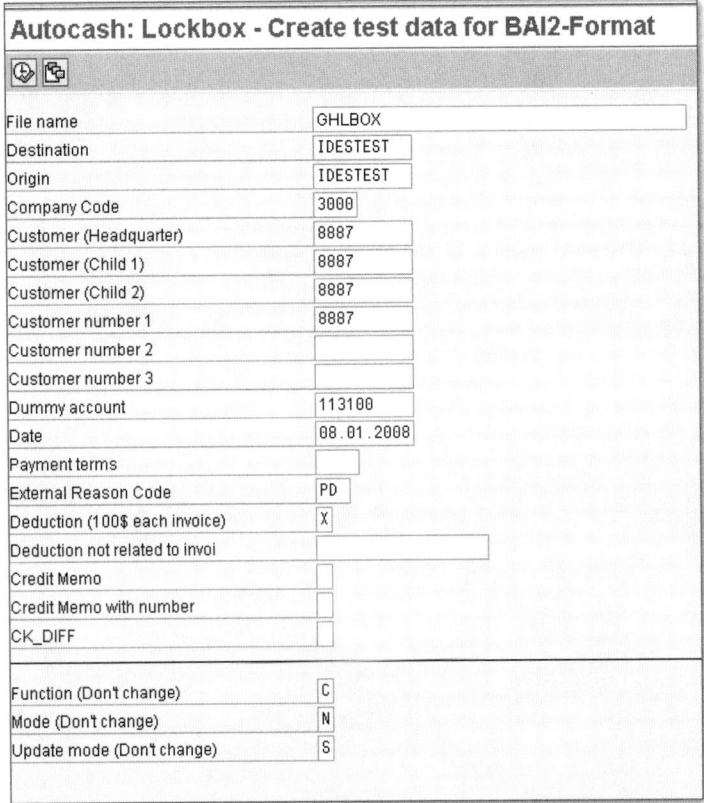

Figure 5.12 Test Data Input for Lockbox Simulation Program RFEBLBT2

The test program also creates an open customer receivable that will create a matching entry in the lockbox file to match and clear against, as shown in Figure 5.13.

C...	Itm	PK	S	Account	Description	Amount	Curr.	Tx	Cost Ce
3000	1	01		8887	Paul Johnson	2.200,00	USD		
	2	50		113100	Citibank Account	2.200,00-	USD		

Data Entry View
Document Number: 1800000027 Company Code: 3000 Fiscal Year: 2007
Document Date: 29.12.2007 Posting Date: 29.12.2007 Period: 12
Reference: Cross-CC no.:
Currency: USD Texts exist Ledger Group:

Figure 5.13 Open Customer Receivable Setup by Test Program

The lockbox file created by the test program is shown in Figure 5.14. The bank administering the lockbox will provide its BAI2 format specifications, which should conform to the format shown in the test example. Any differences can be addressed through the preprocessing program to add or alter any information required to conform to the BAI2 format of SAP ERP for upload purposes.

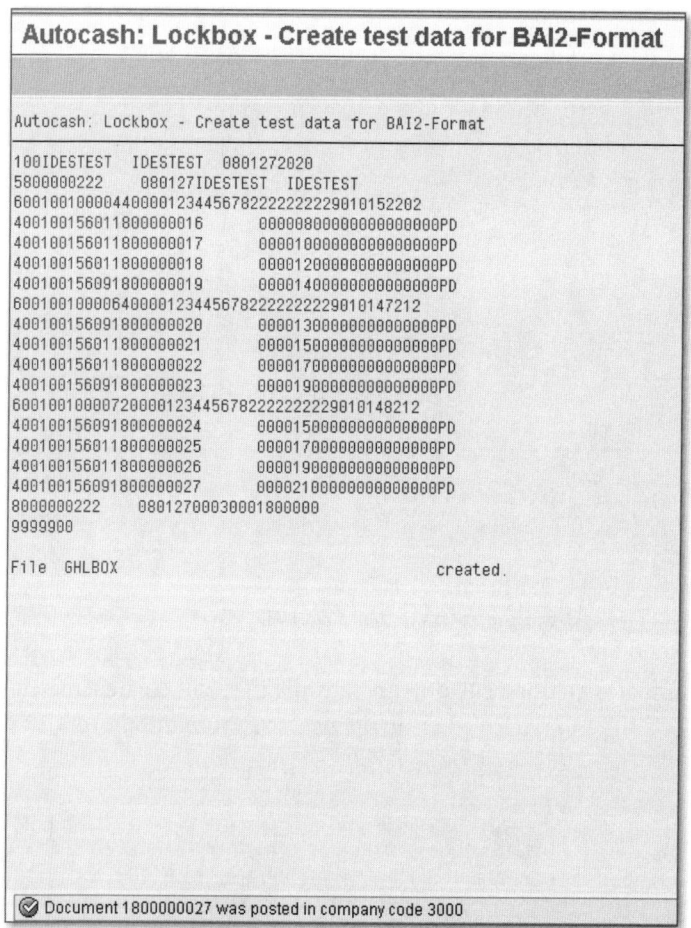

Figure 5.14 Test Lockbox File in BAI2 Format

This file can be saved in a test directory and uploaded using the lockbox program. After running the upload program, SAP ERP provides a posting log of upload results, as shown in Figure 5.15.

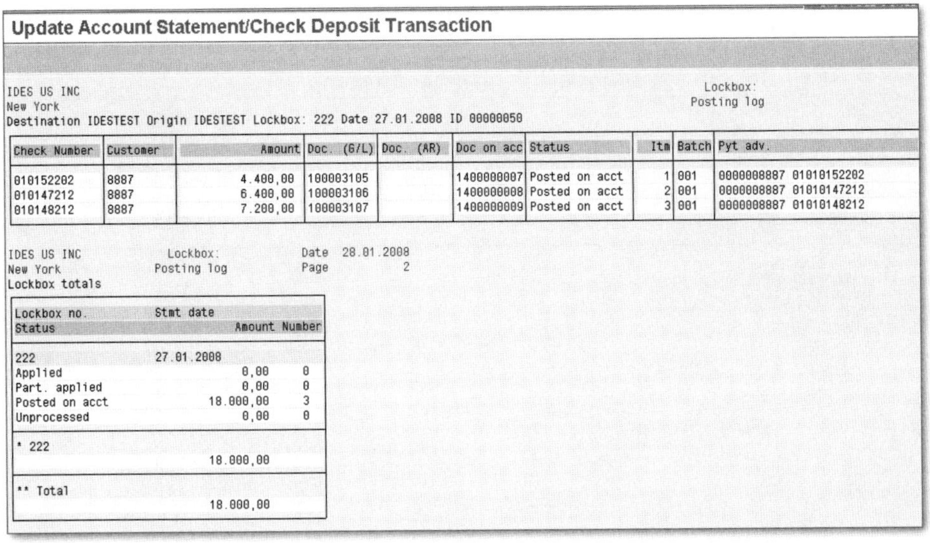

Lockbox Processing | 5.2

Update Account Statement/Check Deposit Transaction									
IDES US INC New York Destination IDESTEST Origin IDESTEST Lockbox: 222 Date 27.01.2008 ID 00000050							Lockbox: Posting log		
Check Number	Customer	Amount	Doc. (G/L)	Doc. (AR)	Doc on acc	Status	Itm	Batch	Pyt adv.
010152202	8887	4.400,00	100003105		1400000007	Posted on acct	1	001	0000008887 01010152202
010147212	8887	6.400,00	100003106		1400000008	Posted on acct	2	001	0000008887 01010147212
010148212	8887	7.200,00	100003107		1400000009	Posted on acct	3	001	0000008887 01010148212

```
IDES US INC           Lockbox:           Date  28.01.2008
New York              Posting log        Page            2
Lockbox totals

Lockbox no.      Stmt date
Status                       Amount  Number

222              27.01.2008
Applied                        0,00       0
Part. applied                  0,00       0
Posted on acct            18.000,00       3
Unprocessed                    0,00       0

* 222
                          18.000,00

** Total
                          18.000,00
```

Figure 5.15 Posting Log of Lockbox Upload Results

The posting log becomes the basis for post-processing and reconciling the lockbox file with the Accounts Receivable subcomponent in SAP ERP. The posting log report provides the breakdown between the type of posting and clearing achieved by the upload program, as shown in Figure 5.16.

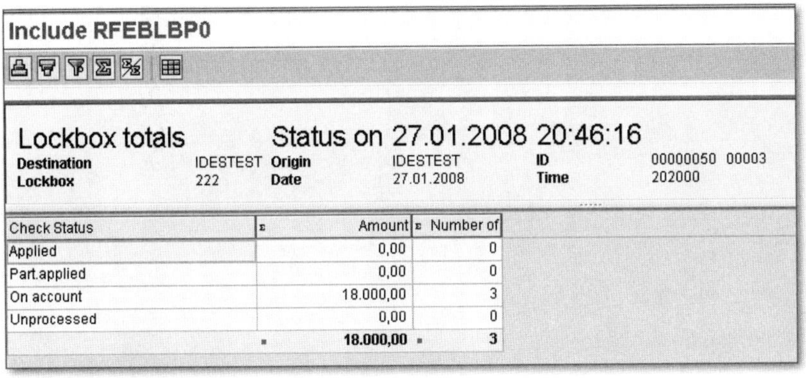

Include RFEBLBP0					
Lockbox totals		**Status on 27.01.2008 20:46:16**			
Destination	IDESTEST	Origin	IDESTEST	ID	00000050 00003
Lockbox	222	Date	27.01.2008	Time	202000

Check Status	∑ Amount	∑ Number of
Applied	0,00	0
Part.applied	0,00	0
On account	18.000,00	3
Unprocessed	0,00	0
	18.000,00	3

Figure 5.16 Summary Report of Lockbox Totals

Further detail is obtained by drilling down into the specific line item. An example of an incoming payment finding the customer, based on the MICR number, is shown in Figure 5.17. This results in the creation of a payment advice that will need to be post-processed.

5 | Positive Pay and Payment Card Processing

```
Destination IDESTEST Origin IDESTEST Lockbox 222 Payment Date 27.01.2008 ID 00000050

 Itm Batch Check number  Customer    Name                    Messages
Messages (2)
Customer Ref.                        Payment Amnt   Deduction Amnt Text

  1 001  010152202     8887      Paul Johnson              Customer uniquely identified with MICR number
Payment advice D 0000008887 01010152202       created.
1800000016                                                 Document found
1800000017                                                 Document found
1800000018                                                 Document found
1800000019                                                 Document found
              Advice Total             0,00
              Check Amount         4.400,00

  2 001  010147212     8887      Paul Johnson              Customer uniquely identified with MICR number
Payment advice D 0000008887 01010147212       created.
1800000020                                                 Document found
1800000021                                                 Document found
1800000022                                                 Document found
1800000023                                                 Document found
              Advice Total             0,00
              Check Amount         6.400,00

  3 001  010148212     8887      Paul Johnson              Customer uniquely identified with MICR number
Payment advice D 0000008887 01010148212       created.
1800000024                                                 Document found
1800000025                                                 Document found
1800000026                                                 Document found
1800000027                                                 Document found
              Advice Total             0,00
              Check Amount         7.200,00
```

Figure 5.17 Posting Log Details of Clearing

Post-processing is carried out using Transaction FEBA_LOCKBOX. The menu path for this function is ACCOUNTING • FINANCIAL ACCOUNTING • BANKS • LOCKBOX • REPROCESS.

The initial screen with the lockbox identifying details is shown in Figure 5.18.

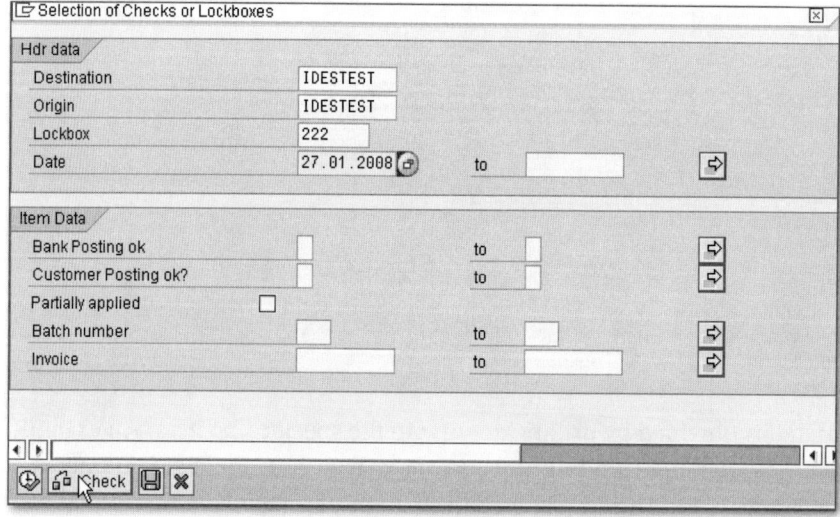

Figure 5.18 Selecting a Lockbox for Post-Processing

The system will identify all transactions that need to be post-processed, as shown in Figure 5.19. It displays a split screen that allows investigation into why the amount did not match and clear the customer receivable completely. In Figure 5.19, you can see that the amount has been identified as a payment on account that needs to be matched with a specific customer invoice.

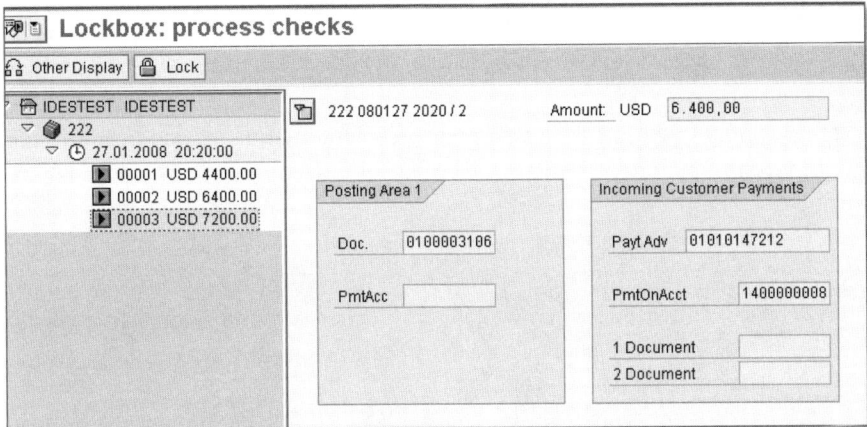

Figure 5.19 Post-Processing Unmatched Items

Posting of the document can be done within the post-processing screen, as shown in Figure 5.20

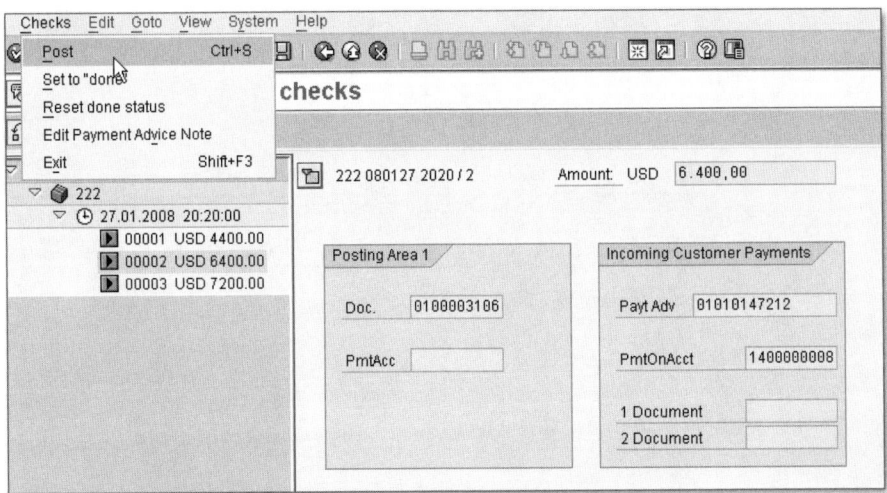

Figure 5.20 Posting an Uncleared Item

Depending on the nature of the uncleared item, the system will propose appropriate clearing functionality. In our example, the system was not able to find an exact match, and displayed the error message shown in Figure 5.21.

Pyt adv.	Messages
0000008887 01010152202	Accounts receivable posting Error: (F5 263) The difference is too large for clearing
0000008887 01010147212	Accounts receivable posting Error: (F5 263) The difference is too large for clearing
0000008887 01010148212	Accounts receivable posting Error: (F5 263) The difference is too large for clearing

Figure 5.21 Example of Explanation of Reason for Unmatched Invoices

The system proposes open item clearing that enables a manual match between the incoming amount and open items on the customer account, as shown in Figure 5.22

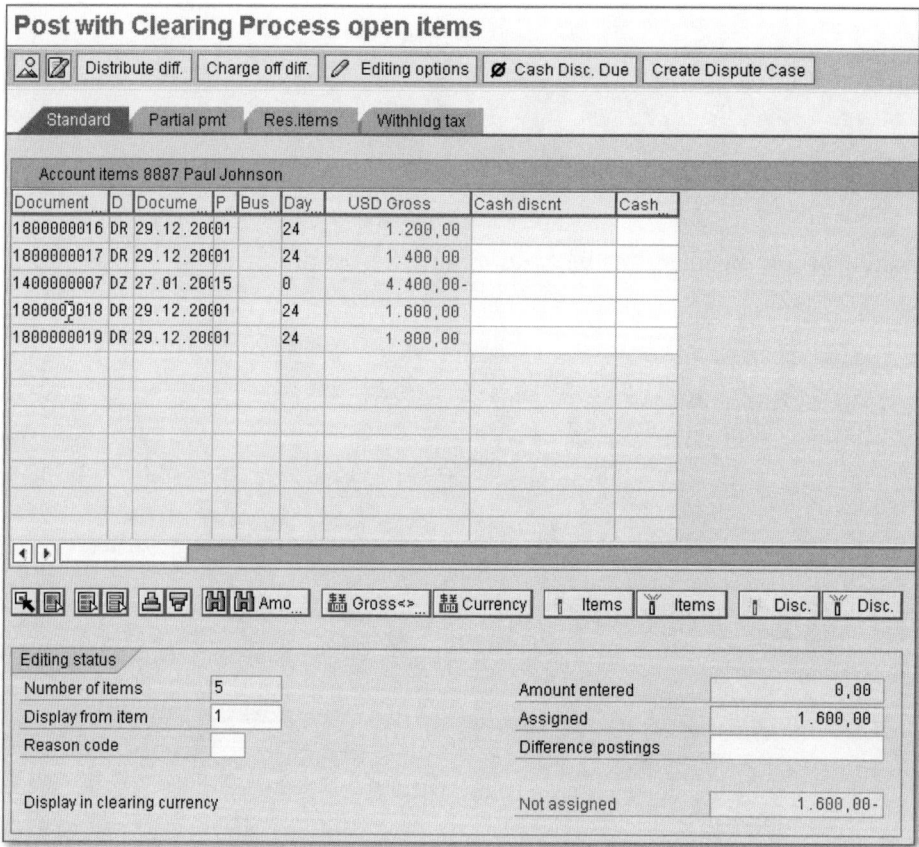

Figure 5.22 Clearing Open Items

When the amount is matched and posted, the record in the post-processing screen turns to green, signifying successful matching, clearing, and posting, as shown in Figure 5.23.

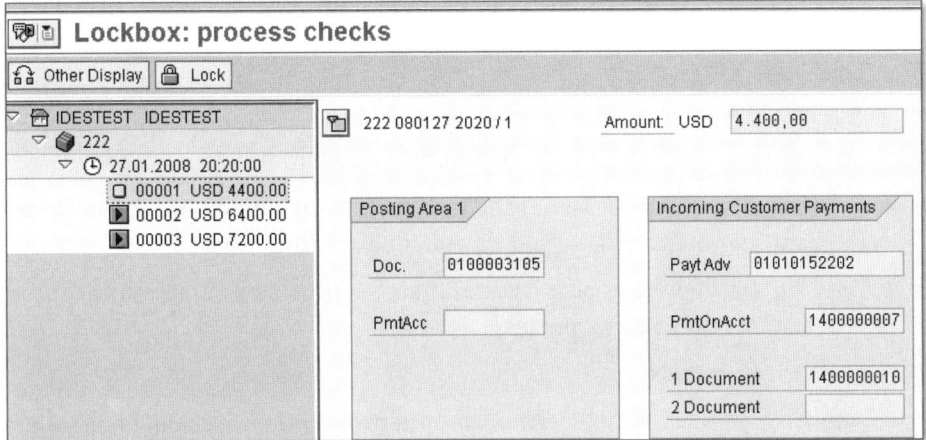

Figure 5.23 Amount Successfully Matched, Cleared and Posted

The accounting document confirming the posting is shown in Figure 5.24.

C...	Itm	PK	S	Account	Description	Amount	Curr.	Tx	Cost Center
3000	1	40		113109	Citibank - customer	4.400,00	USD		
	2	15		8887	Paul Johnson	4.400,00-	USD		

Figure 5.24 Accounting Document Showing Cleared Customer Account

5.2.3 Summary of Key Lockbox Controls

Controls for lockbox are essentially the same as for all inbound electronic file transmissions, but in particular ensure that all receipts were accounted for, cleared the correct customer accounts, and were actually received in full and deposited by the bank into the company's bank account. The following key controls are particularly relevant with respect to lockbox processing:

- **Process controls**
  - Maintain all documentation relating to the setup and operation of the lockbox service between the bank and the company, including legal contracts and SLAs.
  - Establish appropriate lockbox locations that are appropriate for the company's operations, based on cost benefit considerations
  - Develop a list of contact names and information for communication between the bank and the company, and document escalation procedures.
  - Develop and deliver appropriate training for treasury and accounts receivable staff for the lockbox process.

- **File security controls**
  - Implement procedures to ensure monitoring of transmission of inbound lockbox files and batch jobs.
  - Ensure secure file transmission with file encryption and decryption for inbound lockbox files, because the file will contain customer account number, MICR, and other confidential information.
  - Provide appropriate reconciliation staff with logs of SAP ERP batch jobs relating to inbound file transmissions.
  - Ensure that the inbound lockbox file can't be manipulated prior to receipt into the SAP ERP system.
  - Develop and implement backup procedures to protect yourself against failure of an inbound file transmission.

- **Accounting controls**
  - Segregate duties between accounts receivable and treasury staff with respect to customer payment application and bank reconciliation.
  - Ensure adequate controls of customer and bank master data with respect to authorization access, keeping in mind SoD between key handoff points.
  - Ensure daily or otherwise regular reconciliation of lockbox import files to ensure all receipts are accounted for and posted correctly into the accounting ledgers and sub ledgers in SAP ERP.

- Ensure review and post-processing of all unidentified, unmatched, and on account postings, to ensure that the books of financial record are accurate, and to ensure that unauthorized activity has not taken place.
- Conduct daily or periodic bank reconciliation to ensure totals indicated by the lockbox file are actually received subsequently in the bank account of the company.
- **Internal controls**
  - Test process controls periodically to ensure they are working as intended.
  - Create a risk/control matrix for lockbox business processes.
  - Document all procedures and processes to provide evidence and assurance of strong internal controls that can be validated and tested.
  - Ensure independent, periodic review of posting logs, post-processing screens, and clearing accounts to ensure that unauthorized activity has not taken place.
  - Ensure, through regularly occurring reconciliation, that balances or differences do not exist in the lockbox and bank clearing accounts.

5.3 Procurement and Credit Card Processing

Companies are increasingly accepting purchase cards (p-cards) and credit cards as a form of settlement for payment of customer invoices and receivables. Payment and credit card processing adds a new layer of complexity in the form of requirements for security and confidentiality of customer credit card information. Additionally, the Payment Card Industry (PCI) has set certain security standards that need to be complied with, as described in Section 5.3.2, Payment Card Industry (PCI) Data Security Standards. Non-compliance results in fines, additional audit scrutiny, and, possibly, legal ramifications.

5.3.1 Overview of Process

SAP ERP provides a cross-application payment card interface. It is available to various SAP ERP versions and components such as R/3, Customer Relationship Management (CRM), and Biller Direct, a function of the Financial Supply Chain

Management (FSCM) component. The business process involves two components: authorization and settlement.

The authorization process starts with order entry in the Sales and Distribution (SD) component, followed by a request for authorization sent in real-time to the credit card processor or clearinghouse. When the approval is received back, the transaction is processed. Transactions are recorded in SAP ERP using accounts receivable control accounts by card type and merchant identification (ID).

The settlement process starts when all authorized transactions are invoiced and recorded in SAP ERP. The settlement file is sent to the credit card processor, who provides settlement services with merchant banks and financial institutions. The settlement file is received back from the credit card processor, and is uploaded into SAP ERP for clearing, reconciliation, and setting up entries in the bank clearing account for receiving settlement proceeds from banks. The last step in the process is the actual receipt of funds in the company's bank account, and the corresponding reconciliation. Typically, authorization will be in real-time, and settlement in batch mode. Communication takes place through Remote Function Calls (RFCs) out of SAP ERP, with either an Internet or frame relay connection to the payment card processor.

> **Key Term: Remote Function Calls (RFCs)**
>
> RFCs are programs written in ABAP, the programming language of SAP ERP. They drive transactions and functionality within the system.

From a controls standpoint, the key areas you need to address when implementing payment card processing in SAP ERP revolve around security for transactional and master data, integrity of data transmissions (both inbound and outbound), maintenance of confidentiality of customer credit card information, error and exception processing, and daily reconciliation of all control and clearing accounts.

5.3.2 Payment Card Industry (PCI) Data Security Standards

The PCI Security Standards Council is an independent body formed to develop, enhance, disseminate, and assist with implementation of security standards for payment account security. The PCI Security Standards Council was founded by

American Express, Discover Financial Services, JCB International, MasterCard Worldwide, and Visa Inc.

The PCI DSS version 1.1, a set of comprehensive requirements for enhancing payment account data security, was developed by the founding payment brands of the PCI Security Standards Council, to help facilitate the broad adoption of consistent data security measures on a global basis.

PCI DSS requirements are applicable if a Primary Account Number (PAN) is stored, processed, or transmitted. If a PAN is not stored, processed, or transmitted, PCI DSS requirements do not apply.

The core of the PCI DSS is a group of principles and accompanying requirements, around which the specific elements of the DSS are organized. Detailed information is available at the Council's website at *https://www.pcisecuritystandards.org/*. The summary requirements are described in the following list:

- **Build and maintain a secure network**
    - Requirement 1: Install and maintain a firewall configuration to protect cardholder data.
    - Requirement 2: Do not use vendor-supplied defaults for system passwords and other security parameters.
- **Protect cardholder data**
    - Requirement 3: Protect stored cardholder data.
    - Requirement 4: Encrypt transmission of cardholder data across open, public networks.
- **Maintain a vulnerability management program**
    - Requirement 5: Use and regularly update anti-virus software.
    - Requirement 6: Develop and maintain secure systems and applications.
- **Implement strong access control measures**
    - Requirement 7: Restrict access to cardholder data by business need to know.
    - Requirement 8: Assign a unique ID to each person with computer access.
    - Requirement 9: Restrict physical access to cardholder data.

- **Regularly monitor and test networks**
    - Requirement 10: Track and monitor all access to network resources and cardholder data.
    - Requirement 11: Regularly test security systems and processes.
- **Maintain an information security policy**
    - Requirement 12: Maintain a policy that addresses information security.

5.3.3 PCI DSS Requirements and SAP ERP

PCI DSS requirements 3 and 7, relating to the protection and restricted access to cardholder information, are of particular importance when setting up credit card processing in SAP ERP. SAP ERP has the functionality to encrypt cardholder information within the customer master and in the sales order (where card numbers can be selected from a dropdown list based on information contained in the customer master; alternatively, credit card numbers can be entered directly in the sales order).

Access to cardholder data is controlled in SAP ERP through authorization objects that will only allow authorized users to create, change, display, pre-enter, or decrypt the data. To do so, SAP ERP provides authorization objects at the customer and accounting document levels. Credit card types set up in the system will need to be enabled for encryption. The detailed process for this is described in Section 5.3.6, Key Authorization and Encryption Controls.

In instances where the encryption features offered by SAP ERP are not robust enough to ensure compliance with internal corporate requirements or PCI DSS standards, additional security can be configured through Customizing, or by using SAP-certified, third party vendor bolt-on solutions.

SAP ERP provides RFCs, BAPIs, Business Add-Ins (BAdIs), BTCs and user exits for authorization, security (encryption and decryption), and settlement functions that allow for seamless integration with third party-developed bolt-on solutions, and through internally developed customized solutions.

> **Key Terms: BAPIs, BAdIs, BTCs and User Exits**
> Like RFCs, BAPIs, BAdIs, BTCs, and user exits are precoded program function modules written in ABAP or Java code that facilitate functionality and enhancements within the system.

5.3.4 Key Design Considerations

Certain key factors must be taken into account when designing a credit card processing solution that will impact the controls that need to be built to support that process. We will discuss these factors in this section.

Maintaining Credit Card Information

Credit card numbers can be entered directly into a sales order, or stored as part of customer master data and called up when entering an order. If data is entered in the customer master, it needs to be protected per requirement 3 of the PCI DSS standard. SAP ERP lets you encrypt credit card information so that when it is called up in an order, all numbers except the last four or five digits are masked.

Data Transmission

Inbound and outbound credit card information needs to be encrypted when transmitted across open public networks, per requirement 4 of the PCI DSS standard. Due to the real-time nature of authorizations, the links between the company and credit card processor need to be robust and secure. Typically, these are Internet-based ftp or frame relay connections.

Types of Cards and Currencies

The variety of cards and currency of settlement will be an important factor, especially if the implementation is global. It will be important to select a credit card processor who can handle authorization and settlement facilities in the various geographical regions of the world. This will impact the banking structure as well as the design of clearing accounts for the settlement and reconciliation functions.

If multiple currencies are accepted and converted into one settlement currency, special settings in SAP ERP accounting master G/L data will be required.

Level of Detail Transmitted

An important factor to consider is the level of detail that is passed to the credit card processor, because this will dictate the extent of additional configuration or customizing required for extracting and transmitting the fields of information. The details are sent by the merchant's SAP ERP system to the credit card processor, who in turn reports the data to the customer. These details appear on the credit card statement that will require settlement by the customer on the due date agreed upon with the credit card provider. There are three levels of detail that can be passed:

- Level 1 is the basic minimum information required to enable identification and settlement.
- Level 2 provides additional header level information, including purchase order number, other reference numbers, and header level text.
- Level 3 provides the greatest amount of detail, including line item level detail such as quantity, part number, cost, tax, discount, and so on.

Typically, retail customers using regular credit cards receive level 1 data. Corporate or business customers using credit cards or p-cards use level 2 data. Level 3 data is only available for businesses using p-cards. The decision to use level 3 is based on a combination of factors, such as volume of business, need for security, customer requirements, and cost/benefit considerations.

Credit card processors and banks offer a substantial discount on fees if level 3 detail is provided because of the additional fraud protection inherent in this additional detail. These savings are offset by the additional upfront cost of configuring the system and interfaces to handle the complexity that level 3 data entails. Level 3 is primarily used in the U.S. in currency USD.

5.3.5 Key Configuration Steps

The main areas of configuration for credit card processing from a financial and controls perspective revolve around setting up credit cards, enabling encryption, setting up receivable control, settlement, and bank clearing accounts, as well as around inbound and outbound secure file transmission.

The menu path to credit card configuration is IMG • SALES AND DISTRIBUTION • BILLING • PAYMENT CARDS, as shown in Figure 5.25.

5.3 Procurement and Credit Card Processing

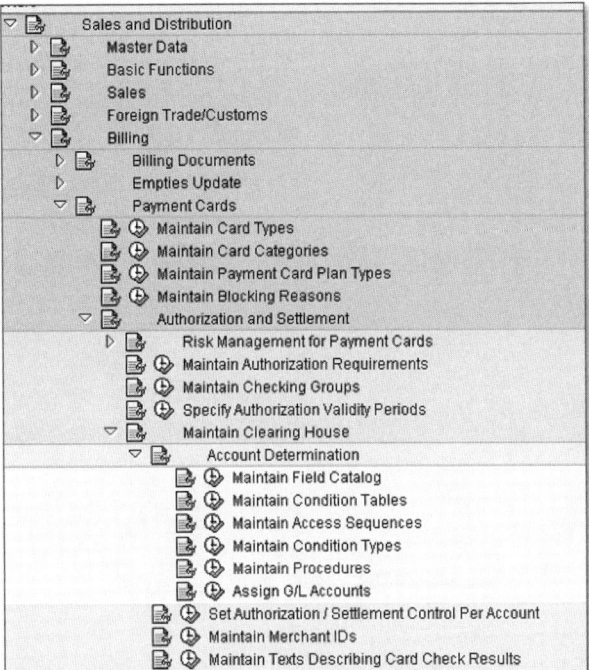

Figure 5.25 IMG Path to Credit Card Configuration

Create Payment Card Type

The first step is to create all of the types of credit cards the merchant will accept, as shown in Figure 5.26. Each card type is linked to specific function modules which may be standard or custom for validation functions.

The menu path for this is IMG • SALES AND DISTRIBUTION • BILLING • PAYMENT CARDS • MAINTAIN CARD TYPES.

Payment Card Type			
Type	Descriptn	Check	Date type
AMEX	American Express	CCARD_CHECK_AMEX	Month
MC	Master-/Euro Card	CCARD_CHECK_MC	Month
PTAM	American Express	CCARD_CHECK_AMEX	Month
PTMC	Master-/Euro Card	CCARD_CHECK_MC	Month
VISA	Visa Card	CCARD_CHECK_VISA	Month

Figure 5.26 Setup of Payment Card Types Accepted by Merchant

213

Enable Payment Card Type Encryption

Encryption of each payment card type needs to be enabled through maintenance of Table CCARDEC_V using Transaction SM30 in maintenance mode, as shown in Figure 5.27.

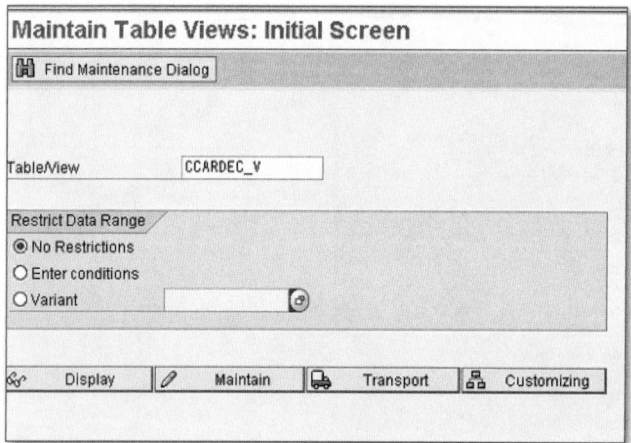

Figure 5.27 Input Screen for Enabling Encryption of Credit Card Type

The resulting screen is shown in Figure 5.28. The cards that need to be encrypted will need to be selected using the ENCRYPTED column checkbox.

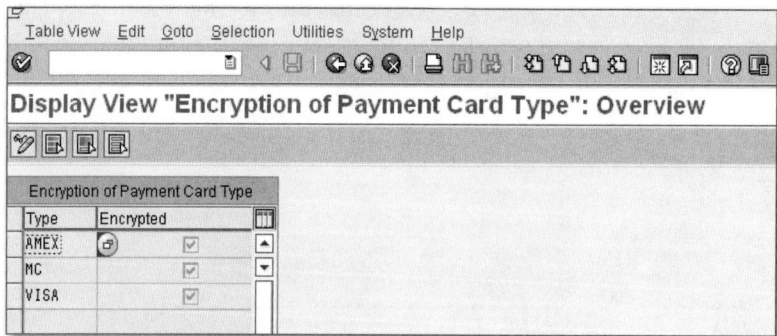

Figure 5.28 Enabling Encryption by Card Type

Create Receivable Control and Clearing Accounts

The payment card types need to be assigned to receivable control and clearing accounts to enable settlement and reconciliation.

Certain features of accounting are unique to credit card processing and settlement. These are explained in the following list:

- Settlement is not possible until an order is invoiced and posted to the receivable control account.
- The individual customer accounts receivable account is cleared of any liability as soon as the invoice is posted to accounting, with the liability being transferred to the issuing card's bank.
- Credit card receivables accounts are posted and cleared in total, and can only be mapped to one merchant ID.
- Typically, one receivable control account is set up per merchant card type.
- One bank clearing account is adequate for reconciling incoming credit card receipts, although this will depend on the banking structure and complexity of the reconciliation process.

The accounting cycle for payment cards is shown in Figure 5.29. The accounting flow starts with recording of the receivable, clearing of the receivable on receiving the settlement file and setup of the bank clearing amount, and finally, settlement and clearing by the bank when the funds settle and are reflected in the inbound EBS that is uploaded into the system.

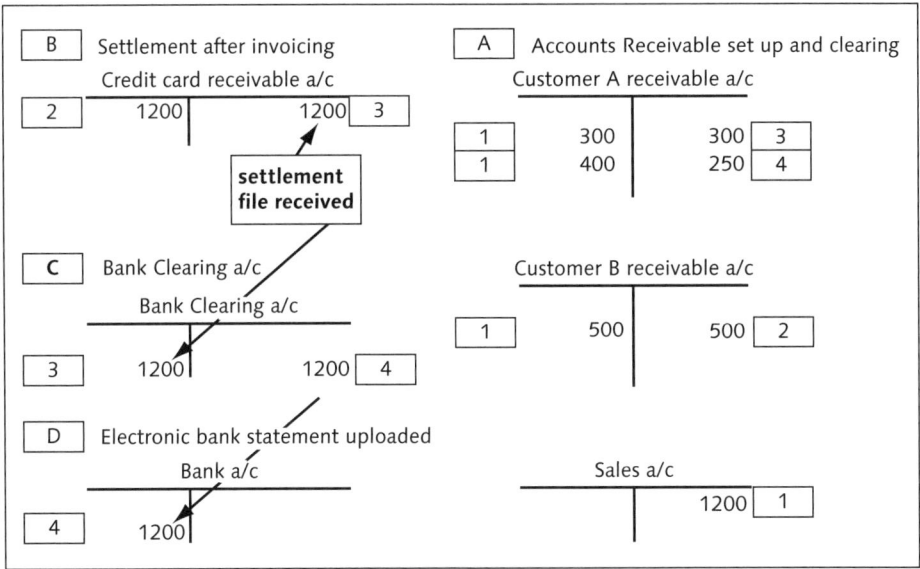

Figure 5.29 Accounting Cycle for Payment Cards

Credit card reconciliation and clearing accounts are assigned to each credit card type, as shown in Figure 5.30. The menu path for this is IMG Sales and Distribution • Billing • Payment Cards • Authorization and Settlement • Maintain Clearing House • Account Determination • Set Authorization/Settlement Control Per Account.

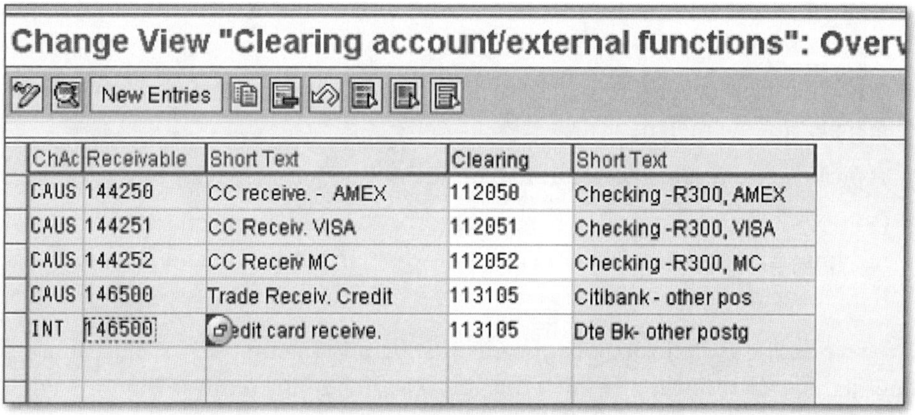

ChAc	Receivable	Short Text	Clearing	Short Text
CAUS	144250	CC receive. - AMEX	112050	Checking -R300, AMEX
CAUS	144251	CC Receiv. VISA	112051	Checking -R300, VISA
CAUS	144252	CC Receiv MC	112052	Checking -R300, MC
CAUS	146500	Trade Receiv. Credit	113105	Citibank - other pos
INT	146500	Credit card receive.	113105	Dte Bk- other postg

Figure 5.30 Assigning Receivable and Clearing Accounts to Card Types

Customer Master Data Setup

Customer-specific card information needs to be entered in the payment card section of bank data in the customer master record, as shown in Figure 5.31. The menu path for this is Accounting • Financial Accounting • Accounts Receivable • Master Records • Change. You can also use Transaction FD02.

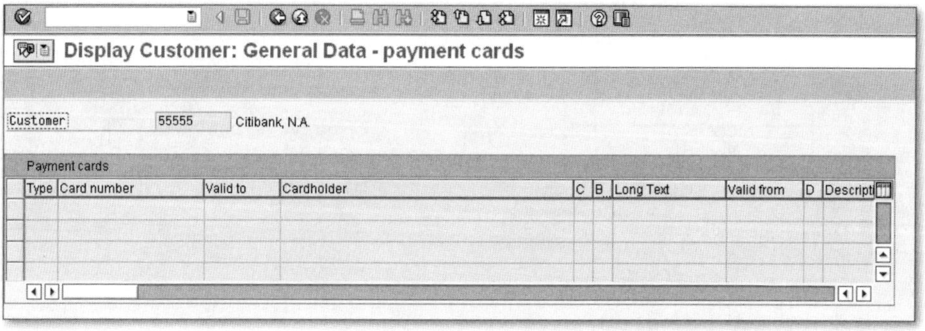

Figure 5.31 Entering Payment Card Information in the Customer Master

Simulation Program for Authorization and Settlement

The link between control and clearing accounts and authorization and settlement is shown in Figure 5.32. SAP ERP has two programs to simulate the authorization and settlement functions without setting up a link to the external credit card processor. These test programs are entered in the screen shown in Figure 5.32. This functionality is available for test purposes only, and needs to be replaced by the card-specific function modules when commencing live testing with the credit card processor.

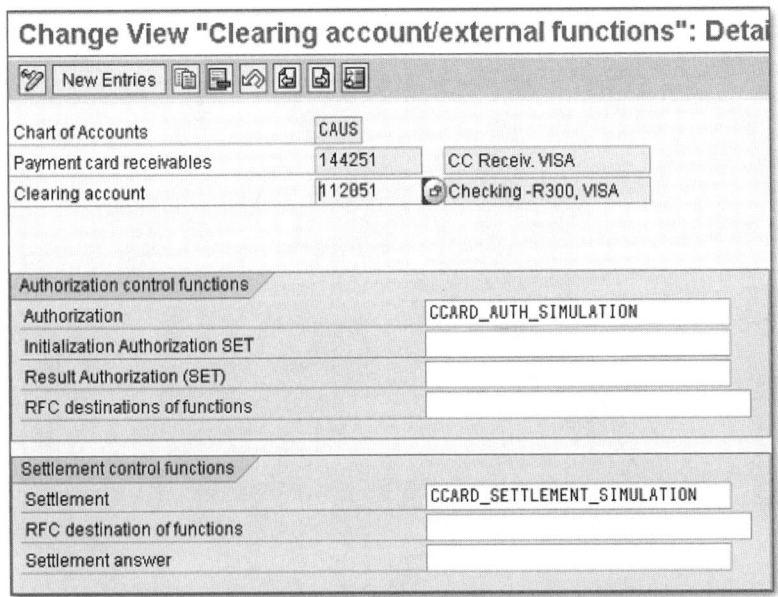

Figure 5.32 Linking Authorization and Settlement to Accounting

5.3.6 Key Authorization and Encryption Controls

Compliance with PCI DSS standards is enabled in SAP ERP through adequate access controls and the ability to encrypt card holder data. This can be accomplished in a variety of ways. However, the primary methods involve the use of authorization objects and enabling encryption functionality in SAP ERP.

Authorization Objects

Authorization objects are used to control the ability of users to create, change, display, and delete master and transactional data within SAP ERP. Specific authorization objects are created for functional tasks in accounting, treasury, and all of the available components within SAP ERP. The key authorization objects relevant to credit card processing and their functionality are explained in this section. All of these objects have certain activities attached to them that are specific to credit card processing, for example C1 MAINTENANCE OF PAYMENT CARDS, and C2 DISPLAY OF PAYMENT CARDS.

Authorization object F_KNA1_GEN controls CUSTOMER CENTRAL DATA screen access, as shown in Figure 5.33.

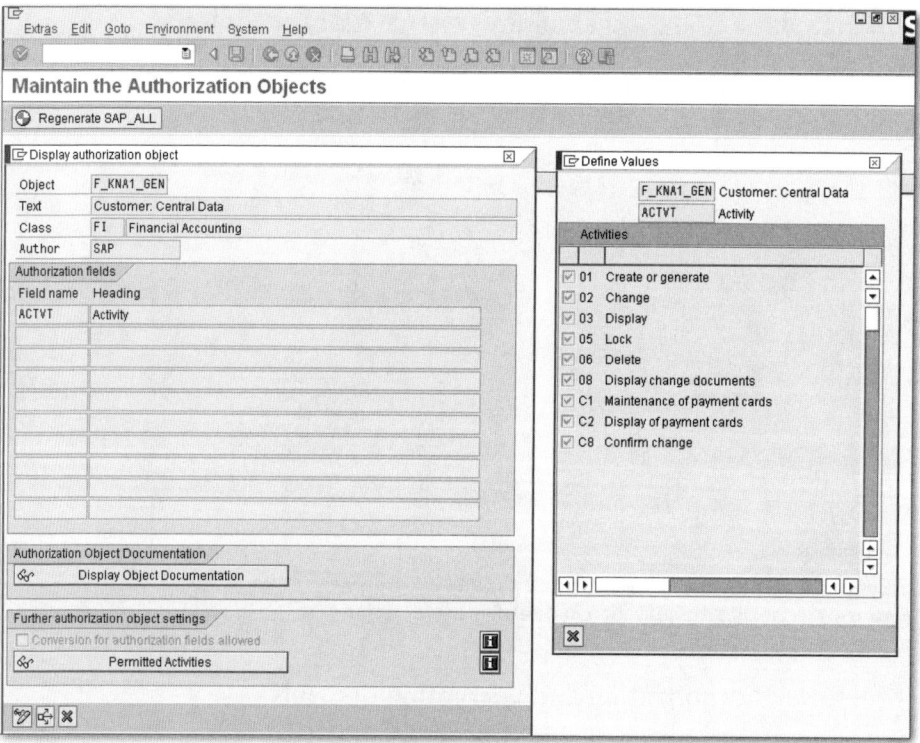

Figure 5.33 Authorization Object F_KNAI_GEN

Authorization object F_KNA1_GRP controls customer account groups, as shown in Figure 5.34.

Authorization object F_KNA1_APP controls authorization to customer and vendor master data, as shown in Figure 5.35.

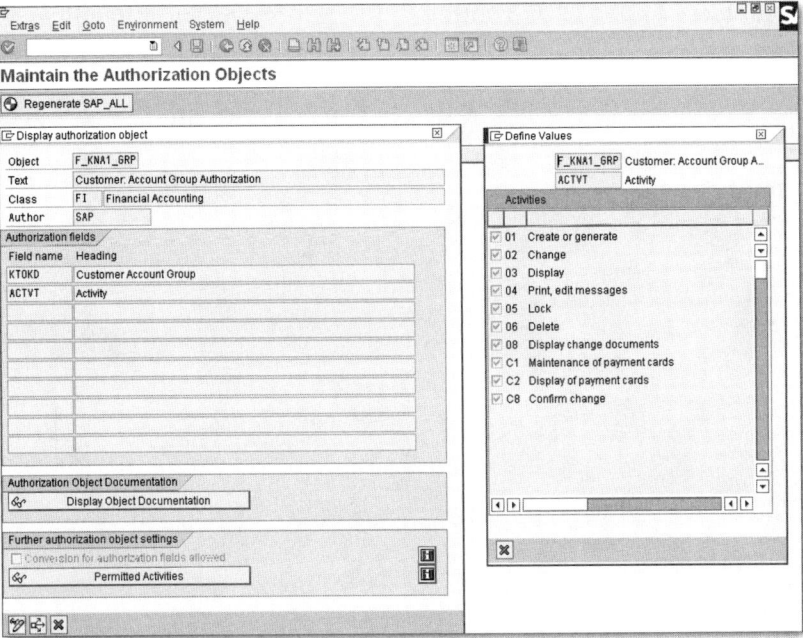

Figure 5.34 Authorization Object F_KNAI_GRP

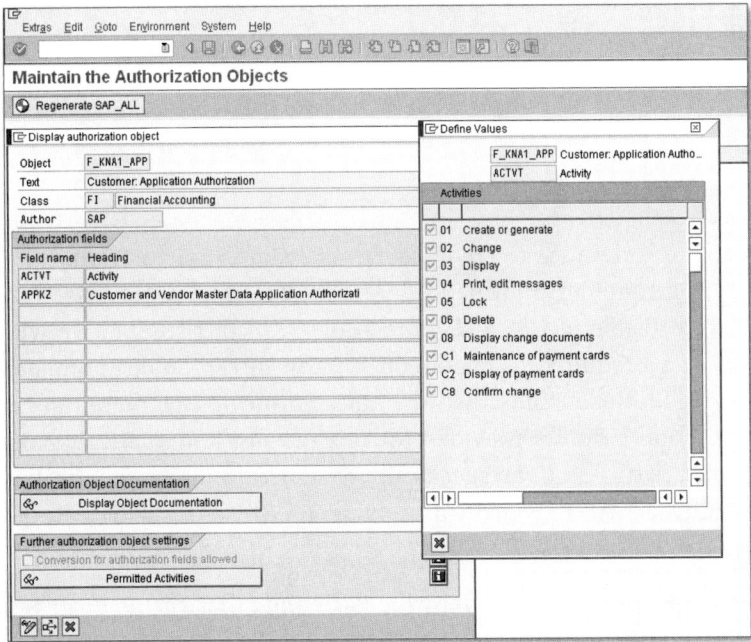

Figure 5.35 Authorization Object F_KNAI_APP

Authorization object F_BKPF_BUK controls authorizations to the accounting, as shown in Figure 5.36.

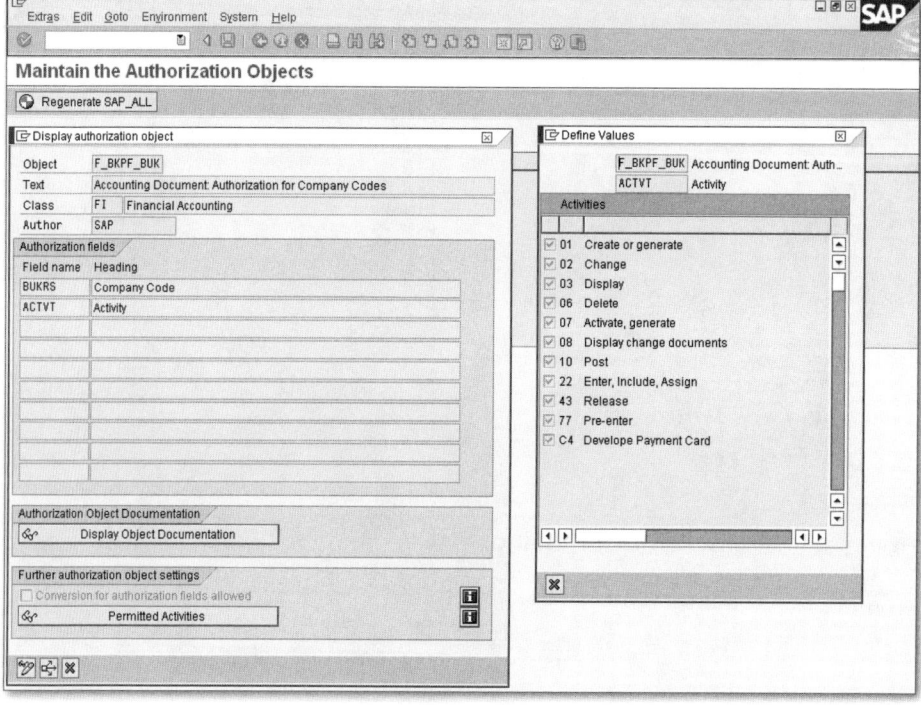

Figure 5.36 Authorization Object F_BKPF_BUK

Encryption

The other main area of relevance to credit card processing revolves around the necessity to encrypt cardholder information. Detailed information on enabling this functionality is available in OSS SAP Note 766703. In this section, we will show you the key steps required to enable encryption of cardholder numbers using standard SAP ERP functionality. As was indicated previously, these can be enhanced using function modules provided for this purpose. Alternatively, you can use bolt-on third party solutions specifically designed to integrate with the standard functionality of SAP ERP that can provide additional security features and functionality.

Most of the initial steps need to be set up by the Basis and infrastructure team, as described in the following procedure:

1. Create a new SSF application using Transaction SSFA for ENCRYPTION OF PAYMENT CARDS IN SAP R/3, and specify security parameters and certificate information as shown in Figure 5.37 and Figure 5.38.

Figure 5.37 Create Encryption Application for Payment Cards

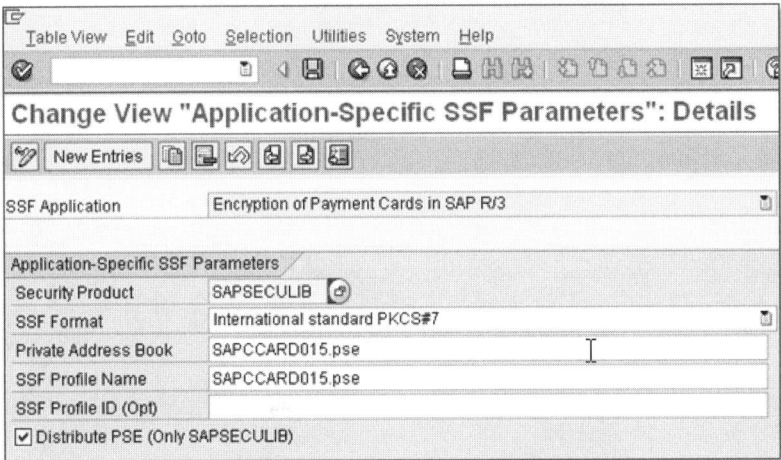

Figure 5.38 Set Up Security Parameters for Credit Card Encryption

2. Generate structures by executing Report SAPFACCG in Transaction SE38. This will also be done by the Basis team.

3. Maintain Table CCARDEC_V, enabling encryption for each card type. This was explained previously in Section 5.3.5, Key Configuration Steps.

4. To verify that the encryption was successful and that the encryption tool is working properly, the Basis team will need to run Report CCARDEC_CHECK. Only the P_TOOLS checkbox should be checked, and the report executed as shown in Figure 5.39.

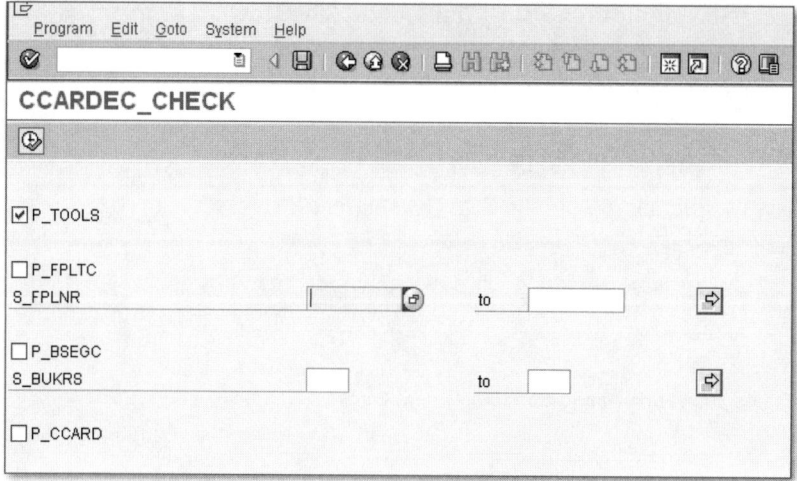

Figure 5.39 Program Check to Validate Successful Encryption

The resulting screen should confirm a successful process for encryption/decryption, as shown in Figure 5.40.

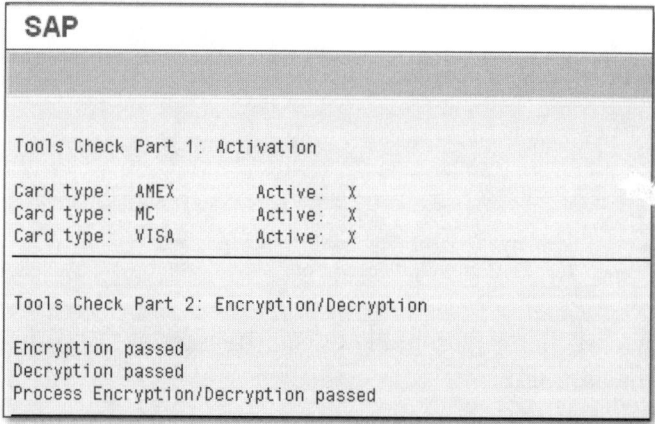

Figure 5.40 Check for Successful Encryption/Decryption

5. The last step is optional, but may be required if you want to convert existing un-encrypted customer card information. Programs CCARDEC_TRANSFORM_SD (Figure 5.41) and CCARDEC_TRANSFORM_FI (Figure 5.42) need to be executed in that order.

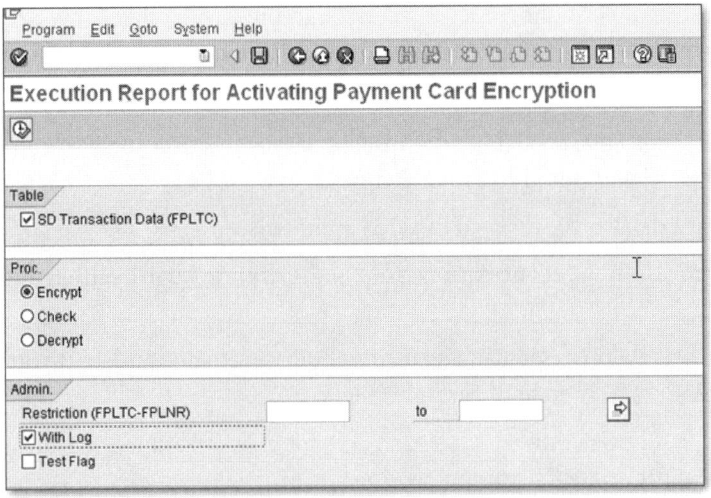

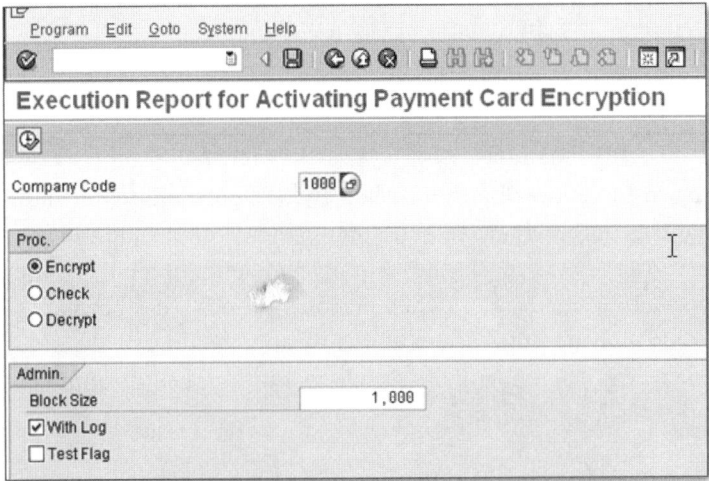

Figure 5.41 Execute SD Report for Encrypting Existing Card Data

Figure 5.42 Execute FI Report for Encrypting Existing Card Data

The resulting report log will display the number of card numbers successfully converted, and will be masked.

5.3.7 Summary of Credit Card Controls

Adequate and robust controls for payment card processing are critical to the successful implementation of a payment card processing system. These are achieved through a combination of systemic, process, access, and financial controls, which, taken together, will add to the integrity and security of the overall process. Key aspects of these controls are summarized as follows:

- Authorization access to master data and transactional data with respect to confidential credit card data limited to as-needed basis.
- Encryption of card data to conform to PCI DSS standards.
- Accounting control and reconciliation for authorization and settlement transactions.
- Documentation of key processes and controls, both internally and with the credit card processor and merchant card providers.
- Standard security and procedures for file transfers for authorization and settlement, including appropriate backup procedures for protection in case of transmission failures.
- Periodic review of all controls, logs, and exception reports to ensure compliance and that unauthorized activity has not taken place.

5.4 Escheatment

When checks are issued to vendors but not cashed and are outstanding for more than six months, they become stale-dated and potentially fall under the category of unclaimed property. In the U.S., most states require companies to report — after a period of time specified by state law — when personal property has been abandoned or unclaimed. With companies, these will most often be uncashed vendor check payments. The process a company has to follow with respect to complying with state regulations is called *escheatment*.

5.4.1 The Escheatment Process

Before an uncashed vendor check payment amount can be considered abandoned or unclaimed, the company must make a diligent effort to try to locate the account owner. If the company is unable to do so, and the account has remained inactive for the period of time specified by state law, the company must report the account to the state where the account is held. The state then claims the account through the process of escheatment and the state becomes the owner of the account. As part of the escheatment process, the state will hold the account in trust, and the former account owner may make a claim.

5.4.2 Company Accounting and Reporting Requirements

Many companies outsource the reporting requirements to third-party companies that specialize in preparing and submitting escheatment returns. However, the information required for filing the returns needs to be prepared by the company. Also, along with the state return, the company needs to transfer the total monies relating to the escheated checks for that state, along with the return.

5.4.3 SAP ERP and Escheatment

There is no standard functionality for escheatment in SAP ERP, but all of the information required for escheatment is maintained in the payment table PAYRQ. It is possible to create a custom program that uses the check processing functionality to mark the checks eligible for escheatment, take them out of the outstanding checks account, place them into an escheatment account, and then transfer the funds with the paper or electronic return to the appropriate state.

The custom program will require a frontend screen that allows for checks to be selected for escheatment. Selection options such as number of days outstanding, check number, amount, vendor, state, and so on need to be provided in the input screen. When the system proposes the checks based on the selection criteria, treasury staff can select the checks for escheatment. On execution the program should a) create an electronic file in the format required by the third party processor, and b) create an accounting entry that takes the selected checks out of the outstanding checks account and transfers the total to an escheatment liability outstanding account. It should also update the check register to match the outstanding checks account. When monies are transferred to the state, the escheatment liability outstanding account is debited and the bank clearing account is credited.

A custom version of Transaction FCHR (online cashed checks) can be used to escheat checks. This transaction enables the online cashing of a check, which in turn updates the check register and posts a debit to the checks outstanding account and a credit to the bank clearing account.

5 | Positive Pay and Payment Card Processing

> **Tip: Identify Escheated Checks with Separate Code**
>
> In the custom version of Transaction FCHR, using the same logic that identifies voided checks, you can identify escheated checks using separate code. This differentiates escheated checks from checks that have cleared the bank or were voided. This greatly helps the reconciliation process, and assists when an enquiry is received from a vendor regarding old or stale dated checks.

This is exactly how you would want an escheated check to clear, except the G/L postings will be different. Table PAYR contains all relevant information with respect to check payments, and this table can be extended to include escheated check information. An extract program can be created to compile an electronic file of escheated checks for transmission in the correct format to the third-party processor responsible for preparing the state returns for submission under the escheatment requirements.

An extract of Table PAYR is shown in Figure 5.43.

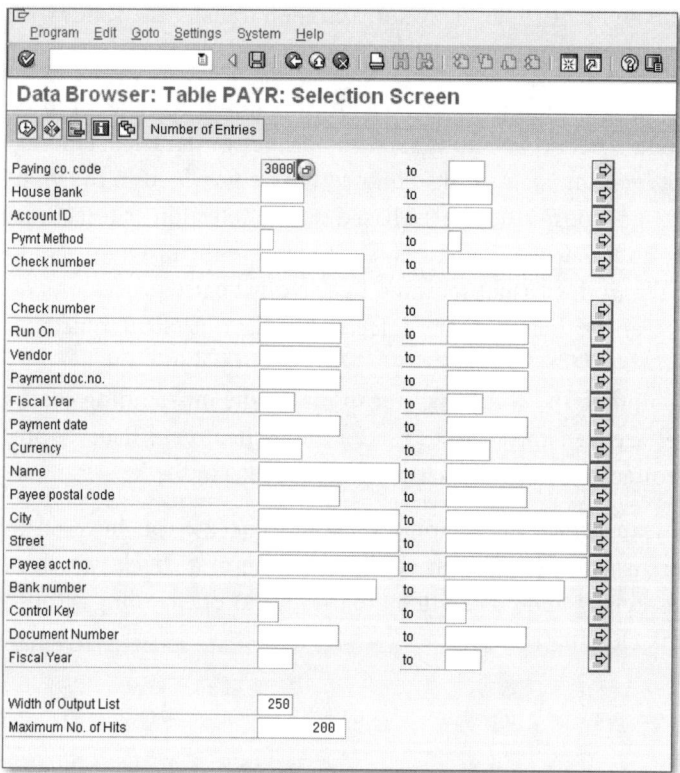

Figure 5.43 Extract of PAYR Table for Use in Escheatment

226

5.4.4 Accounting for Escheatment in SAP ERP

The accounting cycle for escheatment is shown in Figure 5.44. The process starts with removing the escheated check from the checks outstanding account, and placing it in an escheatment clearing amount. The G/L account of outstanding checks is reduced by the amount of the checks escheated. This is an important control feature that ensures that the check register balance of outstanding checks will always be equal to the balance of outstanding checks in the G/L. When the payment is made to the state, the escheatment liability account is debited and the bank clearing account credited. When the EBS is received — reflecting the encashment of the escheated amounts by the state — the bank clearing account is debited and the bank account is credited, completing the process.

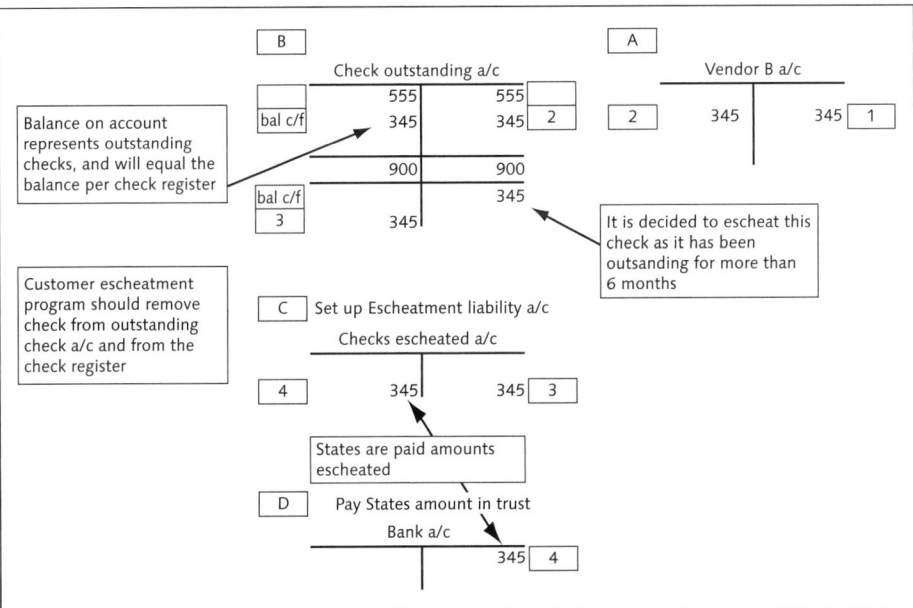

Figure 5.44 Accounting controls for escheatment in SAP ERP

5.4.5 Overview of Key Escheatment Controls

Controls for the escheatment process revolve primarily around the accurate reporting and accounting of property (primarily checks) escheated by the company. These can be summarized as follows:

- Document company policy and procedures for the escheatment process.
- If the compilation of state returns is outsourced, then all relevant contracts, SLAs, fees, and so on need to be maintained.
- The custom program that extracts data from Table PAYR in SAP ERP and maps to the file format specified for state tax returns needs to be tested and validated to make sure that accurate information is provided in the correct format.
- The check register and check and escheatment clearing accounts, and the bank and bank clearing accounts must be reconciled periodically to ensure correct recording and disposition of liabilities with respect to the escheatment process.
- Process reviews must be conducted on a regular basis to ensure that all legal and statutory requirements are met and returns and escheated amounts are submitted to the authorities on or by the due dates.

5.5 Summary

In this chapter we looked at several key electronic banking processes relating to Positive Payee, lockbox processing, payment card processing, and escheatment. We reviewed the business processes, design, setup, configuration, accounting flows, and key controls relating to each of the processes, and we also explained how to implement them. The last three chapters covered most of the key aspects of electronic banking in SAP ERP. In Chapter 6, we will look at how all of these come together in one of the most important treasury functions: cash management and liquidity forecasting.

In this chapter, the concepts of cash management, liquidity forecasting, in-house banking, and intraday bank statement processing are introduced and discussed.

6   Cash Management & Liquidity Forecasting

Cash management and liquidity forecasting is one of the most critical areas in treasury management. With respect to this area, many users find the functionality and flexibility for cash forecasting lacking in SAP ERP. This chapter tries to bridge that gap, describing the key inputs required to create accurate cash management reports for short-term daily cash positioning, as well as long-term liquidity planning and forecasting, and how to leverage the integrated information available within SAP ERP (including the use of intraday bank statements, and in-house banking for intragroup cash management).

Cash management and liquidity forecasting are of critical importance to any organization. No matter how profitable a company is, it needs to be able to pay its bills, plan for its borrowing requirements, invest its surplus cash, minimize its cost of capital, and optimize its return on invested assets. Cash management is typically done using spreadsheet or standalone custom software because of the flexibility provided in working "what if" scenarios, and because of the need to change parameters to reflect constantly changing conditions. The problem with this environment is that a lot of the information has to be entered manually, or the software interfaced with an existing legacy or ERP system of accounting record.

The challenge for cash management functionality in SAP ERP is providing the flexibility that treasury and cash managers have gotten used to working with standalone or workstation-based software.

The power of the cash management functionality of SAP ERP lies in the ability to populate its cash management reports in real-time mode, fully leveraging the integration between all cash-relevant information with which the system is updated. In this chapter, we will review all of the elements required to link cash reports to cash-relevant information within the system. Specifically, we will look at the two key types of cash management reports used in most organizations: the daily cash positioning report and the longer term liquidity forecast.

After all cash-relevant master and transactional data is linked, SAP ERP reports can be customized to reflect any number of views. Reports can be downloaded into Microsoft Excel spreadsheets, if desired.

A key input for daily cash positioning are intraday electronic bank statements. We will review how these can be integrated into the daily cash positioning report.

Finally, we will look at the In-House Cash component that lets organizations manage internal group transactions more cost effectively and efficiently, and with a high degree of automation that allows for STP.

All of this functionality is tightly integrated with all key components in the financial supply chain that allows for a high level of visibility of information across the enterprise and access to online real-time information.

6.1 Cash Management

Daily cash positioning is a key treasury activity that typically takes place early on in the business day. The purpose is to forecast the company's daily cash requirements to ensure that they are met through internal funding, borrowing, or redeeming short-term investments, or to invest any surplus cash, keeping in mind minimum borrowing requirements. One of the most important inputs for the cash positioning report are intraday bank statements. These are polled early in the morning and contain key information relating to inflows such as lockbox deposits, wire and ACH receipts, as well as outflows such as first and second presentment of checks, controlled disbursements, ACH and wire debits, and so on.

In this section, we will build a daily cash position report using inputs from intraday statements as well as other cash-relevant information that is already available in the system. Most organizations performing daily cash positioning will already have existing legacy reports. The goal is to replicate the information contained in these reports in the SAP ERP cash report, with as much STP as possible so that key financing decisions to be executed for the day can be made by the time banks and financial markets open.

6.1.1 Intraday Bank Statements

In Chapter 3, we looked at prior day bank statements that reflect the previous day's actual transactions and that need to be posted to the books of accounts. Intraday bank statements are polled primarily for the purpose of daily cash positioning. Incoming current or intraday bank statements can be automatically uploaded many times during the day for daily cash positioning and forecasting purposes. Intraday statements are polled using the same program as prior day statements but the settings for the upload variant are different. Intraday statements do not post into the financial records; instead, they populate the cash management forecasting reports available in SAP ERP.

Process Overview

Intraday statements are available in BAI (U.S.) or SWIFT MT942 format, and are used for daily cash positioning. The first intraday statement usually contains details of the first clearing of checks, lockbox receipts, available balances, ledger balances, ACH and wire settlements, one day and two day float, and so on. These are uploaded into SAP ERP and posted to the cash forecasting report in the form of planning types. A preprocessing program will almost always be required, and is strongly recommended, to provide the flexibility to select all of the fields of information available in the intraday file. For example, only detail records post into the cash forecast, and it may be useful to download total records as well. Totals information is very important in building a complete cash forecast position, and in validating balances. The program that converts the intraday statement into planning types is Program RFEBKA40.

> **Note: Prior Day vs. Current Day Information in SAP ERP**
> Prior day statements reflect actual transactions form the previous banking day and usually are posted into the books of financial record in SAP ERP. Intraday or current day statements are for cash positioning purposes only. They create memo entries for reporting purposes and are archived or deleted after their value date. They do not create any financial postings within SAP ERP.

It is recommended to create a custom version of program RFEBKA00 — for example, ZRFEBKA00 — to provide flexibility in transferring information from the intraday bank statement to the cash forecast. Furthermore, it may not be desirable to load all of the information in the current day statement. The preprocessing program can act as a means of selecting fields of information in the current day file, specific to the company's cash position reports. Figure 6.1 provides an overview of the process

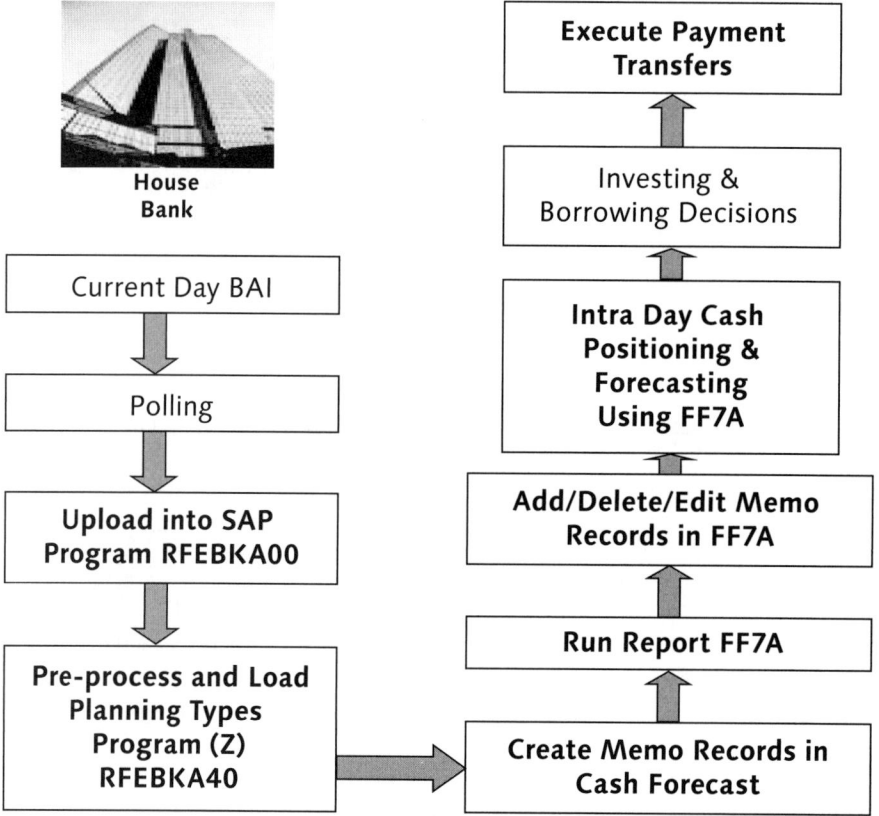

Figure 6.1 Overview of Intraday Bank Statement Processing Cycle

The process for uploading intraday bank statements can be summarized as follows:

1. **Poll file from bank**

    Intraday files use the same transmission process described in Chapter 3 for prior day statements, but with a different variant and preprocessing program on actual upload into the SAP ERP system.

2. **Upload and preprocess bank file**

   The file is uploaded using Transaction FF.5, as part of the bank upload batch job using Program RFEBKA00 with the appropriate variant settings for intraday files. The information that is uploaded is stored in an SAP ERP table awaiting transfer into the cash management report.

3. **Populate cash management report**

   Program RFEBKA40 or, if customized, program ZREFBKA40, is trigerred as the next batch job after the previous step has completed successfully. This program populates the cash management forecast with the planning types based on information contained in the intraday file.

> **Note**
>
> Similar to prior day statements, the polling, preprocessing, and upload of memo records should be automated through batch scheduled jobs to enable STP.

Examples of information available in the intraday statement and identified by the external BAI code are shown in Figure 6.2.

Description	ext code
opening ledger balance	010
opening available	040
closing ledger balance	015
closing collected	045
1 day float	072
2 or more day float	074
current available	060
current ledger balance	030

Figure 6.2 Current Day External Bank Codes

The screen in Figure 6.3 shows the settings required for the upload of intraday statements using Transaction FF.5.

The program is the same that used for uploading prior day bank statements, but the settings are unique to intraday statements. As shown in Figure 6.3, the key differences are that the variant should be set to DO NOT POST, and additional settings need to be made under the CASH MANAGEMENT section of the screen. At a minimum, the checkboxes for CASH MGMT PAYMENT ADVICES and ACCOUNT BALANCE must be checked.

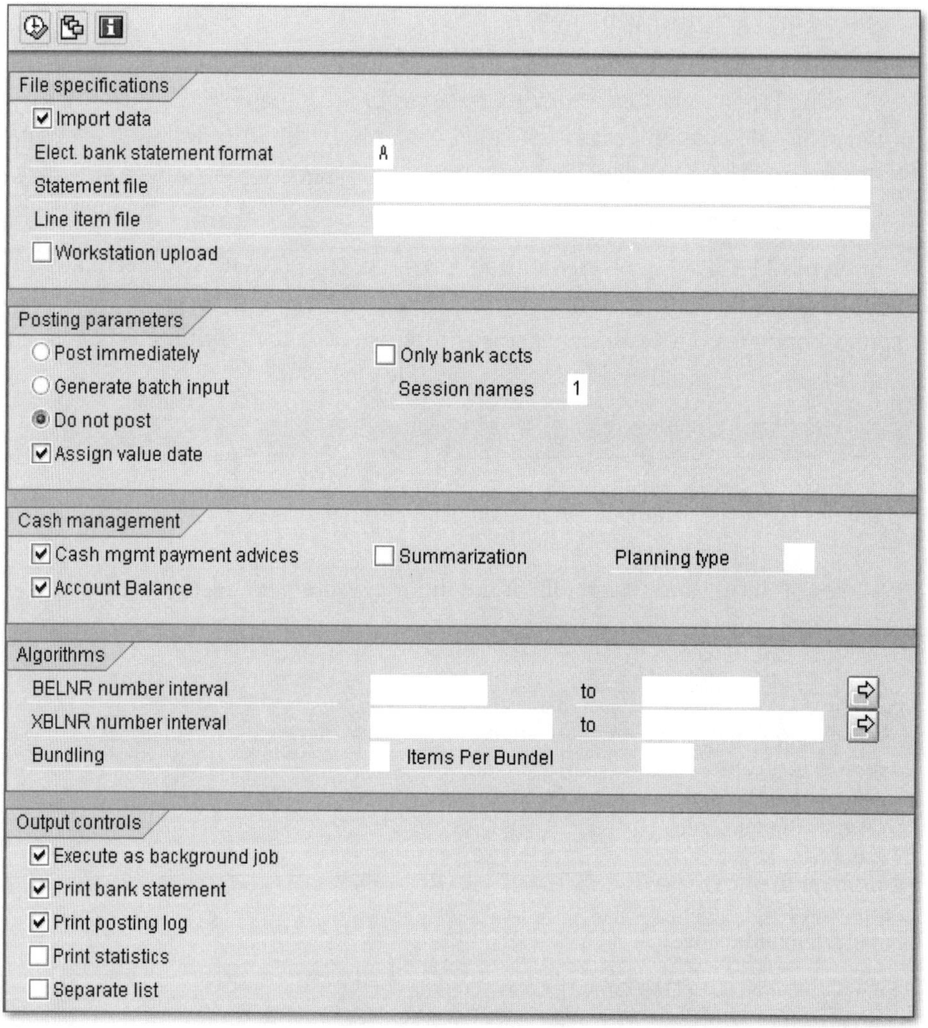

Figure 6.3 Intraday Upload Program Transaction FF.5

Planning types form the link between the cash forecast and transactions in intraday statements, and will populate the cash forecast from the inbound intraday transactions. Planning types will be discussed in detail in Section 6.1.2, Inputs Required for Daily Cash Positioning and Liquidity Forecasting.

In the configuration section of the EBS, under PLG TYPE, the different planning types that can be entered against the external bank transaction codes are listed, as shown in Figure 6.4.

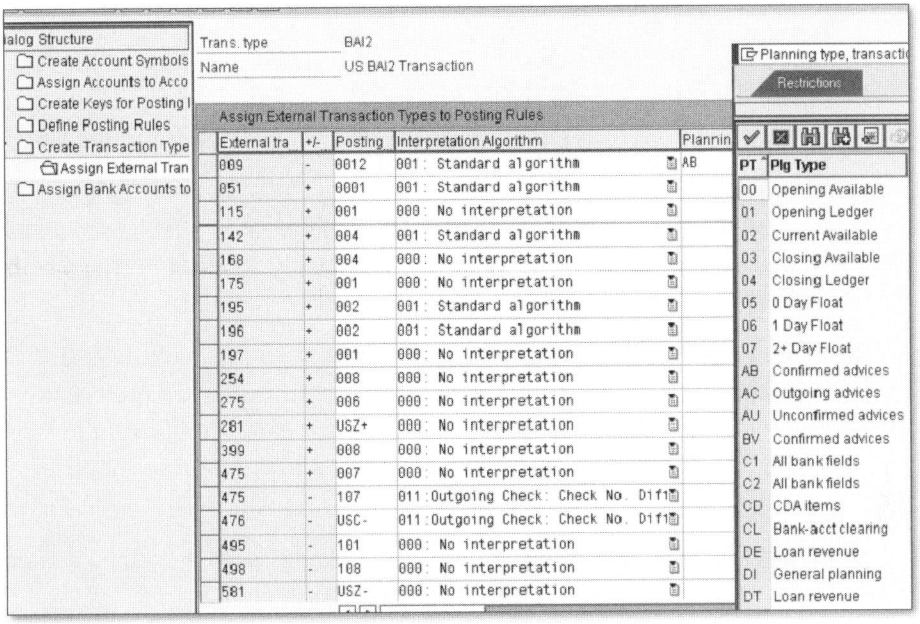

Cash Management | 6.1

Figure 6.4 Intraday Planning Types for Cash Forecast

Manual Posting of Current Day Statements

Manual posting of current day statements is possible through Transaction FPS3. The input screen that displays is shown in Figure 6.5.

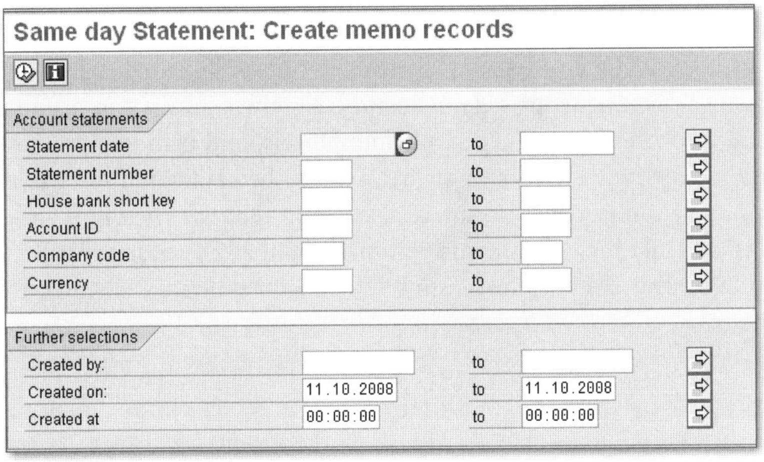

Figure 6.5 Manual Posting of Current Day Statements Using Transaction FPS3

235

Controls for Intraday Statements

Because intraday statements are used primarily for cash positioning and forecasting purposes, the controls that need to be in place need to ensure primarily that data is accurate and complete so that investing or borrowing decisions are based on the latest financial cash positions and balances.

Accordingly, the key control needs to ensure that the intraday posting programs and the resulting cash management reports are thoroughly tested and verified with manual or legacy reports and statements prior to go-live.

Because the intraday statements do not update or post to the books of financial record, the accounting controls are not as critical here. It is important to ensure that access to the variants and preprocessing programs is restricted to authorized persons only, because any change to the settings could result in incomplete or inaccurate data.

All of the same safeguards with respect to controlling access to programs, master data, and configuration discussed in previous chapters apply.

An important control often overlooked is to periodically compare the previous day's cash position report with actual results for that day to validate the accuracy and integrity of the information that is populating the cash forecast.

6.1.2 Inputs Required for Daily Cash Positioning and Liquidity Forecasting

One of the major advantages of using SAP ERP for daily cash positioning and liquidity forecasting is that the system already contains most of the required information. The cash positioning reports are linked to cash flow relevant transactions and master data through planning types, planning levels, and planning groups. In addition, there are several key settings that need to be configured to enable the automatic population of data into the cash position reports. We will review each of these as we build the components that make up the key reports required for cash positioning and liquidity forecasting. The steps required are shown in Figure 6.6.

Cash Management | 6.1

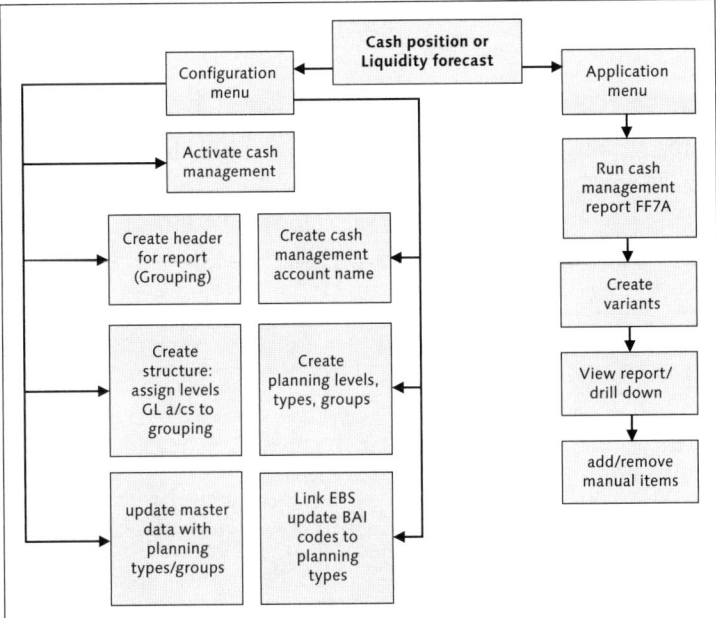

Figure 6.6 Setting up Cash Management in SAP ERP

The IMG path to the configuration area for cash management is shown in Figure 6.7.

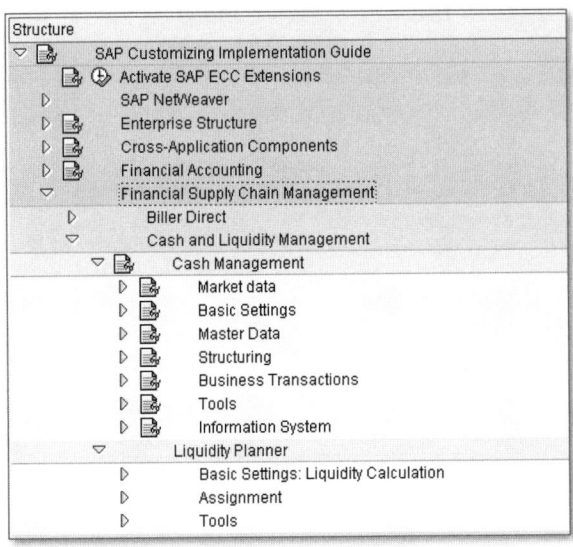

Figure 6.7 IMG Path to the Configuring Area of Cash Management

Activate Cash Management

Cash management functionality needs to be activated in the IMG, by checking the CASH MANAGEMENT ACTIVATED checkbox in the COMPANY CODE GLOBAL DATA settings, as shown in Figure 6.8. The menu path for the setting is FINANCIAL ACCOUNTING • FINANCIAL ACCOUNTING GLOBAL SETTINGS • COMPANY CODE • ENTER GLOBAL PARAMETERS.

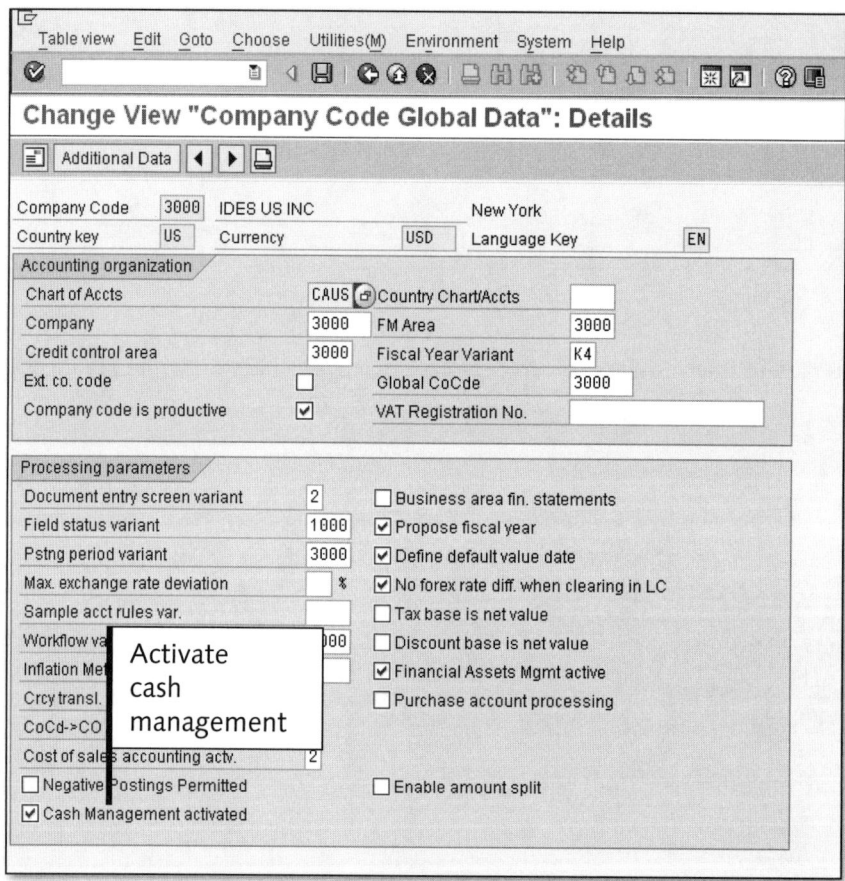

Figure 6.8 Activate Cash Management for Company Code

Configure Source Symbols

Source symbols are system-delivered and identify specific subcomponents within SAP ERP that need to be marked as relevant for cash positioning.

Source symbols are selected for cash positioning purposes using Transaction OT05, or by following the configuration path IMG FINANCIAL SUPPLY CHAIN MANAGEMENT • CASH AND LIQUIDITY MANAGEMENT • CASH MANAGEMENT • BASIC SETTINGS • DEFINE SOURCE SYMBOLS.

The menu path is shown in Figure 6.9.

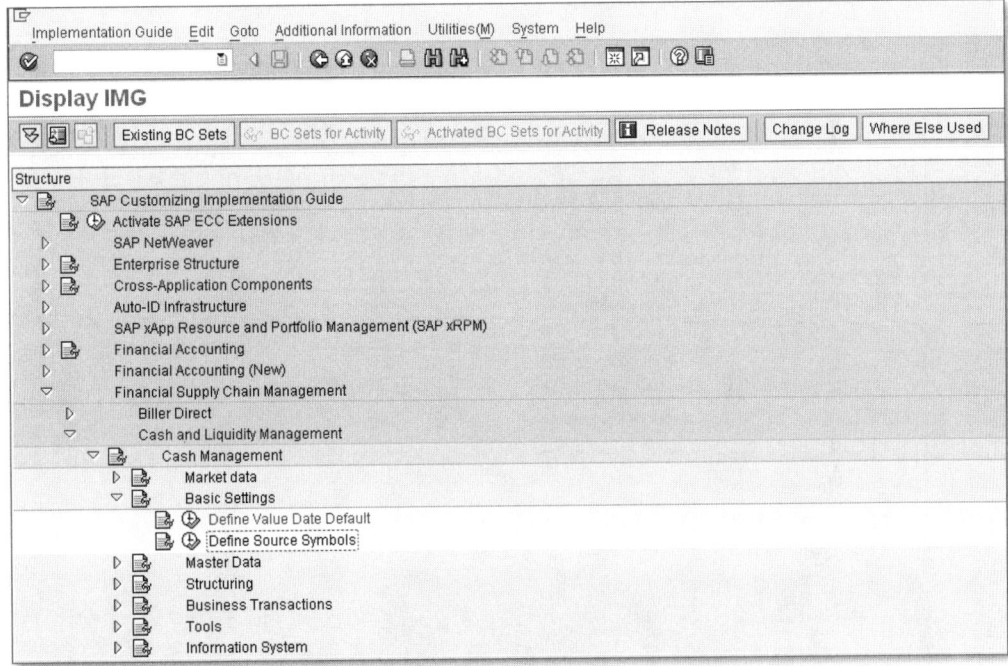

Figure 6.9 Define Source Symbols in the FSCM Application Menu

Source symbols BANK ACCOUNTING (BNK) and IN-HOUSE CASH (IHC) are selected as relevant for cash positioning in the SOURCE SYMBOLS FOR CASH MANAGEMENT screen as shown in Figure 6.10. Source symbols are system-delivered and are automatically linked to specific subcomponents such as MM, SD, and subledger accounting. These source symbols — although not relevant for cash positioning —

will appear on the longer term liquidity forecast, based on the underlying transactions entered in the system. For example, purchase orders (MM), and sales orders (SD) when entered will appear in the liquidity forecast. As these documents move through the financial supply chain, they will change in the liquidity forecast. For example, a purchase order will change to a goods receipt when goods are received, to accounts payable when the invoice is created, to a bank clearing or check outstanding account when the invoice is paid, and then finally be reflected in the bank statement when the check is cashed and the EBS is posted in the books of record. All of these transactions will be reflected as planning levels in the liquidity forecast as well as the cash positioning as soon as cash-relevant transactions such as payment and settlement occur.

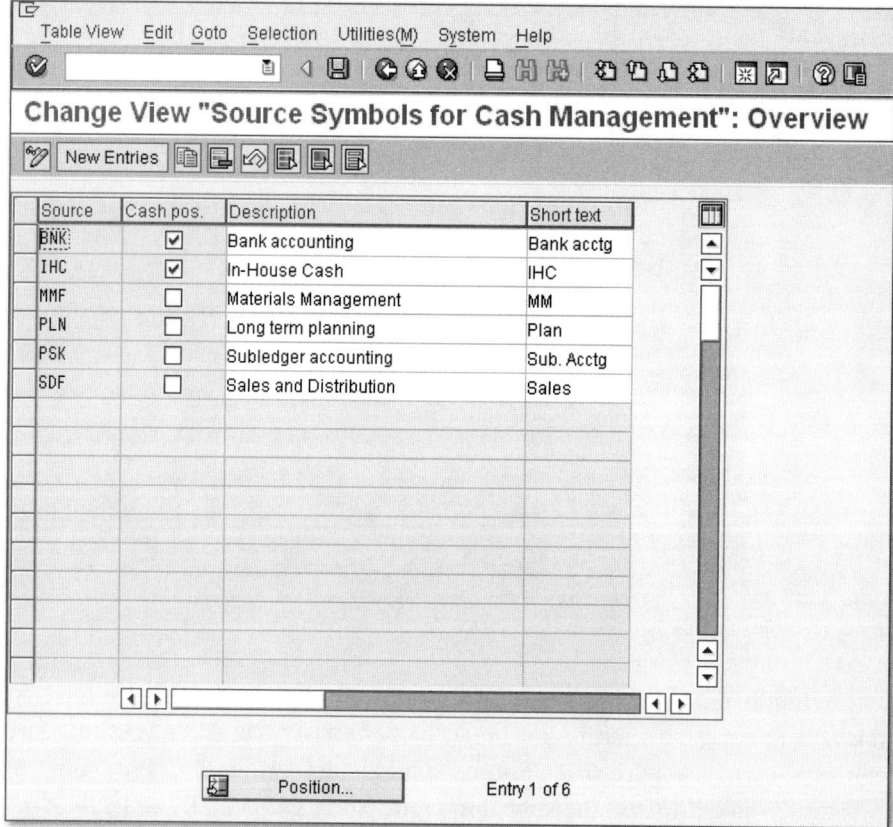

Figure 6.10 Activate Source Symbols for Cash Management

Create Planning Levels

Planning levels are one of the most important elements in the set up of cash management reporting. Planning levels are used to control displays in cash management, and are automatically assigned to each type of transaction when they are created:

- A planning level defines an item's source and how an item was entered in the system. For example, a planning level will identify whether an item in the cash report was based on bank data, based on a payment advice, based on a cash concentration instruction derived from a vendor or customer account, or manually created. Accordingly, for bank data the levels are entered in G/L master data, for manually created items they are entered manually, and for purchasing and sales related data they are entered internally within the system. The cash management reports are automatically updated with planning level assigned to data during posting.

- The naming convention for planning levels allows for a two-digit alphanumeric sequence of characters. To improve the display of the cash position and liquidity forecast, it is recommended to use levels that start with "F" for bank accounts, customers, and vendors, and levels that start with "B" for bank clearing accounts. Planning level F0 is reserved for posting to bank accounts; F1 is usually assigned to posting of purchases and sales, and B1, B2, B3, and so on for bank clearing accounts.

When displaying the cash position, level F0 shows actual balances in the bank account based on postings to that account, whereas the other levels show planned bank account transactions. This could include entered payment advices or postings to bank clearing accounts. Bank clearing accounts will contain cash in transit or pending payments and receipts, and can also be used to create bank reconciliation reports at period end.

Planning levels can be used to identify special situations. For example, all levels beginning with X can represent postings with payment blocking indicators in the liquidity forecast. When displaying the liquidity forecast, these amounts are displayed as blocked for payment purposes.

6 | Cash Management & Liquidity Forecasting

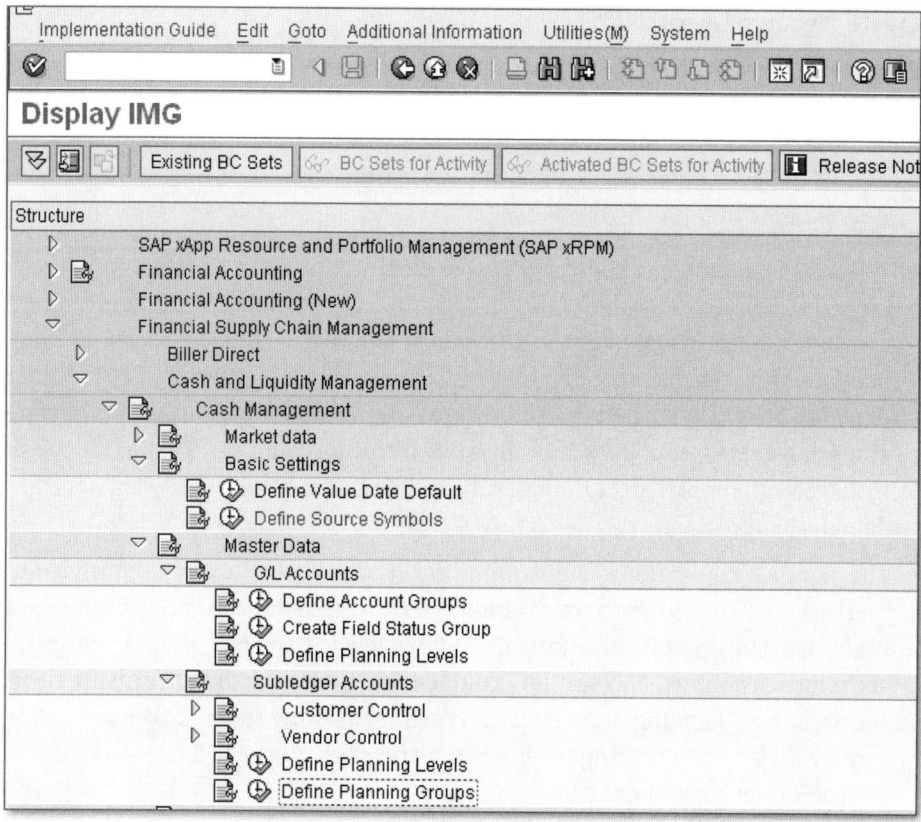

Figure 6.11 IMG Path for Planning Levels and Groups

Planning levels are set up using Transaction OT12 or IMG menu path FINANCIAL SUPPLY CHAIN MANAGEMENT • CASH AND LIQUIDITY MANAGEMENT • CASH MANAGEMENT • MASTER DATA • G/L ACCOUNTS • DEFINE PLANNING LEVELS. The path is shown in Figure 6.11, which also provides a view of other key configuration settings for cash management.

Examples of planning levels for bank accounting are shown in Figure 6.12 As you can see, these are user-defined and can be set up depending on the banking structure relevant to the organization.

Cash Management | 6.1

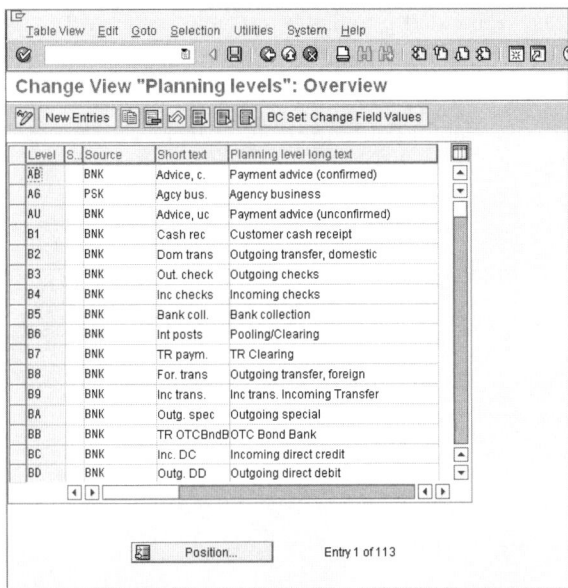

Figure 6.12 Bank Planning Levels

Examples of planning levels for other sources, such as SUB LEDGER ACCOUNTING and SALES AND DISTRIBUTION, are shown in Figure 6.13.

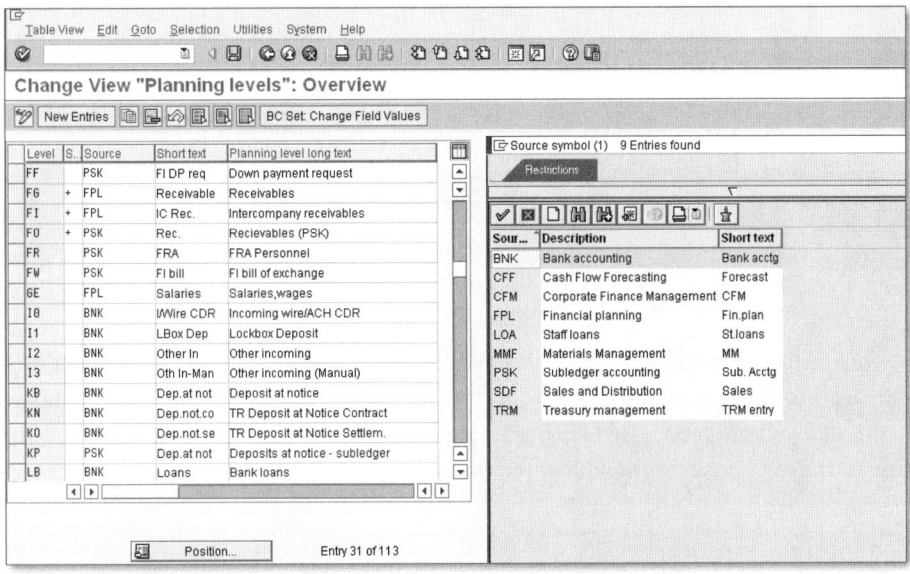

Figure 6.13 Sub Ledger Planning Levels

6 | Cash Management & Liquidity Forecasting

For reporting liquidity forecasting items at the logistics supply chain level, it is necessary to specify the types of documents that need to be viewed as a particular transaction travels through the integrated supply chain. These are configured, as shown in Figure 6.14, through the IMG menu path FINANCIAL SUPPLY CHAIN MANAGEMENT • CASH AND LIQUIDITY MANAGEMENT • CASH MANAGEMENT • STRUCTURING • DEFINE PLANNING LEVELS FOR LOGISTICS.

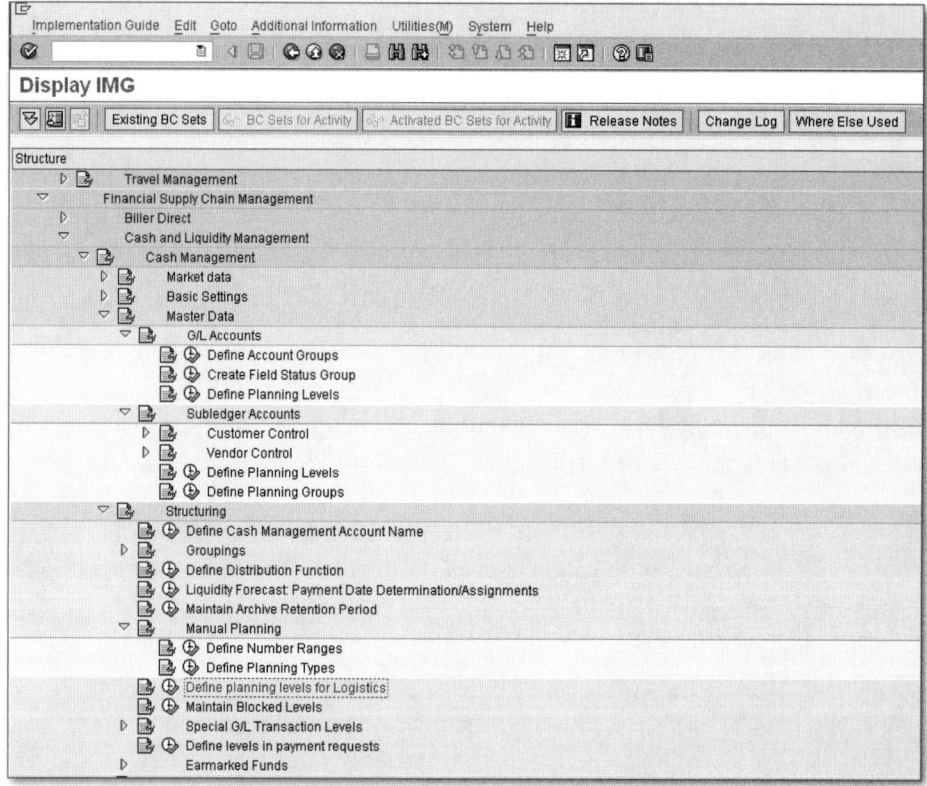

Figure 6.14 IMG Path for Logistics Configuration

The resulting input table allows the selection of specific MM and SD transactions that need to be displayed in the liquidity forecast, through internally designated planning levels and codes, as shown in Figure 6.15. These are not relevant for daily short term cash positioning and forecasting purposes.

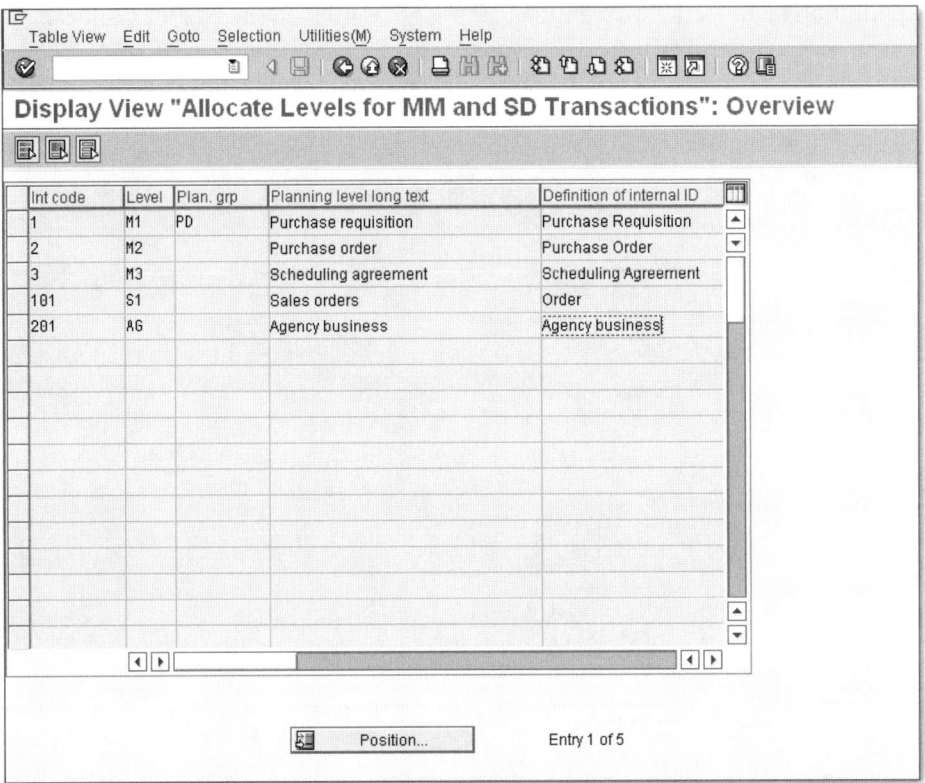

Figure 6.15 Allocate MM and SD Transactions for Liquidity Forecasting

Create planning types

A *planning type* controls the criteria for manually created memo records. Planning types are used to create records that are free form and user defined, and can be entered to reflect any payment or receipt in cash management reporting. Planning types have a one-to-one relationship with a planning level for all manually entered records, because entry criteria for the manually entered planning level is set up through the planning type. Criteria for the setup of planning types include links to a planning level, archiving category, automatic expiry field, and field status variant for screen input settings. The naming convention allows for the standard two-digit alphanumeric sequence of characters. If a new planning level for manual entry records is set up, a planning type with the same name must be created. The application menu path for creating planning types is FINANCIAL SUPPLY CHAIN MANAGEMENT • CASH AND LIQUIDITY MANAGEMENT • CASH MANAGEMENT • STRUCTURING • MANUAL PLANNING • DEFINE PLANNING TYPES.

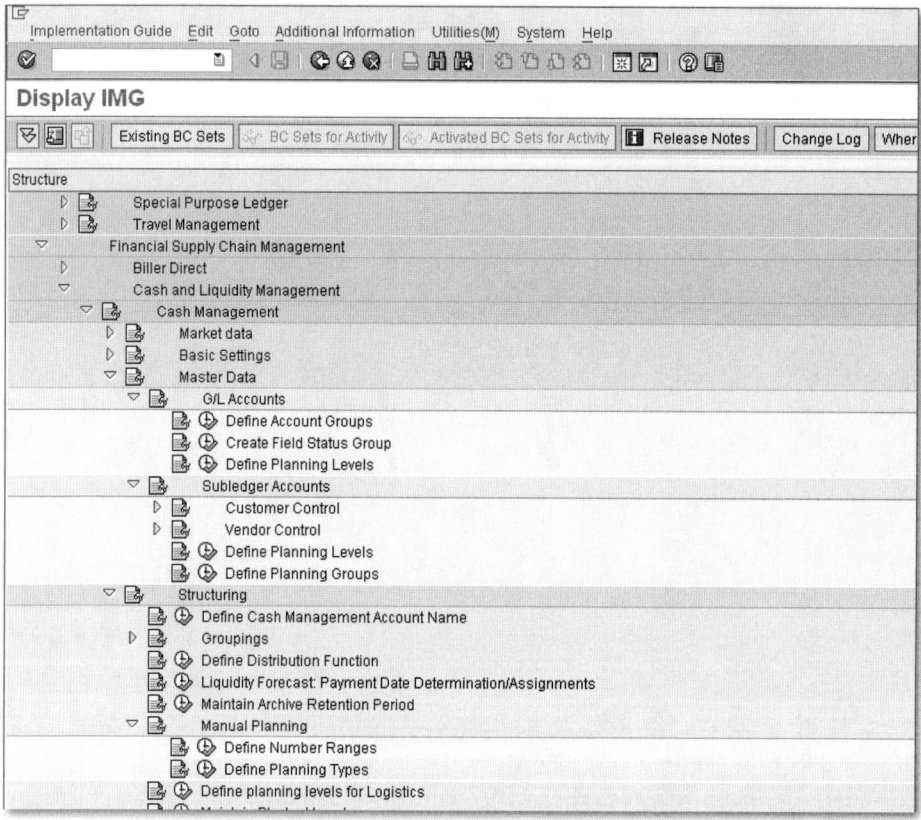

Figure 6.16 IMG Path to Configure Planning Types

The resulting input table allows for the configuration of planning types along with their specific characteristics. The auto archiving feature is particularly relevant for daily cash positioning because the numbers change daily, refreshed by the latest information available. An example of settings is shown in Figure 6.17.

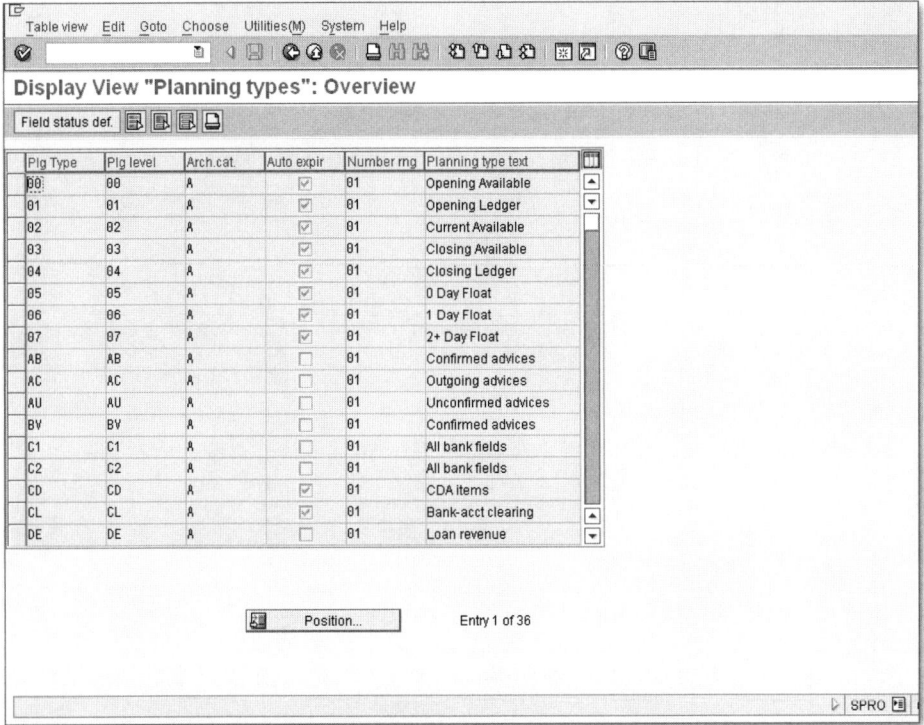

Figure 6.17 Configuring Planning Type Criteria

Create Planning Groups

Planning groups are tied to customer and vendor master data and are used to classify these into user-defined categories. For example, customers can be classified by risk into high, medium, or low. Vendors can be defined as domestic or foreign. These classifications by planning group are available in cash management reports. The accounts receivable amount in the liquidity forecast will drill down to provide a breakdown of the number between domestic and foreign receivables.

Planning groups are configured using Transaction OT13 or IMG menu path FINANCIAL SUPPLY CHAIN MANAGEMENT • CASH AND LIQUIDITY MANAGEMENT • CASH MANAGEMENT • MASTER DATA • SUB LEDGER ACCOUNTS • DEFINE PLANNING GROUPS.

Figure 6.18 provides examples of different forms of classification for vendors and customers.

6 | Cash Management & Liquidity Forecasting

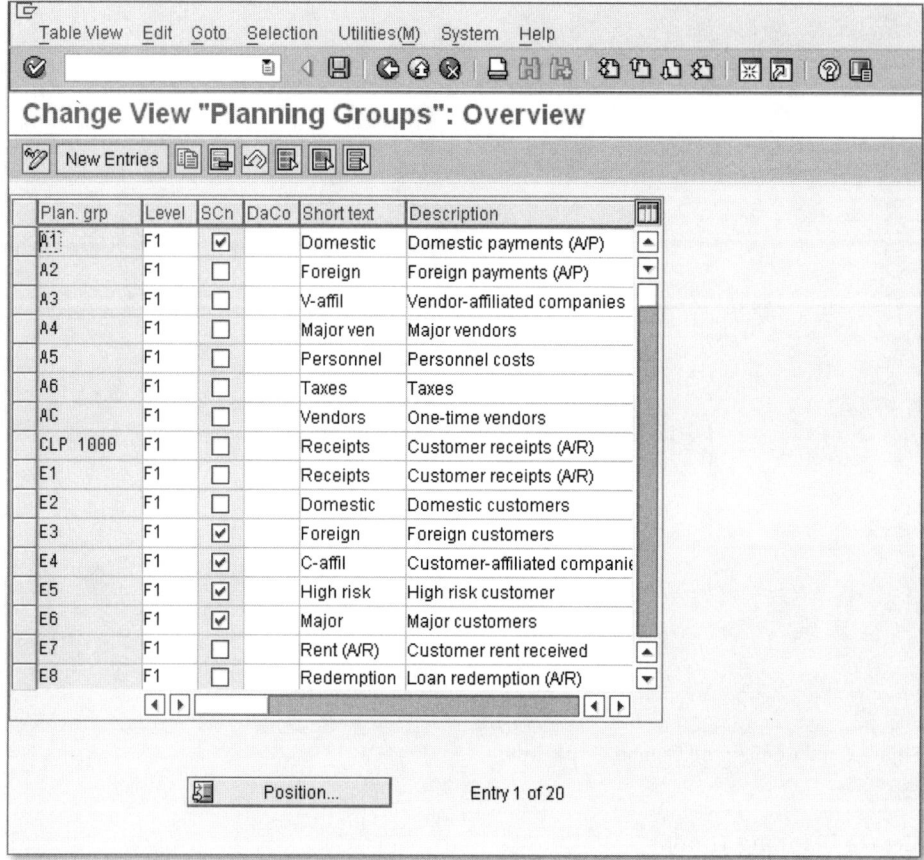

Figure 6.18 Configuring Planning Groups

The next step is to link planning types, planning levels, and planning groups with master data so that they are automatically picked up in the reports reflecting actual transactions entered in the system.

Populate Master Data with Planning Levels

In the customer master, on the ACCOUNT MANAGEMENT tab in the COMPANY CODE view, you will find a field called CASH MGMT GROUP. This is where the planning group is entered, as shown in Figure 6.19.

6.1 Cash Management

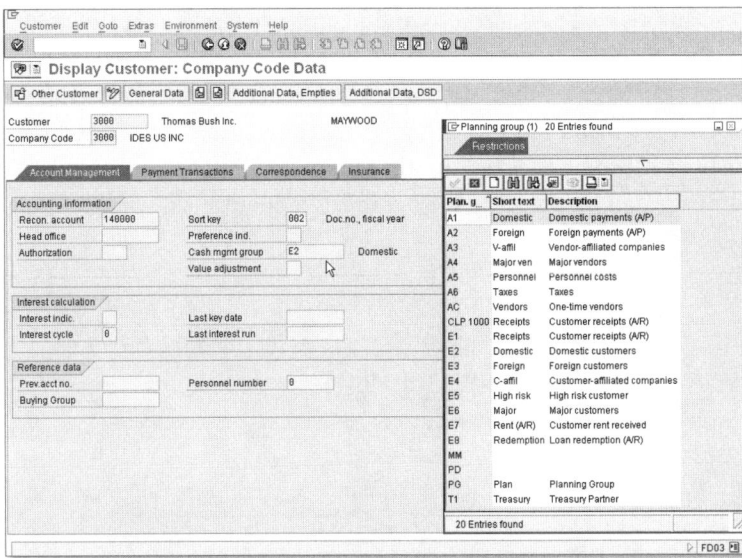

Figure 6.19 Planning Group Entry in the Customer Master

Similarly, in the vendor master, in the COMPANY CODE view under ACCOUNTING INFORMATION, the CASH MGMNT GROUP field is available to enter the planning group specific to the vendor, as shown in Figure 6.20.

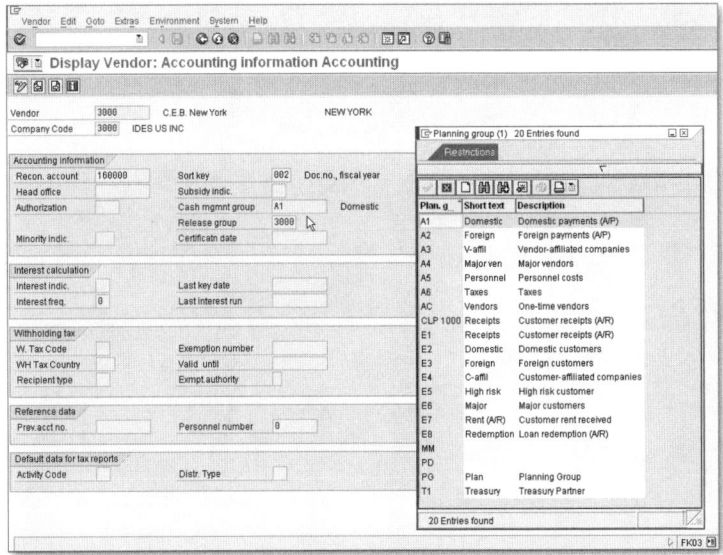

Figure 6.20 Planning Group Entry in the Vendor Master

6 | Cash Management & Liquidity Forecasting

The links between bank-related G/L accounts and planning levels are created in the master data of the G/L account. In the COMPANY CODE view of the G/L account, on the CREATE/BANK/INTEREST tab, you will find a field for PLANNING LEVEL, as shown in Figure 6.21. For all bank and bank clearing G/L accounts, the box named RELEVANT TO CASH FLOW needs to be checked. In this screen, the link to the house bank and bank account is created by entering their respective identifiers.

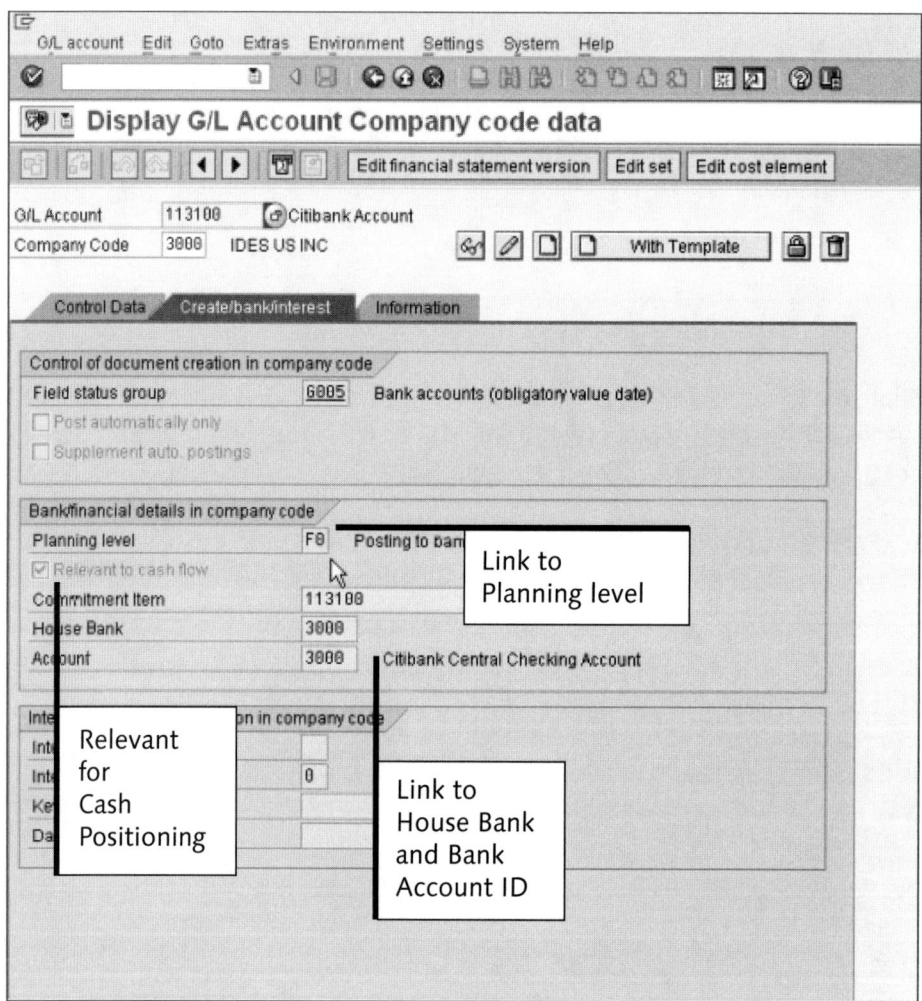

Figure 6.21 Planning Level Entry in G/L Master Data

As mentioned previously, planning level F0 is reserved for actual bank balances, and planning levels B* can be used for clearing accounts and so on, each of which will have a G/L account assigned to them.

Value Dating of Checks and Payment Record History

Value dating refers to planning the expected date of settlement of financial transactions in the bank account. These can be determined for bank and bank clearing accounts if a certain clear pattern can be established. Similarly, settlement dates for accounts receivable and payables can be established based on payment terms. This can be modified if desired, through configuring the system to record payment history that can track actual payments and receipts to/from vendors and customers. This has greater relevance for longer term liquidity forecasting, where a certain element of uncertainty exists in predicting cash inflows and outflows and these techniques help improve the quality of forecasting.

For accounts receivable, in the customer master record, the PAYMENT HISTORY RECORD checkbox can be marked to track payment history in days. The box TIME UNTIL CHECK PAID can be populated in the customer and vendor master to indicate float time in days. This carries over to the liquidity forecast, using the formula "value date = posting date + check cashing time." Both of these boxes are shown in Figure 6.22.

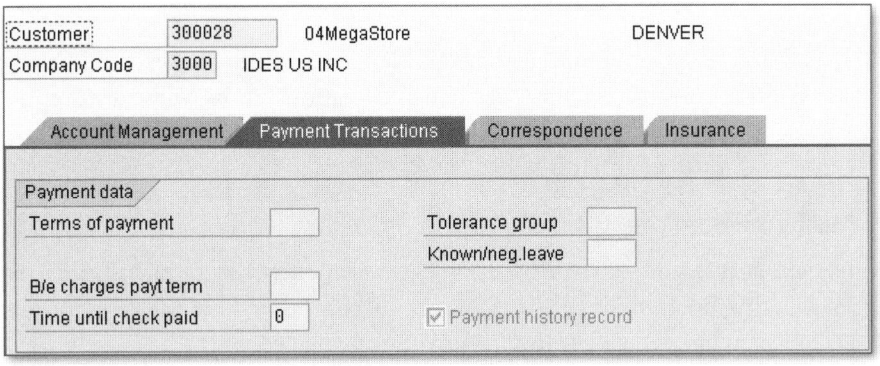

Figure 6.22 Activate Payment History Record in the Customer Master

The payment record for a customer can be displayed using the report displayed in Figure 6.23. It is run through Program RFDOPR20 or Transaction S_ALR_87012177.

Customer	CoCd	Name				Customer Type		
		Street				Backlog	Arrears	
		PostalCode City					Balance Carryforward	Crcy
Month Year	Number	Pmnts with csh disc.		Arrear	Without cash discnt	Arrear		

1000		1000 Becker Berlin				Cash discount taken where possible		
		Calvinstrasse 36				3 Days	0 Days	
		13467	Berlin					0,00 EUR
9 2003	5		0,00	0		16.500,00	24-	
10 2000	1		5.000.000,00	1		0,00	0	
9 2000	1		0,00	0		5.000,00	13-	
2 1997	1		101.053,57	3		0,00	0	
12 1996	2		4.079.225,33	5		0,00	0	
9 1996	1		2.963,45	28		0,00	0	
8 1996	50		1.264.062,40	2		0,00	0	
7 1996	52		1.503.045,76	4		489.395,17	45-	
6 1996	50		1.260.306,82	2		0,00	0	
5 1996	51		1.328.778,45	2		27.942,84	19	
4 1996	47		508.643,30	2		0,00	0	
3 1996	52		570.630,44	1		0,00	0	
2 1996	1		25.136,39	5-		0,00	0	
1 1996	5		51.989,69	15-		58.132,40	331	
10 1995	1		0,00	0		11.759,71	45-	
9 1995	1		0,00	0		23.519,43	14-	

1000		1414 Becker Berlin				Net payer although cash dsct		
		Calvinstrasse 36				45- Days		
		13467	Berlin				395.000,00	USD
3 2008	1		0,00	0		1.000,00	45-	

1001		1000 Lampen-Markt GmbH				Net payer although cash dsct		
		Auf der Schanz 54				18 Days	17 Days	
		65936	Frankfurt					0,00 EUR
3 2003	1		0,00	0		440.820,30	15	

Figure 6.23 Customer Payment History Report

Now that all cash management-related data is identified within the system, it needs to be linked to reporting structures so that information can be viewed in report format to enable decision making based on the results in the reports.

Cash Management Account Name

The first step in this process is to create a cash management account name. These are user friendly mnemonics that link to more technical or numeric descriptions such as G/L accounts, which are in turn linked to bank accounts.

The cash management account names are set up using Transaction OT16 or IMG menu path FINANCIAL SUPPLY CHAIN MANAGEMENT • CASH AND LIQUIDITY MANAGEMENT • CASH MANAGEMENT • STRUCTURING • DEFINE CASH MANAGEMENT ACCOUNT NAME.

An example of cash management account names is shown in Figure 6.20. It is recommended that names are created that are easily recognizable by report users. This greatly facilitates the interpretation of the cash or liquidity forecast items in the report.

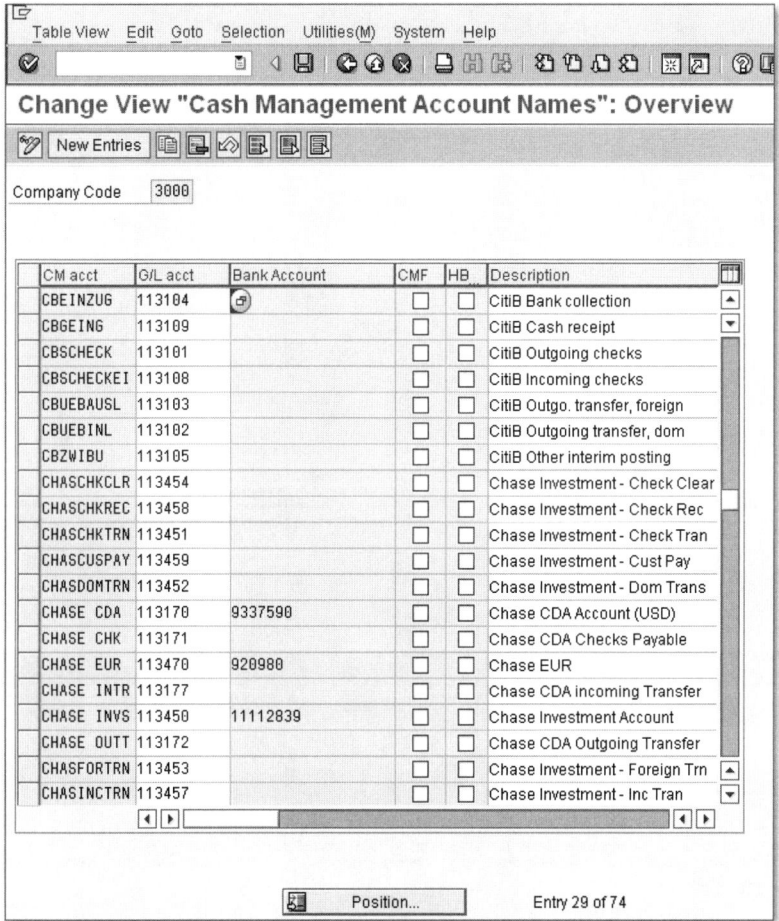

Figure 6.24 Creating Cash Management Account Names

Grouping Structure

Grouping structures are customized views that are required to be displayed in the cash or liquidity forecast. The grouping structure can reflect any combination of planning types, planning groups, and G/L accounts linked to bank and bank clearing accounts. Setting up a grouping structure is a two-step process. First, the structure needs to be named. Again, this should be a user friendly description of the actual report that needs to be displayed. Examples of grouping structure names are shown in Figure 6.25.

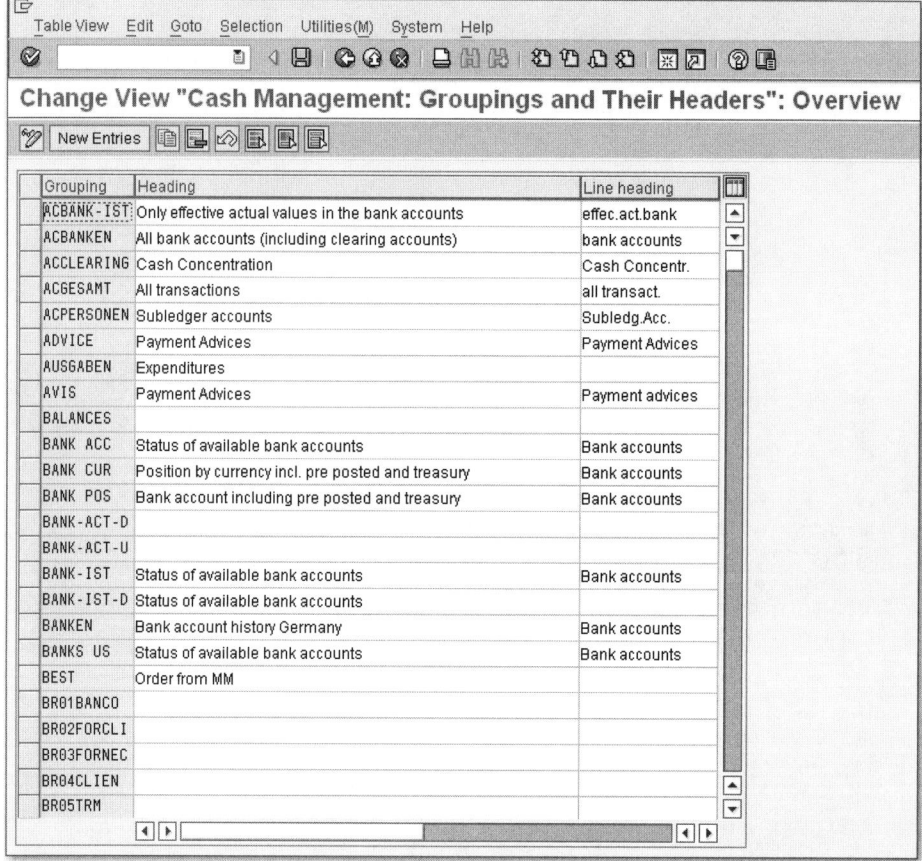

Figure 6.25 Creation of Grouping Structure Names

The second step is to link the grouping name to a specific combination of planning groups, planning types, and bank accounts represented by cash management account names, as shown in Figure 6.26. The IMG menu path to access the relevant configuration area is FINANCIAL SUPPLY CHAIN MANAGEMENT • CASH AND LIQUIDITY MANAGEMENT • CASH MANAGEMENT • STRUCTURING • GROUPINGS • MAINTAIN STRUCTURE.

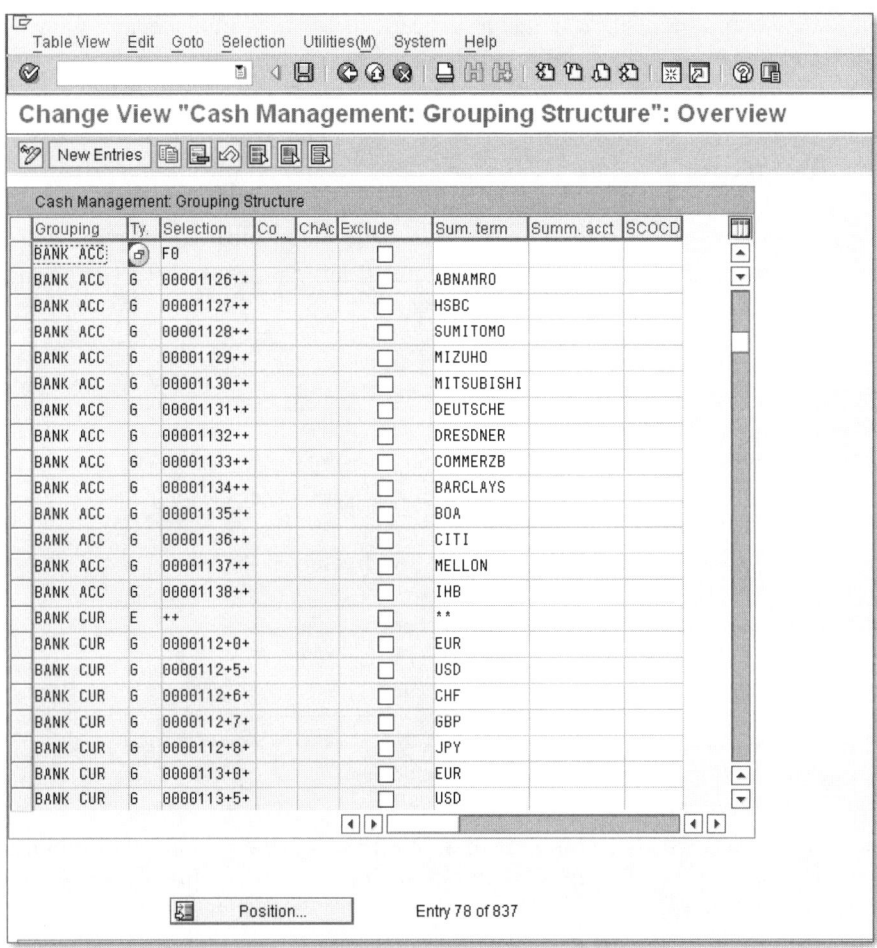

Figure 6.26 Linking Data in SAP ERP to a Grouping Report

There are several optional settings in this screen, enabling the inclusion and exclusion of selected items. Account masking can be used to include complete or partial information using the "+" sign. For example all bank G/L accounts beginning with 100 can be entered as "100+++" if six-digit G/L accounts are used. If the bank account structure has been designed so that all main bank accounts end with "0," the masking to pick up all main bank accounts starting with "1" should be "1+++++0". This grouping could be called "Main Bank Accounts," or, for example, if located in the U.S., "Banks U.S."

All of the key components that make up the reports are now in place, and we will proceed with developing and running the reports.

6.2 Reporting

After all of the steps described in the previous section are executed, the reports are ready to be run. An example of a daily cash positioning report structure showing inputs and sources is provided in Figure 6.27.

Report item	Source
Opening Available - Bank Account A	Intraday File
Maturing Investments	SAP ERP - Money Market
ZBA Transfers in / out	SAP ERP - AP/Treasury Bank Clearing Accounts
Cash Concentration	SAP ERP - AP/Treasury Bank Clearing Accounts
Wires / ACH/ Lockbox in	Intraday File
Presentments - 1st	Intraday File
Presentments - 2nd	Intraday File
Wires / ACH Out	

Figure 6.27 Structure and Sources for Daily Cash Positioning

The required report needs to be built in SAP ERP using the various components described previously. When all of the elements are in place, the report can be executed.

6.2.1 Daily Cash Positioning

Cash positioning reporting is executed through Transaction FF7A. The menu path for this report is APPLICATION MENU PATH: FINANCIAL SUPPLY CHAIN MANAGEMENT • CASH AND LIQUIDITY MANAGEMENT • CASH MANAGEMENT • INFORMATION SYSTEM • REPORTS FOR CASH MANAGEMENT • LIQUIDITY ANALYSES • FF7A - CASH POSITION.

The menu path is shown in Figure 6.28. The report will need to be executed after intraday bank statement files have been uploaded and processed in the system. Typically, prior day files are also uploaded first thing in the morning so that bank G/L balances will also be updated and available in the cash report. These can be reconciled with available bank balances from the intraday information.

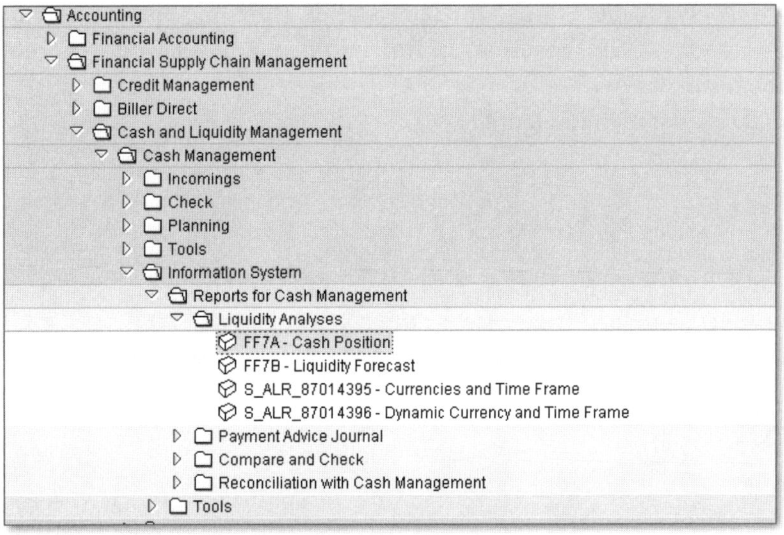

6.2 Reporting

```
▽ 🗁 Accounting
   ▷ 🗀 Financial Accounting
   ▽ 🗁 Financial Supply Chain Management
      ▷ 🗀 Credit Management
      ▷ 🗀 Biller Direct
      ▽ 🗁 Cash and Liquidity Management
         ▽ 🗁 Cash Management
            ▷ 🗀 Incomings
            ▷ 🗀 Check
            ▷ 🗀 Planning
            ▷ 🗀 Tools
            ▽ 🗁 Information System
               ▽ 🗁 Reports for Cash Management
                  ▽ 🗁 Liquidity Analyses
                     ◇ FF7A - Cash Position
                     ◇ FF7B - Liquidity Forecast
                     ◇ S_ALR_87014395 - Currencies and Time Frame
                     ◇ S_ALR_87014396 - Dynamic Currency and Time Frame
                  ▷ 🗀 Payment Advice Journal
                  ▷ 🗀 Compare and Check
                  ▷ 🗀 Reconciliation with Cash Management
            ▷ 🗀 Tools
```

Figure 6.28 Cash Management Reporting Menu Path

The basic selection screen lets you view different combinations of reports that can be created through variants. These can be for daily cash positioning or longer term liquidity forecasting, and can be customized for currency, date range, or time increments such as days, weeks, or months, as shown in Figure 6.29.

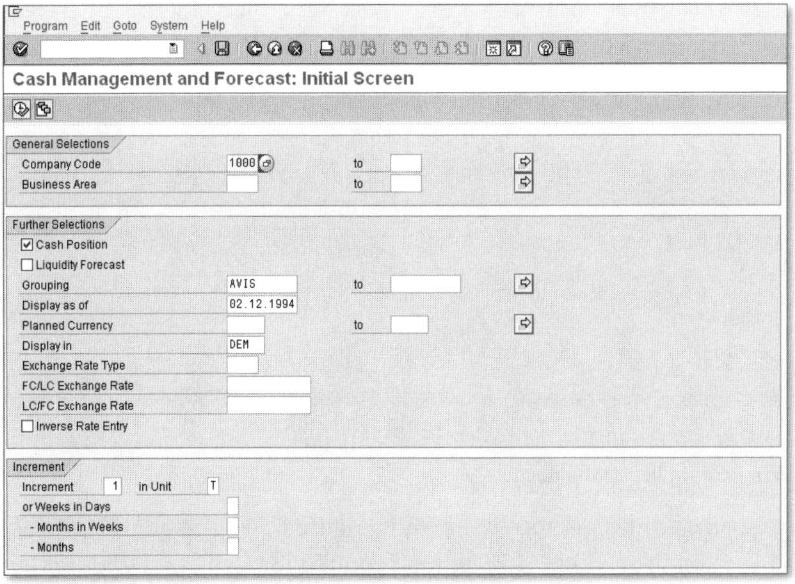

Figure 6.29 Report FF7A / FF7B Basic Selection Screen

257

An extended view is available through the same screen. This screen provides more options with respect to display, output control, and planning for weekends and holidays, through linking with a calendar that can be set up to reflect bank and company holidays, as shown in Figure 6.30.

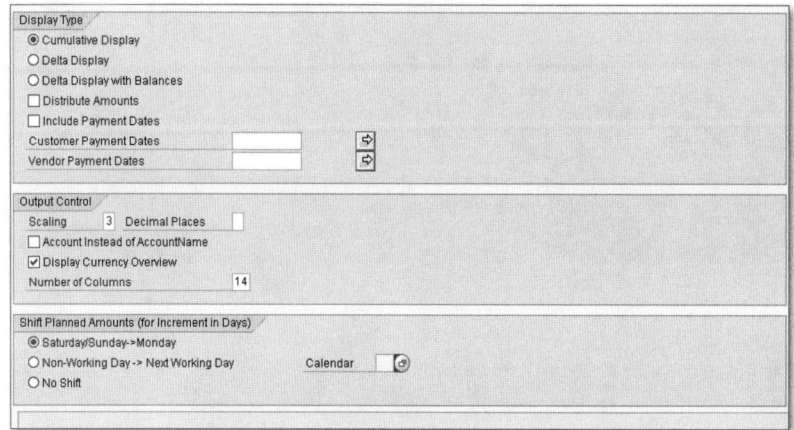

Figure 6.30 Report FF7A / FF7B Extended Selection Screen

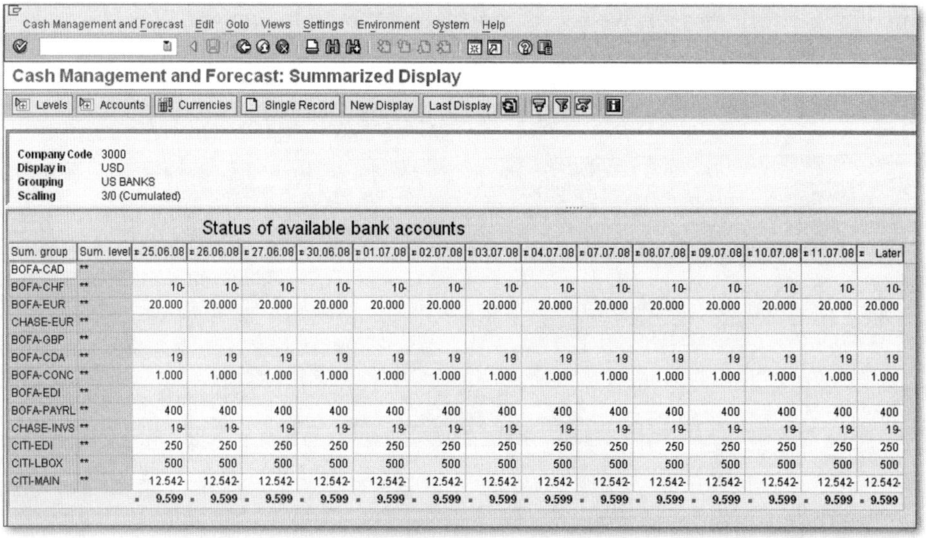

Figure 6.31 Cash Position Report Transaction FF7A

An extract of a bank position report is shown in Figure 6.31. The grouping structure US BANKS set up in Section 6.1.2, Inputs Required for Daily Cash Positioning and Liquidity Forecasting, is reflected in the report, populating all bank balances set up within that grouping structure.

The display by summarization groups can be changed to reflect planning types, planning groups, or currencies. You can also drill down to the individual record level. Manually entered planning types can be created directly from the report screen, which can then be refreshed to reflect the updated cash position or forecast.

6.2.2 Liquidity Forecasting

The longer term liquidity forecast report is available through Transaction FF7B, as shown in Figure 6.32. It extends the cash position view to include cash flow-relevant items such as payables, receivables, commitments, one day or two day float balances, and manually entered planning types.

The liquidity forecast report can be accessed through Transaction FF7B or application menu path FINANCIAL SUPPLY CHAIN MANAGEMENT • CASH AND LIQUIDITY MANAGEMENT • CASH MANAGEMENT • INFORMATION SYSTEM • REPORTS FOR CASH MANAGEMENT • LIQUIDITY ANALYSES • LIQUIDITY FORECAST.

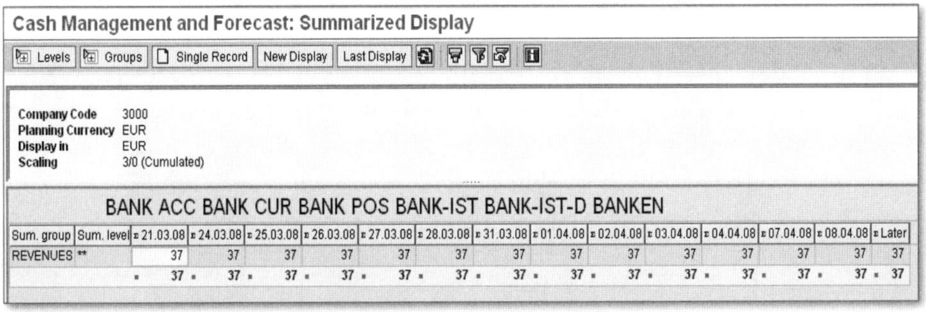

Figure 6.32 Liquidity Forecast Report

For example, as shown in Figure 6.32, the revenue projection for 03/21/2008 of 37,000 Euros is comprised of sales orders, purchase orders and intercompany transactions. The details for this are shown in Figure 6.33.

Cash Management and Forecast: Display Levels															
Company Code 3000															
Planning Currency EUR															
Display in EUR															
Scaling 3/0 (Cumulated)															
REVENUES | **															
Level Short text	= 21.03.08	= 24.03.08	= 25.03.08	= 26.03.08	= 27.03.08	= 28.03.08	= 31.03.08	= 01.04.08	= 02.04.08	= 03.04.08	= 04.04.08	= 07.04.08	= 08.04.08	= Later
F1 FI CN	32-	32-	32-	32-	32-	32-	32-	32-	32-	32-	32-	32-	32-	32-
M2 Order	8-	8-	8-	8-	8-	8-	8-	8-	8-	8-	8-	8-	8-	8-
S1 Order	78	78	78	78	78	78	78	78	78	78	78	78	78	78
	37 =	37 =	37 =	37 =	37 =	37 =	37 =	37 =	37 =	37 =	37 =	37 =	37 =	37

Figure 6.33 Liquidity Forecast Detail

6.2.3 Liquidity Planner

The Liquidity Planner (LP) is a relatively new component in SAP ERP, and replaces the cash budget management component in older versions of SAP R/3. Please note that it does not replace cash management functionality in SAP ERP, but enhances its functionality to facilitate detailed planning at transactional source line item level. The LP has extended a lot of the functionality available in cash budget management and cash management, and liquidity forecasting to enable planning at a detailed level, and integrating it with SAP Strategic Enterprise Management (SAP SEM) and SAP Business Warehouse (SAP BW) reporting. The LP component enables the extrapolation of detailed transactions in the system to create planning forecasts and statement of sources and application of funds, in an integrated environment, across the enterprise. It also allows for decentralized input and planning. The LP component is outside of the scope of this book; however, if you are interested, refer to the SAP PRESS publication *Cash Accounting and Cash Flow Planning with SAP Liquidity Planner* by Stephan Kerber and Dirk Warntje.

6.3 Controls for Cash Management

Cash management is a critical activity that results in key decisions relating to investment, borrowing, and risk management, and the ability of an organization to meet its daily cash and longer term liquidity requirements. From a SOX perspective, an organization must have adequate systems in place to ensure the safeguarding of the company's cash and liquid assets, the accuracy and integrity of its recordings in the books of account, and the protection of its value. In addition, the organization must be able to demonstrate that it has sufficient cash and liquid resources to meet its short term and long term funding commitments.

Because decisions will be made based on the reports, it is important to ensure the accuracy and validity of the information contained in them. As part of this process, it is important to reconcile the reports newly created in SAP ERP with previous legacy reports, as well as with intraday reports available through online banking or hard or soft copy reports from the bank. Because the inputs for reporting in SAP ERP will be automated for the most part, adequate controls must be in place to ensure accuracy and robustness.

The following is a list of key controls that need to be considered:

- Master data should be checked to ensure that planning groups and planning levels are entered where appropriate. This can be checked for all customer and vendor master data, as well as for G/L accounts by company code. Tables KNB1 (customer), LFB1 (vendor), and SKB1 (G/L account) can be viewed through Transaction SE16N. The table name needs to be entered in the table field at the top of the screen input. The required parameters (e.g., customer or planning group) need to be selected and executed as shown in Figure 6.34.

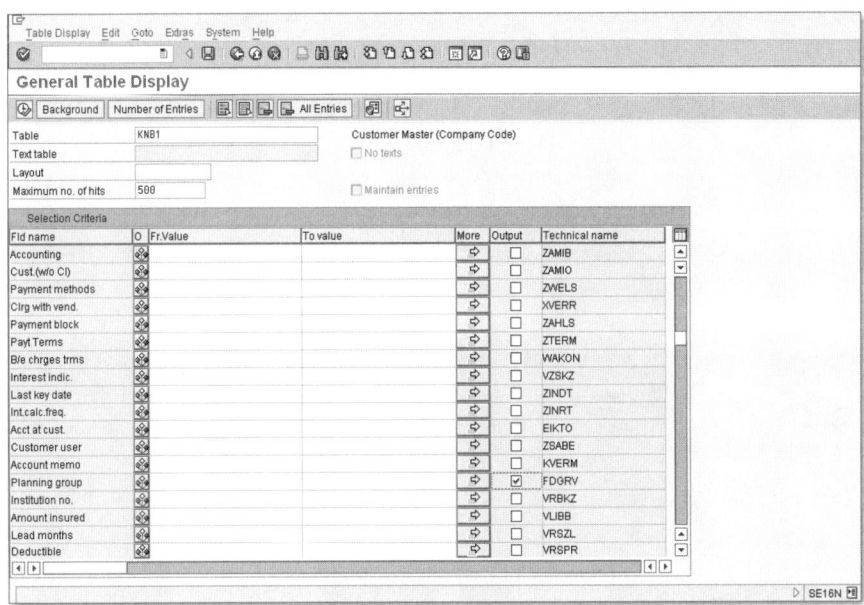

Figure 6.34 View Table KNB1 Using Transaction SE16N

The resulting views are shown in Figure 6.35 (customer), Figure 6.36 (vendor), and Figure 6.37 (G/L accounts).

6 | Cash Management & Liquidity Forecasting

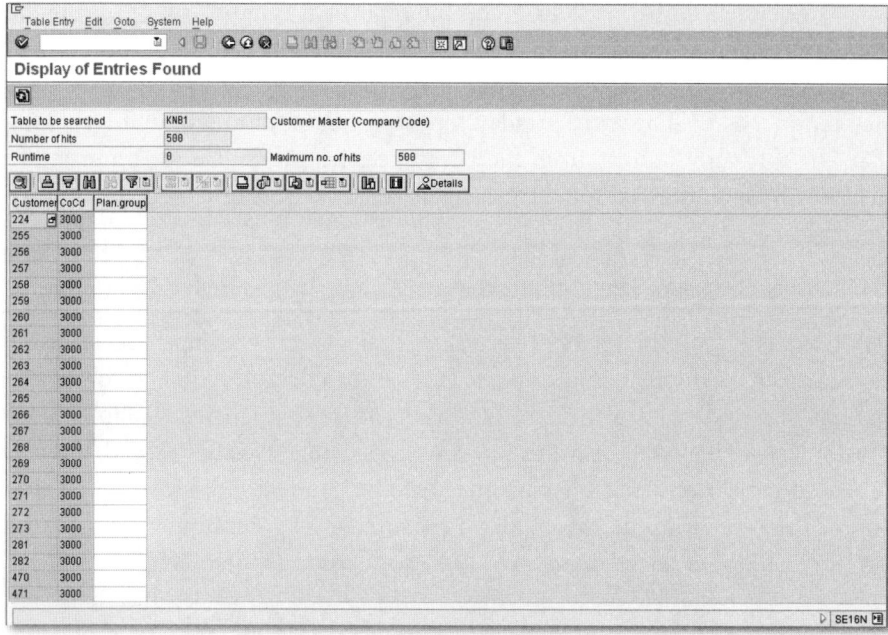

Figure 6.35 Table KNB1 Customer Master Planning Groups

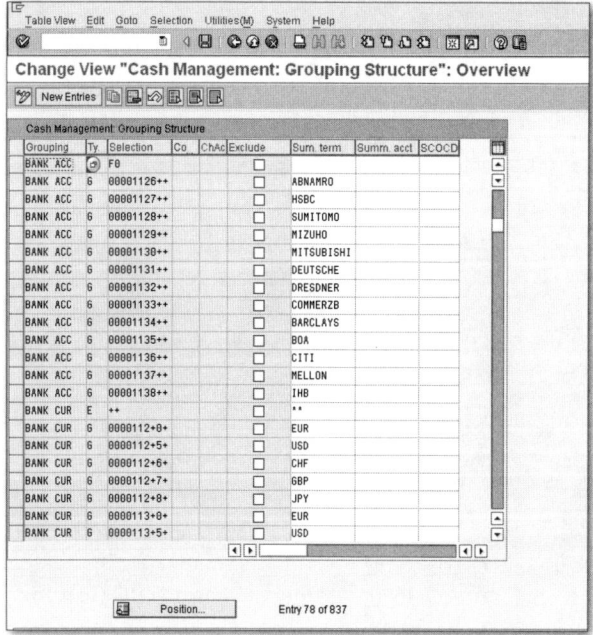

Figure 6.36 Table LFB1 Vendor Master Planning Groups

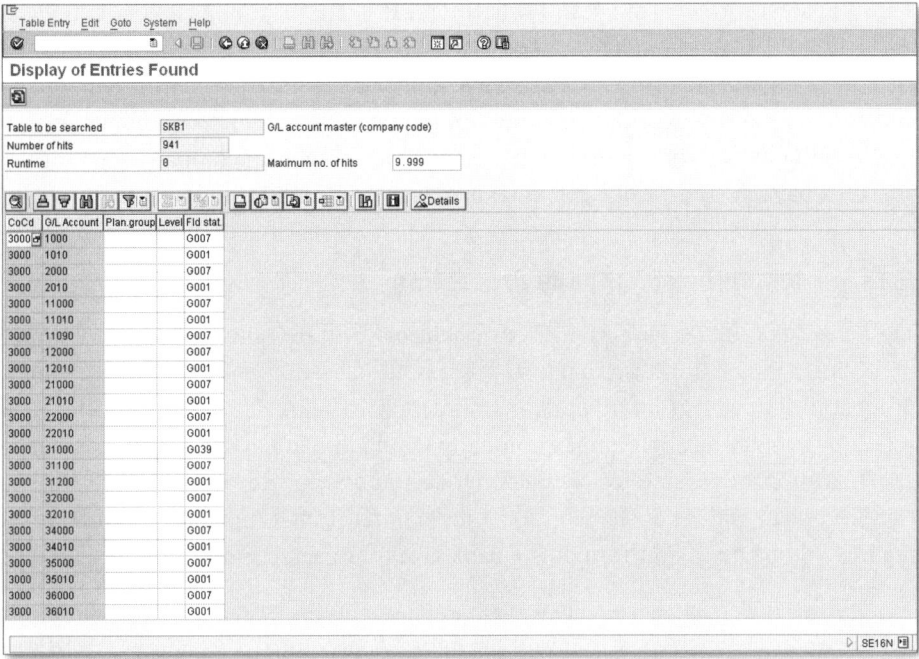

Figure 6.37 Table SKB1 General Ledger Planning Levels and Groups

- Initially, after implementing cash management in SAP ERP, continue legacy reporting if possible until the integrity and robustness of the automated SAP ERP system is validated consistently.
- Ensure standard controls for intraday file transmission and upload into SAP ERP.
- Establish automatic archiving for daily cash positioning planning items, and appropriate date archiving for longer term forecasting items.
- Reconcile prior day forecasts with current day actuals to ensure that the information is accurate within acceptable tolerance levels. If it is not, investigate the cause and ensure corrective action is taken.

6.4 In-House Cash (IHC) Management

IHC is a component in the financial supply chain management suite of applications in SAP ERP. It leverages all of the finance, banking, accounting, and payment processing functionality within SAP ERP to enable intercompany and group transaction processing, recording, and settlement. It is one of the most cost beneficial areas of SAP TRM to implement because of the considerable cost savings available, especially to global corporations that have multiple subsidiaries in different regions and countries of the world. It is tightly integrated with other components in SAP ERP, especially electronic banking, payment processing, intercompany accounting, accounts payable and receivable, cash management, and liquidity forecasting.

6.4.1 IHC and Intercompany Processing

The concept of the IHC in SAP ERP is straightforward. IHC allows a company to set up an internal, or in-house, bank to process all incoming and outgoing payment transactions, as well as intercompany transactions. The In-House Bank (IHB) can be set up by geographical region if a company would like to have individual payment centers, for example one for North America and one for Europe to handle all EU, non-European and Asia Pacific group transactions. Transactions between the two regions will be handled through the bank areas for each region.

The IHB is set up exactly as an external bank, as a house bank, and can have internal bank accounts assigned to it with its own G/L accounts. This allows the IHB to function exactly as an external house bank, with full integration with accounting, payment, and bank statement processing.

The following are the key scenarios that companies typically use with their IHB.

Intercompany Transactions

The IHB can process all intercompany transactions such as purchases, sales, interest and dividend payments, intercompany loans, and other capital transactions. The IHB will act as the internal bank, and account for all of the transactions through intercompany accounts. It can issue internal bank statements in IDoc FINSTA format that can be uploaded by the subsidiaries when transactions are effected, and post into the subsidiary's company code in SAP ERP using external transaction codes and posting rules exactly the same way as external electronic bank statements. Actual cash settlement between the subsidiaries can take place periodically, depending on the laws within the countries or region, and again can be handled through the IHB.

Centralized Payments

With centralized payments, a payment processing center based, for example, in Brussels, can receive requests from all European subsidiaries to make payment to vendors. The IHB can consolidate these requests and make payments to vendors, on behalf of the subsidiaries. Actual cash payments are made out of the IHB's external bank account, with accounting for the transactions taking place internally through intercompany accounts.

Payment On Behalf Of

With the payment on behalf of scenario, a German subsidiary can use the IHB to pay its UK vendor in currency GBP, through a UK subsidiary of the group, without having to incur any foreign exchange currency conversion costs. Again, settlement is achieved internally between the two subsidiaries through the IHB, with actual payment to the vendor being made by a local subsidiary.

Netting and Pooling

The IHB lets the company implement netting and pooling arrangements that are popular in Europe. Because external payments can be executed from the IHB, it lets you maintain fewer bank accounts for disbursement purposes, and allows for timely concentration and consolidation of scarce cash resources.

Centralized Receipts

The IHB can operate as a collection point for the group's accounts receivable, possibly resulting in faster collection, ease of reconciliation, and consolidation of resources at point of receipt, without the need for cash concentration of receipts from different collection points. This can also substantially reduce the number of external subsidiary bank accounts required.

6.4.2 Cost/Benefit Considerations in Implementing IHC

The greatest benefit from implementing the IHC component can be realized through the automation of the process for intercompany transaction processing and settlement. To obtain the greatest benefit, the IHC component is implemented after a company has fully leveraged the finance, cash management, and electronic banking functionality of SAP ERP.

The benefits of implementing IHC are many and most of them are hard savings that considerably enhance ROI and reduce the payback period of the cost of the implementation. These benefits can be summarized as follows:

- Reduction in bank releationships through reduction in number of payment centers and bank accounts.
- Reduction in external bank accounts required for maintaining bank balances and disbursement accounts.
- Savings in bank fees, charges, and currency conversion costs.
- Opportunity for netting and pooling arrangements.
- Reduction in interest and opportunity costs through timely consolidation and concentration of cash balances.
- Ability to have surplus resources invested at higher rates through larger group balances maintained.
- High level of automation enabling STP, which minimizes communication costs, reduces or eliminates manual effort, and automates and simplifies the reconciliation process.

6.4.3 Process Overview

The principle of how IHC works in SAP ERP can be explained using an example of the process for an intercompany transaction for interest payable, showing recording, payment, settlement, accounting, and reconciliation between two subsidiaries through the IHB. As shown in Figure 6.38, the entire transaction between two subsidiaries can be effected without any external interaction. Any cash settlement that may be required at the end of a period because of internal policy or country-specific legal requirements can be made by the IHB through its external banking partner.

We will now review the key components of master data and configuration required to successfully set up an IHB structure within SAP ERP.

6.4 In-House Cash (IHC) Management

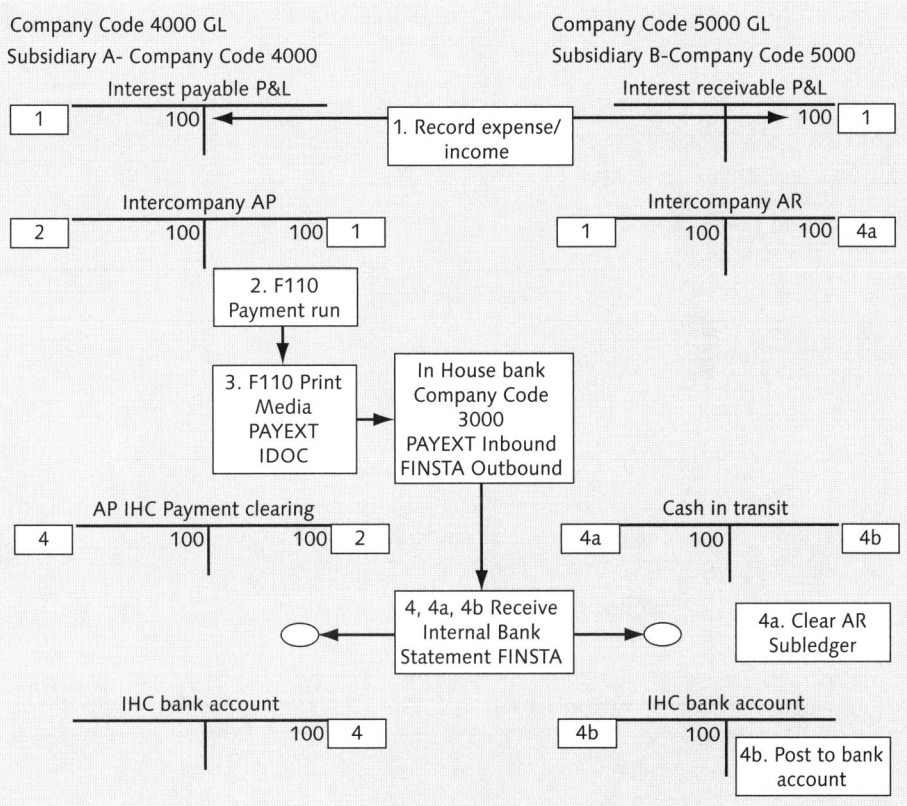

Figure 6.38 Accounting for Transactions Between Subsidiaries Through IHC

6.4.4 Master Data

The IHC component is fully integrated with and uses the banking, finance, and payment program functionality available in SAP ERP. It is also fully integrated with cash management. Furthermore, the component makes use of intercompany accounting and application linking and embedding (ALE) for transferring IDocs, to post internal and external payments as well as internal bank statements. Key master data specific to the IHC component are bank area, bank current account, products, and conditions. The component also uses the BP concept extensively, with organizational subsidiaries set up with appropriate roles for transacting within and outside the group.

In this section, we will review the key components involved in setting up the IHC component, particularly from a controls perspective.

The IMG menu path for setting up IHC is FINANCIAL SUPPLY CHAIN MANAGEMENT • IN-HOUSE CASH, as partially shown in Figure 6.39.

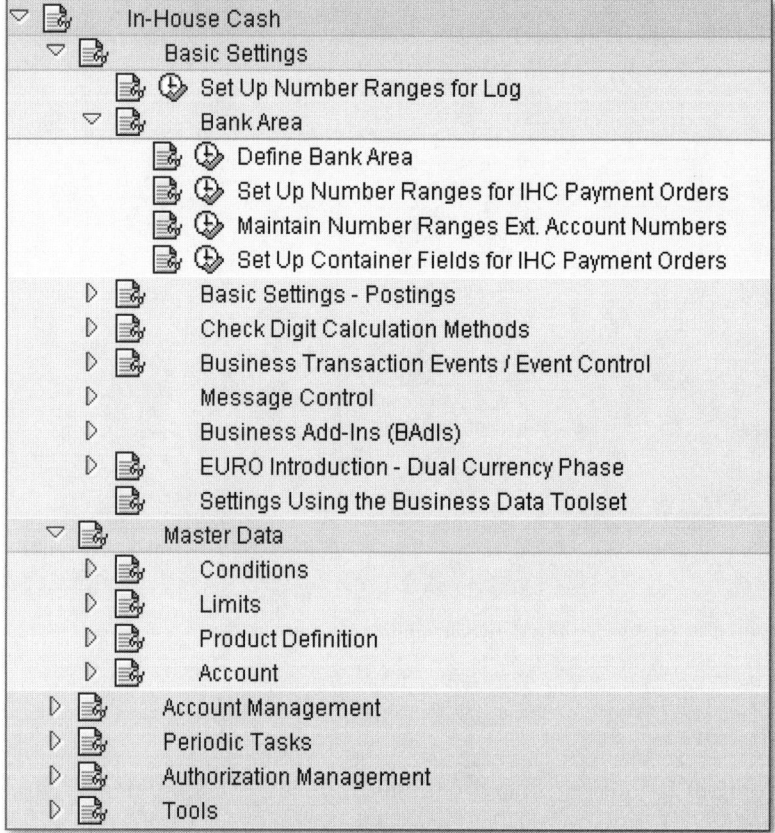

Figure 6.39 The In-House Cash Configuration Menu

Bank Area

The bank area is the internal house bank. It is set up exactly the same way as an external house bank, except that it has an internal identification called the bank area, and an internal bank key or routing number, as shown in Figure 6.40.

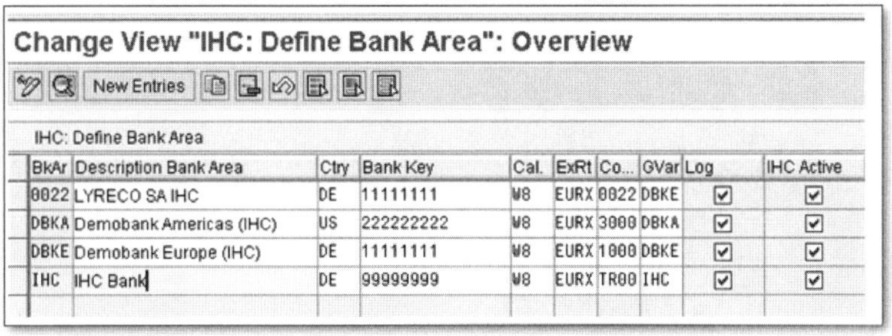

6.4 In-House Cash (IHC) Management

Figure 6.40 Define a Bank Area

The bank area is assigned to a company code, which typically acts as the corporate head office providing internal banking services to its subsidiaries. The detailed input screen for bank area is shown in Figure 6.41.

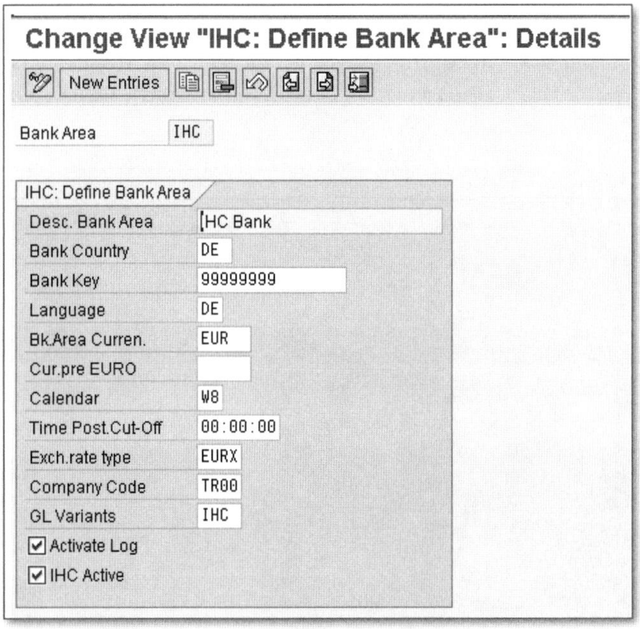

Figure 6.41 Bank Area Input Screen

The IHB will need to have payment methods set up for its internal (I) and external (J) payments. These will need to be EDI-enabled for the payment IDoc files to be transmitted within as well as outside the group, as shown in Figure 6.42.

6 | Cash Management & Liquidity Forecasting

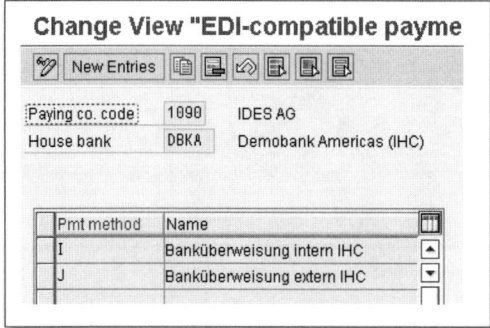

Figure 6.42 EDI-Enabled Payment Methods for In-House Banking

Bank Account

Internal bank accounts — representing the accounts of each subsidiary within the IHB region — are assigned to the IHB under its house bank ID and internal bank key. Similar to the way external bank accounts are set up in SAP ERP, the internal bank accounts are assigned a G/L account to reflect their balances within the G/L, as shown in Figure 6.43.

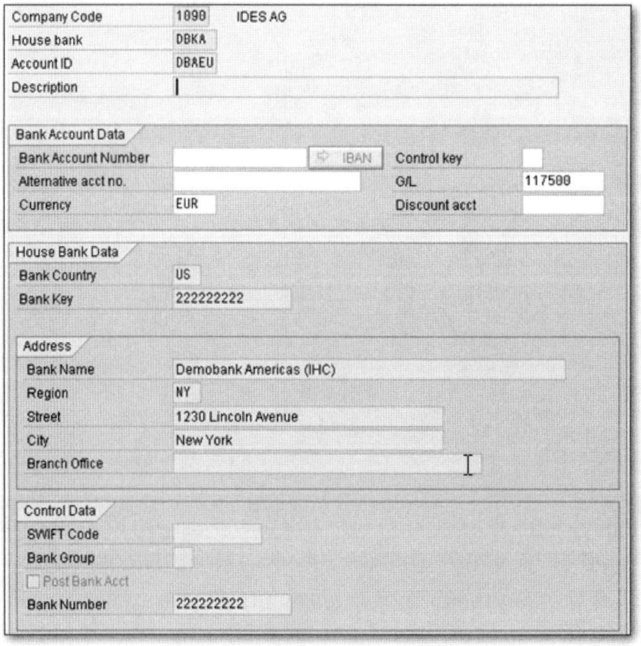

Figure 6.43 IHB Account Setup

In-House Cash (IHC) Management | 6.4

Intercompany transactions are processed through the creation of payment orders, as shown in Figure 6.44.

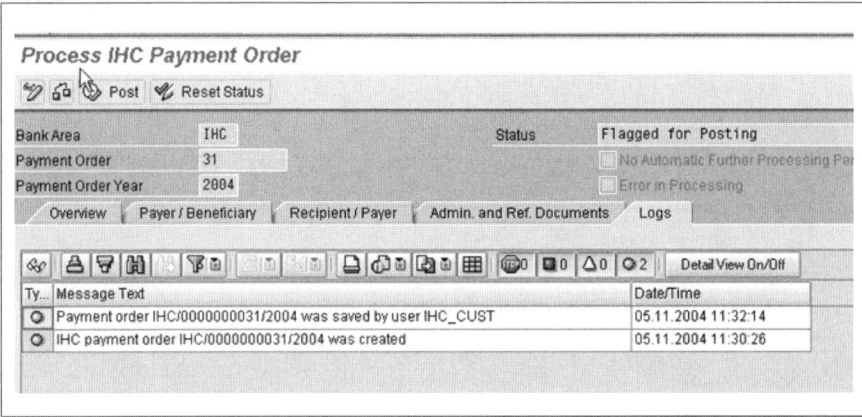

Figure 6.44 Process Payment Order

Payment orders contain all of the detailed information relating to the transaction, as shown in Figure 6.45. These IDocs are transmitted internally or externally, as appropriate.

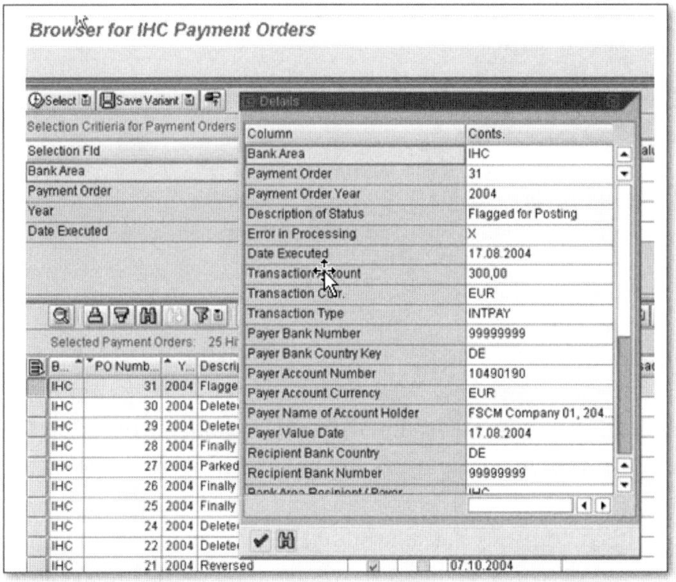

Figure 6.45 Payment Order Detail

Current Account

The bank account that was created for the subsidiary, although internal, has full functionality — as if it was an external account. All of the information relating to the account's transactions are available in the IHC component, as shown in Figure 6.46. This includes all account information, balances, bank statements received, limit management, standing orders, and many other banking features.

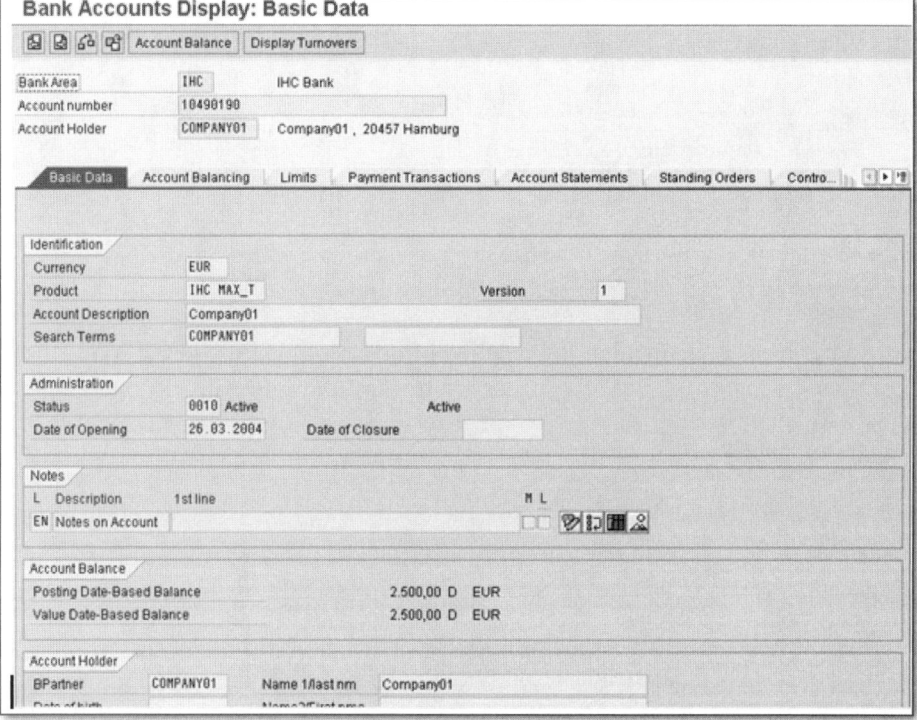

Figure 6.46 Internal Bank Account Setup and Information

Product

Specific banking characteristics of the internal bank account in the IHC component are set up through the product object in SAP ERP. Specific products are set up for each type of transaction, as shown in Figure 6.47. Each bank account is based on a product, and inherits all of the settings relating to that product. This is very important from a control perspective, because products can be set up with specific control features, and then assigned to bank current accounts of subsidiaries, as appropriate to their approved level of access.

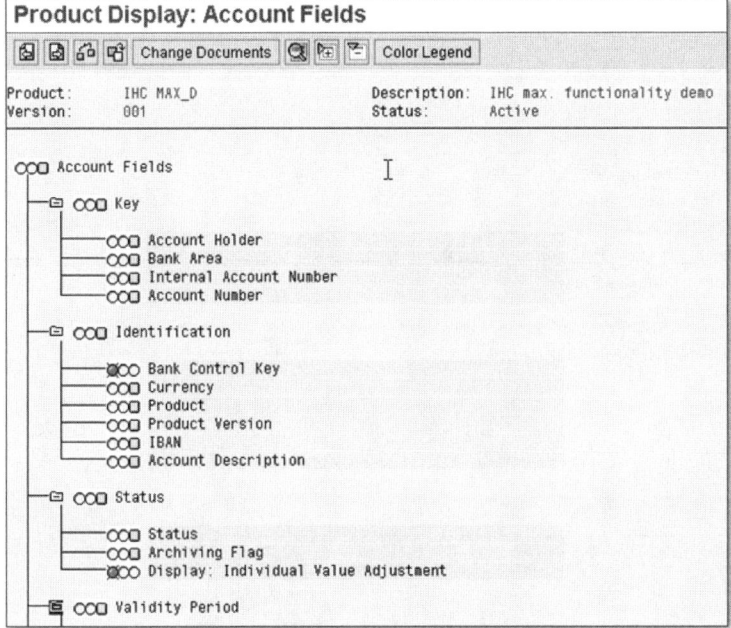

Figure 6.47 Bank Account Product Details

Business Partner

BPs are used in the IHC component to represent subsidiary and affiliated companies within a group. They are assigned various roles, depending on their function within the organization as they relate to IHC. These roles can be, for example, account holder, subsidiary, or counterparty.

6.4.5 Integration with Cash Management

Integration of IHC with cash management is effected through the setup of planning types, levels, and groups, source symbols, and through additional configuration specific to IHC to link the bank area to cash management. We will review these settings in this section.

The path to the configuration area specific to IHC is IMG: FINANCIAL SUPPLY CHAIN MANAGEMENT • IN-HOUSE CASH • PERIODIC TASKS • TRANSFER FINANCIAL STATUS TO SAP CASH MANAGEMENT • SET UP FINANCIAL STATUS, as shown in Figure 6.48.

This screen can also be accessed through Transaction IHCCM0.

6 | Cash Management & Liquidity Forecasting

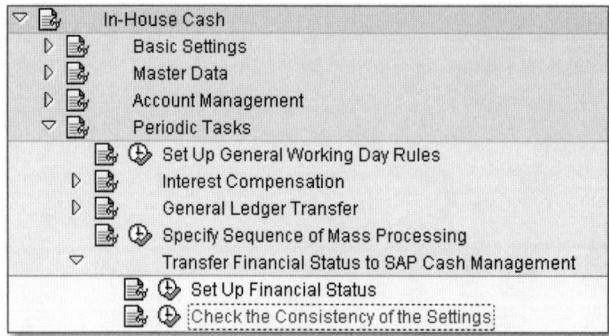

Figure 6.48 Integration with Cash Management

The link to cash management is made through setting up a cash management variant and then linking the variant to the bank area, as shown in Figure 6.49.

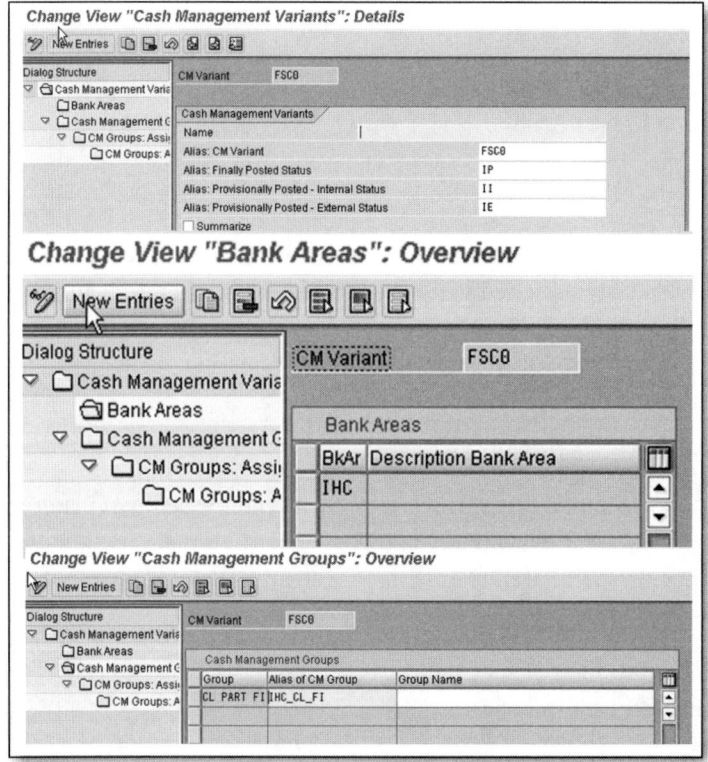

Figure 6.49 Setting up Integration with Cash Management

6.4 In-House Cash (IHC) Management

Further linking to detailed views is configured by setting up group names, which can be linked to individual values. As shown in Figure 6.50, group CL PART FI (clearing partners) is assigned to G/L accounts of specific clearing partner accounts.

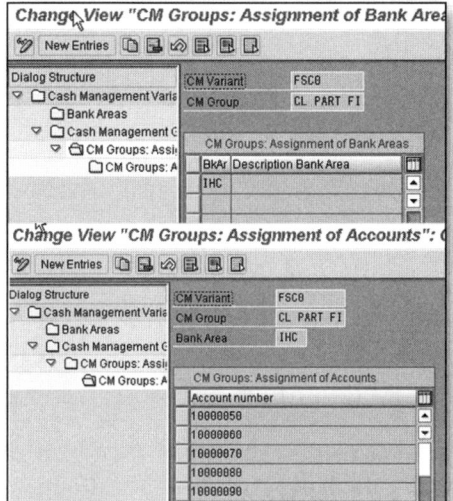

Figure 6.50 Creation and Assignment of Cash Management Groups

Additional settings required are the same as described previously in Section 6.1.2, Inputs Required for Daily Cash Positioning and Liquidity Forecasting, relating to source symbols, planning levels, planning groups, cash management names, defining groupings and creating headers, and maintaining appropriate grouping structures.

A useful feature is a report that lets you run a consistency check to ensure that the configuration that integrates IHC to cash management was successful, as indicated by the green buttons and messages shown in Figure 6.51. You can run this check using Transaction IHCCM3.

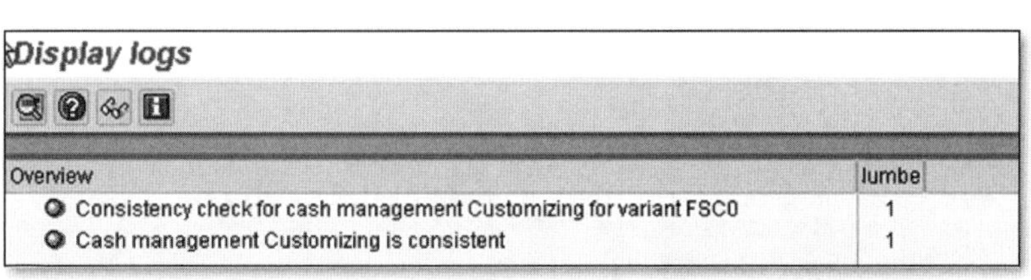

Figure 6.51 Consistency Check for IHC to Cash Management Integration

275

An example of a resulting cash management report is shown in Figure 6.52.

Ebene	09.03.04	10.03.04	11.03.04	12.03.04	15.03.04	16.03.04	17.03.04
I1 IHC-IST	10.318-	11.358-	11.358-	11.358-	11.358-	11.358-	11.358-
I2 IHC-PLINT	10-	1.050-	1.050-	1.050-	1.050-	1.050-	1.050-
I3 IHC-PLEXT	10	1.050	1.050	1.050	1.050	1.050	1.050
Saldo	10.318-	11.358-	11.358-	11.358-	11.358-	11.358-	11.358-

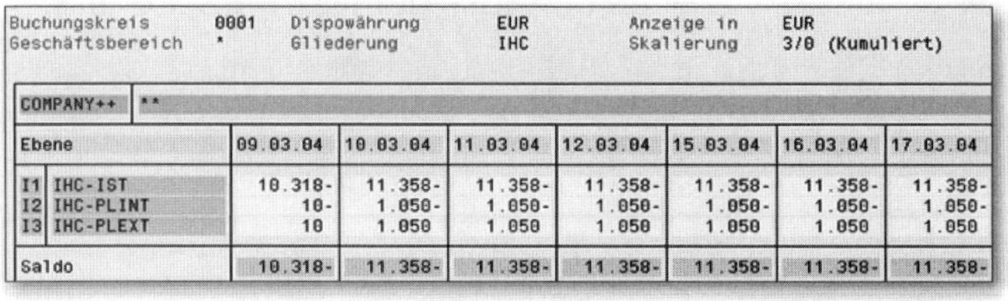

Figure 6.52 Reporting for IHC in Cash Management

6.4.6 Authorization Management

Authorization management in IHC lets you allow or restrict certain actions in the SAP ERP system. The application menu path to configure authorization is FINANCIAL SUPPLY CHAIN MANAGEMENT • IN-HOUSE CASH • AUTHORIZATION MANAGEMENT and is shown in Figure 6.53.

The following options are available for setting up appropriate authorization controls that will strengthen internal controls and facilitate SOX compliance:

- Establish dual control and amount-dependent authorizations for payment orders.
- Create and assign authorization types, a special form of authorization object. Authorization types allow the designation of any fields, and make the assignment of authorizations dependent on the contents of these fields.
- Generate and assign authorization roles.

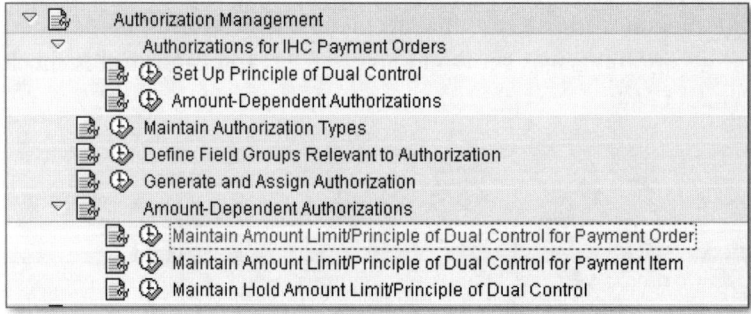

Figure 6.53 IHC Authorization Management

Options for creating authorization types are shown in Figure 6.54.

Name of Activity
Maintain Authorization Types - Account
Maintain Authorization Types - Conditions
Maintain Authorization Types - Payment Order
Maintain Authorization Types - Payment Item
Maintain Authorization Types - Standing Orders
Maintain Authorization Types - Means of Payment Management

Figure 6.54 Authorization Types for Use for IHC

6.4.7 Controls for IHC

Because the IHC component uses all of the functionality relating to regular banking and payment processing, all of the key controls relating to these as discussed in Chapter 3 and Chapter 4 apply. However, a few additional controls need to be considered to ensure full compliance with SOX and country specific requirements:

- Thoroughly test the entire accounting, clearing and reconciliation cycle to ensure that the books of record accurately reflect all of the company's inter-company transactions. The IHC component makes full use of technical and bank clearing accounts for inter-company transactions as well as for transfers to financial accounting.
- Clear all inter-company netting, pooling, and cash concentration arrangements with the organization's legal and tax departments for relevant country-specific regulations.
- Test all inbound and outbound file transmissions to ensure the integrity, security, and accuracy of internal and external transactions.
- Ensure master data is complete and that all transactions are reflected in cash management reports and the financial books of record.

6.5 Summary

This chapter covered all of the components required for putting together a daily cash positioning report, as well as the longer term liquidity forecast. The integrated cash management reports are based on postings from intraday and prior day bank statements, as well as information already recorded within the system, based on planning levels and groups tied to all cash flow-relevant transactions posted in the system. In addition, the forecast can be updated with manual entries through the use of planning types. We also looked at how intragroup transactions are accounted for using the IHC component, and how these can be integrated into cash management reporting.

The last three chapters covered all of the key elements of electronic banking and cash management. The next two chapters will focus on the other major area of treasury management: financial risk management.

This chapter covers foreign exchange (FX) risk management and derivatives. It also covers related transaction management, hedge management and accounting, payment processing, and market data integration.

7 Financial Risk Management: Foreign Exchange and Derivatives

Financial risk management is a major area of responsibility for most treasury departments, where controls, compliance, and decision support are of critical importance and are key drivers for utilizing the full range of functionality available within the SAP ERP system.

We are all familiar with the story of the rogue trader who brought down a 150-year-old bank because he had unrestricted system authority and access, enabling him to execute unauthorized trades and also cover his tracks. In the area of financial risk management, it is of utmost importance that strong controls are built into the entire financial supply chain. SAP ERP is the prime book of accounting record, and the earlier financial transactions are recorded in the system, the greater the opportunity for building in systemic, preventative, and detective controls as they flow through the financial supply chain. By the time a transaction reaches the settlement stage in a bank account, it should only need reconciliation and matching, and action for any exceptional unreconciled items.

Decision support is another area in financial risk management where timely, dynamic, real-time information is required on a daily basis to execute foreign currency and hedging transactions to meet the operating and risk mitigation requirements of the business.

In this chapter, we will review the key controls for foreign exchange management, using examples of forward exchange and currency option transactions to illustrate the functionality available in SAP ERP.

FX Risk Management

With the increasing globalization of business, the financial risk management of FX is becoming an important facet of a treasury department's responsibilities. FX risk management is a daily activity in most global corporations. FX markets are open 24 hours a day and corporations who make, buy, and sell products throughout the world are exposed to changes in currency exchange rates. To mitigate net foreign exchange exposures, U.S.-based companies typically hedge their exposures by purchasing forward or option contracts so that any potential adverse impact of movements in currency exchange rates on non-dollar value denominated revenues will at least be partially offset by an associated increase in the value of the option or forward. Companies also execute spot FX transactions for their immediate FX requirements. Forward exchange transactions are longer dated transactions.

SoD

Relative to other corporate payments such as accounts payable, financial risk management transactions tend to be high-value, low-volume, and typically will need senior level approval prior to execution and payment. SOD between front office, back office, and accounting is of paramount importance in the design and establishment of business process for these transactions.

STP

The execution of financial risk management transactions within SAP ERP is designed for a high level of automation and STP. This also enables a variety of systemic controls to be built into the process to ensure compliance with SOX and other regulatory and financial disclosure requirements.

Hedge Management and Accounting

Accounting for derivatives and financial risk management transactions, and compliance with the related FAS 133 requirements, is an area of ongoing challenge for treasury departments. We will review the functionality available within SAP ERP for compliance with FAS 133 requirements, should the organization decide to use hedge accounting for derivative transactions.

Financial Risk Management: Foreign Exchange and Derivatives | **7**

> **Note**
> FAS 133, issued by the Financial Accounting Standards Board (FASB) in the U.S., establishes accounting and reporting standards for derivative instruments and hedging activities.

Master Data

Master data plays a particularly important role in financial risk management transactions within SAP ERP. The different types of master data are used in conjunction with each other to build in appropriate controls and to provide information that defaults into transactions being processed. This enhances automation and integration.

The next section covers the specific functionality SAP ERP offers with respect to FX management.

FSCM and Risk Management

All of the financial risk management functionality within SAP ERP can be accessed through the FSCM menu, as partially shown in Figure 7.1. The menu path is APPLICATION • ACCOUNTING • FINANCIAL SUPPLY CHAIN MANAGEMENT • TREASURY AND RISK MANAGEMENT • TRANSACTION MANAGER.

The TRANSACTION MANAGER is a section of the FSCM area that enables all transaction management for the different modules, using a standard menu format divided into front office, back office, and accounting functions in addition to utilities, tools, and reporting capabilities.

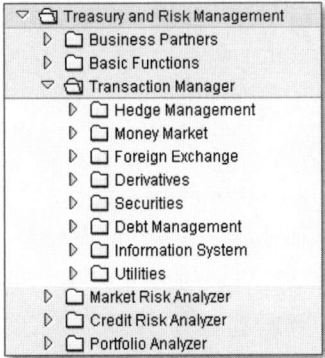

Figure 7.1 FSCM Menu Options

281

FX and Derivatives Functionality in SAP ERP

The menu options under HEDGE MANAGEMENT and FOREIGN EXCHANGE transaction management are shown in Figure 7.2. In this chapter, we will review how the key functionality available in these areas can be used from a controls perspective to enable compliance with SOX as a transaction flows through the financial supply chain.

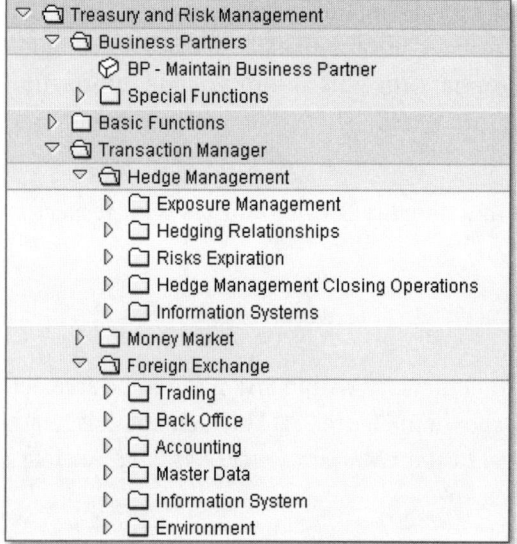

Figure 7.2 Transaction Manager, Hedge Management and Foreign Exchange Application Menu

7.1   Master Data for FX Transaction Management

The master data for FX transaction management comprises all of the key BPs involved in the execution of an FX trade, such as counterparties, brokers, banks, and traders. The actual trade instruments, such as foreign exchange spot, forward transactions, or currency options are called *product types*. Finally, there are certain types of master data required to comply with accounting rules, enable automatic transaction processing, and facilitate reporting functionality. We will now discuss each of these types of master data, and how they are used in transaction processing. The menu path in the configuration menu (IMG) for master data setup and authorization settings are shown in Figure 7.3.

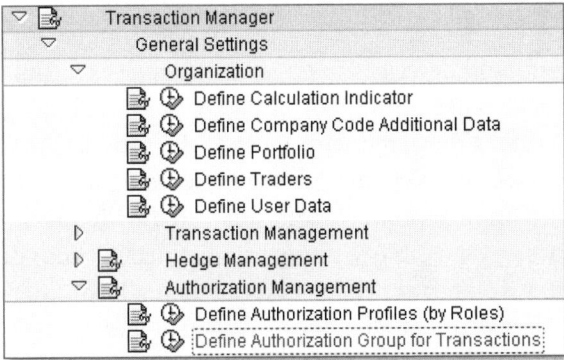

Figure 7.3 Organization Setup for Transaction Management

7.2 Master Data for Transaction Processing

The master data for transaction management is linked through a hierarchical structure that provides for integration and control through assignment and individual settings. This structure is common for all transaction management processing within the FSCM suite of applications, and is shown in Figure 7.13.

7.2.1 Product Categories

The highest level in the hierarchy is called *product category* and is system-delivered with functions and settings that are relevant and specific to the products that can be created under that particular category. A list of product categories is shown in Figure 7.4. For example, all FX products will be automatically linked to product category 600, and will inherit all of the functions and features of that group.

530	Commercial Paper	5
540	Cash flow transaction	5
550	Interest rate instrument	5
560	Facility	5
600	Foreign exchange	4
610	CAP/FLOOR	6
620	SWAP	6
630	FRA	6

Figure 7.4 System-Delivered Product Categories

7.2.2 Product Types

The next level is called product type and describes the treasury products available in the system. Examples of product types are shown in Figure 7.5. Depending on the release version, SAP ERP comes delivered with most of the products that are typically used in treasury transactions. New products are also being added as newer versions become available. Although products come delivered with the system, unlike with product categories, it is possible to create user-defined versions of standard product types, by copying a standard version and re-naming it for internal purposes. For example, you can use the product type called cash flow transaction as a building block to create a custom product type that uses the functionality of the generic cash flow transaction product type. Product types are created under their specific product category.

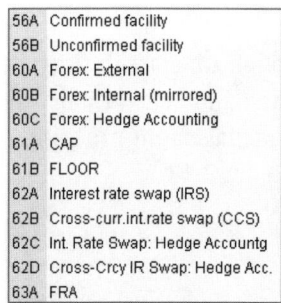

56A	Confirmed facility
56B	Unconfirmed facility
60A	Forex: External
60B	Forex: Internal (mirrored)
60C	Forex: Hedge Accounting
61A	CAP
61B	FLOOR
62A	Interest rate swap (IRS)
62B	Cross-curr.int.rate swap (CCS)
62C	Int. Rate Swap: Hedge Accountg
62D	Cross-Crcy IR Swap: Hedge Acc.
63A	FRA

Figure 7.5 Product Types in FX Management

7.2.3 Transaction Types

Transaction types describe the action being executed with respect to a specific product type, for example the purchase or sale of an FX contract. Transaction types need to be assigned to a product type, as shown in Figure 7.6.

11D	100	Purchase
11D	200	Sale
16A	100	Purchase
16A	200	Sale
51A	100	Investment
51A	200	Borrowing
51B	100	Investment
51B	200	Borrowing
52A	100	Investment
52A	200	Borrowing

Figure 7.6 Assigning Transaction Types to Product Types

Specific settings for each transaction type can be configured through selecting and drilling down into the transaction type, as shown in Figure 7.7.

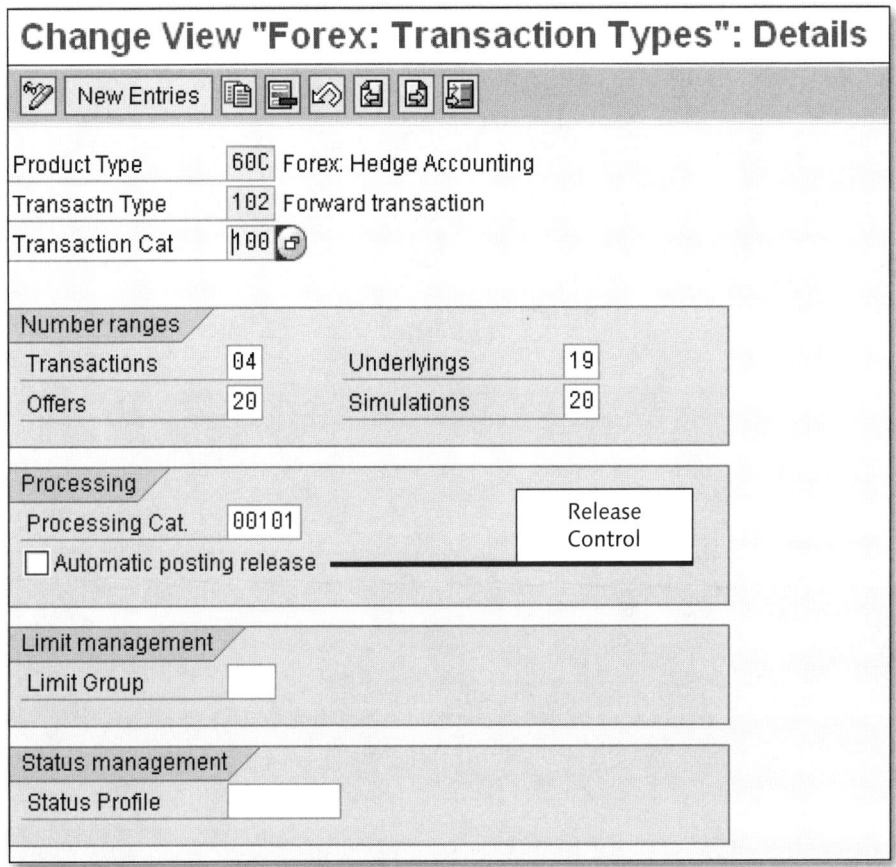

Figure 7.7 Controls for Transaction Type

An important setting is the AUTOMATIC POSTING RELEASE check box shown in Figure 7.7. If this checkbox is unchecked, the system will require a release authorization prior to accounting and payment processing. For example, as shown in Figure 7.8, a contract has been created and settled, and now needs to be released before it can proceed to the next step. Using this feature to build in SOD provides an important control mechanism. The automation and integration of this feature with workflow is discussed in Section 7.7, Transaction Management.

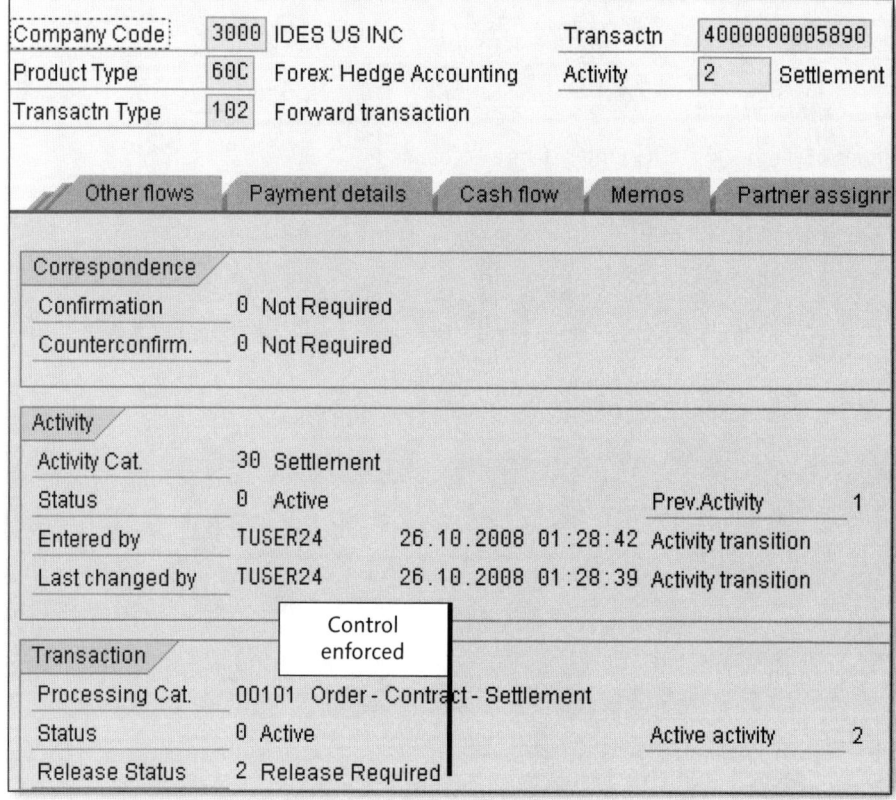

Figure 7.8 Using Release Functionality to Enhance SoD Controls

7.2.4 Flow Types

Flow types describe payment flows that result from transaction execution, valuation, accrual and deferral functions, and transfer postings. For example, the purchase of FX results in payment flows and is designated by flow type (FTYP) 1000, as shown in Figure 7.9.

FTyp	Name	Flow Category
0010	Forex transaction charge	Other Flow/Condition
1000	Buy foreign exchange	Principal Increase
1031	Cash settlement	Cash Settlement
2000	Sell foreign exchange	Principal Increase
2030	Internal flow acc./def. swap	Accrual/Deferral for Diff.Proc
3010	Realized loss (forex)	Realized Forex Loss
3011	Realized gain (forex)	Realized Forex Gain
3020	Create provision	Create Provision
3021	Reverse provision	Reverse Provision
3030	Show unrealized gain	Show Unrealized Gains
3031	Reverse unrealized gain	Write Back Unrealized Gains
3050	Acc./def. swap expenses FET	Acc./Def. Forex Swap Expenses
3051	Acc./def. swap revenue FET	Acc./Def. Forex Swap Revenue
3052	Reverse acc./def.swap expenses	Reverse Acc./Def.Swap Expenses
3053	Reverse acc./def.swap revenue	Reverse Acc./Def.Swap Revenue

Figure 7.9 Flow Types in Transaction Management

Flow types have individual settings to specify their relevancy to cash flow, accounting and valuation, and payment management, as shown in Figure 7.10.

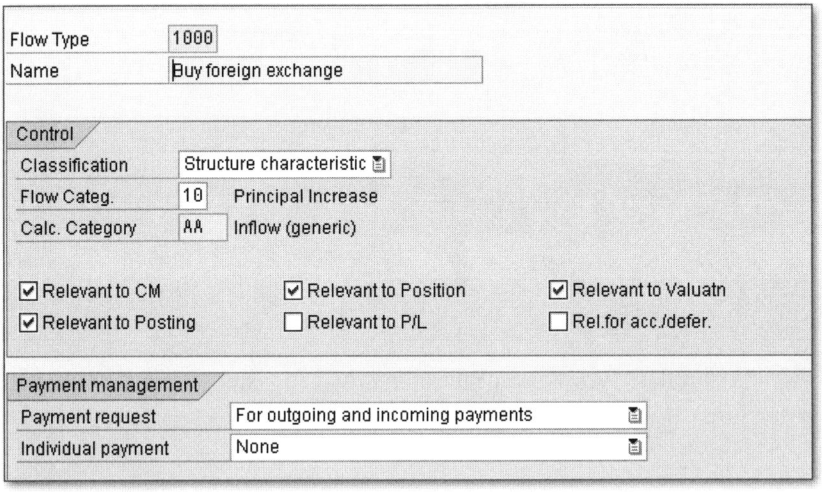

Figure 7.10 Individual Flow Type Settings

Flow types need to be assigned to product types, as shown in Figure 7.11.

PTyp	Prod.type desc.	TTyp	Name of Transaction	FTyp
60A	Forex: External	101	Spot transaction	0010
60A	Forex: External	101	Spot transaction	1000
60A	Forex: External	101	Spot transaction	2000
60A	Forex: External	102	Forward transaction	0010

Figure 7.11 Assigning Flow Types to Product Types

These master data and configuration settings provide strong systemic controls when they are used in transaction processing because they control transaction functionality. For example, if a flow type is not set up for outbound payment requests, any transaction that has that flow type will not be able to generate an outbound payment request.

7.2.5 Update Types

Update types are a key link between transaction management and valuation, accounting, and position management. They can also be identified as relevant for cash management purposes, as shown in Figure 7.12.

Update Type	CM relevant	Update Type Text
DE1000	✓	Forward Purchase
DE1001+	✓	Reverse Repo: Spot Purchase
DE1001-	✓	Reverse Repo: Spot Purchase
DE1002+	✓	Reverse Repo: Forward Sale
DE1002-	✓	Reverse Repo: Forward Sale
DE1010+	✓	Forward Accrued Interest +
DE1010-	✓	Forward Accrued Interest -

Update Type Details

Figure 7.12 Update Type Examples

The links between update types and other elements of master data are explained in the next section.

7.2.6 Links Between Transaction Management and Accounting

Key links between the various elements of master data in transaction processing and accounting are shown in Figure 7.13. These links are created through configuration settings, and enable automation of end-to-end processes. They also facilitate the setup of built-in, systemic, and configurable controls throughout the process. Automatic account determination is one of the key control features available in almost all areas of SAP ERP. The separation of account determination from transaction processing safeguards companies against error and fraud through manipulation of the books of record.

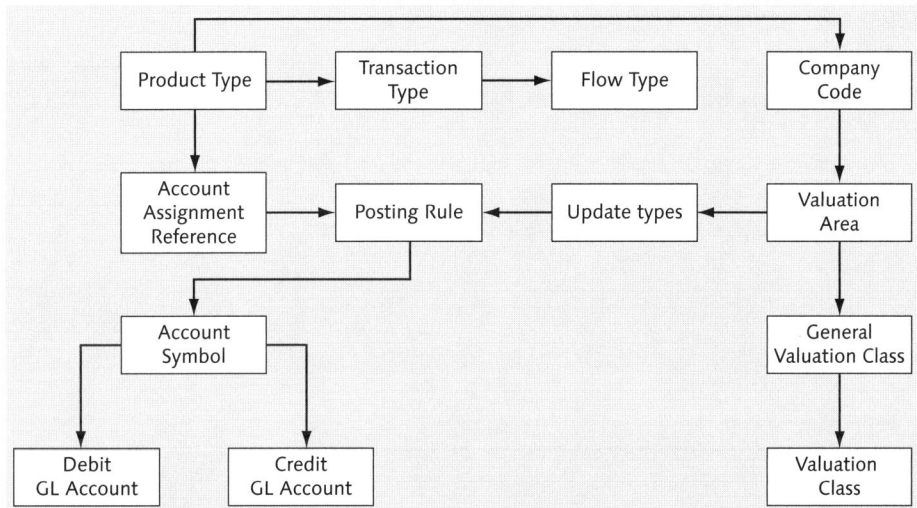

Figure 7.13 Links Between Transaction Management and Accounting

Most of the master data items that are used in the transaction processing flow come delivered with default values. These can be changed or copied to enable a certain amount of customizing specific to organizational requirements.

7.3 Master Data for Transaction Management

The BP is a central component in transaction management processing in SAP ERP, especially in the area of financial risk management. It is set up using roles to call up specific functionality relevant to that role. It is created initially in the role of *general BP* and then extended to other roles, which may be generic or company code-specific.

7.3.1 Business Partner (BP)

The BP concept enables the use of data for different purposes, at the same time enabling the sharing of common data and ensuring that it is only entered once in the system. This eliminates redundant or duplicated data, and eliminates having to maintain different versions of the same master data separately.

Create BP

A BP is created — or can be edited — using Transaction BP. The initial setup of a BP results in the creation of a GENERAL BUSINESS PARTNER, as shown in Figure 7.14.

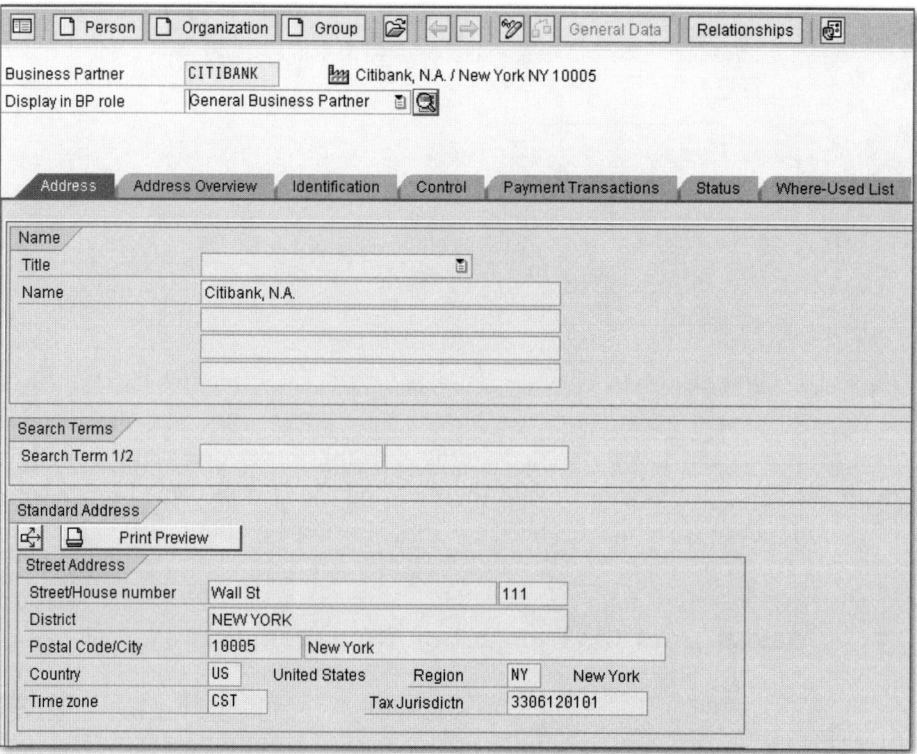

Figure 7.14 Create General BP with Transaction BP

After the General BP has been set up, it can be extended to different roles. Typical treasury roles are COUNTERPARTY, DEPOSITORY BANK, MAIN LOAN PARTNER, and ISSUER, as shown in Figure 7.15. Key roles such as counterparty are company code-specific; thus, different levels of access, payment options, and authorizations can be set up specific to legal entities that are represented as company codes in SAP ERP.

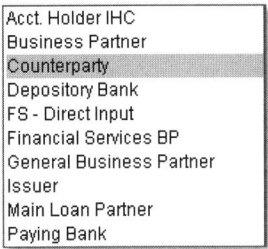

Figure 7.15 Typical Treasury Roles for BPs

Function-specific data is entered on tabs in the BP screen, as shown in Figure 7.16. In this example, the tab PAYMENT TRANSACTIONS is used to enter banking information relating to the GENERAL BUSINESS PARTNER.

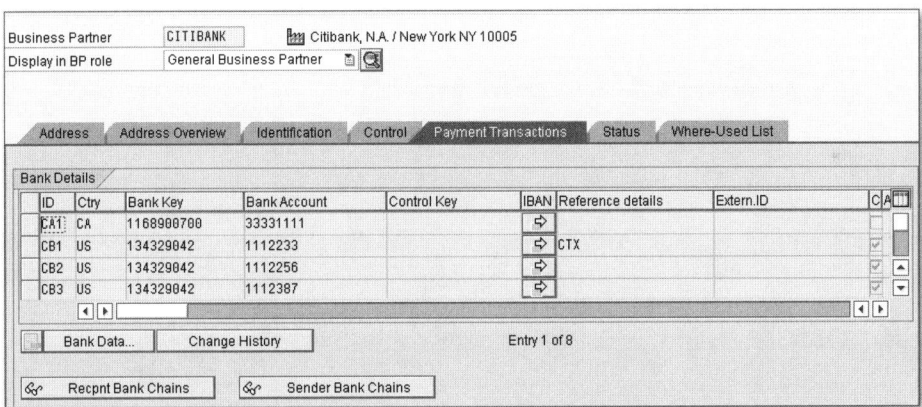

Figure 7.16 Configuring Banking Information in the General BP Screen

The BP can now be extended for specific roles.

Create BP in Role Counterparty

Additional roles are created using Transaction BP. To do so, access the General BP role and then use the change mode to create additional roles, as shown in Figure 7.17.

7 | Financial Risk Management: Foreign Exchange and Derivatives

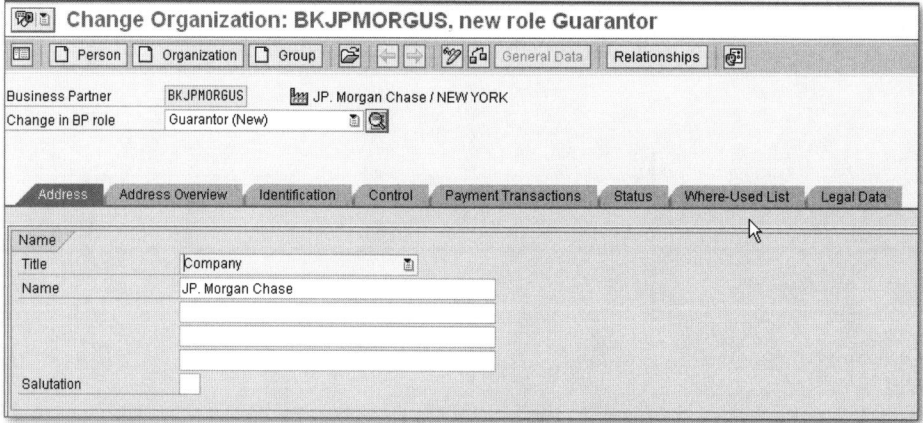

Figure 7.17 Creating a New Role for BP Using Change Mode

After you create the new role, appropriate function tabs for the role will be available to let you configure additional data settings. For example, as shown in Figure 7.18, the role COUNTERPARTY lets you enter company code-specific information, such as payment and banking information, on the PAYMENT DETAILS tab.

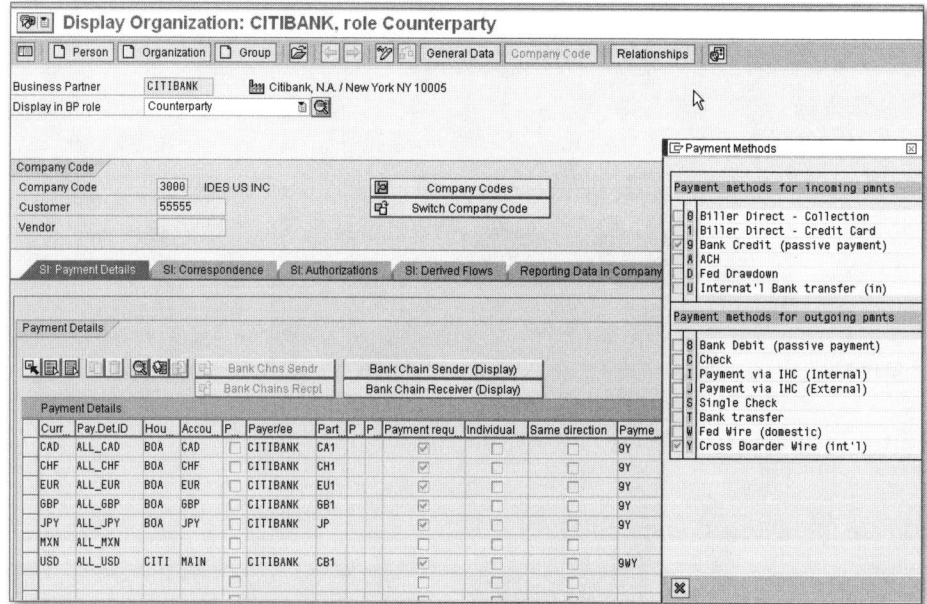

Figure 7.18 Role Counterparty Company Code-Specific Settings

The role counterparty is used for the execution of trade and payment transactions between the company represented by the company code and the BP. Payment information entered here will default into the trade transactions. Segregating duties between persons creating or changing master data and persons executing trade and payment transactions is a powerful control mechanism. For example, as shown in Figure 7.18, banking payment information is set up with specific parameters such as payment methods permitted, or whether payment requests are allowed for that bank account.

Additional BP Control Settings

Because BP counterparties are required for trade execution, additional control features are available that further strengthen controls for transaction processing.

One very important control is the ability to assign bank payment accounts to specific product types. This assignment is only possible at the company code level so that you can establish different control settings for each company code within the same organization. This assignment takes place by selecting a bank account, and then assigning the bank account to authorized product types. The detailed assignment steps were covered earlier in Chapter 2.

It is also possible to assign the BP to authorized product types at a higher level than the bank account, as shown in tab in Figure 7.19.

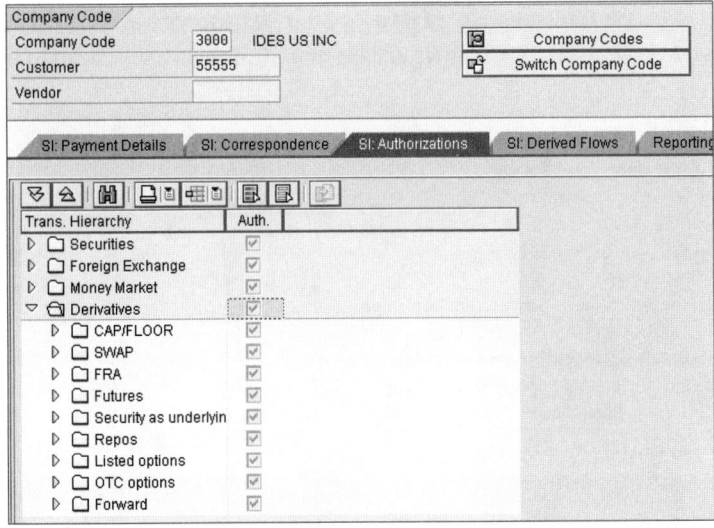

Figure 7.19 Authorize BP for Product Types

Similar functionality is available in other screens, such as setting up CORRESPONDENCE options by product types, as shown in Figure 7.20.

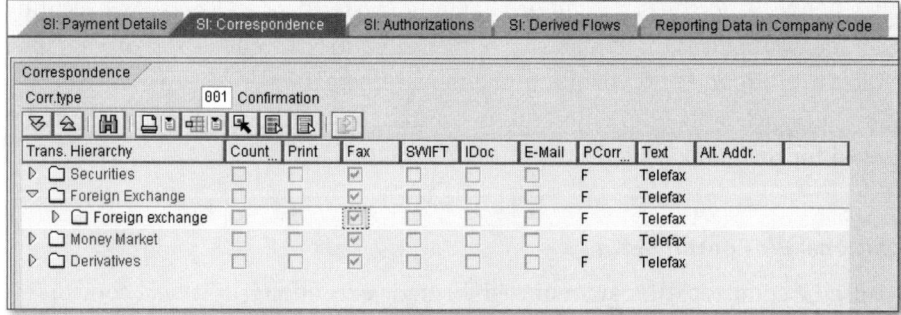

Figure 7.20 Assigning Product Types to Correspondence Options

Create Authorization Group

Authorization groups are available to control access to specific groups of BPs. This topic was covered in detail in Chapter 2.

BP Link to Vendor/Customer

A useful feature in the Application menu is the ability to link BPs with vendors and customers already set up in the SAP ERP system. The menu path for accessing this functionality is APPLICATION: ACCOUNTING • FINANCIAL SUPPLY CHAIN MANAGEMENT • TREASURY AND RISK MANAGEMENT • BUSINESS PARTNERS • SPECIAL FUNCTIONS, as partially shown in Figure 7.21.

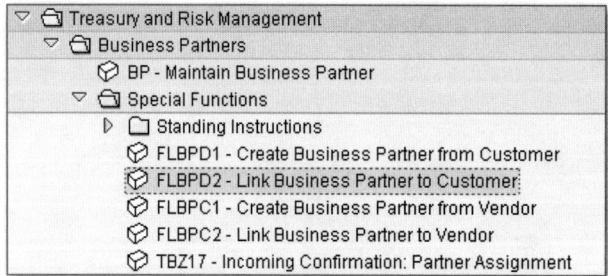

Figure 7.21 Linking BPs to Existing Customer or Vendor

7.3.2 Trader

Traders execute front office functions, and need to be set up and authorized for specific product types and transactions. Strict SOD must be built in to ensure that a trader does not have access to creating or changing master data, or the ability to execute back office or accounting functions.

The creation of a trader and the assignment to product categories and product types was covered in Chapter 2.

7.3.3 Bank-Related Master Data

All financial risk management transactions will involve some form of inbound or outbound payments and banking activity. Appropriate house bank and bank account information needs to be set up. These have been covered in the earlier chapters on inbound and outbound electronic banking, Chapter 3 and Chapter 4.

If wire payments are used for settlement of transactions, repetitive codes will need to be set up for specific combinations of BP and bank account. The creation and assignment of repetitive codes was covered in Chapter 4. The correct setup and release sequence for repetitive codes must be followed, because validation controls will reject a transaction if the release protocols are not followed.

For example, a repetitive code that is released after a trade transaction has already been created will result in an error message. Figure 7.22 shows the release details. The error message that displays when trying to save the transaction is shown in Figure 7.23.

Column	Contents
Repetitive Code	123456
Paying company code	3000
House Bank	3000
Account ID	3000
Business partner reference	CITIBANK
Bank Country	US
Bank Key	134329042
Bank Details	CB2
Bank Account	1112256
Payment Method	W
Currency	USD
Name of Business Partner Category	Central Business Partner
Target Company Code	3000
Created on	23.10.2008
Created by	TUSER24
Release date	23.10.2008
Released by	TUSER24
G/L Account	113402

Figure 7.22 Repetitive Code Release Details

Figure 7.23 Systemic Check and Rejection of a Transaction

7.4 Master Data for Accounting, Valuation, and Reporting

The reporting and classification of transactions is a key element of transaction processing and decision making. This is facilitated by using several types of master data for this purpose.

7.4.1 Portfolio

The *portfolio* is user-defined, and created to match the organization's portfolio of open contracts, investment, debt, and so on. It is set up specific to a COMPANY CODE, as shown in Figure 7.24.

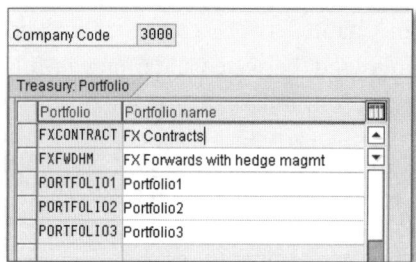

Figure 7.24 Create a Portfolio for Reporting and Classification

7.4.2 Valuation Areas

Valuation areas let you create different versions of accounting, position management, and valuation of transactions, based on the accounting principles in use for a particular country, region, or accounting body for regulatory compliance and reporting purposes. VALUATION AREAS are shown in Figure 7.25.

Valuation Areas	
VA	Valuation area
001	Operational
002	IAS
003	US-GAAP
004	EUR

Figure 7.25 Valuation Areas Based on Accounting Standard Requirements

7.4.3 Market Data

Market data in the form of interest rates, foreign exchange rates, and volatilities will be required on a daily basis for transaction processing and valuation. Market data will be discussed further in Section 7.10, Market Data Management, and in Chapter 8, Investments and Debt Management.

7.5 Workflow Management

Workflow in SAP ERP in the context of treasury management can be defined as a set of tools and technologies that are made available to automate and facilitate control, approval, and processing of transactions electronically, as they flow through the integrated financial supply chain of an enterprise.

Figure 7.29 provides an example of how workflow can be built into an end-to-end process for an FX option contract. Workflow is activated through triggering events, which typically are executed transactions, or when a status change takes place, for example, from status active to released. A release procedure can be defined through IMG configuration as shown in Figure 7.26.

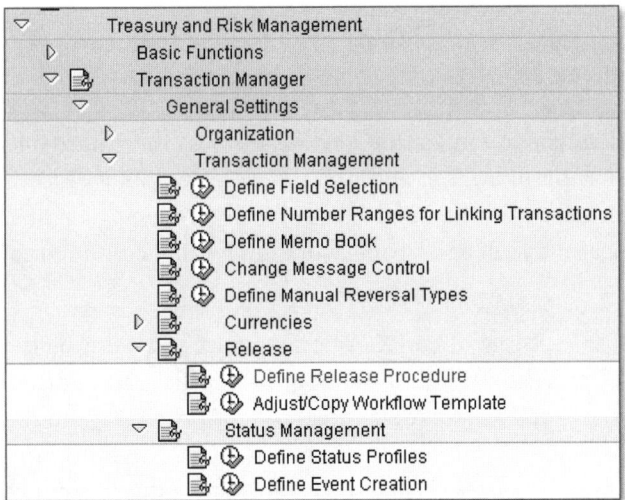

Figure 7.26 Workflow Configuration for Release Procedures

A release condition can be defined for a combination of product type (PTYP) and transaction type (TTYP), as shown in Figure 7.27.

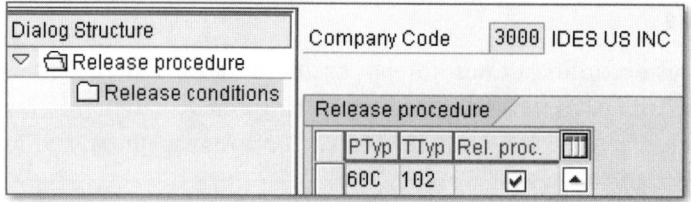

Figure 7.27 Release Procedure by Product Type

The number of release steps (REL. STEPS) can also be defined, depending on how strong the approval chain needs to be, as shown in Figure 7.28.

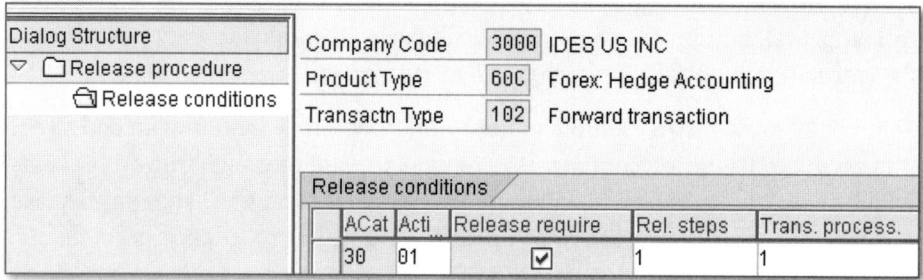

Figure 7.28 Configuring Release Conditions

7.6 Transaction Management

FX processing in SAP ERP lets you automate the key elements of the end-to-end process, allowing for STP. Furthermore, the appropriate use of workflow in this area enables key authorizations to be handled electronically, reducing manual intervention and the physical movement of paperwork, and enhancing internal controls for the process.

In this section, we will use an example of an FX option contract and describe the key steps in the end-to-end process, including trading, back office, accounting, settlement, hedge management, and market data integration. At each stage in the process, we will consider key handoff points, authorizations, SOD, and other controls that need to be built into the process. We will also introduce the concept of using workflow to automate the electronic approval process.

The business process flow consists of the following key steps:

1. The transaction is created.
2. The transaction is approved.
3. The transaction is settled.
4. The payment is approved.
5. The transaction is posted.
6. The transaction is paid.
7. The transaction is reconciled.

The end-to-end cycle of a trade execution using workflow is shown in Figure 7.29.

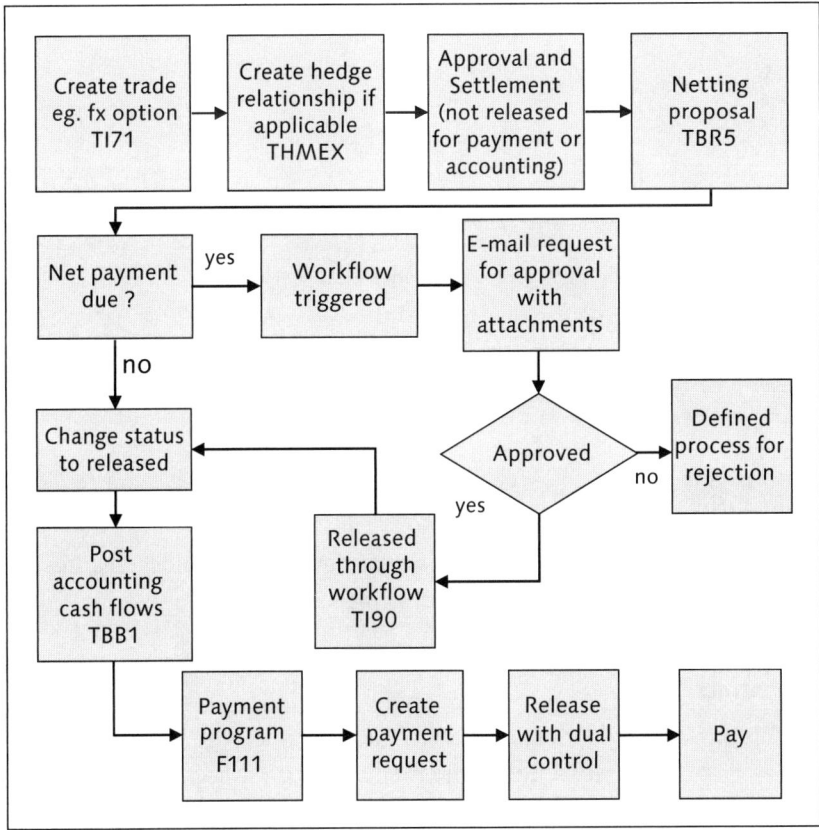

Figure 7.29 Trade Execution with Workflow

7.6.1 Transaction Management Menu

The transaction management menu is standard in the FSCM component in SAP ERP. The functionality is split between front office, back office, and accounting to enable proper SOD. The menu path for the application is shown in Figure 7.30. The common format between all of the different components in FSCM results in consistency and ease of use and training. It also provides opportunities for harmonization, where for example (as covered in the next section), a generic Transaction FTR_CREATE can be used to create transactions across components.

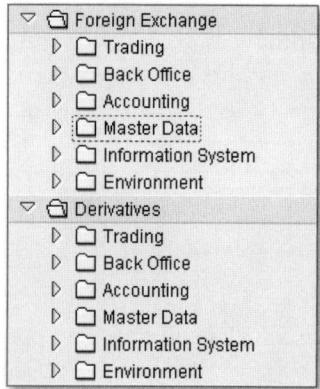

Figure 7.30 Transaction Manager Menu for FX and Derivatives

The functionality and control features that are available in transaction management in FSCM will be illustrated using the example of an FX option and an FX forward contract.

7.6.2 Front Office

The front office is typically responsible for evaluating offers and bids, creating initial FX or option contracts, or converting offers into contracts.

Creating a Contract

In keeping with the standard menu layout, SAP ERP provides a generic Transaction FTR_CREATE for creating transactions. The menu path is APPLICATION: ACCOUNTING • FINANCIAL SUPPLY CHAIN MANAGEMENT • TRANSACTION MANAGER • FOREIGN EXCHANGE • TRADING, as partially shown in Figure 7.31.

The menu option also allows contract-specific transactions to be created.

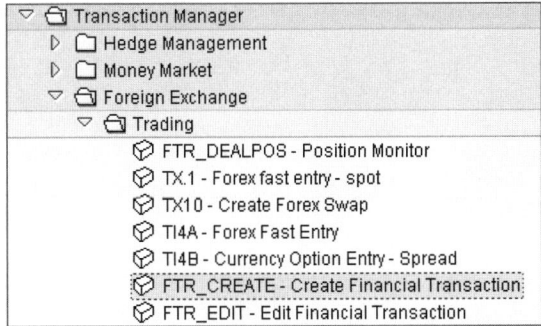

Figure 7.31 Transaction FTR_CREATE Menu Path

Transaction FTR_CREATE results in the initial input screen shown in Figure 7.32. In this example, an FX currency option contract is being created.

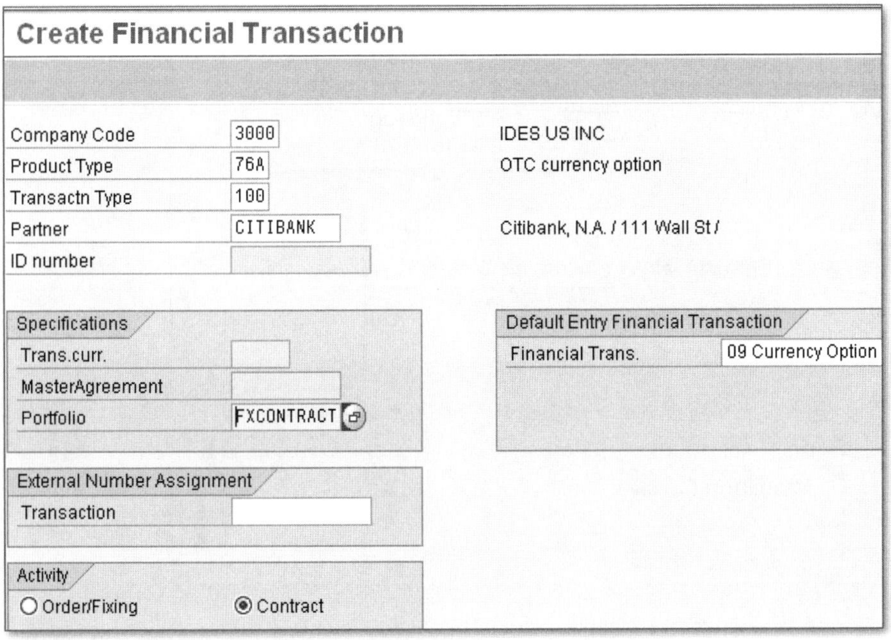

Figure 7.32 Create FX Option Contract with Transaction FTR_CREATE

Certain fields are mandatory, such as COMPANY CODE, PRODUCT TYPE, TRANSACTN TYPE and PARTNER. This enables the system to run the various validation checks that ensure that the transaction is allowed to be created.

Structure Tab

After accepting the initial parameters, the first transaction input area is the STRUCTURE tab shown in Figure 7.33. Here, key information relating to the contract is entered.

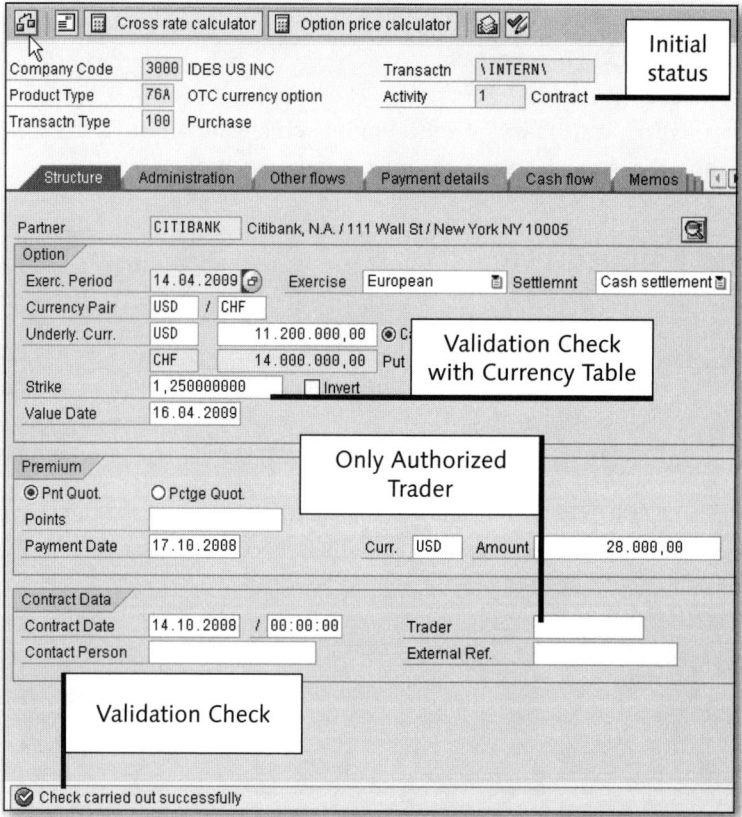

Figure 7.33 Parameters for FX Option Contract on the Structure Tab

After entering all of the parameters, an overall validation check can be run using the scale with boxes icon in the top left corner of the screen.

Administration Tab

The ADMINISTRATION tab controls important fields for entering accounting, classification, and reporting information, as shown in Figure 7.34.

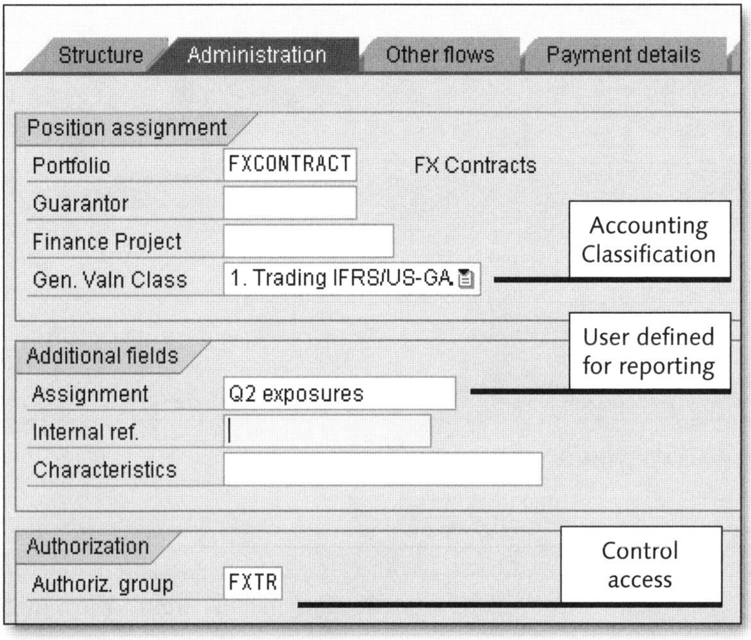

![Administration Tab screenshot showing Position assignment with Portfolio FXCONTRACT, FX Contracts, Gen. Valn Class 1. Trading IFRS/US-GA (Accounting Classification), Additional fields with Assignment Q2 exposures (User defined for reporting), and Authorization with Authoriz. group FXTR (Control access).]

Figure 7.34 Administration Tab Parameters

The transaction can be saved after running the check, as shown in Figure 7.33. This results in a message confirming the creation of the contract, as shown in Figure 7.35. All further references to this contract will be made through reference to this transaction number.

Figure 7.35 Option Contract Created with Transaction Number

Editing the Contract

All further processing of the contract can be accomplished using Transaction FTR_EDIT, using the input screen shown in Figure 7.36.

7 | Financial Risk Management: Foreign Exchange and Derivatives

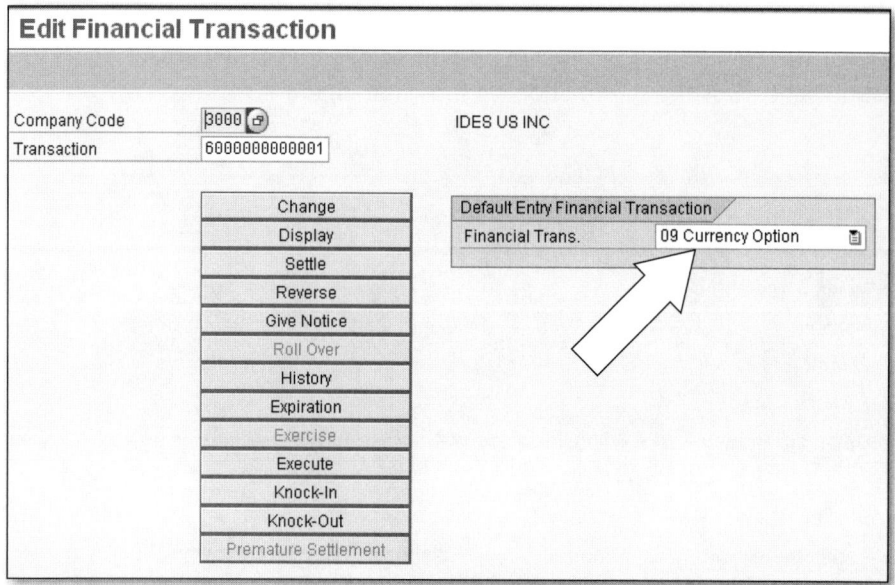

Figure 7.36 Transaction FTR_EDIT Used to Edit a Contract

The DEFAULT ENTRY FINANCIAL TRANSACTION input area (field FINANCIAL TRANS.) lets you select a particular type of contract, in this example CURRENCY OPTION. As a result, only the editing options relevant to that specific contract are highlighted (available). In the example in Figure 7.36, the options ROLL OVER, EXERCISE and PREMATURE SETTLEMENT are inactive and not available for use with CURRENCY OPTIONS.

Payment Details Tab

After the basic parameters are entered, most of the subsequent tabs are automatically populated, taking information from prior screens or defaulting information from master data and configuration settings. As shown in Figure 7.37, payment details for the payment of the currency option premium have defaulted on the PAYMENT DETAILS tab, based on the authorized settings in the BP master data for payments to the counterparty specified.

304

7.6 Transaction Management

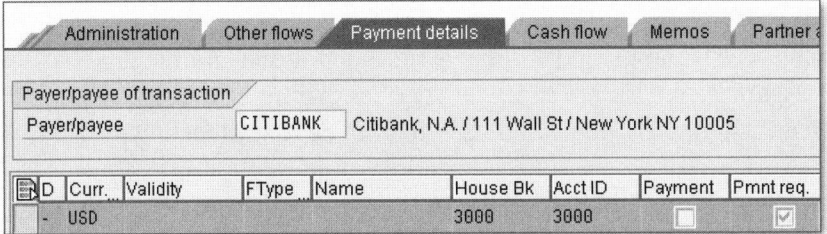

Figure 7.37 Payment Details Tab Information Defaulting From BP Master Data

Selecting the banking information line and double clicking on it provides additional details of the payment that was defaulted in from the authorized BP settings, as shown in Figure 7.38.

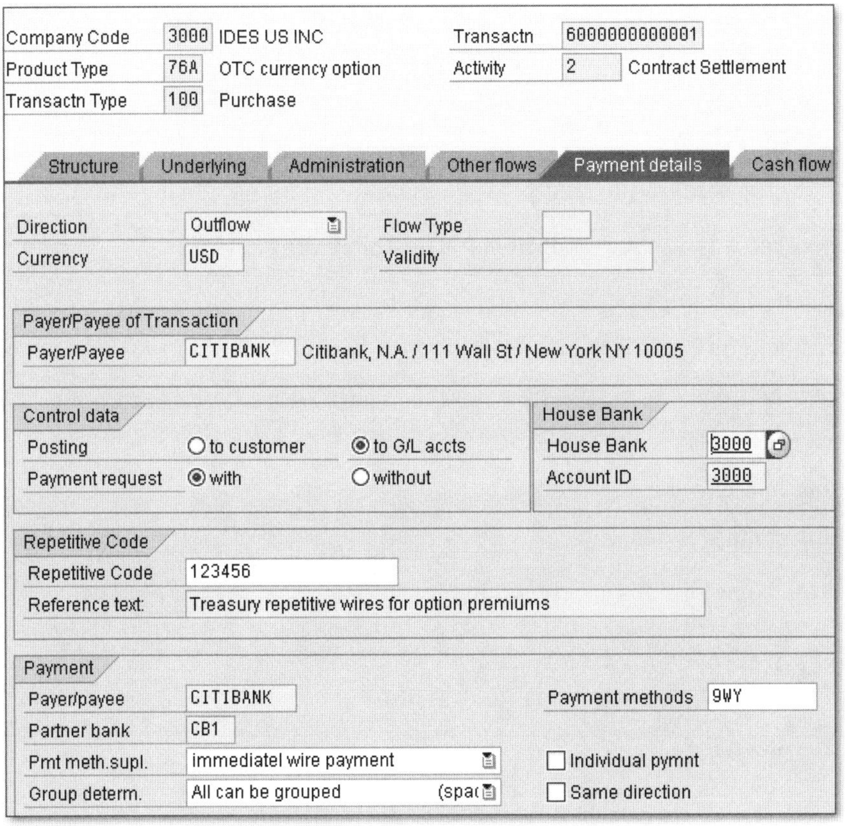

Figure 7.38 Payment Details Defaulted in From Authorized BP Settings

Cash Flow Tab

The CASH FLOW tab automatically displays the amount due and the due date, as shown in Figure 7.39. The lock indicator specifies that no further processing can take place until the transaction is settled. This is a key control feature.

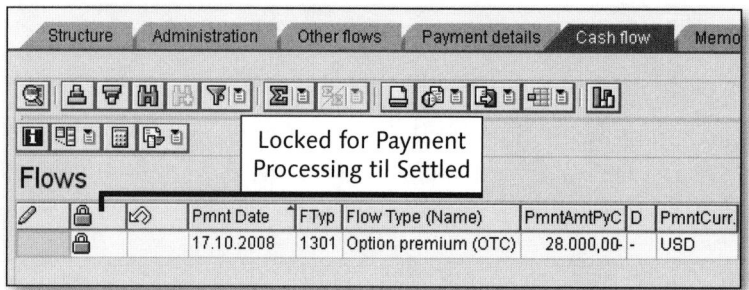

Figure 7.39 Cash Flow Tab Showing Option Premium Due and Date Due

7.6.3 Back Office

Back office processing is the next phase in the transaction processing life cycle.

The back office is typically responsible for the following activities:

- Settlement and control
- Contract and flow release
- Payment netting
- Contract reversals
- Creating references
- Creating confirmations

BACK OFFICE menu options are shown in Figure 7.40.

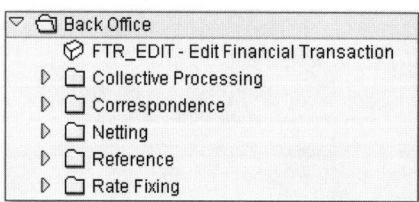

Figure 7.40 Back Office Menu Options

Settlement

One of the key functions of the back office is settling a contract using Transaction FTR_EDIT. When transaction settlement is set up as mandatory, the transaction can't be processed further until it is settled.

Status Tab

The STATUS tab provides information on the status of a transaction and what further actions may be required, as shown in Figure 7.41.

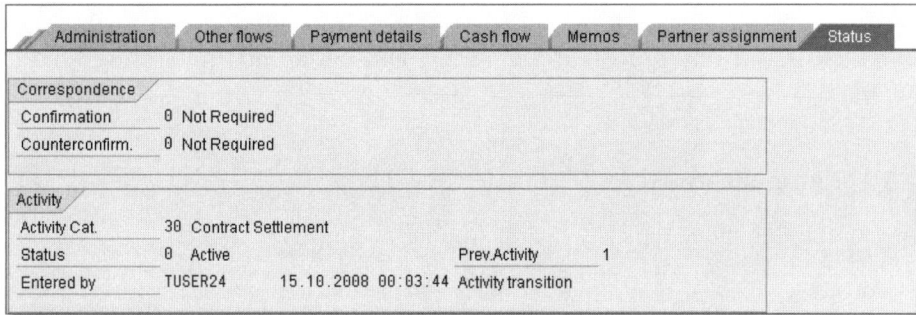

Figure 7.41 Status Management Through the Status Tab

When settlement is executed by the appropriate authorized user, cash flows are released, as indicated by the unlocked lock icon shown in Figure 7.42.

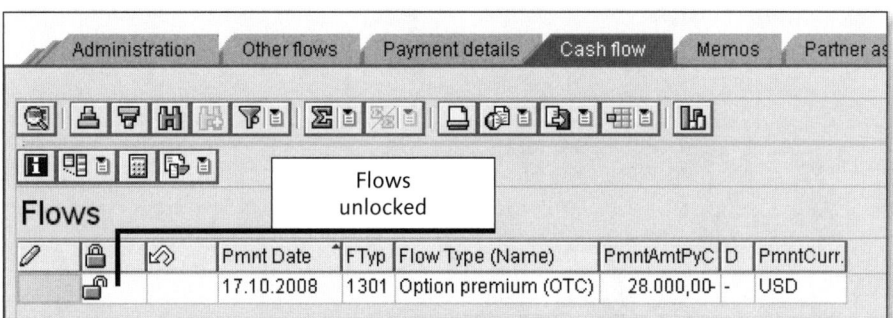

Figure 7.42 Cash Flows Unlocked After Settlement

The status of the transaction also moves to ACTIVITY 2 – CONTRACT SETTLEMENT, as shown in Figure 7.43.

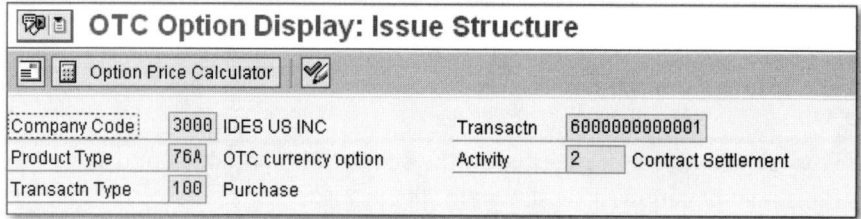

Figure 7.43 Contract Settled Status of Transaction

The final step in the process is accounting and period end processing for the contract.

7.6.4 Accounting

Accounting functions typically include the following key activities:

- Postings
- Payment activities
- Reversals
- Period end processing
- Valuation
- Accounting transfers

The ACCOUNTING menu options are shown in Figure 7.44.

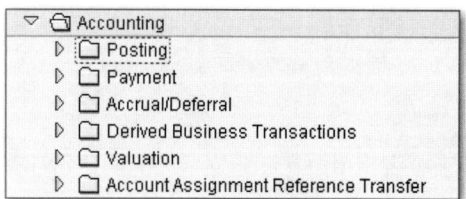

Figure 7.44 Accounting Application Menu Options

Posting

Postings are made through collective processing menu options that allow the system to propose valid postings for accounting and payment processing purposes. This will be covered in greater detail in Chapter 8.

Payment Processing

The FSCM transaction processing and payment program functionalities within the Accounting component in SAP ERP are tightly integrated. Payment processing has been covered in Chapter 4, and the transaction manager uses payment Transactions F110 or F111, depending on whether the accounting (accounts payable) or treasury department is initiating the payment run.

Month End Valuation

Valuation of open contracts at month end is required to comply with accounting compliance requirements that specify that open positions have to be valued at market value. Mark to market calculation and posting is accomplished using Transaction TPM60. SAP ERP uses the discounted cash flow concept to value contracts. Valuation and mark to market concepts will be reviewed in detail in Chapter 8.

A very important aspect of accounting in financial risk management transactions is compliance with hedge accounting rules, where relevant. The next section covers hedge management functionality in SAP ERP.

7.7 Hedge Management

FX options and forward contracts are a form of derivatives used in the context of financial risk management to reduce the possibility of loss, not to make a profit. The process of using a derivative to mitigate the possibility of loss is called *hedging*. Because the primary purpose of FX hedging for risk management is to protect the income statement from adverse fluctuations in exchange rates, companies

7 | Financial Risk Management: Foreign Exchange and Derivatives

using hedging like to use an accounting policy that matches the gain on the option contract with the loss on the underlying asset or cash flow being protected, or vice versa. This accounting policy is defined in FASB Statement 133 (FAS133) on accounting for derivatives, and specifies the conditions under which companies can use hedge accounting. It also specifies the compliance, disclosure, and documentation requirements if they do.

The following hedge management functionality is available in SAP ERP:

- Using exposure management.
- Linking hedging transactions to underlying hedged items.
- Classifying the appropriate hedge type (fair value or cash flow).
- Creating and storing hedge documentation.
- Determining the fair value of linked transactions.
- Tracking hedge effectiveness.
- Applying period end accounting procedures.
- Integrating hedging with cash management and other functional components.
- Providing detailed reporting.

An overview of the business process for hedge management is provided in Figure 7.45.

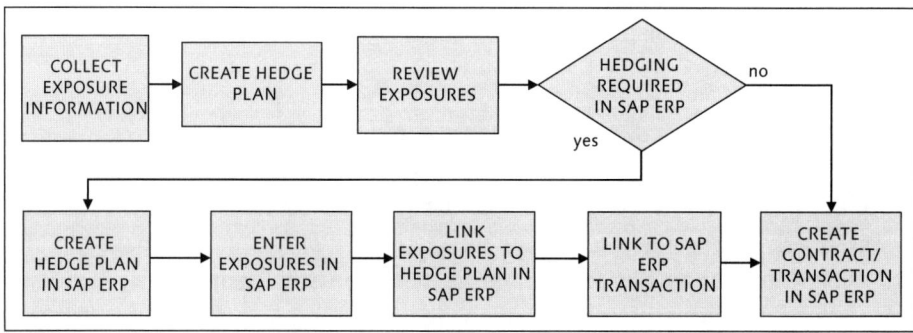

Figure 7.45 Hedge Management Process Overview

310

7.7.1 Hedge Management Menu Options

The menu path to and options under HEDGE MANAGEMENT are shown in Figure 7.46.

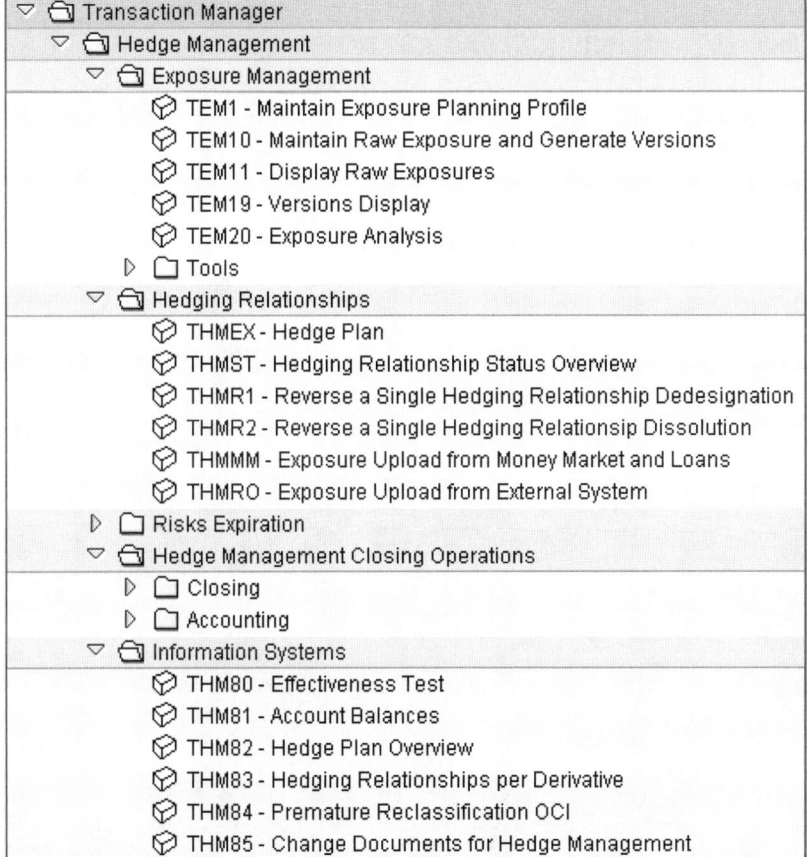

Figure 7.46 Hedge Management Application Menu

7.7.2 Hedge Management Steps

In this section, we will look at the key steps executed for hedge management in SAP ERP, illustrating integration and control features.

Hedge Plan Creation and Integration

Hedge management is accessed using Transaction THMEX. However, some product types such as FX forwards also have the HEDGE MANAGEMENT tab integrated with the Transaction Manager, as shown in Figure 7.47.

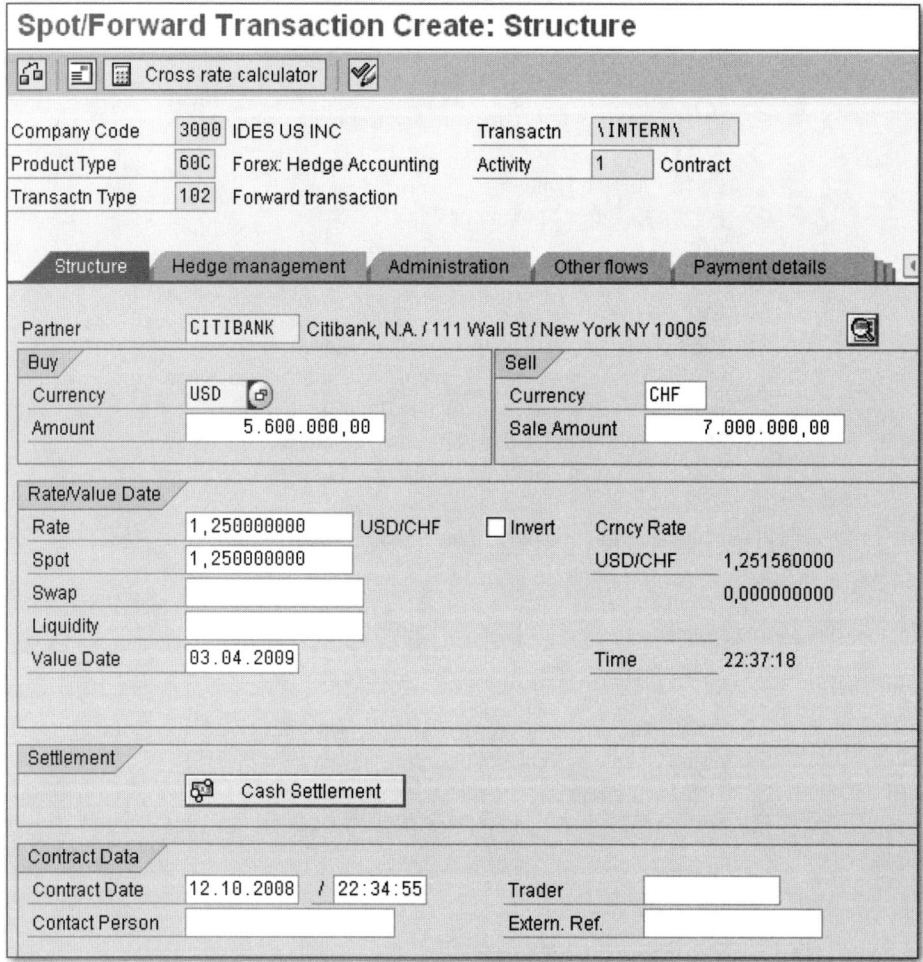

Figure 7.47 Creating an FX Forward with Hedge Accounting

After entering information on the STRUCTURE tab, shown in Figure 7.47, you can use the HEDGE MANAGEMENT tab to create a HEDGE PLAN, and enter EXPOSURE, HEDGE ITEM, and HEDGE RELATIONSHIP information, as shown in Figure 7.48.

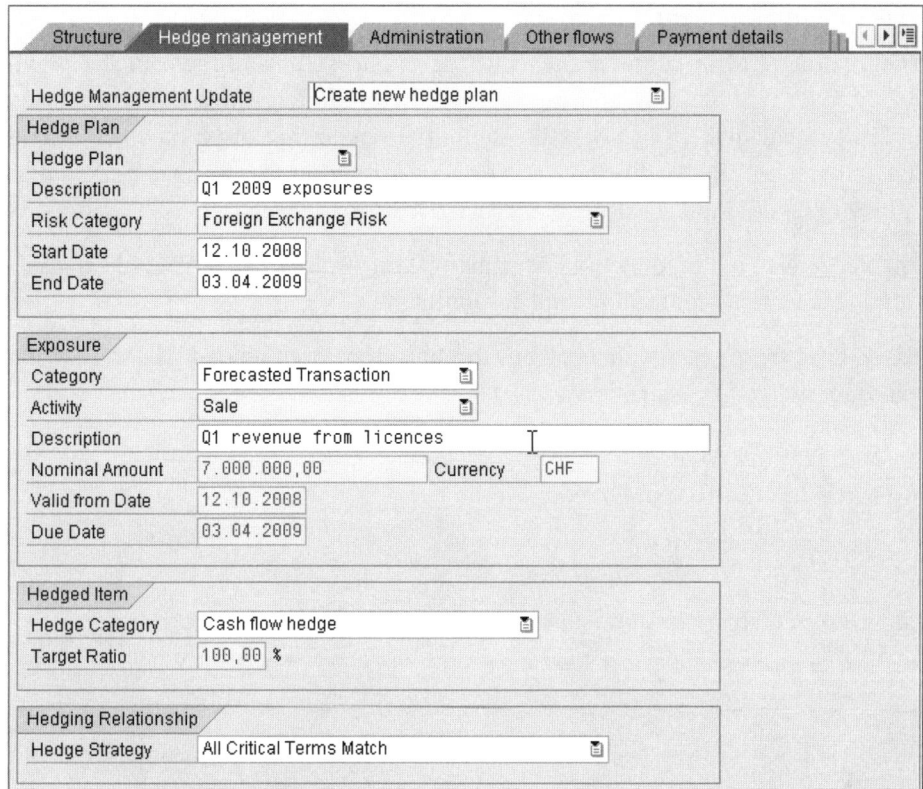

Figure 7.48 Create Hedge Management Information

After saving the transaction, the hedge plan is created with a HEDGE ITEM ID, as shown in Figure 7.49.

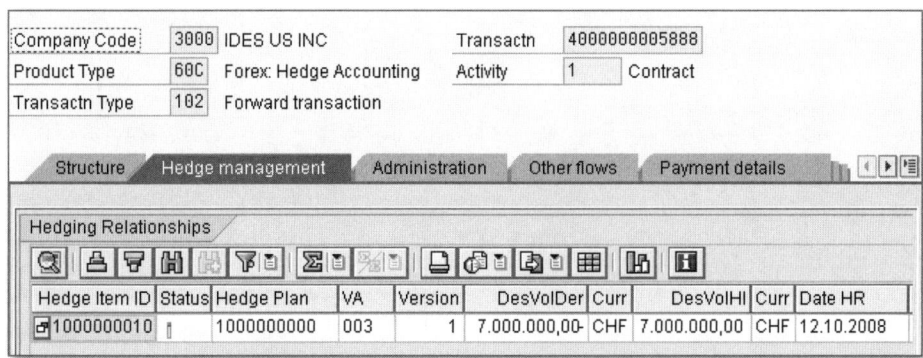

Figure 7.49 Hedge Plan Created for Product Type Forward Contract

Exposure Management

Transaction THMEX contains the same views and steps as shown in the previous product type screens, and can be used for product types that are supported by hedge management in SAP ERP. The initial screen that displays when executing Transaction THMEX, including relevant information that has been entered, is shown in Figure 7.50.

The hedge plan denoted by the hedge plan ID forms the basis for FAS133 transaction management, controlling, and accounting.

Exposures can be entered manually or through automated upload. The transaction exposure categories available are:

- Forecasted transaction: purchase or sale
- Firm commitment: purchase or sale
- Financial Assets/Liabilities

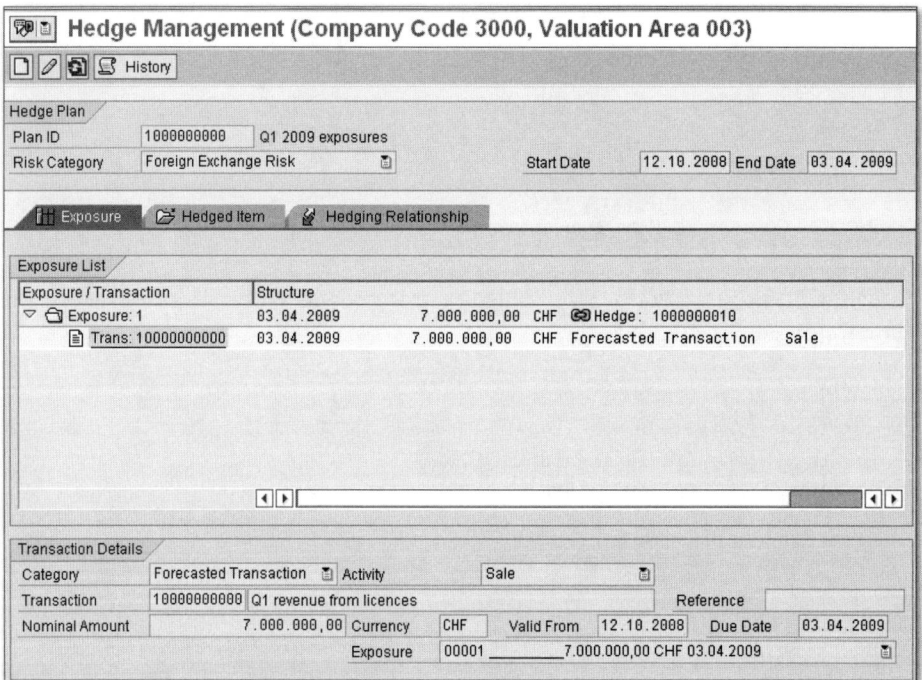

Figure 7.50 Creating a Hedge Plan Using Transaction THMEX

Hedging Categories

The HEDGED ITEM tab is used to enter the underlying HEDGE CATEGORY, which could be a CASH FLOW HEDGE, fair value hedge, or net investment in foreign subsidiary, depending on the type of exposure being hedged. The TARGET RATIO reflects the hedging strategy based on the approved guidelines set by the board or risk management committee of the organization. The actual ratio is calculated when a derivative transaction is created and linked to the exposure. The input screen is shown in Figure 7.51.

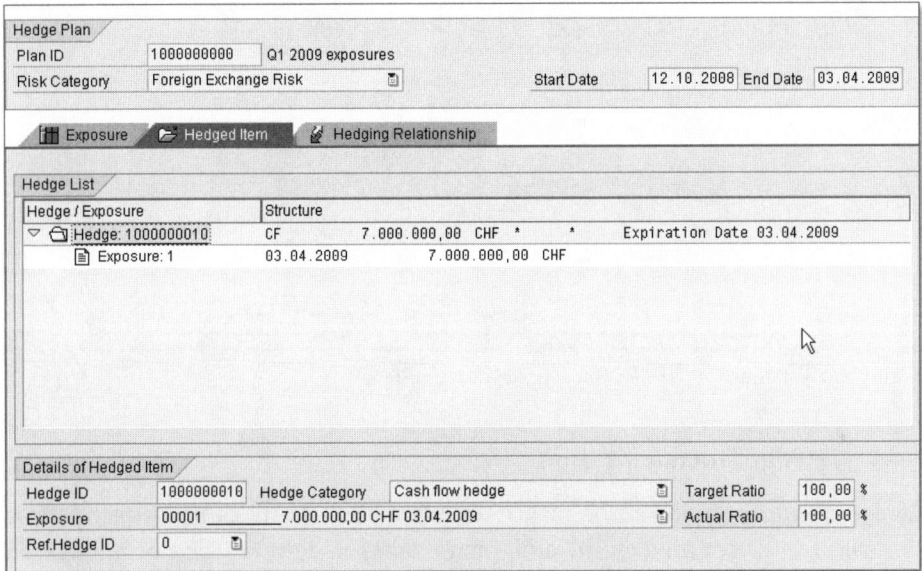

Figure 7.51 Transaction THMEX Hedged Item Tab Entry Screen

Hedging Relationship

The last step in the setup is to create the hedging relationship with the transaction number through the HEDGING RELATIONSHIP tab shown in Figure 7.52.

The SAP ERP system uses the information entered in this screen to calculate effectiveness testing based on the hedging strategy and effective dates.

7 | Financial Risk Management: Foreign Exchange and Derivatives

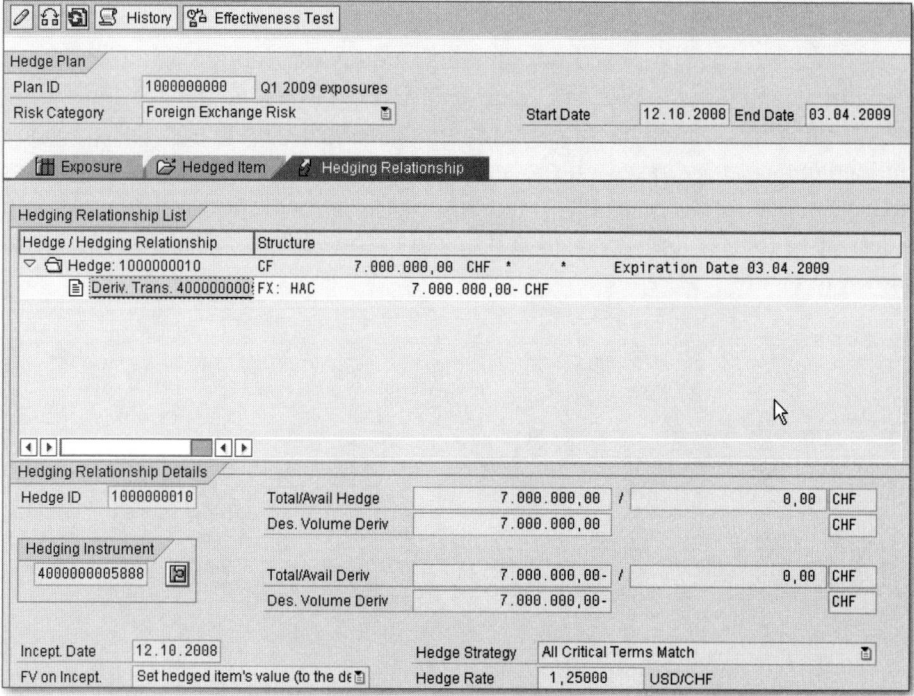

Figure 7.52 Transaction THMEX Hedging Relationship Tab

7.7.3 Hedge Documentation

Hedge documentation can be in PDF or other format and can be attached to a HEDGE PLAN ID for viewing by auditors or other reviewers. The documentation can be imported and attached or directly entered from Transaction THMEX, as shown in Figure 7.53.

Figure 7.53 Entering Hedge Documentation in Transaction THMEX

7.7.4 Hedge Accounting and Periodic Processing

The accounting for hedge management is fully integrated in the transaction management process described earlier. Specifically, the following features are available that create accounting entries based on the parameters entered in the hedge plan ID and the transaction manager:

- Valuation at inception of trade.
- Month end valuation of contracts and mark to market.
- Posting of unrealized gains and losses.
- Transfers between other comprehensive income or equity account (OCI) and P&L, on expiry or dedesignation or dissolution of hedge.
- Posting of realized gains and losses.
- Testing of effectiveness prior to executing accounting valuation.
- Changing the intrinsic value based on the results of effectiveness testing, if applicable.

7.8 Integration with Cash Management

The FSCM components are integrated with cash management reporting for daily cash positioning, as well as longer term cash forecasting and liquidity planning. FSCM uses planning levels the same way the remainder of the components link to cash management, as described in Chapter 6. Specifically, the link between transaction management in FSCM and cash management is made by assigning product types (PTYP) to planning levels (LEVEL), as shown in Figure 7.54.

Company Code	3000			
Treasury: Assign Planning Levels				
PTyp	Sta	ACat	Level (bank known)	Level (bank unknown)
51A	0	10	63	63
51A	0	20	63	63
51A	0	30	63	63
60A	0	10	EB	EP
60A	0	15	EB	EP
60A	0	20	EB	EP
60A	0	30	EB	EP

Figure 7.54 Integration of Product Types with Planning Levels

Examples of planning levels for FX transactions are shown in Figure 7.55.

D1	Cap banks	Cap banks
D2	Cap subledger	Cap SL
D3	Floor banks	Floor bnks
D4	Floor subledger	Floor SL
D5	Swap banks	Swap banks
D6	Swap subledger	Swap SL
D7	FRA banks	FRA banks
D8	FRA subledger	FRA SL
DA		
DB	Forex banks EXTERNAL	FX ext. B.
DC	Forex banks INTERNAL	FX int. B.
DD		
DE	Loan revenue	Loans
DI	General planning	Planned
DP	Forex subledger EXTERNAL	FX ext. SL
DQ	Forex subledger INTERNAL	FX int. SL
DT		
EB	Foreign Exchange (position)	Forex Deal
EP	Foreign Exchange (forecast)	Forex Open
ES	FX Spot transactions	FX Spot

Figure 7.55 Planning Levels in Treasury Risk Management

7.9 Market Data Management

Treasury management — especially in the financial risk management area — is a very dynamic function. Decisions around investing, borrowing, funds transfer, hedging, and foreign exchange transactions rely on real-time data to be able to make the best possible choice based on the most current information available. Typically, the kind of information required includes FX rates, interest rates, FX and interest rate volatilities, swap rates, reference interest rates for yield curve determination, and son on. This information will be required first thing in the morning prior to the opening of the financial markets and banking system so that transactions can be planned and executed as the business day progresses.

SAP ERP provides an integrated interface, SAP NetWeaver XI, that can be set up between external data providers such as Reuters, Bloomberg, or Dow Jones and that can update SAP ERP tables used by the transaction manager for the various functions. The SAP NetWeaver XI interface has data communication and file management capabilities that can provide seamless inbound and outbound data transfer.

After the information is populated in the relevant tables in SAP ERP, it is available for use by the transaction manager, as well as for reporting and evaluation. In Chapter 8, we will review in greater detail how this is accomplished. SAP ERP uses tools called analyzers that enable using this information for the various functions required in treasury management. The integration between transaction management and these analyzers will also be explained in Chapter 8.

7.10 Summary

In this chapter, we covered key functionality available in SAP ERP for FX management and control, including how product types, transaction types, flow types and update types are used in transaction management. We also looked at how workflow and integration can be used to automate the end-to-end financial supply chain process and we reviewed key controls that can be built into the process. Furthermore, we reviewed hedge management functionality and how this functionality can be used for FAS 133 compliance. Finally, we briefly addressed how real-time data can be integrated into the process. The next chapter, Chapter 8, will build on and extend the concepts illustrated in this chapter to another key area in FSCM, that of investment and debt management.

Chapter 8 builds on the financial risk management concepts covered in Chapter 7 and extends them to cover investment and debt management.

8   Investment and Debt Management

Cash positioning and forecasting the liquidity needs of an organization results in cash surpluses and deficits that need to be invested or funded. A major function of treasury departments is to manage the liquidity needs of the corporation. Cash surpluses need to be invested to maximize the return on funds invested, and cash shortfalls need to be funded through borrowing that minimizes the cost of capital. SAP ERP has provided Investment and debt management functionality as part of the FSCM suite of applications. Additionally, it integrates the use of derivatives to hedge interest costs or income through the use of interest rate derivative instruments that can be linked to the underlying security or debt instrument.

The menu for SECURITIES, Money Market, and DEBT MANAGEMENT functionality is divided into corresponding sections. The menu options follow the same structure as described in Chapter 7, as shown in Figure 8.1 below:.

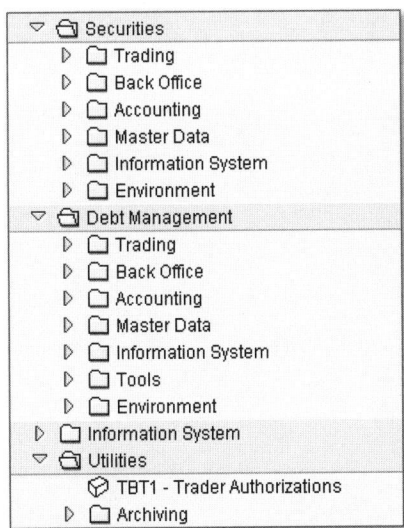

Figure 8.1 Securities and Debt Management Menu Path

8 | Investment and Debt Management

8.1 Master Data Structure

Master data for securities follows the same structure as discussed in Chapter 7; however, two are specific to securities: asset class, and securities account. Although securities investment and debt management are classified as separate sections, they both use the same product types. The transaction type is used to differentiate whether a transaction is an investment or a debt.

8.1.1 Product Types

Product types are available for short-, medium-, and long-term maturities. There is some overlap between product types in the money market (short-term) and securities (medium- to long-term) instruments. The main difference between the two, aside from the term, is that longer-term securities are set up as master data through an asset class (to be discussed in Section 8.1.2, Global Settings for Securities). It is possible, although not typical, to use asset classes in the money market component as well. Furthermore, money market instruments are usually set up as standalone transactions.

Examples of product types in the money market component are shown in Figure 8.2.

PTyp	Name of product type	Product category
51A	Fixed-term deposit: External	Fixed-term deposit
51B	Fixed-term dep: (mirrored)	Fixed-term deposit
52A	Deposit at notice: External	Deposit at notice
52B	Deposit at notice: Int. (mirr)	Deposit at notice
53A	Commercial Paper: External	Commercial Paper
53B	Commercial Paper: Internal	Commercial Paper
54A	Cash flow transact.: External	Cash flow transaction
54B	C. flow trans.: Int. (mirr)	Cash flow transaction
55A	Interest rate instrument: Ext.	Interest rate instrument
55B	Interest rate instrument: Int.	Interest rate instrument
55C	Interest rate instrument: HAC	Interest rate instrument
56A	Confirmed facility	Facility
56B	Unconfirmed facility	Facility
A01	Interest rate instrument: Ext.	Interest rate instrument
A02	Fixed-term deposit: External	Fixed-term deposit
M01	Interest rate instrument: Ext.	Interest rate instrument

Figure 8.2 Money Market Product Types

Product types 54A (CASH FLOW TRANSACT: EXTERNAL) and 55B (INTEREST RATE INSTRUMENT: INT.) are examples of generic product types that can be copied and customized specific to an organization's requirements.

Securities product types are shown in Figure 8.3.

PTyp	Text	Prod. Cate	Cond.gr
01A	Stocks	10	10
02A	Investment certificates	20	30
03A	Subscription rights	30	0
04H	Variable rate bonds	40	42
04I	Fixed-interest bonds	40	40
04J	Zero bonds	40	43
04K	Unit-quoted bonds	40	41
06A	Warrant bonds	60	40
07A	Convertible bonds	70	40
11A	Index warrants	111	0
11B	Equity warrants	112	0
11C	Currency warrants	113	0
11D	Bond warrants	114	0
16A	Shareholdings	160	21
FN1	Funds - Portfolio < 365 days	20	30
FN2	Funds - Portfolio > 365 days	20	30

Figure 8.3 Securities Product Types

8.1.2 Global Settings for Securities

Global settings for securities are shown in Figure 8.4, on the next page.

8.1.3 Transaction Types

Transaction types are used the same way for investment and debt management as was explained in Chapter 7 for financial risk management. However, here, they also serve the purpose of classifying a transaction as an investment or a debt instrument. Both have similar characteristics except that the principal and interest flows will be reversed depending on the transaction type. Examples of SECURITIES TRANSACTION TYPES are shown in Figure 8.5, on the next page.

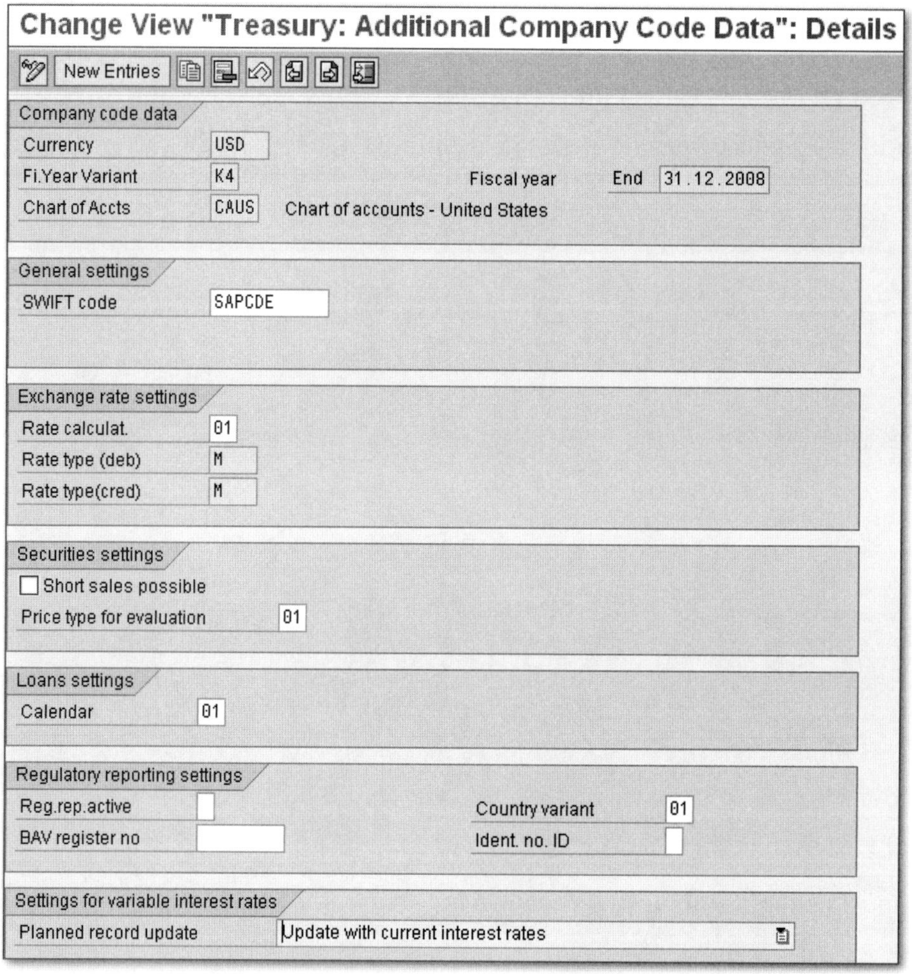

8 | Investment and Debt Management

Change View "Treasury: Additional Company Code Data": Details

Company code data
- Currency: USD
- Fi.Year Variant: K4   Fiscal year   End: 31.12.2008
- Chart of Accts: CAUS   Chart of accounts - United States

General settings
- SWIFT code: SAPCDE

Exchange rate settings
- Rate calculat.: 01
- Rate type (deb): M
- Rate type (cred): M

Securities settings
- ☐ Short sales possible
- Price type for evaluation: 01

Loans settings
- Calendar: 01

Regulatory reporting settings
- Reg.rep.active: Country variant: 01
- BAV register no: Ident. no. ID:

Settings for variable interest rates
- Planned record update: Update with current interest rates

Figure 8.4 Global Settings for Securities

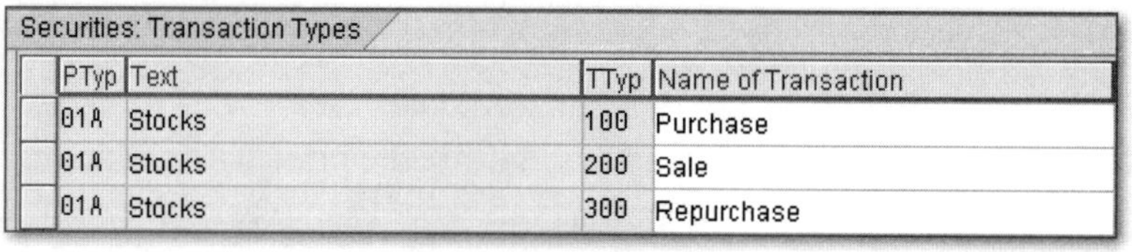

Securities: Transaction Types

PTyp	Text	TTyp	Name of Transaction
01A	Stocks	100	Purchase
01A	Stocks	200	Sale
01A	Stocks	300	Repurchase

Figure 8.5 Transaction Types Linked to Product Type

8.1.4 Securities Account

The SECURITIES account is the actual account at the brokerage firm, bank, or financial institution where the investment or debt portfolio is held. The Securities account setup menu path is shown below.

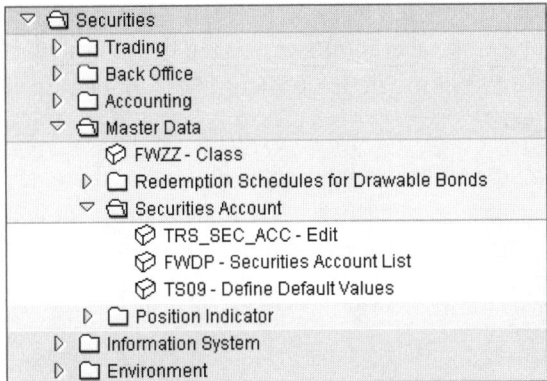

Figure 8.6 Securities Account Setup Menu Path

The setup of the Securities account has been enhanced with the ability to provide payment information, security types, and netting rules, as shown in Figure 8.7.

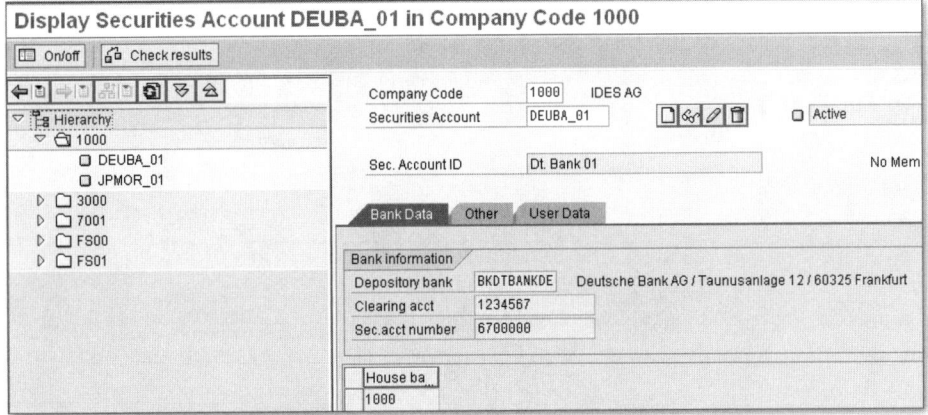

Figure 8.7 Securities Account Setup

8.1.5 Class Data

Class data is master data that is specific to securities or debt instruments. It contains standing data that defines the principal and interest terms, condition, maturity, issue and redemption details, index and ratings data — typically information that is static, or changes only once in a while (such as ratings), and that defaults into the transaction when the security is traded. The system also uses the condition data to calculate cash flows based on principal amounts entered in the transaction. Class data is usually identified in SAP ERP through its CUSIP or ISIN number. Class data is created using Transaction FWZZ.

The initial entries are made on the SEARCH TERMS tab, which allows for the entry of details with respect to type of instrument, securities account the instrument will be held in, CUSIP, ISIN, and other market identifiers, ratings information, and classification for reporting purposes. These entries are shown in Figure 8.8.

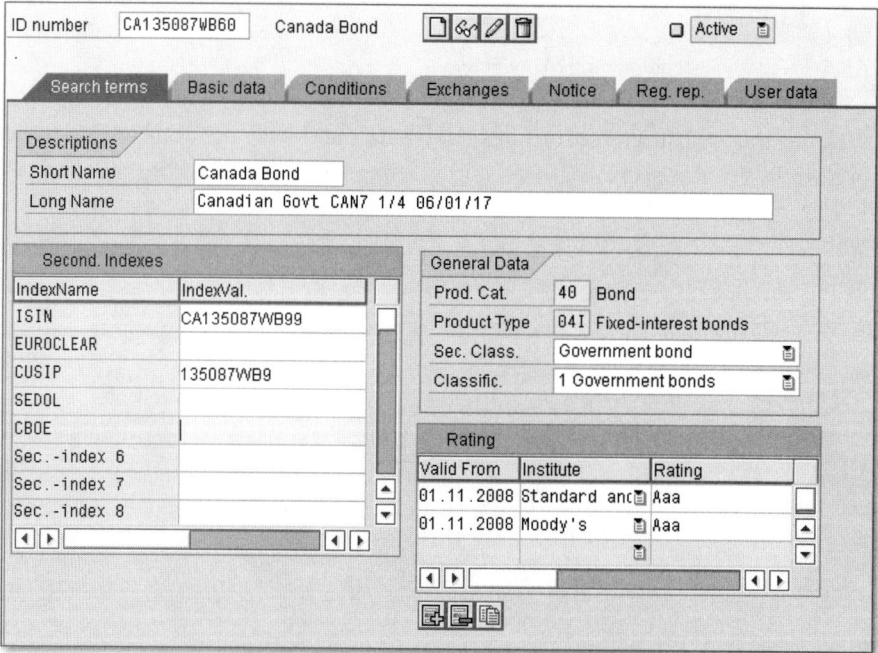

Figure 8.8 Create Class Data Initial Screen

The BASIC DATA tab provides details about the ISSUE and ISSUER, as shown in Figure 8.9. The issuer needs to be set up as a BP in the role of issuer; otherwise, the ISSUER field can't be populated, and will result in an error message.

8.1 Master Data Structure

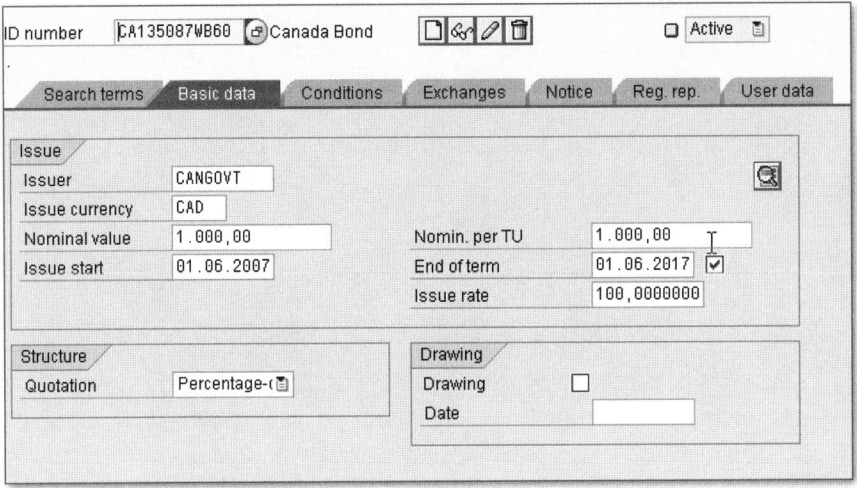

Figure 8.9 Asset Class Basic Data

The CONDITIONS tab contains details of principal and interest terms and conditions, currency details, and calculation methods, as shown in Figure 8.10. The system uses this information to calculate the cash flows and value dates in transaction-specific processing.

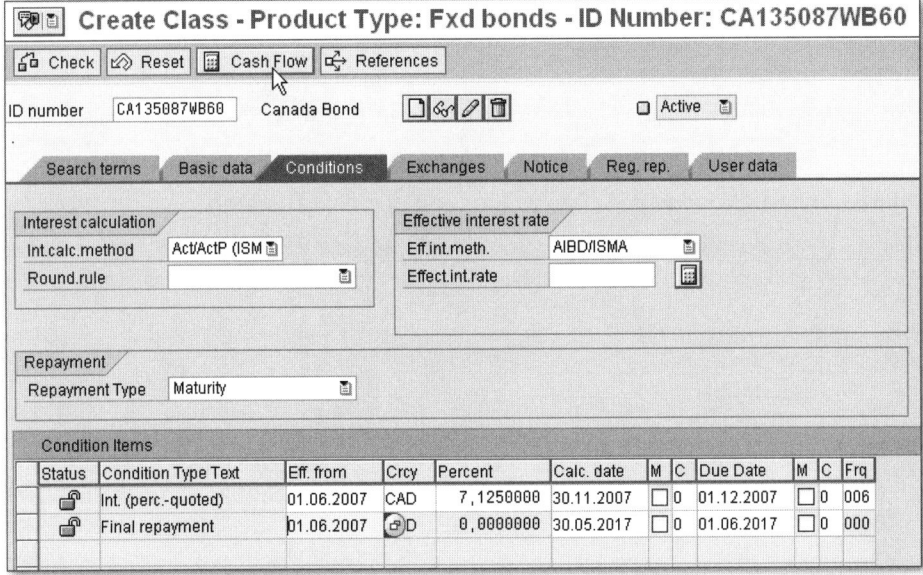

Figure 8.10 Asset Class Conditions Tab

327

Clicking on the CASH FLOW button shown in Figure 8.10 displays the cash flows for the entire life cycle of the transaction, based on the condition parameters entered on the CONDITIONS tab, as shown in Figure 8.11.

Pos.vl.dt	UpdateType	Update Type Text	Status	Units	NomC	Nominal	Amt in PC	Pos.C
01.06.2007	SE1000	Purchase		0,000000	CAD	100.000,00	100.000,00	CAD
01.12.2007	SAM5000	Nominal interest		0,000000			3.543,14	CAD
01.06.2008	SAM5000	Nominal interest		0,000000			3.562,50	CAD
01.12.2008	SAM5000	Nominal interest		0,000000			3.562,50	CAD
01.06.2009	SAM5000	Nominal interest		0,000000			3.562,50	CAD
01.12.2009	SAM5000	Nominal interest		0,000000			3.562,50	CAD
01.06.2010	SAM5000	Nominal interest		0,000000			3.562,50	CAD
01.12.2010	SAM5000	Nominal interest		0,000000			3.562,50	CAD
01.06.2011	SAM5000	Nominal interest		0,000000			3.562,50	CAD
01.12.2011	SAM5000	Nominal interest		0,000000			3.562,50	CAD
01.06.2012	SAM5000	Nominal interest		0,000000			3.562,50	CAD
01.12.2012	SAM5000	Nominal interest		0,000000			3.562,50	CAD
01.06.2013	SAM5000	Nominal interest		0,000000			3.562,50	CAD
01.12.2013	SAM5000	Nominal interest		0,000000			3.562,50	CAD
01.06.2014	SAM5000	Nominal interest		0,000000			3.562,50	CAD
01.12.2014	SAM5000	Nominal interest		0,000000			3.562,50	CAD
01.06.2015	SAM5000	Nominal interest		0,000000			3.562,50	CAD
01.12.2015	SAM5000	Nominal interest		0,000000			3.562,50	CAD
01.06.2016	SAM5000	Nominal interest		0,000000			3.562,50	CAD
01.12.2016	SAM5000	Nominal interest		0,000000			3.562,50	CAD
01.06.2017	SAM1104	Scheduled repayment (final)		0,000000	CAD	100.000,00	100.000,00	CAD
01.06.2017	SAM5000	Nominal interest		0,000000			3.562,50	CAD

Figure 8.11 Cash Flows Based on Conditions Tab Entries

Exchange setup is performed as shown below in Figure 8.12.

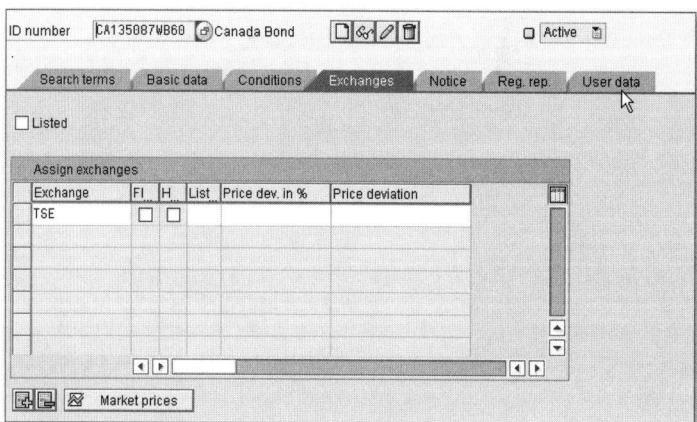

Figure 8.12 Exchange Setup

Class data needs to be maintained in ACTIVE status for transactions to use it, as shown in Figure 8.13.

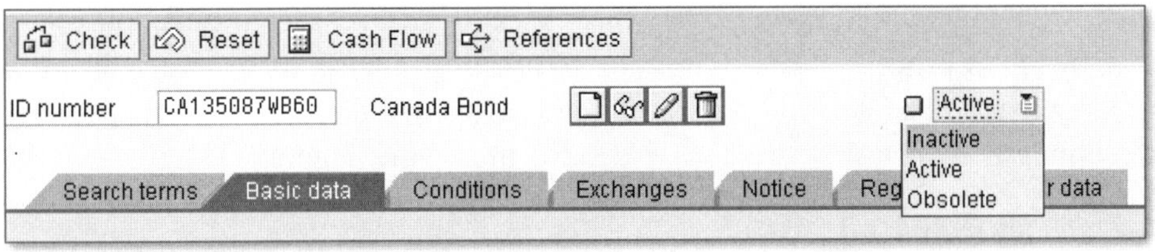

Figure 8.13 Maintain Asset Class in Active Status

8.1.6 Business Partner

The setup of and controls for BPs for FSCM was covered in Chapter 7. Key roles used in investment and debt management are guarantor, issuer, depository bank, and counterparty.

All issuers of securities for whom class data is maintained need to be set up in the role of issuer, as shown in Figure 8.14.

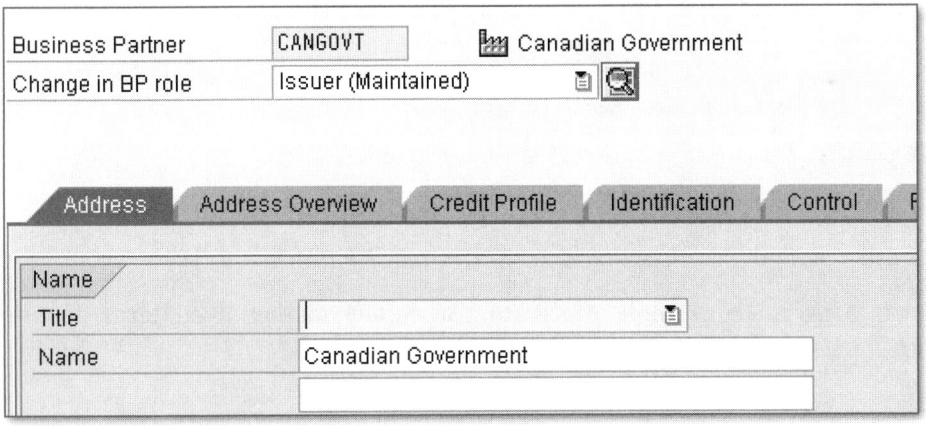

Figure 8.14 Create BP in Role Issuer

8.2 Transaction Management

In accordance with the standard format, transaction management for investments and debt is divided between front office, back office, and accounting. To explain the business process and controls for transaction management, we will use a money market and security/debt transaction. This will illustrate the functionality and underlying controls available in these components (Figure 8.15).

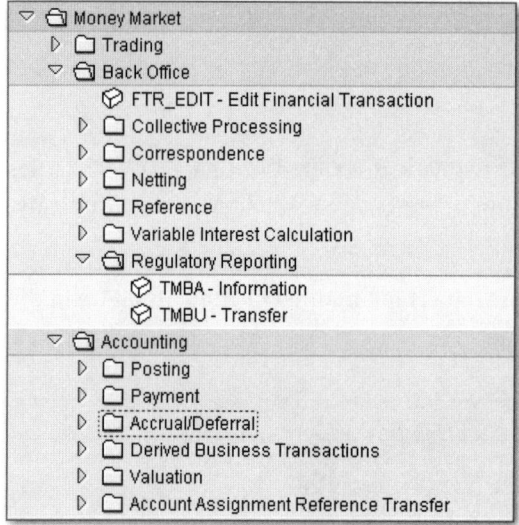

Figure 8.15 Money Market Transaction Management Menu

8.2.1 Money Market Fixed Term Deposit Example

Following is an example of creating a money market fixed term deposit transaction.

Creating a Contract

The front office has created a fixed term deposit transaction in the money market component using Transaction FTR_CREATE, as shown in Figure 8.16.

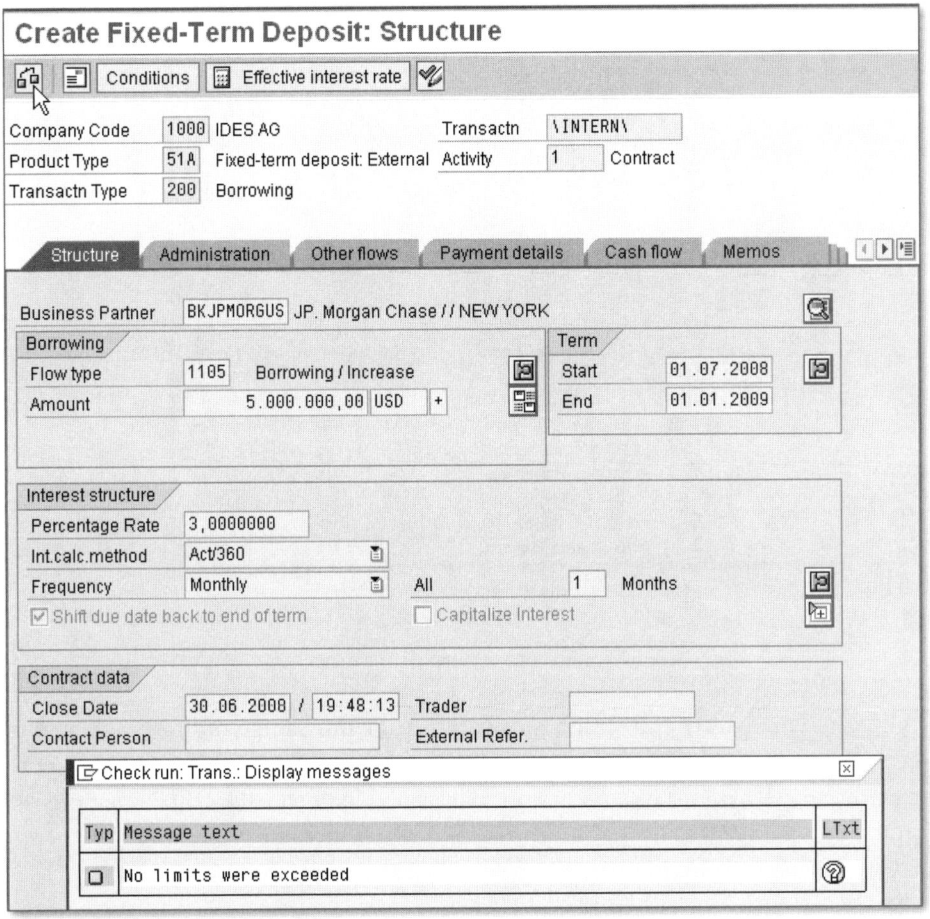

8.2 Transaction Management

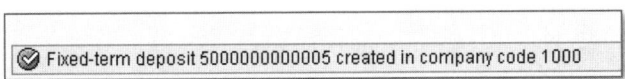

Figure 8.16 Create FTD Using Transaction FTR_CREATE

Successful creation of the FTD results in the following notice (Figure 8.17):

Figure 8.17 FTD Transaction Created

Settling the Contract

The contract flows are settled in the back office after the trade is reviewed and confirmed. As shown in Figure 8.18, the cash flows for the transaction are displayed with the value dates for each inflow or outflow item.

8 | Investment and Debt Management

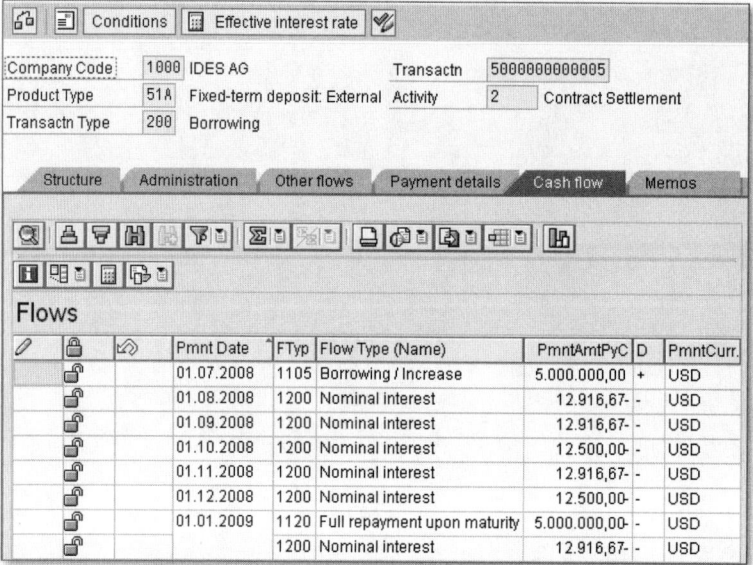

Figure 8.18 Cash Flows for FTD Transaction 5000000000005

Netting of Cash Flows

Where payments are due to or receivable from the same counterparty on the same value date, the flows can optionally be netted to make a net payment to the counterparty. The NETTING menu option is available in all back office functions, as shown in Figure 8.19.

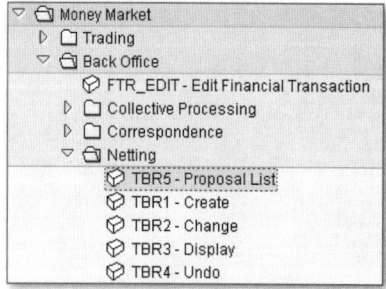

Figure 8.19 Netting of Payments to Counterparty

The screen that displays when executing Transaction TBR5 shows a proposal list of all of the payments eligible for netting, and is shown in Figure 8.20. This is proposed by the system, which will only select items that satisfy the strict criteria for netting eligibility. For example, principal and interest flows due to the same counterparty on the same value date are netted, so that payment request for a net payment is created, for payment purposes, while maintaining and accounting appropriately for all of the individual transactions being netted. The selection and execution completes the netting activity, and the transactions are ready to be posted and paid based on the value dates.

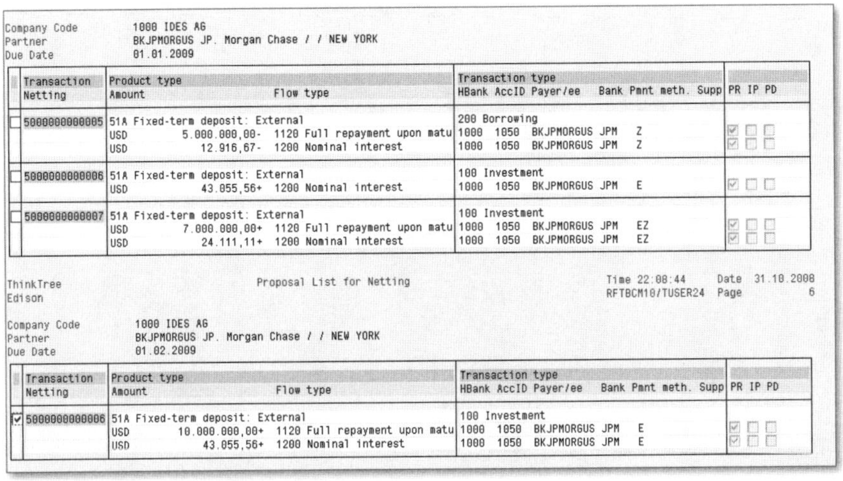

Figure 8.20 Netting Proposal Using Transaction TBR5

Payment Processing and Accounting

After the transaction has been approved for payment and posting, the process moves from the back office to accounting. The functions executed here provide the integration between the treasury and finance functions and components in SAP ERP. The menu options for ACCOUNTING are shown in Figure 8.21.

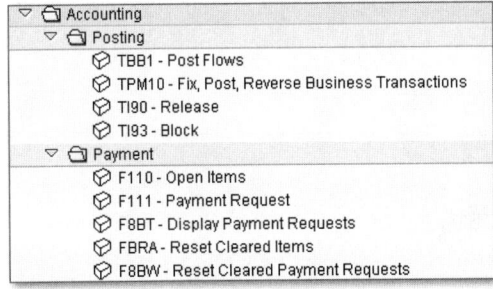

Figure 8.21 Accounting and Payment Controls and Functions

Because cash flows and accounting entries in the books of record will be impacted, additional control functionality is available to accounting to block, release, and reset or reverse transactions that are either erroneous or have not been authorized.

Payment requests are created and related accounting entries made using Transaction TBB1. This transaction is one of many in the FSCM suite that enable collective processing of multiple transactions, as shown in Figure 8.22. Variants can be set up for specific groups of transactions, and can be automated to run daily as a batch job.

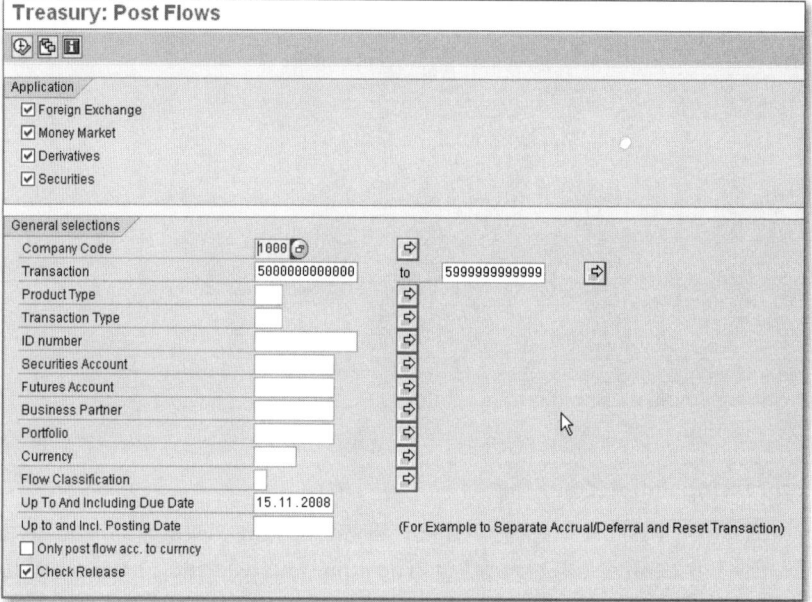

Figure 8.22 Collective Processing of Treasury Flows: Upper Screen Area

The collective processing screen for transaction TBB1 allows for multiple valuation areas, as well as a TEST RUN checkbox you can use if it is being run manually, as shown in Figure 823.

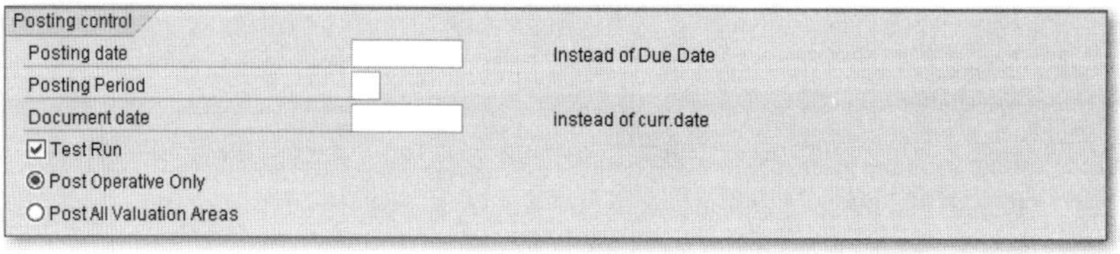

Figure 8.23 Collective Processing of Treasury Flows: Lower Screen Area

Executing Transaction TBB1 results in related LOGS AND MESSAGES, as shown in Figure 8.24. In the POSTING LOG (green square) you will find details of all of the postings made and whether errors were encountered that need to be corrected, and in the MESSAGES (yellow triangle) area, you will find informational-type messages.

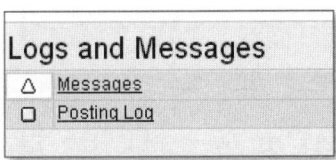

Figure 8.24 Transaction TBB1 Logs and Messages

This is an important control feature and also an audit trail because in the event of hard errors, postings will not be allowed to be created.

The posting log detail is shown in Figure 8.25. If the counterparty is set up for payment requests, and an outbound payment is due, a payment request will be created as shown in the posting log. The asset or income account will be debited and the payment request clearing account will be credited.

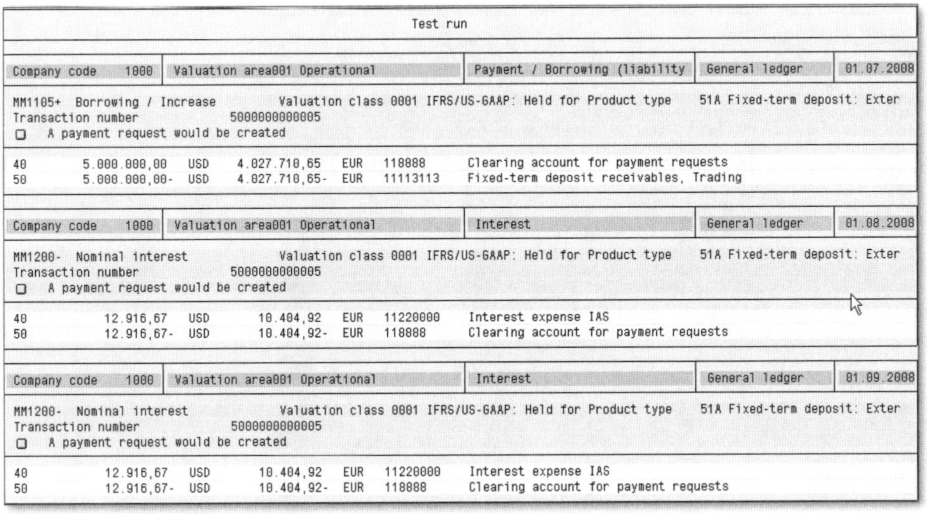

Figure 8.25 Posting Log Showing Creation of Payment Requests

Payment requests that have been created can be viewed using Transaction F8BT, as shown in Figure 8.26. Payment details default in from authorized BP settings.

8 | Investment and Debt Management

```
31.10.2008  21:35:45   Display Payment Requests
```

Key number	CoCd	DocumentNo	Year	Currency	Pymt curr.amnt	AccTy	Partner	Alt. payee
7	1000	1	2008	USD	5.000.000,00	S	118888	
8	1000	2	2008	USD	12.916,87-	S	118888	
9	1000	3	2008	USD	10.000.000,00-	S	118888	
10	1000	4	2008	USD	43.055,56	S	118888	

Figure 8.26 List of Payment Requests Viewed Using Transaction F8BT

Next, the treasury payment program Transaction F111 is executed and creates bank transfers and clearing entries in accounting. The payment program proposes payments based on criteria entered in the payment parameters, as shown in Figure 8.27.

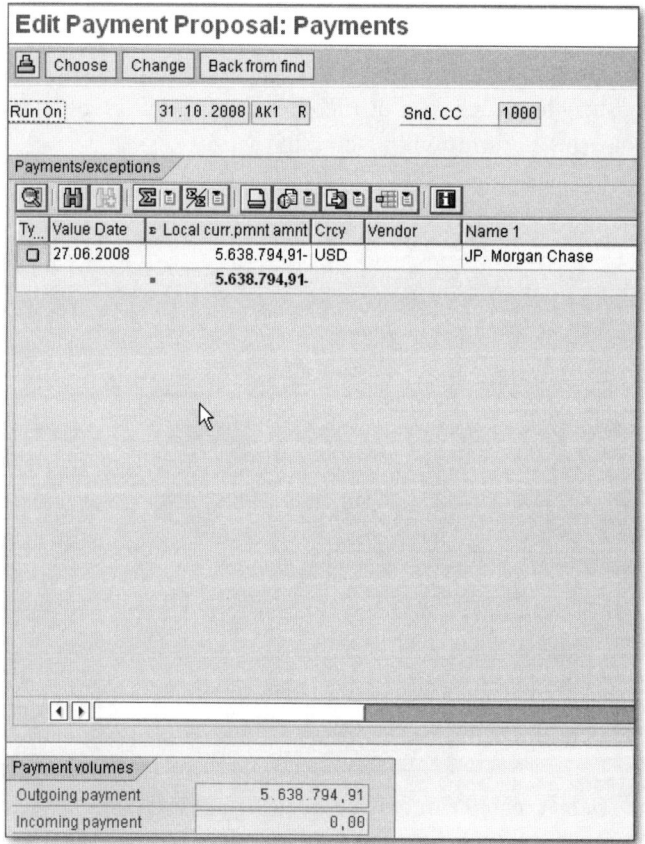

Figure 8.27 Payment Proposal Using Transaction F111

336

When running the payment proposal, the payment request clearing account is debited, and the bank clearing account is credited. The cycle is completed when the payment settles and is reflected in the incoming EBS the next day when the bank clearing account is debited and cleared, and the bank account is credited with the amount of the payment.

Postings made based on user-defined rules are set up in configuration. Because multiple currencies are involved, the accounting can be set up to post to exchange difference accounts, and tolerance limits can be set. The log with details of the accounting posting and accounting document created is shown in Figure 8.28.

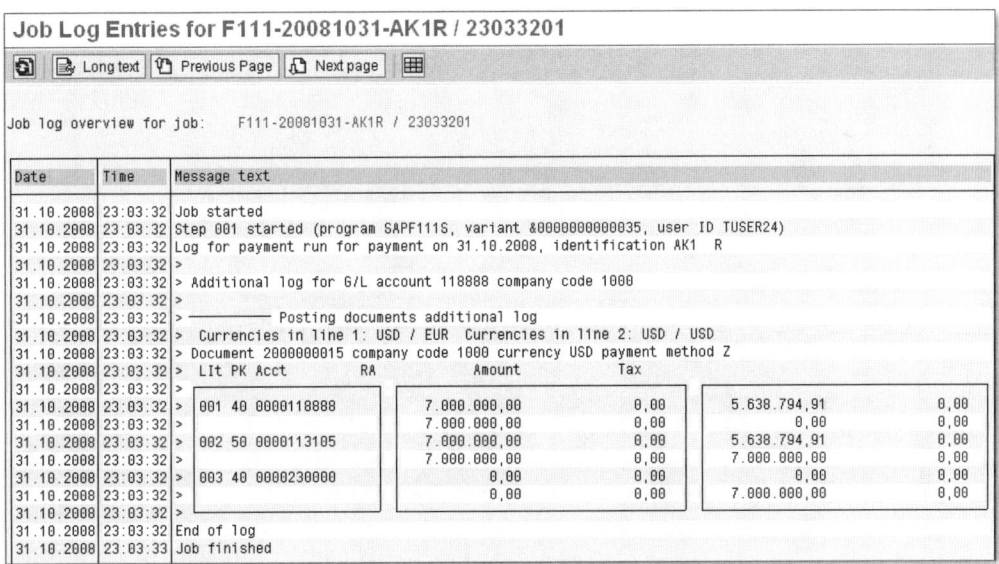

Figure 8.28 Posting and Accounting Document Created After Payment Run

8.2.2 Securities Bond Purchase Example

Transactions in the securities components require the configuration of class data as described in Section 8.1.5, Class Data. In the example shown in Figure 8.29, a fixed interest bond purchase is executed using the class data for the security already configured.

8 | Investment and Debt Management

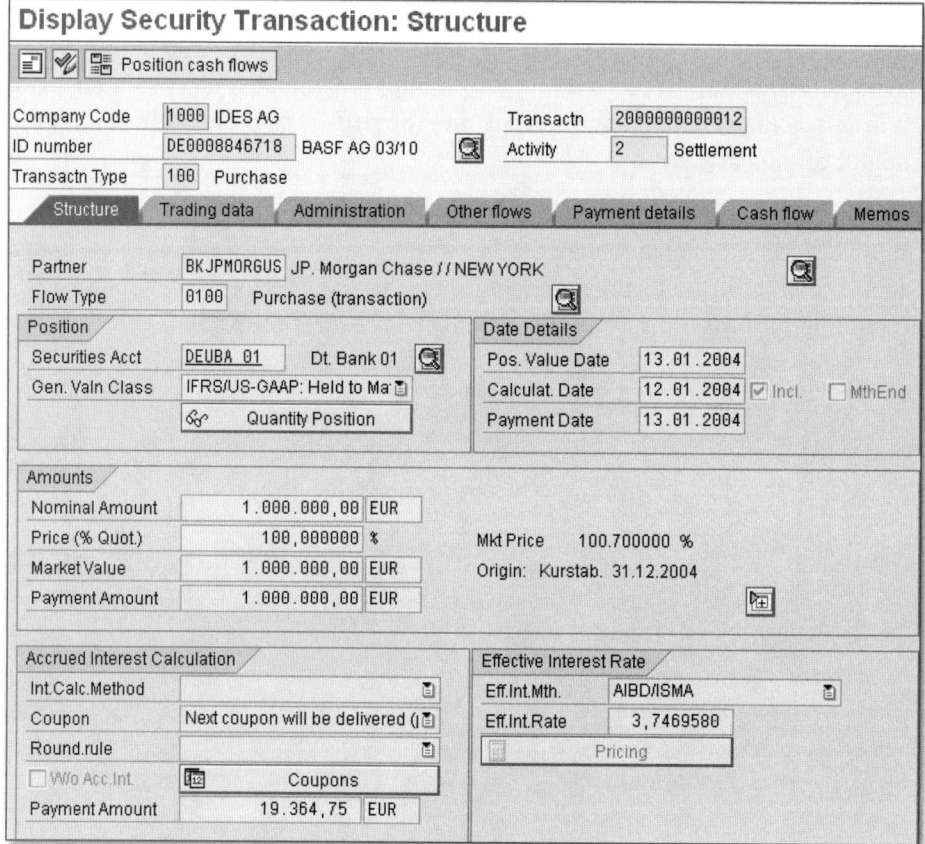

Figure 8.29 Securities Bond Purchase Using Class Master Data

Clicking on the magnifying glass button next to the ID NUMBER lets you view the underlying class data details, as shown in Figure 8.30.

In Section 8.3, Market Data Management, we will look at how class data can be created and updated on a daily basis, especially if an organization has a lot of new securities transactions that are being traded on a daily basis.

Transaction Management | 8.2

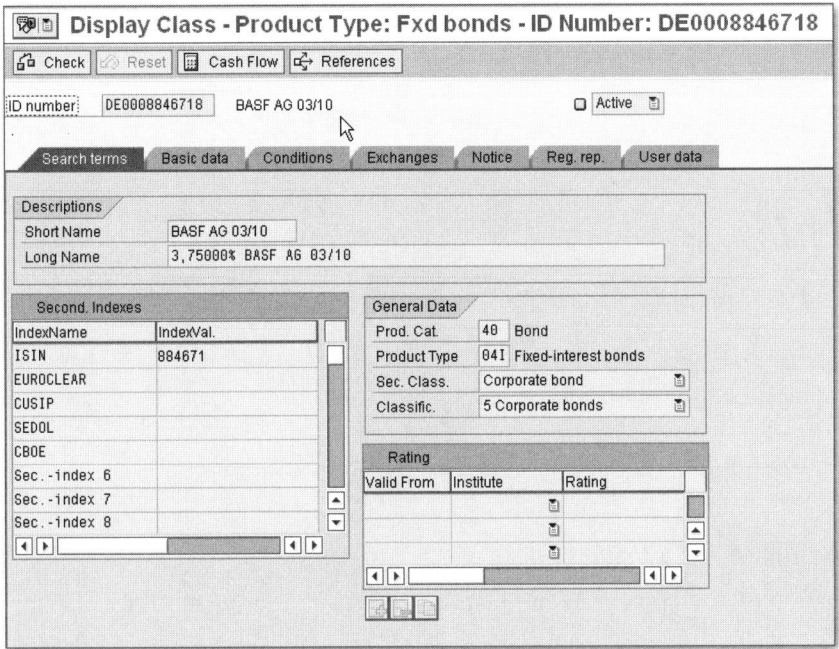

Figure 8.30 Underlying Class Data for Security Purchase

8.2.3 Month End Accounting

Month end and periodic accounting relates to posting interest flows, valuation of positions, mark to market postings, calculation of realized and unrealized gains and losses, accruals and deferrals, and recording permanent impairment. It may also be required to transfer securities between accounts, or between valuation classes.

Key Month End Activities

Table 8.1 summarizes key month end and periodic activities typically executed for FX, investment, debt and derivatives transactions, along with their respective transaction codes:

Transaction Code	Month End and Periodic Activity
TPM1	Key date valuation
TPM60	Mark to market calculation
FWSO	Post interest

339

Transaction Code	Month End and Periodic Activity
FW17	Enter security prices
TPM18	Realized gains and losses
TBB4	Post accruals
TBB1	Post treasury flows
FWDU	Security account transfer
TPM15	Valuation class transfer
TPM 70	Record impairment of position
TPM71	Reverse impairment
TPM73	Impairment table records recovery value

Table 8.1 Key Month End and Periodic Activities and Their Transaction Codes

Valuation and Mark to Market

The valuation of open positions and marking to market is done monthly in accordance with accounting rules that require derivatives to be shown in the balance sheet at their fair value. For derivatives that are quoted on an exchange, the market value can be obtained through existing market data. For contracts that are not traded regularly or that are transacted over the counter and directly between principals, the fair value needs to be calculated. FAS133 refers to statement 107, *Disclosures About Fair Value of Financial Instruments* for guidance on determining the fair value of derivatives. SAP ERP uses the concept of discounted cash flow (DCF) to estimate the value of an open position. The use of DCF techniques for valuation is one of the approaches recommended in statement 107.

> **Note**
>
> SAP ERP uses DCF techniques to value open contracts for monthly mark to market calculation purposes. The basic concept of DCF is that a dollar in hand today does not have the same value as a dollar a year from now, because the dollar now can be invested to earn a rate of interest or the *time value of money* that will make it worth more a year from now. Conversely, the value of the dollar a year from now needs to be discounted by the interest rate to arrive at the current value today. SAP ERP values open positions by discounting future cash flows relating to that contract by a discount rate that is established using a specific yield curve that reflects the organization's cost of capital or discount rate. The data and calculations are provided by the market risk analyzer and are integrated with the transaction manager.

8.2.4 Valuation of an Open Contract

This section uses the example of the forward contract discussed in Chapter 7 to calculate the market value and to create the resulting accounting mark up or mark down postings.

Transaction TPM60 executes the valuation calculation, as shown in Figure 8.31.

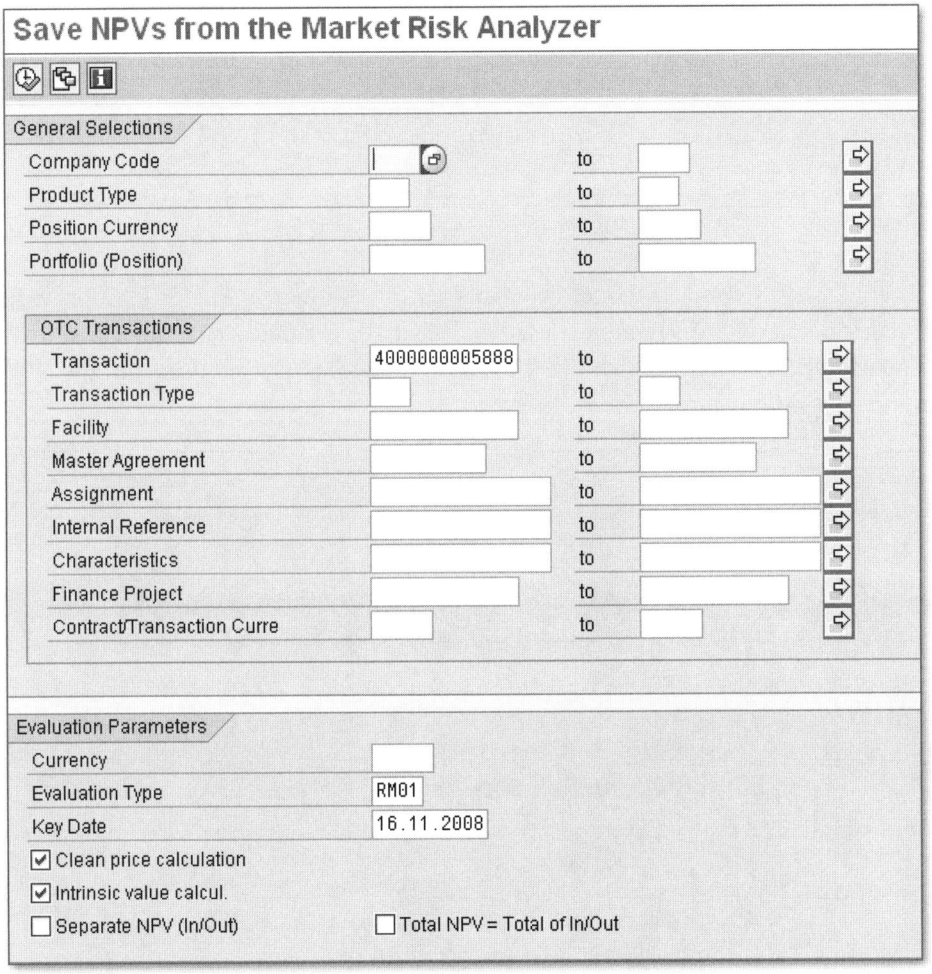

Save NPVs from the Market Risk Analyzer

General Selections
- Company Code: [ ] to [ ]
- Product Type: [ ] to [ ]
- Position Currency: [ ] to [ ]
- Portfolio (Position): [ ] to [ ]

OTC Transactions
- Transaction: 4000000005888 to [ ]
- Transaction Type: [ ] to [ ]
- Facility: [ ] to [ ]
- Master Agreement: [ ] to [ ]
- Assignment: [ ] to [ ]
- Internal Reference: [ ] to [ ]
- Characteristics: [ ] to [ ]
- Finance Project: [ ] to [ ]
- Contract/Transaction Curre: [ ] to [ ]

Evaluation Parameters
- Currency: [ ]
- Evaluation Type: RM01
- Key Date: 16.11.2008
- ☑ Clean price calculation
- ☑ Intrinsic value calcul.
- ☐ Separate NPV (In/Out)   ☐ Total NPV = Total of In/Out

Figure 8.31 Transaction TPM60 Calculates NPV

8 | Investment and Debt Management

The resulting screen, shown in Figure 8.32, shows the NET PRESENT VALUE (NPV) calculation for the contract based on discounting the forward cash flows back to the key valuation date using the discount rate derived from the respective yield curves for U.S. dollars and Swiss Franks (CHF).

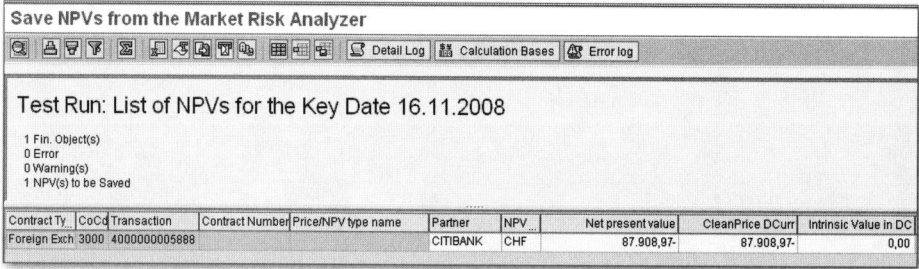

Figure 8.32 NPV Calculation for Forward Contract

The DETAIL LOG and CALCULATION BASES buttons shown in Figure 8.32 provide further detail on the parameters used and the basis for the calculations, as shown in Figure 8.33. The screen shows the discount factor (DISCFAC) used and the NPV of those cash flows.

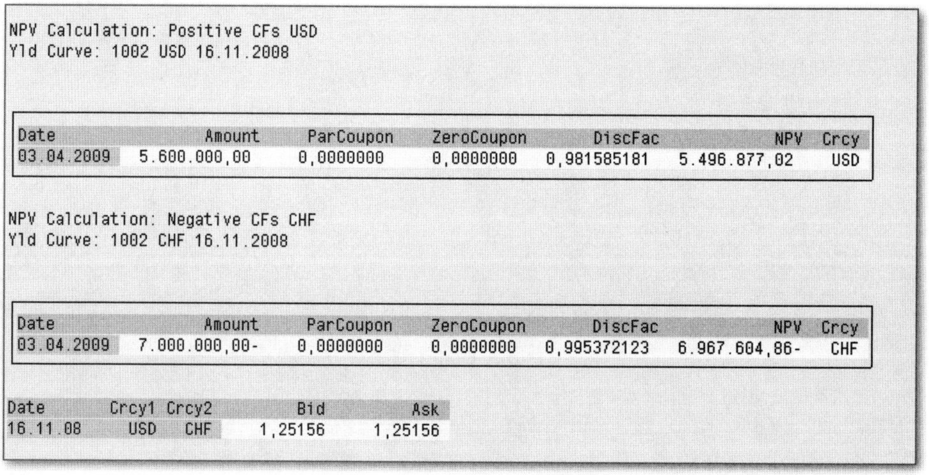

Figure 8.33 NPV Calculation Detail Log: Upper Screen Area

Figure 8.34 shows the netting of the two flows in currency CHF, resulting in the NPV value shown in the Transaction TPM60 valuation screen.

Date	Crcy1	Crcy2	Bid	Ask
16.11.08	USD	CHF	1,25156	1,25156

Value	Crcy	Rate	Value: Displ.Crcy
5.496.877,02	USD	1,25156	6.879.695,89

Date	Crcy1	Crcy2	Bid	Ask
16.11.08	USD	CHF	1,25156	1,25156

Value	Crcy	Rate	Value: Displ.Crcy
5.496.877,02	USD	1,25156	6.879.695,89

Value	Crcy	Rate	Value: Displ.Crcy
6.967.604,86-	CHF	1,00000	6.967.604,86-

Total NPV in Evaluation Currency

Value	Crcy	Rate	Value: Displ.Crcy
87.908,97-	CHF	1,00000	87.908,97-

Figure 8.34 NPV Calculation Detail Log: Lower Screen Area

The Calculation Bases screen shown in Figure 8.35 provides details on the yield curves used for both currencies and discount rates used.

Mkt Data
- Current
  - Yld Curves
    - 1002-CHF-16.11.2008
    - 1002-USD-16.11.2008
  - Exchange Rate

Ref.int.rate	Int.rt.dte	No. of days	Par rate	Zero coupon	ZBDF
CHFLIB01DN	17.11.2008	1	0,7133300	0,7133300	0,999980186
CHFMM_01M	16.12.2008	30	0,9800000	0,9800000	0,999184000
CHFMM_02M	16.01.2009	61	1,0700000	1,0700000	0,998190226
CHFMM_03M	16.02.2009	92	1,1200000	1,1200000	0,997145947
CHFMM_06M	16.05.2009	181	1,3000000	1,3000000	0,993506332
CHFMM_09M	16.08.2009	273	1,5000000	1,5000000	0,988752935
CHFSWP01Y	16.11.2009	365	0,7100000	0,7100000	0,992852839
CHFSWP02Y	16.11.2010	730	1,9479452	1,9600594	0,961403439
CHFSWP03Y	16.11.2011	1.095	2,1205479	2,1330123	0,937820354
CHFSWP04Y	16.11.2012	1.461	2,2324435	2,2460692	0,913799249
CHFSWP05Y	16.11.2013	1.826	2,3165389	2,3318712	0,889656614
	16.11.2014	2.191	2,3687556	2,3850372	0,866362348
	16.11.2015	2.556	2,4209724	2,4392422	0,842730798
	16.11.2016	2.922	2,4733321	2,4945052	0,818741745
	16.11.2017	3.287	2,5255489	2,5505079	0,794569092
CHFSWP10Y	16.11.2018	3.652	2,5777656	2,6073846	0,770192231

Figure 8.35 Yield Curve Details Used in Valuation

The EXCHANGE RATE used in the calculation is available in the same screen, as shown in Figure 8.36.

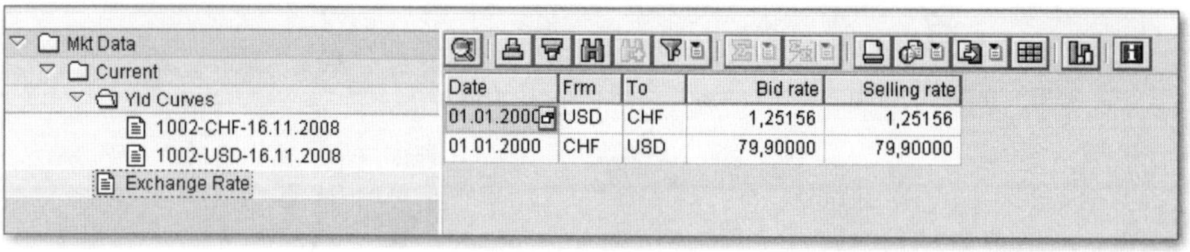

Figure 8.36 Exchange Rate Details Used in Valuation

The mark up or mark down valuation is posted using Transaction TPM1. The resulting screen shows the transaction you can execute for valuation (EXECUTE VALUATION button), as shown in Figure 8.37.

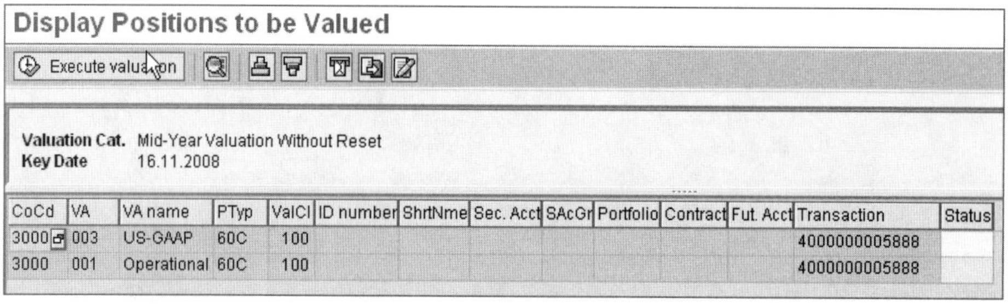

Figure 8.37 Executing Valuation Using Transaction TPM1

The discussed calculations for valuation and other related functionality are made possible through market data feeds and analyzer tools that integrate with transaction management. We will now review these key areas and how they facilitate transaction management.

8.3 Market Data Management

Up-to-date, real-time market data can be made available on a daily or periodic basis using the SAP NetWeaver XI interface or other file communication software to link the SAP ERP system to market data providers such as Reuters, Bloomberg or Dow Jones. Many options are available for bringing in market data, as shown in the application menu options for this functionality shown in Figure 8.38.

The three key options for uploading transactional data required for transaction management are as follows:

- Manual upload through Microsoft Excel
- Datafeed, which can be set up as ad hoc or real-time
- File interface

To fully leverage the integration between market data providers and the SAP ERP system, it is recommended to set up an automated feed through FILE INTERFACES, which will send and receive market data using push/pull file communication commands with middleware such as SAP NetWeaver XI.

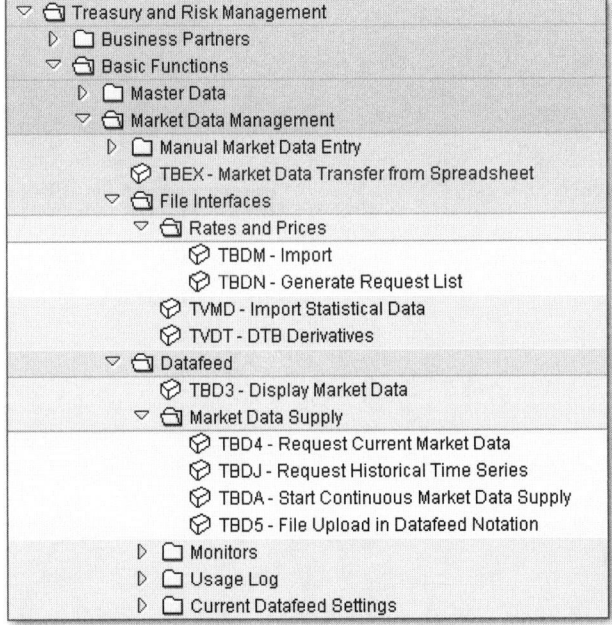

Figure 8.38 Market Data Feed Options

In the next section, will review practical applications of this two-way communication interface.

8.3.1 Transaction Data Feed

Two major areas exist where automatic data feed provides dynamic, real-time data for decision making and accounting purposes. The first is a transactional data feed which will typically be comprised of FX rates, swap rates, interest rates, and related volatilities. These are required for executing foreign exchange transactions and building the yield curves that are used for valuation purposes. Typically, the market data feed is requested daily from the market data provider through an automated request form that is sent through the SAP NetWeaver XI interface, and — based on the parameters entered there — the market data provider will return the requested data. This data is received and brought into SAP ERP by SAP NetWeaver XI, by triggering a function call and populating the various tables in SAP ERP that hold this information. Requests should be automatically scheduled, but authorized treasury users should also have the ability to make one-time or ad hoc requests, for example, if an investment is made after the scheduled job time and master data is required to set up the new transaction. The architecture described here is shown in Figure 8.39.

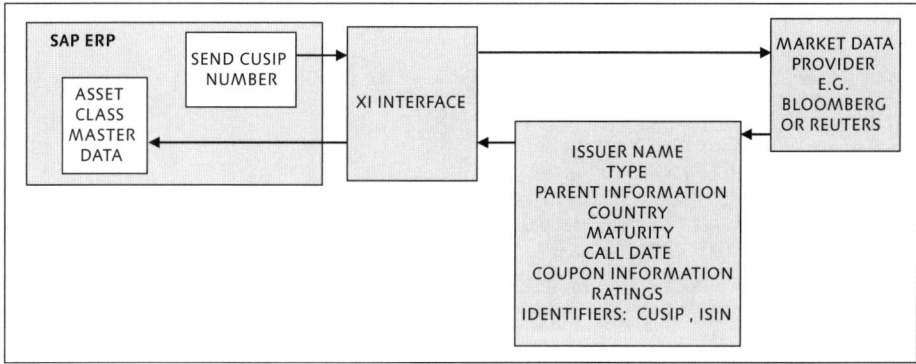

Figure 8.39 Transactional Market Data Interface

8.3.2 Master Data Feed

With the second application, a request can be made for securities master data, based on a CUSIP number sent to the market data provider. The information received will be mapped to fields in the class data. After the class data is set up, the day's transactional activity can be entered in the system either manually or through an automated feed. The SWIFT MT500 series has standard formats for the receipt of securities-related information. As an alternative, the mapping can take place between the market data provider's file format and table fields in SAP ERP.

The following is an example of typical information that can be received to set up securities-related master data:

- Issuer information:
    - Issuer name
    - Type
    - Parent information
- Security information
    - Country
    - Maturity
    - Weighted average life (for ABS)
    - Call date
- Coupon information
    - Coupon
    - Fixed or floating
    - Frequency
    - Day count
    - If floating, coupon frequency (quarterly, semi-annually, etc)
    - If floating, spread to libor
- Identifiers
    - CUSIP
    - ISIN
- Ratings
    - Moody's (short-term and long-term)
    - S&P (short-term and long-term)
    - Combined

The architecture for receiving securities-related master data is shown in Figure 8.40.

The next section reviews how the analyzer tools are used in SAP ERP.

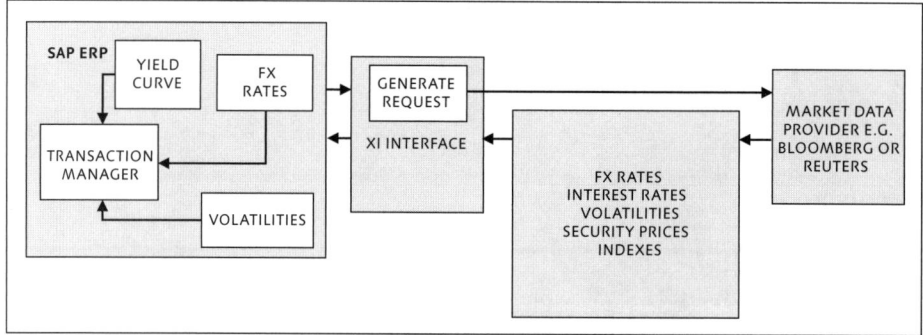

Figure 8.40 Securities Master Data Interface

8.4 The Analyzers

The analyzers are components that support transaction management processing, and that provide analytics, statistical, and measurement tools specific to treasury risk management.

Three analyzers are provided by SAP ERP as part of the FSCM suite of applications:

- Market Risk Analyzer
- Credit Risk Analyzer
- Portfolio Analyzer

The menu path and options for the analyzers are shown in Figure 8.41.

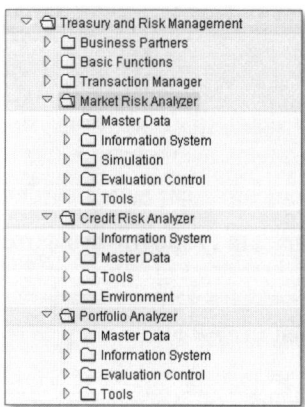

Figure 8.41 Analyzer Menu Path and Options

8.4.1 Analyzer Functionality

Key functionality available in these components for analytics of financial risk management are as follows:

- NPV calculations for valuation
- Value at risk
- What-if analysis
- Simulation
- Limit management
- Market data shifts and scenarios
- Portfolio benchmarking
- Portfolio returns and yield book calculations
- Currency exposure risk analysis

We will look specifically at how the Market Risk Analyzer provides the mark to market valuation calculations functionality described in Section 8.2.4, Valuation of an Open Contract, as well as how the Credit Risk Analyzer provides critical limit management controls for transaction processing in financial risk management, investment, and borrowing activities.

8.4.2 Valuation and Mark to Market

As discussed in Section 8.2.4, Valuation of an Open Contract, valuation for mark to market is calculated using yield curve, interest rate, volatility, and exchange rate information. The link to transaction management is made through an evaluation type that is in turn linked to all of the parameters required to build a yield curve for use in discounted cash flow calculations.

The settings are made through basic analyzer settings in configuration. The menu path is IMG •FINANCIAL SUPPLY CHAIN MANAGEMENT • TREASURY AND RISK MANAGEMENT • BASIC ANALYZER SETTINGS • VALUATION • MAINTAIN AUTHORIZATIONS/PROFILES/USERS, as shown in Figure 8.42.

8 | Investment and Debt Management

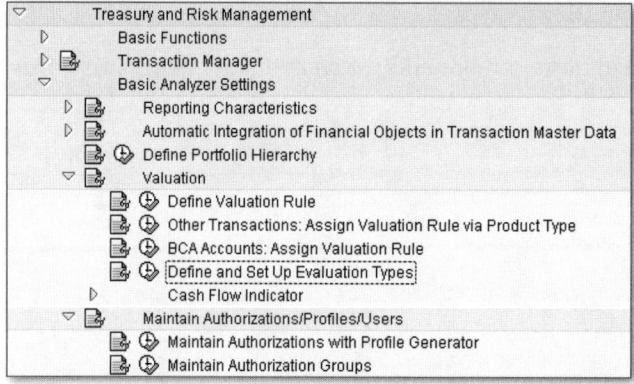

Figure 8.42 Define and Set Up Evaluation Types

The evaluation type is linked to yield curves and volatilities, as shown in Figure 8.43. Additional tabs are available that provide links to DATAFEED, Portfolio Analyzer, and additional securities-related settings.

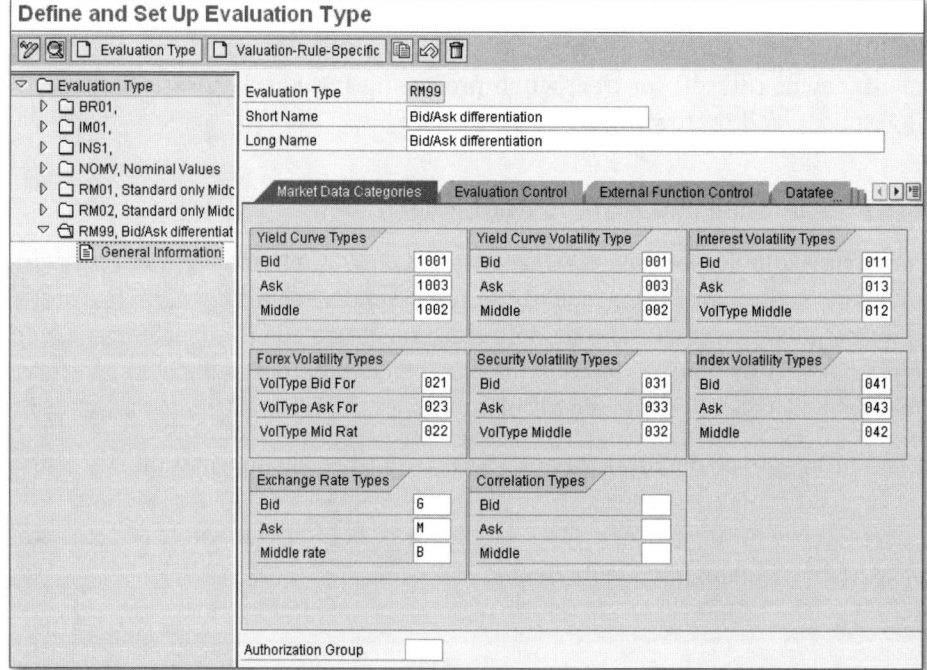

Figure 8.43 Evaluation Type Settings

The path for maintaining master data relating to evaluation type is shown in Figure 8.44.

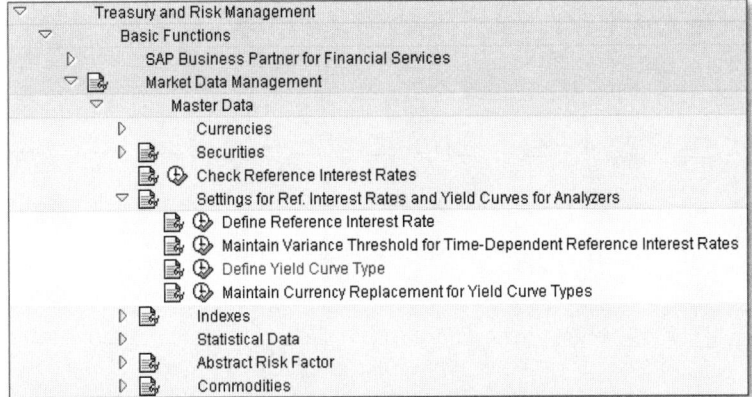

Figure 8.44 IMG Menu Path for Evaluation Type Setup

The YIELD CURVE TYPE is defined for required currencies (CURR.), as shown in Figure 8.45.

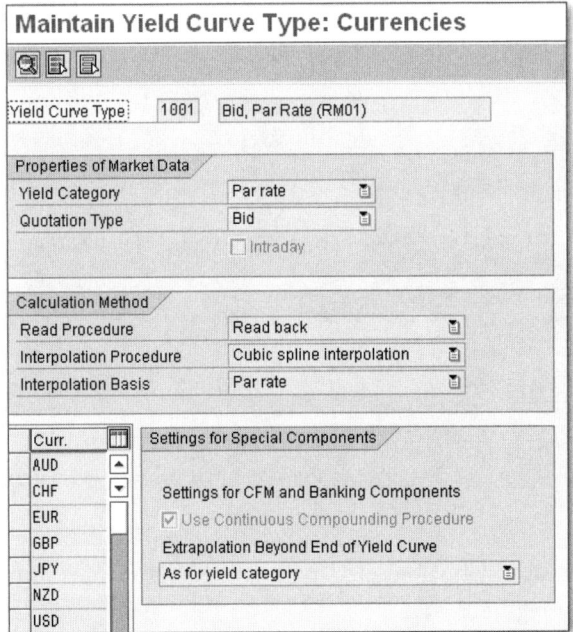

Figure 8.45 Define Yield Curve Type for Multiple Currencies

8 | Investment and Debt Management

Selecting a specific currency enables the creation of the reference interest rates that comprise the yield curve structure, as shown in Figure 8.46.

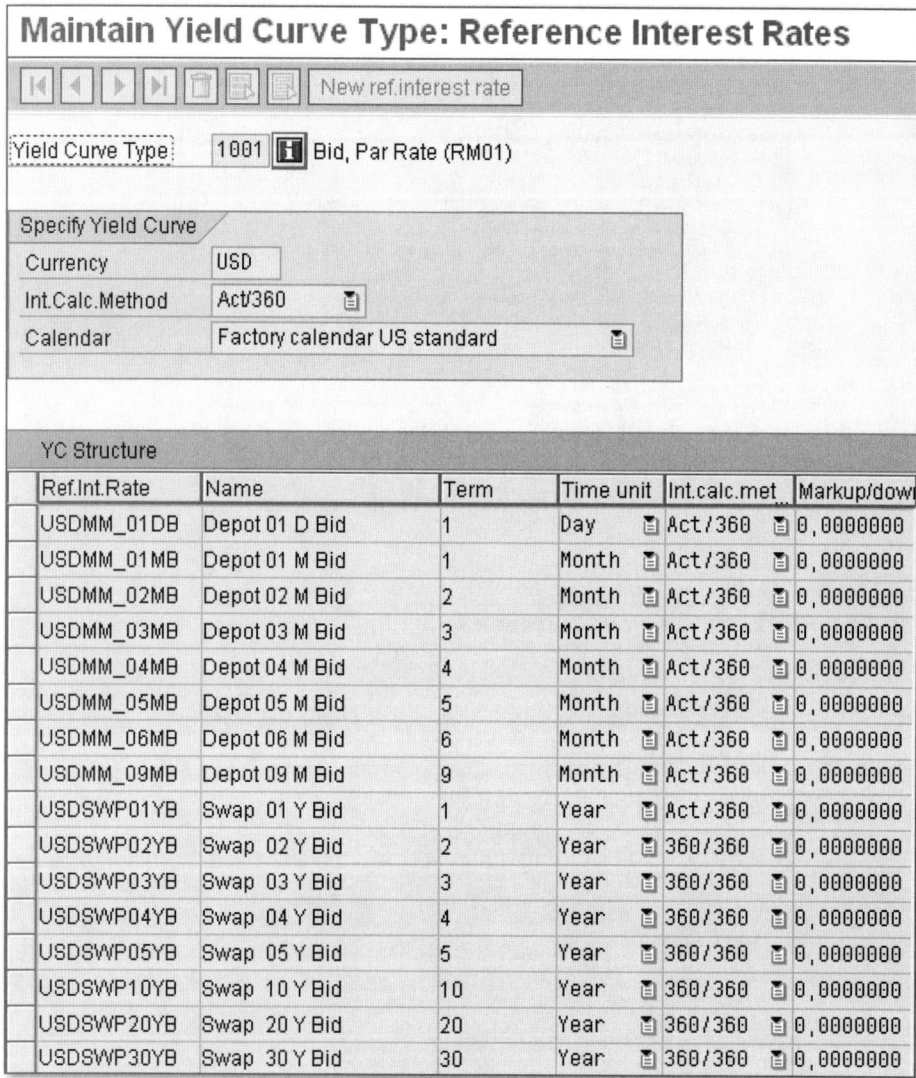

Figure 8.46 Reference Interest Rates for Yield Curve Type

These REFERENCE INTEREST RATES are in turn created with specific attributes and settings as required, as shown in Figure 8.47.

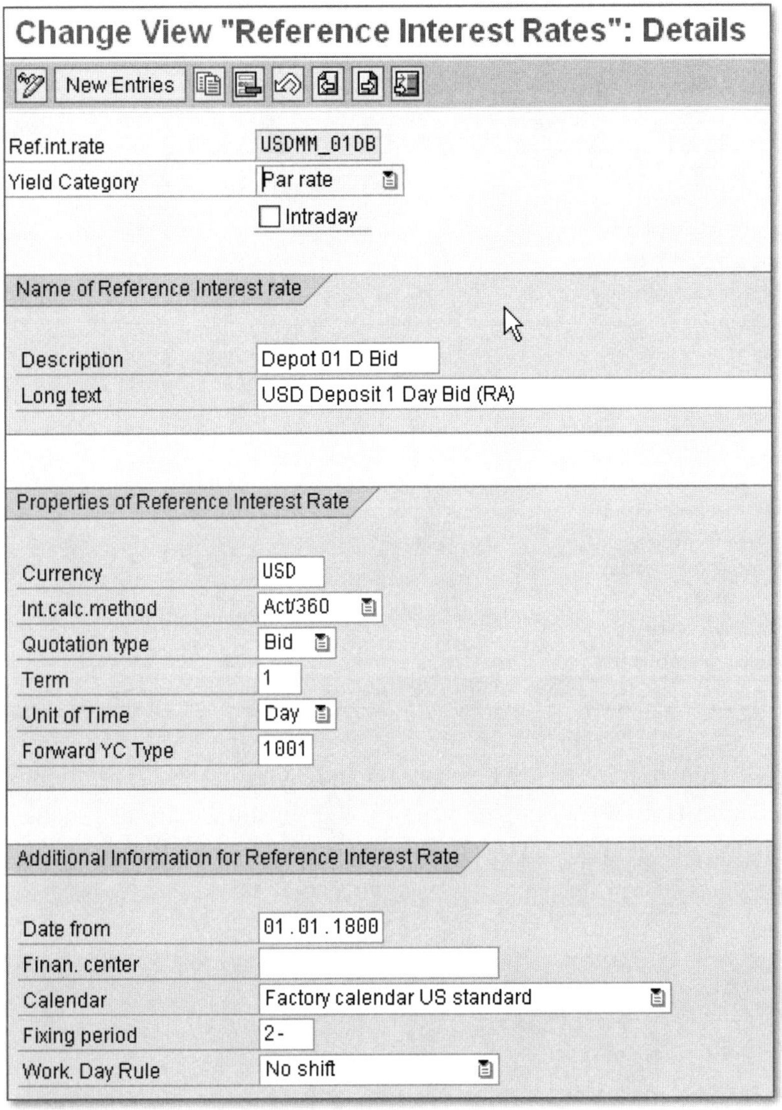

Figure 8.47 Create Reference Interest Rates

Volatilities are set up in the same way, using a VOLATILITY TYPE and related settings. Examples of volatility types used are shown in Figure 8.48.

8 | Investment and Debt Management

Change View "Volatility Type View": Overview

V. Type	V. desc.	V.rate cat	S/A vola	Stat.type
001	Yield Curve volatility bid	3		
002	Yield Curve volatility middle	2		
003	Yield Curve volatility ask	1		
011	Interest volatility bid	1		
012	Interest volatility middle	2		
013	Interest volatility ask	3		
021	Currency volatility bid	1		
022	Currency volatility middle	2		100
023	Currency volatility ask	3		
031	Security volatility bid	1		
032	Security volatility middle	2		
033	Security volatility ask	3		
041	Index volatility bid	3		
042	Index volatility middle	2		
043	Index volatility ask	1		
100	Volatility RiskMetrics			100
200	Volatility Basle directive			200

Figure 8.48 Volatility Types Used

When automatic valuation is not used, you can manually ENTER NET PRESENT VALUES in the valuation table, for example, if the bank or business partner provides valuation data at month end. The application menu path is shown in Figure 8.49.

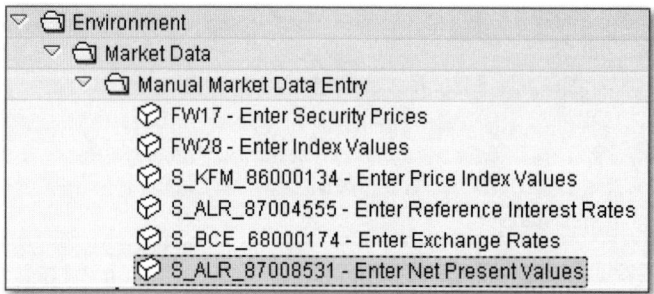

Figure 8.49 Manual Entry of NPV

The table entry in Figure 8.50 shows both the calculated rate shown earlier in Figure 8.32 in Section 8.3.5 and entries that may have been entered manually.

354

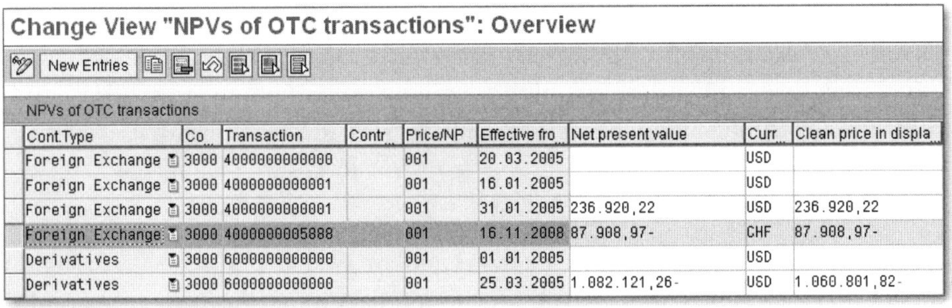

Change View "NPVs of OTC transactions": Overview

NPVs of OTC transactions

Cont.Type	Co	Transaction	Contr	Price/NP	Effective fro	Net present value	Curr	Clean price in displa
Foreign Exchange	3000	4000000000000		001	20.03.2005		USD	
Foreign Exchange	3000	4000000000001		001	16.01.2005		USD	
Foreign Exchange	3000	4000000000001		001	31.01.2005	236.920,22	USD	236.920,22
Foreign Exchange	3000	4000000005888		001	16.11.2008	87.908,97-	CHF	87.908,97-
Derivatives	3000	6000000000000		001	01.01.2005		USD	
Derivatives	3000	6000000000000		001	25.03.2005	1.082.121,26-	USD	1.060.801,82-

Figure 8.50 NPV Table Entries

The link between EVALUATION TYPE and the valuation Transaction TPM60 is shown in Figure 8.51, where all of the previous settings taken together with the market data feed will result in the valuation for mark to market purposes.

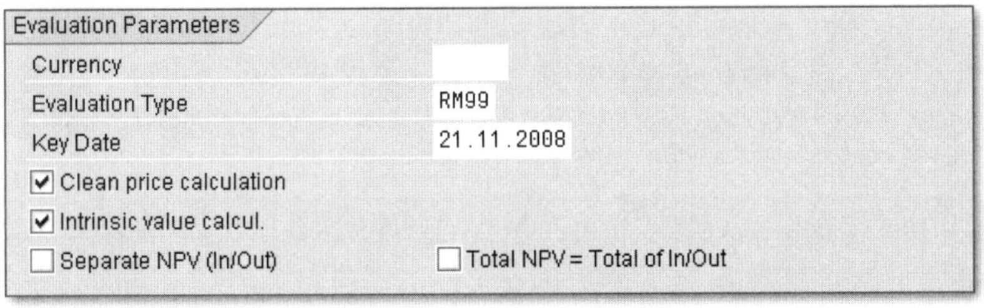

Figure 8.51 Transaction TPM60 Valuation Link to Evaluation Type

In the next section, we will review another key function provided by the analyzers, relating to limit management.

8.4.3 Limit Management

Limit management in the context of transaction management is a critical automated control that provides checks and balances with respect to individual transactions. It also provides overall limits with respect to totals, amounts, percentages by portfolio, amounts allowable by business partner or type of security, and other criteria as set out by the board of directors of the organization, or the investment subcommittee of the board. These guidelines can vary from organization to organization, and can range from fairly simple to highly complex rules that need to factor in sub limits within classes of limits. For example, an organization may have an overall percentage limit for investment in a particular security issued by a company, but may also require a sub limit for investment in any company that has a parent/child relationship with the company at the top of the hierarchy. When the limit structure becomes very complex, it may be advisable from a practical standpoint to leverage the limit management functionality in SAP ERP with user-defined custom ABAP calculation and reporting programs to ensure compliance with the investment guidelines.

Different forms of dynamic limit management are available in FSCM transaction processing. Limit checks can be real-time and proactive, or they can be set up for end of day reporting and notification. Integrated default limit checks for online processing is activated at the company code level.

Workflow in Limit Management

Limit management can make effective use of workflow to ensure that transactions that fail limit checks can be routed to a higher authority, either for approval, or as an alert monitor. The settings to activate these are made in the following IMG path: FINANCIAL SUPPLY CHAIN MANAGEMENT • TREASURY AND RISK MANAGEMENT • CREDIT RISK ANALYZER • BASIC SETTINGS • GLOBAL SETTINGS.

The resulting input screen and settings are shown in Figure 8.52.

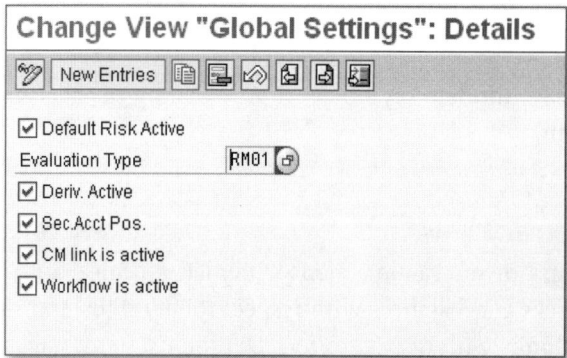

Figure 8.52 Activating Online Limit Checking Settings

Additionally, it is necessary to assign workflow recipients using the following IMG menu path: FINANCIAL SUPPLY CHAIN MANAGEMENT • TREASURY AND RISK MANAGEMENT • CREDIT RISK ANALYZER • BASIC SETTINGS • ASSIGNMENTS • ASSIGNMENT OF SENDERS TO RECIPIENTS • ASSIGN SENDERS OF WORKFLOWS TO RECIPIENTS.

Workflow will be started only when online limit checking is activated. It can't be used with end of day processing.

Limit Per Transaction

Limit checks can be applied at the individual transaction level, using a combination of PRODUCT TYPE and transaction type (TRANSACTN TYPE). An example of a transaction that has failed a limit check is shown in Figure 8.53.

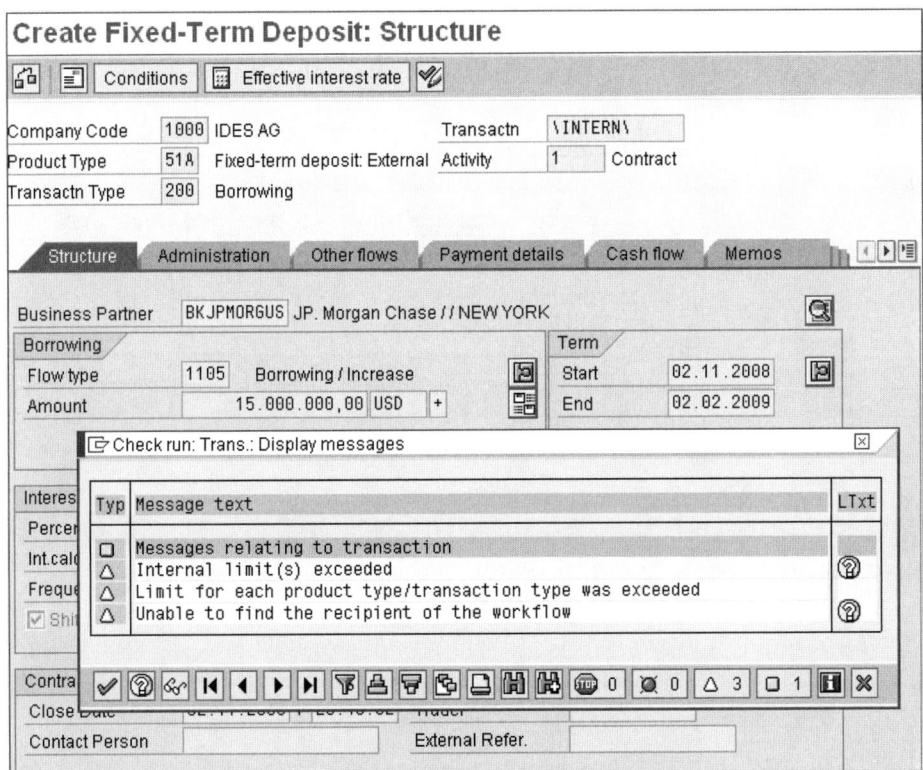

Figure 8.53 Limit Check Activated Message in Transaction Management

This form of limit control is set up using Transaction KLMAXLIMIT, as shown in the application path menu in Figure 8.54.

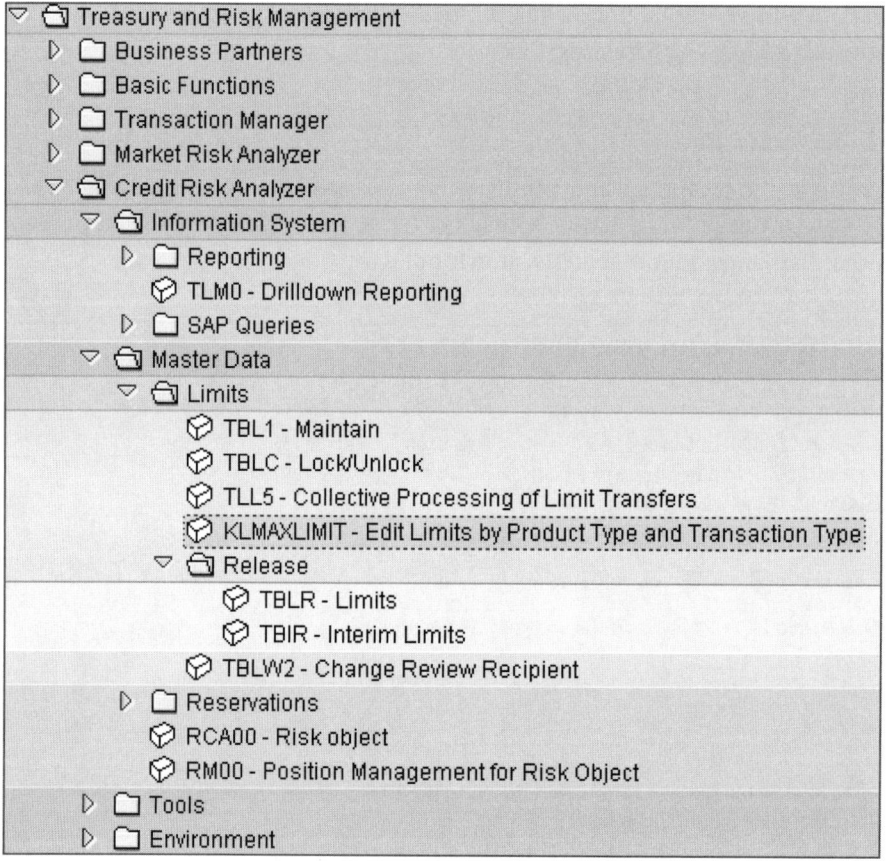

Figure 8.54 Menu Path for Transaction Limits and Release

Limits are set up in the resulting screen by company code (Co...), product type (PTyp), and transaction type (TTyp), as shown in Figure 8.55.

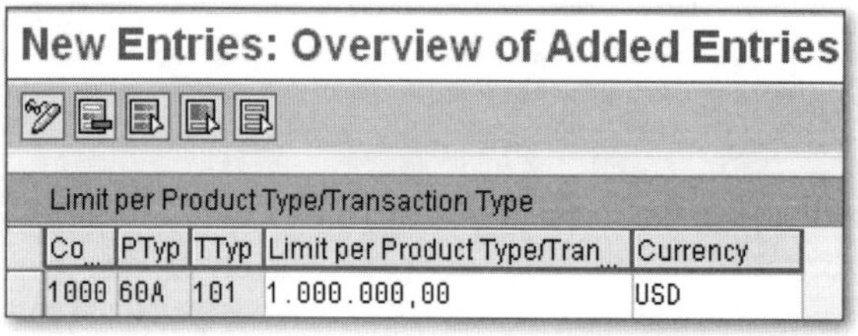

Figure 8.55 Limit Management by Product Type and Transaction Type

Release of limits is available through the same menu path shown in Figure 8.54. The resulting release input screen is shown in Figure 8.56.

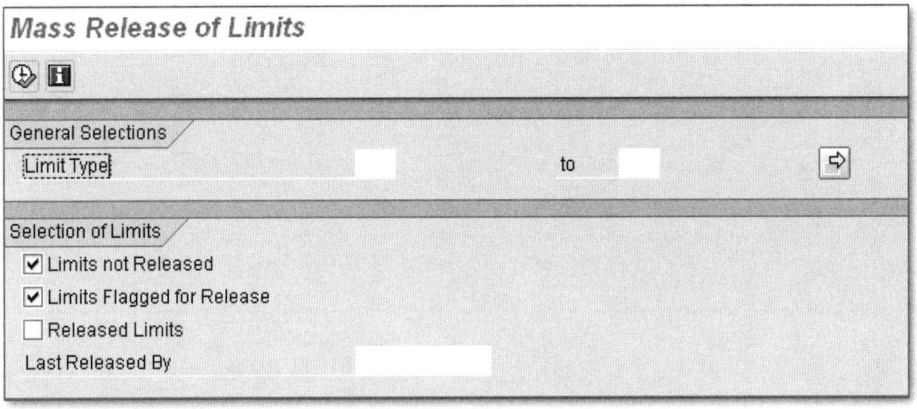

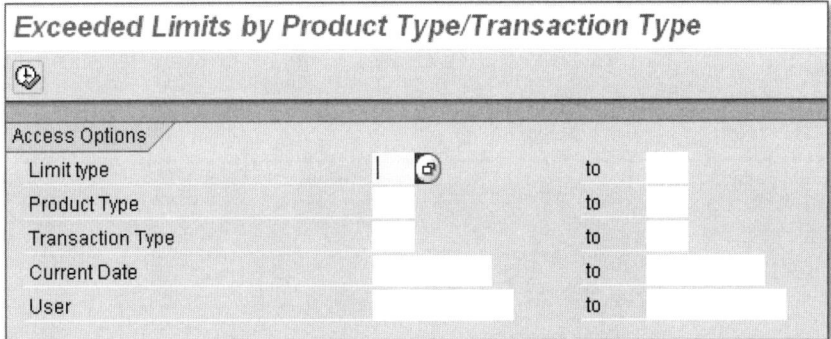

Figure 8.56 Mass Release of Limits with Releaser Information

Reporting on Limit Breach

Transaction KLLE provides a report of exceeded limits per transaction. The input screen for this report is shown in Figure 8.57.

Figure 8.57 Transaction KLLE for Exceeded Limits by Transaction

The resulting report is shown in Figure 8.58.

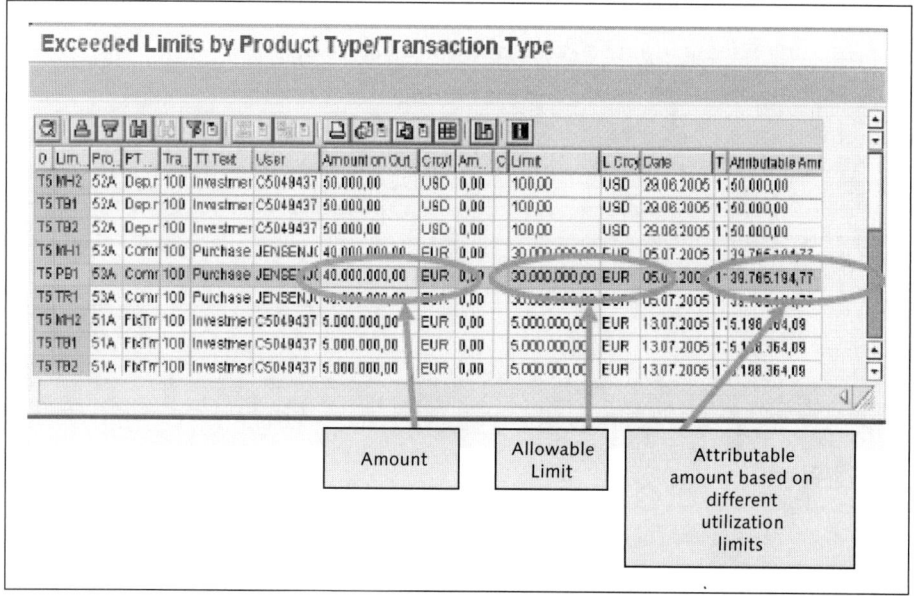

Figure 8.58 Transaction KLLE Report of Exceeded Limits by Transaction

Portfolio-Based Limit Management

The Credit Risk Analyzer has functionality to create limits based on different characteristics that can be linked to portfolios, to monitor compliance with board-related directives for allowable investment criteria. Some of the characteristics and available combinations are shown in Figure 8.59.

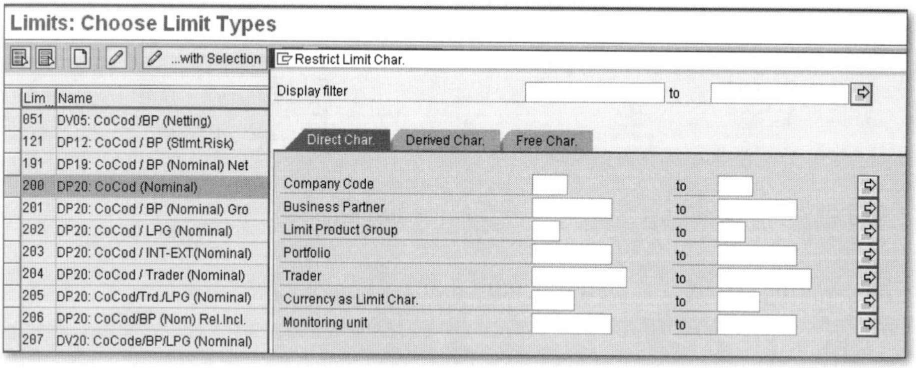

Figure 8.59 Characteristics and Limit Types Available for Limit Management

If parent/child relationships exist between securities in which investments have been made, these can be created through BP master data setup. As shown in Figure 8.60, a subsidiary relationship has been created between two BPs. These relationships can be leveraged to create multi-level limit management capability within the SAP ERP system.

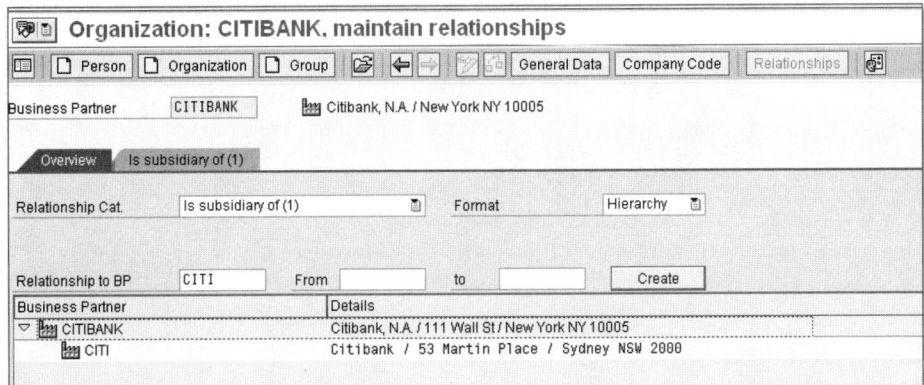

Figure 8.60 Maintaining Relationships for Limit Management

> **Note**
>
> Organizations may want to consider custom programming if the relationships and requirements for limit management become very complex. The existing tables, master data, and transaction codes available in the analyzers and in the transaction manager can be linked through custom ABAP code to fully leverage the functionality and create robust limit management compliance and proactive reporting and audit trails.

8.5 Integration with Cash Management

Securities integration with cash management follows the same steps described in Chapter 7 for the creation of planning types and linking product types with planning types.

One additional step is marking update types as relevant for cash management (CM RELEVANT), as shown in Figure 8.61. This is accomplished through the IMG menu for cash management integration.

8 | Investment and Debt Management

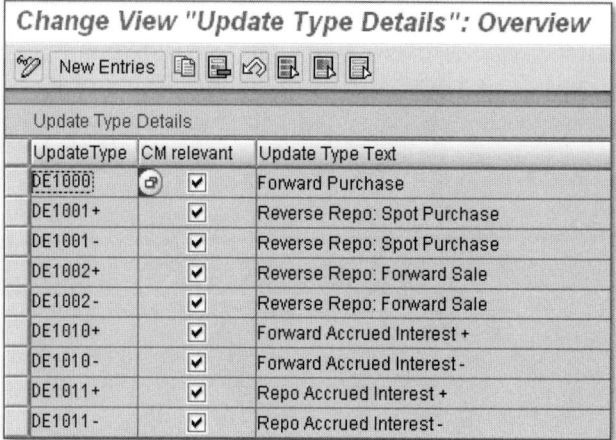

Figure 8.61 Marking Update Types as Relevant for Cash Management

8.6 Reporting

Several reports are available through the application menus so you can view all of the functions executed in transaction management within FSCM. They cover the following:

- Payment information
- Payment due dates
- Posting logs
- Payment alerts
- Accounting information
- Positions
- Financial transactions
- Cash flow
- Posting alerts

Standard reports are accessed through the INFORMATION SYSTEM menu option available in each of the components within the FSCM suite of applications.

8.7 Summary

In this chapter, we covered transaction management for investment and debt, using examples from the money market and securities components, master data, data feed and integration, and how the analyzer tools are used in key areas of valuation and limit management. The last two chapters of this book focus on tools used for SOX compliance and the SOX audit process, as well as special topics such as upgrades and archiving, which are of relevance to existing treasury users of SAP ERP.

This chapter focuses on internal control tools and techniques available in SAP ERP to facilitate compliance with internal controls and regulatory requirements.

9   Tools and Techniques for Internal Controls in SAP ERP

Tools and techniques currently available in SAP ERP that facilitate internal controls through building, testing, and continuous monitoring of the business processes in an enterprise include, for example, Audit Information Systems (AIS) and Management of Internal Controls (MIC). It is important that you make efficient use of these tools and techniques to identify high risk areas and to mitigate them.

SAP ERP is a fully integrated and comprehensive system that covers all aspects of business such as Record to Report, Order to Cash, and Procure to Pay. It has built-in tools you can use to review the risks associated with business processes and the controls associated with each of them.

The following topics will be covered in this chapter:

- MIC
- AIS
- SAP GRC and other SOX compliance systems
- Managing a SOX audit from the treasury perspective
- Reporting, audit trail, and documentation

The effective use of these tools and techniques will enable you to put into place proper SoD and adequate access control for sensitive information assets to provide effective safeguards against potential fraud and mistakes, in the treasury domain as well as in other functional areas.

This will facilitate sound corporate oversight in ensuring compliance with the requirements of internal and external auditors, and help meet regulatory requirements such as SOX.

9 | Tools and Techniques for Internal Controls in SAP ERP

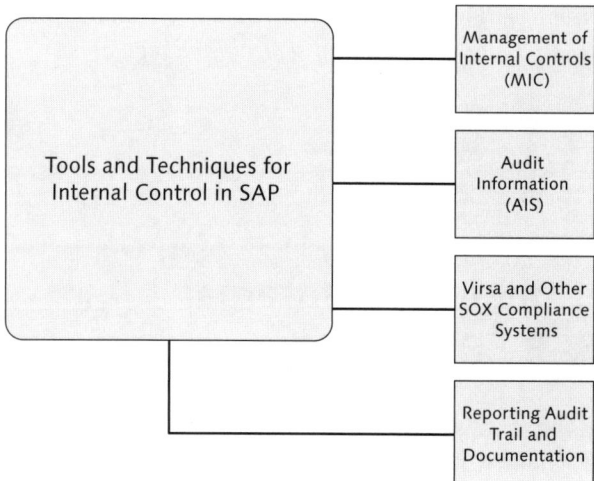

Figure 9.1 Tools and Techniques for Internal Control in SAP

9.1 Management of Internal Controls (MIC)

The MIC component helps you move towards compliance with the software requirements laid out in the SOX act of 2002. MIC can also be deployed in other projects, such as Six Sigma projects for process enhancement. This add-on component is integrated with SAP GRC, but the concepts explained in this chapter refer primarily to the MIC component.

9.1.1 Basic Prerequisites

The basic prerequisites for MIC include the correct design of the accounting setup, banking structure, and proper master data and validations for entering transactions in SAP ERP, coupled with proper SoD and access control for key information assets. These are of utmost importance from a controls perspective, as well as to enable and optimize automated STP. While these are also the most effective safeguards against fraud and mistakes, the list is not exhaustive.

SoD and access control are the most difficult controls to deploy and sustain, given the thousands of users, roles, and processes that require access and authorization, evaluation, testing, and remediation. This is even more true given the globalization of companies, and that they are basic prerequisites for sound corporate oversight required by various regulatory mandates around the world, such as the SOX act.

> **Note: SOX Background**
>
> The Sarbanes-Oxley Act of 2002 — or Public Company Accounting Reform and Investor Protection Act of 2002 — is commonly called SOX or Sarbox and is a U.S. federal law enacted on July 30, 2002 in response to a number of major corporate and accounting scandals, including those affecting Enron, Tyco International, Adelphia, Peregrine Systems, and WorldCom. These accounting scandals cost investors substantial losses when the share prices of the affected companies collapsed and shook public confidence in the nation's securities markets. The act was named after sponsors senator Paul Sarbanes and representative Michael G. Oxley. The legislation establishes enhanced standards for all U.S. public company boards, management, and public accounting firms but does not apply to privately held companies.

The MIC component enables companies to comply with new or enhanced requirements in the areas of corporate governance, financial disclosures, and accountability for fraud established by the SOX act.

MIC primarily enables companies to implement the requirements laid out in sections 302 and 404 of the SOX act (discussed in detail in Chapter 1):

- Section 302 mandates that management must provide — either annually or for each quarter — written assurance regarding the correctness of financial reporting and the effectiveness of the internal controls implemented in the company.

- Section 404 mandates a report by company management regarding the internal controls implemented in the company. This report forms a mandatory part of the annual financial statement and must consist of the following parts:
    - Documented internal controls for the correctness of financial reporting.
    - Documented internal controls that concern the complete and accurate representation of the company for public disclosure.
    - An assessment of the completeness and effectiveness of the internal controls.

These controls are checked and attested by external auditors during the annual audit of year-end financial statements.

9.1.2 MIC Technical Implementation Considerations

While implementing MIC you need to keep in mind certain technical considerations. These are typically addressed by the Basis team. MIC is part of the CGVMIC 1.0 software component that is based on different release statuses of the SAP Web Application Server (SAP Web AS). From a technical standpoint, this component is an add-on to SAP Web AS 6.20. You can install the add-on onto an SAP system with the SAP Web AS Release 6.20 based on Support Package 35 or higher. The only exception to this is with SAP CRM; you can't use MIC on this type of system. Please refer to SAP Note 680118 for more information about the prerequisites for installation.

You can perform Customizing for MIC in a MIC-specific IMG that is automatically inserted into the SAP reference IMG when the add-on is imported. If you are implementing MIC with an SAP BW system, you have to manually include the IMG for MIC in the SAP reference IMG. The details are explained in SAP Note 685018.

9.1.3 MIC Features

The business processes in a company have an impact on financial statements and MIC provides the ability to represent the status of the control activities in these business processes. It applies the recommendations for internal controls indicated in the report by COSO (explained in detail in Chapter 1).

MIC functions are accessed using an HTML start page rather than through the standard SAP Easy Access menu in the SAP GUI. The main reason is that MIC uses web applications in the People-Centric User Interface (PCUI) application window. A unique factor is that the authorizations for access to the applications are assigned to users using the roles and authorizations concept, which is specific to MIC.

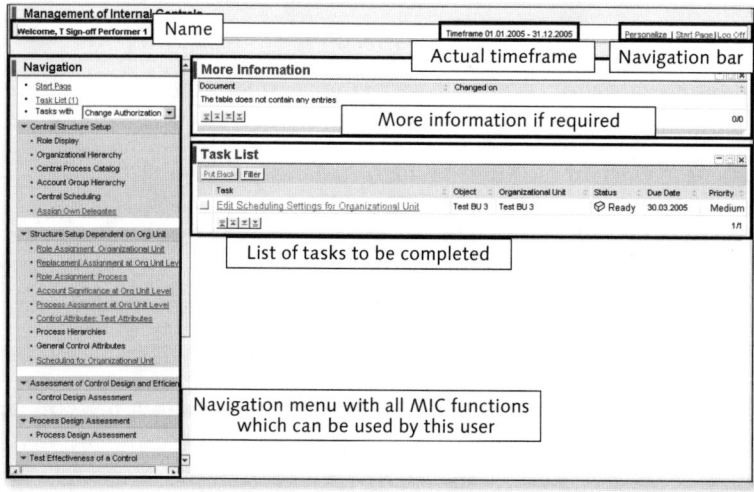

Figure 9.2 MIC — PCUI Interface

MIC helps you to centrally define the following:

- **Organizational hierarchy**
  This is the structure of the organizational units in your company, for internal controls purposes. For example, a corporation may have the holding company PC4YOU, INC. and subsidiary companies such as AMERICAS, EMEA, and ASIA PACIFIC, as shown in Figure 9.3.

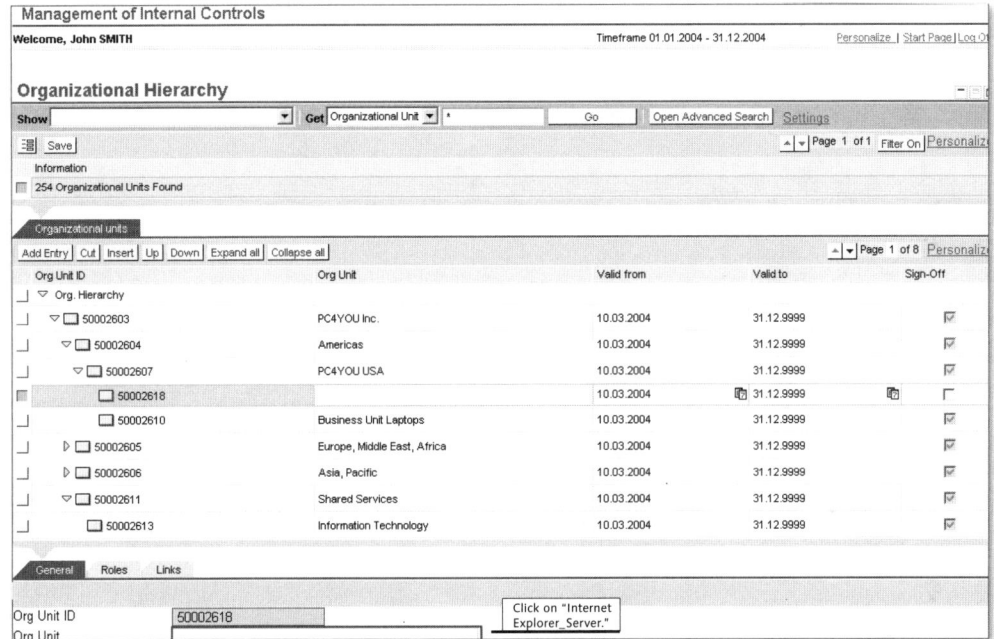

Figure 9.3 MIC Organizational Hierarchy

- **Central process catalog**
  Contains the processes and process steps that are created centrally in the corporate group. They are directly or indirectly related either to financial reporting (to satisfy the requirements of section 404 of the SOX act) or to disclose controls and procedures (to satisfy the requirements of section 302). For example, an organization may have SALES & DISTRIBUTION as the main process, followed by SALES, which, in turn, is followed by sub-processes such as LEAD GENERATION, CONTRACT NEGOTIATION, and ORDER PROCESSING, as shown in Figure 9.4.

9 | Tools and Techniques for Internal Controls in SAP ERP

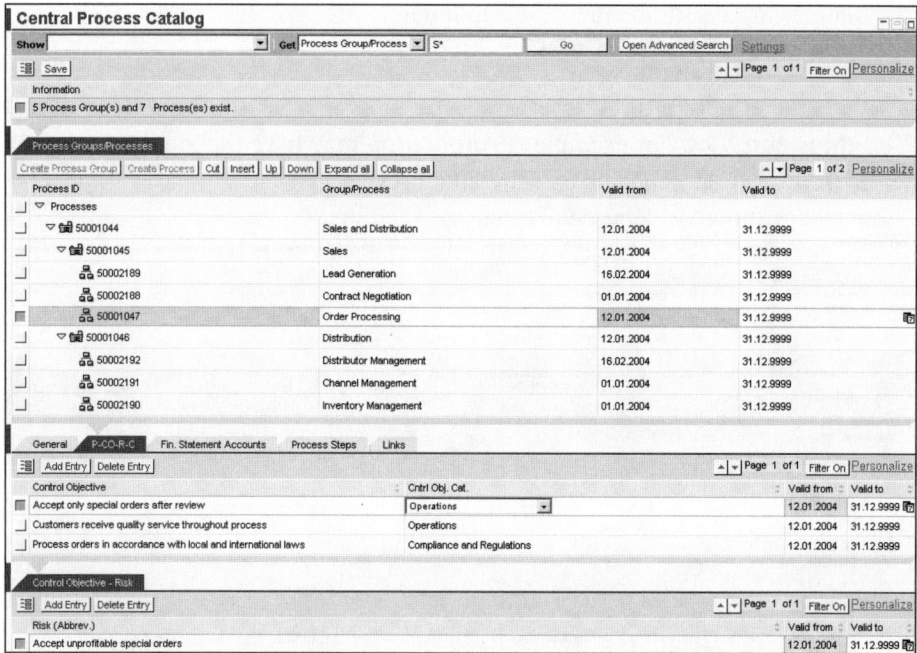

Figure 9.4 MIC Central Process Catalog

- **Account group hierarchy**
  Represents the hierarchical relationships between account groups in a chart of accounts. You identify in the account group hierarchy which account groups of a given chart of accounts are important for the corporate group and you enter into the central process catalog the processes that have an impact on the most significant account groups.

- **Management control catalog**
  Catalogs the controls that are performed at a higher level, that is, at the process group and organizational unit level. The owners responsible for the respective process group or organizational unit (owners at the management level) are responsible for the implementation of these controls. For example, accounts payable is responsible for implementing controls related to the prevention of duplicate payments to vendors.

The organizational units within the organizational hierarchy are automatically included in the project scope. It is possible to document decisions why individual organizational units of the organizational hierarchy fall within the scope of your MIC project.

Each organizational unit can decide locally which business processes, account groups, and management controls are relevant to them and document their internal controls accordingly.

MIC supports a workflow for assessing the documented controls from the control design and efficiency point of view, as well as for testing control effectiveness through assessment. This is used by control owners to provide evaluation of the control and to trigger an improvement process where necessary and test the control. This allows external bodies, such as higher management or internal auditors, to evaluate a control.

Assessments and tests are performed to enable management to identify any potential issues in the internal controls and to ensure that these issues are successfully resolved in a timely manner.

As soon as reported issues have been successfully resolved, the organizational unit owners from the lowest to the highest level of the organizational hierarchy (bottom-up) can sign off in accordance with SOX act section 302, confirming that they acknowledge the status of the internal controls and that they are informed about any existing issues.

After sign-off has been performed at all levels of the organizational hierarchy, the CEO and the CFO perform sign-off for all of the internal controls of the corporate group.

9.1.4 Process Flow for a MIC Project

A project for compliance with the requirements of the SOX act that uses the MIC component usually involves the following steps, divided into three areas:

- **Steps 1 and 2: Setting up the internal controls**
  This can be divided into two parts: central settings and settings for an organizational unit. This helps large companies to set up as many targets as possible centrally, which can then be accepted with minimum effort by the organizational units and adjusted where required. This will considerably reduce the amount of duplicate effort taking place in the company's organizational units.

- **Steps 3 and 4: Reviewing and improving the internal controls**
  Assessments and tests allow any shortcomings in the controls to be identified as issues, and remedied as appropriate.

▶ **Step 5: Analyzing the status of the internal controls**
MIC's reporting functions let you perform a broad analysis of the current status of the internal controls. Management uses this review as the basis for confirming with their sign-off that effective controls are implemented in the organizational unit, and that any shortcomings are known.

9.1.5 Customizing Settings for MIC

The typical Customizing settings for MIC are given for reference only. These are usually configured by an external consultant responsible for the configuration. However, some of these tasks will be performed by the Basis team as well.

1. MIC installation. This will typically be completed by the Basis team. Some of the relevant OSS notes include SAP Note 753547 (Transfer Client Specific Customizing) and SAP Note 517484 (Inactive Services) in the internet communication framework.

2. Deleting or removing old tasks and roles using Transaction SE38 and Program FOPCB_ROLE_CHECK. This will be done by the configuration team. Please refer to Figure 9.5 and Figure 9.6 respectively.

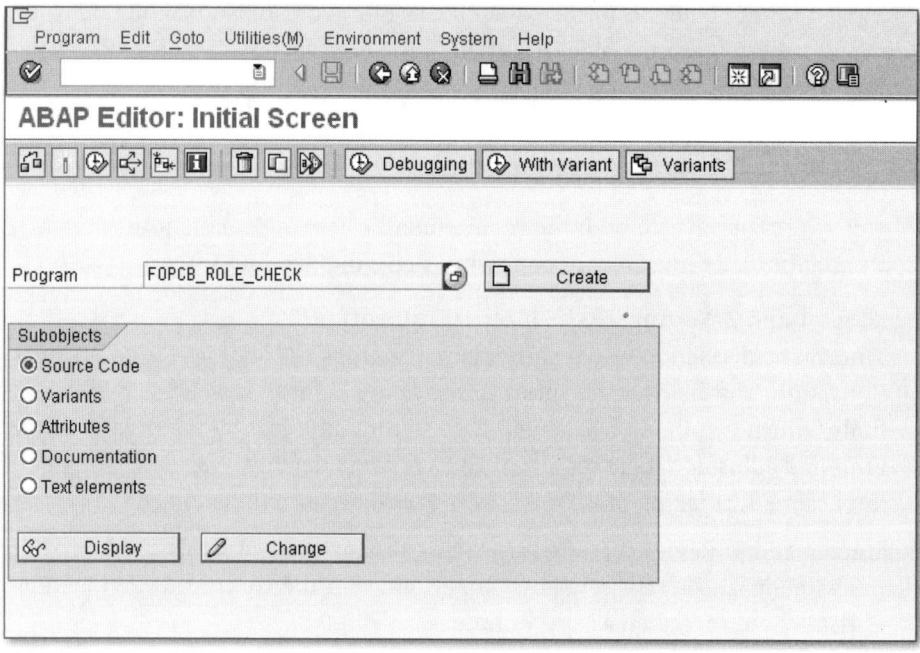

Figure 9.5 Transaction Code SE38 and Program FOPCB_ROLE_CHECK

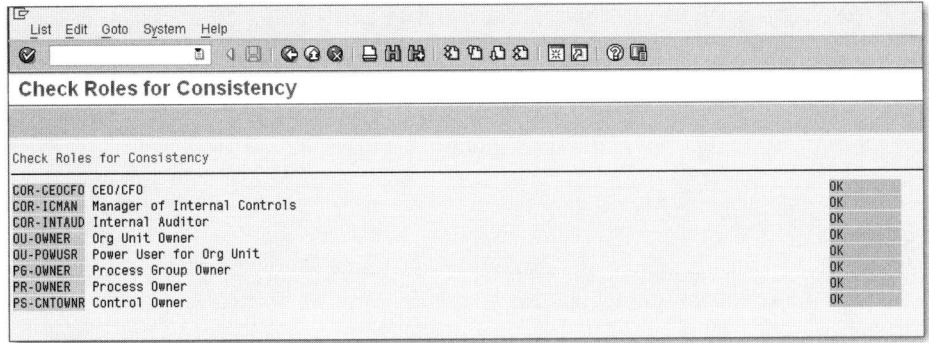

Figure 9.6 Transaction Code SE38 and Program FOPCB_ROLE_CHECK – Output

3. Delete the initial HR data delivered by mistake.
4. Create all roles and task assignments relevant for your organization. In this configuration activity, you enter the roles for MIC and assign tasks to these roles. The tasks are delivered by SAP and can't be changed (see Figure 9.7).

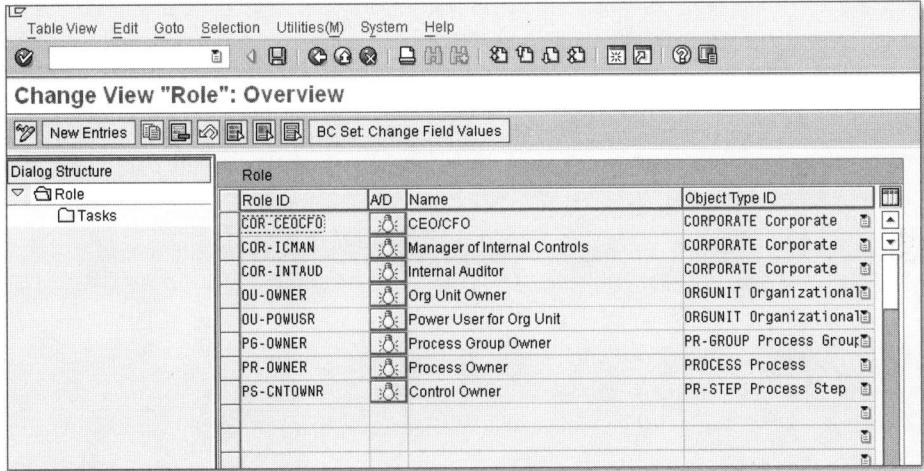

Figure 9.7 MIC Edit Roles

5. Maintain attributes. In this step, the values for attributes of different objects (such as controls or risks) are specified. A distinction is made between the following three types of attributes:

- Attributes with values that you can specify freely.
- Attributes with values that are dependent on other attributes.
- Attributes with values that are fixed and delivered by SAP, and for which you can only change the name, as shown in Figure 9.8.

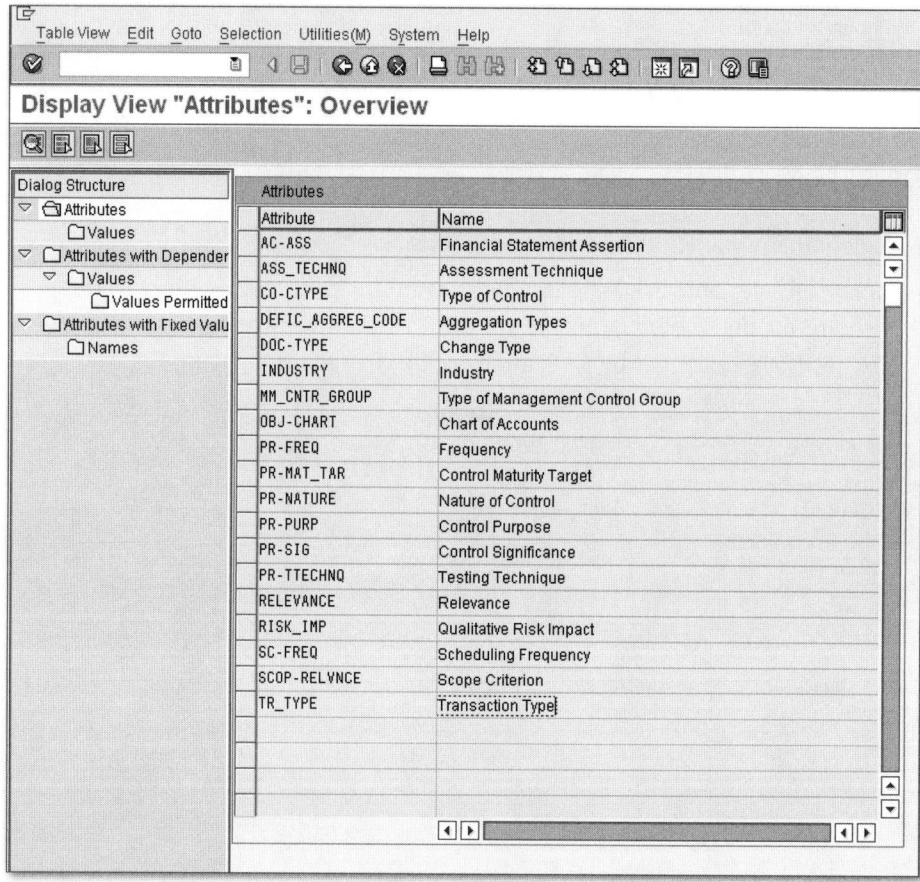

Figure 9.8 MIC Attribute Maintenance

6. Review validation settings. In this step, you can specify whether a given assessment also has to be validated by another person. The assessment is typically

used by the control owner to provide his own evaluation of the control and to trigger an improvement process if necessary:

- For example, we'll look at validation of process design assessment. An assessment for processing payments indicates that a process step has a control issue, is not designed properly, and is therefore ineffective. If you activate the validation setting, this assessment will need to be validated by another person.

- The validation of an assessment refers to the validation of the relevant issues. For the corresponding remediation plans, you can make a separate decision whether they also need to be validated.

- The settings you configure here can be overwritten by organizational units during process assignment. The only exception to this is the validation of the assessment of management controls; the central setting for this can't be overwritten (see Figure 9.9).

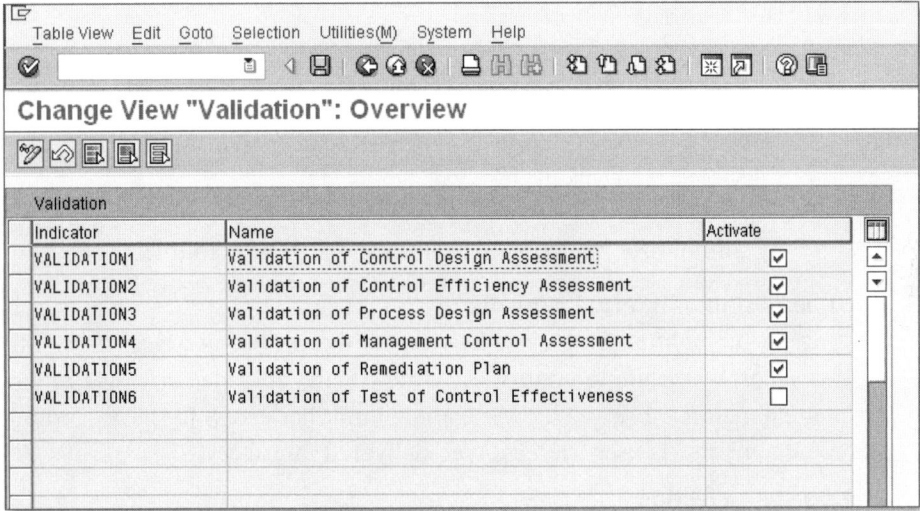

Figure 9.9 Review Validation Settings

7. Review workflow settings. In this step, the workflow configuration is reviewed to ensure workflows are correctly triggered when activities such as assessment, validation, and test are performed in MIC (Figure 9.10).

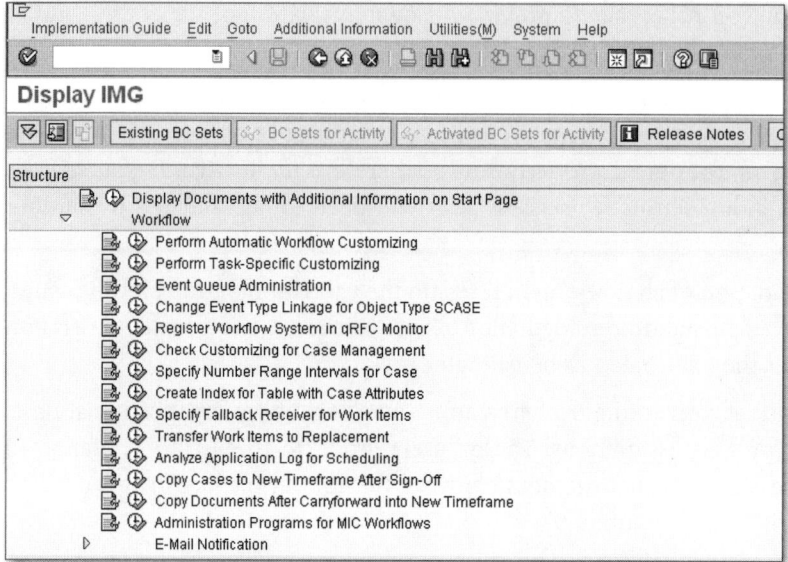

Figure 9.10 IMG for Workflow Settings

> **Note: Workflow Settings**
>
> When encountering general problems related to workflow, refer to SAP Note 322526. It explains several such problems and how to resolve them.

We can briefly summarize the major steps involved in MIC as follows:

- **Documentation of internal controls**

  Existing documentation of processes with their control objectives, risks, and process steps — including control activities — are uploaded to MIC, reducing manual maintenance. Each organizational unit has access to these centrally stored documents via user-friendly, web-delivered interfaces.

- **Process step selection**

  Organizational units use established process steps defined at the corporate level in one of three ways:

  - Referencing default process steps using texts and attributes without changes.

  - Copying process steps from the central default template, which can then be altered as required.

- Creating new process steps without a template.

The source of organizational unit-specific documentation is recorded and is automatically visible at higher levels. An entry screen with a set of control attribute selectors is displayed for high-quality control documentation if a process step represents a control activity. All objects are time- and language-dependent; all changes are recorded in a change log.

- **Assessment and issue remediation**
An HTML-based user interface facilitates data entry during the assessment phase. A web-based user interface means that employees around the world can access MIC without requiring a SAPGUI installation. All involved parties receive automatic notifications triggered by the scheduling functionality. Remediation is linked closely to the relevant issues, and documented remediation plans — including due dates and milestones — are available to management. MIC monitoring minimizes issue resolution time, and the assessment and remediation status is transparent at each stage.

- **Testing**
The test plan (start and end dates, controls, persons involved, and the description of testing techniques and procedures) is maintained in the application; multiple testers can test a single control activity. The MIC's scheduling engine notifies all testers on the start date. Issues are automatically sent to their owners via workflow, and one or more remediation plans can be created to resolve an issue. After resolving the issue, testers are automatically prompted to retest. Reports are available at all levels, showing progress of testing and testing results.

- **Sign-Off**
Management reports provide aggregated dashboard information for global overview of the status of internal control. Individual organizational units perform formalized sign-off procedures covering internal controls in their areas, ensuring that those closest to the business share the responsibility for the internal controls. MIC also facilitates the SOX act Section 404 report attestation by the external auditor via its documentation and analysis functionality.

9.2 Audit Information Systems (AIS)

AIS is an auditing tool used to analyze security aspects of your SAP ERP system in detail. AIS presents its information in the audit info structure (similar to the IMG) to enable you to determine which activities you need to perform and which you have already accomplished. As with other components, SAP AIS provides a collection of pre-defined standard reports to facilitate auditors with limited experience in SAP software.

The following functions are available in AIS:

- Auditing procedures and documentation
- Auditing evaluations
- Audit data downloads

AIS is designed for both business and systems audits. The audit information structure has been designed with these types of audits in mind, and pre-defined views are delivered based on these auditing types. These views can be modified depending on the company's requirements.

You can access AIS with Transaction PFCG (SAP Profile Generator), which is suited to a role-based maintenance environment.

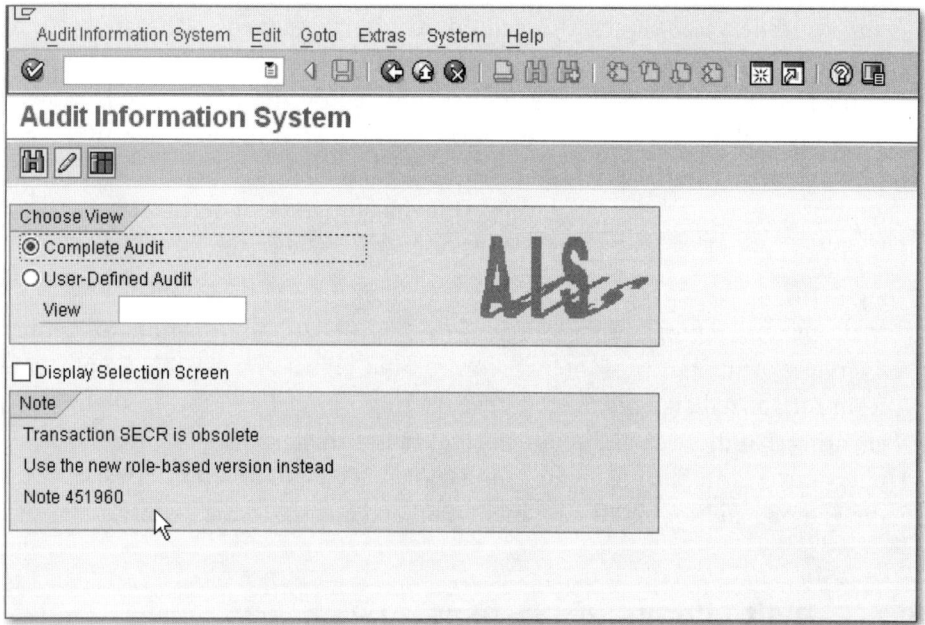

Figure 9.11 Audit Information System – Transaction SECR

9.2 Audit Information Systems (AIS)

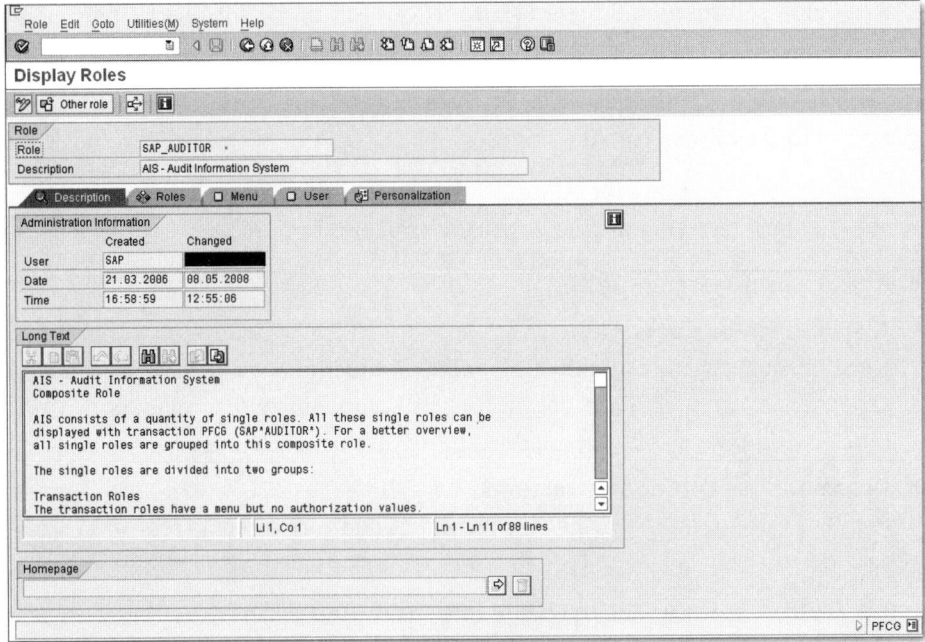

Figure 9.12 AIS – Transaction PFCG

AIS provides a new, more methodical approach for auditing. Using AIS improves the auditing process and its quality.

9.2.1 Areas Supported by AIS

SAP AIS provides a collection of predefined, standard reports that helps auditors who have limited experience in SAP. AIS provides for internal and external business audits, and also facilitates exporting data for external analysis. The following areas are typically supported by AIS within the SAP environment:

- Internal auditing
- External auditing
- Tax checking
- Data protection for HR-related analyses and reports

AIS is typically comprised of a large number of individual roles. Each role usually covers a particular field of auditing. The individual roles are then assigned to the following composite roles:

- AIS: Audit Information System (AIS functions for internal/external auditing).
- AIS: Tax Audit (AIS functions for tax audits/government tax audits).

9.2.2 Process Flow for AIS

The evaluation programs for AIS can be accessed by auditors through the user menu. The business process flow is usually structured as follows:

- **AIS: Perform System Audit**
- **AIS: Perform Business Audit**
  Done through a large number of online evaluations coupled with the data export function. SAP audit data format is compliant with providers of traditional data analysis software used in audits such as IDEA and ACL.
- **Tax Audit: Use Online Transactions**
  Facilitates evaluations that give government auditors direct access to tax-relevant data.
- **Tax Audit: Use Data Transfer/Data Retention Tool (DART)**
  Facilitates external audit by easing data transfer to data medium, and supports SAP audit data format.

Figure 9.13 shows the process flow for AIS.

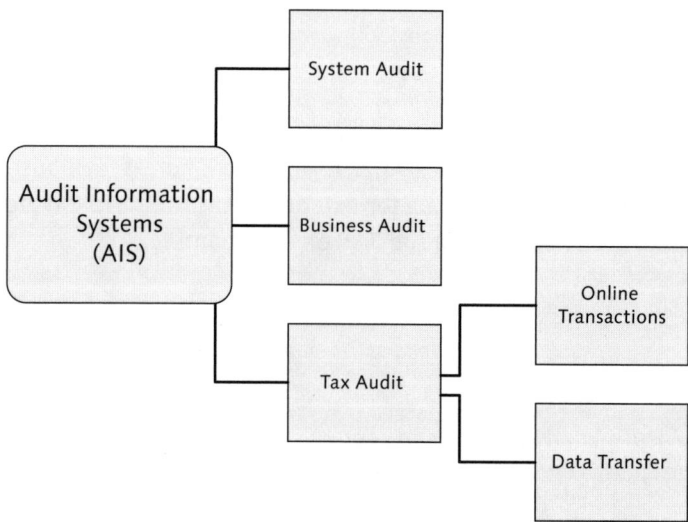

Figure 9.13 Process Flow for AIS

AIS Role Concept

The AIS role concept is the starting point for designing and developing required authorizations. In SAP ERP, different application functions such as treasury and accounts receivable require authorizations. Transactions, activities, tables, programs, and reports are protected by authorization checks in the system. Transactions are the fundamental form of access to SAP ERP. Transactional authorizations protect transactions and their data, and they also restrict functional and organizational elements. Table 9.1 provides an example.

Transaction	Transaction Code	Restricted to
Importing a bank statment	FF.5	Company code

Table 9.1 Transaction FF.5 with Company Code Check

The required authorizations are developed in roles and assigned to individual users. In the previous example, Transaction FF.5 is assigned to the role SAP_FI_BL_INTRADAY_STATEMENT. You can also assign roles at the organizational level of a specific organizational unit, typically by position. For example, Transaction FF.5 is also used by position roles such as Treasurer, Treasury_TRM_Administrator, and Treasury_CFM_Administrator. In these cases, users will receive the relevant authorizations through the organization unit in the form of roles.

In summary, a role typically contains all relevant authorization components and can be assigned to business users individually, or in combination with other roles. AIS consists of a number of individual roles.

It is possible to obtain an overview of the standard roles in AIS in SAP ERP ECC 6.0 system by following these steps:

1. Use Transaction PFCG.
2. Enter "SAP*AUDITOR*" in the ROLE field.
3. Trigger with the F4 key. Then select SINGLE ROLES.

The individual roles are divided into two groups:

- Transaction roles typically contain a menu but don't have authorization values. The role SAP_AUDITOR_BA_CFM provides a menu with the most significant evaluations.

- Authorization roles contain authorization values, but don't have a menu. All roles are delivered without an authorization profile. The role SAP_AUDITOR_BA_CFM_A contains the authorizations for these reports.

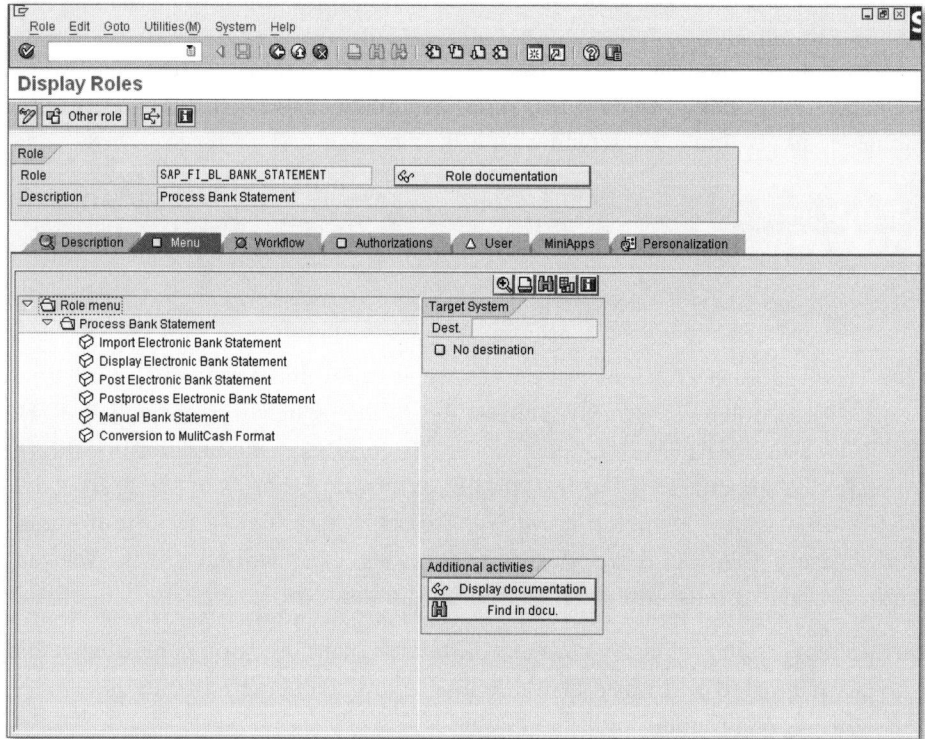

Figure 9.14 Display Roles

Authorizations: Background

Usually, authorizations are generated on the basis of the authorization default values that are adapted to the transactions in the role menu. In the case of AIS transaction roles, however, the authorizations have to be adjusted significantly afterwards (only display authorizations are to be permitted). As a simplified solution, special authorization roles with appropriate authorizations are available for AIS.

9.2.3 Steps to Implement AIS

Six main steps are involved in implementing SAP AIS:

1. **Maintain SAP AIS user roles**
   To make it easier to work with SAP AIS, the auditor will need a user ID that has a large range of display authorization. SAP AIS is a role based maintenance environment and includes a large number of individual roles specifically developed for SAP AIS. SAP_AUDITOR combines all of the individual roles to provide a better overview.

2. **Setting up online help**
   This is required to access SAP AIS help, which is normally stored in the SAP Knowledge Warehouse.

3. **Maintain the selection variables**
   Several reports in SAP AIS usually use variants (prepopulated selection screens) that refer to the standard variables. The variables are stored in Table TVARV. Additional variables can be created.

4. **Import the drill down reports from client 000**
   AIS uses standard drill down reports from the information systems of several components such as G/L, accounts receivable, accounts payable, and so on. The reports are delivered in client 000 and need to be imported in the client if SAP AIS is used extensively.

5. **Activate user exit SQUE0001: ABAP Query – Private storage of data**
   This is typically done by the development team and is required because SAP AIS deals with a large volume of data that needs to be exported to external audit tools. The exported data also requires a description of the data, such as what fields are being exported and their meaning. This standard user exit with sample code enables and optimizes ABAP query so that the data can be exported with field label information. This standard is only available for user group / SAPQUERY/AU and can be extended to other user groups if required. The user exit is implemented with transaction CMOD and the documentation can be reviewed with transaction SMOD.

Please refer to Figure 9.15 for the steps outlined.

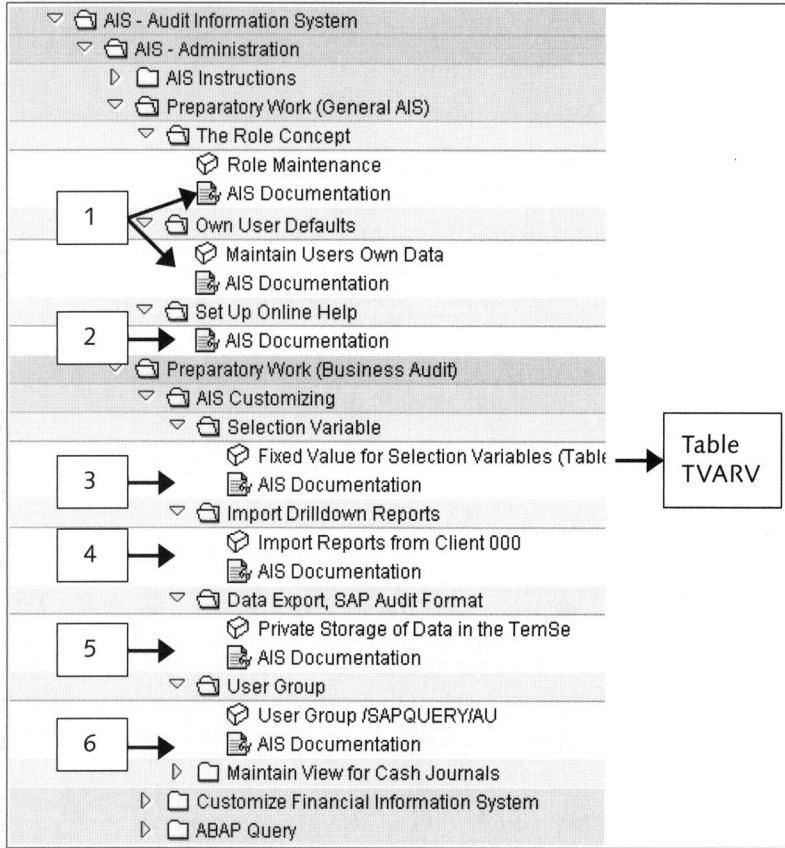

Figure 9.15 AIS implementation Steps

6. Assign User IDs to ABAP Query User Groups (Security Team)

SAP AIS includes several query reports to use along with other ABAP and drill down reports. These reports are logically grouped by target user community such as /SAPQUERY/AU for AIS-specific users and /SAPQUERY/AM for the fixed asset user group, and so on. They can assign users to the respective user groups so that they can execute the queries.

9.2.4 AIS OSS Notes

Please refer to Figure 9.16 for important OSS notes relating to AIS.

Number	Short Text
1011553	Audit Information System (AIS), translation of roles
754273	Availability of the system audit
705197	Audit Information System (AIS) 5.00 – Composite note
680615	Installing SAP CM SOA Release 1.0
544650	Audit Information System (AIS) 4.7 – collective note
498074	PFCG: Creating composite activity group menus
375609	Audit Information System (AIS): Roles for System Auditors
357693	Redundancy avoidance in Easy Access
328019	AIS Structure AUDIT_ALL does not exist
322853	$</R3/RTF/46 46 /0322853/D/00/BC-CCM-USR-PFC /Norbert Hamann
202504	Audit Information System (AIS) 4.6C – composite SAP note
77503	Audit Information System (AIS)

Figure 9.16 Important AIS OSS Notes

9.3 SAP GRC and Other SOX Compliance Systems

The SOX act requires companies to make improvements to their governance model, assuring the existence of effective controls for their business. The SAP compliance calibrator is a useful tool originally created by Virsa Systems that has since been taken over by SAP.

9.3.1 SAP GRC components

The current range of components offered by SAP ERP in its GRC range covers a wide spectrum:

- **SAP GRC Risk Management**
  Balances business opportunities with legal, financial, and operational risks to maximize corporate returns and reduce the market penalties from high-impact events.

- **SAP GRC Access Control**
  Helps with identifying and preventing access and authorization risks in cross-enterprise IT systems, to prevent fraud and decrease the cost of continuous compliance and control.

- **SAP GRC Process Control**
  Ensures compliance and enables business process control management by centrally monitoring key controls for cross-enterprise systems.

- **SAP GRC Global Trade Services**
  Manages all foreign trade processes with the aid of a comprehensive platform to ensure trade compliance, expedited cross-border transactions, and best possible utilization of trade agreements.

- **Environment, Health, and Safety Compliance Management Applications**
  Aligns business processes with environmental, occupational, and product safety regulations, and with corporate policies to ensure proactive compliance.

9.3.2 Other SOX Compliance Systems

Other SOX compliance systems are provided by vendors such as Handysoft SOXA Accelerator, Openpages SOX Express, Paisley Consulting Risk Navigator, Oracle Internal Controls Manager, Stellent Sarbanes-Oxley solution, Protiviti SarbOx Portal, Certus 302/404, Movaris OneClose, IBM Workplace for Business Controls and Reporting, and Peoplesoft Internal Controls Enforcer. This list is not a comprehensive list and is intended to identify some the available options.

9.4 Managing a SOX Audit from the Treasury Perspective

In this topic, we will highlight the following aspects from a treasury perspective, to comply with the SOX audit requirements:

- Suggest organizational best practices to make SAP compliance a vital requirement of the company.
- Best strategies in support of SAP security and controls to leverage these for cost reduction and for deploying automated tools.

Most companies find it difficult to fully meet compliance requirements on their first attempt because they have to deal with a large number of manual processes, limitations of existing tools, lack of in-house expertise, and lack of controls due to outsourcing to different locations, and so on. Working on compliance also wears down the business operations due to restrictive policies and procedures.

9.4.1 SOX Audit

A basic understanding of the audit process will help mitigate the issues that usually arise during an audit. Broadly speaking, two categories of auditors exist: internal and external. Internal auditors protect the interests of management and the board, whereas external auditors protect the interests of shareholders, customers, and other external parties. Furthermore, several types of audits exist, such as compliance, operational, project, financial, and control and technology audits.

For this discussion, we will focus on compliance audits (compliance with internal and external rules), financial audits (reliability and integrity on values indicated in the financial reports), and control audits (effectiveness of the procedures to mitigate the risk).

Benefits of SOX-Compliant Controls

The benefits of SOX-compliant controls are as follows:

- Mapping, documenting, and evaluating all business processes. This also facilitates knowledge sharing.
- Creating a formalized structure to financial close process and providing documentation for the process.
- Improving understanding of business processes and controls at all levels of the organization.
- Increasing employees' appreciation of their role in ensuring the integrity of the organization's financial reporting process.
- Identifying the importance of addressing significant control weaknesses in asset tracking, IT security, and leasing.
- Improving communication between business, IT, and audit personnel.

Lack of controls typically result in undesirable consequences for an organization, such as significant fines, possible financial loss, negative media attention, and potential jail time for management due to non-adherence to various compliance regulations such as the SOX act, the Gramm-Leach-Bliley Act (GLBA) and the Health Insurance Portability and Accountability Act (HIPAA).

Typical SOX Audit Steps

The typical SOX audit steps include the following:

1. **Plan the audit**
   Assess staffing requirements and timing of work to be performed.

2. **Evaluate management's assessment process**
   Review management's project plan and risk assessment process, determine whether all appropriate elements of COSO and standards are addressed, review results of procedures performed by others, ensure that management documentation standard provides reasonable support for the assessment.

3. **Obtain an understanding of internal control for financial reporting**
   Understand the design of controls related to each component of COSO (control environment, risk assessment, control activities, information and communication, and monitoring).

4. **Test and evaluate design effectiveness**
   Identify control objectives in each area and identify controls that satisfy each objective.

5. **Test and evaluate operating effectiveness**
   Determine the timing of tests of controls based on the nature of the control, the frequency of operation, and the importance of the control.

6. **Evaluate the effectiveness of internal control for financial reporting**
   Evaluate deficiencies in internal control for financial reporting, report results to the audit committee, and issue an opinion.

Preparing for a SOX Audit

The SOX act has transformed the way in which auditors look at controls, in turn challenging companies to understand the control requirements and apply compliant processes. We have spent a large amount of time updating and documenting business processes, as well as IT and information security controls, working closely with internal auditors to determine the areas that need improvement. This helped us understand the requirements and successfully complete our first SOX audit. The lessons learned are briefly summarized here to assist with future SOX audits:

- SOX teams typically have two primary responsibilities:
    - Support enterprise-wide compliance efforts (J-SOX and SOX).
    - Ensure that functional teams such as treasury and IT are compliant with internal regulations, documented management processes, structured approval process, SoD, and internal and external audit reports.

It is a good idea to prepare for the SOX audit by "thinking like an auditor." For example:

- Focusing on transactions, processes, and data where things could go wrong and cause the financial reports to be invalid, untimely and inaccurate.
- Identifying loopholes in built-in checks and balances to prevent transactions, processes and data from going wrong — either intentionally or by genuine oversight — by issuing timely alerts.

Key Treasury Control Issues Related to SOX Audit

Five types of key treasury controls exist on which we will focus here from a SOX audit perspective:

- **SAP configuration controls**
  SAP configuration options that are used to support control objectives (e.g., confirmations to master data, BP, customers, and vendors, tolerance groups, substitutions, and validations).

- **Built-in controls**
  System controls that are built into the design of the SAP ERP application and that can't be altered via configuration (e.g., dual entry accounting, which prevents the loading of bank statements twice for the same day).

- **SAP application security controls**
  Security profiles that are built to ensure access to sensitive processing functions and SoD as appropriate (e.g., restricted access to Transaction SE16 to prevent downloading of sensitive or confidential information such as bank account information, SSN numbers, etc.)

- **SAP system-dependent controls**
  SAP exception reports that can be reviewed (e.g., creating and running an exception report in SAP TRM to compare the opening balance of the current day and the closing balance of the prior day for a bank statement, to highlight discrepancies).

- **Manual process controls**
  SAP system-independent controls that are in place under management supervision. They include:
  - **Borrowing**
    Recording in the correct period and with correct contract terms, reconciliation, and compliance with loan covenants.
  - **Managing cash and investments**
    Accurately recording all investment purchases, sales, and maturities, daily reconciliation of cash receipts with G/L postings, and preparing and reviewing bank reconciliation in a timely manner.
  - **Managing derivative transactions**
    Accurately recording all transactions in the correct period, and disclosing off-balance sheet derivative transactions.

▶ **Cash accounting**
Ensuring appropriate SoD is established for input, release, and reconciliation of wire transfers and daily cash activity, appropriate authorizations are implemented for signatories, and opening and closing of bank accounts must be authorized, and necessary approvals obtained.

Useful Treasury Transactions and Reports for SOX Audit

The treasury transactions and reports shown in Figure 9.17 will facilitate installing sufficient controls to prevent fraud and misuse by enabling speedy detection and remediation. The respective individual report trees for MONEY MARKET (TRTG), DERIVATIVES (TRTR), FOREIGN EXCHANGE (TRTV) and SECURITIES (TRTW) provide at a glance the critical treasury-related reports for review.

Treasury and Risk Management Transactions & Reports	
Transaction Code	Description
TRMA	Treasury Information System
TRTG	Money Market Report Tree
TRTR	Derivatives Report Tree
TRTV	Foreign Exchange Report Tree
TRTW	Securities Report Tree
TRTC	Cash Management
FMCB	Cash Budget Management
TRTM	Market Risk Management
TRTD	Loans
FF/1	Compare Bank Terms
FF/2	Compare Value Date
FF.3	G/L Account Cashed Checks
FF-1	Outstanding Checks
F8BT	Display Payment Requests
TBCD	Change Documents
TPM12	Position List
TJ04	Payment Schedule
FF7A	Cash Position
FF7B	Liquidity Forecast
BPCD	Changes to Business Partners
FWDP	Securities Account List
S_ALN_01001151	Overview - Accounting
S_ALN_01001152	Top 5 Positions
S_ALN_01001153	Currency Analysis
S_ALN_01001154	Simulated Valuation
S_ALN_01001155	CFM Key Date Comparison
S_ALN_01001156	Asset History Sheet / HGB
S_ALN_01001157	Position Trend
S_ALN_01001158	Book Value Trend / P&L/ OCI
S_ALN_01001159	Revenues
S_ALN_01001160	Sales Proceeds
S_ALN_01001161	Due Date Grid

Figure 9.17 Useful Treasury and Risk Management Reporting Transactions for SOX Compliance

9.4.2 Best Practices for a Treasury SOX Audit

The following is a brief list of best practices from a SOX perspective for the treasury area:

- Roles should be developed for functions rather than individuals.
- Avoid excessive emergency role access. For example, avoid widespread access to Deletion of Bank Statements or Manual Input of Foreign Exchange Rates.
- Identify SoD conflicts and resolve them as quickly as possible. For example, segregation of deal entry (Transaction TM01) or payment functions (Transaction FRFT) from settlement functions (Transaction TM06), and bank information entry (Transaction FF67) from bank statement posting (Transaction FEBP).
- Use dual approval controls. Segregate between front office and back office. Any manual entry of a deal, payment instructions, counterparty, or bank should have a second pair of eyes to verify the details. For example, facilitated by settlement functionality and confirmation of BP should have dual approval controls.
- Outsourcing of critical and sensitive areas such as treasury should be avoided where possible. This will help prevent sensitive information from falling into wrong hands, avoiding negative consequences. SLAs will mitigate the financial loss to a certain extent but can't salvage the reputation of the company once it is lost.

Strategies for a Successful Treasury SOX Audit

The following strategies can be used to complete a successful treasury SOX audit:

- Consider having a dedicated group within the SAP implementation team focused exclusively on validating end-to-end process controls:
    - Typically an audit occurs long after the implementation has been completed, or late in the implementation process. This prevents the organization from including the suggestions typically provided during the audit regarding the implementation.
    - It is therefore a good idea to get the requirements of a SOX audit early on, and try to incorporate them during the implementation.
- Map and evaluate business processes, IT applications, and end-user tools on an ongoing basis.

- Continuously evaluate IT general controls (change management, operations, security, etc.).
- Conduct extensive SOX training and awareness sessions with the business to reinforce its importance and the vital role it plays.

9.5 Reporting, Audit Trail and Documentation

This section focuses primarily on three tools: reporting, audit trail, and documentation. These enable you to put into place and monitor the internal controls necessary to mitigate potential risks and optimize performance.

9.5.1 Reporting

Reporting in SAP ERP facilitates the following objectives:

- Master data should be correct, complete, and properly validated.
- Transaction data should be correct, complete, and properly validated.
- The system should provide proper and logical processing as per the requirements.

A number of standard reports can be reviewed at periodic intervals to ensure that postings to the financial accounts are correctly made, and to identify changes in master data and exceptions, such as update terminations.

These reports are typically found under the INFORMATION SYSTEM area under the respective components. They must be up-to-date, precise, and customized to meet specific requirements. Typically, reports with current data are connected with the respective database tables and therefore are dependent and limited by the availability of data in the database tables.

Examples of some of the available reports are covered in this section.

Treasury and Risk Management

Treasury reports, such as MONEY MARKET: CASH FLOWS and MONEY MARKET: PAYMENT SCHEDULE can be accessed through the application menu path FINANCIAL SUPPLY CHAIN MANAGEMENT • TREASURY AND RISK MANAGEMENT • TRANSACTION MANAGER • MONEY MARKET • INFORMATION SYSTEM, as partially shown in Figure 9.18.

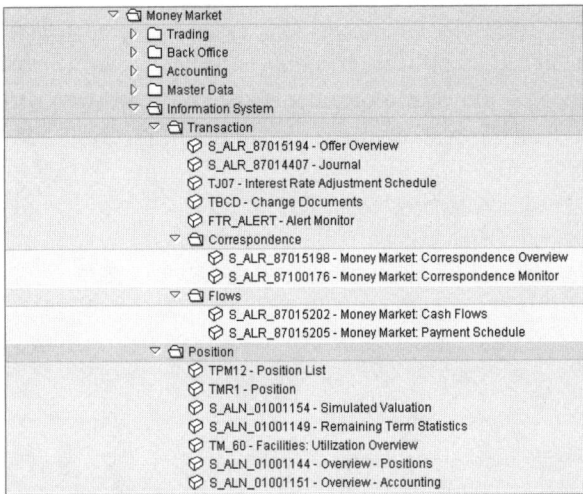

Figure 9.18 Money Market Reports

Derivatives

Derivatives reports can be accessed through the application menu path: FINANCIAL SUPPLY CHAIN MANAGEMENT • TREASURY AND RISK MANAGEMENT • TRANSACTION MANAGER • DERIVATIVES • INFORMATION SYSTEM, as partially shown in Figure 9.19.

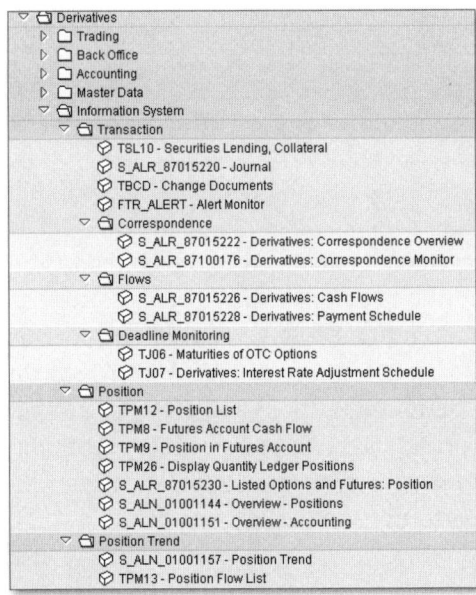

Figure 9.19 Derivatives Reports

Foreign Exchange

FX reports can be accessed through the application menu path FINANCIAL SUPPLY CHAIN MANAGEMENT • TREASURY AND RISK MANAGEMENT • TRANSACTION MANAGER • FOREIGN EXCHANGE • INFORMATION SYSTEMS, as partially shown in Figure 9.20.

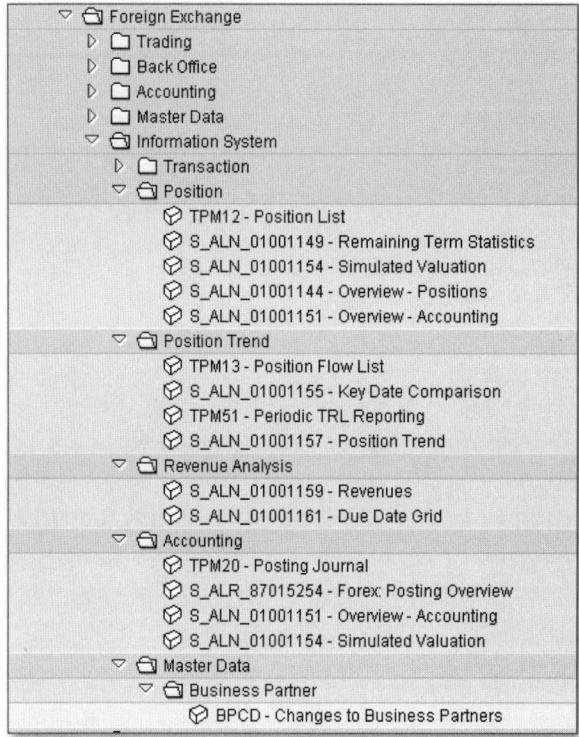

Figure 9.20 FX Reports

A primary task of a financial assets management system is to generate reports on the financial transactions conducted and the positions managed. These reports should be precise, up-to-date, and customized to meet the organization's specific requirements. An example is the alert monitor (Transaction FTR_ALERT), shown in Figure 9.21, which combines several control transactions and provides a broad overview of areas such as settlement, release, payment and posting, correspondence, and interest rate adjustment. This report — when run with variants to save dynamic data entries — enables you to perform period checks very easily.

Type	CoCd	Transaction	Partner	Message Text	Product type/Trans type	Origin
⚠	3000	4000000000001	CITIBANK	Payment is still open (due date 31.03.2005), flow not yet posted	60C - Forex Hedge Accounting / 102 - Forward tran	Payments
⚠	3000	4000000000001	CITIBANK	Payment is still open (due date 31.03.2005), flow not yet posted	60C - Forex Hedge Accounting / 102 - Forward tran	Payments
⚠	3000	4000000000001	CITIBANK	Posting is still open (due date 31.03.2005)	60C - Forex Hedge Accounting / 102 - Forward tran	Posting
⚠	3000	4000000000001	CITIBANK	Posting is still open (due date 31.03.2005)	60C - Forex Hedge Accounting / 102 - Forward tran	Posting
⚠	3000	6000000000000	CITIBANK	Posting is still open (due date 01.10.2007)	62A - Interest rate swap (IRS) / 300 - Payer	Posting
⚠	3000	6000000000000	CITIBANK	Posting is still open (due date 01.09.2007)	62A - Interest rate swap (IRS) / 300 - Payer	Posting
⚠	3000	6000000000000	CITIBANK	Posting is still open (due date 01.08.2007)	62A - Interest rate swap (IRS) / 300 - Payer	Posting
⚠	3000	6000000000000	CITIBANK	Posting is still open (due date 01.07.2007)	62A - Interest rate swap (IRS) / 300 - Payer	Posting
⚠	3000	6000000000000	CITIBANK	Posting is still open (due date 01.06.2007)	62A - Interest rate swap (IRS) / 300 - Payer	Posting
⚠	3000	6000000000000	CITIBANK	Posting is still open (due date 01.05.2007)	62A - Interest rate swap (IRS) / 300 - Payer	Posting
⚠	3000	6000000000000	CITIBANK	Posting is still open (due date 01.04.2007)	62A - Interest rate swap (IRS) / 300 - Payer	Posting
⚠	3000	6000000000000	CITIBANK	Posting is still open (due date 01.03.2007)	62A - Interest rate swap (IRS) / 300 - Payer	Posting
⚠	3000	6000000000000	CITIBANK	Posting is still open (due date 01.02.2007)	62A - Interest rate swap (IRS) / 300 - Payer	Posting
⚠	3000	6000000000000	CITIBANK	Posting is still open (due date 01.01.2007)	62A - Interest rate swap (IRS) / 300 - Payer	Posting
⚠	3000	6000000000000	CITIBANK	Posting is still open (due date 01.11.2007)	62A - Interest rate swap (IRS) / 300 - Payer	Posting

Figure 9.21 Alert Monitor

9.5.2 Audit Trail

Companies are required by statute to retain documents that support the financial transactions recorded in its books of accounts. This requirement imposes a responsibility to ensure that the recorded transactions can be easily traced back to the source documents. The ability to trace a transaction from the books of account back to the original source documents is referred to as maintaining an audit trail.

Audit trails are records of user activity. They are maintained both by the operating system (such as Microsoft Windows for recording user actions [e.g., logins, both successful and failed], resources used, and programs executed), and by application systems such SAP, Oracle, or Peoplesoft (which include the authentication process coupled with a combination of roles or profiles assigned to a user). The roles assigned to a user help the user perform the job roles assigned and restrict access to other areas.

SAP ERP provides an online audit trail for all transactions processed in the system. It is possible to retrieve all existing information through a number of standard reports (available under each component), clearly highlighting any changes made along with the user responsible for making the changes.

Audit trails related to changes made to the financial accounting master data can be regularly reviewed to ensure that the changes are appropriate. For example, any sensitive changes made to BP, vendor or customer master records can be easily identified and traced back.

These can be reviewed using the reports shown in Table 9.2. For each change, you can drill down to display the details of the user who made the change, along with the date and time of the change.

Program Name	Transaction Code	Description
RFSABL00	S_ALR_87012308	Display changes to GL accounts
RFBABL00	S_ALR_87012293	Display changed documents
RFDKLIAB	S_ALR_87012215	Display changes to credit management
RFBKABL0	S_P00_07000008	Display bank changes
RFDABL00	S_ALR_87012182	Display changes to customers
RFKABL00	S_ALR_87012089	Display changes to vendors

Table 9.2 Standard Reports on Master Record Change Logs

Table 9.3 shows a list of standard reports to facilitate an audit from different perspectives, such as table comparison, table changes, table access, and listing of all active users at a given point in time.

Program Name	Description
RSAVGL00	Table comparison between clients
RSDECOMP	Comparing tables between two systems
RSSTAT92	Table changes for a selected month
RSPARAM	Display system parameters settings
RSUSER01	Test SAP_ALL
RSUSR000	List all active users

Table 9.3 Additional Standard Reports

In conclusion, audit trail in SAP ERP lets you log changes applied to business objects such as master data, transactions, and data tables and trace back the flow of a transaction. This topic is also covered extensively in Chapter 2.

9.5.3 Documentation

It is recommended that the following documentation be collected and reviewed to facilitate internal controls:

- The company's organizational chart.
- An overview of the SAP application architecture, preferably through a Visio diagram. This will help you better understand the landscape and resource constraints. The subtopic on upgrading in Chapter 10 highlights the importance of understanding the landscape while planning the upgrade and associated controls.
- A copy of all security policies and procedures. Review these to find possible loopholes.
- Information on the processes for problem resolution, and how a problem is being being resolved and documented.
- Information on proposed system enhancements that are being planned for future implementation through quarterly releases.
- A copy of the application's documentation and development methodology.
- Copies of SLAs currently established for the application.
- Copies of any contingency or disaster recovery plans in place. Review the plans for accuracy, ensure that the plans were recently tested and that backup copies of critical or sensitive data are properly protected.
- Information pertaining to the version of the SAP system and the components that have been implemented, such as level of integration.
- A comprehensive listing of internal and external interfaces in the production sytem and the controls associated with them.
- Information relating to the degree of custom programming done to the system, including ABAP programs and custom data entry screens.
- Information on the overarching SAP system security architecture.
- Information related to the number of client systems running and the geographical locations in which SAP software is currently running. Table T000 provides a listing of all SAP clients and Table T001 provides a listing of all companies.

Treasury-Specific Documentation

A treasury-specific policy document containing the treasury objectives should be maintained at the bare minimum. It should:

- Cover the five financial risks: market risk, liquidity risk, credit risk, settlement risk, and operational risk. It should establish a clear and internally consistent risk management policy with appropriate risk limits.
- Clearly delineate the organizational structure to manage financial risk, including the authority and role each individual or body has. It should include a clear hierarchy or table of delegations.
- Identify the financial instruments that can be used, and their purposes. For example, can the firm invest in options, and if so, under what circumstances can this be done?
- Explain the formal escalation procedures for deviations from the policy and the reporting frequency to the board.
- Clearly state the counterparty limits, credit limits, settlement limits, and investment limits set by the board.

9.6 Summary

This chapter has provided you with an overview of the tools and techniques available in SAP ERP that facilitate better internal controls, including MIC, AIS, Virsa, and SOX-compliant tools. It also discussed standard reporting features together with suggestions on completing a successful SOX audit from a treasury perspective. The last chapter, Chapter 10, covers upgrades, archiving, and other topics of special interest to existing users of SAP ERP.

This chapter covers the topics of upgrading and archiving, which are of particular importance to existing SAP TRM users. The chapter and the book will then conclude with an overview of key new treasury-relevant functionality available in SAP ERP ECC 6.0.

10 Special Topics in Treasury Management

One of the most important and difficult decisions for organizations in general — and treasury departments in particular — is to decide whether to upgrade to a newer version of SAP ERP, specifically to ECC 6.0. As you have seen in the early chapters of this book, SAP ERP treasury functionality has evolved considerably over the years, from bolt-on treasury functionality to extension sets to full integration with SAP ERP ECC 6.0 through the FSCM suite of applications. What makes upgrading a difficult decision is not just the aspect of cost/benefit considerations.

10.1 Upgrading SAP ERP

Upgrading from earlier versions of treasury software or components is a highly technical and complex procedure fraught with problems and pitfalls if not executed properly using the correct sequence of steps. On the other hand, upgrades need to happen at some point, if only because SAP maintenance and support for earlier versions is scheduled to expire. Many different types and combinations of types of upgrades are available, and SAP provides a lot of technical documentation for each possible scenario. In this section, we will provide guidance for the key decision points, as well as practical considerations for the upgrade decision and process.

10.1.1 Key Drivers for Upgrading

The following are some of the key drivers for the decision to upgrade existing SAP treasury systems:

- **Maintenance window**
  The SAP maintenance and support window for the existing version is expiring.

- **Strategic direction**
  The organization may be upgrading their entire SAP system, and treasury may be required to upgrade along with the rest of the organization.

- **New functionality**
  The organization may wish to leverage new functionality available in the latest version of SAP ERP.

- **Technical infrastructure**
  The overall technical environment will play a pivotal role in the decision. Upgrading is primarily a technical function, and can become quite complex, especially when upgrading from the earliest versions of SAP software. The extent of customization in the old system will also be an important factor to consider. In some instances it may make sense to perform a brand new treasury implementation in the new version.

- **Cost/benefit considerations**
  As with any other major investment, cost/benefit considerations will need to be factored into the decision. While the decision to upgrade may be inevitable, it can be undertaken in a phased manner to minimize cost, and through deliberate decisions with regard to what functionality will make the most sense from an ROI perspective. The next section discusses the different approaches an organization can take.

10.1.2 Types of Upgrades

While upgrading may be inevitable, different types of approaches exist, depending on the timing, cost/benefit considerations, and functionality requirements. Three types of upgrade approaches exist, including strategic, technical, and functional. We'll look at each in this section.

Strategic

The strategic approach leverages the latest architecture and functionality offered by SAP ERP, and focuses on improving or revamping existing business processes on the basis of the latest functionality and tools offered by SAP ERP ECC 6.0. It provides the greatest opportunities, but these need to be balanced by cost/benefit considerations.

Technical

The technical approach upgrades the SAP ERP system and adjusts any existing custom programs and configuration as necessary, or uses the old configuration without any adverse impact. The focus is purely on a technological upgrade to the next version, while retaining existing functionality.

Functional

The functional approach provides similar opportunities for improving on or adding new functionality through the upgrade, although the focus is more on simplifying system complexity, for example, if a lot of customization has taken place in the older version. With this approach, the upgrade may not necessarily be to the latest version of SAP ERP. This has benefits that include a simpler and less costly approach to upgrading, as well as reducing the risk of moving too quickly to new functionality that the organization may not yet need or want. Many organizations use this phased approach. In the next section, we will discuss how a phased approach is possible from a technical perspective, and why it may make sense to use this approach.

10.1.3 Using a Phased Approach to Upgrading

Although treasury functionality has improved substantially from version to version, it is the underlying architecture that becomes the critical factor in deciding to which system to upgrade. The NetWeaver architecture has paved the way for a lot of flexibility and integration opportunities in treasury systems management and operations. From a technical perspective, it forms the foundation for future SAP ERP systems. Organizations that are running older versions of SAP ERP on the old architecture should move — at the very least — to the earliest version of SAP ERP that runs on the Netweaver platform.

> **Note**
> The NetWeaver architecture has been available from SAP ERP Enterprise version 4.7 on. Therefore, it is perfectly legitimate to phase the upgrade to this version rather than to upgrade to the latest version, if an organization decides to do so.

The next section looks at some of the key factors that should be considered in arriving at a suitable upgrade strategy and approach

10.1.4 Factors to Consider in the Upgrade Decision

Many factors need to be considered with respect to deciding on an upgrade strategy. Some have more weight than others, depending on the strategic or operational priorities of the organization.

Risk Tolerance

An organization or treasury department may not be able to assimilate rapid changes in technology or functionality, especially if a major reengineering of business processes and integration between treasury and other functional departments is involved. Change management considerations are always an important factor in SAP ERP systems implementations, and upgrade projects are no exception.

Planning Horizon

The time frame involved in implementing an upgrade project, given the treasury department's other priorities, need to be considered. Furthermore, the allocation of scarce resources or budget dollars for competing priorities and projects need to be considered while planning for an upgrade.

SAP ERP Version in Use Prior to Upgrading

The older the current SAP ERP system and related treasury software or components, the greater the impetus to upgrade, especially if the related SAP maintenance and support window is closing.

Upgrade Timing

The planning horizon needs to look at the longer term picture. From an operational perspective, it is important to dovetail the upgrade schedule with other major activities of the organization, such as quarter end, year end, or other key events in the organizational calendar.

System Landscape

The system landscape will be an important factor, given the highly technical nature of all upgrade activities. The treasury upgrade plan must be in consonance with the organizational information technology strategic planning process.

Technical and Functional Support

It is critical to have technical and functional support dedicated and available to ensure that key milestones are being met during the upgrade. These resources need to be available in the post go-live period as well for system stabilization and functional and technical support.

Conversion and Migration Expertise

Upgrading SAP ERP treasury functionality is a specialized skill that requires experience and prior expertise. It is important to obtain the right mix of skills and expertise within the upgrade project team. This includes technical, functional, basis, security, and infrastructure skills in addition to project management and support skills.

Upgrade Complexity

The upgrade complexity is determined by the unique requirements of each company and the type of upgrade undertaken. For companies whose system includes several instances of SAP ERP, or that have a high level of customization, the upgrade process can become very complex. However, the level of complexity can be reduced considerably by documenting issues and their resolution during repeated iterations of the upgrade process, and by diligently following the methodology and required sequence of steps.

Non-Treasury Considerations

Non-treasury considerations may also impact the upgrade decision. For example, SAP ERP ECC 6.0 requires Unicode conversion (see box). Earlier versions, such as SAP ERP Enterprise version 4.7 and SAP ERP ECC 5.0, are Unicode-compatible but database conversion to Unicode is not required to use the system.

> **Key Term: Unicode**
>
> *Unicode* is the international character-encoding standard that allows text data from different languages to be stored in one repository. Prior to Unicode, different standards for assigning numbers to characters existed, and these would often conflict with each other because computer systems needed to support multiple encoding systems. The creation of the Unicode standard was the solution to this problem, but the conversion to the standard in any system is in itself an upgrade project. The Unicode standard has been adopted by all of the major software industry leaders, including SAP.

The next section provides an overview of the upgrade process.

10.1.5 Steps in the Upgrade Process

We'll now look at each of the steps involved in the upgrade process.

Data Clean Up

Prior to any upgrade, it is important to clean up the data in the source system. This will substantially reduce the number of conversion errors encountered during the upgrade process.

The following are steps typically taken to ensure data clean up and error reduction:

- Identify unposted or outdated reversals and correct these as needed using Transaction TBB3.
- Identify open transactions using Transaction TBB1 in test mode and then correct, reverse, or post the flows identified.
- Identify unposted realized gains and losses using Transaction TBB6, and post them using current posting date.
- Run Transactions TBB1, TBB2, and TBB3 to confirm that there are no open items.
- Execute Transaction TBB7 (key date valuation) to ensure all postings have been made.
- Execute Transaction TBB1 again, to post any entries created by previously running Transactions TBB6 and TBB7.

- Check Transaction FF7A and FF7B to ensure that there are no open planning types.
- Repeat the previous steps until all items are cleared, and verify this by running Transactions TBB1, TBB2, TBB3, TBB6, TBB7, TBB8, FF7A and FF7B.

Technical Upgrade

The technical upgrade is performed by the Basis team. Extensive documentation is available from SAP with respect to what needs to be done and in what sequence, and the Basis team will be familiar with the requirements for the technical upgrade. Most important is for the Basis team to apply the latest patches or hot packs available to bring the system to its latest version prior to the upgrade.

Migration of Configuration and Transactional Data

The process of upgrading results in deleting or updating old tables, and also in creating new tables designed to work with the new functionality and Transaction codes available in the new system. For example, the introduction of parallel valuation areas means that the old valuation area methods and related tables will not work any longer. Therefore, data from the old tables and structures has to be migrated into the new architecture, and appropriate changes made to Customizing to enable the new functionality.

The above migration of data, tables, and configuration is accomplished using three key transactions that will be discussed in the next section.

10.1.6 Key Process Steps

Three key transactions drive the upgrade process. These are Transaction TPM_MIGRATION_CAT, Transaction TPM_MIGRATION, and Transaction TS_CONVERT. These will be described in this section.

Transaction TPM_MIGRATION_CAT

Transaction TPM_MIGRATION_CAT is used to capture all Customizing entries within a transport number that can be used to move conversion configuration into other development, test, and production environments. The transaction can be accessed through the IMG menu path FINANCIAL SUPPLY CHAIN MANAGEMENT •

TREASURY AND RISK MANAGEMENT • TRANSACTION MANAGER • GENERAL SETTINGS • TOOLS • CONVERSION • CONVERSION CUSTOMIZING • SET MIGRATION TYPE AND ASSIGN TO CUSTOMIZING REQUEST.

The menu path and options are shown in Figure 10.1.

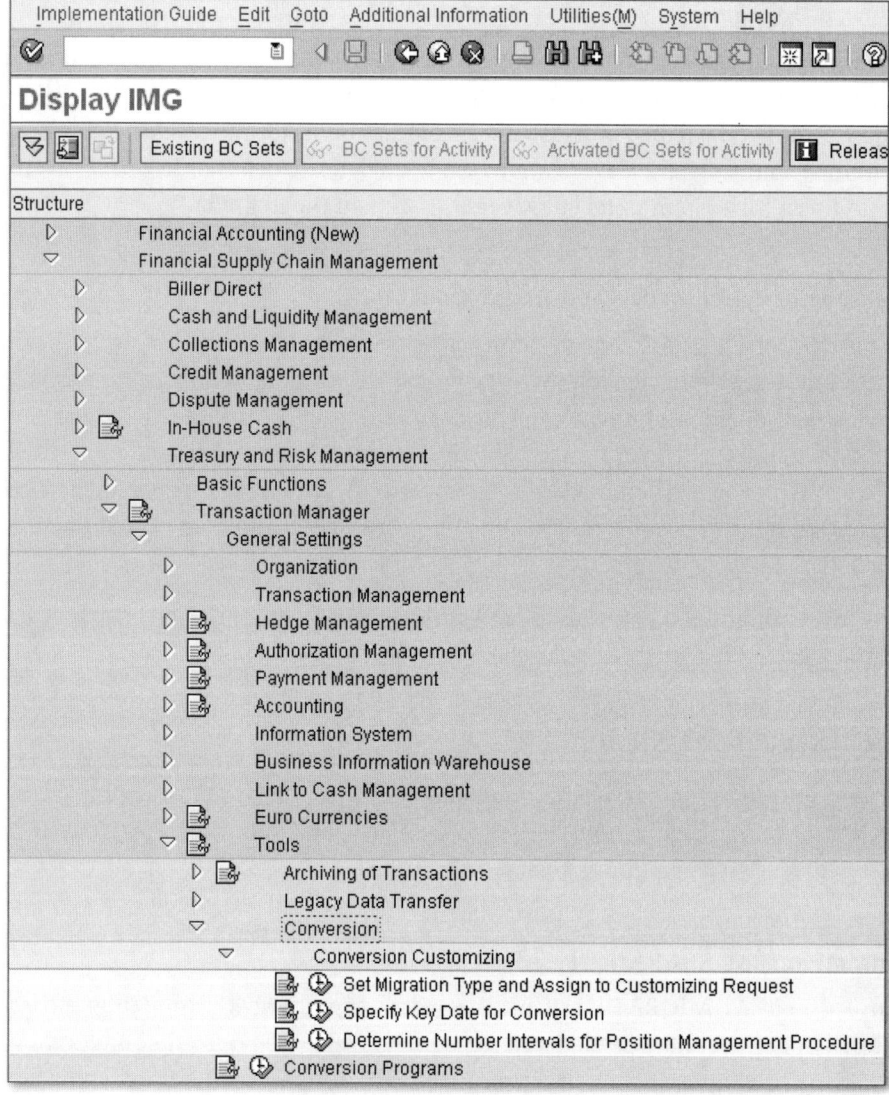

Figure 10.1 Transaction TPM_MIGRATION_CAT Menu Path

The initial screen shown in Figure 10.2 provides the parameters for entering Customizing transport numbers that enable Customizing to move through the landscape. The conversion type is selected from the dropdown box by that name. The source software release version and the target software version define the conversion type.

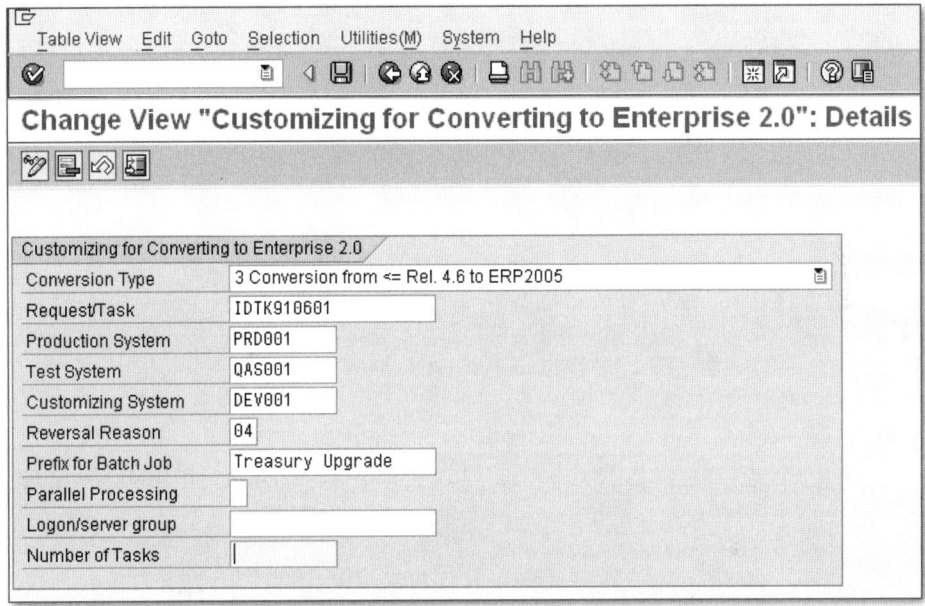

Figure 10.2 Transaction TPM_MIGRATION_CAT

Transaction TPM_MIGRATION

Transaction TPM_MIGRATION provides conversion steps that are divided into Customizing conversion steps and master/flow data conversion steps.

Executing Transaction TPM_MIGRATION results in the screen shown in Figure 10.3. Selecting the Customizing Conversion Options results in the Company Code Independent Steps for conversion, as shown in Figure 10.3.

10 | Special Topics in Treasury Management

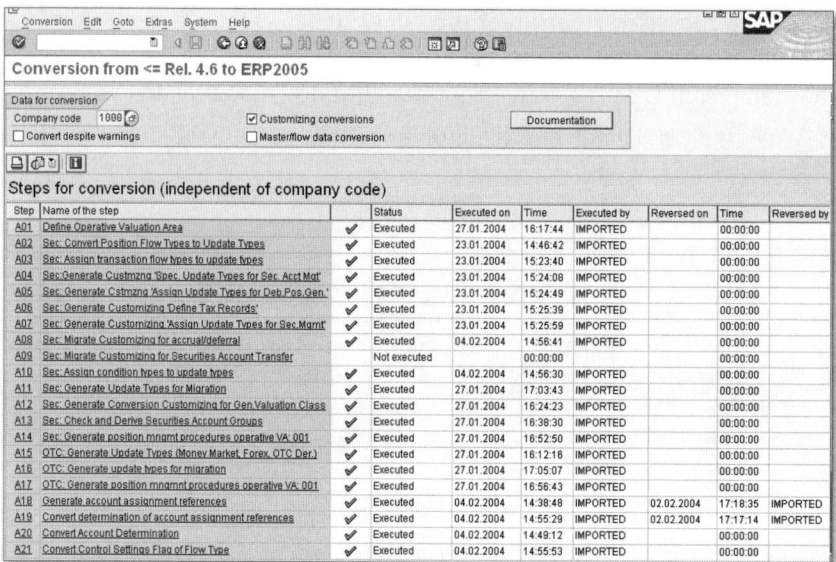

Figure 10.3 Transaction TPM_Migration – Customizing Conversions

The conversion steps for company code-dependent data is shown in Figure 10.4. Each step needs to be executed successfully before the system will allow the next step to be executed.

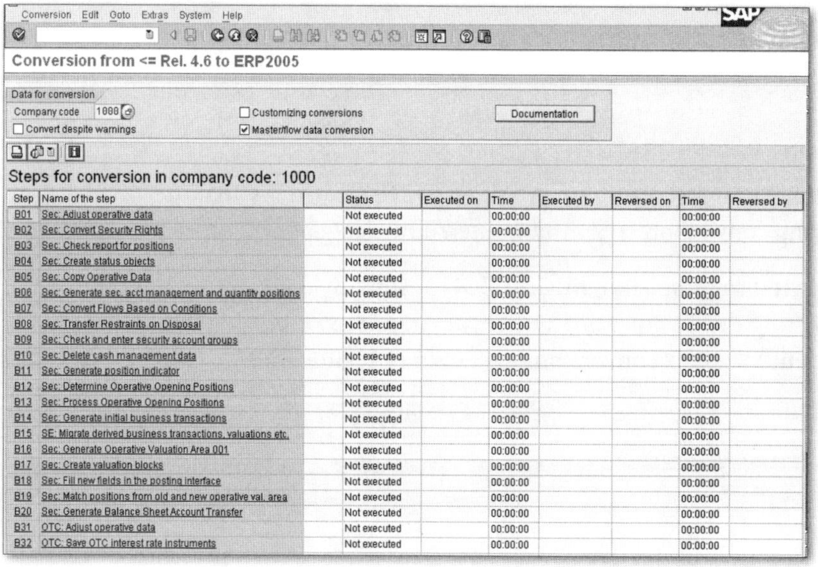

Figure 10.4 Transaction TPM_Migration – Master/Flow Data Conversion

Each step allows execution in test mode, as shown in Figure 10.5.

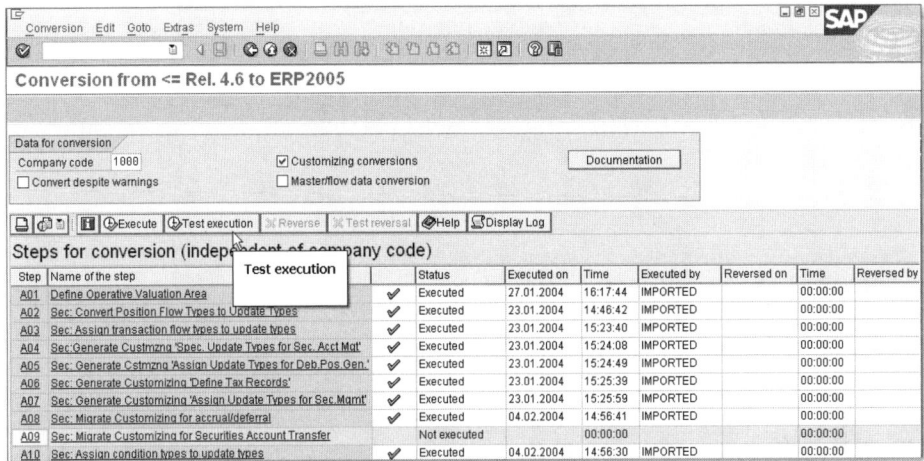

Figure 10.5 Transaction TPM_Migration – Test Mode

Transaction TS_CONVERT

Transaction TS_CONVERT converts specific tables, as shown in Figure 10.6.

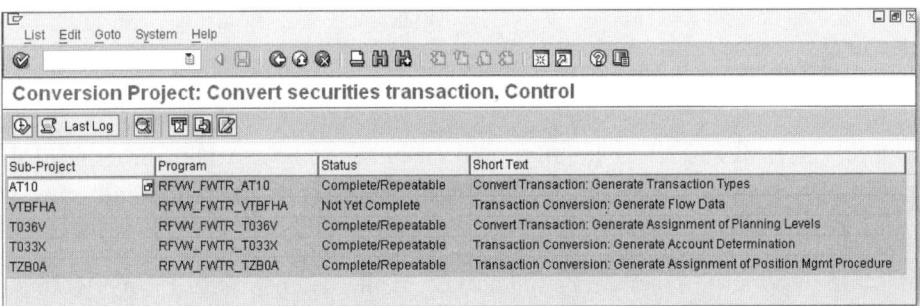

Figure 10.6 Transaction TS_Convert

Conversions can be run in test mode, as shown in Figure 10.7.

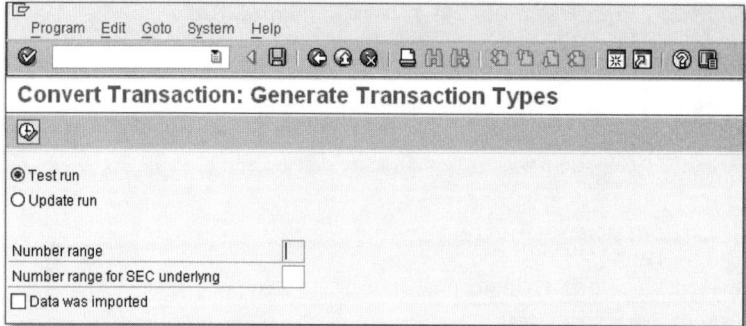

Figure 10.7 Transaction TS_Convert – Test Mode

The resulting log display is shown in Figure 10.8.

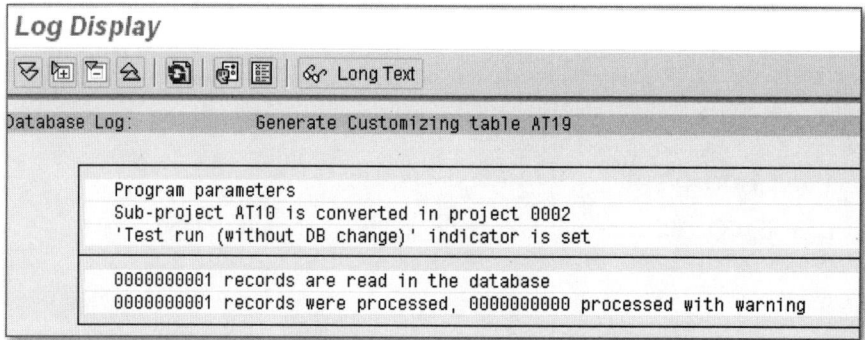

Figure 10.8 Processing Log Display

The processes discussed are iterative, and may need to be run a few times until all errors have been resolved and log messages confirm that the tables and transactions were converted successfully.

It is also important to maintain a full backup of all systems so that recovery can be assured if the upgrade runs into problems, by reverting the system to its original state.

Finally, it is important to test all functionality, programs, and transactions in the upgraded system to ensure they are working as desired. All error messages need to be documented and resolved.

10.1.7 Project Methodology

The suggested project methodology involves three critical phases: plan, build, and run, as shown in Figure 10.9, and the project duration is dependent on critical variables such as the extent of customization, business processes involving testing, and management's commitment. This approach focuses on eliminating modifications that are not used and, where possible, substituting them with standard functionality, as well as on progressively expanding functionality, increasing business value, and preparing the company for the transition to SAP ERP 6.0 while minimizing the risk and adverse impact of the upgrade to the company.

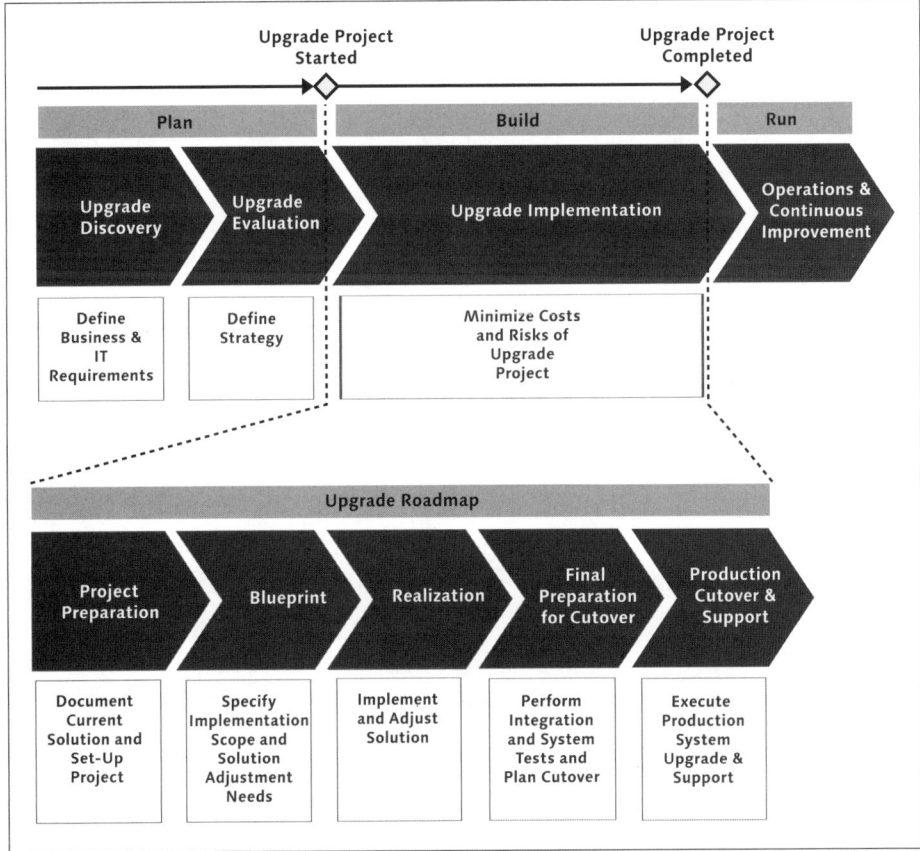

Figure 10.9 Technical Upgrade as a Project – Plan, Build, and Run

Planning Phase

The planning phase can be broadly divided into two steps:

1. **Upgrade discovery**

    During the discovery phase, the business requirements are all discussed. These include:

    - Documenting the current status of the business solution.
    - Assessing the impact of corporate business strategy on the current business solution.
    - Identifying existing gaps and issues.
    - Defining future business needs.
    - Understanding the new functions and features of the SAP target solution, mapping its requirements, and assessing the impact of the corporate IT strategy on the solution (such as outsourcing, hardware, data center, and devising a maintenance strategy for the solution).

    This is an important phase especially if a lot of customization is involved.

2. **Upgrade evaluation**

    For the evaluation phase of the upgrade, you need to define a strategy by identifying and designing possible target solution landscapes (releases and software components) that meet business and IT requirements. For example, it is typical for most companies to have two layers: a production support layer to fix critical production issues and a release layer used to meet new business needs by way of enhancements.

    - Perform a high-level analysis of how changes impact the complete solution landscape (including technical platform, and SAP and non-SAP software), evaluate the migration paths to possible target landscapes, and determine the best option to meet the organization's upgrade needs.
    - You need to provide adequate time for testing in all environments such as development and test client, depending upon the complexity, product types and data volume. This is crucial for the project success.

You also need to concern yourself with data-related issues with respect to master data and transaction data as of the cut off date. Standard reports as of the cut off date can be run to facilitate validation before and after migration. Interface repointing for critical interfaces such as Reuters for FX rates, prior day, and summary day for bank statements should also be considered during the planning phase.

Build Phase

During the build phase, five basic steps need to take place, which include project preparation, blueprint, realization, final preparation for cutover, and production cutover and support.

- During this phase, the upgrade is physically executed in agreement with the project plans and business scenarios identified during the planning phase. This will again differ from company to company, depending the upgrade approach taken.

- With a functional upgrade, the new business processes should work as they were desired. In addition to this, performance and load testing has to be performed to ensure optimal execution. For example, a company may have a business process that updates time on a weekly basis through a web interface. This is a strain on resources as a large number of users are using the system at the same time. The focus with performance and load testing is to minimize project cost and implement procedures that will mitigate the risk of business disruption.

- The duration of the build phase depends on the extent of customization and the number of business processes that require testing. A sample milestone planning project timeline for the build phase is shown in Figure 10.10. The time spent on testing can be reduced by documenting the test scripts and using test tools such as the Test Director.

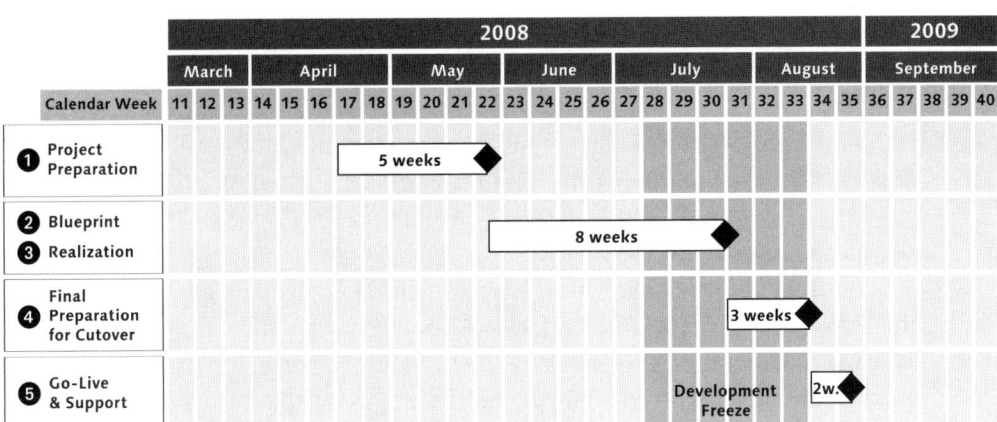

Figure 10.10 Milestone Planning – Technical Upgrade Project

Certain factors should be considered during the build phase, as you'll see next.

Components in Use

You need to consider the number of components currently being used in SAP ERP, and whether all of these components are housed in one client or in different clients (e.g., CFM or MIC being housed in different clients, and integrated to the main system through ALE). The impact of integrating components into one single client needs to be analyzed and evaluated.

The project team — as part of the project preparation activity during the build phase — should be focused on updating company-specific details such as the components used, complexity of user exits, extent of customization, list of Z programs, user exits, and modifications. It should also be focused on evaluating the effort involved in migrating it back to SAP standard functionality, and testing the standard and customized business processes to ensure that they work exactly the same way as they did before the upgrade.

Recommended System Landscape

The recommended system landscape for the upgrade is comprised of two layers: the temporary landscape (which supports production bug fixes), and the productive landscape (which supports the upgrade process). The latter is the release layer, as shown in Figure 10.11. The logic for this is to facilitate bug fixes while working in parallel on the upgrade in the release layer.

Staging the Upgrade

Staging the upgrade is a critical phase that includes testing, user training, system management, and cutover activities, to finalize the organization's readiness to go-live. For example, during this phase, all crucial open issues need to be resolved, end users trained comprehensively, and an SAP ERP help desk set up.

Detailed Cutover Plan

A well thought-out cutover plan — including the steps and sequence in which the cutover activities will be performed, coupled with validation check points at scheduled time intervals — will go a long way in reducing pain points and ensuring a smooth transition to the upgraded system. A sample cutover plan is shown in Figure 10.12 and a sample go-live checklist is shown in Figure 10.13.

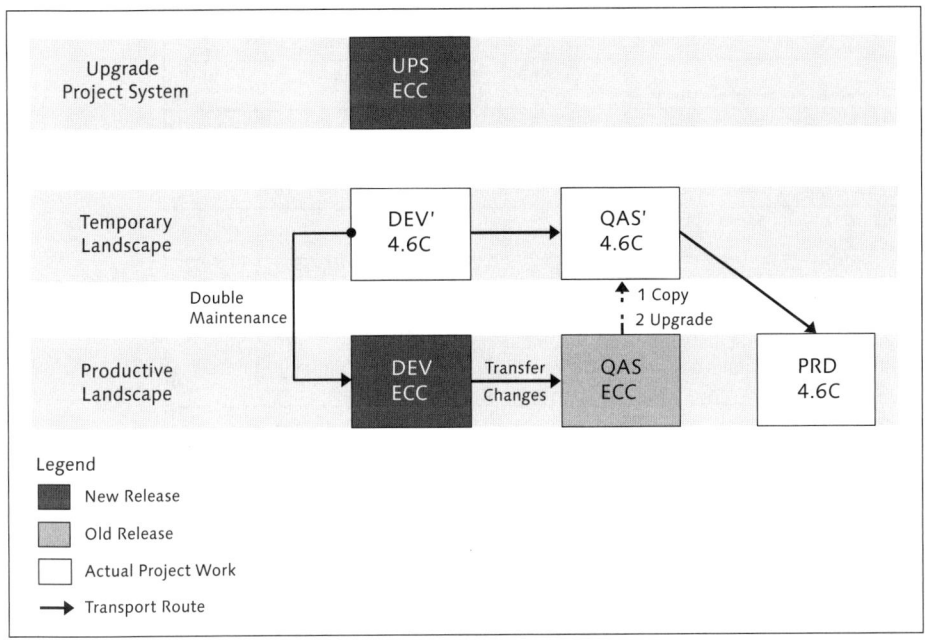

Figure 10.11 Recommended System Landscape for the Upgrade

Task Name	Duration	Start
⊟ AI Cut Over	35 days	10/1/07 8:00 AM
⊟ AI1 Perform Cut Over to Production System	35 days	10/1/07 8:30 AM
AI1.1 Prepare Production Environment	35 days	10/1/07 8:30 AM
AI1.2 Perform Conversions	35 days	10/1/07 8:30 AM
AI1.3 Perform Manual Entries	35 days	10/1/07 8:30 AM
AI1.4 Perform Reconciliations and Obtain Signoffs	35 days	10/1/07 8:30 AM
AI1.5 Deactivate Legacy Systems	35 days	10/1/07 8:30 AM
⊟ AI2 Final Approval for Going Live	5 days	10/1/07 8:00 AM
AI2.1 Define Go Live Criteria	5 days	10/1/07 8:30 AM
AI2.2 Approve the Production System	5 days	10/1/07 8:30 AM
AI2.3 Secure Production Environment	5 days	10/1/07 8:30 AM
AI2.4 Verify Users Are Ready	5 days	10/1/07 8:30 AM
AI2.5 Conduct Quality Check	5 days	10/1/07 8:30 AM
AI2.6 Conduct Go Live Assessment	5 days	10/1/07 8:30 AM
AI2.7 Obtain Approval to Go Live	5 days	10/1/07 8:30 AM
Final Operating Capability checkpoint	0 days	10/1/07 8:00 AM
AI3 Provide Method and Toolset Feedback	5 days	10/1/07 8:30 AM
Go Live	1 day	6/4/01 8:00 AM

Figure 10.12 Sample Project Cutover Plan

Maintain users	Traders are set up for each front office user
Allocate user specific settings	Decimal notation, Working day rule defaults to next day
Check user profiles	
Check user menu trees	
Load SAPGUIs	
Check connectivity	
Check whether User documentation is available	
Set up of variants, ABAP queries and drilldown reports	All variants created for reports, ABAP queries, and drilldown reports need to be re-created
Non-transportable objects need to be input into the productive system direct	Number ranges (transactions, offers, simulations, mirror deals, underlying, planning items.
Posting periods need to be opened in FI	FI document number ranges needed
Activation of the Analysis Structure	To be able to use the Market Risk Analyser
Printer settings should be setup for users	
Enable workflow on business partner changes	
Reports need settting up for use	Reports need to be compiled and if applicable to be imported from client 001. Check reporting tree and run each report

Figure 10.13 Sample Go-Live Checklist

The SAP system will be down and therefore not available to users for a certain period of time during the upgrade. This needs to be planned for according to the company's business operations. You should schedule upgrades on three-day or four-day weekends when possible, such as over the Thanksgiving holiday in the U.S. A fairly accurate estimate of the required downtime can be obtained from past iterations done in sandbox, development, and test clients earlier.

Period End

Upgrades are usually performed after the period end has been completed. It is important to do the following:

▶ Complete month end closing activities, such as opening and closing periods.
▶ Generate external reports, such as financial statements and sales tax reports (through external tax programs such as Vertex or Sabrix), withholding tax reports, and posting accruals/deferrals.
▶ Valuate foreign currency open items and balances.

- Generate normal reports, such as the compact journal, account balances, reconciliation, and open items list.
- Complete year end closing activities such as carrying forward balances, opening and closing posting periods, and so on.

It is recommended to archive documents that are no longer needed in the upgraded system. This will be covered later in this chapter.

Run Phase

During the run phase, emphasis is placed on operations consolidation, continuous improvement in terms of day-to-day operations, and delivering enhancements through periodic releases.

10.2 Archiving

Archiving plays a very important role within an organization. A sound archiving policy is a necessary part of good data management business practice because it enables reducing the volume and growth of data, which in turn results in space and cost savings as well as performance improvements. It also physically removes specific data and documents without compromising legal liability, and while complying with policies and regulations.

> **Key Term: Archiving**
>
> Archiving is the process of migrating data from the online transactional database to a different form of storage while maintaining access to all or part of the data as required by business processes. The Archiving Development Kit (ADK) is used in SAP TRM for archiving its data. The data to be archived is structured in the form of AOs, which facilitates the use of the ADK tool.

The most critical activity for the project team involved in the archiving process is identifying the correct data to archive. It is vital to have knowledge of the company business processes prior to data archiving so that suitable AOs are created. This helps in detecting database table growth and streamlining the process of correctly identifying objects for archiving.

As mentioned, AOs are the building blocks for archiving SAP data. When data objects are combined on the basis of business requirements, a business object is formed. This allows archiving multiple data objects in one business object. The individual data objects can still be logically interpreted when an archived business object is retrieved. AOs also define how the data is archived, its size, customizing linked with AO determines after how much time an object is not required for the day to day system operation and therefore can be archived. AOs instruct the SAP archiving system to use the correct tables when archiving specific business objects. They are defined using Transaction AOBJ, as shown in Figure 10.14.

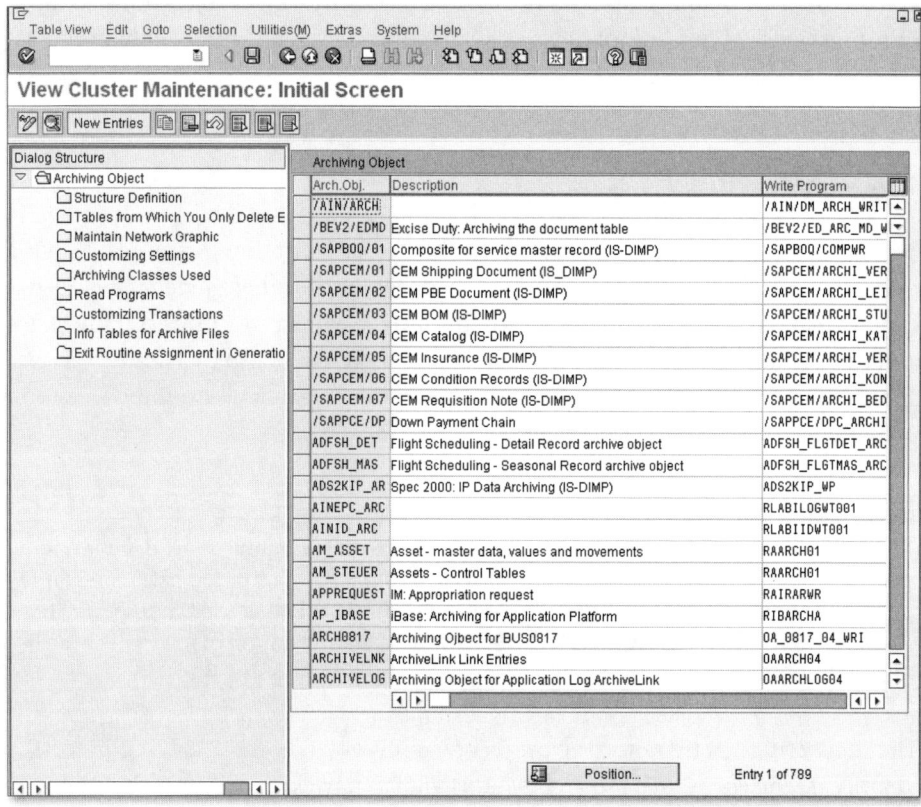

Figure 10.14 Transaction AOBJ – AOs

AOs are defined for different components of an SAP system. For example, financial accounting documents are archived via the AO FI_DOCUMNT, which comprises the document header, company-code-dependent postings, change documents, SAP script texts, and other elements.

The typical AOs associated with SAP TRM are provided in Table 10.1.

Treasury related AOs	Description
TRTM_BPAR	TR-TM BPs
TRTM_FTR	General financial transaction
TRTM_LM	TR limit management – limits, utilization
JB_FOBJ	Financial object
JB_FOCF	Financial object cash flow
JB_FCTY	Facilities
RDBRA_REC	RDB risk analyzer for single records
RM_SVSTATE	Risk management – data pool statuses
RM_BDS	Risk management – report data memory

Table 10.1 AOs Associated with SAP TRM

10.2.1 Archiving Process Flow

The process flow for archiving data consists of three distinct phases as explained in this section

Creating an Archive File

The first phase involves the creation of archived files of data in the SAP database by the Archiving Management System (AMS). AMS reads the data from the database and writes it — in the background — to the archive files. Whenever an archive file exceeds the maximum specified limit, or if the number of data objects in the file goes above the preset limit in the system, the system automatically creates a new archive file.

Toward the end of the process of saving data into the archive files, ADK triggers the system event AP_ARCHIVING_WRITE_FINISHED. This is an indicator to the system to move on to next phase of the archiving process.

Removing the Archived Data From the Database

The second phase of removing the archived data from the database happens simultaneously with the first phase. That is, while AMS writes data to the archive files, another program permanently removes it from the database. The program validates whether the data has been transferred to the archive. This check is critical because it is the last check performed by the system before permanently erasing data from the database. Many deletion programs run simultaneously with the archiving program because it is much faster than the deletion programs. Running deletion programs simultaneously is necessary because this increases the efficiency of the archiving process.

Transferring the Archived Files to a Storage Location Outside of the SAP ERP Database

The third phase, which is optional, saves the archived files to a different storage location outside of the SAP ERP database as soon as AMS has finished with the archiving process. It is possible to achieve this using an automated process in the system, or through a manual process. Most enterprises keep the archived files within the current database; however, the recommended practice is to transfer data to a different location periodically, as part of the data archiving processes. This will also meet disaster recovery process requirements.

10.2.2 Support Tools for the SAP Data Archiving Process

We will now discuss support tools for the archiving process.

SAP Archive Administration – Transaction SARA

The data archiving activities are started by the Archive Administration (AA; Transaction SARA), as shown in Figure 10.15. It controls the overall administration of archiving schedules and enables the archiving sessions. The AA process covers the customization of objects, their conversion to sequential archived files, and overall management. The AA process also retrieves archived files and converts the data through an automated process if there is a change in software, hardware, or the data structure. The data archiving process is streamlined and simplified through the central command of the AA.

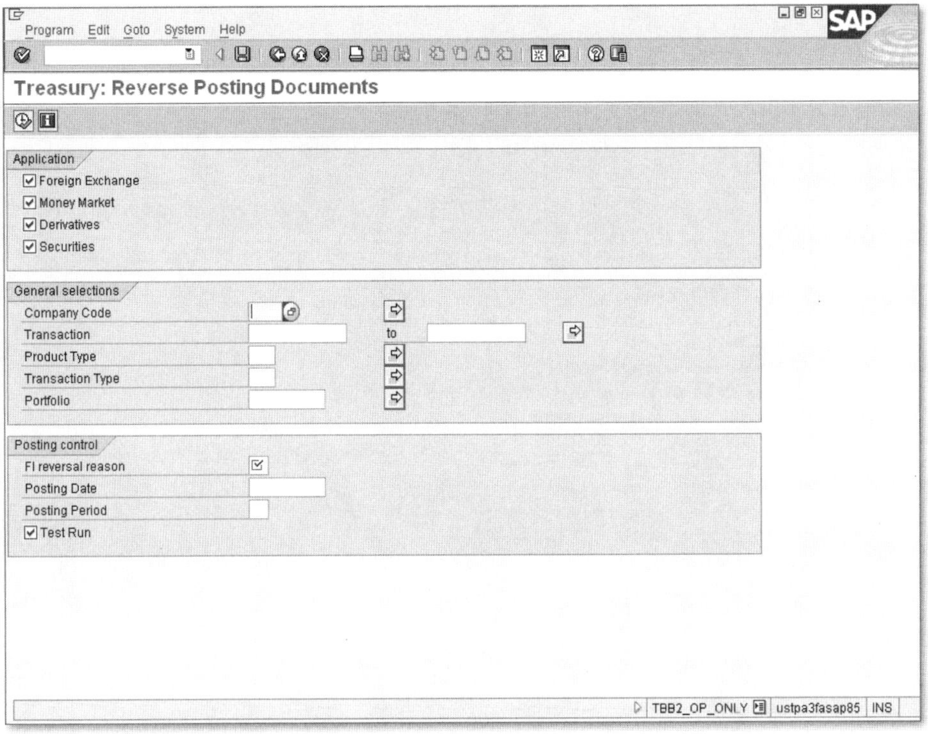

Figure 10.15 AA – Transaction SARA

Data Retention Tool – Transaction FTW0

DART enables the retention of enterprise information for long periods of time. It was designed by Americas SAP Users Group (ASUG), Federal Tax Interest Group, and SAP to meet IRS data retention requirements. It is capable of extracting period-specific data, as well as any supporting information. DART transforms database objects into flat files that can be read by any third-party software designed for flat files, and they are in a flat file format accepted by the IRS. DART is available as an add-on for older versions of SAP R/3, but is an integrated feature of recent versions of SAP ERP.

DART extracts master and transaction level data from multiple R/3 components by copying the contents of predefined fields into the DART application. Here, the data can be opened and viewed or additional queries run against it (see Figure 10.16).

10 | Special Topics in Treasury Management

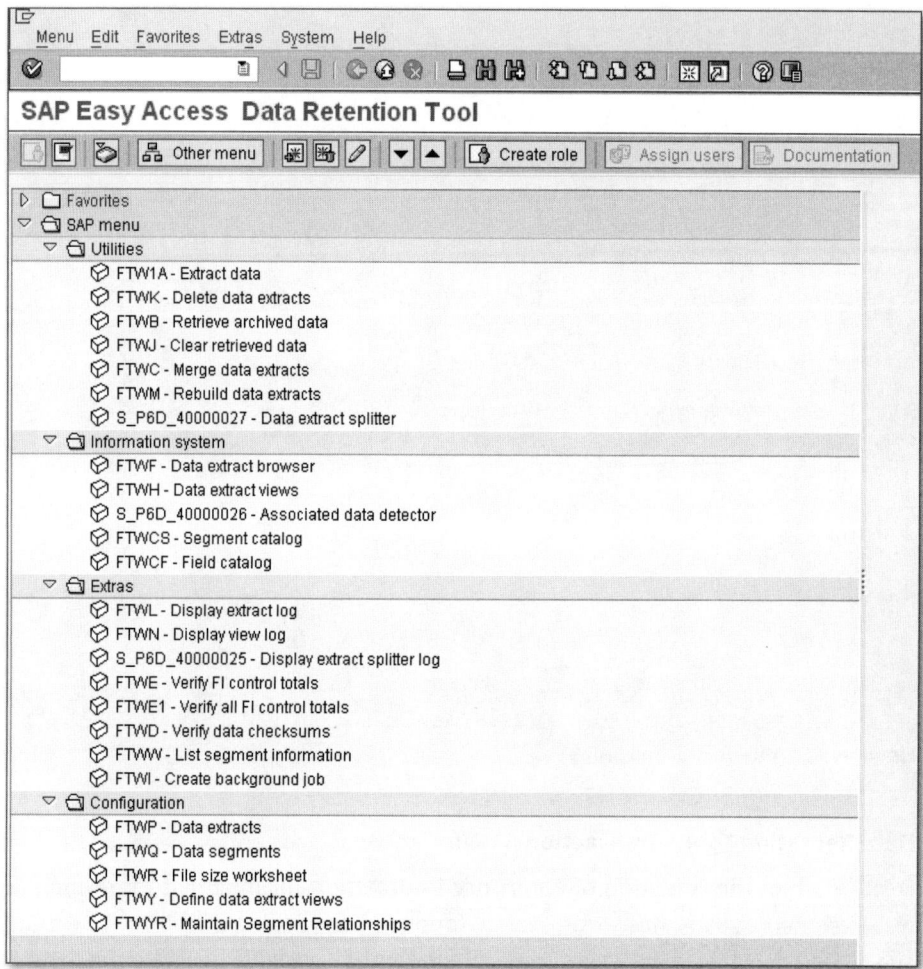

Figure 10.16 DART – Transaction FTW0

SAP Archive Information System – Transaction SARI

The Archive Information System (AIS) is a retrieval tool (Transaction SARI) that provides retrieval capabilities for previously archived data (see Figure 10.17). Data retrieval takes place using archive information structures. AIS requires archive files to be loaded into new tables in the database.

Working with AIS requires detailed, technical knowledge of the database table structure and field layouts. The database structure of an enterprise needs to be flexible and dynamic to be able to quickly adapt to organizational changes.

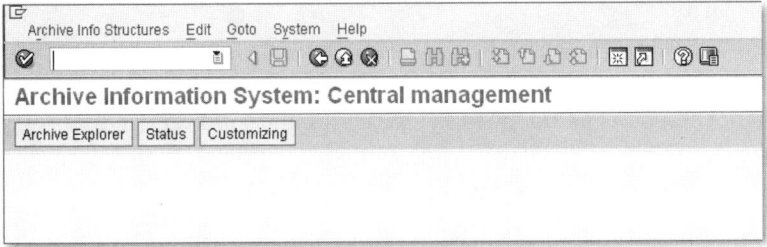

Figure 10.17 AIS – Transaction SARI

10.2.3 The Business Need for Archiving

Several forces drive archiving in any company, as follows:

- Better performance resulting in shorter response times for business users.
- Fast system availability because archiving enables faster backup and shorter run time.
- Effective use of resources because of reduced hardware costs for disks and CPUs, as well as reduced administration costs.
- Assurance of legal compliance by meeting data retention requirements, government regulations, and industry practices.

10.2.4 Potential Control-Related Issues for Archiving

The following potential control issues need to be kept in mind for archiving any type of data, and even more so for archiving FICO and treasury-related data:

- **Compliance considerations**
  A regulatory requirement exists that companies must retain and provide access for x-number of years. The value for which x stands varies depending on country specific regulations.
- **Large data volumes**
  This applies especially in the FICO- and treasury-related areas in interrelated tables such as BSEG, BKPF, BSIK, BSAS, and BSAK. Adequate planning and extra care should therefore be taken for FICO and treasury archiving projects because these are usually the first to be implemented for archiving and are often role models for other areas.

▶ **Specific motivations**

You should make a list of the specific motivations for archiving because this will help in the prioritization of the objects to be archived and to create a logical sequence. Ideally, the first step is identifying the top FICO and treasury AOs from the company's perspective. You can then develop and implement the archiving strategy in manageable phases.

The next step is performing a technical analysis. This forms the base for the success of the archiving project and usually involves performing a technical database analysis using Transaction DB02. Figure 10.18 highlights the largest and fastest growing tables.

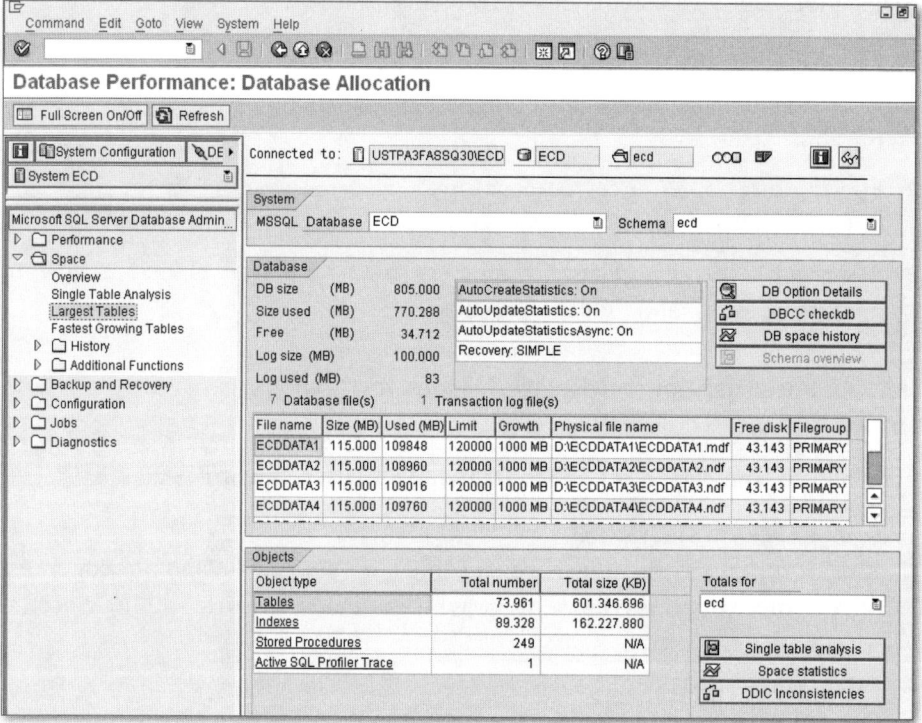

Figure 10.18 Transaction DB02 – Database Performance

The tables are mapped to AOs using Transaction DB15, as shown in Figure 10.19.

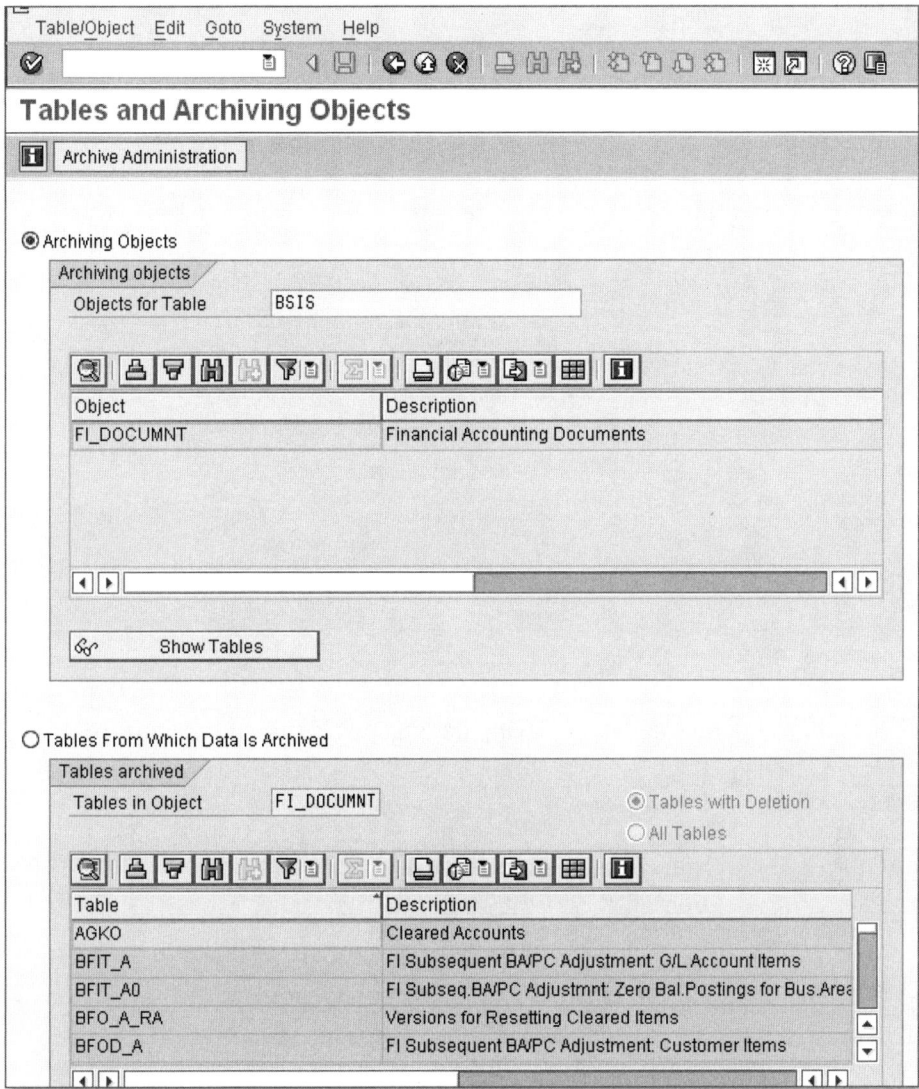

Figure 10.19 Transaction DB15 – Tables and AOs

Data distribution analysis can also be performed using Transaction TAANA (as shown in Figure 10.20), SE11, SE16, optional third-party analysis tools (e.g., PBS™ Analyzer), and SAP Note programs.

10 | Special Topics in Treasury Management

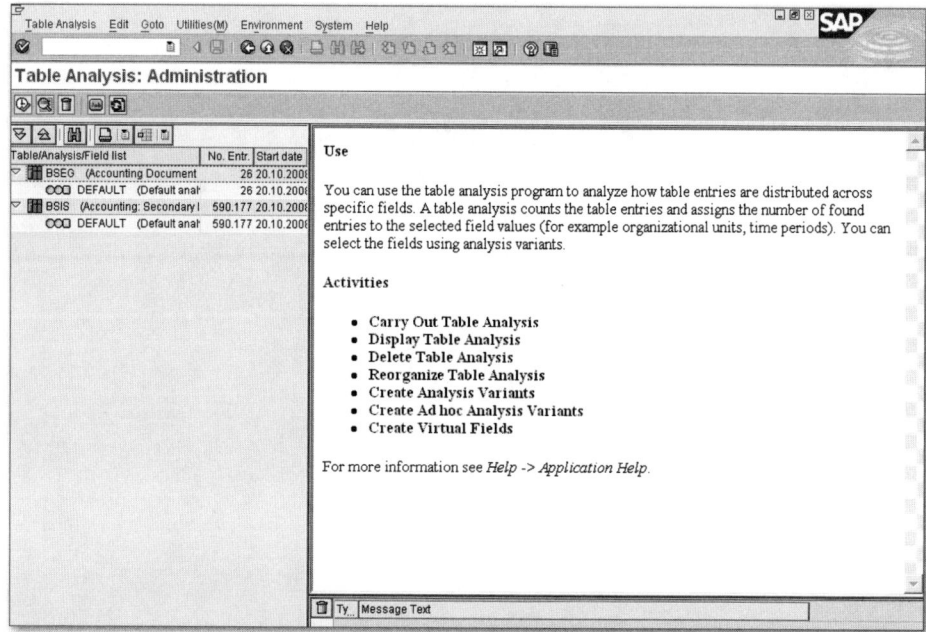

Figure 10.20 Transaction TAANA – Table Analysis

A list of standard SAP data archiving transactions is shown in Figure 10.21.

Transaction Code	Description
AOBJ	View Cluster Maintenance
DB02	Database Performance
DB15	Tables and Archiving Objects
FILE	Logical File Path Definition
OAAD	ArchiveLink: Admin of Stored Documents
OAC0	Content Repositories
OAM1	ArchiveLink: Monitor
SARA	Archive Administration
FTW0	Data Retention Tool
SARI	Archive Info System: Central Management
SF01	Logical File Names, Client-Specific
SM37	Simple Job Selection

Figure 10.21 Data Archiving Transaction List

- **Overall impact and reporting**
  Archiving impacts all departments and regions and therefore care should taken to get buy-in from all affected and potentially affected parties, especially those involved with legal and reporting requirements.

- **Issues specific to multinational organizations**
  Issues include country-specific retention requirements, and synchronizing a mutually convenient time to schedule, archive and delete the jobs. This is critical for global organizations operating in the U.S., and in EMEA and APAC countries.

10.2.5 Access to Archived Data

Being able to access archived data is the most important part of archiving. This is usually accomplished using either standard SAP or third-party tools, as follows:

- **Standard SAP tools**
  Several retrieval options exist in the SAP system, such as the Document Relationship Browser (DRB), AIS, archived enabled transactions, original attached image, DART views, archive-enabled reports, outgoing documents, and print lists.

- **Third-party tools**
  PBS modules are available from 3rd party vendors.

10.3 New Treasury-Related Functionality in SAP ERP

The preceding chapters have been based on and have demonstrated the variety of treasury functionality available in SAP ERP. The concluding section will discuss some new areas of treasury functionality not addressed directly before. It provides a glimpse into the kind of improvements and offerings being developed by SAP that build on existing functionality, and that provide further enhanced integration and controls within the SAP ERP system.

10.3.1 Frontend Trading Platform Integration

Previous versions of SAP ERP — even with the NetWeaver platform and the SAP NetWeaver XI interface available — did not have a robust interface that could enable the system to be used as a frontend trading platform. Instead, it was used primarily as a back office system, recording and processing trades already executed by the front office through standalone trading systems such as the Bloomberg terminal or a bank-provided workstation.

The ECC version of SAP ERP provides integration with the external market place through SAP NetWeaver XI. A special SAP NetWeaver XI format called TreasuryDealNotification is used to collect information with respect to FX spot and forward deals, FX swaps, and generic FX options. The information transmitted through this SAP message type is mapped into SAP ERP through a Business Application Program Interface (BAPI — see box).

> **Key Term: BAPI**
>
> BAPI's are programs provided within the SAP ERP system that have specific functions, and that allow users to define their requirements, using the structure provided by the BAPI. BAdIs and Business Transaction Extensions (BTEs) perform similar functions, and are terms commonly encountered when reviewing SAP ERP functional documentation.
>
> BAPIs are always being added to the programming side of SAP ERP to enable functionality that can be added through plug-and-play capability. Due to the increasingly sophisticated nature of treasury business and its evolving business requirements, these tools are being used more and more often in SAP ERP to provide additional functionality.

The next section describes new functionality for exposure management and hedge management, and provides additional information on how to access documentation that describes specific BAPI functionality.

10.3.2 Exposure Management

A considerable amount of functionality has been added to support exposure and hedge management. Using BAPI TEMExposure, you can upload exposures to an exposure monitor that allows editing and summarization of the data before entering the information into the hedge management component.

The menu path for the exposure monitor is shown in Figure 10.22.

10.3

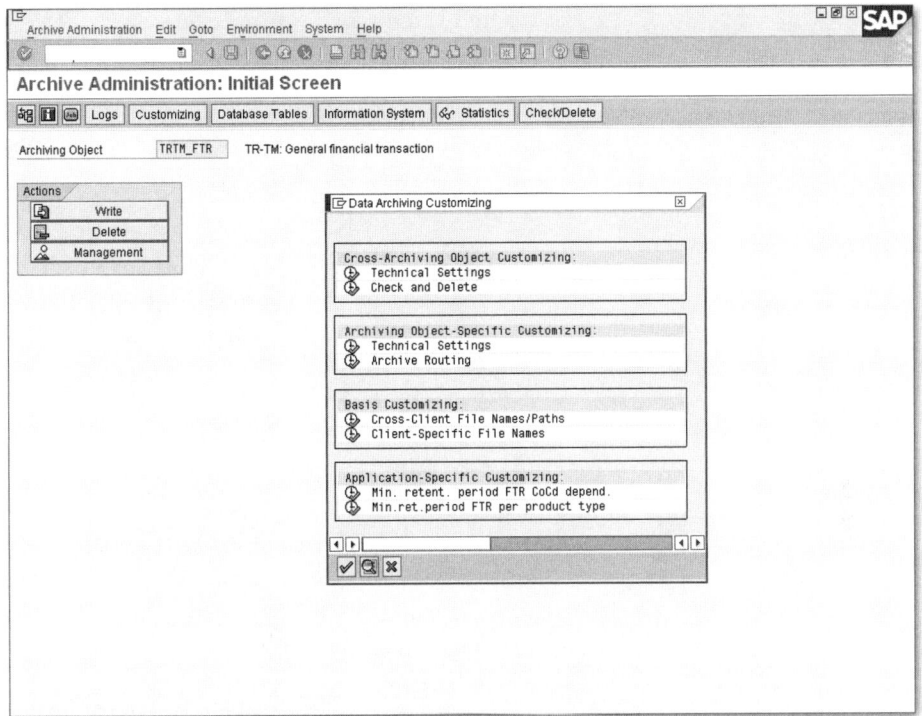

Figure 10.22 Application Menu Path for Exposure Management

Details of the BAPI can be called using Transaction BAPI, as shown in Figure 10.23. The BAPI documentation is also very useful, and provides information about how the BAPI can be used from a functional standpoint. The actual BAPI is a program, and to work, it needs to be set up by a technical resource. However, how it can be used needs to be defined by treasury functional users in the form of a functional specification.

The following are additional BAPIs that have been provided to enhance hedge management functionality:

- THAHedgePlan for hedge plans.
- THATransFX for FX exposures.
- THATransIR for interest rate exposures.

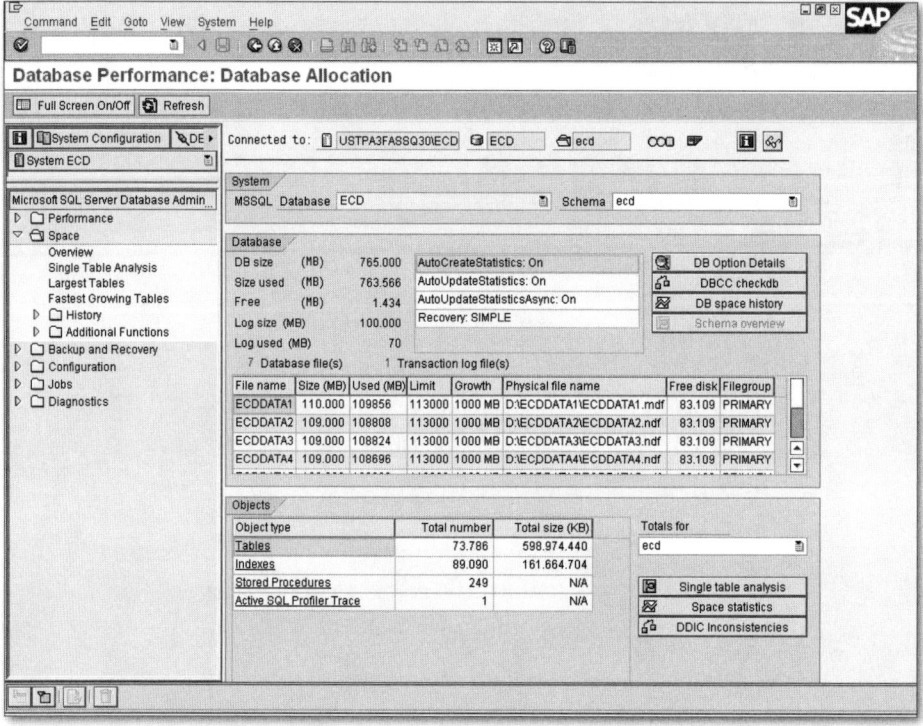

Figure 10.23 Viewing a BAPI Using Transaction BAPI

Additionally, hedge accounting is now available for parallel valuation areas. Therefore, for example, hedge accounting can be run in parallel under the accounting rules of both IAS 39 and FAS 133.

10.3.3 New Product Types

With each new release, new product types and functionality are being added to the core of transaction management in the FSCM suite. Asset-backed securities, syndicated facilities, securities lending, bond issues, forward rate agreements (FRAs), caps and floors, and average rate and basket options are some of the more recent additions. Additionally, FRAs and caps and floors are supported by hedge management in SAP ERP.

10.4 Summary

In this last chapter of the book, we reviewed important decision points relating to the complex area of upgrading SAP TRM, and provided you with practical guidelines for a smooth upgrade process. We discussed key aspects relating to archiving, and also reviewed key new functionality available in SAP ERP ECC 6.0 that is of special relevance to treasury and that was not covered elsewhere in the book.

10.5 Conclusion

The business of treasury is a vast and complex area. We hope that we have been able to provide insight into specific key areas, and how you can leverage the SAP ERP system to optimize and enhance treasury management and its operations. We also hope — and this is most important — that we have been able to show you how you can design the control environment to not only provide compliance with SOX and other regulations, but to also provide the flexibility that enables treasury to run its business efficiently and effectively, using best practice business processes.

The Authors

Arjun Krishnan is a platinum-level SAP ERP Financials and Treasury and Risk Management consultant with over 11 years of implementation experience, specializing in Financial Supply Chain Management. He holds a Canadian Certified Public Accountant designation and is a Certified Treasury Professional (CTP) with over 30 years of experience in treasury, budgeting, financial management, audit, and systems Implementation experience. He is a regular speaker and panelist at treasury and SAP ERP conferences and seminars, and has implemented SAP Treasury and Risk Management projects worldwide. He is President of GlobalSAP Treasury Solutions LLC. He is based in Phoenix, AZ, and can be reached at *support@globalsaptreasury.com*.

Alamanda Balaji Kumar is a certified SAP consultant specializing in the Financial Accounting, Controlling, and Treasury and Risk Management components. He has over 12 years of SAP implementation experience, including managing global implementations. In addition to his 24 years of functional experience in finance, he is a Certified Public Accountant (USA), Certified Treasury Professional (CTP), MBA (Information Systems) and Project Management Professional (PMP). He actively trains business users in SAP Treasury and Risk Management functionality and contributes to ASUG. Currently working as a Senior Manager with a Big 4 professional services firm, Balaji resides with his family in Tampa, FL and can be reached at *saptreasurysupport@gmail.com*.

Index

A

Account Group Hierarchy, 370
Accounting Controls, 196, 206
  for Escheatment, 206
  for Lockbox, 196
Accounting Cycle for Payment Cards, 215
Addenda Record, 150
AIS Role Concept, 381
Alert Monitor, 394
American Institute of Certified Public Accountants (AICPA), 56
ANSI X12, 150
Archiving, 137, 417
Asset Class, 322
Audit Information Systems (AIS), 377
Authorization Check, 69, 381
Authorization Group, 72, 294
Authorization Object, 68, 69, 143, 145, 210, 217-220
  F_BKPF_BUK, 220
  F_FEBB_BUK, 69-71
  F_KNAI_APP, 219
  F_KNAI_GEN, 218
  F_KNAI_GRP, 219
Automated Clearing House (ACH), 149

B

Bank Accounting, 242
Bank Area, 268
Bank Communication Standard, 123
Bank Identifier Code (BIC), 141
Bank Master Data, 100, 143
Bank Polling, 122
Bank Reconciliation, 129
Bankers Administration Institute (BAI), 107,
Basel Accords, 17, 23, 27, 34
Build Phase, 412

Business Partner, 49, 157, 273, 290, 329
Business Partner Access Controls, 78

C

Cash Concentration (CCD+), 149
Cash Management, 230
Central Process Catalog, 369
Committee of Sponsoring Organizations (COSO), 33, 56, 57, 58, 93, 368, 387
Configurable Authorizations, 76-77
Control Objectives for Information and Related Technologies, 33, 58
Corporate Finance Management (CFM), 38, 414
Corporate Trade Exchange (CTX), 149
Counterparty, 49, 78, 273, 290, 291-294, 304, 328, 332, 391, 398
Create Account Symbols, 107
Create Planning Groups, 247
Create Planning Levels, 241
Create Planning Types, 245
Credit Risk Analyzer, 348
CUSIP, 326
Customer Master, 248
Customizing Management of Internal Controls, 372

D

Data Retention Tool (DART), 421
Derivative Instruments, 281
Derivatives, 280, 282, 393
Derivatives Reports, 393
Discounted Cash Flow (DCF), 340
DMEE, 167
Document Control, 85
Document Field Control, 84

Document Relationship Browser (DRB), 427
Dual Approval Controls, 391

E

Electronic Bank Statement (EBS), 95, 106, 132
 Configuration, 106
Escheatment, 224
European Payments Council, 33
Evaluation Type, 349

F

FAS 133, 28, 36, 40, 42, 44, 280, 430
Financial Supply Chain Management (FSCM), 34, 37, 39, 207, 280, 282, 300, 309, 317, 348, 356, 430
Flow Types, 286
Foreign Exchange Reports, 394
Functional Upgrade, 401, 413
FX Reports -> Foreign Exchange Reports

G

G/L Integration with subledgers 86
Go-Live Checklist, 414

H

Hedge Management, 280, 298, 309, 428
Hedging, 315
House Bank, 100

I

IDES_TR_TM_CASH_MANAGER, 75
Information Systems Audit and Control Association (ISACA), 59,
In-House Bank, 100
In-House Cash (IHC), 42, 230, 263
ISIN, 326

J

J-SOX, 388

K

KFMOD, 118

L

Limit Management, 358
Liquidity Forecasting, 41, 111, 236, 259
Liquidity Planner, 260
Lockbox Processing, 193

M

Management Control Catalog, 370
Management of Internal Controls (MIC), 366
Manual Controls, 62, 92
Market Data Management, 318
Market Risk Analyzer, 349
Master Data for Accounting, Valuation, and Reporting, 296
Master Record Change Logs, 396
Money Market Reports, 393
Multicash, 123

N

National Automated Clearing House Association (NACHA), 149

O

Organizational Hierarchy, 369

P

Payment Medium Workbench (PMW), 166

PCI DSS, 210
Planning Types, 111
Portfolio Analyzer, 349
Portfolio-based Limit Management, 360
Positive Pay Cycle, 190
Posting Rules, 111
Prenotification, 152
Product Categories, 283
Program
  CCARDEC_TRANSFORM_FI, 222
  RFCHKE00, 184
  RFDOPR20, 251
  RFEBBU00, 117
  RFEBCK00, 185
  RFEBKA00, 65, 95, 116, 123, 231
  RFEBKA40, 231
  RFEBKA96, 137
  RFEBKATZ, 125
  RFEBLB00, 194
  RFEBLBT2, 198
  RFFOEDI1, 149
  RFFOUS_T, 66, 149-151, 156, 173
  RSPFPAR, 83
  RSTBHIST, 82
Public Company Accounting Oversight Board, 56, 59

R

Recalls, ACH, 154
Risk/Control Matrix, 59, 92
Roles, 289

S

SAP Archive Administration (SARA), 420
SAP Archive Information System (SARI), 422
Sarbanes-Oxley Act (SOX), 29
Segregation of Duties (SoD, SOD), 24, 43, 57, 60, 62, 68, 72, 79, 104, 122, 159, 280, 365
Single European Payments Authority, 23, 33, 141
Straight Through Processing (STP), 51, 96, 112, 280
Strategic Upgrade, 400

T

Table
  CCARDEC_V, 214
  TVARV, 383
  TACT, 71
  TCDOB, 80
  TO12K, 64, 82, 100,
  TO12K-BUKRS, 65
  TOBJ, 71,
  USOBT, 69
  USOBX, 69
Technical Upgrade, 401
Transaction Code
  DB02, 424
  F.13, 96
  F_PAYRQ, 165
  F-04, 96
  F110, 148, 155, 309
  F111, 67, 155, 159, 162-164, 176, 309, 336
  F61A, 137
  F66A, 137
  F8BT, 335
  FEBA_LOCKBOX, 195, 202,
  FEBAN, 64, 74, 96, 113, 128-132
  FEBEP, 119
  FEBKO, 125
  FEBRE, 125
  FF.5, 123, 233,381
  FF.6, 69, 74, 124, 126, 132
  FF67, 133
  FF7A, 62, 256, 405
  FF7B, 259
  FI_BL_BANK, 144
  FI12, 143
  FPS3, 235
  FRFT, 159
  FTR_CREATE, 38, 300, 330
  FTR_EDIT, 303, 307
  FWZZ, 326
  FZBP, 149
  IHCCM3, 275
  KLLE, 359
  KLMAXLIMIT, 357
  OB32, 84
  OT16, 252

OT81, 156
SCU3, 82
SCDO, 80
SE16, 64, 389, 425
SE16N, 261
SE38, 63, 82, 137, 173, 183, 221, 372
SE93, 67
SECR, 378
SUIM, 73
TAANA, 425
TBB1, 334, 404
TBB6, 404
TBR5, 299, 332
THMEX, 312
TPM_MIGRATION_CAT, 405
TPM1, 339
TPM60, 339
XF01U01, 95
ZF01U01, 119
Transaction Processing, 282
Transaction Types, 284

U

Update Types, 288
Upgrade Discovery, 411
Upgrade Evaluation, 412

V

Valuation Areas, 296
Value Dating, 251
Vendor Master, 249

W

ZBA -> Zero-Balance Account, 117
Zero-Balance Account, 97

www.sap-press.com

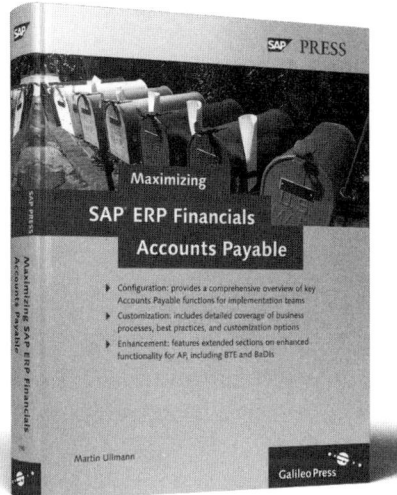

Configuration: provides a comprehensive overview of key Accounts Payable functions

Customization: includes detailed coverage of business processes, best practices, and customization options

Enhancement: features extended sections on enhanced SAP functionality for Accounts Payable, including BTEs and BAdIs, among others.

Martin Ullmann

Maximizing SAP ERP Financials Accounts Payable

Maximizing Accounts Payable in SAP ERP Financials is the definitive, comprehensive guide to implementing, configuring, and enhancing AP for project managers, executives, technical leads, and end-users (functional resources who actually interact on a daily basis with the configured system).Covering the configuration of every AP function, plus strategies for incorporating business processes, best practices, and additional SAP enhancements, this book provides the guidance and experience needed for maximizing the use and potential of the Accounts Payable module.

488 pp., 2009, 79,95 Euro / US$ 79.95
ISBN 978-1-59229-198-4

\>> www.sap-press.de/1754

www.sap-press.com

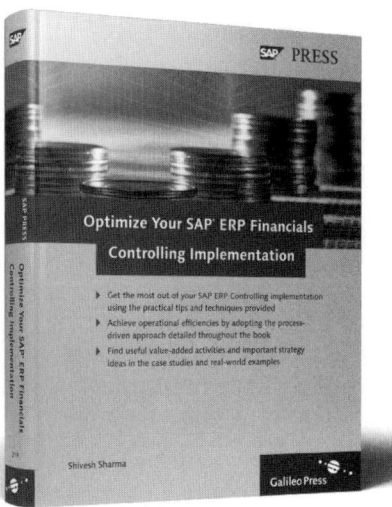

Get the most out of your SAP Controlling implementation using the practical tips and techniques provided

Learn how to make better management decisions by using the Controlling specific information in this book

Discover areas like Investment Management, Funds Management, Product Cost Controlling, and more

Shivesh Sharma

Optimize Your SAP ERP Financials Controlling Implementation

This book will answer the question, What do I do with my SAP Controlling-related requirements once the implementation is complete? Therefore, it begins where implementation guides leave off. Using tested business processes it prepares readers to make the most of their Controlling implementation.

465 pp., 2008, 79,95 Euro / US$ 79.95
ISBN 978-1-59229-219-6

>> www.sap-press.de/1807

Interested in reading more?

Please visit our Web site for all
new book releases from SAP PRESS.

www.sap-press.com